# Cambridge Handbook of Research Approaches to Business Ethics and Corporate Responsibility

Edited by

PATRICIA H. WERHANE
DePaul University
University of Virginia

R. EDWARD FREEMAN
University of Virginia

SERGIY DMYTRIYEV
University of Virginia

CAMBRIDGE
UNIVERSITY PRESS

**CAMBRIDGE**
**UNIVERSITY PRESS**

University Printing House, Cambridge CB2 8BS, United Kingdom

One Liberty Plaza, 20th Floor, New York, NY 10006, USA

477 Williamstown Road, Port Melbourne, VIC 3207, Australia

314–321, 3rd Floor, Plot 3, Splendor Forum, Jasola District Centre, New Delhi – 110025, India

79 Anson Road, #06–04/06, Singapore 079906

Cambridge University Press is part of the University of Cambridge.

It furthers the University's mission by disseminating knowledge in the pursuit of education, learning, and research at the highest international levels of excellence.

www.cambridge.org
Information on this title: www.cambridge.org/9781107150690
DOI: 10.1017/9781316584385



First published 2017

Printed in the United Kingdom by Clays, St Ives plc

*A catalogue record for this publication is available from the British Library.*

*Library of Congress Cataloging-in-Publication Data*
Names: Werhane, Patricia Hogue, editor. | Freeman, R. Edward, 1951- editor. | Dmytriyev, Sergiy, editor.
Title: Cambridge handbook of research approaches to business ethics and corporate responsibility / edited by Patricia H. Werhane, DePaul University, Chicago, University of Virginia, R. Edward Freeman, University of Virginia, Sergiy Dmytriyev, University of Virginia.
Description: New York : Cambridge University Press, 2017. | Includes bibliographical references and index.
Identifiers: LCCN 2017022844 | ISBN 9781107150690 (hardback)
Subjects: LCSH: Business ethics. | Social responsibility of business.
Classification: LCC HF5387 .C3343 2017 | DDC 174/.4–dc23 LC record available at https://lccn.loc.gov/2017022844

ISBN 978-1-107-15069-0 Hardback

# Contents

# Figures

# Tables

# Contributors

**Damian Bäumlisberger** is a doctoral student at the Institute of Economic Education at the University of Münster, Germany. He holds a bachelor's degree in Chinese Studies and Management from the University of Applied Sciences in Konstanz as well as a master's degree in Philosophy and Economics from the University of Bayreuth. In his research, he focuses on the economic and normative analysis of corporate social responsibility, especially on game-theoretic and Kantian analyses of public goods, norms, and governance structures.

**David Bevan**, PhD (King's College London) FHEA, has served the faculties of Schools of Management and Business Schools in the United Kingdom, France, Belgium, Hong Kong, and China, at which he has developed and taught courses in Business Ethics, Corporate Social Responsibility, and Sustainable Business Strategy. David's research interests focus on reconsiderations of his reading of Continental authors (Levinas, Derrida, Badiou, et al.). David and Patricia Werhane have co-authored twelve papers and chapters since 2006, and continue to collaborate.

**Helet Botha** is a doctoral candidate at the Darden School of Business, and a graduate student collaborator at Psychology at the University of Virginia since fall of 2016. She has been interested in ethics ever since teaching Behavioral Decision-Making at the University of Stellenbosch (2012–2014). Like most people, she has been doing experiments since she could crawl. Her scholarly research deals with when and how the individual experience of moral failure facilitates learning and growth. She studies moral failure in the context of organizational settings and interpersonal relationships.

**Norman E. Bowie** is Professor Emeritus at the University of Minnesota. He is perhaps best known for bringing the moral philosophy of Immanuel Kant to bear on issues in business ethics. He is co-editor of the text *Ethical Theory and Business*, now in its ninth edition. His most recent book is *Business Ethics: A Kantian Perspective 2nd Ed.* He is past president of the Society for Business Ethics and former Executive Secretary of the American Philosophical Association. In 2009, the Society for Business Ethics honored him with an award for lifetime scholarly achievement.

**Martin Calkins**, PhD, is Associate Professor at the College of Management of the University of Massachusetts Boston. He earned his PhD from the Colgate Darden Graduate School of Business Administration at the University of Virginia and holds MDiv and ThM degrees from the Weston School of Theology and an MIM degree from the American Graduate School of International Management (Thunderbird). He is also author of more than thirty publications, including two recent business ethics books: *King Car and the Ethics of Automobile Proponents' Strategies in China and India* (2011) and *Developing a Virtue-Imbued Casuistry for Business Ethics* (2014). His academic interests concern the application of the combined use of casuistry and virtue ethics to the resolution of tough business ethics problems.

**Angelo Carlo S. Carrascoso** is Associate Professor of Business Ethics and Director of the Banta Center for Business, Ethics, and Society at the University of Redlands. His research interests include the ethics of firm internationalization, stakeholder theory, and religion, and business ethics education. He received the School of Business and University Excellence in Teaching Awards in 2011 and 2013, respectively. In 2009, he obtained his PhD at the University of Virginia Darden School of Business.

**Wesley Cragg** is York University (Canada) Senior Scholar and Professor Emeritus in the Schulich School of Business and the Department of Philosophy. He is also Project Director and Principal Investigator for the Canadian Business Ethics Research Network (CBERN). Dr. Cragg has published widely on a variety of themes including: business ethics, human rights, environmental ethics, public policy, the extraction of natural resources, Aboriginal issues, the concept of Free, Prior, Informed Consent (FPIC), ethics codes, and social contract theory.

**Katherine (Katy) DeCelles** is Associate Professor of Organizational Behavior at the Rotman School of Management and cross-appointed to the Centre for Criminological Research at the University of Toronto. Katy's research focuses on the intersection of organizational behavior and criminology. She focuses on understanding the micromechanisms involved in topics such as prison work, power and selfishness, inequality, activism, and aggression.

**Richard T. De George**, Distinguished Professor Emeritus at the University of Kansas, is the author of over 200 articles and author or editor of twenty books, including *Business Ethics*, 7th ed. (2010), *Ethics of Information Technology and Business* (2003), and *Competing with Integrity in International Business* (1993). He is Past President of the American Philosophical Association; the International Society for Business, Economics and Ethics; the Society for Business Ethics; and the Metaphysical Society of America.

**Sergiy Dmytriyev** is pursuing a doctorate in Business Ethics at the University of Virginia Darden School of Business. His research interests include supererogation in organizations, stakeholder engagement and responsibility, company success, value from disagreements, and meaning in life. Prior to working at the Darden School, he worked for Procter & Gamble, Bain & Company, and Monsanto in Eastern Europe. As a management consultant at Bain, he conducted multiple projects on strategy development, transformation, and organization redesign for clients in the financial services, airline, oil and gas, FMCG, and real estate industries.

**Thomas Donaldson** is the Mark O. Winkelman Endowed Professor at the Wharton School of the University of Pennsylvania. He has served as Associate Editor for the *Academy of Management Review*, and currently serves as Associate Editor for the *Business Ethics Quarterly*. His writings have appeared in the *Academy of Management Review; Harvard Business Review; Economics and Philosophy*; and *Ethics*.

**R. Edward Freeman** is Elis and Signe Olsson Professor at the Darden School of Business, the University of Virginia, and Senior Fellow at the Olsson Center for Applied Ethics and Academic Director of the Institute for Business in Society. In March 2010, the University of Virginia Board of Visitors named Freeman as a University Professor. Freeman is the first faculty member in the Darden School's history given this rare honor, awarded to fewer than twenty professors among more than 2,200 at UVA. His latest books include, *Bridging the Values Gap* (2015) and *Stakeholder Theory: The State of the Art* (2010). Freeman may be best known for his award-winning book *Strategic Management: A Stakeholder Approach*, originally published in 1984 and reprinted in 2010 by Cambridge University Press. He is the author of more than 100 articles in a wide variety of publications. At its 2010 annual meeting, the Society for Business Ethics presented Professor Freeman with its "Outstanding Contributions to Scholarship Award" for his stakeholder theory work, to which there has currently been more than 50,000 citations. He also serves as co-editor in chief of the *Journal of Business Ethics*.

**Jean-Pascal Gond** is Professor of Corporate Social Responsibility at Cass Business School, City University of London (UK). His research mobilizes organization theory and economic sociology to investigate corporate social responsibility (CSR). His research in economic sociology is concerned with the influence of theory on managerial practice (performativity), the governance of self-regulation, and the interplay of society's commodification and markets' socialization. He has published in academic journals such as *Business and Society, Business Ethics Quarterly, Economy and Society, Journal of Management, Journal of Management Studies, Organization, Organization Science*, and *Organization Studies* and French journals such as *Finance Contrôle Stratégie*.

**Edwin M. Hartman** taught at the Stern School of New York University, the business school and the philosophy department at Rutgers, and the philosophy department at the University of Pennsylvania. He was also a management consultant. He has authored many articles and four books. The latest, *Virtue in Business: Conversations with Aristotle*, was published in 2013 by Cambridge University Press. In 2015 he received a lifetime achievement award for scholarship from the Society for Business Ethics.

**Anna Heikkinen** holds a PhD in Management and Organizations from the University of Tampere where she is currently working as a postdoctoral researcher. Her research areas include corporate sustainability and climate change engagement, stakeholder theory, and discourse analysis. She has published, e.g., in the *Journal of Business Ethics* and *the Business Communication Quarterly*.

**Kathleen M. Higgins** is Professor of Philosophy at the University of Texas at Austin. She is author of seven books (three of them co-authored with Robert C. Solomon), including one on music in relation to ethics. She is also editor or co-editor of numerous other books on such topics as ethics, world philosophy, German idealism, Nietzsche, aesthetics, philosophy of music, and love.

**Sarah M. Jastram** is Professor of International Business Ethics and Sustainability at Hamburg School of Business Administration (HSBA) in Germany. Before joining HSBA, she worked as a postdoctoral research fellow at Humboldt University in Berlin. Her research and her teaching are focusing on Sustainable Leadership, Strategic Corporate Social Responsibility, Private Governance, and Ethical Fashion. She has been published in leading international journals such as the *Journal of Business Ethics*.

**Tae Wan Kim** is Assistant Professor of Business Ethics in the Tepper School of Business at Carnegie Mellon University. He earned his PhD in Business Ethics at the Ethics and Legal Studies Doctoral Program of the University of Pennsylvania in 2012. He has published in *Business Ethics Quarterly, Journal of Business Ethics, Ethics & Information Technology*, and *Academy of Management Learning & Education*.

**Johanna Kujala** is Professor of Management and Organization and a Docent of Business Administration at the University of Tampere, Finland. She is the author or co-author of more than thirty scholarly articles or book chapters in international peer-reviewed publications, and serves as an editorial board member of the *Journal of Business Ethics* and the *Business Ethics: A European Review*. Her current research interests focus on stakeholder value creation, moral decision-making, and case studies on corporate responsibility.

**Matias Laine** works as Senior Researcher at the University of Tampere. In his research, he seeks to understand the role of corporate sustainability accounting and reporting in societies' struggle with the escalating global environmental challenges. Dr. Laine's prior work has been published in various scholarly journals, including *Accounting, Auditing and Accountability Journal, Accounting, Organizations and Society, Critical Perspectives on Accounting, and European Accounting Review*.

**Marion Ligonie** is Assistant Professor in Management Control at IÉSEG School of Management (Paris) where she is involved in the IÉSEG Centre for Organisational Responsibility. Her research projects explore corporate social responsibility (CSR) through practice-based perspectives, with a particular focus on the interactions between CSR and management control. Her doctoral work, defended in 2016, studied CSR practices in a gambling company. Another ongoing research project empirically examines the recent development of CSR in the French healthcare system.

**Irina Lock** is Assistant Professor of Corporate Communication at the University of Amsterdam, the Netherlands. Her research interest is in corporate social responsibility (CSR) communication, digital corporate communication, and public affairs.

**Thomas Maak** is Head School of Management and Chair in Responsible Leadership at the University of South Australia (UniSA). Prior to joining UniSA he was a professor at ESADE Business School, a faculty member at the University of St. Gallen, as well as a visiting professor at The Wharton School, University of Pennsylvania. He is President of ISBEE, the International Society of Business, Economics, and Ethics. His research interests include human dignity, the neuroscience of responsible leadership, and political corporate social responsibility (CSR).

**Hannele Mäkelä** holds a PhD in Accounting from University of Tampere where she currently works as a senior lecturer. Her research interests include social and environmental accounting and reporting as well as accounting for values-based organizations. Her research and publications are primarily in the areas of critical accounting and sustainability accounting studies, examining the relationships between accounting and society, and drawing on literatures from accountability, sustainability, ethics, and critical studies on corporate responsibility.

**Mollie Painter-Morland** is Professor of Ethics and Organization at Nottingham Business School, where she leads the Responsible and Sustainable Business Lab. She is also the part-time Coca-Cola Chair of Sustainability at IEDC-Bled School of Management Postgraduate Studies in Slovenia. She has been active in the business and professional ethics field since 2001, playing leadership roles in various business ethics and sustainability centers and NGOs in South Africa, the United States, Belgium, Slovenia, and the United Kingdom. She is also the Africa Director of the Academy of Business in Society (ABIS), leading a project on Leadership Development for Responsible and Sustainable Business in Africa. She has published multiple research papers in highly ranked journals on business ethics, leadership, accountability, and responsible management education. She is the author or co-editor of five books, amongst which *Business Ethics and Continental Philosophy*, with Rene Ten Bos (2011).

**Bidhan L. Parmar** is Associate Professor at the Darden School of Business, University of Virginia. Parmar's research interests focus on how managers make decisions and collaborate in uncertain and changing environments to create value for stakeholders. His work helps executives better handle ambiguity in their decision making. Parmar is a fellow at the Institute for Business in Society, Olsson Center for Applied Ethics, and the Safra Center for Ethics at Harvard University. Prior to teaching at Darden, Parmar taught at the UVA McIntire School of Commerce.

**Robert Phillips** is David Meade White, Jr. Chair in Business and Professor of Management at the University of Richmond's Robins School of Business and has a joint appointment with the program in Philosophy, Politics, Economics, and Law (PPEL). His work has appeared in *Business Ethics Quarterly, Strategic Management Journal*, and *Academy of Management Review*, among others. He is author of *Stakeholder Theory and Organizational Ethics* (2003).

**John J. Pirri**, PhD, is Senior Lecturer at Webster University Geneva, where he teaches courses in Ethics, Human Rights, and Genocide. Pirri has been Chairman of the Humanities Department at Lebanese American University, Beirut, and Dean for Academic Affairs and Acting President at the American College of Switzerland. He is considered a master teacher and has won teaching awards at the American College, Lebanese American University, and Webster.

**Nicola M. Pless** is Chair in Positive Business and Professor of Management at University of South Australia School of Business, Adjunct Professor at the University of St. Gallen, and holds the 2011 Honorary Jef Van Gerwen Chair from the University of Antwerp for her work in the field of Responsible Leadership. Her research interests include responsible leadership and decision making, relational intelligence, mindfulness, and neuroscience. She is the recipient of the Aspen Faculty Pioneer award for teaching innovation and excellence.

**Filomena Sabatella** is a PhD candidate in Organization Studies and Cultural Theory at the University of St. Gallen and a Research Associate at the Zurich University of Applied Science. She received her BSc and MSc in Psychology from the University of Zurich. Her research focuses on neuroscience, ethical decision making, empathy, and mindfulness. Her current teaching includes Biopsychology and Neuroscience Methods.

**Peter Seele** is Associate Professor of Corporate Social Responsibility and Business Ethics at USI Lugano, Switzerland. He has raised research funds in business ethics covering more than 1 million CHF and his thoughts are published in Metaphilosophy, Journal of Business Ethics, Nature, among others. His research focuses on business ethics as a discipline, CSR reporting, Greenwashing and XBRL.

**Scott Sonenshein** is Henry Gardiner Symonds Professor of Management at the Jones Graduate School of Business at Rice University. He received his PhD in Management and Organizations from the University of Michigan. His research employs field methodologies (primarily involving qualitative data) to explain the resourceful actions of employees in the context of organizational and social/ethical change.

**Patricia H. Werhane** is Wicklander Chair Emerita at DePaul University and Ruffin Professor Emerita at the University of Virginia. Werhane is founding editor of *Business Ethics Quarterly*, a Rockefeller Fellow at Dartmouth, Visiting Professor at the University of Cambridge, and Erskine Visiting Fellow at the University of Canterbury. In 2008, she was listed as one of the 100 most influential people in business ethics by *Ethisphere Magazine*. Professor Werhane is the author or editor of over twenty-five books, including *Moral Imagination and Management Decision-Making*, and over 100 articles and book chapters. She is also the co-producer of an Emmy award-winning documentary series, *Big Questions*.

# Introduction

PATRICIA H. WERHANE, R. EDWARD FREEMAN, and SERGIY DMYTRIYEV

Over the last decades business ethics has established itself as a separate field of study for management and organization scholars. The emergence of academic societies, conferences, and journals focusing on business ethics has led to a drastic surge of scholarship on business ethics issues. The *Journal of Business Ethics* alone received over 2,300 submissions during the year of 2016 on a wide array of business ethics topics. It became a widespread norm to teach business ethics courses in business schools, and some universities started creating dedicated positions for business ethics professors and doctoral students.

While the scholarship on business ethics issues has been growing in number and scope, the discipline of business ethics does not seem to have a clearly formulated set of research approaches that serve its specific needs and purposes. Young scholars, as well as many established ones, when deciding to explore research questions in business ethics, struggle to find what research approaches are available to them in the field and have been often left with no other option but to turn their heads toward other disciplines for finding appropriate research approaches for their projects in business ethics.

For quite some time, the discipline of business ethics has been borrowing research methods from other fields such as philosophy, sociology, economics, and psychology, depending on an academic background the scholar was trained in. Business ethics professors, when teaching their graduate students about research approaches in business ethics, mostly describe their own research methods, while a holistic picture on the research approaches that are available to business ethicists is missing. The lack of clear understanding of their own set of research approaches puts business ethicists at a considerable disadvantage compared to other management and organization scholars who have a long tradition of their research tools and methods.

The book aims to demonstrate that business ethics as an academic field of inquiry has a vast repertoire of research approaches and methods tailored to the specifics of business ethics. This is a first book of its kind and we hope it can serve well to those scholars who are eager to explore research questions in business ethics but are not sure what research approach to apply. While it is possible to apply to business ethics the many research tools and methods used in other academic fields, the field of business ethics has its own peculiarities and it is important to take them into account.

The specifics of business ethics stem from the domain of morality. Unlike scholars in other management and organization disciplines, business ethicists commonly use philosophical and historical methods of inquiry when analyzing business ethics issues. More importantly, a large part of business ethicists' research may be devoted to the normative side of the question of interest that comes from the fact that ethics in business is rooted in philosophical moral theories that are predominantly normative.

Having said that, one of the issues that keeps cropping up is whether there is, or even should be, a research method, or a set of methods in business ethics. There are many extant methodologies including the perspectives of normative ethical approaches, descriptive approaches, behavioral approaches, qualitative and quantitative methodologies, historical perspectives, and case study approaches. Yet because the idea of research methodologies in business ethics is relatively underdefined and because social scientists in the field will have vastly different ideas about methodologies than will the philosophers and theologians, we shall think about this more cautiously as a question of "research *approaches*" that have a broader meaning. Still, within the burgeoning field of business ethics, this is a timely question.

We have collected papers from a wide variety of experts in the field of business ethics, broadly defined, to outline and analyze some of the various approaches to this field. Our goal is not to reach consensus about one approach. Rather, addressing the issue of how one thinks about research in business ethics will be useful in understanding which approach or approaches each of us engages in. For those just entering the field, these ideas present an informative set that should assist them in being clear and self-conscious about their own thinking.

All methodological approaches presented in this volume should be viewed on par with each other, that is their applicability and significance for the field of business ethics are equally prominent. It is the researcher who has the discretion and responsibility to masterfully apply an approach or a set of approaches to her research depending on the specifics of her area of interest. A method is only a tool and not an end in itself, and thus a researcher should pursue her research activities neither with the aim to prove that a particular method is in some way superior compared to the others nor to show off the brilliance of her methodological repertoire. It is too easy to fall victim to the compulsive obsession with the methodological rigor at the expense of the practical reality of the research being conducted. Such research, bred on methodolatry or idolization of methods (Rorty, 1999; Freeman, 2004) rather than on methodology which treats method as a mere tool, turns into an irrelevant display of researcher's cognitive capabilities in the pursuit of the rules of the game set forth by some top-tier academic journals.

In this volume, we aim to reflect the specifics of the business ethics research. Part I of the book is devoted to philosophical approaches of the business ethics scholarship and it consists of history-related thinking that stems from leveraging the legacy of philosophical thinking of the past (Chapters 1–3), and normative dimensions of scholarly inquiry such as a coherence approach and a universalist perspective (Chapters 4 and 5). Part II presents various empirical approaches to business ethics research, including qualitative research approaches (Chapters 6–9), quantitative and experimental research approaches (Chapters 10 and 11), contemporary research approaches (Chapters 12 and 13), and case-study research approaches (Chapters 14–16). The final section of the volume, Part III, provides a finishing touch to the topic of research approaches in business ethics by putting a researcher herself in the spotlight. This part helps a researcher understand her role in research by stressing how important it is for the researcher to be aware of social construction as background for research, to strive for research relevance to practice, to adhere to moral standards in research projects, and to be open to diverse cultural and philosophical perspectives from around the globe (Chapters 17–20). In what follows, we provide more detail as to what a reader can expect from each chapter and delineate how the overarching storyline progresses along the book.

Chapter 1 describes the use of historical figures as a research approach in business ethics. Patricia Werhane, Edward Freeman, and Sergiy Dmytriyev argue that though this method is rarely used in other business disciplines, the use of historical figures has been quite common for the business ethics scholarship from the very inception of the field. Under this research framework, business ethicists analyze the works of great thinkers of the past, often economists or moral philosophers, to find out how the ideas of those historical figures could inform the contemporary research on business ethics issues. The value of using historical figures as a research approach is not as much in referencing historical figures to increase the credibility of researchers' own argumentation, but in holistically comprehending, reconstructing, and applying historical figures' concepts, ideas, and logic from the past to the present challenges. The authors lay down the sequence of steps to be taken within this research approach and demonstrate how to apply it in practice by analyzing how the ideas of John Locke's theory of human rights, Adam Smith's labor theory of value and defense of free enterprise, Karl Marx's labor theory and his critique of capitalism, and John Dewey's meliorism helped advance the contemporary research in business ethics.

Continuing with a historical perspective in research, Chapter 2 outlines history as methodology in business ethics. Here, Edwin Hartman argues that ethics cannot be treated the same way as science, since moral domain cannot provide the same level of precision in measurement and universality in appliance. The histories of ethics and science have different importance for the contemporary knowledge in the respective fields and, differently from science, business ethics can be much better understood by studying the history of ethics. The historical studies show that business ethics is not a matter of simply applying ethical principles to business situations, rather the field often requires a more sophisticated approach. To support his points, Hartman goes back in history to draw from Aristotelian virtue ethics and demonstrates that virtue ethics, though often undeservedly neglected in modern morality, offers much to inform contemporary scholarship on business ethics.

Another approach to business ethics research that builds on historic traditions is the application of the continental philosophy ideas toward present day research questions. In Chapter 3, Mollie Painter Morland explains the distinction between analytic philosophy and continental philosophy and argues that so far, the field of business ethics has been grounded more in analytic philosophy and as such it has largely neglected many important insights from continental philosophy. The author provides an overview of continental philosophy's contributions to contemporary knowledge and shows how it could benefit business ethicists. For instance, continental philosophy can contest many scientific assumptions and instrumentalist reasoning, challenge the positivists' preoccupation with measurements, and provide support to research that stems from practice. The chapter ends with demonstrating how continental philosophy contributes to one of the important topics on the contemporary research agenda such as exploring process, or process-related "becoming," rather than entities in organization studies.

Chapter 4 examines the applications of coherence as a normative research approach in business ethics. Richard De George shows how the use of coherence (internal — within the domain of ethical discourse — and external — with respect to accepted natural and social facts) can be used to discover ethical issues in business, arrive at considered ethical judgments, and test the validity of the obtained results. Although coherence is compatible with using a single ethical theory, he argues for ethical pluralism or using the best from a variety of ethical theories, as the problem, case, or issue requires, and he claims that this combination reflects the way people intuitively make ethical judgments both within and outside of business. Throughout the chapter, the author draws the readers' attention to the instances of when and how the notion of coherence can be applied in their scholarship, and very helpfully uses his own academic works as examples of applying coherence in business ethics research.

Chapter 5 continues to explore normative business ethics; however, differently from the previous chapter that focused on coherence, Norman Bowie analyzes normative business ethics by using the universalist approach. By examining what normative ethics is and what challenges it faces from behavioral ethics, the author argues in favor of using the Kantian approach to normative business ethics and examines in detail the three formulations of Kant's categorical imperative which can be used as research tools in business ethics: the universalizability formulation, the respect for persons formulation, and the kingdom of ends formulation.

Though Chapter 6 continues in the path of exploring normative aspects of business ethics, it marks a transition of the book's focus from philosophical-conceptual research approaches to those that are oriented toward empirical research. Sarah Jastram and Damian Bäumlisberger take the challenge of operationalizing universal normative ethical principles into the practical world of organizations, develop the method of normative assessment, and show the process for applying it in practice. The authors demonstrate that deriving practical indicators, both achievable in reality and logically consistent with overarching abstract moral principles, can serve as a much-needed connection between normative ethics and its implementation in practice.

Chapter 7 analyzes the use of descriptive ethics which lies between normative and empirical domains of research and whose findings contribute to both domains of scholarship and, thus, similarly to the previous chapter, serves as a bridge between them. Wesley Cragg argues that human behavior cannot be explained merely by social science or simply by normative power of values, and we need descriptive ethics to help us understand and interpret organizational phenomena. By conducting four on-ground studies of Canadian resource-based companies, the author, relying on descriptive ethics methodology, examined how different values guide people's decisions at work and analyzed the role of values in causing and solving conflicts among stakeholders.

Bearing some features of descriptive research discussed in the previous chapter, Chapter 8 reviews in detail what it means to do research by using grounded theory. David Bevan and Angelo Carlo Carrascoso show how grounded theory, being an inductive qualitative research approach, can be applied to both qualitative and quantitative data to yield a conceptual core category. They then outline practical steps for its application in business ethics scholarship. To better illustrate the application of grounded theory in practice, the authors provide many exemplary studies from management as well as from their own scholarship in business ethics that feature grounded theory as a research method.

The analysis of qualitative research methods in business ethics continues in Chapter 9. This chapter provides a comprehensive overview of the research process in discursive studies and describes how to use discourse analysis for different datasets. Anna Heikkinen, Johanna Kujala, Matias Laine, and Hannele Mäkelä argue that the analysis of discourses provides a powerful tool for studying phenomena in organizations as it can help explain how a set of ideas produces meanings that lead to a better understanding how people act. The authors provide practical insights on applying the discursive approaches in empirical studies; this is complemented with examples from management scholarship to demonstrate how discourse analysis can be applied in business ethics and corporate responsibility thinking.

Chapter 10 continues reviewing the use of the analysis of textual and graphical evidence in scholarly research, but considers its application not in qualitative studies as it was discussed in the previous chapter, but rather from a quantitative research perspective. Emphasizing the importance of not restraining business ethics scholarship only to conceptual and qualitative studies, Irina Lock and Peter Seele elaborate on how to apply quantitative content analysis in business ethics by building on the best research practices in communication sciences, given that the scope of research interests in both fields often overlap. The authors review different approaches to coding – human vs. software – and analyze available coding tools for business ethics and corporate social responsibility (CSR) such as codebooks and software applications, as well as provide visual illustrations of software outputs.

Chapter 11 gives a detailed account of one of the fast-growing methods in the field – experiments in business ethics. Helet Botha analyzes the extent to which experimental methods have been used in business ethics up to now, and discusses the relevance of using experiments in the field. The author explains when and how experiments can be of help to business ethicists in addressing their research questions and describes the key features of properly conducted experiments: hypothesis generation, treatment conditions, statistical analysis, and the assimilation of the outcomes that may or may not lead to the generation of new hypothesis. To illustrate said experimental features, Botha outlines studies that have made exemplary use of experimental methods. Since the design of the experiments is the critical component in experimental research method, the author, aiming to facilitate the design of high quality experiments, provides a list of questions that a business ethicist needs to answer to evaluate the validity of the results.

Chapter 12 steers the book's focus from traditional research to more contemporary approaches. Scott Sonenshein and Katherine DeCelles provide an overview of the most common research methods used in empirical studies on ethical issues – such as experiments discussed in the previous chapter, as well as ethnography and surveys – and argue that each of these methods, if used separately, has limitations that may undermine generalizability and interpretation of the study results. To address these limitations, the authors offer a quasi-full-cycle research approach to exploring business ethics questions whose application presupposes the use of multiple methodologies toward analyzing the same phenomenon. As a result, applying the combination of mixed methods toward the phenomenon of interest, where the sequence of collecting and analyzing quantitative and qualitative data may vary, can help achieve both external and internal validity of the findings. Despite indisputable scientific advantages in using the quasi-full-cycle approach to research, there are several unnecessary barriers that prevent business ethicists from using it, and this resonates with the problems in academic research raised in Chapter 18 on a pragmatist approach to business ethics.

As a part of the section on contemporary research methods, Chapter 13 reviews the advancements in neuroscientific research tools, such as fMRI and EEG, which have been widely used in neuroscience to explore neuronal activity of the human brain. Filomena Sabatella, Nicola Pless, and Thomas Maak demonstrate how neuroimaging technologies can be incorporated in business ethics scholarship and argue for applying neuroscience to business ethics. Paying a proper attention to the advantages, disadvantages, and concerns of applying neuroscientific tools in research, the authors show how neuroscience can be of help to business ethicists, especially in exploring the role of emotions and reasoning in ethical decision making. As an example of applying neuroscientific methods in business ethics scholarship, the authors examine how the concept of mindfulness can affect managerial decision making through the mechanism of reperceiving, considering both cognitive and emotional processes in individuals.

Chapter 14 opens the section devoted to case-based research approaches to business ethics. Here, Patricia Werhane analyses the use of wide reflective equilibrium (WRE) in scholarship and argues that exploring multiple cases in business ethics can link theory and practice, enrich our understanding of the ethical problems, advance our understanding beyond major moral theories, and help set tentative conclusions for evaluating reoccurring analogous cases. The author provides an overview of how WRE was developed and uses several real-life cases to better illustrate how WRE can contribute to business ethics scholarship.

Another case-based approach to business ethics research is casuistry which is the focus of Chapter 15. A casuistic approach derives guiding ideas for current research by analyzing previous successfully resolved ethical cases. Demystifying the dubious reputation of casuistry from the past for its lax reasoning, sophistry, and equivocation, Martin Calkins demonstrates that casuistry can help define and understand different aspects of moral sentiments and argumentation, and formulate defensible moral judgments in scholars' own research. The author explains the differences between casuistry and related approaches to research such as reflective equilibrium, applied principles, and the business case method; and argues that casuistry works best if it is paired with virtue ethics, and this tandem – virtue-imbued casuistry – creates an effective tool for moral deliberation in research.

The section on case-based approaches to research ends with Chapter 16 that describes how actor-network analysis can be helpful for scholarly work in business ethics, and for studying CSR in particular. Jean-Pascal Gond and Marion Ligonie show that actor-network theory (ANT) can explain how the diverse network actors get to work and continue working together, what actors' connections are, and how actors' activities affect networks. The most common use of ANT is found in empirical research through case studies where researchers analyze organizational networks and their actors' behavior based on the three key assumptions: the assembling of actor-networks, materiality, and performativity. The authors discuss methodological implications of using ANT assumptions to study CSR, provide several exemplary studies that used ANT to advance CSR scholarship, and elaborate on what ANT can offer for scholars' future research in CSR.

Chapter 17 marks an important transition of the book storyline: after offering a review of different research approaches, we would like to turn readers' attention to the role of a researcher in research projects. John Pirri and Patricia Werhane emphasize that it is essential to acknowledge that social construction is a part of business ethics scholarship. The authors argue that when we embark on our research projects in business ethics, we already have established mindsets and mental models that frame our thinking. These are socially created, which inadvertently leaves an imprint on our research design and the analysis of its outcomes. Oftentimes we are driven in our research by the dominant societal logics and we may not be aware of our blind spots that prevent us from discerning important, conspicuous, and yetoften-missed insights in our analysis. Recognizing the very fact that blind spots are present in business ethics studies is the first step that helps us pay more attention to the need to overcome these spots; and moral imagination can be one of the effective tools in this process.

Another important decision that researchers need to consider in their business ethics scholarship is the relevance of their work to practice, and this topic is the focus of Chapter 18. Building on the ideas of the philosophical school of pragmatism, Bidhan Parmar, Robert Phillips, and Edward Freeman argue that theories should stem from experience, that most dichotomies are artificial, and that the language we use to frame problems matters. The authors criticize research that has little relevance to practice and argue that theories should be actionable tools that could help make the world a better place for all of us. Applying the ideas of pragmatism in business ethics means that researchers should care and be able to show how their theoretical and empirical contributions can make a real difference to practice.

Continuing with the focus on the role of a researcher in business ethics scholarship, Chapter 19 challenges positivists' belief in the separation of values from research. Based on their analysis of academic papers in management, Tae Wan Kim and Thomas Donaldson argue that moral epistemology oriented toward objectivity-seeking research can positively contribute to management scholarship. The authors demonstrate that providing room for moral standards in scholarship can guide the practice of research (e.g., ethical norms on data gathering, experimentation, and research quality and meaningfulness in business ethics), provide clues for empirical hypothesis (e.g., corporate or stakeholder responsibility in business ethics), and add prescriptive power to empirical theories (e.g. "objective" or normative aspects of business ethics).

Finally, in the last chapter in Part III, we turn to the work of Kathleen Higgins, who challenges researchers as well as managers to think differently about commerce, particularly in nonwestern contexts such as China. The author walks us through a Chinese traditionalist Daoist perspective on business and business relationships, an approach that is prevalent in the mindsets, if not explicitly, of most Chinese managers and executives. The idea of "negative capability" challenges managers to truly think "out of the box" into the mind sets of the strangers with whom they interact rather than impose our own ways of doing business unilaterally in all global commerce. "Guanxi," a term which many of us are familiar with, is important for us in the West to understand, not as providing an excuse for bribery, but as an indicator that positive interpersonal and family relationships ground much of the Chinese way of business. A Daoist approach also questions what Higgins finds to be a Western habit of thinking in binary either-or terms, since it invites researchers and managers to imagine new possibilities that had not been considered initially.

We are far from claiming that this volume presents an exhaustive list of research methods available for business ethics scholarship. Yet the twenty chapters covered in the book can provide the core arsenal of research approaches to be applied by business ethicists in their research projects. Each of the chapters considers the specifics of business ethics research and provides examples of how a research method could be applied. This volume should help scholars appreciate a rather broad variety of research tools for exploring business ethics phenomena, enrich methodologically the breadth of their business ethics research and inspire more scholars to join the field.

Each chapter has been written by an expert in the respective area and we thank all the contributors to this volume for their understanding of the importance to methodologically expand the field of business ethics and for all their valuable efforts in this endeavor.

## References

Freeman, R. E. 2004. Book review essay: the relevance of Richard Rorty to management research. *Academy of Management Review*, 29(1): 127–144.

Rorty, R. 1999. *Philosophy and social hope*. London: Penguin.

PART I

# Philosophical Approaches

# Historical Approaches

CHAPTER 1

# The Use of Historical Figures as a Research Approach

PATRICIA H. WERHANE, R. EDWARD FREEMAN, and SERGIY DMYTRIYEV

It is for a certain reason that we start the book on research approaches in business ethics with the chapter on the use of historical figures. While business ethics may be regarded by many as a relatively new field of inquiry, the roots of contemporary thinking go well into the seventeenth century.[1] It is the great thinkers of the past who laid down the foundation for economic thoughts while all along speculating on the role of ethics in business; and it is the moral philosophers of the past whose ideas continue to be quite relevant for today's business practices. Indeed, the awareness of the invaluable heritage left for us by historical figures opens a horizon for multiple research possibilities in business ethics, and provides a specific framework, a research approach, for the business ethics scholarship. As an illustration of this research approach, this chapter attempts to cover the relevant works of John Locke, Adam Smith, Karl Marx, and John Dewey, though of course there are many other historical figures who could serve well for research projects in business ethics. Business ethics scholars of today regularly take to this methodological framework both to develop new full-scale theories and to analyze an array of pertinent business ethics concepts and phenomena. Thus, philosophical teachings of the past continue to inform the present-day scholarship of the field.

The use of historical figures as a research approach is typically not included in books on social research methodology. The inspection of about a dozen books on qualitative research methods in social sciences (Barbour, 2008; Roth, 2005; Ritchie & Lewis, 2003; May, 2002; Bernard, 2000; Silverman, 1997; Sarantakos, 1994) revealed that none of them described the methodological approach to research that we are going to cover in this chapter. Some social research books briefly touch upon the work with historical documentary data (Punch, 1998), culturally or historically significant phenomena (Ragin, 1994), or they briefly talk about historical-comparative methods (Luker, 2008). However, all these methodologies are different from the use of historical figures as a research approach whose variations might sometimes be included in business ethics textbooks (e.g., Donaldson & Werhane, 2008).

The use of historical figures method may share certain tools and logic building with other methodologies, nevertheless we see this way of doing research as a standalone approach with its unique research framework. The word "historical" in the research approach of using historical figures may suggest that it is a part of a historical field of research. However, this is misleading as the research method of using historical figures does not reside in the historical research domain. History looks at particular events in the past, and historical methodology focuses on the collection of evidence and on the communication of evidence (Shafer, 1980; Subrahmanian, 1980), and the goal of history is to present a body of established facts to understand what happened and why (Krentz, 2002). Differently from it, the research approach of using historical figures focuses more on influential, far-reaching ideas of great thinkers, though of course placed in a historical perspective, and the relevance of those ideas to the contemporary development of the field. As Luker (2008: 191) put it, "if you just wanted to tell a story, that is, craft a narrative of what happened, you would have found yourself

[1] However, historians can trace some business codes of ethics to the 1800 BC ruler, Hammurabi (see Carroll et al., 2012, chapter 1).

more drawn to history." Differently from historians, business ethicists who use historical figures in their research write not stories per se, but try to build theories and narratives that are applicable to the present-day business world.

It is in its attempt to generate theories that this historical figures approach is similar to historical-comparative methods used in social sciences. However, what makes this approach different from the set of historical-comparative methods is that the latter aim to attend to the two main questions – "either (a) what events in the past shaped how this turned out in the present? or (b) why did things turn out this way in one place and another way in another place?" (Luker, 2008: 191) – and try to find the causation effects to create explanations why particular things may also happen in other places and times. We are not arguing that doing real history is not important in business ethics. In fact, understanding the causes and effects of historical events in business is central to building narratives. For instance, the investigation into the Panic of 1837 and the consequent long-lasting economic recession in the United States can apply when analyzing the global financial crisis of 2007–2009. On the one hand, a research approach of using historical figures in business ethics may draw on particular events in the past and analyze the elements of causation; on the other hand, this research framework also goes beyond explaining the causal links between ethics and business, and often centers around normative aspects of business ethics by grounding itself in the logic of argumentation.

Logical argumentation in developing one's points of view and the room for encompassing normative aspects make the research approach of using historical figures in business ethics similar to philosophical inquiry. In other words, though the use of historical figures as a research approach in business ethics has some similarities with the historical research methodology and with the historical-comparative methods of research used in social sciences, it is the philosophical methodology where it primarily belongs to due to the similarity of some key tools (e.g., philosophical inquiry and logical argumentation), the ability to go beyond empirical causal links, and openness for normative aspects. Yet, unlike pure philosophical inquiry, the use of historical figures as a research approach is more oriented to practical applications, such as the role of business ethics in business. Moreover, in normative business ethics the use of historical figures is often utilized to give substantive and substantiated grounds for a point of argumentation or justification, say, for the rights theory or (Smith's) free enterprise (see Bowie's Chapter 5 on Kant as an example).

## Specifics of Applying the Historical Figures Research Method

Business ethicists using historical figures as a research method typically derive their research questions or find support for their arguments from one of the two sources. First, scholars in business ethics analyze the works of great economic thinkers who laid down the foundations for the contemporary economic system and try to find their perspective on ethical aspects of doing business as "many of these economists were moral philosophers (and vice versa)" (Wicks, 1995: 603). It is often the case that the academic proponents of "cowboy capitalism" draw on particular parts of economic works of historical figures but miss, unintentionally or not, on the bigger context which provided the grounding and general moral directions for these very works. Torn out of context, these works breed a litany of academic misinterpretations and misunderstandings. For example, Werhane (1991) compellingly showed that Adam Smith's views on economic systems, with the emphasis on egoism and greed, were often misinterpreted. Rather, Smith's widely read *The Wealth of Nations* should be viewed together with his *Theory of Moral Sentiments*, as the latter clearly points to the difference between individualism and egoism, as well as pinpoints the fact that competition takes place in the environment of mutual cooperation and coordination.

Secondly, business ethicists may draw on the ideas of moral philosophers who were not necessarily writing about business and economics, but whose ideas about morality in the society can be interpreted and analyzed to apply well to business. Edwin Hartman (2015; 1996) did an amazing job of bringing Aristotelean virtue ethics to business, as well as Norman Bowie who applied Kantian moral theory to business settings (Bowie, 1999). No matter what particular source (economic or philosophical) business ethicists choose to consider, approaching business ethics research from a historical perspective and tracing its roots to the philosophical gurus of modern capitalism allows to strongly connect and ground the business ethics research in the work of some traditionally recognized, established philosophical figures and at the same time to critique those contemporary approaches to business ethics that have neglected some fundamentally important aspects of the discipline.

The research approach of using historical figures includes taking the contemporary theories in business ethics and juxtaposing them with the stream of thoughts of the great thinkers of the past. What would Adam Smith say about stakeholder theory? How would Karl Marx react to the call to create a new story of business different from "cowboy capitalism" and instead focused on the joint value creation – will the new story of business resolve many of Marx's concerns? Would John Dewey see the importance of moral imagination in business settings the same way business ethics scholars see it today?

One way to see the methodological approach of using historical figures is through the search for the answers to the sequence of questions which taken together lead to a new perspective on a particular issue:

1. What is the problem in issue X that is at stake?
2. How would particular historical figures A and B have seen this issue X given their established viewpoints on a variety of issues? How appealing would their arguments be in strengthening one's contemporary justification for addressing X?
3. What is the context (historical, political, philosophical) of their views?
4. What are the insights that we can gain from A and B on X? How would they differ?
5. What are the limitations of A and B's views?

Another way to apply the research approach discussed in this chapter is to consolidate the thoughts of a historical figure on the topic of interest. Most great thinkers were prolific writers who often touched upon a multitude of topics briefly across multiple works, here and there, again and again. Thus, great research opportunity opens up for any scholar willing to go through many works of a particular historical figure, seeking and consolidating his or her thoughts pertinent to a particular topic while at the same time adding one's own interpretation and triangulation where different pieces do not fully fit together: reconstructing as if from puzzle pieces one holistic view of that historical figure on this or that topic. Gregory Fernando Pappas's work *John Dewey's Ethics* (2008) is one of the recent thoroughgoing research projects written in this way. In his work, Pappas provided a comprehensive overview of Dewey's thoughts on moral experience that came as a result of Pappas's analysis of Dewey's numerous works, including *Democracy and Education (1916), Reconstruction in Philosophy (1920), Human Nature and Conduct (1922), Three Independent Factors in Morals (1930)*, and *Ethics (1932)*. Another example of a strong and successful application of this method would be McVea's work (2007) in which he relied on Dewey's philosophy to pave the way for bridging business ethics and American pragmatism.

Contemporary forms of business ethics are grounded in the free enterprise system (or in some cases, opposition to elements of that system), so referring back to historical figures sheds light on the understanding of many challenges we face today. In this chapter, we take four great thinkers from the past – John Locke, Adam Smith, Karl Marx, and John Dewey – and show how using historical figures can serve well for the research agenda of business ethics scholarship. We trace the beginnings of the free enterprise system from John Locke's defense of human rights and property rights, through Adam Smith's analysis of the importance of industrialization and free markets to economic growth, and Marx's idea of the alienation of labor, the precursor of employee rights, and the critique of slave and child labor. We end with John Dewey's pragmatic approach to moral judgment and decision making.

## The Importance of John Locke for Business Ethics

Much of the contemporary literature in business ethics is built on rights talk. We begin, then, by going back to the seventeenth-century philosopher, John Locke, because it is Locke who developed the notion of what he called "natural" rights and that included rights to liberty, to work, to be remunerated for one's work, and the right to privately owned property, cornerstones of any free enterprise system. In brief, in his well-known book, *Two Treatises on Government*, and in particular, *The Second Treatise*, Locke proposes what is today a very basic and standardly accepted view of human rights. Locke argues that because we are human beings, which, he assumes, is a unique and superior species (although Locke predates studies of species), human beings have basic rights. He calls these "natural rights," because he was convinced that these rights are innate – part of who we are as human being, and God-given. Today, because of various religious complications with the term "natural rights," we call these human rights or, better, "moral rights," more secular terms. Moral rights are rights all human beings should have, as human beings, but rights that are not always recognized, operationalized, or defended.

However one names them, as Locke argues and rights theorists continue to argue, rights are those claims to which all humans have, inalienably, and equally, even if and when they are not acknowledged and violated. According to Locke, because we are born as human beings, we have, equally, all of us, the right to life. Because of that right, we have rights to survival. Additionally, as human beings, we are each unique individuals and thus have the right to liberty. That much seems natural today but it was not obvious at that time. Locke argues further that the rights to survival and liberty entail the right to work, and work, in turn, because it belongs to the worker, should be remunerated. He calls this archaically, receiving the "fruits of one's labor." Today we call that getting paid, and paid fairly, for one's contributions. From this position, Locke then argues that one has rights to property one improves with one's labor (the "fruits"). Note that in Locke's day there was a great deal of unowned property, particularly in "America," the underexplored and vast new continent where one could develop unowned property to one's advantage. As ownership expands and as we develop political economies to protect our rights including property rights (Locke proposed forms of legislative democracy), property ownership expands beyond what is merely improved through one's own labor, trade develops, and money becomes a means to trade and to pay workers.

It is from Locke that we appeal for the justification of free enterprise and private property, principles that are essential for capitalism. This too seems obvious, but its grounding in basic rights gives credence to free enterprise, a system often challenged by questioning the normative viability of property ownership, particularly as it has developed and expanded to large corporate and institutional holdings.

Locke also realized that the gain of property, even through one's own labor, has limits and there should be enough good quality property left for others. In Locke's words, "for this labour being the unquestionable property of the labourer, no man but he can have a right to what that is once joined to, at least where there is enough, and as good, left in common for others" (Locke, 1980/1690: 19). Later Nozick referred to this as 'Lockean proviso' (1974) and went on to set it as a criterion to determine whether some particular property acquisition could be judged as just or not.

Locke's thinking is important for a number of reasons. Not only is it the basis for the continuing arguments defending the liberty of each individual and basic rights to property, it is also used against slavery. Locke's thinking is the basis for what today is a plethora of rights declarations including the United Nations *Universal Declaration of Human Rights*, which includes worker rights, and the 2000 the United Nations Global Compact, specifically aimed at global interactions, including those of commerce. More recently, in 2011, United Nations developed the *Guiding Principles on Business and Human Rights*, often referred to as the Ruggie Principles, for its principal author, a set of principles that argues that corporations have specific obligations to respect human rights throughout their fields of operation. All of these proposals, each of which is voluntary with no specific sanctions, come out of Locke's original theory. Thus standards for global corporations and international trade evolve from Locke's original theories.

Given the importance of Locke's ideas to business ethics, a number of management scholars continue to build on his ideas in their research. Hartman (1996: 70) mentions that "Locke is the most famous of many who have argued that there is a kind of contract between the individual and his or her community and that this contract provides the basis for individuals' rights and obligations with respect to one another." Locke, along with other historical figures such as Plato, Hobbes, and Rousseau, as cursorily admitted by Donaldson and Dunfee (1994: 259), provided "the methodology of social contract" used by them for creating integrative social contract theory. Similar historical figures – Hobbes, Locke, and Rousseau – were considered by Hsieh (2016: 437) when analyzing the origins of "traditional" social contract theory in comparison to "contemporary (as opposed to traditional) applications of social contract theory" in business ethics. Solomon and Higgins (1996: 199) summarized that "[a] number of philosophers, not only Locke but Hobbes and later Hume, Rousseau and Kant defended the conception of society as a 'social contract', further destroying traditional authority ... and supporting the new emphasis on individual will and self-rule."

Locke's contribution to the contemporary human rights and the concept of justice is widely acknowledged in business ethics (Shaw & Barry, 1998; Santoro, 2010). De George (1982) admitted that John Locke's theory on the natural rights had an impact on the American Founding Fathers, and private property became a cornerstone of capitalism. Locke's ideas influence business ethics scholarship directly or through the works of contemporary philosophers who based their theories on Lockean principles such as Robert Nozick in *Anarchy, State, and Utopia* (1974). Solomon (1993: 98), when analyzing "what a theory in business ethics is supposed to look like," proposed to design a course on business ethics where the concept of justice would be "a natural introductory section, and John Locke on natural property rights is an appropriate inclusion."

## The "Father" of Free Enterprise: Adam Smith

Adam Smith is an eighteenth-century Scottish moral philosopher, widely read not only in the philosophical circles, but also by political theorists, economists, and social scientists. Because of his widespread influence, particularly to contemporary economics, it is well worth considering his thinking and approach when doing research in business ethics. Smith wrote only two books, the *Theory of Moral Sentiments* (1767) and the *Wealth of Nations* (1776), and many would claim it is the latter that is important to economics and business ethics.

Smith comes out of a Scottish tradition that accepts Locke's theory of rights with one exception. Although adopting Locke's labor theory of value – that laboring creates value, and thus should be rewarded – Smith argues that property rights are not inalienable rights, but rather conventional rights that are defined differently in different societies. Thus accepting that each of us has property rights, what that means and how that is spelled out depend on the political economy in which each of us dwells. This point is important for contemporary research on transnational corporations, since such companies often operate in communities where the idea of property is different from a Western, post-Lockean view. Unless one understands these differences, serious negative consequences can preclude successful global development. For example, Shell's oil exploration in the Ogoni region of Nigeria failed to acknowledge ancient but unwritten tribal property rights, and initially Shell could not understand why the Ogoni were so against their oil development in that region.

The labor theory of value, initiated by Locke's theory of natural rights, is amplified by Smith. Smith locates economic growth through labor. He recognizes that because labor can create value, organizing and mechanizing labor (the thinking behind the industrial revolution) can create value for a community and thus wealth for a nation. Indeed, since the industrial revolution, of which Smith is the philosophical "father," economic growth in the now-industrialized world has

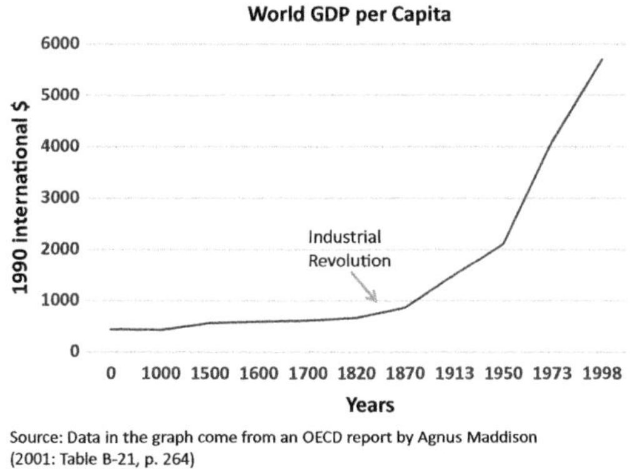


*Figure 1.1* Economic growth after industrialization.

increased exponentially since 1776. Industrialization can also free workers from serfdom when labor is paid a living wage and when laborers are allowed to choose and change jobs at will. It was Smith who recognized the importance of free and industrialized labor as the key factor in economic growth. Indeed, according to Deirdre McCloskey, and Smith would agree, without industrialization a society cannot provide enough jobs, goods, and services to reduce endemic poverty and achieve economic well-being for the majority of the population (McCloskey, 1985). Indeed, since the industrial revolution beginning in the late nineteenth century, economic growth in those countries who adapted this methodology has been and will continue to be exponential (see Figure 1.1). Going back to Smith for such grounding arguments is important, particularly as an antidote to those who question the capitalist system (Smith, 1776).

Smith himself never used the word "capitalism," and he has often been misidentified as a laissez-faire economist, what today we might label as libertarian capitalism. But that is a misreading of Smith. For Smith, free exchanges work best when they are restrained by parsimony (rather than greed), when these exchanges are conducted fairly, when basic rights and the rule of law are respected and enforced, and when money is used as investment to create more value, not as an end in itself. If money accumulation becomes an end in itself, economic growth will be stunted and the economy will atrophy. It is worth rereading Smith for these reasons alone, as we live in a society where value is often measured by money rather than wealth creation (Smith, 1776).

Interestingly, Smith is also the father of the Separation Thesis, the critique of dividing business from ethics. Smith was a philosopher and a political economist and he could not imagine dividing these subjects into separate categories in inquiry.

There is one other useful point to be gleaned from Smith, his notion of the self as he develops that idea in his earlier book, *The Theory of Moral Sentiments*. In analyzing the idea of the self in that text, Smith argues that we are not merely behavioral beings. Rather, as human beings, we are capable of making moral judgments, both about oneself and others, and thus creating moral change. Because a human being is a conscious being who is also conscious of oneself, we are able to mentally step back from ourselves and our social interactions, taking what Smith calls an "impartial spectator" perspective. No one can completely disengage nor ever be completely impartial, but we are able to step back from our social, political, or economic situation, obtain what Michael Walzer calls a "critical distance" (Walzer, 2002), and be self-critics, thus the source of conscience, and critics of others and their behavior. This phenomenon accounts for individual and social change (Smith, 1767). The idea is important in business ethics, because it accounts for the fact that companies can examine themselves, revise their mission, goals, and direction, and reinvent themselves. This is not to conclude that all companies do this, nor is it to recognize that sometimes these changes are disastrous. However, this idea is very useful in understanding corporate atrophy or change, and provides tools for those who imagine that such changes are not possible.

The impartial spectator is also the source of thinking of the business ethicist as a social critic. According to Scott Sonenshein, "organizational members can use principles of morality within their business communities to practice moral criticism. ISC [internal social criticism] emphasizes discussions among organizational members geared toward unearthing thick moral principles and any contradictions between those principles and practices" (Sonenshein, 2005: 476). Sonenshein gets this idea from a contemporary political philosopher, Michael Walzer, but it originates with Smith. This is because the ability to be a social critic both within an organization and as an outside business ethicist depends initially on one's ability to disengage, to get at a critical distance from the organization or political economy, that is, to engage oneself as an impartial spectator.

Among business ethicists who use historical figures as a research approach, Adam Smith is perhaps one of the most popular protagonists. The research on Adam Smith in business ethics has been actively growing over the last thirty years and by now there are at least several dozen studies in the area. Apart from Werhane's above-mentioned book, *Adam Smith and His Legacy for Modern Capitalism* (1991), and her previous works on Adam Smith, where the ideas of Adam Smith were thoroughly reinvestigated and applied to business ethics, there is a whole body of scholars who have explored Smith's ethical foundations for capitalist activities (Sen, 1987; Rothschild, 1992; Sen, 1993; Collins, 1994; James & Rassekh, 2000; Bragues, 2009; Wells & Graafland, 2012). Wilson (1989: 70) showed in his analysis of Smith's works that "Adam Smith provides us with a far richer and deeper assessment of the ethical aspects of capitalism than can be found in the writings of most present-day critics." He mentions that "the Adam Smith who invented capitalism, described the useful effects of the invisible hand, and showed how the free pursuit of self-interest would lead to greater prosperity than any system of state-controlled exchanges was also the Adam Smith who, more deeply than anyone since, has explored the sources and power of human sympathy and the relationship between sympathy and justice" (Wilson, 1989: 66).

Gonin (2015: 221) presented Smith's "integrative conception of business and its contributions to the development of integrative theories of organizations and of business-society relations in the twenty-first century" where, referring to Adam Smith, "the business enterprise [is] primarily … the endeavor of an individual who remains fully embedded in the broader society and subject to its moral demands." Huhn and Dierksmeier (2016: 119) conducted an extensive review of the secondary literature written on Adam Smith by economists, business ethicists, and philosophers and concluded that "Smith, far from being an advocate of a value-free or even value-averse conception of economic transactions, stood for a virtue-based and virtue-oriented model of business."

Overall, as long as we continue to explore the merits and drawbacks of our capitalistic society, we will inevitably continue to reinterpret Adam Smith.

## Why Study Karl Marx?

Often in business ethics one ignores the work of Karl Marx, who, after all, was the founder of communism, an anathema to capitalism. However, we suggest that Marx is important in business ethics research for a number of reasons. First, Marx agrees with Smith that to create economic growth, a society must industrialize. Without that development, nations will continue to be mired in agricultural abject poverty for most of its population. But capitalism, spawned by the industrial revolution, has serious downsides, particularly for the worker whom, Marx contends, is promised independence through being able to choose her job, get paid in money, and is free to quit at any time. In fact, Marx points out, with a plethora of labor, companies can with impunity offer low wages because they can replace any worker with another. Thus, workers are not paid fully for the value of their labor input, and in factories they become alienated or distanced from what they produce, since their input is measured quantitatively and as merely measurable input rather than as the contribution of a person. Workers become alienated from their work, which seems to be no longer theirs; they are underpaid, and it is difficult to change jobs. Thus, the industrial revolution, while necessary to create jobs and expand worker pay, is only a stepping stone to what he imagines as a fairly anarchical communism where workers own the means of production (Marx, 1844). While most of us will not buy into what he sees as an inevitable outcome of capitalism, historically, his critique of worker mistreatment and alienation has served as ongoing arguments in defense of worker rights. These arguments continue today, particularly in communities where there is virtually slave labor and/or where workers are not paid adequately for their contributions nor respected as human beings in the workplace.

Marx also worried that capitalism would evolve into economies that were focused on money as an end in itself rather than its value in creating wealth (see Marx, 1867, Part III). These arguments, later revitalized by thinkers such as Michael Walzer (1993), are invaluable both for questioning the worship of money and in helping us rethink the purpose of free enterprise, which was originally to create widespread economic well-being. Reading Marx does not entail buying into his systemic prognosis, but rather leads one to mine some of his particular arguments that are still relevant today.

Initially, as the field of business ethics was just emerging, some scholarly studies built around Marxism referenced the great philosopher to highlight what these scholars considered to be the cynicism of the business ethics world. For instance, Massay (1982) speculated on Marx's would-be response to the newly sprung phenomenon of business ethics. He argued that Marx would probably claim that business ethics was conceived by employers who, driven by declining profits and the desire to maintain legitimacy for capitalistic system, decided to "discipline individual members of the bourgeoisie so that they will refrain from pursuing their individual interests when these conflict with the interests of their class" (Massay, 1982: 301).

With further development of the field, Marxian philosophy served to explain important business ethics concepts. Corlett (1998), admitting that Marx does not provide sufficient reasons for building a comprehensive theory of business ethics, nevertheless underlined that Marxian philosophy could provide a number of important contributions to business ethics. As a starting point, it could serve to outline a more comprehensive description of capitalist political economies by admitting employee-related problems, e.g., their alienation and oppression, and struggles for power among business people. Further, it could help build better communities by analyzing "socio-economic and political power internal and external to business communities and devote attention to matters of justice (retributive and distributive) and fairness" (Corlett, 1998: 100) and help with fostering "the commitment to a community-oriented sense of moral and legal responsibility" (Corlett, 1998: 101). Along similar lines, Linz and Chu (2013) analyzed the relationship between work values and economic environment comparing Marxian views with those of Weber. Their empirical study showed that values are determined by the economic environment, thus reasserting the Marxian link between work values and economic environment (Linz & Chu, 2013: 444). De George (2006), in his critique of Rorty's views on philosophic contribution to business ethics, which also discussed the role of Marx, mentioned that "Marx got much of the problem right; he got the solution wrong . . . [t]hose in business ethics focus on business and see it not only as one of the causes of the ills that Marx described but as one of the key players in the amelioration of those ills" (De George, 2006: 389). Shaw (2009: 565) analyzed "some links, and some tensions, between business ethics and the traditional concerns of Marxism," attempting to explore whether Marx was right in his considerations that business ethics was an improbable entity in capitalistic environment due to its strong inclination to greed, and thus a tendency to produce unethical behavior. The examination of Marx's works and the contemporary development in the field of business ethics allowed Shaw to conclude that "far from being impossible, business requires and indeed presupposes ethics and that for those who share Marx's hope for a better society, nothing could be more relevant than engaging in the debate over corporate social responsibility" (Shaw, 2009: 565).

Overall, Marx-inspired research in the area of business ethics, to a large extent, tends to outline challenges within capitalism. Some business ethicists go beyond this stage and try to tap into Marxian philosophy to seek an array of potential solutions to meet these challenges. Yet, most management scholars, though agreeing with Marx's criticism of capitalism, do not offer or see any feasible alternative to the present capitalistic system. As Kerlin (1998) put it, while using the Marxism ideas to criticize capitalism, "the answer may be that no other economic system is viable at this moment in history" (Kerlin, 1998: 1717). Many Marx's tenets resonate well with business ethicists and have been widely adopted in the business ethics field, especially when it comes to the evaluation of the contemporary economic landscape. As Joanne Ciulla (2011: 338) said in her Presidential Address for the Society of Business Ethics, "you do not have to read Karl Marx to understand this problem," referring to the issue of work and wages, when some businesses may get advantage from the work of others by underpaying their employees.

## Dewey's Meliorism at the Heart of Business Ethics

John Dewey's contributions are well acknowledged in the areas of education and philosophy. However, in business and business ethics, Dewey remains largely unexplored, especially if compared to John Locke, Adam Smith, and Karl Marx. We believe that Dewey's philosophical pragmatism has much to add to the contemporary business ethics discussion.

Dewey argues that evaluating each situation through the prism of some selected single highest end meant to perfectly fit all human endeavor – be it self-realization, holiness, happiness, or something else – is misleading, if not to say counterproductive. The world is complex and multifaceted and there is no one unique panacea for the plethora of moral problems we encounter. Instead, there are multiple factors that require our consideration any time we face a morally puzzling situation. In Dewey's words:

> Morals is not a catalogue of acts nor a set of rules to be applied like drugstore prescriptions or cookbook recipes. (Dewey, 1920: 169)

> The blunt assertion that every moral situation is a unique situation having its own irreplaceable good may seem not merely blunt but preposterous. Let us, however, follow the pragmatic rule, and in order to discover the meaning of the idea ask for its consequences. Then it surprisingly turns out that the primary significance of the unique and morally ultimate character of the concrete situation is to transfer the weight and burden of morality to intelligence. It does not destroy responsibility; it only locates it. A moral situation is one in which judgement and choice are required antecedently to overt action. The practical meaning of the situation – that is to say the action needed to satisfy it – is not self-evident. It has to be searched for. There are conflicting desires and alternative apparent goods. What is needed is to find the right course of action, the right good. (Dewey, 1920: 163)

Where morality can help is with providing methods of inquiry which are to be used to identify issues specific to each situation and to create some working hypotheses to deal with those issues. This inquiry is based in intelligence and is coupled with moral traits such as "wide sympathy, keen sensitiveness, persistence in the face of the disagreeable, balance of interests enabling us to undertake the work of analysis and decision intelligently" (Dewey, 1920:164). We need to realize that each situation is unique and requires a more scrupulous attention to its context than just the mechanical appliance of generalized conceptions. Similarly, the abundance of ethical issues we observe in business settings deserve individualized attention. Each ethical problem has its specific individualized context, which we should attend to when developing our attitude to it.

Pappas, in his *John Dewey's Ethics* that analyzed and put together Dewey's thoughts on ethics from many of his writings, mentions that in Dewey's view, "[s]ituations in their qualitative immediacy and uniqueness are primary and prior to any distinction between subject and object" (Pappas, 2008: 86). When we talk about morality, "moral qualities and moral decisions are context-dependent and have their home and meaning in a particular situation" (Pappas, 2008: 85). A moral problem takes place when a person starts struggling with the situation as her previous experience does not help resolve the current problem in a proper way. When a moral problem occurs, "[t]he fluidity of everyday life is blocked and experienced as a unique ambiguity, confusion, disharmony, conflict, or pain that pervades one's situation" (Pappas, 2008: 90). It does not take much to realize when ethical issues are at the core of the problem as "insofar as a situation is experienced as morally problematic then it really is problematic" (Pappas, 2008: 91).

Dewey mentions that "inquiry, discovery take the same place in morals that they have come to occupy in sciences of nature." The problem is that "remote and abstract generalities promote jumping at conclusions" which may not reflect a situation adequately. According to Dewey, past decisions and old principles cannot be used to justify an action so "shifting the issue to analysis of a specific situation makes inquiry obligatory and alert observation of consequences imperative" (Dewey, 1920: 174). Pappas explains it in his analysis of Dewey's works that moral deliberation, involving analysis and synthesis, and moral imagination as a dramatic rehearsal are needed to resolve a morally puzzling situation:

> In any process of inquiry we can make a functional distinction between phases of doing and undergoing as well as phases of analysis and synthesis . . . Analysis is what we do when inquiry is centered on making some finer discrimination of the parts that make up our problematic situation. Synthesis takes place when we are concerned with weighing how the parts contribute to making an overall judgement . . . The final judgement about what we ought to do is a synthesis that results from the analysis of the situation as a whole, but it is only the final step in a series of tentative overall judgements that have occurred throughout the entire process of deliberation. (Pappas, 2008: 96)
>
> Reasoning provides us with the inferences needed to go beyond what we have, or it helps us elaborate our suppositions in light of other beliefs. Imagination in the form of a dramatic rehearsal helps us survey and test our options. (Pappas, 2008: 97)

Dewey argues that many moral problems arise because we treat worthy things as instrumental and not intrinsic. As he states, "every case where moral action is required becomes of equal moral importance and urgency with every other" (Dewey, 1920: 175). Extrapolating his example on health to business, if the need of a particular situation shows that some of the company employees require improvement of health, "then for that situation health is the ultimate and supreme good. It is no means to something else. It is a final and intrinsic value. The same thing is true of improvement of economic status, of making a living" (Dewey, 1920: 175).

For Dewey, the highest importance in morality is the direction along which a person is currently moving along, not the previous accumulation of good and bad deeds.

> The bad man is the man who no matter how good he has been is beginning to deteriorate, to grow less good. The good man is the man who no matter how morally unworthy he has been is moving to become better. Such a conception makes one severe in judging himself and humane in judging others. (Dewey, 1920: 176)

This sends two strong messages to contemporary corporations. First, no matter how good a particular company was in the past, it still has to keep up with ethically praiseworthy behavior, here and now. Second, even if a particular company was suspect in wrongdoing, there is still a chance to restore its reputation by wholeheartedly moving in a positive direction.

The ultimate aim, for Dewey, is not static, but about the growth per se toward a positive end. It is a never-ending progress without a limit, "it is the active process of transforming the existent situation. Not perfection as a final goal, but the ever-enduring process of perfecting, maturing, refining is the aim of living" (Dewey, 1920: 177). Business organizations should constantly strive to improve in all directions, as the "[g]rowth itself is the only moral 'end.'" Dewey was a strong proponent of meliorism, "the belief that the specific conditions which exist at one moment, be they comparatively bad or comparatively good, in any event may be bettered" (Dewey, 1920: 178).

Though not accepting utilitarianism in all its manifestations, Dewey appreciated that it "insisted upon getting away from vague generalities, and down to the specific and concrete" (Dewey, 1920: 180). Dewey combined meliorism and utilitarianism in a way that doing good should bring a pleasant experience, "goodness without happiness, valor and virtue without satisfaction, ends without conscious enjoyment – these things are as intolerable practically as they are self-contradictory in conception." Dewey rejected Kant's view of doing good as of a pure duty, and believed that it should be enjoyable by a doer. Yet, Dewey cautions us that meliorism should not be mixed with optimism which, in his view, is "the consequence of the attempt to explain evil away." Saying that "the world is already the best possible of all worlds" could be considered as "the most cynical of pessimisms". (Dewey, 1920: 178)

Dewey was a pragmatist who saw the meaning of ideas in their consequences. In his *Reconstruction in Philosophy*, Dewey framed the direction for the development of our society and business. For Dewey's time, those ideas may have been too progressively radical to be easily accepted; and though nowadays we are a bit closer to their full implementation, there is still a way to go, for social institutions in general and business in particular:

> Government, business, art, religion, all social institutions have a meaning, a purpose. That purpose is to set free and to develop the capacities of human individuals without respect to race, sex, class or economic growth.
>
> Democracy has many meanings, but if it has a moral meaning, it is found in resolving that the supreme test of all political institutions and industrial arrangements [business] shall be the contribution they make to the all-around growth of every member of society. (Dewey, 1920: 186)

Dewey mentioned business as one of the key responsible parties for fostering moral values. A hundred years ago, Dewey already anticipated conversations that we are having nowadays about the purpose of business: should it be rendered as a financial metric only or is there anything beyond that? We expect that the role of Dewey in business ethics will significantly grow over time incorporating the idea of focusing on the context of each moral situation instead of using shelf-ready universal guidelines, the concept of melioration, the elevation of the current direction of moral development and his questioning of economic gains as the primary purpose of business and his appeal to business to develop human capacities, primarily and foremost. Dewey's prioritization of a situation over a subject and object means that "[w]e need not choose between deontology, virtue ethics, and consequentialism" (Pappas, 2008: 2) as a universal wand that can solve any morally problematic situation and "the quality of the problematic situation determines which rules of the total system are selected" (Pappas, 2008: 97). Dewey's ethics allows us to depart from the myopic view of moral problems through only one possible lens, and makes business ethics much more realistic, and much more varied and interesting.

## Conclusion

In this chapter, we attempted to describe the research approach of using historical figures as well as to outline some possible directions for research that relies on the philosophies of established historical figures. This research approach has been relevant in the business ethics field since the inception of the field. Contemporary business ethics thinking often breeds on the influential thoughts of the great thinkers of the past. First, business ethicists look at the great economists – e.g., Adam Smith and Karl Marx – who laid down the foundations for the current economic system, and examine their attitude (as expressed directly in their works or reconstructed through some kind of analysis) toward the moral side of business. Second, business ethics scholars look at the moral philosophers – e.g., John Locke and John Dewey – whose ideas on ethical behavior and morality in general can be well adapted to fit the ethics of business organizations as social institutions.

It is impossible to imagine the development of business ethics without the use of historical figures. This research approach goes beyond referencing historical figures to create a line on the literature review page; rather, it is a holistic reconstruction of the concepts, arguments, and logic that eventually create a picture of a certain moral philosophy that bridges the past with present research seeking to explain the contemporary business world.

## References

Barbour, Rosaline S. 2008. *Introducing qualitative research: a student guide to the craft of doing qualitative research*. London: Sage Publications.

Bernard, H. Russel. 2000. *Social research methods: qualitative and quantitative approaches*. Thousand Oaks, CA: Sage Publications.

Bowie, Norman E. 1999. *Business ethics: a Kantian perspective*. Blackwell Publishers.
Bragues, George. 2009. Adam Smith's vision of the ethical manager. *Journal of Business Ethics*, 90: 447–460.
Carroll, Archie, Lipartio, Kenneth, Post, James, Werhane, Patricia, and Goodpaster, Kenneth. 2012. *Corporate responsibility: the American experience*. New York: Cambridge University Press.
Ciulla, Joanne B. 2011. Is business ethics getting better? A historical perspective. 2010 Society for Business Ethics Presidential Address. *Business Ethics Quarterly*, 21(2): 335–343.
Collins, Denis. 1994. The fall of business ethics in capitalist society: Adam Smith revisited. *Business Ethics Quarterly*, 4(4): 519–535.
Corlett, J. Angelo. 1998. A Marxist approach to business ethics. *Journal of Business Ethics*, 17, 99–103.
De George, Richard T. 1982. *Business ethics*. New York: Macmillan Publishing Co., Inc.
2006. The relevance of philosophy to business ethics: a response to Rorty's "Is philosophy relevant to applied ethics?" *Business Ethics Quarterly*, 16(3): 381–389.
Dewey, John. 1920. *Reconstruction in philosophy*. New York: Henry Hold and Company.
Donaldson, Thomas, and Dunfee, Thomas W. 1994. Toward a unified conception of business ethics: integrative social contract theory. *Academy of Management Review*, 19(2): 252–284.
Donaldson, Thomas, and Werhane, Patricia H. 2008. *Ethical issues in business: a philosophical approach*. (8th ed.) Upper Saddle River, NJ: Pearson/Prentice Hall.
Freeman, R. Edward. 1994. The politics of stakeholder theory: some future directions. *Business Ethics Quarterly*, 4(4): 409–421.
Gonin, Michael. 2015. Adam Smith's contribution to business ethics, then and now. *Journal of Business Ethics*, 129: 221–236.
Hartman, Edwin M. 1996. *Organizational ethics and the good life*. New York: Oxford University Press.
2015. *Virtue in business: an Aristotelian approach*. New York: Cambridge University Press.
Hsieh, Nien-hê. 2016. The social contract model of corporate purpose and responsibility. *Business Ethics Quarterly*, 25(4): 433–460.
Huhn, Mattias P., and Dierksmeier, Claus. 2016. Will the real A. Smith please stand up! *Journal of Business Ethics*, 136: 119–132.
James, Harvey, and Rassekh, Farhad. 2000. Smith, Friedman, and self-interest in ethical society. *Business Ethics Quarterly*, 10(3): 659–674.
Kerlin, Michael J. 1998. The end of history, specters of Marx and business ethics. *Journal of Business Ethics*, 17(15): 1717–1725.
Krentz, Edgar. 2002/1975. *The historical-critical methods*. Eugene, OR: Wipf & Stock Pub.
Linz, Susan J., and Chu, Yu Wei Luke. 2013. Weber, Marx, and work values: evidence from transition economies. *Economic Systems*, 37: 431–448.
Locke, John. 1980/1690. *Second treatise of government*. Indianapolis: Hackett Publishing Company, Inc.
Luker, Kristin. 2008. *Salsa dancing into the social sciences: research in an age of info-glut*. Cambridge, MA: Harvard University Press.
Maddison, Agnus. 2001. *The world economy: a millennial perspective*. Development Centre of the Organization for Economic Co-operation and Development. Retrieved on June 18, 2017 from http://theunbrokenwindow.com/Development/MADDISON%20The%20World%20Economy–A%20Millennial.pdf.
Massey, Stephen J. 1982. Marxism and business ethics. *Journal of Business Ethics*, 1: 301–312.
McCloskey, Deirdre N. 1985. *The rhetoric of economics*. Madison, WI: The University of Wisconsin Press.
McVea, John F. 2007. Constructing good decisions in ethically charged situations: the role of dramatic rehearsal. *Journal of Business Ethics*, 70(4): 375–390.
Marx, Karl. 1963/1844. *Early writings*. Trans. T. B. Bottomore. New York: McGraw-Hill.
1990/1867. *Capital: volume I*. Trans. Ben Fowkes. London: Penguin Classics.
May, Tim (ed.). 2002. *Qualitative research in action*. London: Sage Publications.
Nozick, Robert. 1974. *Anarchy, state, and utopia*. New York: Basic Books.
Ragin, Charles C. 1994. *Constructing social research: the unity and diversity method*. Thousand Oaks, CA: Pine Forge Press.
Ritchie, Jane, and Lewis, Jane. 2003. *Qualitative research practice: a guide for social science students and researchers*. London: Sage Publications.
Roth, Wolff-Michael. 2005. *Doing qualitative research: praxis of method*. Rotterdam: Sense Publishers.
Rothschild, Emma. 1992. Adam Smith and conservative economics. *Economic History Review*, 45.

Pappas, Gregory Fernando. 2008. *John Dewey's ethics: democracy as experience*. Bloomington: Indiana University Press.

Punch, Keith F. 1998. *Introduction to social research: quantitative and qualitative approaches*. London: Sage Publications.

Santoro, Michael A. 2010. Post Westphalia and its discontents: business, globalization, and human rights in political and moral perspective. *Business Ethics Quarterly*, 20(2): 285–297.

Sarantakos, Sotirios. 1994. *Social research*. Basingstoke: Macmillan.

Sen, Amartya. 1987. *On ethics and economics*. Oxford: Blackwell.

1993. Does business ethics make economic sense? *Business Ethics Quarterly*, 3: 45–54.

Shafer, Robert Jones (ed.). 1980. *A guide to historical method*. Homewood, IL: Dorsey Press.

Shaw, William H., and Barry, Vincent. 1998. *Moral issues in business*. New York: Wadsworth Publishing Company.

Silverman, David (ed.). 1997. *Qualitative research: theory, method and practice*. London: Sage Publications.

Shaw, William H. 2009. Marxism, business ethics and corporate social responsibility. *Journal of Business Ethics*, 84: 565–576.

Solomon, Robert C. 1993. *Ethics and excellence: cooperation and integrity in business*. The Ruffin Series in Business Ethics. New York: Oxford University Press.

Solomon, Robert C., and Higgins, Kathleen M. 1996. *A short history of philosophy*. New York: Oxford University Press.

Sonenshein, Scott. 2005. Business ethics and internal social criticism. *Business Ethics Quarterly*, 15(3): 475–498.

Smith, Adam. 1966; 1776. *Wealth of nations*. Oxford: Oxford University Press.

1976; 1767. *Theory of moral sentiments*. Oxford: Oxford University Press.

Subrahmanian, N. 1980. *Historical research methodology*. Madurai: Ennes Publications.

Walzer, Michael. 2002. *The company of critics: social criticsm and political commitment in the twentieth century*. New York: Basic Books.

Wells, Thomas, and Graafland, Johan. 2012. Adam Smith's bourgeois virtues in competition. *Business Ethics Quarterly*, 22(2): 319–350.

Werhane, Patricia H. 1991. *Adam Smith and his legacy for modern capitalism*. New York: Oxford University Press.

Wicks, Andrew C. 1995. Business ethics movement: where are we headed and what can we learn from our colleagues in bioethics? *Business Ethics Quarterly*, 5(3): 603–620.

Wilson, James Q. 1989. Adam Smith on business ethics. *California Management Review*, fall.

CHAPTER 2

# History as Methodology in Business Ethics

*Lessons from Aristotle*

EDWIN M. HARTMAN

## Introduction

### Learning from History

Studying history may seem an odd way into thinking about business ethics. Philosophers do study the history of philosophy, but usually in the style of archaeologists rather than geologists. Their interest is antiquarian, the sort of interest in the history of philosophy that scientists have in the history of science, which is of limited importance to scientific research and theorizing.

We might think that the reason for studying any sort of history is that otherwise we are condemned to repeat it. So, for example, if I am ignorant of the history of philosophy and in particular of Aristotle's and others' criticisms of Plato, I might adopt something like the theory of Forms as a theory of meaning. I doubt it. Today's philosophers of language have arguments for their theories that do not require taking Plato into account. But even if they profit from Aristotle's destruction of Plato, that destructive chore is one that they do not have to undertake, or even consider. So they may stand on Aristotle's shoulders, but they do not need to fight his battles over again or explain his criticisms of Plato while arguing for their theories.

Philosophers believe that they have made progress; in particular, moral philosophers believe that they have sound arguments that are superior to the claims of even such majestic figures as Plato, Aristotle, Kant, and Bentham. But why bother to engage them at all? What can they know that we don't?

Business ethicists may seem to have even less reason to look to the past. Ancient business has little to teach us about management, finance, and the other business-related disciplines. So how can the study of any kind of history shed light on contemporary thinking about our pressing issues in business ethics?

### What Can Go Wrong?

We can learn from the past if we understand that moral philosophy has taken a wrong turn at some point, with the result that by now we have lost sight of some of the essential features of ethics that past philosophers understood better than we do. We can profit from looking again at some methods and insights that should not have been abandoned. It is my view that, in part because of the highly successful scientific revolution and the Enlightenment, moral philosophers prematurely embraced the ethics of principles and abandoned the ethics of character. Reconsideration is in order.

We might have noticed the deficiencies of principle-based ethics without attending to history. Though Aristotle offers an extraordinarily sophisticated exposition and defense of virtue ethics, today's moral philosophers might have done the same without his help. But they did not, even with his help, until G. E. M. Anscombe propounded her influential pro-virtue argument in 1958. Like many other Oxford philosophers, she read Aristotle as an undergraduate at Oxford. Unlike them, she took Aristotle seriously. Nor did business ethicists take virtue seriously until Robert Solomon did so more than thirty years after Anscombe.[1]

I thank an anonymous reviewer for useful suggestions.

[1] See G. Anscombe, "Modern Moral Philosophy" and R. Solomon, *Ethics and Excellence*. I admit to a little oversimplification here.

Aristotle offers us an example of what moral philosophers can learn from history. I consider him an excellent example for several reasons that will become clear, but he is not the only good example. We can learn some lessons about the uses of history if we note how easily we misunderstand apparently time-honored claims and theories when we do not consider their historical context carefully. Consider how Adam Smith has been misused by some of his would-be followers: they abstract what they take to be his most famous principle from the whole of the work and from the world in which they have their meaning, and implausibly infer that the eighteenth-century author of *A Theory of Moral Sentiments* would approve of Ayn Rand.[2]

This essay is about the importance of attending to history as a way of understanding ethics. I am focusing on Aristotle not only because virtue ethics is a good example of how we can learn from history but also because an Aristotelian perspective is useful in understanding change itself, for better or worse, through the history of ethics.

I shall pay particular attention to utility, a staple of utilitarianism, of economics, and of management. Here Aristotle's views are superior to some that are in play now; the message about how much progress we have made in ethics is therefore not an entirely positive one. The natural sciences have sometimes misled not only moral philosophers and business ethicists but also economists and management theorists.[3]

## An Example of How Aristotelian Ethics Works

Consider Norman, a person of intelligence and good character. His boss, Patricia, has proposed a course of action that Norm has good reason to believe based on his expertise would be a disaster. As a person of high professional standards, he believes he has an ethical responsibility to try to avert the disaster. But he hesitates to approach Pat with his misgivings, since, like many managers, she does not like being shown to be wrong, particularly since some men in her company are quick to see signs of deficiency in women. How should Norm deliberate about this situation?

If he has great faith in moral principles, he might set out to bring about the greatest possible net happiness for the greatest possible number of stakeholders. He might then figure out who the stakeholders are and how to maximize their benefit. Or he might act on a maxim that could be made a universal law, and thus try to treat all the affected parties fairly. Or he might reflect that his employer has a right to expect him to help enrich the stockholders, and he might think that other stakeholders have rights too.

Or he might take a somewhat different approach. He might decide that he needs to act courageously – to show some spine. He might decide that he must effectively convey a message that will help Pat make a crucial decision for the company and for her. He knows that she has an ego, but also that she cares about the company's success. So he must not be afraid to speak up; he must not be content to say something so cautious and vague that she doesn't get the message. On the other hand, he must not denounce her plan as stupid in the presence of others, especially her boss. He must try to understand her position, too, as he would want her to do if he were in her place. If he feels upset, he must try to be calm.

This is recognizably virtuous thinking in an Aristotelian mode. Norm is trying to be truly courageous, to do what must be done despite some risks. He must try to find a mean between the extremes of cowardice and foolhardiness. And Aristotle adds in discussing the mean that it is necessary to take account of the details of the case. So Norm's actions, and his feelings as well, should be appropriate to the time, to the issues, to the people concerned, and to the correct purpose of his action. (See *Nicomachean Ethics* II 6 1106b16-22 and III 7 1115b17–19.)

Utilitarians and advocates of justice and rights may object that their concerns are being ignored here. Not so. Considering what courage requires does not keep Norm from taking utility into account as he considers the interests of the

[2] For a thoughtful and nuanced account of Smith, see P. Werhane, *Adam Smith.*

[3] For an account of my views on Aristotle on business ethics, see E. Hartman, *Virtue in Business.*

company and by extension the other stakeholders and the whole economy, and taking rights into account in believing that the company has a right to his most effective efforts. Norm brings in justice in trying to put himself in Pat's position: he sees her interests as counting for something, just as his do. In speaking the language of virtue we often invoke utilitarian and broadly deontic considerations. Aristotle puts great emphasis on the good life, which includes autonomy, and on justice. Nor does he abjure principles, but there are no algorithms to guide Norm in prioritizing or weighing those factors, or in applying them to complex cases. He has wisdom born of experience, but he has no rulebook to consult.

Insofar as he is a good person, Norm not only has the capacity to figure out what is the right thing to do. He values being a good person and acting accordingly. According to Aristotle, good character is not only about doing the right things but also about enjoying doing the right things (*NE* II 3 1104b5-9). Norm not only wants to do the right thing in this and similar cases; he wants to do so willingly, to have the right desires. So being a person of good character involves wanting to be a person of good character, wanting to have the desires and emotions associated with good character, taking it to be in one's best interests to be a person of good character. In the well-known words of Harry Frankfurt, one has the right second-order desires.[4]

Notice the importance of Norm's feelings: he tries not to be upset. This is not because in general he strives to be unemotional. Rather he wants to have appropriate emotions, to be pleased about things worth being pleased about, to be angry at what deserves anger, and so on. (See *NE* IV 5 1125b26-1126a3.) In this case he would be disappointed if Pat made a bad decision, and he would be right to be disappointed.

### *Some Lessons*

The story suggests some important lessons about virtue ethics, and this essay will elaborate on them. First, character as well as principle has a place in ethics, and the right emotions are a part of good character. Second, the doctrine of the ethical as a mean between extremes is substantive and useful as a way of dealing with ethical problems. Achieving the mean requires a clear view of the essential details of the situation, though it offers no theory for gathering those details into an understanding of the situation. Third, ethics is not a science and does not generate algorithms. Fourth, Aristotle's view of human motivation is more accurate than that of many of today's standard economists and organization theorists, in part because it avoids immodest claims about precision, in part because it is hospitable to a wide range of possible reasons for action, including ethical reasons.

## The Lure of Science

### *Science and the Humanities*

The history of ethics is important to our contemporary understanding of ethical theory and practice – more important than is the history of science to modern science. We should take Aristotle's ethics seriously as we should not take his natural science seriously. Why? The answer has something to do with the difference between the humanities and the hard sciences. Einstein represents progress over Democritus. Crick and Watson understood biology better than Aristotle did. In fact any intelligent undergraduate who takes a survey course in physics or biology is far ahead of Democritus and Aristotle in scientific knowledge.

By contrast consider literature. We would surely not say that authors of fiction have made so much progress through history that we cannot profitably read Shakespeare, or even Sophocles. Great literature contributes to our ethical deliberation in cases like the one faced by Norm, and in many others as well. It helps us develop an intuitive understanding of human nature, including our own, and a capacity for recognizing the subtleties of morally significant situations that is crucial to ethics. According to Aristotle, this capacity helps us understand a situation or a contemplated action for what it really is. For example, a good person

[4] See H. Frankfurt, "Freedom of the Will and the Concept of a Person." Aristotle seems to countenance second-order desires at *NE* IX 4 1166b7-14.

can understand that in a certain situation punishing Jones is a vindictive act rather than a just one. So this capacity is essential to character. Aristotle usually calls it perception; Werhane and others call it moral imagination.[5]

## How Scientific Progress Has Misled Us

History shows that ethical theory can regress. It does so when science and its progress have misled moral philosophers by offering an inappropriate model of knowledge and how we acquire it. If the accomplishments of Newton and other scientific giants impress you for the wrong reasons, you may think that whatever is worth talking about is precisely measurable, at least in principle. But ethics is not a precise science, even in principle. We cannot give an exact account of happiness or say with certainty what *the* maxim of any action is. As Aristotle says, it is a mark of erudition to demand of any subject matter no more precision than it allows (*NE* I 3 1094b23-27). This in no way supports relativism or nihilism. Ethics is real; it admits of true and false, though it does not admit of precision. Norm can deliberate wisely and be pretty sure that he is doing so; he cannot be wholly sure that he is going to do exactly the right thing.

Enlightenment figures influenced by the universal nature of scientific theories characteristically believed that ethics too ought to be universal – bound to no particular community.[6] If scientific laws were good models for principles in ethics, ethical principles would be portable: they would apply across a vast range of events, as the laws of physics do. So medical ethics would be a matter of applying ethical principles to what doctors and nurses do and generating statements about what they ought to do, while business ethics would be a matter of applying those same principles to what businesspeople do to get statements of what they ought to do. But it is difficult to think of any but the most general and vague principles that apply to both medical ethics and business ethics, and those principles are of little help in addressing difficult ethical issues in either field. Business ethics is not a matter of applying ethical principles (supplied by philosophers) to facts about business (supplied by businesspeople and management professors).

As we have noted, Aristotle claims that contextual details help determine the rightness or wrongness of an action. Among other things, the identities of the stakeholders matter, as do the relations between them and the agent. In part for that reason, what is acceptable in one community may be unacceptable in another not because relativism is true but because different communities may have different social contracts. Some social contracts are profoundly immoral, but more than one social contract may be morally acceptable.[7]

## Does Science Leave Room for Ethics?

Aristotle thinks of his psychology and his ethics as being continuous with his physics and metaphysics. Human beings are substances with essences and accidents. To understand the essence of human beings is to know a great deal about ethics: human beings are essentially (which is not to say always) rational and sociable, and working out the implications of that essential fact is much of what the study of ethics is about. Aristotle does not worry about the place of human beings, conscious creatures, in nature in part because he believes that all substances have natural purposes toward which they tend.

The scientific revolution raised questions about the place of consciousness in nature, in which events seemed to be subject to unexceptionable laws governing material events. Where does consciousness fit in? How can mental entities like

5 P. Werhane, *Moral Imagination*; P. Werhane et al., "Social Constructivism." In at least one passage (*NE* III 5 1114a32-b3) Aristotle uses the term *phantasia*, which is normally translated imagination. Elsewhere he uses *aesthesis*, perception. See *NE* III 5 1114a32-b3 and VII 3 concerning the ethical importance of this sort of perception.

6 Here I am one of many influenced by A. MacIntyre, *After Virtue*, especially chapters 4–6.

7 For much more on this issue, see T. Donaldson and T. Dunfee, *Ties that Bind: A Social Contracts Approach to Business Ethics*. They are more optimistic than I about so-called hypernorms, which are supposed to justify (or not) local norms.

desires and reasons be effective? What basis can there be for ethics?

Aristotle sees no problem because his science encompasses psychology and ethics. He is mistaken in thinking of science as broadly teleological; he holds that nonhuman states and events admit of explanations that resemble reasons in some ways: so a substance may have a property that we can explain because it has a useful purpose. Today there are scientists and others who make roughly the opposite mistake: they believe that anything other than a scientific explanation – for example, an explanation that invokes intentions – is not worth much unless it can be reduced to an explanation that invokes some entities acting measurably according to some natural law. So mental entities must be reduced in some way to physical events and states. Science has made progress, but the assumption that all useful knowledge can be reduced to scientific knowledge is not progress. Both sides seem to make the mistaken assumption that we need to explain the physical universe and human behavior in the same way.

The positivists, influenced by science and inclined to consider imprecision a fatal flaw, saw that the propositions of ethics were not verifiable or falsifiable scientifically; so they inferred that they were not meaningful propositions at all, but only expressions of emotion.[8] Some moral philosophers have argued that ethical language is evaluative rather than factual, that one cannot infer an "ought" from an "is." Most of them do not embrace relativism or nihilism, but they do seem to demote ethics to second-class citizenship – something not within the scope of science.[9]

Some economists have tried to deal with this supposed problem by taking the view that utility and other ethical concepts can be measured and even monetized. Now and then some organization theorist will demand that ethicists operationalize their concepts or provide something that can be measured. We cannot. We need not. We create needless problems if we try.

Some of the reasons for rejecting natural science as a model for moral philosophy are also reasons for being careful about drawing inferences from economics to ethics. This is not surprising, since some economic theorists seem to think that their field has many of the characteristics of science and tells us something about ethics.

## Economics, Management, and Ethics

### *Free Market Morality*

Some of our ethical views are in large part a result of our having embraced capitalism. In many respects capitalism is ethically praiseworthy, but we should be conscious of its influence on our values and of its presuppositions.

We can make a case that competitive markets are good from the point of view of utility, fairness, and autonomy. They are certainly productive. They involve willing buyers trading items for other items that they desire more; hence those on both sides of the deal are better off for acquiring these items. They are fair in that the fair price of an item is the market-clearing price in a competitive market: it is the price at which many traders can trade for a more desirable item. The market is fair in the additional sense that what you as a participant get out of the market is closely related to what you put into it. Finally, the participants are autonomous in that they are free to buy and sell, or not, as they please.

But the conceptions of utility, justice, and autonomy at work here are much influenced by a preference for free market capitalism. Aristotle would not embrace them, nor should we do so uncritically. To understand ethical change in history is to see that what we presuppose without argument, without challenge, sometimes without awareness,

[8] Strangely, many positivists appeared to think that stating an ethical proposition must involve a positive emotional reaction. It would be a contradiction to say, "That would be the right thing to do, but I don't care."

[9] In *Principia Ethica* G. E. Moore famously makes this argument, against Aristotle and others. Aristotle believes that a correct description of human beings as rational and sociable has strong ethical implications. For a view more in line with Aristotle's, see H. Putnam, *Collapse of the Fact/Value Dichotomy*. He claims that our language is shot through with irreducible normative assumptions and implications.

is not always true and can be difficult to correct. Why, once we think of it, is the market-clearing price necessarily the just price? Does every bargain to which we consent get us what we want in the end? For that matter, is getting what we want always good for us? Is the standard assumption that participants in markets act based on adequate information always true? And what if it isn't?[10]

## Homo Economicus

In the social sciences, and in ethics as well, the search for the precision characteristic of hard science often leads to fatal oversimplification, as Ghoshal argues.[11] In ethics based on economics it leads to *homo economicus*, that rationally selfish and knowledgeable model human being. *Homo economicus* is rational not by virtue of working out what is best from some well-considered point of view: instead what is best is just whatever *homo economicus* prefers, and we can deduce preference as well as belief from action, as *homo economicus* is a behaviorist construct. Nothing could count as evidence that *homo economicus* has chosen something that is not in fact preferable.[12]

If you believe that people are *homines economici*, then ethics has nothing to do with the sort of person one is, since everyone is the same sort of person. It would follow that ethics is primarily about the acts that you perform rather than the sort of person you are, much as science is about events rather than things. It would also follow that no description of what human life is or can be could generate any conclusions about how to live, or even about what makes it possible to be ethical. So the work of psychologists, including evolutionary psychologists and even brain physiologists, would be irrelevant to ethics.

## Utility, Autonomy, and Motivation

A discussion of human autonomy, much prized in most versions of ethics, requires an understanding of human motivation. The standard economic model can mislead us into assuming that it is human nature to be naturally selfish. The arguments for that view are weak, but it is not based on arguments or evidence, and it is certainly not based on any familiarity with Aristotle's views, or those of most other philosophers ancient or modern about human nature and the good life. Nor is based on any consideration of the possibility that some people regularly have inappropriate desires and lives unworthy of a human being.[13]

Economists can respond that the view of utility embedded in the *homo economicus* model is handy for computation and prediction at a macro level, despite its contestable assumption of a certain hard individualism. In the theory of neoclassical economics there is no problem about individual selfishness: in the aggregate it is a win-win for everyone, good from the point of view of utility, justice, and rights.

But it is not, especially in organizations. If people are *homines economici*, it will be difficult to preserve the commons in organizations and elsewhere. If each employee can get away with acting in a narrowly selfish way, he or she will be better off whether the others do so or not. But then the organization as a whole will suffer from free riding, to the disadvantage of all.

Many factors other than individual financial gain can motivate employees. In a well-designed organization, the success of the whole may motivate you if you believe others are similarly motivated. There is evidence that trust and trustworthiness make organizations more productive. One would expect that, since I am more likely to cooperate with you if I can trust you to cooperate with me. This sort of trust is based on what Aristotle considers a weak form of friendship: we are friends of convenience.

[10] Fairness requires me to note that excellent work has been done on information asymmetry, though there is more work to be done in considering its moral implications.

[11] S. Ghoshal, "Bad Management Theories . . ."

[12] Psychological egoism in most versions is trivially true. In *Principia Ethica* G. E. Moore criticizes philosophers who fail to distinguish the preferred from the preferable. *Homo economicus* recognizes no such distinction.

[13] A possible response to my point is this: "Oh, so you think you or someone else or the state should determine what I should desire?" That is an example of the cheap rhetorical trick of attributing an extreme position to an opponent who is trying to find the mean.

Strong friendship, characteristic of virtuous citizens of good communities, is a matter of taking one's friend's interests as a reason for action. In true friendship I aim to benefit you. And research has shown that this genuine as opposed to transactional friendship has a productive role in organizations.[14] This should come as no surprise to anyone who takes the notion of social capital seriously. No less important, we should recognize as Aristotle does that genuine friendship is a good thing in itself, a necessary component of the good life.

The fact remains that our usual way of explaining human behavior, which has not advanced much since Aristotle, is imprecise. Aristotle offers a teleological explanation of human behavior because his natural science is teleological. It explains the actions of individual substances, which have potential for movement and growth. It explains an event or state by reference to the actualization of a substance. That kind of explanation often invokes some end or goal toward which the substance tends. According to Aristotle, a human being is a substance, characteristically rational and sociable, so we explain what a person does by reference to some reason for action. We not only justify but explain the actions of a good person by reference to ethical reasons.

Our explanations of behavior, which typically invoke reasons for action instead of laws covering events, originate in teleological, hence problematic, science. Our psychological theories postulate first- and second-order desires, beliefs, feelings, traits, and other entities that are elusive: we usually cannot observe them directly or even infer them from an action. A certain action may indicate what Jones desires, given what he believes; or it may indicate what he believes, given what he desires. Other cases may be still more complicated. No case isolates a necessary and sufficient condition for the action it explains. To make matters more difficult, we usually base our explanations on the assumption that the agent is rational to some degree. This is not always so, nor can we readily see how rational the agent is. Folk psychology is not a hard science. When we invoke intentions to explain behavior, we are abandoning natural science, for reasons Davidson famously offered a generation ago: we cannot understand intentions or intentional behavior without invoking rationality, which is not always present.[15] In any case, we cannot always know whether an agent has a certain reason or whether that reason motivates an action.

Explaining some human behavior without postulating mental entities of this sort is not impossible. Survey research can indicate how likely subordinates are to confront their bosses and how much more likely they are to be successful under these rather than those circumstances. That is worth knowing. Arguably that kind of information helps explain Norm's behavior and even gives him some clues as to what to do. Some social psychologists and philosophers argue that the environment is the determining factor of the agent's action, that character is not an independent variable, if it is a variable at all.[16] The Milgram and Zimbardo experiments are offered as evidence.

That argument is based on a form of behaviorism, which has some problems. An action may be evidence of a desire given a belief, or a belief given a desire, but no independent evidence indicates what the desire is, or the belief. Social psychologists typically assume that the agent's belief is true; so a desire reduces to a disposition to act. No internal state need be postulated; the independent variable is in the environment. But how do we explain the subjects, rare though they are, who defied Milgram? Norm may be rare too: Aristotle himself does not believe that many people are very virtuous, and he is a good person. If he offers us

[14] So argue M. Sommers in "Useful Friendships" and M. Drake and J. Schlachter in "A Virtue-Ethics Analysis of Supply Chain Collaboration." Aristotle discusses friendship in books VIII and IX. Beyond the transactional sort of friendship there is true friendship, which includes taking the friend's interests as one's own. Here is the basis for a possible response to MacIntyre's claim in *After Virtue* that virtues are being crowded out of business.

[15] See D. Davidson, "Actions, Reasons, and Causes." J. Haidt argues in both "The Rational Dog" and *The Righteous Mind* that we often act on intuition or impulse and rationalize afterwards, so that the stated reasons for the act did not in fact cause it.

[16] See especially J. Doris, *Absence of Character*.

plausible and detailed reasons for his choosing a certain course of action, we surely do not have a good basis for just dismissing what he says. And we would surely not advise him not to bother deliberating seriously about this issue because his environment will determine what he does.

Some questions that managers ask do presuppose that employees are rational and sociable creatures who are motivated at least in part by ethical considerations, such as concern for the success of their colleagues and the organization. In deciding how to deal with Norm or someone like him, a manager might take a cue from Aristotle and treat him as citizens in a good *polis* treat one another.[17] On the other hand, for the purpose of making a policy for a large group of employees it might make more sense to assume that money is a primary motivator. But even in that case it is not a good idea to assume that money is the only possible motivator.

Managers sometimes embrace the more facile notion of self-interest to motivate employees to be productive for the organization by offering incentive compensation based on desired individual results. Quite aside from ignoring the great range of reasons people may have for doing whatever they do, these managers will find it very difficult to find the right financial sticks and carrots to motivate what is needed. Too often an incentive compensation scheme becomes a license for employees to game the system. To put the point in terms that Aristotle would not find unduly harsh, treating people as though they were largely mercenary is self-fulfilling.[18]

## The Good Life and Ethics

There are moral as well as practical issues about *homo economicus* as a model of self-interest. It does not consider Aristotle's notion of well-being (*eudaimonia*) or much of anything else Aristotle says, since Aristotle takes self-interest to be complex and elusive, and subtly related to ethics. It takes a pretty stubborn libertarian to hold that well-being is just preference satisfaction.

Aristotle does not believe that utility is a matter of the satisfaction of just any old preference. He certainly does not believe that being a good person requires sacrificing one's interests. On the contrary, he argues that the good life entails being ethical, which in turn entails having and satisfying desires of a certain kind. He rules out first-order desires that are inconsistent with second-order desires, desires that offer short-term gain for the price of long-term loss, desires that stunt one's intellectual or moral development, desires that stand one in poor stead as a family member, a friend, or a citizen of a good *polis* – or, we can suppose, an employee of an ethical organization. Some desires are unworthy of an adult human being and incompatible with a good life. In that sense they are irrational. So if Aristotle is right, the great Enlightenment figure Hume and others are wrong in suggesting that rationality is a feature of the means we choose to achieve our ends, and not of our ends.[19]

More broadly speaking, as a human being you have good reason to be a person of integrity in the sense that your desires, your emotions, your interests, and your capacity to reason form a coherent whole consistent with your sociable and rational human nature. If that is true of you, you enjoy the well-being that only an ethical person can experience.

I am not claiming that the views of Aristotle on what the good life looks like are acceptable in all respects, though they are attractive. At the very least, we need to consider what economists, managers, and others take for granted about the good life and see whether history offers any alternatives.

[17] How to make an organization more like a *polis* is an important issue, but beyond the scope of this essay.

[18] J. Heath's "The Uses and Abuses of Agency Theory" is especially forceful on this issue. His arguments will not come as news to all economists. Having myself had extensive experience in trying to create incentive compensation systems, I strongly agree with Heath.

[19] At the very least an explanation of behavior cannot get off the ground if it involves a wholly irrational end. To say that Jones has always wanted to help the unfortunate assists us in understanding why he has chosen to become a social worker. To say that Jones has always wanted to drink paint does not assist us in understanding why he hangs around hardware stores.

And it does, at least in the form of Aristotle's conception.

But not all old forms of morality are as sophisticated as that of Aristotle.

## Morality Now

### *Individuals and Communities*

We may think we have made moral progress because we embrace a version of modern morality as opposed to the traditional sort, which we may be tempted to consider radically different and worse. Traditional moralities emphasize in-group loyalty, tradition, and purity. Modern or liberal moralities emphasize the welfare of the individual, broad-gauged justice with a presumption of equality, and autonomy. If you are a typical reader of this essay, you may think that traditional morality is stifling, that you don't need a tribe to tell you what to do. You may also think that Aristotle is too much mired in the traditional camp.[20]

Part of modern morality has been a search for principles that give us some perspective on all the parochial versions of ethics, ancient and current, so that we can assess them from the sunlit uplands of objectivity, or at least clarity.[21] As I claimed earlier, this was an attractive prospect to many figures of the Enlightenment. One of them, Friedrich Schiller, wrote "All people become brothers," and Beethoven famously set his words to music. Let the world unite in joyful understanding of what is good for all humankind! But it is not clear that Schiller's ideal is psychologically possible or that it would be useful as a way of dealing with ethical issues. Edmund Burke, a more conservative and less enthusiastic thinker, saw ethical development as a matter of learning to play an appropriate role in one's community – "our little platoon," as he put it.[22] We can then extend this love for our platoon and work out how to treat people in other platoons.

Yet Burke too was unduly optimistic, in his way. Joining hands and singing about how the tender wing of joy unites us was indeed unattainable. But at the other extreme lay events like the Thirty Years' War, which was essentially mass murder in the name of religion – in fact, two branches of the same religion. Loyalty to our own platoon may generate contempt for other platoons, including (some would say especially) those rather like our own.

We should look for a mean between these extremes, Aristotle would say. Modern western moralities do not ignore the importance of family, friends, and community. We understand the importance of loyalty as well as exit and voice. Traditional moralists typically consider loyalty an essential aspect of the good life for an individual, and so do we. How loyal we should be and to whom depends in part on social arrangements that differ from those in which our ancestors lived. For example, unlike the Greeks of Aristotle's time, we must have extensive and productive dealings with people far outside our tribe. At the extreme of communitarianism there is murderous religious fanaticism and honor killing. At the extreme of individualism there is mindless greed and the kind of isolation that mass communication does little to alleviate. If we have come to either of these extremes, what we have achieved is not ethical progress. That modern life in the West frays our ties of community and friendship does not show that these ties are now unimportant; it shows that we have a problem about how to balance the values of autonomy against those of community. Problems of this sort are not easily solved – in particular, there are no principles that will do it – but we must try. We can begin by pondering the questionable aspects of individualism in our society and

[20] Most of what I say here is based on J. Haidt, *The Righteous Mind.* Haidt has told me that he thinks Aristotle's views fall between the traditional and modern conceptions.

[21] T. Donaldson and T. Dunfee argue in *Ties that Bind* that there are cross-cultural norms, which they call hypernorms, that enable us to judge local norms. Sometimes they do. A hypernorm like "the right to personal autonomy is fundamental" does not much help us assess political arguments about regulation, but "all men are created equal" does seem to condemn slavery, ironically.

[22] This is an oft-cited point. See K. Appiah, *Cosmopolitanism,* and J. Haidt, *The Righteous Mind.*

asking ourselves whether our modern view of ethics has caused us to undervalue the associative virtues. They are surely undervalued in certain areas, including areas of business.[23]

### *Business and Moral Progress*

Whether and how business affects moral progress is a complex issue. That it is by nature competitive is a matter of moral significance, but competition is not all there is to it and not always a bad thing. Consider a multinational firm which, in the interests of effectiveness, imposes a strong egalitarianism on its employees, including the local ones, so that people of any race and gender will be hired based on qualifications and promoted because of performance. The resulting diversity will likely make this workplace a school for getting along with a broad swath of people and outlooks and for developing attitudes of respect and empathy toward them and their kith. So says Timothy Fort,[24] and Burke might agree if he would accept that an organization can be a platoon. So two cheers for capitalism, different in many crucial ways from the economic arrangements of Aristotle's time. It encourages certain personal traits related to individual autonomy, which we and Aristotle value. At least it is better than feudalism.

We may be inclined to believe that business demands its own forms of virtue; we may even think that these forms are dissociated from virtue as we normally understand it. I doubt this. Consider how important social capital is, how important it is for employees to be trustworthy and trusting, and unselfishly so. What I do not doubt is that some vices may help individuals in certain businesses succeed; but any business, any organization, is ethically problematic when it supports selfishness and a narrow notion of the good life. Capitalism encourages vices as well as virtues, and it is our task to sort them out.

[23] I would not go so far as MacIntyre's *After Virtue* in claiming that profit regularly drives out the associative virtues, but that does sometimes happen.

[24] T. Fort, *Prophets, Profits, and Peace.*

## A Final Word

Old ethics, like old literature and unlike old science, can shed light on the new kind. That can happen when we discover unnoticed value in Aristotle and other ancients. At the same time, in seeing how and why the great moral philosophers of antiquity have gone wrong, as well as how and why we have forgotten their valuable lessons, we learn something about how moral philosophy and people too can change, sometimes for the better, over time.

We also learn something about the nature of moral philosophy. One inference we may draw, a cautionary lesson, is that there is always more progress to be made. We have only begun to sort out our problems about autonomy and community, made immeasurably more complicated by barely predictable technological and therefore economic change. To put the matter another way, we do not know whether our moral philosophy can adequately address the challenges of modernity. Principles will be of limited help in addressing them. But wisdom, integrity, courage, and similar virtues will not go out of style.

## References

Anscombe, G. "Modern Moral Philosophy." *Philosophy* 33 (1958), 1–19.

Appiah, K. *Cosmopolitanism: Ethics in a World of Strangers*. New York: W. W. Norton, 2006.

Aristotle, *Ethica Nichomachea*. Edited by I. Bywater. Oxford: Clarendon Press, 1962.

Davidson, D. "Actions, Reasons, and Causes." *Essays on Actions and Events*, 3–19. Oxford: Clarendon Press, 1982.

Donaldson, T., and T. Dunfee. *Ties that Bind: A Social Contracts Approach to Business Ethics*. Boston: Harvard Business Press, 1999.

Doris, J. *Lack of Character: Personality and Moral Behavior*. New York: Cambridge University Press, 2002.

Drake, M., and J. Schlachter. "A Virtue-Ethics Analysis of Supply Chain Collaboration. *Journal of Business Ethics*, 82 (2008), 851–864.

Dunn, E., and M. Norton. *Happier Money: The Science of Happier Spending*. New York: Simon and Schuster, 2013.

Fort, T. *Prophets, Profits, and Peace: The Positive Role of Business in Promoting Religious Tolerance*. New Haven: Yale University Press, 2008.

Frankfurt, H. "Freedom of the Will and the Concept of a Person." In G. Watson (ed.), *Free Will*, 81–95. New York: Oxford University Press, 1981.

Ghoshal, S. "Bad Management Theories are Destroying Good Management Practices." *Academy of Management Learning and Education*, 4 (2005), 75–91.

Haidt, J. "The Emotional Dog and its Rational Tail: A Social Intuitionist Approach to Moral Judgment." *Psychological Review*, 108 (2001), 814–834.

*The Righteous Mind: Why Good People Are Divided by Politics and Religion*. New York: Pantheon Books, 2012.

Hartman, E. *Virtue in Business: Conversations with Aristotle*. New York: Cambridge University Press, 2013.

Heath, J. "The Uses and Abuses of Agency Theory." *Business Ethics Quarterly*, 19 (2009), 497–528.

MacIntyre, A. *After Virtue*. 2nd edition. Notre Dame: Notre Dame University Press, 1985.

Moore, G. E. *Principia Ethica*. New York: Cambridge University Press, 1903.

Putnam, H. *The Collapse of the Fact/Value Dichotomy and Other Essays*. Cambridge, MA: Harvard University Press, 2002.

Solomon, R. *Ethics and Excellence: Cooperation and Integrity in Business*. New York, Oxford University Press, 1992.

Sommers, M. "Useful Friendships: A Foundation for Business Ethics." *Journal of Business Ethics*, 16 (1997), 1453–1458.

Werhane, P. *Adam Smith and his Legacy for Modern Capitalism*. New York: Oxford University Press, 1991.

*Moral Imagination and Management Decision-making*. New York: Oxford University Press 1999.

Werhane, P. L. Hartman, D. Moberg, E. Englehardt, M. Pritchard, and B. Parmar. "Social Constructivism, Mental Models, and Problems of Obedience." *Journal of Business Ethics*, 100, (2011), 103–118.

CHAPTER 3

# The Role of Continental Philosophy in Business Ethics Research

MOLLIE PAINTER-MORLAND

## Introduction

In this chapter, we will explore a few intricately related questions regarding the role of "continental" philosophy in business ethics research. The first most basic question is whether "philosophy" itself can be considered a "research method" or "research approach". The second is whether continental, otherwise also sometimes described as "European" philosophy, has a distinct role to play as a research approach among others. The last, but perhaps most important question, pertains to the contemporary scholarly opportunities for business ethics researchers in pursuing continental philosophy as a research approach, focusing for the purposes of this chapter, on its employment within process studies.

There was a time in history when the first question, i.e. whether philosophy can be considered a research approach, would have been oxymoronic. In ancient times philosophy was very much a mode of investigation of all issues related to society, politics, economics, and ethics. It was also a style of engagement between people, a practice of particular ways of existing and relating. Philosophy and what we now call "science" were part of the same search for truth and wisdom. In fact, the distinction between these two terms was not at all as pronounced as it has become in contemporary academe. As such, ontological questions about what exists and epistemological debates about how we best come to know it was part of all enquiry, and philosophical engagement our access to it. These assumptions were debated as part of societal discussions of the best ways to live, rather than being positioned as the privy of a separate theoretical discipline called "philosophy." We believe that it would serve us well to restore this intimate relationship between philosophy and scientific practices, and as such we will not spend too much time focusing on whether philosophy is indeed a research approach but instead show what kind of research it allows us to pursue.

The second question calls for a consideration of what may be the unique contribution of "continental philosophy." To answer this question, we will have to start by exploring what lies at the heart of the somewhat contentious distinction between analytic philosophy and continental philosophy (Friedman, 2002; Gordon, 2004). The distinction is important because historically, the field of business ethics seems much more grounded in analytic philosophy than in continental philosophy. It is only relatively recently that research drawing on continental philosophy has become more prominent in business ethics journals (Jones, 2007; Ladkin 2006; Deslandes 2012; Ibarra-Colado, Clegg and Rhodes, 2006; Byers and Rhodes, 2007; Painter-Morland, 2010, 2012, 2013), and a few books have appeared claiming to take this approach to the field of business ethics (Jones, Parker and Ten Bos, 2010; Painter-Morland and Ten Bos, 2011).

To address the third question, we will firstly discuss continental philosophy's general theoretical contribution, before turning to its unique potential for enhancing new fields of research. In this latter regard, we discuss the increased interest in studying process rather than entities within organization studies and other management disciplines. As we will explain, a growing interest in understanding "process" has prompted an interest in developing ways to conduct empirical studies that do not undermine process philosophy's most central assumptions. In this regard, continental philosophy's ontological commitments offer important insights regarding how research into becoming can and should be done. Scholars who will be able to find meaningful ways to do process research, both theoretically and empirically, may find that their business and society research is valued far beyond the traditional business ethics journals. This partnership between continental philosophy and process studies also holds much promise for mainstreaming ethics and sustainability concerns into other disciplines – something which is increasingly a priority given the systemic challenges that we face globally in the area of business and society.

## The "Analytic" versus "Continental" Divide

Nobody knows exactly who is responsible for the distinction between "analytic" and "continental" philosophy,[1] though a meeting at a conference in the small Swiss city of Davos in Spring 1929 is often seen as the event that engendered this distinction. At this conference, two very influential German philosophers, Martin Heidegger and Ernst Cassirer, engaged in a discussion about the Enlightenment philosopher Immanuel Kant (1724–1804). One of the attendants at the meeting was a young Austrian philosopher called Rudolf Carnap. This young man, who was already on his way to becoming one of the most famous analytic philosophers of his time, accused Heidegger, who is widely seen as perhaps the single most important continental philosopher of the twentieth century, of talking only "mumbo-jumbo." This accusation has led, at least among logicians, positivists, and other scientifically inclined philosophers, to either mirth or downright contempt. But it is not just a meeting between two philosophers that helped to bring about such a distinction. Carnap actually read Heidegger quite closely and remarked, in an article published in 1931, that Heidegger is driven by only one truly "big question," to wit, "the question of Being and nothing more." But what is the meaning of such a big question? Carnap (1932, 1959) frankly admitted he could not make much sense of such a question and offered some arguments that need not concern us here. The point that is interesting in the present context is that Carnap (1932, 1959) claims that Heidegger is a "metaphysical" philosopher. He is adamantly clear about what this means: Metaphysical philosophers do not offer us "propositions," that is to say, statements that describe the world and that are as such either false or true. They rather offer us something entirely different, something that might be an expression of our attitude to life, something that comes closer to poetry than to exact logical thinking.

The allegation that metaphysical philosophy expresses pure artistry rather than logical ingenuity has haunted what came to be known as "continental" philosophy. In the wake of Carnap, many analytic philosophers have claimed to abhor the "metaphysics" that seems to underpin continental philosophy. There has been a lot of debate about whether the analytic portrayal of metaphysics is correct, but we will not enter into that here. There were also times that it was taken for granted that metaphysics is the most important kind of philosophy since it allegedly asks the most basic questions that human beings can ask: What is the essence of life? What is the essence of being? Does the human soul exist and is it immortal? Carnap's way of denouncing all these questions as poetry, artistry, or pseudo-science was widely seen as challenging and provocative. The discussion between Carnap and Heidegger became emblematic of the divide between analytic and continental philosophy. Analytic philosophers think that not just Heidegger, but all continental philosophers are at best metaphysical poets or artists.

How did continental philosophers respond? Most of them simply ignored all these allegations and continued with the kind of work they were doing. But underneath this superficial indifference, it is clear that many continental philosophers think that analytic philosophers lack depth, are not rigorous, and engage in their own kind of metaphysics. Such a different kind of "metaphysics" implies, for example, a naıve belief in the idea that science has straightforward access to objects in the world and does not experience any difficulties in phrasing unequivocal propositions about these objects. In fact, scientists operate in a world where hard facts

[1] This section is partially derived from the editors' introduction of "*Business Ethics and Continental Philosophy*," edited by Rene Ten Bos and Mollie Painter-Morland, Cambridge University Press, 2011.

have become increasingly exceptional. What however becomes more and more apparent, is that issues such as globalization or sustainability are hardly ever uncontested and do not have the clear factual status some people may long for. Many continental philosophers alert us to the difficulties we may experience in accessing the world. More importantly, the implicit belief that only that which can be quantitatively established is meaningful and important, may undermine many important agendas such as environmental responsibility, because it embraces an exclusively instrumentalist logic (see, e.g., Painter-Morland and Ten Bos 2016).

These insights however do not mitigate the extent to which analytic philosophy has become associated with "factual" research, whereas "continental philosophy" has altogether been seen as unhelpful to scientific research, perhaps even more so in the case of business ethics research. The reason lies in the way in which "science" is perceived, and in the way the various approaches to philosophical writing has been described. As seen from the perspective of analytic philosophy, analytic philosophy is superior because it engages in language analysis, is concerned with developing disciplined, logical argumentation, making scientific claims, is politically neutral, methodological. Analytic philosophy is committed to the belief in the progress of knowledge. Many analytic philosophers believe that continental philosophy is more interested in literary, poetical analysis. In fact, that continental writing is poetry itself, artistic at best, even nonsensical wild, unruly, anarchistic, chaotic, and rhetorical. Continental philosophy has also developed the reputation of being politically leftist and relativistic in its embrace of particularity, contingency, and as such pluralistic conceptions of truth.

Having looked over the distinctions drawn above, you may now have lost interest in reading this chapter. After all, what is wrong with disciplined, politically neutral, methodological texts that offer "real" philosophical perspectives on business? And why would one want any alternative to this? As indicated above, the distinctions drawn above explained the perspective of analytic philosophy, but one could easily redraft it to cast a more positive light on the continental perspective, and be more dismissive about the contributions of analytic philosophy. Many of the commitments of the analytic philosophers, especially their commitment to science, progress, and politically neutral analysis, have been questioned by the continentals. Some of this has its contextual origins in the political events in Europe during the first half of the twentieth century. Especially the events of the Second World War were pivotal in shaping the concerns of many continental thinkers. In fact, Auschwitz has been described as "the collapse of reason." Therefore, one can detect a distinct disillusionment with reason, science, and technology in the writings of many continental thinkers. The events of the war and the demise of humanity and morality during this time made it eminently clear that science, technology, and the desire for progress is neither politically neutral nor unequivocally "good." Continental philosophers made clear that some critical questioning in the realms of science, politics, and philosophy were desperately called for. One cannot continue, as analytic philosophers would propose, to venerate science as a bulwark of reason and objectivity.

The purpose of this chapter is to illustrate how specific continental philosophers do research and introduce you to just some of the basic issues that concern continental philosophers. One example of such an issue is "truth." Thinkers like Nietzsche or Heidegger, who are often seen as the precursors of many of the key figures you will encounter in this chapter, had a problem with the big claims to "truth" that we find within science or history. Nietzsche proposed that there are always very specific interests of power lurking behind these seemingly "objective" claims. Heidegger agreed with Nietzsche in the sense that he also thinks that language does not straightforwardly correspond to reality. Many continental philosophers would subsequently address the issue of truth, arguing that truth is not a state of affairs, but rather an ongoing *process*. Others argued that instead of looking for all-encompassing explanations of reality, we should rather focus on *specificity* and *particularity*. In some cases, this led to a reevaluation or downright condemnation of what came to be known as "grand narratives" or "big stories." An example of such a big story would be the self-portrayal of science as a heroic quest for truth, or the history of humankind as a march from tyranny to more and more liberty. Jean-Francois Lyotard, an influential French philosopher, proposed that philosophers and scientists should be more modest and only tell "small stories." Historians, for example, should henceforward not focus on the great events in our history (the battles, the revolutions, or the deeds of the big heroes) but on how all of this might have impacted on the lives of smaller communities (particular trades, villages, or families). Small stories, so the argument goes, are taken from real life, whereas big stories lack any connection with it.

The skepticism regarding big and all-encompassing "truths" led other continental figures such as Jacques Derrida to rethink the very *nature of language*. His idea of "deconstruction" suggested that meaning and sense in language can be very slippery. Indeed, texts and words can obtain a significance that was initially not anticipated. In this chapter, we will see that many concepts used in business ethics – globalization, responsibility, value, or sustainability – have undergone a constant shift in meaning. Another key figure in this chapter, Gilles Deleuze, proposed to replace what he understood as "transcendental" reason with a kind of "vitalist empiricism" that would take concrete *bodily affections* and *experiences* as the point of departure. Like Nietzsche, Deleuze reminded us of the importance of emotion and embodiment. As such, it allowed us to radically reframe what we understand by human agency and notions such as "decision-making." We will return to this later on in the chapter. For the moment, it suffices to note that many continental philosophers do not think that the pursuit of knowledge is or should be an entirely reasonable and disembodied endeavor. And what counts for knowledge, in this regard at least, also counts for language.

This very brief exposé of some of the issues that continental figures engage with should, however, not be read as a "position statement," which all continental philosophers would subscribe to. On many issues they do not agree with one another at all. Therefore, they should most certainly not be portrayed as all singing the same tune, as if they are putting forward a homogeneous, coherent position. For instance, the German philosopher Peter Sloterdijk responds to the fragmentation that the rejection of big stories might entail by deliberately constructing a new "big story," which narrates how human beings have always been in the business of constructing and destroying the kind of communities he refers to as "spheres." The Slovenian philosopher Slavoj Zizek dismisses Deleuze's vitalism as a philosophy that merely incites people to indulge in their own feelings rather than to be concerned about real problems in the world. Against this conceitedness, he hopes to reinvigorate a revolutionary zeal and clearly argues that big truths are needed for that. Only big stories engage people, not small stories. But this has, in turn, led Sloterdijk to accuse Zizek of flirting with the possibility of violence. If there is one lesson to be drawn from history, Sloterdijk argues, then it is that big stories can be dangerous, especially when they turn out to be political.

This debate among Deleuze, Zizek, and Sloterdijk serves to show that "continental philosophy" is not a name for a unified tradition. However, what seems important to many of these thinkers – in spite of all their mutual differences – is to engage critically with the tradition that informs their own work, and with each other's work. Contemporary continental philosophers still take their inspiration from earlier philosophers who played an important role in the history of philosophy: Aristotle, Plato, Descartes, Spinoza, Hume, Kant, Hegel, Marx, and many others. They also reflect on thinkers who can be seen as their immediate predecessors: Nietzsche, Bergson, Blanchot, Batailles, and even Ludwig Wittgenstein's later work (he is a prominent name in analytic circles as well based on his earlier work). All these philosophers cast doubt on some central tenets and values not only of philosophy but also of modern culture as such. However, it is important to note that continental philosophers never envisaged a radical rift with the history of philosophy. If, for example, Derrida talks about "deconstruction," we should not forget that he never envisaged a wholesale attack on the heroes of ancient or modern philosophy. In fact, it is a distinct characteristic of continental philosophers that they take the history of Western thought very seriously. Subtle and precise textual analyses of classical philosophical texts are the hallmark of much continental philosophy, something that has tempted commentators to label this philosophy as difficult and obscure.

We want to reiterate that the distinction between continental and analytic philosophy remains opaque and contentious. Also, we should never forget that the very notion of "continental philosophy" has been created in the Anglo-Saxon world. Just a few philosophers in the continent would actually endorse the distinction even though many of them might deem "analytic" philosophy to be boring, superficial, and overly rigid. Be this as it may, business ethics seems to have emerged as rooted in the analytic tradition and has largely ignored continental philosophy for many years. This is not to say that it does not add meaningful perspectives. Indeed, business ethics has embraced the analytic agenda and offered clear normative perspectives on important issues. It has, for example, formulated codes of conduct for business practitioners, it has developed new and important insights in the business environment (in terms of stakeholders, politics, and so on), and it has also raised important issues about worldwide processes such as capitalism and globalization and what businesses can do about them. Despite the advances made, however, we do believe that research in this area can be so much richer when it opens up to a long but neglected continental tradition of thought.

Continental philosophers suggest that one should always start from where one is. We will start with a critical perspective on the basic assumptions operative in certain parts of the business ethics field. What do we mean by "critical reflection"? It is clear that the discipline of business ethics has always been reflective, but in a somewhat different kind of way than what we will be proposing here. The field of business ethics reflects issues that are topical in the corporate world. Yet, we maintain that it hardly ever discusses its own assumptions. Instead, business ethics has always been intent on improving the status quo, but is, in our opinion, much less inclined to questioning the status quo. This made it impossible to question commercial motivations such as profit maximization, limiting liability, or building reputational value from a normative perspective. The central question seems to have been how ethics could make business more profitable. The result is that it forecloses critical discussions of the idea of "profit" and what it might mean for our society. In the process, many business ethicists neglect the most basic ethical question: How should we live? Ethics should always remain questioning; if it fails to do this, it ceases to be ethics. Ethics is not primarily about answers, or solutions, but about questions, puzzles, or dilemmas. This does not mean that solutions cannot emerge, but they should always be submitted to the process of critical questioning. We would argue that this is an important lesson that can be drawn from continental thought.

## Continental Philosophy's Contribution to Research

### *Philosophy as the Practice of Questioning Assumptions*

In what follows, we argue that continental philosophy allows us to critique some of business ethics' most central assumptions. We argue that the implicit "scientific" commitment to Enlightenment assumptions about the existence of foundationalist truth and rational agency, have severed the intimate relationships between philosophy, our material and discursive becoming and the everyday practice of questioning. As such, we have largely abandoned philosophy as a legitimate method of enquiry into what we can know about our becoming and about our ongoing attempts to make sense of "ethics."

We seemed to have replaced philosophical practices concerned with the questioning of assumptions with a preoccupation with positivistic measurement, which often imply an uncritical acceptance of implicit assumptions as well as blindspots for existing power relations. We may for instance reconsider why the rational transcendental subject with his (sexism intended) objective calculative decision-making capacities implicitly became the accountable "agent" of all action, and as such, of much of our research. If we implicitly or explicitly subscribe to this view of agency, it also influences our epistemological strategies, because the raw material that this agent needs to take these decisions is objective facts, determined through positivistic modes of enquiry. These days it seems as if taken for granted assumptions exist that make it impossible to realize how what we believe on an ontological level is in fact disputable. Limited understanding of epistemological assumptions also makes it impossible to enquire about the world in new ways. Such enquiry is urgently needed, as we live in an age in which our current understanding comes up short in addressing the challenges of increased insecurity, on political, economic, social, and environmental fronts. In this context, avoiding a political analysis of business ethics issues seems a serious oversight (Rhodes, 2014; 2016).

An example that will be used to illustrate many of the points made in this chapter relates to the large number of research articles focused on establishing the "business case" for corporate responsibility, as well as for ethics and compliance programs. The centrality of this research question indicates the preoccupation with utilitarian calculation as a central mode of theoretical and practical engagement in the field of business ethics. An acceptance of instrumentalist means-to-an-end reasoning seems to predominate in business ethics research. Our understanding of decision-makers as utility-maximizers inform our understanding of "corporate agency" as a specific type of utility maximization; managers employ "natural capital" and "human resources" within "industrial ecologies" to the benefit of their principals.

Since financial outcomes are the easiest to measure and calculate, they typically become the focus of our attention. As Polanyi (1947) highlighted, our preoccupation with utilitarian calculation requires the perpetuation of two fallacies: on an individual level it is a belief that all incentives operating in everyday life are material incentives, and on the societal level it implies that social institutions are necessarily determined by the economic system. As such, to pursue a "rational" scale of material ends, efficacy could only be calculated on the basis of scientific "fact." One of the central distinctions that much of our efforts to "measure" and "manage" relies upon, and implicit in our means-to-an-end reasoning, is the "facts" versus "value" distinction. We can see here that we are dealing with very specific ontological and epistemological assumptions.

As part of our preoccupation with utilitarian calculation, we have also inherited multiple problematic metaphysical binaries, which many continental philosophers have been debunking since the late nineteenth century. "Fact" versus "value," "body" versus "mind," "reason" versus "sentiment," "means" versus "ends" have been exposed as damaging to understanding ourselves and our understanding of truth and morality. Nietzsche's "On truth and lie in the extra/ nonmoral sense" is perhaps one of the most elegant treatises in this regard. But we see it equally well-articulated in Martin Heidegger's *Letter on Humanism*, in Gilles Deleuze and Felix Guattari's playful experimentations in *Anti-Oedipus* and *A Thousand Plateaus*, as well as Jacques Derrida's extended oeuvre, to name but a few.

Over the past few years, the insights of these philosophers have been slowly but surely making their way in the business and society field. For instance, quite a number of scholars have been offering critical perspectives on the nature of business ethics (Jones, 2003; Painter-Morland, 2008; Pérezts, Bouilloud and Gaulejac, 2011; Pérezts and Picard, 2015;), while others focus their critical analysis on management practices (Alvesson and Spicer, 2012a; Clegg, Kornberger, and Rhodes, 2007; Rhodes, 2009; Fleming, and Sturdy, 2011; Spicer, 2013). This kind of philosophical analysis has much more to offer the field of business ethics, both in terms of critique and gesturing toward alternatives. The challenge for process research however lies in *living* these insights, which means participating in the emergence of new truths about reality.

## *Engaging: Philosophy as Dwelling Rather than Building/Functioning*

It must be acknowledged that most research that draws on continental/European philosophy for inspiration tend to favor critique, rather than proposing alternatives. For instance, the process philosophical movement within organization studies has gone some way toward drawing on Heidegger, Derrida, Deleuze and Guattari, Levinas, Spivak, etc. to shed critical light on our attempts to "manage" ethical challenges, environmental responsibility, sustainable development etc., but many of these attempts struggle to articulate viable alternative courses of action. Heidegger for instance offers rich resources toward a critique of the instrumentalist preoccupation with utility-arguments in sustainability discourses, which objectifies the environment and all that form part of it as mere means toward our ends. This critique targets the predominance of a kind of "pay-off argumentation" – arguments which include: the environment must be protected because doing so limits the corporation's legal liability, or because green innovations/buildings save us money in overheads, or because it builds reputation, or as an ultimate pay-off, it safeguards humanity's future livelihood (Painter-Morland and Ten Bos, 2016). Heidegger would insist that paradoxically, this kind of instrumentalist reasoning estranges us from what makes us human beings, Dasein. It makes us incapable of thinking, because we cannot contemplate that which makes us capable of dwelling. We are always rushing to "make things work." Even in research. Such is the nature of the inevitable "so what" question that faces all philosophical research in business and society. To ask the question, "How would Heidegger make things work better?" clearly seems to be the ultimate performative contradiction– or is it? Is there an answer to the "so what" question that is not couched in utilitarian terms? How can we speak of this non-instrumental way of being in the world in terms that are meaningful to business ethics?

To explore this possibility, let us go one step further in investigating again the prominent discourse in the business ethics field, i.e. the "business case" for corporate responsibility and sustainability. If we take up the challenge of formulating a noncalculative response to this discourse, what would it look like? In the first place, we can dispute the terms within which the calculation takes place. The evidence for the "business case" comes in many different forms: the pursuit of triple bottom-line reporting, the "balanced score-cared," the strategic imperative of creating "shared value," or the calculation of an organization's "true value." What these initiatives have in common, is the conflation of all types of value. In some cases, it attempts conflation to a single, economic scale. For example, KPMG's new "True value" methodology encourages organizations to internalize their externalities to create clearer picture of the "true value" of the corporation. The Global Reporting Initiative's (GRI) triple bottom-line reporting guidelines offer detailed performance indicators to help organizations display their social, environmental, and economic performance. Though business ethics and sustainability experts debate whether GRI in fact makes an aggregation claim, i.e. whether it is possible to translate incommensurable goods to a single scale, a more important interrogation of the assumptions behind all such strategies lies latent, unexplored, uncomfortably silent. It is the assumption that only that which can be measured, can be valued. Only the calculable, comparable, containable is worthy of pursuit. Is it because of our desire for control, for "management"? How many times have business ethicists had to deal with deans, directors, politicians scrambling for data on teaching, research and service because "only what can be measured can be managed?"

But could it be that this pursuit of "measurement" for the sake of "management" mismanages precisely because it destroys moral agency as such? By drawing on Derrida (Jones, 2010; Painter-Morland, 2010), Foucault (Ahonen et al, 2014; Jones, 2002), Heidegger (Bakken, Holt and Zundel, 2013; Blok, 2014; Holt and Mueller, 2011, Ladkin, 2006; Painter-Morland and Ten Bos, 2016), Levinas (Jones, 2007), Kierkegaard (Deslandes 2011), Pascal (Deslandes, 2012a), Ricoeur (Deslandes, 2012b), Spivak (Jones, 2005) and others, critically explored the implications of management interventions on ethics in organizations. Painter-Morland (2008) came to the conclusion that ethics management via codes and other management tools often undermines ethics as practice. Others, like Bevan and Corvellec (2007), challenge the simplistic use of Levinas in stakeholder theory and objects to the idea of "corporate moral agency," precisely because corporations cannot have an embodied response to the face of Other. If moral agency, as Levinas and Derrida in conversation with Levinas, describe it, is about openness and responsiveness to the face of the Other, and grappling with the specific iteration of the general in order to give it meaning through the particular, we can understand why measurement is the antithesis of moral responsiveness (Painter-Morland, 2010). It generalizes, it aggregates, and in the process it effaces, it loses the principle in its contextless inarticulability. The conception of moral agency that emerge through my reading of my favorite continental philosophers is a far cry from the calculating rational subject operating on the basis of generalized principles. It is an embodied subject bound, yes, held hostage by the ambiguity that messy, nonaggregated relationships entail. And yet this subject must act, and does act. This subject is not indecisive – instead, "undecidability" means realizing that any action is haunted by all the relationships that cannot be severed even if the action taken will strain and constrain them. When experiencing life in this way, we may find that our current conceptual apparatus fall short in helping us describe and relate to this experience. In fact, our concepts can trap us in our previous assumptions, reassert its binary oppositions and perpetuate its agentic beliefs. These perspectives are helpful in telling us what we cannot assume in the business and society discourses, but does it help us go beyond critique? It is in this respect that another important employment of continental philosophy often remains unexplored, i.e. the crafting of new concepts.

## *Continental Philosophy as the Crafting of Concepts*

Continental philosophy often combines the questioning of assumptions with the recrafting of concepts. Yet it is up to us to not just borrow their critiques, or to adopt the new concepts they coin to obscurify our own texts, but to actively become the crafters of concepts ourselves and rethink our hermeneutic engagement with the various "texts" we engage with in our research (not only written ones). Deleuze in fact suggested that one of the most important philosophical tasks is the crafting of new concepts, or making the concepts that may be emerging from experience or new experiments explicit. As the perfect partners in crime, Deleuze and Guattari (1983 [1992]), were of course the masters of this technique. Shifting their concepts so frequently that it continued to disrupt a sense of mastery, instead eliciting a playfulness, intrigue, responsiveness, and tentativeness. In my mind the trap that many of us fall in when drawing on these philosophers' work, is to become preoccupied with the "correct" interpretation. We waste time engaging in debates about the exact meaning of Derrida's "*differance*," or Deleuze and Guattari's "rhizomes," "war machines," "lines of flight," etc. – disputes about we can call the fetishization of figures and texts. Let us leave this for the hardcore philosophical journals! One of the pleasures of working in business and society research is to start with practice first, and return philosophy to this practice.

Instead of fetishizing philosophers and texts, we should be enticed to experience practice in a way that calls for new concepts, and playfully coin them – not just to reframe and critique existing concepts, but to render alternative ways of being and acting legitimate and desirable. Can we therefore draw on the critics of capitalism to argue for new business models? Can we draw on Marxist concepts to inform proposals around sustainable consumption? We would argue, yes, in fact, we should. Sometimes it is indeed necessary to draw some Trojan horses into capitalist fortresses, and aim to employ them toward the reformation and transformation of our business engagement, rather than its mere destruction.

Let us take one concept, central to our preoccupation with utilitarian calculability, i.e. that of *homo economicus*: Over the past decades, the existence of *homo economicus*, the calculating agent maximizing his or her self-interest, has indeed come under scrutiny. A number of other alternative proposals were made: *homo reciprocans*, *homo ludens*, *homo ecologicus*, etc. What these alternatives suggest is an embodied, relational agent who lives outside of strict economic calculation – who in fact needs to defy such calculation in order to be fully human. By using these alternative concepts more frequently, and exploring its meanings in various contexts, we may succeed in transforming the business and society discourse.

## Process Philosophy as an Emerging Research Method

One of the most exciting research agendas that continental philosophy has been contributing to within the field of organization studies in recent years is that of process studies, and we believe this area holds much potential for business ethics researchers. The increased interest in studying process rather than entities (Helin, Hernes, Hjorth and Holt, 2014) has prompted an interest in empirical methods that do not undermine process philosophy's most central assumptions. In this regard, continental philosophy's ontological commitments hold much promise to inform how research into process-related becomings can and should be done. Studies that can serve as an example of what is possible are emerging from the organization studies literature (Clarke and Holt, 2016) the entrepreneurship literature (Hjorth, Holt and Steyaert, 2015; Popp and Holt, 2013), leadership (Ladkin, 2012; Rhodes, 2012; Painter-Morland and Deslandes, 2014; Blom and Alvesson, 2015; Bouilloud and Deslandes, 2015), as well as gender studies (Pullen, 2006; Pullen, Rhodes and Thanem, 2017; Phillips, Pullen and Rhodes, 2014). However, studies that draw on philosophical insights to study the impact of process thinking in business ethics remain few and far between.

As explained above, continental philosophers critique the ways in which certain Enlightenment assumptions have become fixed, unquestionable truths, which now form the basis of our laws, or economic system and our understanding of morality. Some of these assumptions undermine research into process, because it is primarily focusing on describing, measuring, and predicting specific entities in their relationship to each other. Our ontological assumptions must be revised, not just by articulating and critiquing them, but by actively experimenting with alternatives that would allow us to gauge processes, rather than entities, focusing not so much on what "is," but on what is "becoming."

Examples of authors that use philosophical insights to reframe our understanding of available epistemological approaches include: Alvesson and Kärreman (2007), Garrick and Rhodes (2000); Rendtorff (2016) and Zwier, Blok and Lemmens (2016). Others focus on the philosophical assumptions that underpin our approach to management education (Alvesson and Gabriel, 2016; Painter-Morland, 2015).

### *A Process-Driven Conception of Agency*

This sense of always already starting from within a provenance (Vattimo, 1997), is key to every inquiry that approximates any truth. Nietzsche and Heidegger are central thinkers in the process of progressing this narrative of Being as a becoming. This, process philosophers, pragmatists, and hermeneuticians alike, describe as weak ontology, resisting what they would call a "metaphysics of presence," i.e., some hidden assumptions around what a person "is" as a fixed essence. Philosophically inspired reflections on agency abound in the field or organization studies (Jones, 2010a; Green and Li, 2011; Ibarra-Colado, Clegg, and Rhodes 2006; McMurray, Pullen and Rhodes, 2011; Painter-Morland, 2012, 2013; Spicer, 2011), and have important insights to offer business ethics.

These insights have been acknowledged as critical in furthering reflective methodologies for doing empirical research. For example, Alvesson and Skoldberg (2010) articulated the research implications that emerge from the destabilizing of the subject within poststructuralism and postmodernism. However, a more nuanced understanding of how this influences the way in which we study process is still only in its cradle (cf. Bennett and Checkel, 2015). Process research requires that we rethink the language we use when engaging and writing in and through our research, precisely because we are always already becoming in and through the terms that we use. Continental philosophers can help us in conceptualizing and describing our own becoming and the ongoing processes of sense-making that we engage in. For example, in describing the "passive syntheses" that inform what we previously understood as "rational decisions," and explaining the multiplicities that lie at the heart of any self-concept, Deleuze and Guattari (1987 [2007]) have much to offer a reconceptualization of terms such as "responsibility," "accountability," and moral "decision-making" (Painter-Morland, 2012, 2013).

### Critical Reflection on Process ... Processual Critique

In organization studies, the notion of critical performativity has been rigorously interrogated (Fleming and Banerjee, 2016; Spicer, Alvesson and Kärreman, 2009: Alvesson and Spicer, 2012b), and these insights can be fruitfully applied to the business ethics field. For example, Hjorth proposed the term "critique nouvelle" to describe a performative-affirmative critique that is not so much interested in the impossibilities as in how new possibilities for living can be opened. "Critique nouvelle" oriented research practice can no longer, as did critical thinking, get away with disavowing its own inventiveness as much as possible, so as to produce the effect of not being part of the world that is criticized. It would instead have to recognize its own inventiveness and move to affirmative methods. There is great potential for this kind of philosophical practice to inform research into social entrepreneurship, for instance. Since entrepreneurship also seeks to find limits to transgress, one can see an affinity between critique nouvelle, and indeed the affirmative (vitalist) philosophy of Foucault, Deleuze, Nietzsche and Spinoza, and the practice of entrepreneurship. In both cases, the undefined work of freedom is a desire that produces the subject of creation, the transgressing subject. The art of making space for newness always includes a formation of a self, but a self forms in desubjugation, a practice "that seeks to yield artistry from constraint" (Butler, 2002).

### Process-Driven Hermeneutics

As Friedrich Nietzsche (1886[1973]) already explained in the late 1800s, our most central concepts are essentially metaphors. These concepts cover over some hidden assumptions, and trap us in the status quo (Rhodes and Garrick, 2002; Painter-Morland and Slegers, 2017).

Nietzsche challenged us to explore the ways in which hidden truths become fixed in faded metaphorical dictionaries, of which the meanings lie forgotten, allowing truth to be wielded by whoever has an interest in maintaining the status quo. An analysis of the metaphors operating in the business and society discourse, reveals the dominant logic of utilitarian calculation. So much so, that it is hard to speak about morality in any other way. As George Lakoff and Mark Johnson explain in "*Philosophy of the Flesh*" (1999), much of our moral language is embedded in the utilitarian structure that views wellbeing = wealth, and that therefore, whatever maximizes wealth, maximizes wellbeing, and must therefore be morally good. We "invest" in friendships, I "owe you a debt" of gratitude, and criminals "pay the price" for their deceit. From this perspective, everything of worth must be measured as a cost or benefit. If we therefore employ metaphors such as "natural capital" and "human resources," we inevitably employ entity thinking rather than process thinking. Being aware of the impact of the assumptions hidden within metaphors, don't just help us reveal the tacit beliefs of our key stakeholders and help us to engage in more meaningful conversations (Painter-Morland and Slegers, 2017), but may also allow us to understand the metaphors that are more descriptive of the processual nature of many of the issues that business ethicists are interested in.

Concepts are signs derived from our sensory and neurological processing, they are material and sensory in and of themselves – as embodied utterances when speaking, as visual script when writing, as shared patterned neurological cognition when relating. As such, we have to challenge ourselves to dare to coin now concepts to highlight our experience of process when we engage in qualitative empirical work. They do not have to be "correct," as there is no such thing, but they have to be real, they have to ring true in the relational space we share with others. The philosophers' concepts were their response to the set of relationships that they participated in – our only authentic option would to be to respond to ours. It is in this regard, that philosophically informed qualitative empirical work will make an important contribution to our understanding of process.

## Conclusion

From this chapter, it becomes clear that continental philosophy need no longer be the neglected step-daughter of business ethics research. In fact, publications in the field of organization studies indicate that philosophy can insert inspiring perspectives to discuss all kinds of topics that as yet, have eluded business ethicists. Consider, for instance, the fascinating studies on magic (Rhodes and Pitsis, 2008), literature/fiction (Rhodes and Westwood, 2016; Holt and Zundel, 2014), slow food (Van Bommel and Spicer, 2011), rock music (Rhodes, 2007), and coaching (Clegg et al, 2005). More narrowly defined "business ethics" research drawing on continental thought may perhaps still be in its infancy, but it has much to offer a new generation of business ethics scholars as well as to a broader field of management scholars interested in process studies. As such, publication opportunities in more mainstream journals such as *Organization Studies*, *Organization*, *European Management Review*, *Human Relations*, *Journal of Management Inquiry*, and *Leadership*, to name but a few, now extend the reach of business ethics research into other disciplines. This is an important development in mainstreaming business ethics research and allowing it to reach a readership in other management fields. The challenge, however, will be to do this research well, which means pursuing rigor and clarity, while never compromising continental philosophers' love of beautiful sentences.

## References

Ahonen, P., Tienari, J., Meriläinen, S., and Pullen, A. (2014). Hidden contexts and invisible power relations: A Foucauldian reading of diversity research. *Human Relations*, *67*(3), 263–286. doi:10.1177/0018726713491772.

Alvesson, M., and Kärreman, D. (2007). Constructing mystery: Empirical matters in theory development. *Academy of Management Review*, *32*(4), 1265–1281. doi:10.5465/AMR.2007.26586822.

Alvesson, M. and Skoldberg, K. (2010). *Reflexive Methodology: New Vistas for Qualitative Research*. London: SAGE.

Alvesson, M., and Spicer, A. (2012a). A stupidity-based theory of organizations. *Journal of Management Studies*, *49*(7), 1194–1220. doi:10.1111/j.1467–6486.2012.01072.x.

(2012b). Critical leadership studies: The case for critical performativity. *Human Relations*, *65*(3), 367–390. doi:10.1177/0018726711430555.

Alvesson, M., and Gabriel, Y. (2016). Grandiosity in contemporary management and education. *Management Learning*, *47*(4), 464–473. doi:10.1177/1350507615618321.

Bennett, A. and Checkel, J. T. (Eds.) (2015). *Process tracing: from metaphor to analytic tool*, Cambridge: Cambridge University Press.

Bevan, D., and Corvellec, H. (2007). The impossibility of corporate ethics: For a Levinasian approach to management ethics. *Business Ethics: A European Review*, 16(3), 208–219.

Bakken, T., Holt, R., and Zundel, M. (2013). Time and play in management practice: An investigation through the philosophies of McTaggart and Heidegger. *Scandinavian Journal of Management*, *29*(1), 13–22. doi:10.1016/j.scaman.2012.09.003.

Blok, V. (2014). Being-in-the-world as being-in-nature: An ecological perspective on being and time. *Studia Phaenomenologica*, *14*, 215–235.

Blom, M., and Alvesson, M. (2015). All-inclusive and all good: The hegemonic ambiguity of leadership. *Scandinavian Journal of Management*, *31*(4), 480–492. doi:10.1016/j.scaman.2015.08.001.

Bouilloud, J., and Deslandes, G. (2015). The aesthetics of leadership: Beau geste as critical behaviour. *Organization Studies (01708406)*, *36*(8), 1095–1114. doi:10.1177/0170840615585341.

Butler, Judith (2002). What is critique? An essay on Foucault's virtue. *The Political*, 212–228.

Byers, D., and Rhodes, C. (2007). Ethics, alterity, and organizational justice. *Business Ethics: A European Review*, *16*(3), 239–250. doi:10.1111/j.1467–8608.2007.00496.x.

Carnap, R. (1932). Uberwindung der Metaphysic durch Logische Analyse der Sprache. *Erkenntnis* 2, 219–241.

(1959). The elimination of metaphysics through logical analysis of language, in Alfred Ayer (ed.), *Logical Positivism*, Glencoe, IL: The Free Press, 60–81.

Clarke, J. S., and Holt, R. (2016). Vivienne Westwood and the ethics of consuming fashion. *Journal of Management Inquiry*, *25*(2), 199–213. doi:10.1177/1056492615592969.

Clegg, S. R., Rhodes, C., Kornberger, M., and Stilin, R. (2005). Business coaching: Challenges for an emerging industry. *Industrial and Commercial Training*, *37*(5), 218–223. doi:10.1108/00197850510609630.

Clegg, S., Kornberger, M., and Rhodes, C. (2007). Business ethics as practice. *British Journal of Management*, *18*(2), 107–122. doi:10.1111/j.1467–8551.2006.00493.x.

Curtis, R., Harney, S., and Jones, C. (2013). Ethics in a time of crisis: editorial introduction to special focus. *Business Ethics: A European Review*, *22*(1), 64–67.

Deleuze, G. and Guattari, F. (1992/ 1983) *Anti-Oedipus.: Capitalism and Schizophrenia*. Translated by Hurley, R; Seem, M. and Lane, H. R., Minneapolis: University of Minnesota Press.

(2007/1987). *A Thousand Plateaus: Capitalism and Schizophrenia* Translated by Brian Massumi, Minneapolis: University of Minnesota Press.

Deslandes, G. (2012a). In search of individual responsibility: The dark side of organizations in the light of Jansenist ethics. *Journal of Business Ethics*, *101*, 61–70. doi:10.1007/s10551-011–1173-6.

(2011). Indirect communication and business ethics: Kierkegaardian perspectives. *Business and Professional Ethics Journal*, *30*(3), 307–330.

(2012b). Power, profits, and practical wisdom: Ricoeur's perspectives on the possibility of ethics in institutions. *Business and Professional Ethics Journal*, *31*(1), 1–24. doi:10.5840/bpej20123111.

Fleming, P., and Banerjee, S. B., (2016). When performativity fails: Implications for critical management studies. *Human Relations*, *69*(2), 257–276. doi:10.1177/0018726715599241.

Fleming, P., and Sturdy, A. (2011). "Being yourself" in the electronic sweatshop: New forms of normative control. *Human Relations*, *64*(2), 177–200. doi:10.1177/0018726710375481.

Friedman, M. (2002). Carnap, Cassirer, and Heidegger: the Davos disputation and twentieth century philosophy. *Journal of Philosophy*, *10*(3), 263–274.

Garrick, J., and Rhodes, C. (2000). *Research and knowledge at work: Perspectives, case-studies and innovative strategies.*

Gordon, P. E. (2004). A Continental Divide: Ernst Cassirer and Martin Heidegger at Davos, 1929: An Allegory of Intellectual History. *Modern Intellectual History*, *1* (2), 219–248.

Green Jr, S. E., and Li, Y. (2011). Rhetorical institutionalism: Language, agency, and structure in institutional theory since Alvesson 1993. *Journal of Management Studies*, *48*(7), 1662–1697. doi:10.1111/j.1467–6486.2011.01022.x.

Helin, J., Hernes, T., Hjorth, D., and Holt, R. (eds.) (2014). *The Oxford Handbook of Process Philosophy and Organization Studies*, Oxford: Oxford University Press.

Hjorth, D., Holt, R., and Steyaert, C. (2015). Entrepreneurship and process studies. *International Small Business Journal*, *33*(6), 599–611. doi:10.1177/0266242615583566.

Holt, R., and Mueller, F. (2011). Wittgenstein, Heidegger and drawing lines in organization studies. *Organization Studies (01708406)*, *32*(1), 67–84. doi:10.1177/0170840610394299.

Holt, R., and Zundel, M. (2014). Understanding management, trade, and society through fiction: Lessons from *The Wire*. *Academy of Management Review*, *39*(4), 576–585. doi:10.5465/amr.2014.0087.

Ibarra-Colado, E., Clegg, S. R., and Rhodes, C. (2006). The ethics of managerial subjectivity. *Journal of Business Ethics*, *64*(1), 45–55.

Jones, C. (2002). Foucault's inheritance/inheriting Foucault. *Culture and Organization*, *8*(3), 225.

(2003). As if business ethics were possible, "within such limits." *Organization*, *10*(2), 223.

(2005). Practical deconstructivist feminist Marxist organization theory: Gayatri Chakravorty Spivak. In C. Jones, and R. Munro (Eds.), (pp. 228–244) *Sociological Review Monographs series*; Malden, MA and Oxford: Blackwell.

(2010a). The subject supposed to recycle. *Philosophy Today*, *54*(1), 30–39.

(2010b). Editorial introduction: Derrida, business, ethics. *Business Ethics: A European Review*,

*19*(3), 235–237. doi:10.1111/j.1467–8608.2010.01594.x.
ed. (2007). Special issue: Levinas, business, ethics /. *Business Ethics: A European Review*, *16*(3), 196–321.
Jones, C. Parker, M. and Ten Bos, R. (2006). *For Business Ethics*. Routledge.
Ladkin, D. (2006). When deontology and utilitarianism aren't enough: How Heidegger's notion of "dwelling" might help organisational leaders resolve ethical issues. *Journal of Business Ethics*, *65*(1), 87–98.
(2012). Perception, reversibility, "flesh": Merleau-Ponty's phenomenology and leadership as embodied practice. *Integral Leadership Review*, *12*(1), 1–13.
Lakoff, G. and Johnson, M. (1999). *Philosophy in the Flesh: The embodied mind and its challenge to Western thought*, New York: Basic Books, Kindle edition.
Nietzsche, F. (1886/1973). On truth and lie in the extramoral sense. In: W. Kaufman (ed.) *The Portable Nietzsche*. New York, Viking Press.
McMurray, R., Pullen, A., and Rhodes, C. (2011). Ethical subjectivity and politics in organizations: a case of health care tendering. *Organization*, *18*(4), 541–561. doi:10.1177/1350508410388336.
Painter-Morland, M. and Slegers, R. (2017). Strengthening "Giving Voice to Values" in business schools by reconsidering capitalist metaphors. *Journal of Business Ethics* (forthcoming).
Painter-Morland, M. J. and Ten Bos, R. (2016). Should environmental concern "pay off"? A Heideggerian perspective. *Organization Studies*, DOI 10.1177/0170840615604502.
Painter-Morland, M. J. 2015, Philosophical assumptions undermining responsible management education. *Journal of Management Development*, *34* (1): 61–75.
(2013). The relationship between identity crises and crises of control. *Journal of Business Ethics*, 114, 1–14.
(2012). Rethinking responsible agency in corporations: perspectives from Deleuze and Guattari. *Journal of Business Ethics*, *101*(10), 83–95.
Painter-Morland, M. J. and Ten Bos, R. (2011). *Business Ethics and Continental Philosophy*, Cambridge: Cambridge University Press.
(2010). Derrida and Business Ethics: Ethical questioning (and)(or) questioning ethics. *Business Ethics: A European Review*, 9(3), 265–279.
(2008) *Business Ethics as Practice: Ethics as the everyday business of business*, Cambridge: Cambridge University Press.
Painter-Morland, M., and Deslandes, G. (2014). Gender and visionary leading: rethinking "vision" with Bergson, Deleuze, and Guattari. *Organization*, *21*(6), 844–866. doi:10.1177/1350508413488636.
Pérezts, M., Bouilloud, J., and Gaulejac, V. (2011). *Serving Two Masters: The contradictory organization as an ethical challenge for managerial responsibility* Springer Science and Business Media B.V. doi:10.1007/s10551-011–1176-3.
Pérezts, M., and Picard, S. (2015). Compliance or comfort zone? The work of embedded ethics in performing regulation. *Journal of Business Ethics*, *131*(4), 833–852. doi:10.1007/s10551-014–2154-3.
Phillips, M., Pullen, A., and Rhodes, C. (2014). Writing organization as gendered practice: Interrupting the libidinal economy. *Organization Studies (01708406)*, *35*(3), 313–333. doi:10.1177/0170840613483656.
Polanyi, K. (1947). On belief in economic determinism. *Sociological Review*, *37*(1), 96–112.
Popp, A., and Holt, R. (2013). Entrepreneurship and being: The case of the Shaws. *Entrepreneurship and Regional Development*, *25*(1), 52–68. doi:10.1080/08985626.2012.746887.
Pullen, A. (2006). Gendering the research self: Social practice and corporeal multiplicity in the writing of organizational research. *Gender, Work and Organization*, *13*(3), 277–298. doi:10.1111/j.1468-0432.2006.00308.x.
Pullen, A., Rhodes, C., and Thanem, T. (2017). Affective politics in gendered organizations: affirmative notes on becoming-woman. *Organization*, *24*(1), 105–123. doi:10.1177/1350508416668367.
Rendtorff, J. D. (2016). Philosophical foundations of business ethics: French philosophy and social theory in relation to ethics and philosophy management. *Philosophy Study*, *6*(2), 96–102.
Rhodes, C., and Garrick, J. (2002). Economic metaphors and working knowledge: Enter the "cogito-economic" subject. *Human Resource Development International*, *5*(1), 87–97. doi:10.1080/13678860110018803.
Rhodes, C. (2007). Outside the gates of Eden: Utopia and work in rock music. *Group and Organization Management*, *32*(1), 22–49.

Rhodes, C., and Pitsis, A. (2008). Organization and mimetic excess: Magic, critique, and style. *International Studies of Management and Organization*, *38*(1), 71–91. doi:10.2753/IMO 0020-8825380104.

(2009). After reflexivity: Ethics, freedom and the writing of organization studies. *Organization Studies (01708406)*, *30*(6), 653–672. doi: 10.1177/0170840609104804.

(2012). Ethics, alterity and the rationality of leadership justice. *Human Relations*, *65*(10), 1311–1331. doi:10.1177/0018726712448488.

(2014). Ethical anarchism, business ethics and the politics of disturbance. *Ephemera: Theory and Politics in Organization*, *14*(4), 725–737.

(2016). Democratic business ethics: Volkswagen's emissions scandal and the disruption of corporate sovereignty. *Organization Studies (01708406)*, *37*(10), 1501–1518. doi:10.1177/ 0170840616641984.

Rhodes, C., and Westwood, R. (2016). The limits of generosity: Lessons on ethics, economy, and reciprocity in Kafka's the metamorphosis. *Journal of Business Ethics*, *133*(2), 235–248. doi:10.1007/s10551-014-2350-1.

Spicer, A., Alvesson, M., and Kärreman, D. (2009). Critical performativity: The unfinished business of critical management studies. *Human Relations*, *62*(4), 537–560. doi:10.1177/00187267 08101984.

Spicer, A. (2011). Guilty lives: The authenticity trap at work. *Ephemera: Theory and Politics in Organization*, *11*(1), 46–62.

(2013). Shooting the shit: The role of bullshit in organisations. *M@n@gement*, *16*(5), 653–666.

Van Bommel, K., and Spicer, A. (2011). Hail the snail: Hegemonic struggles in the slow food movement. *Organization Studies (01708406)*, *32*(12), 1717–1744. doi:10.1177/0170840611425722.

Vattimo, G. (1997). *Beyond Interpretation: the meaning of hermeneutics for philosophy*, Cambridge: Polity Press.

Zwier, J., Blok, V., and Lemmens, P. (2016). Phenomenology and the empirical turn: A phenomenological analysis of postphenomenology. *Philosophy and Technology*, *29*(4), 313–333. doi:10.1007/s13347-016–0221-7.

# Normative Approaches

CHAPTER 4

# Research in Normative Business Ethics

## *A Coherence Approach*

RICHARD T. DE GEORGE

### Introduction

How does one do research in normative business ethics? One way of answering this question is to present and defend an abstract approach, or set of steps or rules. Another is to follow the example of expert systems, and try to capture the steps that a practitioner in the field uses. My answer will be closer to the latter than the former. I will briefly describe how I do research in business ethics in traditional abstract terms. It is not the only way to do it, as the other chapters in this book will demonstrate. But it is an approach that I will defend and perhaps more importantly that I have found fruitful. I will then illustrate it in some detail with two examples; and finally, I will draw some conclusions about the approach.

In answering the question of what a method of research in business ethics is, we must get clear what the purpose of the research is. Is it to analyze a case, to resolve a moral dilemma, to uncover the moral dimensions of a business practice (such as using child labor), to answer meta-ethical questions (such as whether corporations can have moral responsibility), to answer broad questions (such as whether capitalism is morally justified), or to develop a new theory? The use of the method is arguably different depending on the nature of the issue.

The method of discovery is different from the method of exposition, although exposition is usually the final stage of research broadly conceived. Among the more interesting, important, and difficult aspects of research in normative ethics is discovering, uncovering, and bringing to light new dimensions of ethics, new issues, new challenges to conventional morality, the status quo, and the received body of ethical doctrine.

A short description of ethics is that it is a systematic study of morality. Every society, if it is at all stable and functional, has a set of rules, norms, taboos and prohibitions, punishments, and ideals in accordance with which members (at least for the most part) interact with each other and carry on daily life. Without these, which I shall call the contents of conventional morality, life, in Hobbes's terms, would be "nasty, brutish and short." (Hobbes, 1651/2017) Societies tend to arrive at similar basic moral norms – norms against killing the members of one's own society, against theft, against violations of personal security, against breaking trust, and so on. They do so because those basic rules have been found to be necessary if a society is to exist, be relatively stable, and be sufficiently productive to support its members. Conventional morality is what a society tries to inculcate into it members and tries to get them to internalize. It is what mothers teach their children and is passed on from generation to generation, sometimes unchanged and sometime modified (especially if conditions change or pertinent knowledge increases). This forms the primary data that ethics studies. Descriptive ethics tries to capture the conventional morality of a society as it is found in both institutionalized form in law and teachings of churches and schools, and more informally in its portrayal in novels and plays, newspaper articles and other media, and as it is lived or not lived by the members of the society. Such work is empirical and those engaged in it use the methods of the social sciences, especially anthropology, sociology, and social and individual psychology.

## Normative Business Ethics

I take normative ethics, which is my focus here, to be a systematic attempt to make sense of morality (both conventional and critical) and to determine the rules that ought to govern human behavior, the goods and values worth seeking in life, and the virtues that lead to a good life worth living. Normative ethical theories are measured in large part by how successfully they capture and make sense of the moral experience of individuals and societies. All of them take as part of their task separating out the parts of conventional morality that can be and should be preserved and justified, and those parts that do not cohere well with whatever criterion or criteria of justification the theory proposes. It should come as no surprise, then, that almost all of them agree that murder, theft, perjury, fraud and so on are morally bad, and that helping others, respecting people, and developing some set of accepted virtues are morally good.

Business ethics is a part of general ethics, composed of a subset of ethical problems and issues. As a subset, it is a systematic attempt to make sense of morality in our individual and communal experience in business and economic life. Business and economic life are parts of our broader moral experience and should not be dealt with as if they were independent of them. Aristotle emphasizes that we can only meaningfully talk about ethics in a reasonably moral society, and only in such a society can the accepted moral practices be a plausible starting point for critical analysis.

Normative ethics is in part dependent not only on the data and results supplied by descriptive ethics, but also on the data supplied by all the other social sciences, by the physical sciences, by history, and by the insights supplied by literature, the arts, and religion – as I shall briefly argue later. It is partly critical and partly constructive.

### *Why Is Research in Business Ethics Necessary?*

The ordinary person knows that murder is wrong, stealing is wrong, fraud and deceptive advertising are wrong, and so on through the catalog of actions that are wrong both in and out of business. If those in academic business ethics did nothing more than make such pronouncements, its value would be questionable, and any discussion of the method it uses would carry little interest for any but the students who might have to answer questions about method in a class on ethics. The *academic field of business ethics* can be distinguished from *ethics in business* on the one hand and the *business ethics movement* on the other. Ethics in business consists of the everyday awareness of morally right and morally wrong actions in business as exemplified in newspaper stories of corruption, in the articles by public pundits, the sermons in churches, the complaints of many about business abuses and wrongdoing, and the everyday judgments people in a society make about business and its practices. The business ethics movement includes attempts by government and NGOs to reign in violations of the law through proactive actions by business such as businesses adopting codes of conduct, hot lines, and the like, as well as responding to demands that they adopt socially responsible practices. The two are related to the academic field, and the three areas each influence one another.[1]

Philosophers in general, and so those involved in business ethics, have no more privileged access to morality than the ordinary citizen and the ordinary business person. What those in normative business ethics have, in addition to knowledge about business, is training in ethical theory, in ethical analysis, and in ethical argumentation. They approach morality systematically, impartially, and critically, uncovering and analyzing hidden presuppositions, mistaken beliefs, invalid arguments and seeking ways of fruitfully defending values, rules, and actions deserving of defense by showing why they should be accepted. Those involved in normative business ethics examine business and business practices from an informed moral point

[1] See my "The History of Business Ethics" (De George, 2006a) for a detailed account of the three and of their interrelations. See also my reply to Richard Rorty's paper which claims that ethics has nothing to add to business or to anything else (De George, 2006b).

of view. Doing so involves not only reflection but also careful investigation and research and an appreciation of the fact that controversial and novel moral issues are usually complex and demand the careful investigation that research provides. The most difficult part of engaging in ethical research is not analyzing a particular case, but in much that goes on before one approaches cases at all.

## Coherence

Methods are not true or false. They are useful for whatever purpose they are intended to serve. Scientific method, for instance, is different from any theory in physics. In all of them coherence as a method is appropriate, where coherence means evaluating how well the theory fits and makes sense of the phenomena with which it is concerned and how well it leads to successfully accomplishing the task for which it was chosen. Normative ethics is not an empirical science insofar as it seeks to determine what one *should* do, how one *should* act, which actions are right and which are wrong. Yet, in attempting to determine this, one starts out with moral phenomena – individual and collective moral experience. A good deal of what is called research in normative business ethics consists of taking a critical stance to some existing literature– to an article or book or theory – or to an existing practice or argument. Philosophers are notorious for criticizing one another's positions as a way of advancing an argument, clarifying a point, or demonstrating that a position leads to a contradiction or to a dead-end to be avoided. As opposed to critical research constructive research breaks new ground and goes beyond the negative work of criticism, and I shall be primarily concerned with the latter. The emphasis in the ethics literature on ethical theory usually leads to discussing a particular method based on the theory in question. The method of coherence takes a step back from the methods of particular theories and can be used to choose which theory is applicable and to test the validity of individual theories and the results they prescribe by evaluating the degree they cohere with the rest of morality and more broadly the rest of the social and natural world of which they are a part.[2]

The method involves a three-step process. It starts with coherence as the method for selecting problems and selecting ethical theories or parts thereof. It then uses the selected theory or theories, each of which may specify a method of analyzing cases or problems in the light of the values and views the theories prescribe. Thus, utilitarianism presents in detail a method for determining which of the available actions in a given situation will produce the great amount of good, however that is defined. Considering results is certainly part of ordinary approaches to moral problems. There is no need for us to reinvent a systematic approach to doing so, since that has already been developed. But there is the need to decide whether the specific ethical problem can best be solved by using utilitarianism, and whether that provides a solution that coheres with our other moral judgments and in fact satisfactorily fits into the context. If rights are also involved, we may wish to use a Kantian approach to the rights issues and then must balance the two results in such a way that the solution is internally coherent and coherent with the other factors relevant to the context and specific situation. Since the coherence method is open to using a variety of ethical theories in specific applications, when it is so used it is pluralistic. My approach to business ethics research consists of combining coherence as a method with the methods of appropriate ethical theories for analyzing cases and problems. The latter can be considered a set of tools available for making moral evaluations. Coherence as a method can be used for choosing the tools it employs to analyze or solve problems, for testing the fit of the various tools it employs with each other, and for testing the results with the other relevant external and internal considerations, both as the research goes along as well as once it is completed.

Coherence is widely ignored in the literature of business ethics, although, as I shall argue, it is

[2] See my papers "Ethics and Coherence" (De George, 1990) and "The Place for Coherence and Moral Rules in Ethics: Richard De George and Bernard Gert" (De George, Gert, and Magnell, 1994).

implicitly widely used and has intuitive appeal among nonphilosophers. The reason for its being ignored, is, I suggest, because historically coherence has been viewed as a theory rather than as a method, and is identified with the coherence theory of truth – a theory which has been widely criticized, identified with the German Idealists of the nineteenth century, and rejected by those who adopt the correspondence theory of truth.[3] Its major defect as a theory of truth is that competing coherent systems can be built, but coherence within a theory does not show it is true. In the hands of idealists, the world of ideas replaces the physical world as the basis of reality. I agree with the view that the everyday world of experience is what morality and ethics are or should be concerned with. But using the method of coherence does not commit one to any specific theory of truth, nor, in ethics does it imply that one is necessarily a realist.

Among the more interesting, important, and difficult aspects of research in normative ethics, I suggested earlier, is uncovering, discovering, bringing to light new dimensions of ethics, new issues, new challenges to conventional morality, the status quo, and the accepted body of received ethical doctrine. Coherence can help one find problems needing analysis, suggest solutions, and guide both research and action. I suggest this search for coherence is the way that moral progress has historically been made, if we mean by progress the enlargement of the moral community to include women as equal to men, to condemn slavery, to acknowledge that the way we use nonrenewable resources and the way we use the natural environment have moral implications, and so on. Each starts with anomalies and ends with a balanced view that better coheres with the uncovered reality.

The method of coherence makes sense of our individual and moral experience by including the diversity of ethical theories as part of that experience. The major ethical theories each seize some part of the whole and privilege it. The search for coherence among them does not yield a supertheory. Rather it is an approach that emphasizes the commonalities of theories and where they yield conflicting judgments, it provides a means of deciding between or among them by asking which coheres best, not only with a coherent pattern internally, that is with respect to other elements of the theory, but also externally.

External coherence means coherence with established or accepted facts including facts of science and those widely accepted as being established by the social sciences, including psychology, sociology, and anthropology. Coherence with widely accepted social norms is an argument in favor of a practice or judgment, although not the last word. In some ways a coherence approach is similar to Rawls's notion of reflective equilibrium.[4] It involves a balancing of one's moral judgment in a particular case with one's carefully considered moral principles; the result of that balancing should be tested for coherence with principles and moral judgments of others in one's own society, culture or tradition; and most broadly, if we seek universal validity for a moral judgment or claim, it must be balanced against the principles and values of other societies. Balancing involves being open to other views and principles, but allows that some of these may be unacceptable and cannot be made to cohere

[3] A good description and defense of coherence as a theory of truth in ethics can be found in Dorsey (2006). In the paper he deals with method, although his major concern is with truth within a system. Thagard (1998) develops what he calls "a multicoherence theory of ethical thinking that involves a "computationally implemented theory of ethics." For a critical "rebuttal" of that theory, see Guarini (2007). For coherence without moral theory, see Engel (2012). In the applied ethics area, DeGrazia (2003) critically evaluates James Childress and Tom Beauchamp's methodology in their *Principles of biomedical ethics* (2001). He briefly describes their use of coherence and then is critical of their abandoning moral theories in favor of relying exclusively on "common morality." Joseph P. DeMarco presents his theory of "dynamic coherence" in his article "Coherence and applied ethics" (1997). My own emphasis is on coherence as a method, not as a theory competing with ethical theories but as useful in evaluating them, choosing the best parts of each, and utilizing the results in solving ethical problems. Nonetheless, I agree with much of what is developed in these and other articles about coherence as a method. I know of no work in business ethics that deals explicitly with coherence either as a method or as a theory.

[4] For Rawls's notion of reflective equilibrium see his *A theory of justice* (1971: 49) and "The Independence of Moral Theory" (1974–1975).

with the predominance appropriately given to judgments, values, and principles with which it is incompatible. A view intolerant of other views cannot be made to cohere with them, although it raises the issue of what terms of mutual coexistence are morally acceptable. Coherence reminds us that the aim of ethics is to make sense of individual and collective moral experience. The experience or moral phenomena come first. A collective moral judgment made by a society may be the result of mistakes about facts, or of considering only expected consequences (and not what actually happens), and it may not cohere with lived reality in many other ways. Mistakes are often failures to realize discrepancies between held beliefs or values and accepted practices. A society may have correctly applied its principles to a set of conditions, and failed to reevaluate the differences that changed conditions make. Hence the coherence approach requires us to be constantly open to the claim that our considered moral judgments are mistaken, no longer appropriate or applicable or deficient in other ways. Not all such claims are valid or can be substantiated or defended in such a way as to deserve sustained consideration. And many of a society's basic principles have been challenged and tested in a variety of ways over time. The more solidly entrenched, the more they cohere with large segments of our experience, the greater the difficulty in overturning or replacing them.

Wide reflective equilibrium[5] should at some point connect with and involve coherence not only with our moral experience but also with reality as it is. If it stops at a theoretical level, it might provide what is sometimes called an ideal theory – a goal to be approached or an end by which to measure existing conditions or practices. But if a decision is needed as to how to act now in a real-world situation, it should yield an actual action plan, given actual conditions.

Some version of utilitarianism and some version of Kantianism may each be internally consistent and coherent. That shows that internal coherence is not the only test of an ethical theory. Any such version that one picks has its critics. If the critics mount their criticism from the point of view of an opposing theory, it presupposes the correctness of the opposing view and so will be rejected by the defender of the theory under attack. A more successful attack can be launched by showing the theory fails to account adequately for some aspect of our moral experience or fails to cohere with some widely accepted moral principle, e.g., that act utilitarianism justifies condemning an innocent man if doing so in an instance produces more good overall than not doing so. The argument is based on showing a lack of coherence with a widely accepted moral principle that it is unjust to condemn an innocent person. There are various ways the utilitarian might respond. But the point is that coherence is a technique that is widely used even by those who adhere exclusively to one ethical theory.

The coherence approach is equally applicable on the international level as it is on the national, corporate, and individual levels. For example, two countries may have different views of justice. If neither interacts with the other each may criticize the other, whether or not such criticism affects the other's actions. But if the two wish to interact, not by intervention to change the other and not by force, but by voluntary trade or commerce, then they will do so only if each side seeks to benefit by the interaction. Each side will seek a relation that

[5] Several philosophers have commented on the relation of reflective equilibrium and coherence. Daniels (1979) develops his version of the notion as a method of theory acceptance. DePaul develops his position in two articles "Two conceptions of coherence methods in ethics" (1987) and "The problem of the criterion and coherence methods in ethics" (1988). In the first he distinguishes between what he calls conservative and radical reflective equilibrium and he opts for the second. One starts with one's considered judgments, then moves to an explanatory theory, modifying each until one reaches an equilibrium point. The radical version looks further at alternative moral theories and one's other non-moral background beliefs. In the second paper he defends what he calls full coherentism as comparable to Rawls' wide reflective equilibrium, which allows for modifying one's particularist beliefs and one's moral theory in the light of one's pertinent non-moral beliefs. This is similar to my position, if the latter includes, for instance, the facts of science among one's non-moral beliefs, and if one allows for going beyond belief to experience of a non-epistemic nature.

fits in with or coheres with its own perception of what it takes to be just or fair. To be just, any agreement must also cohere with the other realities of the world scene if it is to succeed and be sustainable. This involves justice as reciprocity, which means that the agreement is fair if representative persons of various groups with a stake in the matter would accept it as fair whatever conception of justice they hold. The test of the acceptability of the new agreement is whether it coheres with each groups' other agreements, commitments, values, and so on. Any such agreement may involve negotiation and compromise, but to be morally acceptable it must cohere with each side's moral principles. In some cases, this may involve widening one's perspective of what is just. If no such accommodation is possible, the transaction will not take place. Agreement on global issues is even more difficult than bilateral or multilateral agreements, since they involve so many different views of what is fair or just or necessary, what the facts are, and how commitments to any global agreement cohere with the values, institutions, and good of each of the agreeing entities.

Coherence, thus, operates on all levels. What must be tested for coherence, at what level, and with what it must cohere, depends on the case or problem, the circumstances, and the purpose of using the method for the analysis or investigation in question. This fits nicely with the notion that moral analysis is an art as much as a science, that it requires judgment, and that it is not amenable to any simplistic algorithm.

## Coherence and Pluralism

The coherence view of ethics I use is pluralistic. It is pluralistic not only for the reasons I have already given about ethical theories, but because American society is pluralistic. I distinguish ethical pluralism on three levels: the level of principles, the level of practices, and the level of values or lifestyles.

On the level of principles, not all principles or approaches to morality are compatible, and so not all of them can be embraced in a coherence approach. In particular, principles that are totally exclusive or that justify torture or slavery or intolerance of all other views are excluded. Developing a business ethics based on a coherence view must be amenable to the variety of moral principles found in a pluralistic society, at least to the extent of respecting them and, less strongly, of tolerating them. In my own work, I find no difficulty in reconciling utilitarian and deontological principles together with Aristotelian and other principles, although in each case I reject the claim that the principle in question is the sole basic one. To the extent that this is the case, my view is not utilitarian or Kantian or Aristotelian, even though it embraces insights from them and others.

The second level is the level of practices. On this level, I do not mean that contradictory practices are both justifiable, but that with respect to the basic practices of society, they can be justified from a variety of principles. Murder, for instance, is recognized as morally wrong. Some people may not ask why it is wrong, and just treat it as self-evident or intuitive or one's gut reaction to it. But all the major ethical theories give accounts of why murder is wrong, and the accounts are often different from one another. From the point of view of coherence, what is important is not the different rationales given but the agreement on the wrongness of the action. To some extent it is like Rawls's notion of an overlapping consensus (Rawls, 1987; Rawls, 1993: 134–1949; Rawls, 1999: 340).

There are, however, in American society some differences on the morality of certain practices. They may arise from different principles, or from differences of facts or perception of facts, or from differences in the weight people assign to conflicting principles or values. In such cases coherence does not claim to have a definitive solution or method of reconciling all differences. It requires openness to all reasonable contenders and seeks the solution that is best supported by the arguments presented in its behalf and the related facts. Where the facts are in dispute, then all theories are in the same position. A nonpluralistic position with a single basic moral principle may be used to come to a decision, but even here not all moral disputes are decidable, although many – I believe most – are. And if the principle does resolve the problem for its adherents, it may not for those who do not accept the principle as the ultimate authority and as the only means of evaluating moral practices. Some moral issues are poorly framed. Some require knowledge of facts that are not available.

The third level of moral pluralism – the level of choice of values and lifestyles – is again a fact of American society and one which coherence accommodates. Pluralism with respect to values is compatible with agreement that certain practices are immoral from a variety of principles. As with practices, not all lifestyles are equal and coherence is not committed to accepting all of them. Only those that are co-possible with other choices can form a coherent moral community to which moral norms are appropriate. The choice of bank robber or hit-man is not acceptable. But within the bounds set by broadly agreed upon moral principles, the coherence approach tolerates and can accommodate a great many lifestyles that might not be acceptable in a homogeneous society.

Now each of the different theories of ethics may propose a different method for determining the rightness or wrongness of whatever is being analyzed. And one can in that sense speak of the utilitarian or the Kantian method of doing moral analysis. But since the method of analyzing problems or cases using the theory's method is a method internal to the theory, Aristotle or Kant or Mill had to have an external method that preceded their theory and that they and others could use to test the theory. I believe that, if by method in this latter sense one means some systematic way of approaching moral phenomena and testing the adequacy of a theory, the method they implicitly used and we can explicitly use is coherence: how well does the theory proposed fit the facts and explain them, that is, how well does it cohere with the phenomena being investigated and cohere with everything else pertinent that we know? The more of what we think we know that must be jettisoned by a theory to achieve coherence, the more difficult it is for a theory to achieve acceptance by the respective community of practitioners (or scientists or scholars) and eventually by the public.

If we use coherence with ethical experience as our guide to theory evaluation., we can make sense of the variety of ethical theories and see their usefulness in dealing with ethical issues. As one studies the various theories and thinkers in ethics, one sees that each of them had grasped something important. They all say and articulate an important part of morality. It is because they do so that they are still read and that we still learn from them. One can hold this while admitting they all had weak points. Coherence helps us evaluate theories by seeing how well they cohere with the general and our own moral experience, and how well they make sense of it. This is not a task that we each must do individually, however, for all the great theories have been studied and analyzed and the literature surrounding them points up their strengths and weaknesses. A frequent criticism of a theory is that when applied to some cases it yields a judgment that goes against some widely held belief or principle. To that extent it fails to cohere with it, either one must give up the belief or principle, or one must give up – or more usually – modify the theory. No ethical theory so far developed has mustered acceptance by all philosophers, and, most often, bright thinkers can be found on each side of the argument. One conclusion one might draw is that the conflicts are irresolvable and none of them is worth pursuing. But that would be too strong a conclusion. Because no one theory coheres perfectly with our moral experience and adequately captures it all is no reason to jettison what does cohere and that does help us understand and make sense of morality. A second reaction of some is to choose the theory that seems to them to best do the whole job. Often, they are motivated by the desire to choose and work with one theory to preserve internal consistency. They argue that different theories have different presuppositions that are usually incompatible with those of another theory. Pluralism, which uses each of the various theories – or a subset of them – as the user deems appropriate, is a third alternative.

Using coherence as a method is compatible with using a single moral theory. Yet, although using a pluralistic approach to moral theory is not required by a coherence approach, it arguably best coheres with our moral experience. If a case involves rights, why not use a theory of rights to analyze to it? Why should one try to analyze it by using a consequentialist theory? And similarly, if a case involves conflicts of consequences, why try to force the actions into rights talk? On the coherence view, it is possible to see the insights of each of the great theories as describing or accounting for a portion of our moral experience. One might compare it to the story of the blind men each feeling a different part of the elephant. Each of them gets part of the description of the elephant right; they err in extrapolating from that to a theory of the whole. The individual descriptions by themselves will all fit together or cohere and none is incompatible with the others because they all describe the same elephant. Similarly, if various parts of one ethical theory cohere with our experience, there is good reason to preserve the insight we derive from it. We can use each of the insights insofar as they fit or make sense of or cohere with moral experience, without being required to accept generalizations or claims to completeness that do not fit or cohere. If each is a valid insight, it expresses part of the same whole–the totality of moral experience, including the variety of moral values that make it up. This approach to ethics makes it possible to learn from all the great ethical theories. Each of the great thinkers had remarkable insight into a part of moral experience and captured and articulated an important part of it. They were generally correct in what they affirmed but mistaken in their claim, if they made it, to be either a complete account of morality or the only correct one.

Thus, from Aristotle one can learn the importance of virtue and how to fruitfully think about it, and one can also appreciate and evaluate his practical, empirical approach to ethical issues, the importance of seeing ethics as a social institution, and the crucial role of judgment. From Aquinas, one can come to appreciate that human beings have a certain structure, just as other natural beings, and that there is something valuable to be learned from looking at what are called human nature and natural law. From Bentham, Mill, Sidgwick, and Moore one can learn how to consider consequences in a systematic way, considering the effects of actions on all those affected. From Kant and Ross, one can find a way to understand duties, rights, and justice. From Hegel, one can come to appreciate dialectics, the usefulness of negative thinking, the interplay of the positive and the negative, and the need to look for and to resolve contradictions. From Marx, one can learn not to take moral problems at their face value, but to cut below the surface to find root causes and to realize that the solution to problems may lie on a level other than the one at which they appear. From Hume, one can learn the importance of emotions. From analytic philosophers, one can learn the need to break problems down into their component parts, to be as clear and precise in moral reasoning as it allows. Negatively one can learn from them the need not only to be critical but also to be constructive. From the existentialists and phenomenologists, one can learn the importance of description, context, and responsibility for what one is and becomes.[6] If these are all valid insights, it seems foolish to feel one must reject them because of their failure to cohere with one's preferred theory. That insight constitutes the pull and attraction of pluralism.

If it is correct that each of the authors I mentioned above have something that resonates and reflects people's moral experience, that coheres with their personal and social moral experience, then one is better off being able to include that in one's analysis or approach to solving problems or issues or cases than one would be without being able to access them. The purpose of being able to use different theories and types of moral argumentation does not require a super theory. Nor does using them together require a global argument to show in advance of what is being used together how they all cohere. Rather one can proceed based the knowledge that to the extent they accurately reflect our collective moral experience they all cohere because each describes, captures, reveals, or highlights in an exemplary way an aspect, facet, or part of moral experience. That is why their contributions continue to be pertinent. Together

[6] The list is arbitrary and the readers can add their own figures from whom they have learned and whose approach they follow. The list includes ethical thinkers often included in anthologies of ethics whose views many teachers of ethics think are still worth reading and who may have something to say to their students. The list does not include contemporaries or near contemporaries. The point is that unless one was brought up in or trained in only one school of thought, one's thinking about ethics has probably been influenced by the views of a number of different philosophers.

they show that moral experience is not simple but a rich, thick, multifaceted phenomenon that has not been adequately and fully captured by any one of the competing ethical theories. Different kinds of questions require different approaches, but the answers all should cohere, on the one hand, with one another (internal coherence), and, on the other hand, with the rest of reality, with the facts that science provides, and at least initially with the values and the social structures that we all find ourselves in (external coherence). Insofar as different theories propose different techniques for determining the morality of whatever is being investigated, it seems to make sense to utilize each of them as and when necessary.

Resolving moral issues is a practical endeavor. Judgment is always necessary both in developing general principles from cases and in applying general principles to these cases. Pluralists see that all – or at least the clear majority – of ethical theories have much more in common than the arguments raised by their attackers would lead one to suspect. After all, they all attempt to make sense of our individual and collective moral experience, and do so with varying degrees of success.

There are several practical reasons for adopting pluralism in doing business ethics, although the arguments do not singly or together lead to the conclusion that it is the only proper way to do it. First, we live in a pluralist world and in the United States in a pluralist liberal society. Pluralism allows one to take all the different values into account.

A second reason for adopting a pluralistic approach is pragmatic or strategic. One can use theory to help one think through a moral problem or resolve a moral case or decide on a collective level to adopt a practice or policy, e.g., for a firm. But one may be called on to justify one's position if it affects others, and, if one wishes to convince others that a policy is the right one to adopt, simply stating one's preference is not enough. The results that best explain and cohere with individual and collective moral experience are the most likely to be convincing to the general population including, in the case of business ethics, to customers, workers, and executives alike. Arguments that depend on consequences, that consider rights and justice, and that exemplify integrity and compassion are more likely to be understood and accepted than arguments that rely on understanding and accepting a Kantian or a utilitarian or any other specific theoretical approach. Not all customers, workers or managers are Kantians or utilitarians although they all probably understand arguments that speak of duty or rights or consequences.

Adoption of both coherence and pluralism with respect to ethical theories and values enables one to take advantage of any theory that has something positive to contribute to whatever topic, issue, problem, or case one is investigating. This method has the advantage of being able to accommodate the best each theory offers and to explain where each falls short.

A search for coherence can help one become sensitive to moral issues as well as provide suggested solutions. When theories and facts don't cohere, the lack of coherence is a starting point for research. When proposed values do not cohere with each other or with accepted practices, that offers a starting point for research. A test of the moral acceptability of a solution is how well it coheres with the overall situation for which it is proposed. The approach excludes nothing a priori except contradictions, known factual errors, and the like. It encourages imaginative and novel approaches, is open to different cultures and norms, yet provides the tools for sorting out fanaticism from morality, the morally acceptable from the unacceptable, which is determined not a priori but a posteriori.

That is the broad picture. Judgment is crucial in deciding what to investigate, what issue or topic to tackle and which approach or approaches is or are appropriate for investigation and then for presentation. Where different approaches lead to different results, judgment is required to decide which side has the better arguments or which results cohere better with other pertinent considerations. Sometimes one gets an idea about what is missing in an ongoing discussion or what has been overlooked or what needs to be brought to light. As one develops the arguments in support of one's thesis and considers the possible counterarguments, one's position may change or shift or be modified. Judgment is critical in choosing which approach to use to solve a problem.

In doing normative ethics it is helpful to use some general rules of thumb (but they should not be taken as a method): determine all the relevant facts; break large questions down into small units; see if analogies are useful; look for additional alternatives in questions or issues that are seemingly either/or; use one's moral imagination; be conscious of the fact that what appears as a moral issue on one level, for instance the individual level, may have an appropriate moral resolution only on a higher level, for instance the corporate level; examine one's own presuppositions as well as those of others in stating the question; look for logical errors and inconsistencies; use the resources of moral reasoning developed over the centuries, testing your intuitions against counterexamples. Once you have tentatively come to a moral evaluation, consider arguments that someone who disagrees with you might raise, and consider whether you can give a satisfactory reply. Intuitions are not enough, nor is conventional morality, although they both provide starting points and raw material. Investigation involves false starts, dead ends, mistakes, and revisions, change of thesis as facts emerge. It is messy and not straightforward, unlike the presentation of results, which usually appears as a linear development of an argument which leads to a conclusion.

In keeping with the notion of coherence, if one wishes what one does in business ethics to possibly have an impact beyond academic journals, what one writes will be most accessible if one avoids both technical jargon (to the extent possible) and reliance on the authority of some historical figure or figures. If one learns something from Kant, and if one uses a Kantian type argument, whether the argument is valid and effective depends on the strength of the argument and not on acceptance or even knowledge of Kant. The reader should not have to be a Kantian to accept an argument, for instance, on rights, or for the claim that people should be treated with respect, or that if x is morally obligatory for me, it is morally obligatory for everyone else similarly situated. As one defends one's position to one's business colleagues one doesn't have to refer to Mill or mention utilitarianism to argue that one option is morally preferable to another based on considering the consequences of each.[7] Moreover to the extent possible, when arguing for a policy or a position or the moral evaluation of a case, it is most likely to be accepted if one defends one's statements or position or policy by presenting arguments from more than one point of view, for instance both from a consequences and from a rights point of view to show that the conclusion is not dependent on the acceptance of one approach to the exclusion of others. When different approaches reach opposite conclusions – which, I suggest, is rare – then one should provide an argument as to why one is preferable to the other. Rights tend to trump consequences most of the time, but sometimes consequences can trump rights, especially less fundamental rights. A pluralist has more leeway in this situation than someone committed exclusively to a particular ethical theory. This does not mean that the pluralist has no principles and is a relativist or an opportunist able to justify all conclusions. To be credible a pluralist must take arguments seriously, weigh them all impartially, seek the best reasons available for choosing, and should be able to defend his choice of one ethical theory or one argument over another in the consideration at hand.

## Applying the Coherence Method: Two Examples

I noted at the beginning that I would discuss method in normative business ethics not only in the abstract, but also by trying to describe how I do business ethics. I shall first describe my approach to defining the field of business ethics by presenting my attempt at this in my book *Business Ethics* (De George, 2010), as an example of a large research project; and then look in more detail at a single chapter, as an example of the analysis of a particular issue.

I came to business ethics from my work in general ethics, and when I first started in this area there was no such field as business ethics. Business ethics as an academic field did not exist before the

[7] Of course this does not imply that in scholarly research one should not give appropriate credit or cite the existing literature when appropriate.

latter part of the 1970s. So, part of the task I decided to tackle was to help define the problems and the overall structure of the field. What approach did I use?

Before business ethics emerged as a field, there were of course, as I noted earlier, moral judgments made about business practices – workers could tell when they were being exploited, customers could tell when they were being cheated or when products were misrepresented, mothers taught their children the virtues of honesty, thrift, charity and so on as applied to life, including business or economic life. Some business schools had courses in social issues in management. Those of us in philosophical ethics who had an interest in the periodic scandals in business, the charges make against the military-industrial complex, in the disputes about equal opportunity, discrimination, and the like, saw the need for a systematic, coherent approach that could make sense of them, evaluate them, develop the links between them, and offer a reasoned and intelligible way to discuss them and to open fora where they could be further discussed. The time must have been ripe for such a field to emerge because several philosophers all independently started on developing what would become the field of business ethics. In doing so we all used the method or methods we had used in doing general ethics. There was nowhere else to turn.

If the study of business from a moral point of view was to be systematic, and the aim was to structure a coherent view of business ethics as a field, how does one go about such a process? The hardest part was determining where to start and what the issues of the proposed field were. I took a hint from the last of the great system builders in philosophy, Georg W. Hegel. The first task was to lay out the field of business, that is, choose a starting point and see how each part leads rationally or naturally to the next part. With that framework, then view both the whole and each of the successive parts from the moral point of view. Where one starts from the ethical perspective is where one is at a given time and place. For me that initially was business and conventional morality as applied to business in the United States. Since normative ethics is both constructive and critical, I envisioned the task as articulating a defense of those parts of the system that withstood ethical scrutiny and arguing for the need to change those parts that failed such scrutiny. In a somewhat Hegelian vein, I tried to achieve objectivity by considering the strongest arguments I could against the positions I would attempt to defend and the practices I would attempt to justify.

The starting point for both investigation and presentation had to be conventional morality as applied to business and business practices. How does one start? Coherence as a method suggests that one might well look for what Thomas Kuhn (1962) called anomalies or what Hegel called contradictions in actual practice. What I found when I looked at business and the public view of it, was a wealth of business bashing for moral failures and attacks on the military-industrial as well as a variety of movements – the civil right movement, the women's rights movement, the beginning of an environmentalist movement. All involved criticism of business and business practices to some extent. Could the attacks and the replies, and the strong support for the U.S. economic system vs. the communist alternative all be fit into a coherent field, one that could account for them all and cohere internally as well as externally with a strong implicit acceptance of business and a proud commitment to the American system of which it was a part? There was a disconnect or incoherence between the two. People complained about business, especially big business, yet embraced it. People complained about crookedness in business, yet they often accepted it as inevitable and with a shrug would say "Business is business, what do you expect? Business should not be confused with morality, which is personal." If business ethics as a field was to do justice to all of this, it had to include all the diversity people experienced while providing a coherent umbrella under which it could all be brought together. That became the aim I proposed to achieve in writing my book, *Business Ethics*, which I began with an analysis of what I called "the myth of amoral business."

The technique of identifying and analyzing social myths I adapted from Claude Lévi Strauss. His technique of analysis consists of first of describing the parts of social reality that society acknowledges and then bringing to light the parts that are shielded from view, obscured, or covered over by the myth. That notion perfectly fit the American phenomenon of the general population's seemingly inconsistent moral appraisal of business. The rest of my book turned out to be an extended argument to the effect that the myth captures part of reality and conceals a good deal that needed to be brought to the surface, and that ethics not only did indeed apply to business but was a necessary part of its functioning. It was the glue that held the system together as well as the oil that allowed it to run efficiently. My book turned out to be a long argument to try to uncover the validity of the ethical imperatives for needed change that are present in society, that were necessary to justify the system, that could and should be incorporated into business practice, and that would render the system coherent with perceived reality.

The structure of the work I adopted led me to start with the broad picture first, and again I found a striking anomaly or apparent contradiction of moral views. The American view of capitalism or free enterprise or whatever other name one gave to the system found in the United States was in many ways schizophrenic. The 1970s were in the middle of the Cold War years, but they were also the Vietnam War years. Americans were often fierce in their opposition to the Soviet Union and communism, yet many were opposed to the U.S. war in Vietnam, to the military-industrial complex, and to big business. Because of the Cold War mentality, capitalism and the American way of life were diametrically opposed to the Soviet Union and the communist way of life. Yet there was little actual defense of capitalism, which in the U.S. was simply accepted unquestioningly as the economic system. If business ethics was to develop as a field, and if it was to deal primarily with business in a capitalist or free enterprise system, then it made sense to me that capitalism or free enterprise had to be analyzed, critiqued, and if appropriate, defended. This led me to a moral examination of capitalism, the system in which American business operated, and of the values that existed together with the economic system. But here the first meta-ethical question arose. I mentioned earlier that the method of investigation differs from the method of presentation. The question was: can one talk sensibly about an ethical evaluation of an economic system? Are economic systems comparable to mathematical systems? It makes little sense to speak about mathematical systems being moral or immoral. Morality deals with people, with right and wrong actions of individuals, with moral virtues. Does any of this apply to economic systems, and if so, do the moral terms mean the same thing when applied to economic system? In searching for an answer, I looked to coherence – coherence with common morality which evaluated economic systems, to discussions by philosophers of morally evaluating collectives, and to economic theory. The solution I arrived at was to side with those economists who saw economics as essentially a study of relations among people mediated by commodities, exchange, money, and so on. This was more in the tradition of political economy than of econometrics.

Criticism of economic systems fell into two different models. One was what I termed a structural analysis: namely what are the basic, essential components of the system? If any of them can be shown to be inherently immoral, then the system could be judged immoral. The clearest case was slavery. An economic system based on slavery could be morally condemned because slavery could be shown to be inherently immoral. There was a general agreement on the immorality of slavery and that was enough to make out the case against it and show that economic systems could be morally evaluated. How did this apply to capitalism? My analysis of capitalism drew on the then-standard descriptions of it, including Marx's. Drawing on these I distinguished three necessary components – industrially available capital, private ownership of the means of production, and a free-market system, which includes competition and the free movement of capital and labor. For the ethical analysis, I used both a utilitarian and a deontological approach, since they were the most generally used theories. If any of the necessary components could be shown to be inherently immoral – as slavery was – using either of the theories, then the system could not be morally justified. I did the same for socialism, which I saw as a more plausible alternative to capitalism than communism, which neither the Soviets nor anyone else claimed had been achieved. The result I reached was that neither was inherently immoral.

I called the second model an end-state approach. It consisted of analyzing the results for a society of adopting the economic system in question. But this could only be done by looking at actual societies, not simply economic models. Capitalism as found in many countries in Western Europe was mixed with some elements of socialism, and capitalism in the United States was different from capitalism in Japan, or in Germany. So, I examined capitalism as found in the United States, that is, capitalism as it had evolved within the context of American law, history, and social institutions. The task here consisted in comparing the results of adopting the American system as found in the United States with socialism as found in socialist societies. The criteria I used, based on the existing literature of both sides, were primarily standard of living and satisfaction of those subject to the system. I did not compare the U.S. results with imagined results under some other alternatives which had never been tried in a society, and made no claims that the U.S. system was the best that could be achieved. As the basis for the comparison. I could not rely only on ethical theory but had to bring in a good deal of empirical data. The task involved answering Marx's charges as well as evaluating the current defenses of the U.S. economic system. The conclusion I reached was that the U.S. system, considered from an end-state point of view, was not immoral. It was not a defense of capitalism in general and it showed that capitalism had many tendencies and aspects that could be criticized from a moral point of view.

In my view, my analysis of the American system was an example of an approach that could be used in evaluating any embedded economic system. That cohered nicely with my earlier analysis of the myth of amoral business. The structure of the field then emerged. One of its central tasks was to help rectify the ills of capitalism by systematically asking and answering questions such as: what moral norms were missing in American capitalism that, if adopted, could help put a human face on rapacious capitalism, and how could one make capitalism a system that benefited all in a society and not just the capitalist class? The rest of my book spelled out what I argued could be defended and what deserved criticism if one wished to improve the system from a moral point of view. As I worked through issue after issue I came to realize that the task I saw for business ethics was to help improve the system by helping businesses improve themselves, and, when necessary, by suggesting legislation to rein in business excesses when businesses failed to do so.

My point was not to present the final word on any of the topics but to demonstrate how one could argue for a position and reach a conclusion after considering the arguments on the other side as well. By showing that in the clear majority of cases one could argue to a conclusion that was supported by various supposedly competing ethical approaches, I tried to exemplify the truth of the claim that on many issues one could come to a conclusion that was not only justified by one's preferred ethical theory, but one that had broad support from many theories.

The outlines of the field of business ethics now became apparent. From an analysis of American system of capitalism as a whole one could pass seamlessly on to an analysis of its parts. Business in America is varied, but from a moral point of view the major actors and the major objects of criticism were big business corporations, even though small and medium-size enterprises numerically outnumbered them by far. An unanticipated question I encountered and felt forced to discuss was whether one could morally evaluate the actions of corporations as well as of the individuals within the corporation. G I turned to coherence for a solution. I searched for a position that would account for ordinary usage, corporate law, the arguments in sociology about methodological individualism, and the meaning of moral terms as generally found in ethical theories. As a metaethical question, it did not depend on one's normative moral view, even though the results had normative implications. The solution seemed to be that corporations were moral actors insofar as one could morally evaluate the actions of corporations, but that they were not moral agents, at least not in the same sense that human individuals are.

The division of chapters of *Business Ethics* was dictated by the systematic relations of production, exchange, marketing, labor, and finance, and the values that underlay them and the practices prevalent in each, which for the most part roughly corresponded to the areas of business as found in business schools and in corporations. Briefly put, there are moral issues raised by the structure of a corporation, issues about corporate governance, including its relation to shareholders, its suppliers, workers, customers, and the public. If the corporation produces goods, there are moral issues connected to the way production is carried on and to the externalities it produces. Pollution and responsibility for environmental damage have a moral dimension. After producing a product, the corporation makes a profit by selling it. Marketing raises clear moral issues about deceptive advertising, monopolistic practices, price gauging, and so on. The products are produced by workers, and there are a host of moral issues related to labor – including the doctrine of employment-at-will, the ethics of downsizing, hostile takeovers, unions and strikes, and the like. Corporations require financing, and there are many moral issues about banks, interest rates, loans, stock s and bonds, and other commercial instruments. Each stage involves consideration of specific issues and cases and alternatives, using all the techniques of moral reasoning and argumentation that I mentioned as my influences. But the treatment of each topic had to cohere with what went before and what followed, if it was to be a coherent whole. To be accepted by others it also had to cohere with much of conventional morality and be consistent with accepted business practices to the extent possible. If it was to be critical, the criticism had to cohere with the positive values broadly accepted in American society, while at the same time being open to change and revision.

That is an overview of how coherence structures a large research project, but it leaves out the false starts, the internal revisions to achieve internal and external coherence, and the fact that clarity on the project and on details emerges only as one starts working though the project in detail.

To show how the method works on a more limited piece of research I shall use an article I wrote in 1980 (De George, 1981) that I revised for a chapter of my book and that deals with the responsibilities of engineers in large organizations. The article itself was a revised version of a paper I presented at a National Conference on Engineering Ethics in 1980. At each iteration, I made changes, some based on feedback by others and some required by the different purposes the material was to serve. In searching for a topic for the conference paper I noticed as I looked through the literature a puzzling discrepancy between the view of whistleblowers as heroes presented by those in applied ethics and the fate that the whistleblower frequently suffered for his or her heroic act. They often lost their jobs, and were considered traitors by fellow employees. How could one explain this seemingly contradictory phenomenon? In a search for a solution I hit upon doing an analysis of the Ford Pinto case, which was topical at the time. I chose that because I found the discussions of the case at the time simplistic, starting with the article on the case in *Mother Jones* (Dowie, 1977). The account was that Ford did a cost benefit analysis of correcting a defect they knew about. They could have prevented fires from rear end collisions if they inserted an $11.00 baffle, but decided to put people's lives at risk because a cost benefit analysis showed it was cheaper to pay the few law suits that would arise from deaths than insert the baffle. Moreover, Ford continued to leave off the baffle even as it redesigned parts of the car in later versions. If the facts were as presented, it was a clear case of Ford acting unethically. The question it raised for me was: how could this happen? The facts presented did not seem to make as much sense or cohere as might first appear. Does a company like Ford really make its decisions based on one cost benefit analysis, which obviously is incomplete? It does not take a managerial genius to realize immediately that the analysis does not consider the reputational damage that such law suits cost. It also gave the impression that no one at Ford cared about saving lives or about safety, and that the engineers, quality control people, and a great many others were all complicit with management at many levels up to the CEO, Lee Iacocca, to kill people. That seemed unlikely, which led me to research the case a little deeper, and in the process forced me to ask and try to answer many questions including: how much safety can and do consumers expect from the products they use, including cars? Do they have a right to safety and if so how does one justify that right and what exactly does it amount to? Do they have a right to be informed of risks they are taking? What are the obligations of manufacturers in the way of safety, and what role does strict liability play? Does failure to come up to state of the art with respect to safety constitute a moral failure? In the Pinto case, who made the crucial decisions and on what basis? Was the case one of willful negligence, criminal intent, or something else? Who was responsible for decisions along the line and in the end? How can one explain the fact that it took so long for anyone in the company to blow the whistle? Were all those who did not blow the whistle and knew what was going on morally culpable for not blowing the whistle? The questions are complex and not easy to answer. But must we really know the answer to all of them to decide what seems like a simple case? The answer requires research. The first step in pursuing such research is to get all the facts, or as many as possible. If not all the pertinent facts are available, then one's moral evaluation is necessarily incomplete and conditional, given the available facts. If more pertinent information becomes available, then one's analysis and conclusion might have to be revised. The case started with a trial in Winamac, Indiana, in which Ford was charged with three counts of reckless homicide, a criminal offense. On March 16, 1980, a jury returned the verdict of not guilty.

I gathered as many facts about the case as I could from whatever sources I could find – primarily news articles, court testimony, and whatever corporate documents and statements were available. I did not second guess the jury decision, which given the facts of the case they were presented with, I think made the proper decision. I did not feel the court case answered the question of the moral responsibility of Ford or of its managers. But it did supply some bits of information that were helpful. Francis Olsen, the assistant chief engineer in charge of design at Ford testified that he had bought a 1973 Pinto for his 18-year-old daughter. He was an informed buyer and thought the car safe enough for his daughter. There were no National Highway Traffic Safety Administration standards for gas tanks until 1977. The State of Oregon sold its fleet of Pintos for safety reasons it said. Yet it considered the cars safe enough to sell to other buyers. They went at auction for as much as $1800, even though they cost only $2000 new. Evidently at least some drivers thought them safe enough at that price. The case upon further investigation proved more complicated than it first seemed. I published my analysis, but it turned out to be a minor part of my conference paper and of the article and an even smaller part of the chapter on whistle blowing in my book. Doing research on the Pinto case led me to another question: were the engineers and others who knew about the defect complicit in any possible wrongdoing for not blowing the whistle on Ford? Did they have an obligation to do so?

There was growing interest in whistle blowing at the time, but little in the way of ethical analysis. The research I did on the Pinto case led me to research on whistle blowing. I read the available material on whistle blowing. Part of the method I used was to see what the existing scholarly literature said and how well that cohered with ordinary views on whistle blowing. Most whistle blowers were not looked upon favorably by their peers, yet they were presented as courageous role models by many academic writers. That disconnect between the two helped guide my research, as it had helped guide me to choose the topic in the first place. The issue in the literature, as far as I could determine because there was not a great deal of it, was between those who claimed that loyalty to one's employer trumped any justification for going external, and those who claimed that safety issues trumped all other considerations and were in addition an instance of the exercise of free speech. At the extremes one side held whistle blowing was never justified; the other that even a slight concern was adequate grounds for morally requiring that one blow the whistle. Did loyalty always trump free speech, or did free speech always trump loyalty? In analyzing the strongest arguments presented by each side, I concluded that each of the extreme positions was too strong and did not cohere with all the relevant considerations. Yet each side had something positive to contribute to the discussion. If any conclusion I arrived at had to cohere with moral experience, it could not arbitrarily exclude the views held by many people. Any adequate account had to take such views into account and give them their due.

In attempting to reconcile the strengths of each side while avoiding the weaknesses, the arguments led me to make distinctions that were not typically made. There were many kinds of actions that went under the name of whistle blowing: internal and external, personal and impersonal, governmental and nongovernmental. The arguments for and against each were different. Much of the difficulty in the literature came from conflating different types of whistle blowing. Rather than attempt to analyze all of them, I chose to analyze nongovernmental, impersonal, external whistleblowing. My point was to show readers that one type on which there was great agreement could be analyzed from a moral point of view, and that anyone who wanted to think further about other types had a model from which to start. This is an example of breaking a complex problem into smaller parts.

As I tried to give both sides of the argument their due, I saw that I had to divide up the issue still further. Sometimes whistle blowing was indeed morally impermissible. Sometimes it was morally obligatory. Could I come up with some general rules for when the kind of whistle blowing I was examining was morally prohibited, when it was permitted but not morally obligatory, and when it was morally obligatory? In each case I looked at the arguments presented by others, presented them in their strongest light, added any I could think of that supported either side, and tested them for coherence with moral theories and with pertinent facts. Against those who argued whistle blowing is never justified there were obvious cases in which lives could have been saved at what arguably was little cost to the company (which was the *Mother Jones* argument in the Pinto case). Neither obedience to one's corporate superiors nor loyalty to one's employer could offset imminent danger to human life. But not every case reached that threshold. Obedience and loyalty could be defended in some cases and an argument could be made that internal whistle blowing was consistent with both and could be defended as a necessary first step that had to be taken before one had the obligation to blow the whistle externally. Since blowing the whistle externally would produce harm for the firm, it seemed the fairest, the quickest, and the easiest way to prevent deaths was to attempt to get the firm to take corrective action. Until that was done, going public would be morally prohibited. I similarly analyzed when the whistle blowing was permitted but not morally required and the conditions under which it was morally required. From a utilitarian point of view, I looked at the consequences, but I also looked at the rights of all involved in and affected by the action. I argued, as I indicated, that the conditions I outlined applied only to one specific type of whistle blowing and I claimed that my analysis suggested a way for analyzing other types of whistle blowing. The conditions, I argued, did justice to both those who extolled and those who disparaged whistle blowers, and that the solution involved a weighing of various rights, obligations, and consequences. It also acknowledged that blowing the whistle externally required a certain amount of moral courage on the part of the whistle blower because they were not protected by law at the time. I used a variety of approaches because they were called for. The right of free speech was pertinent, but also pertinent was the obligation to save lives, as was the possible often claimed obligation of loyalty to one's employer. The conditions I ended up with came from balancing the various claims in such a way that did justice to all of them – which involved arguing that some of them were exaggerated and were reasonable only if modified. The result seemed to satisfy the intuition that sometimes whistle blowing is morally required and also the intuition that most workers are not under a constant moral obligation to externally blow the whistle for every perceived wrong they are aware of on the job. Coherence with one's intuitions or one's "gut feeling" is not an adequate test of the correctness of one's conclusions, but failure to achieve such coherence can be taken as an indication that more work is required, if only to account for and explain that lack of coherence.

My hope in presenting these two cases is that they might more concretely illustrate how coherence operates at each stage of investigation: that anomalies suggest issues requiring investigation or research; that although the answer to some moral questions are easy, some are by no means easy; that in research one should get all the pertinent facts of a case, issue, or problem; that one should take into account existing literature on a topic as well as current opinion to the extent that can be gauged; and that one has to bring to bear the resources supplied by whatever theory is necessary to do justice to the issue at hand – including rights, consequences, virtues, and obligations. The method does not claim to be a straight and sure guide to research, the conclusions of which are often unclear until the final results take shape. When recast for presentation they may appear linear and straight forward. Research is rarely that way.

I have outlined the systematic way I approached the question of what constituted the field of business ethics when the field was new. Since then the issues I have chosen to deal with have been dictated by changes in business.[8] Where is there a poor fit, an anomaly, an inconsistency between theory and practice? What are the new practices, the innovations in business, and can one analyze them from a moral point of view? Indeed, unless business is dynamic, innovative, and changing, after a while there would be little new to analyze and little need for people trained in such analysis. Both the globalization of business and the union of business with computers and information technology have raised many issues to which our intuitions, based on previous conditions, may or not be reliable indicators of the moral permissibility or impermissibility of the new practices.[9] Recently we have been hearing about the right to be forgotten. Is that really a right, and if so, what kind or right, how is it defended, what are its limits, and what are the implications for business? The financial industry has developed many new derivatives. Are they morally defensible? What are the moral implications of the increasing use of big data by corporations? The questions, I suggest, require careful examination, are complex, and are not easy to answer. They are the sorts of questions that require research and the sort for which those trained in business ethics are in a position to tackle.

[8] Each new edition of *Business ethics* incorporated new issues and topics, for the project of that book was open-ended and never claimed to be complete or all-inclusive. Most research projects are more limited and reach closure.

[9] For my attempt to deal with some issues in this area, see my book *The ethics of information technology and business* (De George, 2003).

## Conclusion

In sum, my view of method is that it is complex and many faceted because the interesting moral issues are complex and many faceted, and coherence is an approach to research in business ethics able to encompass the many other approaches and yield defensible results compatible with common sense and ordinary experience.

As a method of research in business ethics the coherence approach has much to recommend it. It enables one to take what is helpful and useful from a variety of theories. As a method coherence is intelligible to the nonexpert in ethics, e.g., to the ordinary person both in and out of business. For a practical endeavor, such as I take business ethics to be, this is a plus rather than a minus. At the same time, it preserves for business ethics the critical edge that adopting conventional morality does not. Business ethics should not be restricted to descriptive ethics. As normative, it prescribes how business should act insofar as it wishes to act morally. Its prescriptions, however, will be seriously considered, and more importantly acted on, only if they are shown to be coherent with a wide range of existing and morally accepted business practices, with existing economic, social and legal structures (insofar as they are justifiable), and with the existing principles and institutions such as free markets, fair competition, and reasonable profits (all of which are arguably morally defensible).

Coherence in business transactions from a moral point of view involves companies being conscious of their values, of the values of their constituents and customers and potential partners. Moral coherence in a business involves seeing each of its activities in conjunction with each of its other activities. A company that wishes to be moral is well served by looking for dissonance between its stated values and its actions. Coherence provides a guide to striving for ideals as well as for evaluating existing or proposed practices.

Coherence as a method provides a guide to the problems demanding research when both intuitions and every-day or conventional morality fail to produce clear evaluations. It is a guide to conducting the research process, and a guide to evaluating the results at which the investigation arrives. In the process stage a pluralistic adoption of ethical theories provides the basic approaches to evaluation and an important part of what can be called the tools of ethical analysis. Moreover, both coherence and pluralism are part of the approach to moral judgments used almost intuitively by people making moral judgments. What separates those who do research in academic business is that they use the approach consciously and deliberately in a disciplined way; that they have a deep knowledge of ethical theory, of the techniques of ethical analysis, and of the canons of criticism; that they are conscious of the pitfalls of analysis and ways to avoid them; and that they have the training to pursue research in a systematic, objective, professional manner. Coherence as a method, joined with a pluralistic approach to ethical theory and moral values, provides an intuitive, useful, and underappreciated approach to research in normative business ethics.

## References


Childress, James F., and Tom L. Beauchamp. 2001. *Principles of Biomedical Ethics*. Oxford University Press, USA.

Daniels, Norman. 1979. Wide Reflective Equilibrium and Theory Acceptance in Ethics. *The Journal of Philosophy*, 76(5): 256–282.

De George, Richard T. 1981. Ethical Responsibilities of Engineers in Large Organizations: the Pinto case. *Business and Professional Ethics Journal*, I: 1–14.

1990. Ethics and Coherence. *Proceedings and Addresses of the American Philosophical Association*, 64(3): 39–52.

2003. *The Ethics of Information Technology and Business*. Oxford: Blackwell Publishing.

2006a. The History of Business Ethics. In Marc Epstein and Kirk Hanson (eds.) *The Accountable Corporation*. Vol. II, p. 47–58. Westport, CT: Praeger.

2006b. The Relevance of Philosophy to Business Ethics: A Response to Rorty's "Is Philosophy Relevant to Applied Ethics?" *Business Ethics Quarterly*, 16(3): 381–389.

2010. *Business Ethics*. (7th ed.) Englewood Cliffs, N.J.: Prentice Hall. (1st, 2nd, 3rd eds., N.Y.: Macmillan and London: Collier, 1982, 1986, 1990; 4rd-6th eds., Englewood Cliffs, N.J.: Prentice-Hall, 1995, 1999, 2006.)

De George, Richard T., Bernard Gert, and Thomas Magnell. 1994. The Place for Coherence and Moral Rules in Ethics: Richard De George and Bernard Gert (Dialogue moderated and edited by Thomas Magnell). *The Journal of Value Inquiry*, 28(3): 463–479.

DeGrazia, David. 2003. Common Morality: Coherence, and the Principles of Biomedical Ethics. *Kennedy Institute of Ethics Journal*, 13(5): 219–230

DeMarco, Joseph P. 1997. Coherence and Applied Ethics. *Journal of Applied Philosophy*, 14(3): 289–300.

DePaul, Michael. 1987. Two Conceptions of Coherence Methods in Ethics. *Mind*, 96: 384, 463–481.

1988. The Problem of the Criterion and Coherence Methods in Ethics. *Canadian Journal of Philosophy*, 18(1): 67–86.

Dorsey, Dale. 2006. A Coherence Theory of Truth in Ethics. *Philosophical Studies*, 127: 493–523.

Dowie, Mark. 1977. Pinto Madness, *Mother Jones*, September/October, 24–28.

Engel, Mylan Jr. 2012. Coherentism and the Epistemic Justification of Moral Beliefs: A Case Study in How to Do Practical Ethics Without Appeal to a Moral Theory. *The Southern Journal of Philosophy*, 50(1): 50–74.

Guarini, Marcello. 2007. Computation, Coherence, and Ethical Reasoning. *Minds and Machines*, 17: 27–46.

Hobbes, Thomas. 1651/2017. *Leviathan*. Part I, chapter 13. Web site www.bartleby.com/34/5/13 .html retrieved April 10, 2017.

Kuhn, Thomas. 1962. *Structure of Scientific Revolutions*. Chicago: University of Chicago Press.

Rawls, John. 1971. *A Theory of Justice*. Cambridge, MA: Harvard.

Rawls, John. B. 1974–1975. The independence of moral theory. *Proceedings and Addresses of the American Philosophical Association*, XLVII, 5–22.

1987. The Idea of an Overlapping Consensus. *Oxford Journal of Legal Studies*, 7(1): 1–25.

1993. *Political Liberalism*. New York: Columbia University Press.

1999. *A Theory of Justice*. Revised ed., Cambridge, MA: Harvard University Press.

Thagard, Paul. 1998. Ethical Coherence. *Philosophical Psychology*, 11(4): 405–419.

CHAPTER 5

# The Universalist Approach and Kant in Business Ethics

NORMAN E. BOWIE

## General Methodological Background for any Normative Ethical Theory

Normative ethics does not describe the world; it stands in judgment of the world. That makes normative ethics very different from the economic, psychological, and sociological research that characterizes business school research. (Although I note in passing that a lot of what passes for economic research is mathematical modeling and thus analytic and not empirical until the model is operationalized and tested.) Saying that normative ethics does not describe the world does not mean there is not an empirical element to normative ethics research. It is empirical in the sense that normative reasoning about business is about the actual practices and behaviors of businesses and business people. When judging the world, one is judging something about the world. Thus, nothing in these remarks should be taken to imply there is a chasm or even a gap between the empirical and the normative. Describing and judging are different ways of dealing with one and the same world. Normative ethics is empirical in another way as well. Once a normative theory judges the world and finds it wanting, the question arises as to what can be done to make the world better, to have it conform to the way the normative theory says the world ought to be. Thus, if a normative theory finds a business, a business practice, or a business person to fall short of what the normative ethical theory requires, what should be done about it? At that point, one can use and should use sound psychological, sociological, and economic theory to get to where you want to go. For example, if a human resource practice is found to be morally wanting, knowledge from psychology and economics is required to come up with an alternative practice. The normative theory judges the world but the theory itself does not provide the alternative. What the normative ethical theory does do is judge the suggested alternative to see if it is morally better than the practice it replaces. A normative ethical theory is about judging and justification for making business and the world a better place; those are its primary reasons for being.

The analysis above implies that normative ethics research is interdisciplinary. You cannot judge something if you do not know a lot about the object of the judgment. You cannot justify something if you do not know something about what you are trying to judge. And you cannot suggest alternatives to a current practice unless you know something about the alternative practice. Good normative research in business ethics is a shining light for what interdisciplinary research should be. Many bemoan the fact that academic research has become too specialized. More comprehensive and integrated approaches are needed, it is argued. More specifically the Kantian approach is not designed to impose moral universal rules on business. The Kantian approach is a part of the interdisciplinary project of business ethics. Kantian ethics can be an important part of business ethics research but it is not the only part.

## Kantian Normative Ethics Research

Kantian ethical theory is universal but it is universal in a very narrow sense. It is important to emphasize the narrowness of the universal claim, because there is considerable misunderstanding, even among accomplished ethical theorists, as to what Kant's universal claim involves. For example, in his excellent introductory text, *The Elements of Moral Philosophy*, the late James Rachels titles one of his two chapters on Kant, "The System of Absolute Moral Rules." There is only one absolute rule in Kant's ethical theory, the categorical imperative. The categorical imperative does have three formulations. I paraphrase them below:

1. Always act on a maxim that could be a universal law of nature. This is commonly called the universalizability formulation.
2. Always treat the humanity of a person, whether yourself or another, as an end and never merely as a means. This is commonly called the respect for persons formulation.
3. Always act as if you were a member of a kingdom of ends in which you were both sovereign and subject. This is commonly called the kingdom of ends formulation.

The first and second formulations resonate as universal principles because the first formulation of the categorical imperative bears some similarity to the "Golden Rule" which in one version says, "Do to others as you would have them do to you." It has been pointed out that all the world's major religions share some version of the "Golden Rule." The second formulation seems to describe a moral demand that one finds in every culture. Persons demand respect. You hear that either explicitly or implicitly in the demands of the "Black Lives Matter" movement, in the voices of Syrian refuges trying to enter Europe or other countries, and in pleas of those Africans who wish to preserve their culture and share it with others around the world. In practice, what respect requires in various cultures is a matter of controversy. However, the demand for respect does seem to be universal. As for the universality of the third formulation, more will be said about that later. At this point I assert that the first two formulations entail the third.[1]

Why base a normative theory on these three very abstract formulations of a universal rule? The common answer is because the categorical imperative is a requirement of reason, indeed it may be that properly understood, the first, and perhaps all, the formulations of the categorical imperative are just statements of the principle of reason itself. If such an approach were successful, then Kant's ethical theory rests on the power of reason itself.

Kant's theory is a bit more complicated than that since the ultimate ground of his ethics is freedom or human autonomy. Reason is possible because we are free beings. Kant distinguishes two kinds of freedom, negative freedom which is freedom from the causal laws of nature and positive freedom which is freedom to act on a law of our own making, the freedom to act based on a reason. Now Kant's account of freedom is hard to explain as are all accounts of free will. Indeed, many social scientists have become skeptical of "free will." Central to Kant's argument for free will is that we must see ourselves as free, that freedom is a requirement of the rational and moral life.

Kant believes that human beings act on incentives-something often translated as desires. If one is hungry one seeks food; if one is thirsty one seeks water. But not all action is like that. Even when an incentive is present, one can take up and act on a reason. Acting on a reason is what constitutes human freedom. Reasons are different from incentives, desires, and the like that are in the causal chain. Freedom in its full sense is the ability to act based on a reason.

## A Digression into Behavioral Ethics

Recently, behavioral ethics has used empirical findings in psychology to challenge any normative account like Kant's that uses ethical theory as an account of how people make decisions.[2] A brief description of behavioral ethics is in order.

Trevino, Weaver, and Reynolds (2006: 92) defined behavioral ethics as the study of "individual behavior that is subject to or judged according to generally accepted norms of behavior." That definition was adopted by the editors of a special issue of *Business Ethics Quarterly* (BEQ) on behavioral ethics in 2010. Although I shall return to this commonly accepted definition shortly, the

[1] I avoid the dispute as to whether the three formulations of the categorical imperative are identical.

[2] This discussion of behavioral ethics is an abbreviated account of my discussion in N.E. Bowie, *Business ethics: a Kantian perspective* (Cambridge: Cambridge University Press, 2017)

definition as it stands does not give sufficient information as to what constitutes behavioral ethics.

Of special interest, here are the behavioral experiments related to ethical decision making. Indeed, for my purposes I will look at behavioral ethics as the study of how people make ethical decisions. The results of those studies show that people {usually} do not make ethical decisions by thinking about them, by applying rules to behavior. Ethical decision making is usually not rational. People especially do not make ethical decisions by formulating maxims of action and then seeing whether those maxims pass the categorical imperative test.

Many behavioral ethicists then use these results to argue that philosophical ethics or ethical theorizing is useless. They argue that teaching business students the basics of the classic ethical theories such as virtue theory, utilitarianism, and Kantianism will not improve ethical decision making in business. And if proof beyond the actual experiments is needed, they argue that one need only look at the fact that despite all the teaching of ethics in business schools, unethical behavior in business continues unabated.

The findings of behavioral economics are interesting and certainly should not be ignored by philosophers. If the traditional philosopher's goal is to help individuals make good ethical choices and psychologists show that psychological biases and unconscious or semiconscious processes get in the way, then we do need to deal with those biases and processes if our goal is to be achieved. In our teaching and training we may need to start with behavioral ethics. In other words, the relevant findings of behavioral ethics should be a part of every business ethics course, unless there are multiple business ethics courses where one would focus on behavioral ethics and the other on traditional philosophical normative ethics.

However, the leap from how people behave to the uselessness of philosophical ethics in general and Kantian ethics in particular is not warranted. Behavioral ethics does not pose as great a challenge to Kantian ethics as it might to some other ethical theories such as utilitarianism for example. Recall that Kant thought the categorical imperative technique was to be used as the default for making ethical decisions. Most of the time we knew what was the right thing to do and we did it. Rather the categorical imperative was designed for difficult decisions when determining what was right was difficult. That is clear when one considers the examples in the Groundwork (1785). Of course, Kant was unaware of many of the factors that psychologists show affect ethical decision making. One would hope that psychology had made some progress since the eighteenth century. However, there is one psychological insight that Kant was well aware of: we tend to make an exception of ourselves in moral deliberation. The most that the behaviorists have shown is that we may not use normative theory including the categorical imperative as often as previously thought.

What behavioral ethics ignores are issues of justification. And this is not just an oversight. Behaviorists cannot offer a theory of justification because the psychological causes of a decision are different from the justification of a decision. This is implicitly recognized in the Trevino, Weaver, and Reynolds (2006: 92) definition that is commonly recognized and was the basis for the BEQ special issue. To repeat behavioral ethics is the study of "individual behavior that is subject to or judged according to generally accepted norms of behavior." Generally accepted norms of behavior are taken as the starting point. But are such generally accepted norms morally right? The behaviorists cannot answer that question. That is the job for moral philosophy.

Behavioral ethicists start off with certain assumptions about what is right or wrong. In their book Brazerman and Tenbrunsel (2011) speak of troubling decisions such as Enron, cooking the books, going to war in Iraq, and making loans to indigent borrowers and passing the risk off to others. The authors seem to think these decisions were wrong or at least morally troubling. But why? The authors never say. Saying why something is wrong is the job of the normative philosopher and that is what ethical theory in general and Kantian ethics in particular is about. Indeed, the authors believe that the value of their work is to point out the hidden processes and biases that interfere with or even prevent people from doing the right thing. Once those hidden processes and biases are known, presumably they can be counteracted. You can see that in the subtitle of the book. But how do we know what the right thing is? Bounded ethicality will not determine whether the war in Iraq was right or wrong. Knowledge about the biases that affect ethical decision making will help us avoid making ethical errors but that knowledge does not tell us what is right or wrong.

Even when people act inappropriately due to bounded ethicality, we need to show why the act was inappropriate. After all, once an ethical decision is made, one can always ask whether the decision was justified. Insights into how people behave is of limited value as to whether their behavior is justified. (The major exception here is any findings that people cannot act in a certain way. If they cannot act differently that means that we cannot morally require that they act in that way. Ought implies can, as the saying goes.)

We have long known that human beings have a desire to seek revenge when they perceive that they have been treated wrongly and we also know that a number of those people will act on their desire for revenge. But political philosophers like Hobbes and Locke have argued that we need institutions like the state to control this desire for individual revenge. This is a classic case where people use institutions to control how people would otherwise behave.

Kant's ethical theory provides a basis for evaluating behavior as we will see in the use of the first formulation of the categorical imperative for evaluating the maxims of behavior. The consistency test of the categorical imperative provides a means for evaluation. Thus, Kantian ethical theory is extremely valuable as a means for justification and has nothing to fear from the work of behavioral ethics. Indeed, insights into how people behave should provide grist for the Kantian ethical mill. Such psychological knowledge just might indicate that more so called ethical behavior might require more justification than previously thought. That would come as no surprise to Kant.

## The Universalizability Formulation of the Categorical Imperative as a Research Tool in Business Ethics

The first formulation of the categorical imperative says, "Act only on that maxim by which you can at the same time will that it should become a universal law."[3] (Kant, 1785: 38) Kant wants to show that some principles (maxims) upon which actions are based are inconsistent or self-defeating. An inconsistent or self-defeating principle is one where it is impossible for everyone to act based on the principle; that is why the principle could not be accepted as a universal law. If an individual acted on a principle that it would be impossible for everyone to follow, that individual's action would be wrong. That is precisely what is wrong with the idea of making a promise with the intention of breaking it.

Thus, the research value of the categorical imperative is that it functions as a test to see if the principle (maxim) upon which an action is based is morally permissible. So long as the principle for one's action passes the test of the categorical imperative, then the action may be undertaken. A business manager who accepts Kantian morality would ask, for any decision, whether the principle on which the decision is based passes the test of the categorical imperative. If it does, then the decision would be morally permissible. The first formulation of the categorical imperative also functions as a test for the morality of business practices. A practice that if universally adopted by business in general would be self-defeating is one that an individual business could adopt only on pain of being unethical.

It is important to reemphasize here that this research use of the categorical imperative is not a description of how business people, or anyone else for that matter, makes ethical decisions ordinarily. Kant along with most everyone else believes that an action like lying is usually morally wrong and that deep philosophical analysis was not required to show that it is. The universalizability test is the appropriate tool to use in cases where people do deliberate about what ought to be done. Kant thought that the contribution of his moral philosophy was to show what one ought to do in hard cases-those cases where it was hard to know what

[3] The explanation of the three formulations of the categorical imperative is a much-abbreviated version of the explanations given in *Business ethics: a Kantian perspective*.

was right. That is why in his example the person only considers making a promise with no intention of keeping it when he is under extreme financial distress. He desperately needs money but knows he cannot repay it.[4]

To answer to the question as to whether a person in desperate financial straits is morally permitted to make a promise to return borrowed money with no intention of doing so, Kant would instruct the person to construct a general principle, (maxim) that captured the action. In this case the general principle would be, "It is morally permissible to make a promise with the intention of breaking it." Kant then asks us whether such a maxim could become a universal law. The answer is "no" because that maxim is contradictory. It is contradictory because if everyone could break a promise, promises would never get made. If such a maxim were universalized, the very notion of promises would make no sense. As Kant says,

> And could I say to myself that everyone may make a false promise when he is in difficulty from which he cannot escape? Immediately I see that I could will the lie but not a universal law to lie. For with such a law there would be no promises at all, inasmuch as it would be futile to make a pretense of my intention in regard to future actions to those who would not believe this pretense or – if they over hastily did so-would pay me back in my own coin. Thus my maxim would necessarily destroy itself as soon as it was made a universal law. (Kant, 1785: 19)

The use of the first formulation of the categorical imperative as a research tool can be seen by applying it to business. The making of promises is a practice. It is important to note with Christine Korsgaard (1996: 85) that the self-contradiction interpretation of the categorical imperative works well for the violation of the rules of a practice: "a practice has a standard purpose and if its rules are universally violated it ceases to be efficacious for this person, and so ceases to exist." Since business consists, at least in part, of many practices with standard purposes, we might expect Kant's universal law formulation of the categorical imperative to work well in business and so it does.

Consider the breaking of contracts. A contract is an agreement between two or more parties, usually enforceable by law, for the doing or not doing of some specific thing. A contract is one of the more formal ways of making a promise. The hiring of employees, the use of credit, the ordering and supplying of goods, and the notion of warranty, to name but a few, all make use of contracts. If a maxim that permitted contract breaking were universalized, there would be no contracts (contracts would cease to exist.) No one would enter into a contract if he or she believed the other party had no intention of honoring it. A universalized maxim that permitted contract breaking would be self-defeating.

Kant's point here is subject to empirical validation. It could even by stated as a hypothesis.

> *H1 If business people try to find loopholes in honoring contracts, attempts will be made to close those loopholes. As a result contracts will become increasingly complex to the point that they become so unwieldly that they lose their purpose.*

We can see places where this hypothesis is confirmed. Regulations are notorious for their complexity because they try to cover every loophole. Eventually the regulations become so complex they no longer function in the ways intended and instead act as a burden on legitimate business, a burden that can become so great that that type of business might cease. It is not hard to imagine ways to test whether this hypothesis can be substantiated. Thus, Kantian ethics can generate empirical hypotheses. Good empirical research would see if there are so called tipping points where trying to gain an exception for oneself leads to behavior that ultimately undermines the practice

[4] This discussion enables me to dismiss a criticism of Kant based on a major misunderstanding of his work. Some have argued that Kant only thinks that one is moral if doing the right thing is hard. The examples in the *Groundwork* are cited as evidence. However, that is a misunderstanding. Kant uses examples such as whether one should commit suicide when one if painfully ill or whether one should make a promise with no intention to keep it when one is in desperate financial straits because he believes that nearly everyone would agree that in general a lying promise is wrong. Kant's argument works for the general case but in the examples, Kant is showing that his analysis works in the tough cases.

and thus defeats the purpose of the person trying to gain an exception for himself.

Another example is the practice of lining (queuing) up. There is nothing inconsistent about a society that does not have such a practice. However, in a society that does have the practice, cutting into line is morally wrong. The maxim on which the act of line-cutting is based cannot become a universal law. An attempt to universalize line-cutting destroys the very notion of a line.

It is important to note that the categorical imperative works for the rules of any institution or practice and thus is universal in that sense. Indeed, the test of the categorical imperative becomes a universal principle of fair play. One of the essential features of fair play is that one should not make an exception for oneself.

With this notion of fair play, we can use Kant's first formulation of the categorical imperative to show that whenever someone, including someone in business, agrees to follow the rules for cooperative behavior and then violates those rules for personal gain, such a violation is morally wrong. A maxim that permitted universal violation of the rules is self-defeating. A universally violated rule is not a rule.

This kind of analysis shows that free-loading is morally wrong. A free-loader is one who accepts the advantages of the rules of cooperative behavior, but then either violates the rules or fails to contribute his share in supporting them. Most of us would characterize free-loading as unfair or unjust. Kant's universalizability formulation of the categorical imperative explains why it is unjust. If free-loading were universalized then the rules that make cooperative activity possible could not exist.

Another way of putting this is as follows: What's wrong with freeloading? You are not contributing to the institution that relies on the contributions of those participating in the institution-a contribution which you agreed to make when you agreed to participate in the institution. That is what it means to be a free-loader. If for some reason a maxim permitting free-loading were universalized, the institution itself would be undermined, but the participants in the institution want the institution to exist, so free-loading must be immoral.

These Kantian–type arguments apply to almost all competitive situations as well. Capitalism is a system of economic competition but even competitive activity requires rules regulating competition. As Adam Smith and all after him have realized, capitalism requires rules protecting property rights, enforcing contracts, and settling disputes; otherwise business activity would be impossible. Some describe the business world as a jungle, but if it truly were a jungle, business itself would not survive.

Someone who enters a competitive activity and violates the rules regulating that competition acts immorally. Why? Because if the rules regulating competition were universally violated, those "rules" would no longer be rules. If regulatory rules are universally violated, regulation is impossible. Such activity would be self-defeating in two senses. Universal violation of the rule would make the rule nugatory. And since the rule is one that is required to keep competition from degenerating into chaos or a war of all against all, the universalized violation of rules would make welfare enhancing competition itself self-defeating. Although this point is often lost on business people who are adversely disposed to regulation, more enlightened business people recognize that some regulation is necessary in a capitalist system. The issue for these business people is to be sure that regulation is beneficial in promoting fairness and stability, rather than being counterproductive.

The first formulation of the categorical imperative can, when combined with certain empirical facts about the means to make a profit, tell a manager what is morally required. We can illustrate this by considering trust. Strategy professors, among others, have already done a lot of empirical work to show how trust contributes to profitability.

Management theorists seem to be endorsing the following hypothetical imperative:

> *H1 If one wants to achieve profitability in one's business, then one must establish trust with one's various corporate stakeholders.*

What will need to be shown is that business practice requires trust, so that one who acts in ways that violate trust or make trust on the part of others impossible is inconsistent. The argument for this claim can be stated as follows:

1. Managers have a contractual obligation to manage the firm in the best interests of the corporation.
2. Managers can manage the firm in the best interests of the corporation only if they build trusts among the corporate stakeholders.
3. Therefore, managers have an obligation to build trust among the corporate stakeholders.

The first premise is a normative claim regarding the obligation of managers. To this normative claim you add a factual statement regarding how managers manage in the best interests of the corporation. Since the manager has made a promise (has a contractual obligation) to manage in the best interest of the corporation, and since building trusting relationships among the corporate stakeholders is necessary to fulfill that promise, then a manager has a moral obligation and not merely a prudential one for building those trusting relationships. The normative claim is widely accepted, although what counts as the interests of the corporation varies as to whether one holds to a traditional stockholder finance model of the firm or to a more contemporary stakeholder theory.

What the Kantian research methodology can add to the analysis is a justification of the first premise. The universalizability formulation of the categorical imperative can be used to show that a denial of premise 1 involves one in a contradiction, although in this case the contradiction is pragmatic rather than logical. According to Christine Korsgaard (1996) we can distinguish between logical (conceptual) contradiction and pragmatic contradiction. On the logical interpretation, a self-contradictory universalized maxim is one that proposes an inconceivable action or policy. On the pragmatic interpretation, a contradictory maxim is one that proposes an action that would be inconsistent with your purpose if everyone acted on it. Korsgaard (1996: 96–97) provides some additional explanation as to what constitutes a pragmatic contradiction.

> If a thwarted purpose is a practical contradiction, we must understand the contradiction in the will test in this way: we must find some purpose or purposes which belong essentially to the will, and in the world where maxims that fail these tests are universal law, these essential purposes will be thwarted, because the means of achieving them will be unavailable. Examples of purposes that might be thought to be essential to the will are its general effectiveness in the pursuit of its ends, and its freedom to adopt and pursue new ends.

The Kantian strategy is to show that trust is essential in most business relationships if business is to achieve its ends. We need to show that trust is essential to business practice, so essential that a universalized maxim that undermines trust can be shown to be pragmatically (volitionally) self-defeating. Following Korsgaard, I seek to show that actions that violate trust are inconsistent with the essential purposes of business. In other words, in the absence of trust, business as we know it, would be impossible. I will not provide the detailed arguments here because they are not germane to Kantian ethics per se. The arguments are empirical ones provided by colleagues in the various management disciplines. The interested reader should see K. Boulding, (1967), F. Fukuyama (1995) P. Bromiley and L. Cummings (1995) among others. What these facts establish is the truth of premise 2 and that premise in conjunction with the normative obligation created by the contractual obligation leads to the conclusion that managers should establish trust among the corporate stakeholders. Denial of the conclusion involves one in a pragmatic contradiction because it would undermine the business practice of profit seeking.

Thus, the first formulation of the categorical imperative has several functions as a research tool. It can show that the maxims or principles for certain actions are self-contradictory when universalized and thus would not be rational. To make an exception of oneself in such a situation would be unethical. Practices that would undermine the institution on which the practice depends are also irrational and the continuation or pursuit of such practices is immoral. These claims are intended to be universally true since they are grounded in reason itself. Also, as an empirical matter, if people did act on self-contradictory practices, a tipping point would be reached and the practice or institution upon which the practice depends would be undermined and no longer exist.

## The Respect for Persons Formulation of the Categorical Imperative as a Research Tool in Business Ethics

If the average person has a second moral principle to supplement the Golden Rule, it is probably a principle that says we should respect people. Just as the first formulation of the categorical imperative provided a more rigorous formulation of the Golden Rule, Kant's second formulation of the categorical imperative, "Always act so that you treat the humanity in a person, whether in your own person or in that of another, always as an end and never as a means only" is a more rigorous formulation of the principle that one should respect people. (Kant, 1785: 46)

Respecting people is thoroughly interwoven into the fabric of contemporary life. A "respect for persons" principle, like a "golden rule" principle could claim the status of a universal moral principle. People demand respect and when they don't feel respected, the results can be tragic as we have seen. In the United States, there are numerous instances where people have been shot dead because they allegedly felt disrespected by the person they shot.

Yet ironically, many of the moral criticisms of business practice are directed against policies that do not respect persons, e.g., that business human relations policies often invade privacy or relegate people to dead-end jobs where they cannot grow. But there is considerable controversy, even among ethicists, as to what a respect for persons principle requires.

To get at this question, we need to consider Kant's rationale for the respect for persons principle. Kant (1785) did not simply assert that human beings are entitled to respect; he had an elaborate argument for it. Human beings ought to be respected because human beings have dignity. For Kant, an object that has dignity is beyond price. But, first, why do persons possess a dignity that is beyond all price? They have dignity because human beings are capable of autonomy and thus are capable of self-governance. As autonomous beings capable of self-governance, they are also responsible beings, since autonomy and self-governance are conditions for responsibility. A person who is not autonomous and who is not capable of self-governance is not responsible. That's why little children or the mentally ill are not considered responsible beings. Thus, there is a conceptual link between being a human being, being an autonomous being, being capable of self-governance, and being a responsible being.

Autonomous responsible beings are capable of making and following their own laws. Anyone who recognizes that she is autonomous should recognize that she is responsible for her actions and thus she should recognize that that she is a moral being. From this Kant (1785: 52) argues that the fact that one is a moral being enables us to say that such a being possesses dignity.

> Morality is the condition under which alone a rational being can be an end in himself because only through it is it possible to be a lawgiving member in the realm of ends. Thus morality, and humanity, insofar as it is capable of morality, alone have dignity.

Just as with the universalizability formulation of the categorical imperative, the respect for persons formulations is also based on consistency. What we say about ourselves, we must say about similar cases, namely about other human beings. To do otherwise is to make an exception of ourselves and we have already shown that such exceptions are contradictory and thus unethical. The respect for principles formulation of the categorical imperative is a universal moral principle.

In a business context, what specific obligations follow from that general obligation and what is permitted under that general obligation? In other words, how does the respect for persons principle function as a research tool? I follow contemporary Kantian scholarship in arguing that respect for persons requires two steps.

## Not Using Employees: Neither Coercion nor Deceit

The first step to respect the humanity in a person requires that a person should not be used as a means only. With respect to business ethics that means that a business relationship should be neither coerced nor deceptive. The general point against coercion and deception has been made by Korsgaard (1996: 140–141).

> According to the Formula of Humanity, coercion and deception are the most fundamental forms of wrongdoing to others-the roots of all evil. Coercion and deception violate the conditions of possible assent, and all actions which depend for their nature and efficacy on their coercive or deceptive character are ones that others cannot assent to ... Physical coercion treats someone's person as a tool; lying treats someone's reason as a tool. That is why Kant finds it so horrifying; it is a direct violation of autonomy.

Kant's point about the immorality of coercion and deception is accepted by nearly all regardless of their political persuasion. Coercion and deception are a violation of one's negative freedom because they block a person from choosing ends she would have chosen had the coercion or deception not occurred.

Let us see just what the respect for persons principle can tell us and what it cannot tell us about one of the most controversial and complicated issues in business ethics-layoffs and downsizing. What the analysis will show is that Kantian moral philosophy is helpful in the analysis but it is not sufficient in providing an answer as to what managers ought or ought not to do.

Economic actions are considered free actions voluntarily entered into. If both parties are fully informed, then business transactions are neither coerced nor involve deception. They thus pass the two tests for negative freedom. Using the standard assumption that the employment relationship is a contractual one and further assuming that the employee has all the relevant knowledge regarding the relationship, then one could argue that the employee has accepted the fact that if the price of machinery becomes cheaper compared to the price of labor, then she has agreed that the manager is morally permitted to substitute a machine for her labor. This is because one could say that employees know that they can be laid off if their labor becomes more expensive compared to machines. They accept the job knowing that and thus there is a sense in which layoffs are something that has been agreed to. The employees are not used as a means merely because they have freely consented to the conditions of their employment. There is neither coercion nor deception and thus the employees have not been used.

Is the argument that employment contracts, especially contracts that permit massive layoffs, are voluntary agreements sound? One way to get at this issue is to shift the focus to the institution of capitalism as it is currently practiced rather than on the specific transactions between an individual employee and the firm she works for. This approach has in fact been taken by Onora O'Neill (1989: 122–123):

> What could be more paradigmatic of an offer that can be refused than an offer of employment that is, as they say in wage negotiations, "on the table"? If we argue that such offers are coercive or deceptive, we must take a broader view of maxims, and judge not the principles that particular would-be-employees have in mind but the principles that guide the institution of employment in a capitalist system. The underlying principle of capitalist employment, whatever that may be, might be judged to use some as means or fail to treat them as persons, even where individuals' intentions fail in neither way.

There are many issues here which show that Kantian ethics as a research tool must be supplemented by an adequate analysis of other ethical terms-an analysis where Kantian ethics may be necessary but not sufficient. At issue here is what counts as coercion? If employment contracts are freely accepted and not coercive, involuntary layoffs might pass the Kantian respect for persons test. However, under other accounts of coercion, employment contracts would not be freely made. There is a second issue. O'Neill's argument, and ones similar to it, presupposes that a coherent account can be given of the notion of institutional coercion. Whether a coherent account of institutional coercion can be provided is certainly controversial. Moreover, discussions of institutional coercion pose special challenges for Kantian ethics. Social scientists emphasize the importance of being clear about one's level of analysis. The three levels are the individual level, the organizational level, and the macro-economic level. Issues in business ethics can occur at any one of three levels and some business ethics issues-such as the employer/employee relationship can be discussed on all three levels. The key is to be clear as to what level you are working on. O'Neill's discussion, for example, of the institution of capitalism occurs at the macro-economic level. Kant himself operated almost exclusively at the individual level. He provided an ethics for individuals. Contemporary Kantian ethicists and particularly Kantian business ethics have had to wrestle with trying to provide a Kantian account of organizational coercion and/or cultural coercion.[5] What is significant for this discussion is the realization that Kantian ethics is not sufficient as a research tool, nor is any other general ethical theory. The value of the respect for persons principle in this case was that it got the discussion focused on the right issue – whether or not the employment relationship is truly free. One does not simply start off with the assumption that it is.

Since I am maintaining that business ethics is primarily an interdisciplinary research project let me show how Kantian moral philosophy and economics can work together; consider the notion of information asymmetry. Information asymmetry occurs when one party in a business relationship has information that the other party does not, and in some instances cannot, have. Doctors are in an asymmetrical relationship with their patients-although less so now in the age of the Internet. Asymmetrical information causes a tension in the notion of a free contract or mutually advantageous business relationship because at least one party does not have the information needed to make an informed decision. Information asymmetry is likely to contribute to coercion. Knowing this the business ethicist can then endorse many business techniques that would reduce information asymmetry and thus would reduce the likelihood of coercion and increase the opportunity for managers to show respect consistent with the respect for persons principle.

One such management technique developed by Jack Stack is called open book management. Open book management greatly enhances opportunity for employee participation while simultaneously increasing employee autonomy and reducing problems of information asymmetry. The underlying philosophy of open book management is that persons should be treated as responsible autonomous beings. A precondition of such treatment is that employees have the information needed to make responsible decisions. John Case (1995) calls this, "empowerment with brains."

Under open book management employees are given all the financial information about the company. They are also under a profit sharing plan where what they make is in large part determined by the profit of the company. With complete information and the proper incentives, employees behave responsibly without the necessity of layers of supervision.

> How does open book management do what it does? The simplest answer is this. People get a chance to act, to take responsibility, rather than just doing their job ... No supervisor or department head can anticipate or handle all ... situations. A company that hired enough managers to do so would go broke from the overhead. Open book management gets people on the job doing things right. And it teaches them to make smart decisions ... because they can see the impact of their decisions on the relevant numbers. (Case, 1995: 45–46)

The adoption of practices like open book management would go far toward correcting the asymmetrical information that managers possess and that gives rise to the charge that the employment contract is often deceptive. Any time the firm faces a situation that might involve the layoff of employees, employees as well as managers would have access to all the relevant information. Deception in such circumstances would be much more difficult.

[5] A few articles reflecting the attempts to provide such an account include P. A. French, The corporation as a moral person, *American Philosophical Quarterly*, 16 (1979), 207–215, D. G. Arnold, Corporate Moral Agency, *Midwest Studies in Philosophy*, 30 (2006), 279–291, and K. M The free will of corporations (and other collectives), *Philosophical Studies* 168, (2014) 241–260, K. M. Hess, Because they can: the basis for the moral obligations of (certain) collectives," *Midwest Studies in Philosophy* 38, (2014) 203–223,

Open book management also greatly increases employee autonomy including autonomy with respect to company ethics programs.

Does Kantian ethics require companies to adopt open book management? "No." There may be other management techniques that eliminate information asymmetry and/or enhance employee autonomy. Some may choose to try those techniques rather than open book management. What Kantian ethics does require is that companies not violate employee autonomy nor deceive them. However, there may be several morally permissible ways to structure business practice to achieve that goal.

## *Respecting People's Freedom in an Active Way*

Lack of coercion and deception is not always sufficient for treating those in a business relationship with respect. On occasion, we are obliged to act positively to further their humanity. This is because we not only must not use people but we must treat them as ends in themselves. To treat a person as an end itself sometimes requires that we do more than merely refrain from coercion or deception; it requires that we take some positive action to help a person.

For textual support, I cite two examples of moral duties from the *Foundations of the metaphysics of morals* (Kant 1785), specifically the imperfect duties to develop one's talents and give aid to the needy. There Kant explicitly says that being indifferent to someone does not treat him as a means merely (merely use them). But being indifferent does not treat the person as an end in itself. That is why, for Kant, not using people is not sufficient for respecting them in the way morality requires. In part two of the *Metaphysics of Morals* (1797), Kant develops his theory of our obligations of virtue, that is, of our obligations of perfection to oneself and a duty to promote the happiness of others. He asks, "What are the ends which are at the same time duties? They are these: one's own perfection and the happiness of others." (Kant 1797: 43) In an elaboration on our duty to promote the happiness of others Kant argues that each must be concerned with the physical welfare of others and with their moral well-being (Kant 1797).

An obvious research agenda is for Kantians to join with researchers in the management area to examine those management practices that are most consistent with the moral obligation to respect the positive freedom of employees. Kantian ethicists are looking for ways to help employees achieve self-realization. Given the vast amount of time that people spend on the job, human resource management is an obvious area where Kantian ethics can be applied. This interdisciplinary research area has as one of its foci, meaningful work. Despite the vast amount of time spent at work, far too many workers find their work life to be one of drudgery where they follow orders delivered from on high. Our language reflects this reality with TGIF (Thank God It's Friday.), Hump Day, and Blue Monday. Kantian business ethicists would insist that morality requires that managers treat work to the extent possible in a different way, in a way where workers find meaning and purpose in what they do. Identifying those practices through careful empirical research has usually fallen to others. But Kantians not only encourage management practices that provide for self-realization in work but act as a negative check as well. Frequently management is tempted to act in a paternalistic manner on the grounds that management knows better than the employee about what is in his or her best interest. We know that employees do not save enough for their retirement. One way to alleviate that problem is for management to mandate that a certain percentage of each worker's salary be set aside in a retirement account. But such mandatory practices are suspect from a Kantian perspective. A good way to avoid this overt paternalism and still get employees to contribute a sufficient amount to their retirement is to use social science research which shows the following: If you make employees opt in to putting aside money for their retirement, many will not do so. However, if you make employees opt out of having money put aside, most employees will not opt out and thus more will save more for their retirement. This "nudge" as it is called is more consistent with respecting an employee's freedom than the use of an overt directive to set money aside for retirement (Sunstein and Thaler, 2008).

Research on meaningful work is progressing on many fronts. Kantian moral philosophy is relevant.

However, research in this area is truly interdisciplinary and social science research and organizational theory research each have crucial roles to play. The best Kantian research is carried on by partnering with other researchers from other fields who share an interest in meaningful work.

## The Kingdom of Ends Formulation of the Categorical Imperative as a Research Tool in Business Ethics

The third formulation of the categorical imperative is usually called the kingdom of ends formulation. Loosely put this formulation of the categorical imperative says that you should act as if you were a member of an ideal organization in which you were both subject and sovereign at the same time.

What did Kant mean? Kant recognized that human beings interacted with other human beings (ends). The arena of interaction was called the kingdom of ends. A business organization, like any other organization, is composed of individual persons and since persons are moral creatures, the interaction of persons in an organization is constrained by the categorical imperative. This means that an organization, whatever its purpose, should be governed by morality. Because an organization is a community of persons, whatever else an organization is, it should be a moral community.

What are the laws which govern these interactions? Kant maintained that since those interactions were the interactions of human beings the laws that govern the interactions of persons should be self-legislated. Any self-legislated law for human beings must be capable of being universal in the sense described in our discussion of the first formulation of the categorical imperative and must treat the humanity of those with whom one interacts as an end and not as a means merely. In an organizational setting this requirement means that any law (rule or principle) a person proposes to govern the interactions of the organizational members in some sense must be acceptable to all.

A first pass enables us to interpret the phrase "acceptable to all" as follows: When the rules that govern the organization are acceptable to all, everyone in the organization would be sovereign with respect to the law. However, since the laws that govern the interaction of the members of the organization apply to all persons, members of the organization are also subject to the law. Thus, an organization passes the formal tests of morality if the rules which govern the interactions of the members of the organization are consistent with the first two formulations of the categorical imperative and can be publicly advocated and accepted by all. As Kant (1785: 50) said:

> For all rational beings stand under the law that each of them should treat himself and all others never merely as a means but in every case also as an end in himself. Thus there arises a systematic union of rational beings through common objective laws. This is a realm which may be called a realm of ends ... because what these laws have in view is just the relation of these beings to each other as ends and means.

What Kant suggests is that we ask moral beings to act from laws that are publicly acceptable in the sense that they can be objective for every rational being. Since all persons in economic affairs are moral agents, they are equal with respect to possessing dignity and intrinsic value. Thus, in a business firm, organized as a moral community, the interests of every member of the community are equal to the interests of every other member. Our task is to go from a purely formal analysis to some specific suggestions for management theory and organizational design. Borrowing from the title of a collection of essays by Christine Korsgaard (1996), the task is to show how managers should and could create the kingdom of ends within a business firm. Consistent with our focus on the interdisciplinary aspect of the Kantian research agenda we will weave together insights from Kantian moral theory and some of the empirical work from organizational studies.

A Kantian must reject a purely instrumental view of organizations. I believe this follows from Kant's notion of the kingdom of ends and his theory of respect for persons. The best quotation distinguishing an instrumental view of organizations from a moral view of organizations as a means for carrying out the shared purposes of persons is from John Rawls. What I am referring to is Rawls's concept of a social union in the last third of *A theory of justice*. Rawls (1971: 521–523) argues as follows:

> Thus we are led to the notion of a private society. Its chief features are first that the persons comprising it, whether they are human individuals or associations, have their own private ends which are either competing or independent, but not in any case complementary. And second institutions are not to have any value in themselves, the activity of engaging in them not being counted as a good but if anything a burden. Thus each person assesses social arrangements solely as a means to his private ends . . . The social nature of mankind is best seen by contrast with the conception of private society. Thus human beings have in fact shared final ends and they value their common institutions and activities as goods in themselves. We need one another as partners in ways of life that are engaged in for their own sake, and the successes and enjoyments of others are necessary for and complimentary to our own good.

Institutions that embodied these common activities and shared final ends were called social unions and the just society should be a social union of social unions. There does seem to be a great similarity between Kant's notion of the kingdom of ends and Rawls's concept of a social union, whatever the other differences in their philosophies. When an organization is viewed as an instrument for the achievement of one's own ends, then it appears that a person is simply using the organization, and thus using the people in the organization for their own ends. This would violate the second formulation of the categorical imperative. To avoid such a violation, the members of the organization would have to agree on the norms that are to govern the enterprise and their treatment of each other. But such an agreement transforms the organization into a sphere of cooperative activity-at least to a minimal extent. The association of persons is no longer simply a private society. In the context of the business enterprise part of what it means for a business to be a kingdom of ends is that it should be viewed as a social union, or a moral community.

What I am suggesting here is that business organizations need to be viewed as cooperative enterprises that add value to their stakeholders. You do not get the synergies from cooperation if each stakeholder simply sees the business as a means to his or her end. Business schools recognize the importance of cooperation with their emphasis on teamwork. From the side of Kantian morality, an appropriate way to look at a business is to see it as a kingdom of ends, as a social union. In a social union, each stakeholder is to be treated with respect.

So far nothing has been said about leadership in businesses viewed as cooperative enterprises. The kingdom of ends formulation of the categorical imperative has implication for conducting research on leadership.[6] From a Kantian perspective the leader must view the corporation as a cooperative enterprise rather than as a means to his own financial enhancement. Otherwise there is a misfit between the company culture and the values of the leader. Of course, agency theorists have looked at leadership as an agency problem where incentives should be aligned so that the self-interest goals of the leader are in tune with the interests of the stockholders. However, a Kantian looks at leadership in a very different way. A Kantian leader cannot look at the organization she leads as simply instrumental for her own interests. A genuine moral action must be done from the proper motive – out of duty or because it is right. But there is more to Kantian leadership than that.

A Kantian leader supports the development of autonomy both in his followers and in himself. The implementation of such a commitment requires that the leader turn followers into leaders. In other words, the leader transforms the relationship in an organization so that those who had been followers could now be considered leaders.

This account of leadership can be grounded in the kingdom of ends formulation of the categorical imperative. As we have said there is a sense in which the rules that govern an organization must

[6] This account of Kantian leadership and the summary of the ABB Relays case is an abbreviated version of N. Bowie A Kantian theory of leadership, *Leadership & Organization Development Journal* 21 (2000) 185–193. A version of that article also appears in N. E. Bowie, *Business ethics: a Kantian perspective, Cambridge University Press, 2017.*

be acceptable to all. Many think of the leader as the boss – as the person who makes the decisions. A Kantian does not accept that view. To be consistent with the kingdom of ends formulation of the categorical imperative, the leader is a decision proposer rather than a decision imposer. The leader in an organization can propose ends as well as the means for reaching those ends. He or she can propose decision – making rules as well. But the leader should not order these things or impose them based on his or her power. In management terms, the leader creates the conditions for participative management. In less scholarly terms, the Kantian leader gets buy-in. But the buy-in is not based on charisma. Neither is it based on the power of the position. Rather it is based on the merits of the proposal. The rules that govern human interactions should be rules that are acceptable to all.

The Harvard Business School case ABB's Relay Business (1993) is often used as a case study for the development of the matrix organization but it can also be used as a case study for a Kantian theory of leadership. Here is how the case unfolds: the CEO of Asea Brown Boveri (ABB) is Percy Barnevik. In this case, Barnevik is the person who exemplifies leadership. Yet after page two, Barnevik disappears and is never heard from again. However, this HBR case is twelve pages long excluding appendices. If this case is about Barnevik's leadership, where is he? In an important sense Barnevik is always there because all the others became leaders through his leadership style. By page two, the actor on center stage is Goran Lindahl, Asea's executive vice-president. As the case unfolds, it is clear that Barnevik has made Lindahl a leader. For example, Lindahl is responsible for communicating the new philosophy and principles including the guiding principle of decentralization. He also wanted to emphasize the importance of individual accountability. He delegated a series of tasks to managers at lower levels. By page six, Lindahl disappears and Ulf Gundemark who becomes ABB's business head for the world-wide relay business is at the center of action. Leadership is being pushed down the organization chart. A focal point event in the case centers on the allocation of export markets. The Swiss company has been given responsibility for coordinating sales into Mexico, but a dispute arose concerning shortening the company's lines to its customers and minimizing the nonvalue added work in the system. Gundemark delegated this to a team of four marketing managers. After much negotiation, they reported back to Gundemark that they could not reach a decision. Rather than make the decision himself, Gundemark sent them back for further discussion. Several days later, after exhausting negotiations, they reported that they had reached a majority decision of three to one. Gundemark wanted a unanimous decision and sent them back yet again. Finally, after three more days of intense negotiation, the marketing team came back with a unanimous recommendation. Talk about a decision where you are subject and sovereign at the same time. A Kantian leader, contrary to popular stereotype, is not one to whom you look for a decision. The Kantian leader empowers others in the organization to take responsibility for making a decision. In so doing Barnevik, at least in part exemplifies what it means to be a Kantian leader.

## A Concluding Example of Interdisciplinary Research with a Kantian Overlay

I have argued that Kantian ethics has an important role to play in interdisciplinary business ethics research – the only research that can really help us understand a successful business with integrity. It is an argument that endorses certain universal values for a business with integrity and is an ethical argument that can generate testable hypotheses. This essay concludes with an interdisciplinary argument to show how that can be done.

One can give a straightforward Kantian argument for three universal ethical norms. A maxim that permitted bribery violates the first formulation of the categorical imperative and is thus morally wrong. A maxim that permits discrimination on such grounds as race, religion, sexual orientation, and ethnicity etc. violates the first and second formulations of the categorical imperative and is morally wrong. A maxim that encourage lack of trust in business relationships violates the first formulation of the categorical imperative and thus is morally wrong. This latter maxim involves a practical contradiction as we have already shown. The argument to show that bribery and discrimination are wrong needs to proceed in two steps. At the organizational level, in a society where bribery is considered morally wrong, a maxim that permitted an organization to bribe would put it in a competitive disadvantage because it would pay more to obtain business than others who won contracts based on cost and or quality. And a bribe taker would pay more than necessary for a product or service. In both cases such a maxim to be a bribe taker or briber giver puts the business at a competitive disadvantage and eventually bribe giving and bribe taking undermine the firm. Now in a society where bribery is common, we need to go to the societal level rather than the organizational level to make the point. At that level, it is the bribe taking and bribe giving society that is at a competitive disadvantage. The relative poverty of corrupt societies provides empirical evidence for this point. The same kind of argument can be used about firms or societies that discriminate on grounds such as race, religion, ethnicity, or sexual orientation. None other than Milton Friedman has provided the grounds for this argument. Thus, a straight forward application of Kantian ethics provides an argument as to the universal validity of an antibribery, antidiscrimination, and trust building multinational business culture.

But there is an economic argument that would also give the same results. The first step in the argument is limited to those MNC's that believe that their core ethical values are an essential part of their brand. For example, being a socially responsible corporation is part of the Johnson and Johnson (J & J) brand. J and J believes that its reputation as a socially responsible corporation gives it a competitive advantage. Companies like J and J could give the following argument for applying their own ethical values universally:

An Argument for Universal Ethical Values[7]

1. Certain ethical values are believed by the management of a MNC to provide the MNC with a competitive advantage.
2. Those ethical values which provide a durable competitive advantage abroad will tend to be knowledge based, be embodies in individual employees or firm routines and be characterized by high asset specificity.
3. Highly specific assets associated with high return should not be diluted.
4. If ethical values are such assets, they should not be diluted.
5. If ethical values vary among subsidiaries, these assets will be diluted due to the phenomenon of cognitive dissonance.
6. Therefore, an MNC should have common ethical values in all its subsidiaries.

This argument is based on transaction cost economics and the psychological phenomenon of cognitive dissonance. The notion "high asset specificity" is a key concept in transaction cost economics. From the transaction cost economics perspective, assets that have high asset specificity are unique and thus cannot be easily copied. Using the terminology of transaction cost economics, premise two asserts that the nature of a moral climate is such that it has high asset specificity and thus cannot be easily copied. Given premises 1 and 2, we have MNC's that believe that their ethical values are a competitive advantage and if the transaction cost economics story is right, then these MNC's have a competitive advantage that is hard to copy. For one doing corporate strategy, this is an ideal situation.

The soundness of premise 5 is based on the psychological concept of cognitive dissonance. Suppose an MNC considers adopting the "When in Rome, do as the Romans do," philosophy with

[7] This section which includes two arguments for universal values and three hypotheses based on those arguments are based on a much more extended analysis in N. E. Bowie, *Business Ethics" A Kantian Perspective*, Cambridge University Press, 2017. The argument in that volume is in turn based on work presented in N. E. Bowie and P. Vaaler, Some arguments for universal moral standards in *International business ethics: challenges and approaches* G. Enderle, (ed.). (South Bend, IN: University of Notre Dame Press, 1999) 160–173 and P. Vaaler and N. E. Bowie, "Transaction cost economics, knowledge transfer and universal business norms in multinational enterprises" *International Journal of Strategic Change Management*, 2 (2010) 269–297.

respect to ethical values. In other words, if bribery is widely practiced in a country where it does business, the company policy would be that it is permissible to bribe in those countries. However, employees could not bribe in countries where bribery was forbidden and not practiced. Since employees on track to be senior executives at a MNC do multiple postings abroad, in such an environment they would suffer from the psychological phenomenon of cognitive dissonance. Cognitive dissonance is a state of discomfort or tension that results when people hold or are asked to hold incompatible beliefs. In our example of the MNC that adopts the "When in Rome, do as the Romans do," strategy with respect to bribery, up and coming senior managers would be told that with respect to bribery it is morally permissible to bribe and it is not permissible to bribe according to the circumstances. Strictly speaking there is no logical contradiction here since whether the employee should bribe or not bribe depends on the laws and practices of the countries where the MNC does business. However, as a matter of psychology, there is a tension, because if people think that bribery is wrong (or right), they would tend to that that it is right or wrong universally. Most people cannot contextualize their core ethical values.

Adding the knowledge regarding cognitive dissonance to the knowledge about the nature of the competitive advantage of ethical values, gives us the conclusion that a MNC of that type should impose its ethical values universally in all its subsidiaries. Interestingly transaction cost economics gives us an argument why a firm like Johnson and Johnson should not bribe.

Up to this point, the argument is based on a premise that the MNC believes that its ethical values give it a competitive advantage. Suppose that the belief expressed in premise 1 is true. In fact, the ethical values do give the company a competitive advantage. In other words, the beliefs of those companies identified in premise 1 are true beliefs. We could then rewrite premise 1 as follows:

1. Certain ethical values of a MNC provide the MNC with a competitive advantage.

What should the response be of a MNC that adopts the "When in Rome, do as the Romans do," strategy? Such a MNC could hold to its relativistic strategy. However, other things being equal, economists would say that such stubbornness would have to end in failure. If the MNC's that do not have the relativistic "When in Rome, do as the Romans do," strategy really do have a competitive advantage, then eventually those companies will win out in the competitive struggle. A company that has the relativistic strategy will eventually, other things being equal, go bankrupt. In that case the wise strategy is to try to develop an ethical culture with ethical values that are adopted universally. In other words, the appropriate strategy is to make a universal commitment to certain ethical values, as part of the MNC's brand. This strategy is rational even though it is hard to achieve. It is hard to achieve because an ethical culture with universal values has high asset specificity and is, therefore, hard to copy. Nonetheless, the company's strategy should be to try.

An Argument for Truly Universal Standards of Business Ethics

1. Certain ethical values provide a competitive advantage for MNC's and contribute to the MNCs economic success.
2. Thus, other things being equal, MNCs will be driven by market forces to adopt those ethical values which are necessary to provide a competitive advantage and economic success.
3. Thus, other things being equal, market forces will favor the development of at least a common core of ethical standards. Thus, all MNCs will ultimately adopt nearly identical standards whatever their beliefs of the competitive advantage of ethical commitments.

This argument provides an argument for the adoption for a common core of ethical values that MNC's will impose across all their subsidiaries. But what will those values be? They will be the same antibribery, antidiscrimination, and trust building values, that a Kantian using the categorical imperative would endorse as morally required maxims for multinational corporate action. An endorsement of these values is subject to empirical verification. Consider the following three hypotheses:

*H1 As international business increases, the amount of bribery in international business will decrease.*

*H2 As international business increases, the amount of discrimination in business practice will decrease.*

*H3 As international business increases, the level of honesty and trust among business participants will increase.*

This case for multinational corporations to act as nonbribers, nondiscriminators, and trust builders is based on a truly interdisciplinary research model. Crucial to that model is the guiding hand of Kantian ethical theory. This example is meant as verification of R. Edward Freeman's insistence that there is no separation thesis between business and ethics. The two are wound together. This is exactly what a Kantian who endorses the respect for persons principle would expect in an organization of persons.

## References

Bartlett, C. A., "ABB's Relays Business: Building and Managing a Global Matrix," Harvard Business School Case 394016 (1993).

Bazerman, M. H. and A. E. Tenbrunsel, *Blind Spots: Why We Fail to Do What's Right and What To Do About It*, Princeton University Press, 2011.

Boulding, K. E., "The Basis of Value Judgments in Economics," in *Human Values and Economic Policy*, S. Hook (ed.), New York University Press, 1967.

Bromiley, P. and L. Cummings Transaction Costs in Organizations with Trust," in R. J. Bies, R. Lewicki, and B. Shepard (eds.) *Research on Negotiations in Organizations*. Bingley, UK: Emerald Group Publishing Limited, 1995.

Case, J. *Open Book Management*, New York: HarperCollins Publishers, 1995.

Fukuyama, F., *Trust*, New York: The Free Press, 1995.

Kant, I., *Foundation of the Metaphysics of Morals*, 1785 L.W. Beck Trans. New York: Macmillan, 1990.

"Metaphysical Principles of Virtue," *The Metaphysics of Morals, 1797 in Kant's Ethical Philosophy*, 2nd ed. James W. Ellington 1994. trans. Indianapolis: Hackett Publishing, 1994.

Korsgaard, C., *Creating the Kingdom of Ends*, Cambridge University Press, 1996.

O'Neill, O., *Constructions of Reason*, Cambridge University Press, 1989.

Rawls, J., *A Theory of Justice*, Harvard University Press, 1971.

Sunstein, C. R., and R. H Thaler, *Nudge: Improving Decisions About Health, Wealth, and Happiness*, Yale University Press, 2008.

Trevino, L. K., G. R. Weaver, and S. J. Reynolds, "Behavioral Ethics in Organizations: A Review," *Journal of Management*, 32 (2006) 951–990.

PART II

# Empirical Approaches

# Qualitative Approaches

CHAPTER 6

# Normative Assessments in Empirical Business Ethics Research

## *Toward a Methodological Bridge across the Ontological Gap*

SARAH M. JASTRAM and DAMIAN BÄUMLISBERGER

### Introduction

The application of deontological theories – such as those by Immanuel Kant and Jürgen Habermas – in normative assessments of economic institutions, business processes and/or individual business conduct has become increasingly popular. The corresponding research inquires, for instance, whether the involvement of companies in new forms of policy making is legitimate (Gilbert & Rasche 2007; Jastram 2012) or what it means to organize companies in line with Kantian ideals (Bowie 1998; Reynolds & Bowie 2004). Using the said theories in such analyses is fruitful, but is not without pitfalls. Their reliance on abstract normative principles, like Kant's *Categorical Imperative* and Habermas' *Discourse Principle*, makes them independent from a particular historical or cultural context and applicable to all possible empirical cases. But this universality comes at a price. The corresponding principles tend to be so unspecific that their use in normative analyses of factual circumstances requires their translation into more tangible criteria. In contemporary business ethics research, the methodology behind this translation is often neglected or remains implicit. This exposes any new research project to methodological criticism.

In response, this chapter outlines and refines a methodological procedure for the more systematic and rigorous development of such indicators. It takes a particular normative principle as given and shows how the major difficulties in applying it to a normative assessment of the status quo can be conquered. Thus, it supports scholarly efforts of pragmatically linking normative ideals and empirical reality without collapsing them into each other or committing the category mistake of deriving an "ought" from an "is" (Hume, 1896 [1739]).[1] It is designed to help researchers make sure that their operationalization of a deontological principle is methodologically driven, intersubjectively comprehensible, and embedded in theory.

The chapter illustrates methodological aspects in view of Kantian ethics as a particular class of deontological theories frequently used in contemporary business ethics research. It highlights the methodology of operationalizing the abstract universal principles formulated by Immanuel Kant and Jürgen Habermas as two important proponents of the Kantian tradition in ethics.[2] Internationally, the moral philosophy of Kant has been popularized by Norman Bowie who was one of the first to make sense of Kant's three formulations of the *Categorical Imperative* in the context of business organizations. His *Theory of Meaningful Work* is comprised of six criteria for the application of Kant's overarching moral principle to the workplace and the treatment of employees has inspired and guided a host of impactful contributions to the scholarship on business ethics (Bowie, 1998; Bowie, 1999; Reynolds & Bowie, 2004). Habermasian *Discourse Ethics* (Habermas, 1993 [1991]) has found its way into

Both authors contributed equally to this book chapter.

[1] This angle on the methodology in business ethics is unorthodox as most methodological discussions seem to focus on the methods that are (or should be) used in developing moral theories themselves (Jamieson, 1993).

[2] As an umbrella term, Kantian ethics stands for a whole array of contemporary approaches to ethics regarding themselves as being in the tradition of Kant and drawing on his original ideas (O'Neill, 1993, p. 175).

contemporary business ethics research via the scholarly debate on political CSR where it continues to play a pivotal role. It has been used for the justification of the political role of the firm (Scherer & Palazzo, 2007) and the normative analysis of private regulation efforts in multistakeholder initiatives (Matten & Crane, 2005; Mueckenberger & Jastram, 2010).

Kant and Habermas adopt similar approaches to moral philosophy by grounding ethics in the autonomy of reasonable beings. From their respective accounts of autonomy and reason,[3] both philosophers derive universal ethical principles for the moral guidance of human (inter) action. Both moral principles are designed as formal mechanisms for testing the generalizability of the formal and informal rules at heart of human (inter)action. In both approaches those rules are in line with the overarching ethical principle when they can be willed and accepted by all reasonable and autonomous beings. While Kant's *Categorical Imperative* is designed to test the maxims of individuals, meaning their action-guiding rules or heuristics, Habermas' *Discourse Principle* captures the ideal conditions for the discursive development of shared norms.

In sections 2 and 3, the moral philosophies by Kant and Habermas will be outlined in more detail along with their reception in empirically oriented contributions to contemporary business ethics research. Both strands of the literature will be analyzed with a special focus on the underlying methodology. Section 4 is dedicated to the development of a more rigorous method of translating abstract ethical principles into benchmark criteria for the normative assessment of economic or political institutions, business organizations, and individual business conduct. In section 5, the chapter will be rounded off with a short conclusion, where other application areas of the method and potential for further refinement will be pointed out.

[3] While Kant focuses on the capacity of humans to pursue self-imposed goals, Habermas puts more emphasis on their ability for discursive deliberation.

## Methodological Lessons from Kantian Approaches to Business Ethics

This section focuses on the challenges of applying the *Categorical Imperative* to the modern business context. It discusses these challenges in light of Norman Bowie's Kantian *Theory of Meaningful Work* as one particularly suitable example from contemporary business ethics research. The focus will be on describing the ways in which Bowie translates Kant's universal principle into more concrete criteria for the normative guidance of organizational development and institutional reform. A first methodological rule for the development of abstract normative principles into tangible benchmark indicators will be explained in view of Bowie's approach and the need for a second methodological criterion will be highlighted. But first, a brief account is given of the key concepts of Kant's moral philosophy.

### *Theoretical Foundations of Kant's Ethics*

Max Weber categorized Kant's moral philosophy as an "ethic of attitude" (in German: *Gesinnungsethik;* sometimes also translated as: *ethic of ultimate ends*). This is the case because for Kant, the moral quality of an action is conditional on the underlying motivation (Weber, 2004 [1919]). In his "Groundwork of the Metaphysic of Morals", where he lays out his moral philosophy, Kant insists that "there is nothing it is possible to think of anywhere in the world, or indeed anything at all outside it, that can be held to be good without limitation excepting only a good will" (Kant, 2002 [1785], p. 9 (emphasis removed)). This good will, understood as respect for the moral law, is conceived as a necessary condition for the consideration of an action as ethical. In addition, the maxim, meaning the internal guideline or heuristic at heart of the action, has to be in line with the *Categorical Imperative* as the overarching normative principle of Kant's moral philosophy. As an expression of the moral law, the *Categorical Imperative* serves as a touchstone for all possible action-guiding maxims.

The ability of human beings to act upon self-chosen maxims follows from their endowment with reason. As rational and autonomous beings they can set themselves targets and choose the appropriate means for their pursuit. This is to say that they have the ability to be a law unto themselves. But their targets are subject to hypothetical imperatives prescribing that willing y implies willing all x required for achieving y. This means that the pursuit of a goal like the goal of becoming a doctor requires specific means for its achievement, such as the attendance of medical school. While hypothetical imperatives capture the physical constraints on possible goals (or that which can be willed) the *Categorical Imperative* reflects the constraints of reason. It narrows the set of all possible maxims down to those maxims that all reasonable beings would endorse.

The most basic formulation of the *Categorical Imperative* requires individuals to "act only in accordance with that maxim through which [they] can at the same time will that it should become a universal law" (Kant, 2002 [1785], p. 37 (italics removed)). This overarching normative principle of Kant's moral philosophy requires the agent to put him/herself into everybody else's shoes when deliberating on a particular course of action. The underlying maxim is only morally desirable when all reasonable beings can will it. A maxim that permits theft, for instance, will be revealed as inconsistent by this test, largely because the universalization of stealing undermines the property rights which are the precondition for the possibility of stealing something in the first place.

For Kant, reasonable beings have a duty to act in accordance with the requirements of the *Categorical Imperative*. Duty is defined as "the necessity of an action from respect for the law" (Kant, 2002 [1785], p. 16 (italics removed)), meaning the moral law embodied by the *Categorical Imperative*. For Kant, reasonable beings have a perfect duty not to act according to maxims that are self-defeating when tested on the basis of the *Categorical Imperative*. Furthermore, they have an imperfect duty to act on those maxims that are consistent with it. An action that is performed out of reverence or respect for the universal requirements of the *Categorical Imperative* is an action *from duty*. An action that is in line with the *Categorical Imperative*, but performed instrumentally in pursuit of other goals, is merely an action *in conformity with duty*. For Kant. only the former action has moral value.

Kant describes several formulations of the *Categorical Imperative* reflecting different angles on the same moral principle. The formula of *An End in Itself* (in German: *Selbstzweckformel*) requires individuals to "act so that [they] use humanity, as much in [their] own person as in the person of every other, always at the same time as end and never merely as means" (Kant, 2002 [1785], pp. 46–47 (italics removed)). This formula articulates the moral requirement of respecting the personhood and dignity of all rational and autonomous beings. It is pivotal to Bowie's *Kantian Theory of Meaningful Work*, which is applied at the level of business organizations. The *Kingdom of Ends* formula (in German: *Reich-der-Zwecke-Formel*), as another important formulation, asks every rational being to "act as if it were through its maxims always a legislating member in a universal realm of ends" (Kant, 2002 [1785], p. 56). By virtue of its explicit focus on shared social norms, the *Kingdom of Ends* formula offers a bridge to macro-level interpretations of the *Categorical Imperative* such as Walter Eucken's Kantian conception of a social market economy (Eucken, 1948, 2004 [1952]; Wörsdörfer, 2010), which had a considerable impact on the organization of the German economic system in the aftermath of the Second World War. We will now turn to the methodological analysis of contemporary applications of Kant's moral philosophy with a specific focus on Bowie's contribution.

## Applications of the Categorical Imperative to the Modern Business Context

One of the biggest strengths of Kant's universalist approach to ethics is its high level of abstraction. In virtue of its generality, it is timeless and applicable to an assessment of any society in any historical period with any economic system. However, the application of Kant's ethics to modern society and a modern business context is anything but straightforward. Kant's abstract formulations of the *Categorical Imperative*, focused on individual action and based on examples from eighteenth century premodern Prussian society, offer little practical guidance on how to organize a company or an economy in line with the requirements of universalized reason.

That is why many scholars have addressed the task of exploring the implications of the *Categorical Imperative* for the modern firm and the ground rules of (globalizing) markets. They substantiated Kant's overarching ethical principle at different levels of aggregation: the individual (manager), the organization, and the economic system. Denis Arnold and Jared Harris, for instance, developed a conception of a Kantian personality (Arnold & Harris, 2012). Norman Bowie and Scott Reynolds drew the implications of Kantian ethics for ethics programs and the organization of meaningful work in companies (Bowie, 1998; Bowie, 1999; Reynolds & Bowie, 2004). And scholars like Walter Eucken and John Rawls offered Kantian justifications of the principles at heart of the basic institutions of a capitalist system (Rawls, 1971; Wörsdörfer, 2010).

All those approaches derive, more or less, concrete benchmark criteria from the *Categorical Imperative* as Kant's overarching principle, which are designed to facilitate its application to economies, firms, and managers. Bowie's application of the *Categorical Imperative* at the level of (business) organizations is particularly suitable for a methodological analysis because his approach is both well-known and nicely draws on one of the two methodological criteria to be outlined.

Bowie derives the implications of Kantian ethics for the organizational structure of firms. In his Kantian *Theory of Meaningful Work*, he develops six criteria that are designed to guide managers in their efforts to fulfill their Kantian duty to provide meaningful work to their employees. Reflecting a concretion the second formulation of Kant's *Categorical Imperative*, they specify that, meaningful work is (1) freely entered into, (2) allows workers to exercise their autonomy and independence, (3) enables workers to develop their rational capacities, (4) provides a wage sufficient for physical welfare, (5) supports the moral development of employees, and (6) is not paternalistic in the sense of interfering with the workers' conception of how they wish to obtain happiness.

Methodologically, the respective publications put great emphasis on the coherence of those criteria with Kant's overarching normative principle.

In a first step, it is argued that the *Theory of Meaningful Work* is consistent with Kant's writings in general. On the basis of suitable quotes from Kant's comprehensive oeuvre, it is shown that Kant did not just put great emphasis on the notion of self-respect, but tied it to a person's professional life. More specifically, Bowie retrieves primary references for Kant's belief that "work is necessary for the development of selfhood understood as the development of one's ability to act autonomously" (Bowie, 1998, p. 1084). From a methodological standpoint, this approach is very similar to the historical-critical method used in literary and historical studies as well as theology (Krentz, 1975). A body of basic works such as the novels of a particular writer or the key texts of a religious or philosophical tradition is interpreted from a contemporary perspective and in consideration of the (historical) conditions of their genesis. But in line with Kant's motto of "sapere aude" (in English: *dare to think for yourself*), Bowie goes beyond this historical analysis of a given text that has been written or revealed by an authoritative figure.

In a second step, he meticulously establishes the coherence between Kant's moral philosophy and the six criteria of meaningful work at a conceptual level, sometimes drawing on contemporary interpreters of Kant. He argues that employers who want to fulfill their Kantian duty to treat humanity in themselves and others "always at the same time as end and never merely as means" (Kant, 2002 [1785], p. 47) must organize work in their companies in ways that do justice to the human nature of their employees. Following Thomas E. Hill, he identifies this nature with positive freedom, as the "autonomy persons have to be a law unto themselves" (Bowie, 1998, p. 1085) and systematically shows that his six principles can promote the same.

This logical consistency of the formulated criteria of meaningful work with the *Categorical Imperative* can be considered as the first methodological criterion for the operationalization of abstract normative standards. It reflects a variation of the foundationalist method in moral theory. Foundationalism refers to "the view that systems of belief are justified in virtue of the logical relations that obtain between beliefs that require justification, and other beliefs that themselves are in no need of justification" (Jamieson, 1993, p. 480). In Bowie's account the *Categorical Imperative* is considered as the foundational belief that does not require any justification, whereas the six criteria of meaningful work are justified in virtue of their logical connection to it.

Even though the logical consistency of the six criteria of meaningful work with Kant's supreme ethical principle is of crucial importance, it should not be forgotten that they fulfill another important function: they mediate between Kant's normative ideal and empirical reality by pointing to normative deficits of the status quo and guiding its reform. For this purpose, they have to live up to a second methodological requirement, necessitating their practicability at the margin of the (physically) feasible. The feasibility constraint in this requirement is captured by the (Kantian) formula of "ought implies can" (Kant, 1998 [1781]), demanding the physical feasibility, and thus the verifiability, of all serious normative desiderata. Bowie implicitly demonstrates his commitment to this aspect by discussing his six principles in view of selected case studies from a modern business context and by citing "examples of companies that at least come close to providing their workers with meaningful work in a Kantian sense" (Bowie, 1998, p. 1090). By this he indicates that it is, in principle, possible to live up to his interpretation of the Kantian ideal.

However, the systematic assessment (i.e. beyond selected case studies) of business reality in light of his six criteria of meaningful work does not seem to be Bowie's main focus. In order to become fully operational for an assessment of an organization's closeness to the ideal of meaningful work, the criteria would have to be translated into much more tangible performance indicators.[4]

Some applications of Habermas' *Discourse Ethics* to contemporary business ethics research offer additional insights with regard to this twofold nature of the second methodological criterion. As they are better at capturing the field of tension between the feasibility of benchmark criteria, on the one hand, and their idealistic ambition, on the other hand, they will play a key role in the next section.

## Methodological Lessons from Habermasian Approaches to Business Ethics

This section explores the method of applying universal ethical principles in normative evaluations of empirical reality from a Habermasian perspective. As a neo-Kantian research program (Gottschalk-Mazouz, 2004, p. 8) Habermasian *Discourse Ethics* adopts Kant's approach to moral philosophy by grounding ethics in the autonomy of reasonable beings. *Discourse Ethics* also hinges on an abstract universal principle, the *Discourse Principle*, in need of interpretation when applied to the business context.[5] However, while Kant's moral philosophy tests the generalizability of

[4] It could, for instance, be said that a job is started and done voluntarily when it is based on a contractually documented declaration of intention by the employee. This declaration in the form of a signature has to be made in the absence of physical force and in light of all relevant information, i.e. without fraud or manipulation. Indirect measures like the labor turnover rate or the average number of applicants per job advertisement, possibly in consideration of the overall economic situation, could also serve as indications for the desirability of a company or a particular position in that company. Second, a particular position would allow for a certain degree of autonomy and independence when company processes are organized in a way that leaves their executers with scope for autonomous decisions. This criterion could, for instance, be captured by indicators for the number, complexity and variety of decisions to be taken in a particular job. Third, the degree to which employees' rational capacities are being developed might be reflected by their opportunities to practice job rotation, to participate in trainings or to move up the corporate ladder. Fourth, a job could be considered as yielding a living wage as soon as the remuneration permits the acquisition of a certain basket of basic material goods. This basket of a minimum level of food, clothing and housing could be defined on the basis of existing measures of absolute or relative poverty. Comparable benchmark indicators are conceivable for the remaining two criteria of meaningful work.

[5] As we will see, Habermas develops two principles, the *Principle of Universalization* and the *Discourse Principle*, but scholars disagree whether they are separate principles

maxims on the basis of an internal monologue *Discourse Ethics* evaluates it in the course of a dialog between real individuals trying to convince each other on the basis of rational argument. Unlike Kant's Ethics, *Discourse Ethics* integrates the articulated interests and values of real people as well as the intended and unintended consequences of proposed norms into the process of norm justification. In this sense it systematically links normative aspirations and empirical reality. Participants in discourses will only give their approval to the norms under consideration when they reflect their actual preferences and perspectives. This link builds the ground for our analysis of a second methodological criterion for the operationalization of universal ethical principles, as the following sections will show.

After an introduction to Habermas' *Discourse Ethics* as the moral foundation of his later developed *Theory of Deliberative Politics*, the next section discusses recent examples of normative analyses of corporate behavior and governance processes based on Habermasian theory (Scherer & Palazzo, 2007; Gilbert, Rasche, & Waddock, 2011; Gilbert & Rasche, 2007). It makes implicit methodological procedures explicit and refines them, where appropriate.

## *Discourse-Ethical Foundations of Habermas' Theory of Deliberative Politics*

Habermas' extensive oeuvre ranges from contributions to social-political theory and critical theory to legal theory and the philosophy of religion.[6] Pivotal to his theoretical work is the belief in the importance of the autonomy of the people (also: popular sovereignty).[7] Habermas is convinced that any law or social norm will become more acceptable and legitimate if those affected by it have had the chance to participate in the process of developing it. Like Kant, rather than focusing on the material content of norms, Habermas is interested in the (democratic) processes of norm-building.

In contrast to Kant, Habermas develops an integrative account of the relationship between law and morality (Bohmann & Rehg, 2014, chapter 3.4). His writings culminate in two interlinked principles, the *Principle of Universalization* and the *Discourse Principle*. The former systematically relates the Kantian requirement of putting oneself into the place of (all) others (i.e. adopting the "moral point of view") to factual circumstances. It considers a moral norm to be valid "just in case the foreseeable consequences and side-effects of its general observance for the interests and value-orientations of each individual could be jointly accepted by all concerned without coercion" (Habermas, 1998 [1996], p. 42 (italics removed)). It is flanked by the *Discourse Principle*, which is the centerpiece of Habermas' outlook on law and ethics and captures his dialogical conception of the justification of ethical norms. The principle states that "only those norms can claim to be valid that meet (or could meet) with the approval of all affected in their capacity as participants in a practical discourse" (Habermas, 1990 [1983], p. 197). Habermas understands the *Discourse Principle* very broadly as an "overarching principle of impartial justification for all types of practical discourse" (Bohmann & Rehg, 2014, chapter 3.4). For him, it applies to ethical and political discourses alike. As such it constitutes a yardstick for the normative assessment of both moral and legal norms.

A condition for the realization of a true consensus via discourse is described by Habermas in

or whether the latter implies the former (Gottschalk-Mazouz, 2004).

6 Some of his most received publications include "Structural Transformation of the Public Sphere" (1989 [1962]), "The Theory of Communicative Action" (1984 [1981]), and "Between Facts and Norms" (1996 [1992]).

7 In this context he explains: "The principle of popular sovereignty states that all political power derives from the communicative power of citizens. The exercise of public authority is oriented and legitimated by the laws citizens give themselves in a discursively structured opinion- and will-formation. [. . .] The rational acceptability of results achieved in conformity with procedure follows from the institutionalization of interlinked forms of communication that, ideally speaking, ensure that all relevant questions, issues, and contributions are brought up and processed in discourses and negotiations on the basis of the best available information and arguments." (Habermas, 1996 [1992], p. 169)

terms of the so called "ideal speech situation" (Habermas, 1990). The ideal speech situation can be considered as a concretion of the *Discourse Principle*. It requires that all participants of a discourse must have equal chances to initiate a discourse, to speak, and to present arguments without constraints. It must be possible to dispute, to justify, or to disprove any statement. No other motive should influence the discourse but the search for communicative and rational consensus and there shall be no other influencing power in an ideal speech situation but the power of the better argument (Habermas, 1984; Habermas, 1990).

It is, of course, impossible to fully meet those ideal conditions, especially in political discourses. Yet, they function as a benchmark towards which practical discourses can strive. They enable a comparison of actual discourses in terms of their closeness to the ideal state of a rational discourse. Thus, in contrast to Kant, Habermas takes the first steps toward a translation of his supreme normative principle(s) into concrete benchmark indicators himself.

Habermas further developed his thoughts about the rational and consensus-oriented discourse in his *Theory of Deliberative Politics* (1996 [1992]).[8] This theory has gained widespread attention, particularly among political scientists with an interest in searching for new forms of legitimate (global) governance beyond the level of nation states (Dingwerth, 2007; Zürn, 2004). In a situation with partly limited regulative powers of individual nation states and cross-border political challenges, deliberative democracy can be a suitable approach to democratic will-formation beyond national institutions.[9] Again, it is not necessarily a national institutional system but the *process* of discursive will-formation that creates legitimacy and this process can take place in any setting within national borders or at the transnational level.[10]

Concerning the concrete, formal requirements of a deliberative process, Habermas refers to the conditions of an ideal democratic process as described in Robert Dahl's "Democracy and its Critics"(1989).[11]

Dahl's conditions can be seen as an operationalization of the *Discourse Principle* in the context of new forms of *Deliberative Politics*. As such they fulfill a similar function as the ideal speech situation in the context of *Discourse Ethics* (ibid., p. 109 et seq.):

[8] The book has been influenced by authors like John Dryzek (1990) and Joshua Cohen (1989; 1997a; 1997b). In this context, the term deliberation refers to nonhierarchical, discursive discussions based on a rational exchange of justified arguments aiming at convincing others and at reaching a well-grounded consensus (Cohen, 1989). The idea of deliberative democracy is grounded in the ideal of popular sovereignty where the source of legitimacy is the collective judgment of the people. Therefore, proponents of a deliberative democracy believe that a justified consensus among those who are affected by a decision will lead to perceived legitimacy and thereby positively affect norm-compliance (Jastram, 2012).

[9] As Habermas puts it: "According to discourse theory, the success of deliberative politics depends not on a collectively acting citizenry but on the institutionalization of the corresponding procedures and conditions of communication, as well as on the interplay of institutionalized deliberative processes with informally developed public opinions. Proceduralized popular sovereignty and a political system tied into the peripheral networks of the political public sphere go together with the image of a decentered society. At any rate, this concept of democracy no longer has to operate with the notion of a social whole centered in the state." (1996 [1992], p. 298).

[10] In one of his most influential publications Between facts and norms, he states that "the law receives its full normative sense neither through its legal *form* per se, nor through an a priori moral *content*, but through a *procedure* of lawmaking that begets legitimacy" (Habermas, 1996 [1992], p. 135).

[11] Dahl's criteria are based on the fundamental principles of fairness, liberty, and autonomy, which are expressed in the general condition that those affected by a decision must be involved in the decision-making process. The fundamental assumption, as in the work of Habermas, holds "that each member of the association is ... a better judge of his or her interests than others would be"(Dahl, 1989, p. 108). The corresponding discourses should be nonhierarchical and not discriminate against particular moral inclinations and viewpoints. Participants have to convince each other based on arguments alone. The quality of an argument is rationally assessed by every individual in view of his own interests (which is why differences in intellectual capabilities are believed to be negligible).

(1) **Effective participation:** All citizens must have adequate and equal opportunities to develop and to articulate their preferences and decisions and to place questions on the public agenda.
(2) **Voting equality at the decisive stage:** All citizens must have equal voting rights at important stages of the process.
(3) **Enlightened understanding:** All citizens must have adequate and equal opportunities to make enlightened decisions in their own best interest.[12]
(4) **Control of the agenda:** The demos must have the exclusive chance to decide about which political matters to be on the agenda of the process.
(5) **Inclusion:** The demos must include all adults who are affected by a binding decision.

It becomes clear that Dahl's criteria of an ideal democratic process and Habermas' deliberative theory are interlinked and complement each other. Transparency, inclusion, and egalitarian deliberations play crucial roles in both approaches. Habermas as well as Dahl stress that in an ideal and legitimate democratic process, all participants must have equal chances to influence the results of the process, to access relevant information and documents, and to evaluate different arguments in view of their own particular interests. The goal of a deliberative process is to enable autonomous and democratic as well as consensus-oriented decision-making, thereby creating legitimacy and public acceptance.

The following section will illustrate how Habermas' theories and Dahl's contributions and supplements to it have been applied in contemporary business ethics research. Special attention will be given to the implicit methodology behind the translation of the *Discourse Principle*, the ideal speech situation, and Dahl's principles into even more tangible empirical indicators.

## *Applications of Habermas' Theories to the Modern Business Context*

Scherer, Palazzo, and Baumann (2006), as well as Scherer and Palazzo (2007), were among the first to discuss Habermasian ideas in the context of management science and business ethics. Based on the concept of *Deliberative Democracy*, the authors develop a notion of the political role of the firm. They distinguish this perspective from positivist, instrumental perspectives on CSR and from "monological" approaches to business ethics (Scherer & Palazzo, 2007). Drawing on Habermas' analysis of the "postnational constellation" (2011) they argue that globalization diminishes "the ability of the nation-state to regulate business activities" (2007, p. 1101). As a consequence, they posit, corporations have to deal with changing and more complex societal demands and must "replace implicit compliance with assumed societal norms and expectations with explicit participation in public processes of political will formation" (Scherer & Palazzo, 2007, p. 1108). The underlying rationale holds that "instead of being regulated by their governments, corporations have a considerable impact on the formulation of national economic policy and international negotiations over economic issues due to their increasing power" (Scherer et al., 2006). According to the authors, this raises serious questions relating to the democratic legitimacy and accountability of corporate political activities. In response, they develop a new communicative theory of CSR based on joint reasoning and deliberation. It forms the basis for the normative assessment of the legitimacy of the new political role of the firm (Scherer & Palazzo, 2007, p. 1109).

Their conceptual groundwork inspired a variety of *empirically oriented* research endeavors. Many of those studies are aimed at normatively assessing (the involvement of private companies in) current initiatives, processes, and standards of CSR

[12] Most of Dahl's criteria are formulated in an explicit and unambiguous manner. The condition "enlightened understanding", however, needs further clarification. Dahl explains: "This criterion implies [...] that alternative procedures for making decisions ought to be evaluated according to the opportunities they furnish citizens for acquiring an understanding of means and ends, of one's interests and the expected consequences of policies for interests, not only for oneself but for all other relevant persons as well"(Dahl, 1989, p. 112).

Governance in view of the Habermasian ideal.[13] In one of the first studies, Gilbert and Rasche (2007) use the *Discourse Principle* in a normative analysis of the international social accountability standard SA 8000, which defines minimum requirements for workplace conditions (ibid., p. 189). Like Bowie and in line with the first methodological criterion, they put great emphasis on establishing the logical consistency of their approach with the overarching *Discourse Principle.* They achieve this by means of a comprehensive and in-depth discussion of different forms of practical reason and the *Discourse Principle* and by highlighting the conceptual link to their specific adaptation of the ideal speech situation in the context of SA 8000.

However, they do not develop their account of the ideal speech situation into a set of clearly defined and empirically verifiable indicators. Nor do they elaborate on or make explicit quantitative or qualitative empirical methods of data collection to determine the status quo with regard to the realization of SA8000. This methodological gap is common in earlier studies of this kind. The development of more tangible benchmark indicators and their combination with empirical methods occurred later in an incremental manner.

In analyses of ISO 26000 and the UN Global Compact, Mückenberger and Jastram (2010) as well as Jastram (2012, p. 51), for instance, gradually formulated more explicit indicators for the normative assessment and comparison of the legitimacy of various multistakeholder initiatives and governance processes. These are presented in Table 6.1.[14]

In the original study, the indicators served as normative reference points in confrontation with qualitative empirical data collected through interviews, document analyses as well as through participatory observations (Jastram, 2012). These triangulated data were used to assess the empirical status quo in order to determine to what extent the ISO 26000 process approached the Habermasian ideal.

**Table 6.1 Set of indicators for the assessment of ISO 26000.**

| Criterion | Indicator |
|---|---|
| **Inclusion** | **Indicator I1:** All relevant stakeholders have, in principle, equal rights to participate in the governance process. |
| | **Indicator I2:** The selection of the participating stakeholders is based on transparent criteria. |
| | **Indicator I3:** All participating stakeholder representatives have been elected and can possibly be deselected by their constituency. |
| **Transparency** | **Indicator T1: All documents concerning the governance process are freely accessible.** |
| **Deliberation** | **Indicator D1:** All participating stakeholders have an equal opportunity to make proposals for the agenda. |
| | **Indicator D2:** All participating stakeholders have equal opportunities to contribute arguments, questions, and other statements to the discourse. |
| | **Indicator D3:** All participating stakeholders have equal voting rights at all relevant stages of the process. |
| | **Indicator D4:** The goal of the process is a consensus between all participants. |
| | **Indicator D5:** The rules of the process itself can be subject to deliberation. |

*Source:* Jastram, 2012, p. 51

For this purpose, the indicators in Table 6.1 have been formulated in line with the "ought implies can" requirement, as the first aspect of the second methodological criterion. The normative demands of the indicators can, in principle, be met and in light of this (physical) feasibility, their (non-) fulfillment in actual governance processes is verifiable. It is, for instance, possible without difficulty to ascertain whether all documents on the governance process have been made available in ISO 26000 (indicator T1).

In virtue of their empirical orientation, especially their verifiability, the developed benchmark criteria

[13] In this context, the term CSR-Governance relates to the sum of processes, stakeholders and instruments that are involved in an attempt to address social and environmental issues in the field of CSR (Jastram & Schneider, 2015).

[14] Detailed explanations of the criteria and their theoretical derivation can be found in Jastram and Prescher (2014).

can also be used for the systematic comparison of different empirical phenomena of the same type. Jastram and Prescher (2014), for instance, used the mentioned set of indicators in a comparative study of ISO 26000, the European Multistakeholder Forum on CSR, and the National CSR Strategy of the German government. Again, qualitative data was assessed in view of the normative legitimacy indicators. The subsequent comparison of the different multistakeholder processes revealed clear variances in the legitimacy of the different CSR governance approaches (Jastram & Prescher, 2014). Most notably, results show different levels of stakeholder representativeness, transparency, or inclusion and therefore illustrate different types and democratic qualities of multistakeholder governance processes. The challenges in conducting such comparative assessments point to further methodological and conceptual issues as well as to the need for further refinements of the discussed method.

The first issue is related to the verifiability of indicators, as one of two important aspects of the second methodological criterion. The realist claim that the legitimacy criteria can be fulfilled and are fulfilled by some multistakeholder initiatives does not imply a fine-grained measurement scale. Consequently, it remains open if and under which conditions indicators are binary,[15] representable by an ordinal scale[16] or even compatible with a cardinal[17] scale. This issue of how fine-grained and quantifiable an indicator can and should be requires further analysis and/or argument.

The second issue relates to the idealism of indicators, as another important aspect of the second methodological criterion. It is unclear whether the margin of the (physically) feasible, meaning the highest possible level of indicator fulfillment by empirical cases, can always be determined. It is not even clear whether it has to be determined in order to make an indicator useful.[18] This issue also requires further scholarly attention.[19]

In sum, Habermas' *Discourse Ethics* as well as his theory of *Deliberative Politics* have been stimulating a paradigmatically new perspective in business ethics and new forms of normative analyses of empirical cases. Even though an ideal theory of the Habermasian type might never be completely fulfilled, possibly for systematic reasons, it can be adapted to assessments and comparisons of governance processes and the corresponding political discourses. Both theories can guide the search for fair and democratic governance and decision-making. The indicators discussed make the overarching but abstract theories concrete and applicable in a practical context and therefore serve as a guiding set of best practice principles for actors involved in the organization and implementation of governance processes and of stakeholder discourses. In the following section,

[15] E.g., being either "fulfilled" or "not fulfilled".

[16] E.g., level of fulfillment: "not fulfilled" – "hardly fulfilled" – "a little bit fulfilled" – "completely fulfilled".

[17] E.g., level of fulfillment: 1 – 2 – 3 – 4 – 5 – 6 – 7 – 8 – 9 – 10.

[18] This is connected to fundamental discussions on the status of ideal theory (Simmons, 2010), which, in fact, combine this issue with the previously discussed coarseness of the measurement scale. In relation to our methodological analysis this debate raises the question of whether the benchmark indicators

(i) Merely reflect the highest possible standard without enabling the normative comparison of different data points (i.e. the height of the mountain is known, but until climbers reach the top it is unclear where they are (in relation to each other))
(ii) or merely enable the normative comparison of different data points without specifying the highest possible standard (i.e. it is possible to say which climber is higher up the mountain, but the height of the mountain is unknown)
(iii) or reflect the highest possible standard and enable the normative comparison of different data points (i.e. the height of the mountain is known and it is possible to determine how far up the mountain the climbers are)

[19] Those who are skeptical about the moral realism at heart of the described methodology would actually favor a fourth scenario. They would argue that it is not possible to develop benchmark criteria that capture the highest possible standard or enable objective comparisons of different empirical cases (i.e. for them, the top of the mountain is unknown for systematic reasons and it is impossible to say which climber is higher up the mountain).

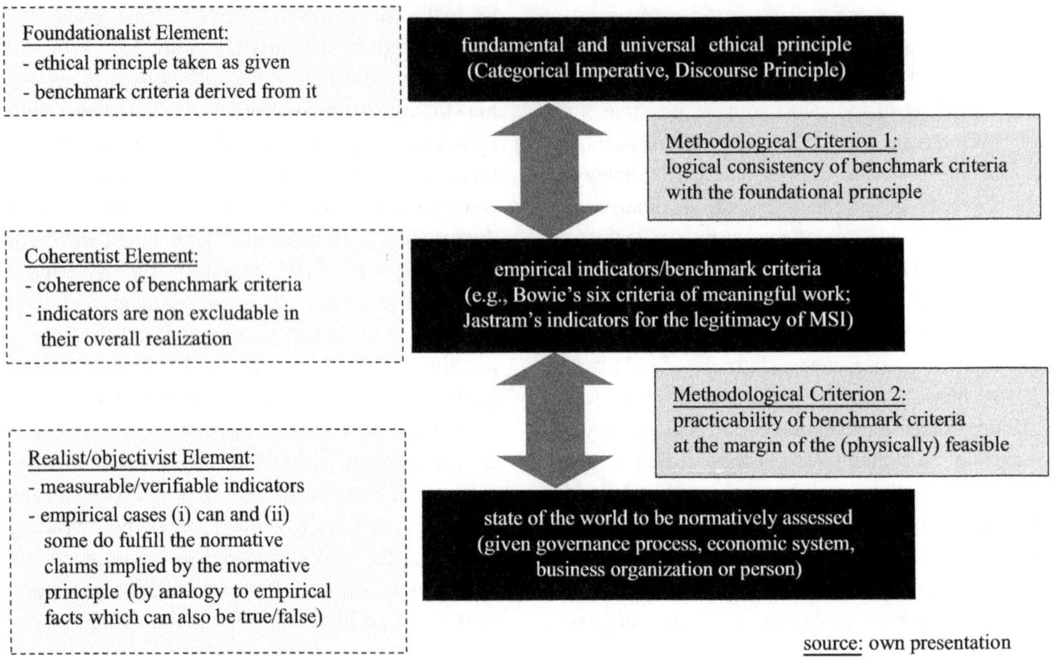
Foundationalist Element:
- ethical principle taken as given
- benchmark criteria derived from it
fundamental and universal ethical principle
(Categorical Imperative, Discourse Principle)
Methodological Criterion 1:
logical consistency of benchmark criteria
with the foundational principle
Coherentist Element:
- coherence of benchmark criteria
- indicators are non excludable in
their overall realization
empirical indicators/benchmark criteria
(e.g., Bowie's six criteria of meaningful work;
Jastram's indicators for the legitimacy of MSI)
Methodological Criterion 2:
practicability of benchmark criteria
at the margin of the (physically) feasible
Realist/objectivist Element:
- measurable/verifiable indicators
- empirical cases (i) can and (ii)
some do fulfill the normative
claims implied by the normative
principle (by analogy to empirical
facts which can also be true/false)
state of the world to be normatively assessed
(given governance process, economic system,
business organization or person)
source: own presentation

*Figure 6.1* Method of normative assessment.

the methodological insights from the preceding two sections will be brought together.

## Toward a Method of Normative Assessment

Based on the preceding analyses of selected applications of Kant's *Categorical Imperative* and Habermas' *Discourse Principle*, a refined "method of normative assessment" can now be formulated. It is designed to guide the translation of universal ethical principles into benchmark criteria for an assessment of empirical cases in the business context. As depicted in Figure 1, those empirical indicators occupy an intermediate position between the actual state of the world to be normatively evaluated and the ideal state of the world implied by the universal ethical principle.

The described method requires the benchmark criteria to meet two methodological conditions. First of all, they have to be logically consistent with the foundational principle. This means that those who wish to apply the *Categorical Imperative* or the *Discourse Principle* to empirical cases have to explain how the fundamental principle leads to the mediating indicators.[20]

While the first methodological criterion applies to the relationship between the benchmark criteria and the normative universe, the second methodological criterion is designed to structure its link with the empirical world. In the spirit of the "ought implies can" principle, it requires indicators to be realizable and verifiable. In order to capture the idealistic spirit of universal ethical theories, such as those by Kant and Habermas, the indicators should be located at the margin of that which is physically feasible (under current technological conditions). Only then will they be able to offer

[20] To avoid confusion, this justification effort should not apply to the fundamental ethical standard itself, which is simply accepted as sufficiently well-justified. This process of highlighting the coherence of the benchmark criteria with the foundational ethical principle bears resemblance to the foundationalist methodology in moral philosophy (Jamieson, 1993).

normative guidance on how to improve the status quo in line with the ethical ideal.[21]

The quality of the developed set of benchmark criteria themselves can be assessed in virtue of their inner coherence. This can be seen as a weakly coherentist trait of the described normative assessment method.[22] When each of the indicators is logically consistent with the overarching normative ideal, they should not contradict each other at a conceptual level. Furthermore, the complete realization of all benchmark criteria should be possible. This would not be the case when the full realization of a subset of the indicators in the defined set systematically excludes the realization of another subset.

The methodology can be applied in six consecutive steps, illustrated in Figure 6.2.

In a first step, the process of indicator development should begin with the search for a deontological theory that relates to or provides answers to the core research question.

Once a suitable normative theory has been selected, in a second step, the original writings of the preferred theorist should be scrutinized for a full-fledged set of indicators or hints on how to develop them. This guarantees that the ethical principle used is applied according to the ideas of its originator and minimizes the risk of misinterpreting the adopted normative framework.

In a third step, the applicability of those hints or indicators to the considered empirical context should be tested. If a set of criteria for the concrete interpretation of the ethical principle is available, e.g., in the form of Habermas' ideal speech situation, the main challenge consists in its adaptation to the research question and the empirical phenomena it relates to. The indicators used should be systematically linked to the applied normative theory as shown in various Habermasian studies (see section 3.2). If no concretion of the ethical principle in a specific context is available, as is typical for Kant, empirical indicators have to be developed from scratch. As in Bowie's *Theory of Meaningful Work* (see section 2.2). they should be based on logical deductions from and/or semantical interpretations of the original normative content.

In a fourth step, the systematic relationship and logical connection between the indicators used and the applied ethical principle should be explained in a sufficiently detailed way. In their Habermasian assessment of SA 8000, Gilbert and Rasche (2007) provide a nice example how the linkage of a set of indicators with the original normative theory can succeed. The same can be said for Bowie's (1998) six criteria of meaningful work.

The fifth step consists in establishing the verifiability of the developed indicators. If they systematically escape empirical scrutiny, they are still too close to their normative origins and will not be able to fulfill their purpose of enabling a reliable normative assessment and/or comparison of similar empirical phenomena. An indicator is verifiable as soon as its binary or gradual (non-)fulfillment can be ascertained when it is applied to the qualitative or quantitative empirical data it is designed to assess. The theorist should make sure that the highest possible level of indicator fulfillment is possible and does not violate natural laws or clear economic and technological constraints.

In a sixth step, researchers should make sure that the verifiable indicators are not just achievable, but also sufficiently ambitious. Only when they are both attainable and sufficiently aspirational will they be able to guide the way toward the ethical ideal from which they have been derived.

[21] Applied to benchmark criteria this twofold requirement, capturing the Rawlsian notion of a "realistic utopia" (Rawls, 1999, p. 7), reflects the commitment to a certain type of moral realism. It presupposes that the normative claims implied by a universal ethical principle (i) can be and (ii) sometimes are true, and, most importantly, that this can be empirically verified (in an objective way).

[22] Coherentism can be summarized as "the view that beliefs can be justified only by their relation to other beliefs" (Jamieson, 1993, p. 41). The Rawlsian notion of a "reflective equilibrium" is one of the most familiar examples of the coherentist approach (Daniels, 2013). It takes a number of "considered beliefs" as a starting point and requires the formulation of general principles, such as Rawls' principles of justice, "to account for" the considered beliefs (Jamieson, 1993, p. 41). The beliefs and principles are justified as soon as their iterative, mutual revision leads to a state of equilibrium or coherence. In our discussion, the requirement of coherence does not apply to the relationship between moral judgments and the universal ethical principles, but to the indicators for normative assessment themselves.

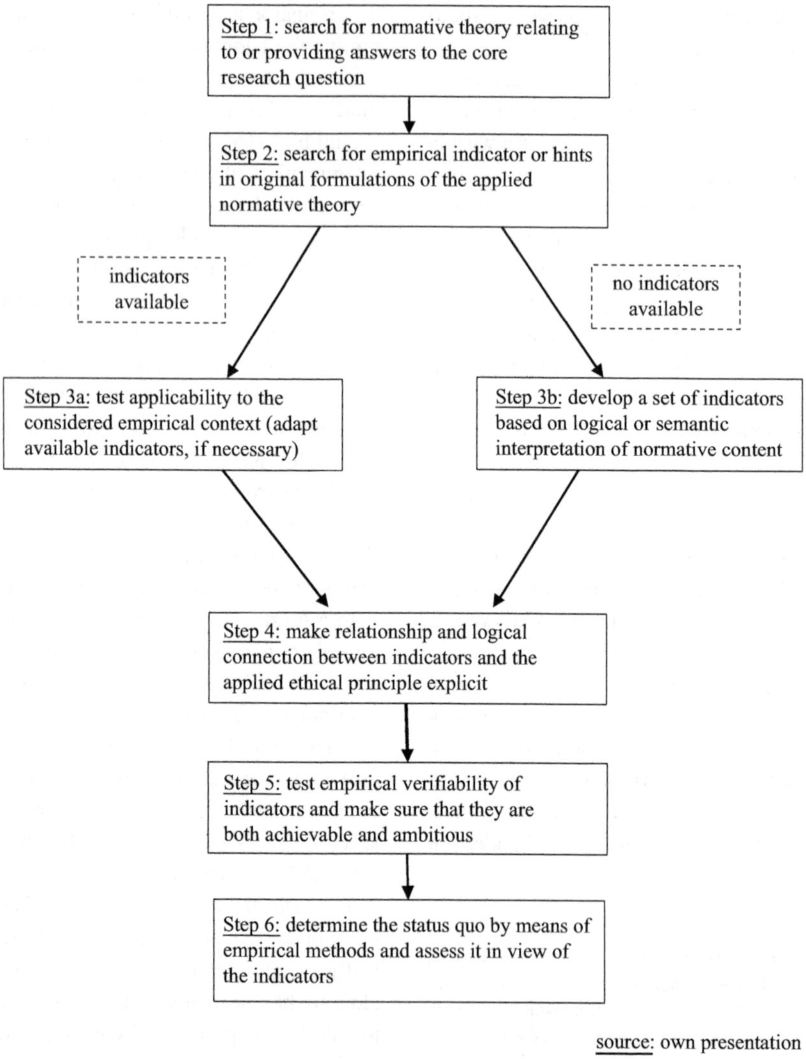
Step 1: search for normative theory relating to or providing answers to the core research question
Step 2: search for empirical indicator or hints in original formulations of the applied normative theory
indicators available
no indicators available
Step 3a: test applicability to the considered empirical context (adapt available indicators, if necessary)
Step 3b: develop a set of indicators based on logical or semantic interpretation of normative content
Step 4: make relationship and logical connection between indicators and the applied ethical principle explicit
Step 5: test empirical verifiability of indicators and make sure that they are both achievable and ambitious
Step 6: determine the status quo by means of empirical methods and assess it in view of the indicators
source: own presentation

*Figure 6.2* The process of applying the method of normative assessment.

The method can be seen as a response to three major criticisms of ideal theory. First of all, it facilitates the formulation of concrete benchmark criteria for the gradual reform of the status quo in light of ideal ethical principles like the *Discourse Principle* and the *Categorical Imperative*. In doing so, it attenuates the criticism that ideal theory with its abstract principles is unable to guide action. Secondly, a "method of normative assessment" ensures that ideal theory does not violate the basic (Kantian) standard of "ought implies can." It can be viewed as a litmus test for the feasibility of universal ethical principles. They will only be the "realistic utopia" they claim to be, if they logically imply physically feasible and verifiable benchmark criteria (such as Bowie's six principles of meaningful work). Thirdly, the benchmark criteria, to which the method leads, are crucial for an analysis of the realizability of the overarching normative principle in an economic system, a company, or a person's professional life. In virtue of the last two characteristics, the "method of normative assessment" helps to avoid overexerting moral requirements (Homann, 2006). It does so by showing the way to concrete indicators for the design of individual, organizational, and societal rules that foster the realization of the supreme moral principle. Furthermore, the concrete benchmark criteria are helpful for identifying the tradeoffs and complexity associated with the task of applying abstract universal principles to real life. Thus, the "method of normative assessment" contributes to maintaining the authority of morality. This authority would be jeopardized by unrealistic, conflicting and/or individually harmful normative demands.[23]

## Conclusion

The previous analysis formulated a "method of normative assessment" for applying abstract normative standards to the business context. It revealed the implicit adoption of this method in selected applications of the *Discourse Principle* and the *Categorical Imperative* to economic systems, business organizations, and individual economic actors. This chapter made the adopted methodology explicit and suggested refinements.

The method formulates quality attributes for the process of translating the overarching principle into a set of mediating benchmark criteria designed to bridge the ontological gap between "is" and "ought" without falling victim to it. For this purpose, benchmark criteria have to meet two quality attributes. On the one hand, they have to be logically consistent with the fundamental ethical principle. On the other hand, they have to be achievable without being automatically identical with the status quo.

Both methodological criteria are designed as scientific quality conditions for benchmark criteria that are derivative of a given universal ethical principle. Consequently, and in contrast to conventional ethical methods, they do not aim at the construction and justification of universal moral theories themselves.

Despite this difference in purpose, the described "method of normative assessment" combines elements of foundationalism and a weak form of coherentism (Jamieson, 1993). It is foundationalist in considering the applied normative principle as sufficiently well-justified and accepting it as given. The concrete benchmark criteria have to be derived from this foundational principle. At the same time the method is coherentist in requiring the logical coherence between the concrete benchmark criteria themselves.

[23] The described methodological approach hinges on a range of presuppositions. The notion that normative desiderata are translatable into measurable empirical indicators might not be compatible with all possible philosophical world views or accounts of the nature of moral claims. The impulse to develop clear-cut methodological criteria for the application of universal ethical principles to empirical reality is driven by a conception of science that associates scientific activity with a systematic approach and specific procedures for knowledge production. For alternative philosophical and/or methodological positions see, e.g., Smith (1993); Feyerabend (1975).

## References

Arnold, D. G., & Harris, J. D. (2012). *Kantian Business Ethics: Critical Perspectives*. Cheltenham: Edward Elgar.

Benz, A. (2004). Einleitung: Governance: Modebegriff oder Nützliches sozialwissenschaftliches Konzept? In A. Benz (Ed.) *Governance: Regieren in komplexen Regelsystemen: Eine Einführung* (11–28). Wiesbaden: Gabler.

Bohmann, James, & Rehg, William (2014). Jürgen Habermas. *The Stanford Encyclopedia of Philosophy, Fall 2014 Edition*, Edward N. Zalta (ed.), http://plato.stanford.edu/archies/fall2014/entries/habermas/.

Bowie, N. E. (1998). A Kantian Theory of Meaningful Work. *Journal of Business Ethics, 17*, 1083–1092.

(1999). *Business Ethics: A Kantian Perspective*. Malden, MA: Wiley.

Cohen, J. (1989). Deliberation and Democratic Legitimacy. In A. Hamlin, & P. Pettit (Eds.), *The Good Polity: Normative Analysis of the State* (pp. 18–34). Oxford/New York: Basil Blackwell.

(1997a). Deliberation and Democratic Legitimacy. In J. Bohmann, & W. Rehg (Eds.), *Deliberative Democracy: Essays on Reason and Politics* (pp. 67–92). Cambridge, MA: MIT Press.

(1997b). Procedure and Substance in Deliberative Democracy. In J. Bohmann, & W. Rehg (Eds.), *Deliberative Democracy: Essays on Reason and*

*Politics* (pp. 407–437). Cambridge, MA: MIT Press.

Dahl, R. A. (1989). *Democracy and its Critics*. New Haven, London: Yale University Press.

Daniels, N. (2013). Reflective Equilibrium. *The Stanford Encyclopedia of Philosophy, Winter 2013 Edition*, Edward N. Zalta (ed.), http://plato.stanford.edu/archives/win2013/entries/reflective-equilibrium/.

Dingwerth, K. (2007). *The New Transnationalism - Private Transnational Governance and Its Democratic Legitimacy*. Basingstoke: Palgrave Macmillan.

Dryzek, J. S. (1990). *Discursive Democracy: Politics, Policy, and Political Science*. New York: Cambridge University Press.

Eucken, Walter (1948). Das ordnungspolitische Problem. *ORDO*, *1*, 56–90.

(2004 [1952]). *Grundsätze der Wirtschaftspolitik*. Edited by Edith Eucken and K. Paul Hensel. UTB: Tübingen.

Feyerabend, P. K. (1975). *Against Method: Outline of an Anarchistic Theory of Knowledge*. London: New Left Books.

Gilbert, D. U., Rasche, A., & Waddock, S. (2011). Accountability in a Global Economy: The Emergence of International Accountability Standards. *Business Ethics Quarterly*, *21*(1), 23–44.

Gilbert, D. U., & Rasche, A. (2007). Discourse Ethics and Social Accountability: The Ethics of SA 8000. *Business Ethics Quarterly*, *17*(2), 187–216.

Gottschalk-Mazouz, N. (2004). *Perspektiven der Diskursethik*. Würzburg: Königshausen & Neumann.

Habermas, J. (1971 [1962]). *Strukturwandel der Öffentlichkeit: Untersuchungen zu einer Kategorie der bürgerlichen Gesellschaft* (5th ed.). Neuwied/Berlin: Luchterhand.

(1981). *Theorie des kommunikativen Handelns (Band 1: Handlungsrationalität und gesellschaftliche Rationalisierung; Band 2: Zur Kritik der funktionalistischen Vernunft)*. Frankfurt am Main: Suhrkamp.

(1984). *Vorstudien und Ergänzungen zur Theorie des kommunikativen Handelns*. Frankfurt am Main: Suhrkamp.

(1984 [1981]). *The Theory of Communicative Action (Vol. 1: Reason and the Rationalization of Society)* (T. McCarthy, Trans.). Boston: Beacon.

(1989 [1962]). *The Structural Transformation of the Public Sphere: An Inquiry into a Category of Bourgeois Society*. Cambridge: Polity.

(Ed.). (1990). *Discourse Ethics: Notes on a Program of Philosophical Justification - Moral Consciousness and Communicative Action* (C. Lenhart, S. Weber-Nicholson Trans.). Cambridge, MA: MIT Press.

(1990 [1983]). *Moral Consciousness and Communicative Action* (C. Lenhardt, S. Weber-Nicholson Trans.). Cambridge, MA: MIT Press.

(1992). *Faktizität und Geltung: Beiträge zur Diskurstheorie des Rechts und des demokratischen Rechtsstaats*. Frankfurt am Main: Suhrkamp.

(1993 [1991]). *Erläuterungen zur Diskursethik*. Frankfurt am Main: Suhrkamp Verlag.

(1996 [1992]). *Between Facts and Norms: Contributions to a Discourse Theory of Law and Democracy*. Cambridge, MA: MIT Press.

(2001). *The Postnational Constellation: Political Essays*. Cambridge, MA: Polity Press.

Homann, K. (2006). Competition and Morality. *Discussion Paper of the Wittenberg Center for Global Ethics*, (4), 1–20.

Hume, D. (1896 [1739]). *A Treatise of Human Nature*. Reprinted from the original edition in three volumes and edited, with an analytical index, by L. A. Shelby-Bigge. Oxford: Clarendon Press.

Jamieson, D. (1993). Method and Moral Theory. In P. Singer (Ed.), *A Companion to Ethics* (pp. 476–487) Wiley-Blackwell.

Jastram, S. (2012). *Legitimation privater Governance - Chancen und Probleme am Beispiel von ISO 26000*. Wiesbaden: Gabler Verlag.

Jastram, S., & Prescher, J. (2014). Legitimizing Corporate Social Responsibility Governance. In: C. Frederiksen, C. Strue, S. O. Idowu, A. Y. Mermod, & M. E. J. Nielsen (Eds.), *Corporate Social Responsibility and Governance: Practice and Theory* (pp. 39–61). Cham. Springer International Publishing.

Jastram, S., & Schneider, A.-M. (2015). Sustainable Fashion Governance at the Example of the Partnership for Sustainable Textiles. *Umweltwirtschaftsforum. 23(4)*, 205–212.

Jastram, S. (Forthcoming). Habermas' Theorie und die Legitimation von Multi-Stakeholder-Verfahren in der Praxis. In M. Scholz & M. Czuray (Eds.), *ISO 26000 und ONR 192500: Leitlinien und Normen zur Unternehmensverantwortung*. Berlin/Heidelberg: Springer Gabler.

Kant, I. (1998 [1781]). *Critique of Pure Reason*. In P. Guyer & A. W. Wood (Eds.) *The Cambridge Edition of the Works of Immanuel Kant*

(P. Guyer & A. W. Wood Trans.). Cambridge: Cambridge University Press.
(2002 [1785]). In Wood A. W. (Ed.), *Groundwork for the Metaphysics of Morals* [Grundlegung zur Metaphysik der Sitten] (A. W. Wood Trans.). New Haven and London: Yale University Press.
Kobrin, S. J. (2008). Globalization, Transnational Corporations, and the Future of Global Governance. In A. G. Scherer, & G. Palazzo (Eds.), *Handbook of Research on Global Corporate Citizenship* (pp. 249–272). Cheltenham: Edward Elgar.
Krentz, E. (1975). *The Historical-Critical Method.* Philadelphia: Fortress Press.
Matten, D., & Crane, A. (2005). What is Stakeholder Democracy? Perspectives and Issues. *Business Ethics: A European Review*, *14*(1), 6-13.
Mueckenberger, U., & Jastram, S. (2010). Transnational Norm-building Networks and the Legitimacy of Corporate Social Responsibility standards. *Journal of Business Ethics*, *97*, 223–239.
O'Neill, O. (1993). Kantian Ethics. In P. Singer (Ed.), *A Companion to Ethics* (pp. 175–185). Oxford: Wiley-Blackwell.
Rawls, J. (1971). *A Theory of Justice*. Cambridge, MA: Harvard University Press.
(1999). *The Law of Peoples*. Cambridge, MA: Harvard University Press.
Reynolds, S. J., & Bowie, N. E. (2004). A Kantian Perspective on the Characteristics of Ethics Programs. *Business Ethics Quarterly*, *14*(2), 275–292.
Sayre-McCord, G. (2015). Moral Realism. *The Stanford Encyclopedia of Philosophy, Spring 2015 Edition*, Edward N. Zalta (ed.), http://plato.stanford.edu/archives/spr2015/entries/moral-realism/
Scherer, A. G., Palazzo, G., & Baumann, D. (2006). Global Rules and Private Actors: Toward a New Role of the Transnational Corporation in Global Governance. *Business Ethics Quarterly*, *16*(4), 505–532.
Scherer, A. G., Palazzo, G., & Baumann-Pauly, D. (2013). Democratizing Corporate Governance: Compensating for the Democratic Deficit of Corporate Political Activity and Corporate Citizenship. *Business & Society*, *52*(3), 473–514.
Scherer, A. G., Palazzo, G., & Matten, D. (2009). Introduction to the Special Issue: Globalization as a Challenge for Business Responsibilities. *Business Ethics Quarterly*, *19*(3), 327–347.
(2014). The Business Firm as a Political Actor: A New Theory of the Firm for a Globalizaed World. *Business & Society*, *53*(2), 143–156.
Scherer, A. G., Rasche, A., Palazzo, G., & Spicer, A. (2016). Managing for Political Corporate Social Responsibility: New Challenges and Directions for PCSR 2.0. *Journal of Management Studies*, *53*(3), 273–298.
Scherer, A. G., & Palazzo, G. (2007). Toward a Political Conception of Corporate Responsibility: Business and Society Seen from a Habermasian Perspective. *Academy of Management Review*, *32*(4), 1096–1120.
Simmons, J. A. (2010). Ideal and Nonideal Theory. *Philosophy & Public Affairs*, *38*(1), 5-36.
Smith, M. (1993). Moral Realism. In P. Singer (Ed.), *A Companion to Ethics* (pp. 15–37). Oxford: Wiley-Blackwell.
Weber, M. (2004 [1919]). *The Vocation Lectures*. Translated by R. Livingstone. Edited by D. Owen & T. Strong. Illinois: Hackett Books.
Wörsdörfer, M. (2010). On the Economic Ethics of Walter Eucken. In Konrad Adenauer Foundation (Ed.), *Sixty Years of Social Market Economy: Formation, Development and Perspectives of a Peacemaking Formula* (pp. 21–42). Sankt Augustin: Konrad Adenauer Foundation.
Zürn, M. (2004). Global Governance and Legitimacy Problems. *Government and Opposition*, *39*(2), 260–287.

CHAPTER 7

# Descriptive Ethics

## *A Neglected Methodological Domain in Business and Applied Ethics*

WESLEY CRAGG

### Introduction

Applied ethics is now widely recognized as a sub-discipline in philosophy. As such, it has three distinguishing characteristics. It uses normative tools, techniques, and theories in an effort to address ethical concerns to which human activity gives rise. It is resolutely practical in as much as its goal is to shed light on the ethical resolution of those concerns. Finally, it is unavoidably interdisciplinary since addressing practical ethical concerns requires an understanding of all aspects of the contexts in which ethical concerns are generated.

Applied ethics is also typically normative not descriptive in character. For the most part, its goal is find the values that *ought* to guide the resolution of moral concerns, not the values that typically *do* guide it.

What seems to be missing from this picture is serious analysis of the normative logic of the actual positions people take in response to the ethical concerns to which their lives give rise. Such a venture would be both descriptive and normative. It would be descriptive because its focus would be the beliefs and the application of those beliefs to the resolution of specific concerns. It would be normative because its purpose would be to describe the values that people believed ought govern their responses in particular situations, why those values were viewed as appropriate in the circumstances and the implications of relying on them in response to the concerns in question.

This task of accurately identifying the positions people and organizations take on ethical issues and their reasons for taking those positions is in fact a traditional, though in recent years a largely neglected, domain of moral philosophy, including applied ethics as branch of moral philosophy and in business ethics as a branch of applied ethics as practiced by analytic or Anglo-American philosophers and business ethics academics.[1] Its goal is to identify in an empirically accurate fashion the values governing the positions being taken on ethical issues by decision makers, commentators and analysts confronted with practical ethical issues and then provide an accurate account of the normative logic that frames, explains and explicitly or implicitly justifies those positions for those whose position they are. I propose to label this domain of applied ethics "*descriptive ethics*" because its function is to provide a description or map that is both empirical and normative in nature. It might also be described as moral geography.[2]

[1] Moral philosophy or ethics, which are treated as synonyms in this chapter, has a number of branches or domains including meta ethics, moral theory and applied ethics. Applied ethics has in turn a number of branches or domains which focus on different topic areas of interest and importance, for example environmental or medical or professional or business ethics. These branches of applied ethics often intersect in important ways. The focus of this chapter, as will become evident as the discussion proceeds, is the general field of applied ethics but with a particular focus on business and environmental ethics as branches of applied ethics.

[2] The expression "descriptive ethics" as it is generally used fails to differentiate between what is essentially an empirical task, namely what Wikipedia describes as "empirical research into the attitudes of individuals or groups of people," and what I am describing here as the task of identifying empirically the values guiding decision making or human behaviour in specific settings and then describing their normative characteristics. One of the goals of this chapter is to expose and critique the fact that for the most part the distinction between empirical and descriptive ethics is ignored by post war ethics related research or analysis.

The reasons for resuscitating this domain of descriptive ethics are legion. Values play a pivotal role in human choices, decisions, and actions. They provide the rational for advice and recommendations, explain and justify actions and decisions, structure the creation and the implementation of public policy and justify the strategies and day to day operations of business. They range from the trivial – will it be chocolate or a vanilla ice cream – to the profound – is capital punishment a morally justifiable response to murder; from the aesthetic – the late string quartets of Beethoven represent his greatest musical achievement – to the personal – should I take this job offer or continue my education? Values underpin our assessments, evaluations, judgments, criticisms, and commitments. For example: Many of the people who support the extension of marriage rights to single sex couples do so because they believe restricting marriage to unions between a man and a woman to be discriminatory. Many of those who disagree believe that morality requires for a variety of reasons respect for the traditional heterosexual character of marriage. The push for sustainable development is anchored on a framework of morally grounded values that many believe ought to govern all economic development. Resource extraction companies propose projects because among other things they believe they will provide a good return on investments which they have a moral obligation to secure for investors. People become involved in environmental disputes because they believe something of value is at stake, old growth forests, an endangered species, jobs for loggers, access to a rich mineral deposit, peace and quiet, and so on. What that something is may well vary from individual to individual or from group to group. However, if they are asked to explain or justify their interventions or their protests or their political positions, they will do so by appealing to the values and relevant facts that motivate their involvement.

The influence of values goes beyond what we do. Values impact also what we see and what we know.[3] It is true that the work that values do is less obvious where perception, learning, and knowledge are concerned. Nevertheless, values have an impact on these aspects of human lives as well. What we see, for example, is not a function simply of what is there to be seen. A trained forester will see varieties of trees and other kinds of vegetation that will not be noticed by someone brought up in an urban environment. People can train themselves to identify bird calls that the untrained ear will not differentiate. This is equally true of business managers, staff, and employees. A key purpose of management education is to sensitize students to dimensions of business that would otherwise likely remain invisible to them.

What lies behind these acquired skills and capacities in each case are values. Foresters learn to differentiate and name different kinds of trees and vegetation because learning to do so is an important part of being a forester. This knowledge and the attendant skills are acquired because of their value or importance for foresters. Bird watchers value the ability to differentiate bird calls. Managers value the ability to identify elements in their business environment that allow them to make sound business decisions. It is for this reason they acquire the perceptual skills they acquire.

Even scientific research whose goal is acquiring knowledge and which is often thought to be value free is influenced by values. The topics scientists and social scientists research are chosen because they are seen by the researchers in question to be important or worth researching, though the reasons for seeing a research topic as important or of value may well vary from researcher to researcher. Research projects that are topical or seen as related to national priorities or important needs or goals are more likely to be funded. What we know or learn, after all, is a function of what we decide it is important to know or learn. If an area likely to be impacted by industrial waste disposal plans is regarded as waste land and therefore of no value,

[3] I argue for this view in Teaching business ethics: the role of ethics in business and business education, *Journal of Business Ethics*, 16, 3, Feb 1997. For a more recent discussion, see Kim, T. W. & T. Donaldson. J Bus Ethics (2016). The discussion that follows also intersects with an extensive discussion about the roles of values in social science and business management research including: Wicks, A. C. (1996); Wicks, A. C., & R Freeman (1998); Werhane, P. H. (1994); Scanlon, T. M. (2014).

the impact of the waste on that area is less likely to be studied. Resulting impacts are therefore likely to remain unknown until they begin to engage values to which importance is attached, human health, for example.[4]

In summary, then, values permeate everything that human beings do. Behind all human activity lie judgments that something is worth doing or not worth doing, justifiable or unjustifiable, ethical or unethical, useful or useless, desirable, undesirable or indifferent, of value, no value or negative value. Understanding the values driving what people do and the positions they take is central to understanding what people are doing, why they are doing it and therefore their justification for doing what they are doing. We cannot understand human behavior if we ignore the values that are people's reasons for doing what they are doing.

Ignoring this descriptive domain of applied ethics also ignores the fact that for the most part the resolution of normative and ethical issues, is carried out by practitioners, the people who face issues that can only be resolved by coming to conclusions about what is worthwhile, obligatory, ethically appropriate or acceptable, and so on. Yet, in spite of this fact, ethicists have paid little attention to mapping the systems of values that lead people including business managers to the conclusions on which their actions are based. So have other analysts in crucial ways. Two important recent examples revolve around the election of Donald Trump as President of the United States and the "Brexit vote" in the United Kingdom. One insightful pattern of analysis argues that a key reason for these failures to predict important political outcomes or address them in the run up to the US election or the United Kingdom referendum was a failure to understand the values/concerns of a significant proportion of the American and British electorates that led them to vote as they did. And this, I am suggesting, was a failure of descriptive ethics.

Ignoring the normative positions people and organizations take, for example on public policy issues, is also important because, as we shall see, it ignores the role that values play in shaping conflicts and the role that descriptive ethics could play in resolving values based conflicts.

Finally, ignoring the domain of descriptive ethics or the value of mapping the values people and organizations bring to public debate and that ground disagreements and conflicts also ignores the need to construct bridges between social science based research focused on the values that guide people's choices, decisions, and actions and its normative counterpart. The gap between what for the purposes of this discussion I propose to call empirical ethics and the domain of normative research is significant. It is true that persuasive arguments have been offered in support of the view that there is no gap at all.[5] However, these arguments and appeals by business ethicists have done little to impact the shape or values that dominate the field of business research in the United States, for example.[6] As a result, empirical studies of for example the cultural and causal origins of values frequently have the effect of dismissing or negating normative justifications of those same values. Normative accounts in contrast, dismiss empirical studies as descriptions of what people **believe** to be right, or morally required, or of value, when what we really want and need to know, it is frequently asserted, is the validity or justifiability of what is believed or thought to be right, or good or morally justifiable or required. The result is that domains of empirical and normative research continue to be examined in relative isolation from each other.

## Descriptive Ethics: Methodological Issues

How then is the moral logic or justificatory structure of positions people or organizations take on moral issues discerned? This should not be a difficult question to answer in as much as both as an academic and as a practical matter, discerning the position that people are taking on moral issues is or should be a fundamental feature of both

[4] This thesis is argued most recently in Kim et al., 2016.

[5] See for example the research cited in note (iii) above.

[6] Evidence for this observation is set out in some detail by Kim et al., 2016.

understanding those positions and evaluating them. Further, as a practical matter, the importance of understanding the reasons for the positions people take on moral or ethical issues is embedded in the moral wisdom of ethical traditions. A typical example is the North American Aboriginal aphorism: never judge a person until you have walked a mile in his or her moccasins. To understand where someone is coming from on values-based issues, you have to put yourself in that person's shoes, to cite an alternative description, or see things through his or her eyes.

For academics, the importance of assuring that one has an accurate understanding of the positions being taken on moral issues is reflected in the history of moral philosophy of which Socrates is an exemplar. Socrates confronted influential Athenians in the agora and pushed them to justify the positions they were taking on issues of moral importance. He then engaged in conversation and dialog designed to analyse those positions and the justifications offered for their flaws.

As a matter of scholarly practice, the analysis of the positions on ethical issues by others virtually always begins by laying out their positions and their justification for those positions before subjecting their positions to critical analysis. It could be argued, that stakeholder analysis is a contemporary counterpart to the Socratic model, although it has not led applied ethicists to give priority to the kind of descriptive accounts or the moral geography of positions being taken on ethical issues to which I am pointing.

How then to proceed? The purpose of what follows is to provide an initial and partial answer to that question. The account is initial and partial just because the domain of descriptive ethics is largely unexplored in the contemporary literature. In making this claim, it is important to be clear that what is not at issue is the thesis that values and reasons are the building blocks of decision making and human action. This is a metaethical thesis that has been the subject of extensive study.[7] The challenge rather is to identify what descriptive ethics or values mapping actually requires. What are the methodological issues that mapping values or descriptive ethics require be addressed.

How best to meet this challenge? The answer offered in what follows is an attempt to answer just this question. Its focus is environmental issues, specifically those generated by resource extraction, which tend not to get the attention of business ethicists that they deserve. Many of the most profound challenges that business faces today are environmental challenges. This is because both the extraction and use of natural resources are key to economic development in almost any form. It is also true because a core existential challenge faced by humanity today is the environmental crisis of climate change. Equally important, the environment and environmental protection are subjects of intense public debates that have pushed those involved to stake out and defend contrasting positions and track their varying implications for public policy.

In what follows I outline the findings of a research project focused on resource extraction, a subject area of importance in Canada whose economy is to a considerable extent grounded on the extraction and export of natural resources. Because of its importance for the Canadian economy, its controversial character, and the fact that virtually all proposals for new activity require extensive and detailed environmental assessments, resource extraction has generated a rich data base of studies, and position justifications by government, business, and civil society organizations with an interest in resource extraction-based economic development proposals.

What was required for this research was a small number of cases where interest groups were staking out distinct and contrasting positions on development projects that were generating debate and disagreement. Also required were examples of projects that had not become highly politicized. Our concern was to avoid conflicting positions that were so deeply entrenched that the primary interest of those articulating conflicting positions was their rhetorical impact and not a defense of the foundational values on which positions were based. Wanted also were cases that had been through some kind of public environmental assessment that had resulted in a substantial paper trail that

[7] See for example Thomas Scanlon's (2014) *Being realistic about reasons.*

could then be examined in detail. A final characteristic was cases with a cross cultural component. One research objective was to examine the extent to which cross cultural factors influenced the complexity and character of resulting debates, disagreements, and conflicts.

## *Mapping Values: Four Environmental Ethics Case Studies*

Four cases were identified that fit these requirements. Each of the cases had Aboriginal, i.e., First Nation, stakeholders.

The first of our cases was a timber management plan governing the use of the timber resources in a broad area south and east of the town of Sudbury, located in mid-northern Ontario. Access to timber in this area was important to several forest product companies operating in that area of the province. The land in question was also used extensively for recreation purposes: camping, canoeing, hiking, cottages, fishing, and hunting. All of these uses involved private and public, commercial and noncommercial interests. The plan was the subject of a public government review of the existing timber management plan. The land covered by the plan embraces the traditional territory of a First Nation.

The second case took as its focus the use of the timber resources in Algonquin Park, Canada's oldest and best known provincial park. The area has a rich natural, recreational, and commercial history. It is a wildlife preserve, has an interesting and varied geology and geography, and is a popular destination for campers, cottagers, canoeists, hikers, bird watchers, wild life enthusiasts, and scientists. It is also an important source of soft and hardwood lumber and has been the scene of intensive logging for more than one hundred years. Finally, the area is the subject of a land claim by a First Nation, the Golden Lake Band. Hence, as with the Trout Lake area, private and public commercial and noncommercial interests are involved. The timber management plan which governs logging in the park has over recent years attracted increasingly vigorous challenges. The most prominent among the challengers is the Wildlands League, an environmental group that wishes to see logging in the park prohibited. Control over park management has also been challenged by the First Nation who are laying claim to a large area that includes Algonquin Park to which, they argue, they have never relinquished title. A decision by the provincial government to allow First Nation members to resume limited hunting within the park boundaries is also matter of controversy among the non-Native stakeholders.

Our third case was a proposed open pit copper mine development planned for northern British Columbia by Placer Dome, Inc. that was at the time of the study a major multinational Canadian gold mining company.[8] The issues this case raises are characteristic of mining developments: the potential for ground water pollution from tailings sites; the opening of wilderness areas to nonnatives for recreational uses including hunting and fishing through road construction; wildlife habitat destruction; and so on. Prior to developing its proposal, Placer Dome identified possible stakeholders including two First Nation Bands and invited their participation in the planning process. The resulting plan has subsequently won consensus approval following extensive environmental review by the stakeholders involved and by the provincial government authorities in so far as their involvement was required for planning purposes. To date, no development has occurred since detailed cost studies have failed to establish that the project is economically viable.

Our last case involved a proposal to redevelop four dams that harness water draining into James Bay via the Moose River Basin. This was the most complex of our studies because of the wide area affected, the number of stakeholders, and the importance of the interests at stake. At the time of the study, the proposed hydroelectric developments were a part of a Twenty-five Year Supply Demand Plan developed by Ontario Hydro and subsequently submitted for review under Ontario's Environmental Assessment Act. Over $50 million were disbursed to interested parties to finance their evaluation of the plan in preparation for environmental assessment hearings.

[8] Placer Dome, Inc. was purchased by Barrick Gold Corporation in 2006.

The plan itself was subsequently withdrawn by Ontario Hydro in light of dramatic reductions in the demand for power resulting from the economic recession of the late nineteen eighties and early nineties. The focus of our study was the redevelopment of four dams on the Mattagami River, a major river in northeastern Ontario draining into James Bay. Project stakeholders included a First Nation coalition, the Ontario public, several government ministries, a forest products company, several municipalities, hunters, trappers, tourist operators, and several environmental groups, to name just a few.

### *Developing a Research Plan*

We decided to approach our study in three phases. The first phase consisted of site visits and document analysis. The purpose of the site visits was to meet stakeholders and familiarize ourselves with the cases in a concrete way. Document analysis was undertaken by graduate research assistants at York University drawn from the business school, environmental studies, and philosophy. A complex coding scheme was constructed whose purpose was to allow us to build a values inventory and explore the logic of the values in that inventory. Our final task in phase one was to build vignettes that captured what our document analysis and site visits suggested were the salient ethical features of each case. We proposed to use these vignettes in the second and third phases of the project.

The second phase, never successfully completed, called for a survey of stakeholders in each of the four cases under study. One of our goals was to test the reliability of questionnaire survey methodology for building values maps of stakeholders in and around environmental issues. Unfortunately the team was unable to construct an adequate survey instrument in the time available with the funds available. The second phase of the project was subsequently abandoned.

Phase three of the research project involved interviews with case stakeholders. Five people from each group having a direct stake in a case under study were interviewed. Over eighty interviews were completed. People interviewed were asked first to respond to questions about the case in which they had a direct stake. They were then asked to answer questions about the other three cases under study. Transcripts of the interviews were prepared. Analysis of the interviews was undertaken by a research team consisting of four PhD level graduate students working both from recordings of the interviews and interview transcripts.

## Phase One: Site Visits and Document Analysis

### *Goals and Objectives*

The specific goal in phase one of the study was to build values profiles of the stakeholder groups that had taken public positions in discussions and debates generated in and around the four cases we had chosen to study. Our purpose in building the profiles was to determine as clearly as possible the nature of the positions being taken, the key values on which the positions were based, and the justificatory logic supporting those positions.

In this important respect, the task we were setting for ourselves had a focus quite different from the focus of a typical empirical or social scientific study. A significant question, therefore, was the extent to which data gathering methodology typical of social science research, for example the use of coding protocols for purposes of document analysis as well as questionnaires, interviews, and interview analysis techniques, could assist in answering the questions that were at the center of our research.

The reason for thinking that data gathering and data analysis tools developed by social scientists might be of value was the fact that the proposed analysis did have a descriptive purpose. Our goal was to set out the justifications or what might be described as the normative logic of the actual positions of the groups involved. What we needed, therefore, was a methodology for **describing** the values stakeholder groups wanted taken into account in decisions about resource use. That is to say, the research objective of this phase of the study was to describe, not evaluate the merits of the values being put into play by the various actors.

The analysis was not designed to evaluate whether the values that people wanted in play were sound, or justifiable or the values that ought to structure the decisions of eventual decision makers. Rather, the goal was to **describe** the values that the various stakeholder groups wanted in play and their interrelationships and identify as accurately as possible the justificatory structure of the resulting positions being taken.

The research plan required as a first step that we analyse the documents that had been generated by public environmental assessment hearings on the part of various stakeholder groups with three goals in mind. Our first goal was to identify the values the documents indicated the groups involved wanted to be taken into account in resolving the issues being generated in each of the cases. Our second task was to build an inventory of stakeholder values by stakeholder group. Our third task was to build a values profile of each stakeholder group participating the environmental assessment process.

## *Lessons*

Much of what we learned from the document analysis phase of the project emerged from the process of constructing a coding scheme to guide the document analysis process. We wanted to create values inventories. We also wanted to describe and characterize the values in the inventories in ways that would allow us to build profiles that would provide insight into the disagreements that resource use projects and proposals were generating.

### Identifying Values

For the purpose of identification, we agreed that worth, desirability, or usefulness were the indicators of value. No *a priori* limits were placed on what could count as a value. No *a priori* limit was placed on the categories or types of thing that could said to be values, or carry value or be valued. States of affairs, states of mind, states of being, things, virtues, principles, rules, goals, purposes, objectives, actions, activities were identified as examples of what could be valued or be thought to carry or have value. Our inventory had room in it, as a consequence, for such things as beaver, logging, recreation, a good standard of living, the land, a way of life, winning, succeeding, surviving, and so on. This approach, we concluded, was both philosophically defensible but also consistent with the prevailing vocabulary and rhetoric of practical environmental debate and its accompanying literature which now routinely refer to such things as objects and systems not simply as having value but as values.[9]

Our second task was to characterize or categorize the values entering into environmental dialogs, debates, disputes, and conflicts. Here a number of significant lessons emerged as we analyzed the public submissions that the four cases under study had generated.

### Characterizing Values: Building an Appropriate Values Typology

The idea of characterizing values by type is not a novel one. Most studies of values sort values either implicitly or explicitly into categories for both descriptive and explanatory purposes.[10] Furthermore, virtually all discussions of values develop from an explicit or an implied typology. This, we discovered, is certainly true of discussions of environmental values. Our own study was no exception.

Two types of values were obviously central to our study. The first was environmental values. Clearly, one of our tasks in the study was to identify what and how nature and the natural environment were valued by those concerned about resource use and development. Second, our study was premised on the assumption that economic values also had an integral role in environmental disputes including those which were integral to the four cases we were studying. We were as a consequence working with a two component typology. Further, not only was this typology evident in the

9 Such inventories, we discovered, were and are quite common where natural resources and the environment is under discussion by resource managers, environmentalists and so on.

10 Two examples are in Rokeach (1973), *The Nature of human values*, p. 24 ff. and Kilby (1993), *The study of human values*, chapter 1.

assumptions on which our own study was built, it was also central to wider discussions about the structure of environmental conflict. It seems to be widely assumed, that is to say, that environmental conflicts are in large part generated by clashes between economic and environmental values. This view typically provides the framework for commentary in the popular press. It is also widely assumed to be true in scholarly discussion.

One of the early findings that emerged from document analysis of the four cases we were studying was that the frequent categorization of values in environmental disputes as either environmental or economic was a seriously misleading over simplification. What our analysis revealed was an additional thirteen types of values that stakeholders wanted taken into account in the four cases under study: aesthetic, educational, ecological, economic, environmental, health, legal, moral, personal preference, political, recreational, religious/ spiritual, scientific, social, and subsistence values.[11] Marking this fact turned out to be crucial to setting out the logic of the positions of the stakeholder groups involved. This is because identifying the type of value being put into play by a stakeholder or stakeholder group revealed in important ways the reasons that supported the view that the value was important and should be taken into account. It therefore turned out to be crucial step in understanding the nature of the positions being taken on the environmental and commercial issues in play.

One or two examples will illustrate this point. In the Trout Lake case, some of the most important values that Trout Lake cottagers wanted respected related directly to their own personal and family history. The lake itself, surrounding forest lands, picnic and camp sites, portages and trails were valued because of their association with lake traditions and past activities and events of great significance for those involved.[12] Discussion that focused exclusively on economic or environmental values might well miss, ignore, or distort in important ways values that the cottagers wanted taken into account. Misunderstanding the values in play was a significant source of resulting conflicts, our study revealed.

In the case of the debate over the Mattagami extension, of key importance to aboriginal stakeholders was the subsistence value attached to wildlife, fish, and vegetation in the area likely to be affected by the proposed redevelopment. That is to say, the natural environment was seen by the aboriginal inhabitants of that region as of value in part because of their traditional dependence on the land for food. An exclusive focus on economic or environmental values would inevitably marginalize a set of values that were central to the thinking of a key stakeholder group, as our analysis confirmed. In the case of Algonquin Park, concern with logging was motivated in part by aesthetic values associated with a forest wilderness. Logging interfered with this because of its impact on a sense of being in a wilderness and because of its physical impact on the forests themselves. Aesthetic values were in turn connected to recreational values since one reason for visiting the park was the sense of renewal which many indicated resulted from the call of a loon or sun rising through mist, or an encounter with an old growth forest in a wilderness setting. To try to understand the debate over logging in the park without factoring in aesthetic values understood as such would therefore be to miss an important factor motivating the involvement and guiding the recommendations of a number of stakeholders.

Creating the appropriate typology of value types therefore quickly emerged as an important task. We wanted a comprehensive values typology comprising conceptually distinct categories. This did not mean that something might not be valued for different reasons. For example, many Algonquin Park Ministry of Natural Resources staff valued the park both because it was a source of employment thus identifying the park as having economic value, and because they enjoyed the recreational opportunities it created for themselves, their families, and park visitors, thus identifying the park as having recreational value.

[11] A list with definitions is appended to this chapter.

[12] For a detailed study of values associated with place see "Your Place or Mine?: The Effect of Place Creation on Environmental Values and Landscape Meanings" Brandenburg et al., 1995).

A key methodological requirement for our study was ensuring that the values categories we created were conceptually distinct. That is to say, a lake, for example, might well have recreational value as a destination for fishing and economic value for tourism. However, whether it had both recreational and economic value were distinct, empirically grounded questions. The answer to the one should in no way imply logically the answer to the other.

Finally, the typology also had to link empirically to the practical concerns and the reasoning patterns that characterized the value positions represented in our case studies and emerge from empirical study of those concerns. Otherwise its practical value for understanding the logic of the positions being taken by stakeholder groups would be questionable.

### Characterizing Values by Function

A second way of characterizing values and things valued is by reference to their function as means or as ends. Evaluating things as means is something everyone understands. It is an essential element in everyday life. This kind of evaluation occurs every time someone goes shopping, considers how to get from one place to another, or undertakes virtually any task. Determining the best way to get where we want to go is a process of evaluating the value of various options as a means of arriving at our chosen goal or objective.

This kind of evaluation has been traditionally called instrumental evaluation. The value that attaches to things as means has traditionally been called their instrumental or use value. Tools are a good example because their value lies in their usefulness or utility. A knife is for cutting. A good knife is a knife that cuts well. The reasoning involved in instrumental valuations is called instrumental reasoning. Instrumental rationality is the name given to reasoning processes designed to identify the best way to accomplish a desired end. Its focus is typically efficiency and effectiveness.

Instrumental rationality is highly prized in western cultures. It is the form of rationality that is embedded in technology whose purpose is to provide new and more effective ways of doing what people want to do or achieving goals people want to achieve. For this reason it is closely associated with economic analysis or any activity that is associated with the efficient use or acquisition of wealth. Indeed, the association is so close that for many people, including many economists, the concepts of instrumental rationality and economic rationality are synonymous. It is also a form of rationality that can be assessed objectively. Whether something is useful, or efficient or effective is always a matter of fact that ought to be decidable empirically at least in principle.[13] A moment's thought indicates, however, that not all values are instrumental values. Things acquire instrumental value because of their value for pursuing ends that carry their own distinct value. For logging companies, forests have value for the logs that can be harvested from them. A forest that is not a potential source of logs will therefore have no instrumental value as a source of logs. Logs in turn are valuable for making lumber. If lumber lost its value, so would logging. Lumber in turn is useful for constructing houses, making furniture, and so on. Thus, instrumental values always point to some end from which they derive their value. They are in this sense pointer values whose value depends on the value of that to which they point.

Underlying instrumental evaluation is the assumption that some things are worth doing not for the sake of something else but for their own sake. It is things that are worth doing for their own sake that give instrumental reasoning its point and anchor any process of instrumental reasoning. For the purpose of our analysis we decided to characterize these values as core values.

For a variety of reasons, our research in its early stages focused on mapping the core values that people were bringing to the environmental disputes under discussion. That is to say, we began the task of mapping values with the assumption that the values we would encounter in our analysis of stakeholder positions would be either instrumental values or core values. Instrumental values, we

[13] In practice, complexity or lack of research or imperfect scientific knowledge may block an actual determination. These are practical obstacles, however. They are by their nature the kind of problems that can in principle be resolved.

assumed were significant for our study only for their value as pointers, pointing to core values which gave them their instrumental value. Methodologically, this seemed a reasonable assumption. At the level of value theory, the distinction between instrumental and core values is uncontroversial and accepted as fundamental. Nomenclature varies, it is true. What we decided to label core values are called "terminal values" by some,[14] fundamental values, existence values,[15] and intrinsic values[16] by yet others. However, much of this terminology is closely related to theoretical assumptions. We wanted to avoid those theoretical linkages and so decided to talk of core values.

In everyday life, people, e.g., students, are often urged to work out what they *really* want, or what they are really after in life, or to choose what they really want to do. In the business world, it is now widely assumed that to compete successfully requires that a corporation decide what their core values, or goals or objectives are. These are then frequently articulated in the form of a mission statement or a statement of core values. Confusion, lack of direction, lack of motivation is often linked to a lack of clarity about core values. We expected, therefore, that the positions people were taking in our cases on environmental issues would be organized around the core values they wanted respected in resolving the issues in which they were involved. We assumed further that value based conflicts and disagreements about the use of natural resources would derive from differences in core values.

[14] Rokeach 1973, p. 11, for example.

[15] A term favoured by economists and used to describe those things that people say they want protected or conserved for non-utilitarian reasons. They are valued, that is to say, just because they exist.

[16] Philosophical commentary typically distinguishes between instrumental and intrinsic values. We decided not to use that terminology. The concept of intrinsic values is closely tied to normative philosophy, sometimes called axiology and connotes things which have what might be described as absolute worth or merit. We were unable to determine that the values we identified as core values had that status for the stakeholder groups whose values we were mapping or the individuals making up those groups. Hence we avoided that terminology.

Responding to these considerations, we defined core values as any value around which a position was structured. Things, goals, principles and so on were properly described as having core value if they were high priority values whose value was not linked to their utility for achieving something further of value. This is not to say that things that were properly identified as having core value would always be devoid of utility value. To the contrary, things seen as having core value were often also recognized as having instrumental value as well. For example, many of those who wanted environmental conservation and protection to be given over-riding priority in any decisions about logging, did so because for them Algonquin Park was a wilderness worth protecting for its own sake.[17] Most of these people also recognized the Park's value as a source of logs for the surrounding lumber mills. However, these two reasons for seeing the Park as having value were logically distinct.

As it turned out, we were able to identify core values around which the positions that groups were taking in the four cases under study appeared to be organized. Core values were set out as fundamental goals and objectives in some cases. In other cases, they were reflected in the reasons offered by the stakeholder groups for getting involved. It was clear from position statements, moreover, that the public participation in the environmental assessment process was motivated by a desire to ensure that the core, fundamental, or over-riding values they wanted respected in the decision making process were noticed and respected. For the most part, it was also possible to determine how stakeholder groups were prioritizing the core values being advanced.

Algonquin Park documents illustrate these observations. For example, three core values were clearly central to the master plan developed by the Algonquin Forest Authority for logging in Algonquin Park. The first was the **long term economic health of the communities surrounding the Park**. The second was **wilderness experience**.

[17] For these people, Algonquin Park had what some would describe as existence value, something worth protecting not for its use value but just to ensure that it goes on existing.

And the third was preserving **the environmental quality of the park**. Sustainable forestry was identified as of value because of its perceived importance to achieving the long term economic health of the communities around the Park that relied on logging for jobs and local investment. Wilderness experience was projected as being of value both because of the value attached to it by park users and also for its value for attracting tourists and thus contributing to the economic welfare of the surrounding communities. Protecting the environmental quality of the Park emerged from document analysis as a core value. Authority documents emphasized the importance of protecting the environmental quality of the Park for its own sake. It was this that justified the identification of environmental quality as a core value. Forest Authority documents also made it clear, however, that protecting environmental quality was important for its instrumental value both by way of ensuring a long term supply of saw logs and for its value for attracting tourists.

In contrast, the core values of the Wildlands League[18] were identified as: wilderness, wilderness experience, and the enhancement of human well-being. Document analysis revealed just one core value for the Golden Lake Band: respect for the creator. The documents available to us indicated, that is to say, that the position of the Golden Lake Band on the appropriate use of the Park's natural resources revolved around their understanding of what "respect for the creator" required.

## *Findings*

Our focus on differentiating core and instrumental values led to two conclusions followed by a number of other significant findings about the nature and function of the values stakeholders were putting in play in the cases under study. Our first conclusion: Differentiating between core and instrumental values was both possible and revealing. It provided important insights into the nature of the values around which positions of those involved in public debate were structured.

A second and significantly more surprising finding also emerged from our analysis, however. What we discovered was that an assumption implicit in our own analysis and also in the literature, namely that values functions either as core values or as instrumental values, was excessively simplistic. The problem lay not with the concept of core values. Rather it lay with the assumption that all noncore values or what in the literature are often described as use values were instrumental values.

The problem here lay not with the concept of instrumental evaluation itself. We had no difficulty identifying instrumental values. Where resource extraction is involved, natural resources, for example forests, or rivers, are bound to be evaluated from an instrumental perspective. Mineral deposits are mined and forests logged because of their instrumental value for a great variety of purposes. Iron ore is useful for the manufacture of steel, gold for its investment value, logs for their value as lumber and so on. Modern western societies value natural resources in part and in large measure because of their utility and therefore their instrumental value.

The assumption that all noncore or use values are instrumental values is very significant for understanding the nature of at least some environmental conflicts. There are a number of reasons for this. Things identified as means to ends by virtue of their instrumental value, tools for example, are typically seen or treated as replaceable. When an instrument, or tool wears out, a replacement can normally be found, constructed, or purchased, etc. Normally, the comparative instrumental value of things is also relatively easily calculated. Thus, if someone has a job to do, various ways of doing that job can be compared and their relative value determined. For related reasons, the instrumental value of things also can be and frequently is calculated or measured in monetary terms, particularly where the use of natural resources is in question. Thus, the decision to develop or extract a resource will be made in the light of the monetary value of

[18] It is important to add a caveat here. The positions we were analyzing were those set out in the documents available to us. The values mapped were therefore the values contained in those documents. What we learned therefore applies only to those documents and the positions being taken by the stakeholders groups in question at that time as reflected in those documents.

the resource in question, the cost of machinery to extract it, the wages to be paid, the risks likely to be encountered and so on. Finally the process of determining the instrumental and therefore the monetary value of things typically requires experience and expertise. Engineers are experts of this sort. So are managers, professionals, trades people, and so on.

What gradually became clear as we engaged in document analysis, however, was that instrumental values were just one of three kinds of noncore values, that is to say, values that derived their value from a "use" or "means" relationship to a core value. Symbols were a second kind of "use" or "derivative value" value that we discovered playing an important role in the cases we were studying. The concept of a symbol is not esoteric or obscure. However, symbols are not typically identified as use values or means to an end in the sense in which we are now speaking. Yet that is certainly what they are. Symbols have value for those for whom they are symbols. Their value lies in their usefulness in symbolizing things that are themselves important and have significant meaning for those for whom they are symbols. Furthermore, their value is derivative. They have value because what they symbolize has value. If what they symbolize loses its value, the symbol in turn ceases to be of value.

In our western, industrialized culture, symbols are rarely seen as playing a role in debates generated in and around environmental issues impacting business decisions. That is not to say that symbols are relatively rare in our culture. To the contrary, they are quite common. They are, however, typically associated in people's minds with social or cultural artifacts, such things as flags, or wedding rings or objects associated with religious observance. To our surprise, however, our analysis of documents and later our interviews uncovered symbolic values playing significant roles in all of our four cases.

Accurately mapping values, we discovered required, therefore, the identification of things whose value derived from their function as symbols. This is because symbols or things having symbolic value have characteristics which are quite different from instruments or things whose value derives from their usefulness or utility as instruments. Typically they are not replaceable in the way in which tools or instruments are replaceable. Their value cannot be measured or calculated in monetary terms in a manner characteristic of things whose value is instrumental in nature. Finally their use and application is not typically the preserve of experts.

What we discovered was that while symbolic values were clearly evident in the statements of stakeholder groups in the cases we were studying, including companies with development objectives, identifying symbolic values was considerably more difficult in most cases than identifying instrumental values. That is to say symbols can be and frequently are hidden from view in ways not characteristic of instrumental values. This seems particularly true of values associated with the natural environment, and even more true where resource use issues are under discussion by people immersed in a western culture. In contrast, documents emanating from native groups were replete with symbols relatively easily identified as such. Animals, trees, places, events were described frequently in symbolic terms. However, frequently, their symbolic significance was missed or simply ignored by business and government stakeholders.

Ignoring the symbolic values of things revealed itself as a potent source of misunderstanding and conflict. Treating things of symbolic value as though their value was purely instrumental was also a significant factor in exacerbating disagreements. For these reasons, we came to realize that differentiating symbolic from instrumental use values was important for understanding values based conflict.

A third kind of "use" or derivative value that we discovered as we analyzed the documents we were studying was what, for lack of a better name, we decided to call "prerequisite use values." That is to say, what emerged from our study was the fact that in some cases, the value attached to things derived from their noncausal, internal, or logical relationship to the core value to which they were connected. The clearest example of a value of this sort emerged from the Algonquin Park case where several of the stakeholders identified wilderness experience as a core value. Wilderness experience requires wilderness. In this case, wilderness derives its value from the value placed on wilderness experience. However, wilderness in this instance is not a tool or instrument, replaceable by say "virtual" wilderness. Neither is its role that of a symbol. Rather wilderness experience presupposes access to wilderness. You cannot have one without the other. The one is a necessary condition of the other. Yet they are distinct and have related but distinct value.

Clearly, this kind of value too has the characteristics of a "use" value. If wilderness experience lost its value, so too would wilderness at least as a prerequisite of wilderness experience. In this context, therefore, its value is derivative. On the other hand, values of this sort differ from instrumental values. That is to say they have a noncontingent relationship to that from which their value is derived, something that is not true of instrumental values. The relationship between instrumental and core values is always contingent and causal. That something has instrumental value for some purpose is always a matter of fact that can change with circumstances. Prerequisite values do not have this character. They are not replaceable. Their value in relationship to other use values cannot be established comparatively. And working with prerequisite values is not the domain of experts or expertise.

We discovered that specific instances of things having core value are a second type of prerequisite use values. That is to say, their value is logically or integrally, not causally related to that from which they derive their value. Thus, for some stakeholders, the value of Algonquin Park derived directly from the fundamental value they saw in preserving wilderness. Because Algonquin Park was seen as a wilderness area by some people and, more important, the only protectable example of wilderness within reach of people in southern Ontario[19], great value was attached to it by them for that reason.

Clearly, in this kind of situation, the value of an instance of wilderness like Algonquin Park is derivative; it is not, however, instrumental in character. Some stakeholders involved in the forest management plan assessment process for Algonquin Park valued the park in this way. They saw Algonquin Park as an instance of something they saw as important, namely wilderness. Furthermore, its value for them derived in large measure from this fact.

Finally, we discovered things being identified as having value because they were an integral part of something which was seen as having value. Thus, if wilderness has value, the flora and fauna characteristic of that wilderness will have value also. Once again it became clear to us that values of this sort needed to be distinguished from instrumental values if the logic of the positions being taken by those involved in the cases under study was to be understood and if constructive dialog responsive to the logic of the positions being taken was to be possible.

### Negative and Positive Values

A final characteristic of values also emerged as significant in understanding the values under riding the positions people were taking. Values, it became quickly apparent, could be either positive or negative. The conceptual structure of this observation is not complex, unlike those discussed above. However, it is significant. The concept of "value" is essentially positive. It is equally the case that the connotations normally attached to the word are also positive. Thus, when we think of values or look for them in the words or behavior of others, we are typically looking for something positive. Examination of the position statements of the stakeholder groups involved in our four cases, however, also revealed negative as well as positive values. Furthermore, negative values revealed as much about the values a stakeholder group was putting in play as positive values.

What we discovered in our analysis was that negative values typically did not function as core values. They were typically negative instrumental values. Their role largely was to identify impediments or obstacles to the realization of something of value, an end, goal, or objective, for example. Thus, for those who identified the preservation of wilderness as a core value, roads had a negative value since roads functioned to open wilderness

19 Some people may and in our study did find that the concept of a wilderness accessible to large numbers of people less than coherent.

to a variety of uses many of which (logging for example) were seen as incompatible with wilderness preservation. Negative value was also attached to things that contributed to an undesirable state of affairs. For example, road construction in Algonquin Park was assigned a negative value by the Wildlands League not simply because roads created access but because their construction caused silting which damaged the environmental quality of the streams affected.

For all of these reasons, identifying negative as well as positive values turned out to be important for identifying and describing accurately the values the various stakeholder groups were putting in play.

**Resulting Coding Scheme**

Arising out of these methodological considerations emerged a coding scheme designed to capture the following information: (i) the values in play by case and stakeholder group (this being the values inventory); (ii) the negative or positive character of each of the values identified (iii) the categorization of each value identified by value type; (iv) categorization of values in the inventory as core or "use" values; (v) the value structure linking "use" values to core values: and (v) in the case of "use" values, the kind of use value involved (i.e. instrumental, symbolic, or prerequisite).

## Stage Three: Conducting Interviews

### *Goals and Objectives*

As was the case for document analysis, the purpose of our interviews was to determine the value profiles of stakeholder groups.

Three interview goals were as follows:

- We wanted to determine the extent to which the publicly articulated positions of the stakeholder groups reflected the actual values to which the group was committed or reflected a rhetorical stance articulated for strategic reasons. To put the matter another way, were the values being defended in the documents designed to disguise or justify a position whose real foundation was of a self-serving or self-interested variety.
- We wanted to examine the role of information and the extent to which stakeholders were working from different informational assumptions.
- We wanted to determine the extent to which the values the various stakeholders thought should guide decisions in the case in which they were involved were case specific or influenced by the particular interests of the stakeholders in the case in question.

Interviews were guided by a detailed interview protocol that was common for all interviewees and all four cases under study

### *Research Findings*

A key result of our research was a much richer appreciation of the role of values in generating and resolving conflicts. Three are particularly relevant for an understanding of environmental conflict and its resolution.

**Lesson One**

Typically, environmental conflict is described as a conflict between environmental and economic interests. Economic interests are described as the driving force behind proposals for the extraction or use of a natural resource, a mineral deposit for example, or a forest or a river with hydroelectric potential. Conflict is generated when the pursuit of economic interests poses a threat to environmental values which are typically championed by environmental groups.

The first lesson to be drawn from our research is that this is a vastly over-simplified picture or values typology of values based conflict involving the natural environment impact of economic development. The effect of this over simplification is to highlight two types of values that without question play a central role in environment/economic conflict while ignoring a range of other values whose role, we discovered, is equally, and in some cases more important for understanding environment/economic conflict than the two that normally are focused on.

Reliance on this simplified typology distorts analysis in revealing ways. It creates a binary framework that implies two related things. First, it implies that all environmental disputes are disputes involving what are in effect two parties, those whose priority is to sustain or enhance economic activity, and those whose priority is environmental protection or enhancement. This largely tacit assumption leads in turn to a tendency to lump what are in fact distinct stakeholder groups together. For example, aboriginal stakeholders were typically grouped with environmentalists and therefore assumed to be hostile to economic development. And groups like loggers were typically assumed to be allies of economic interests with a primary interest in jobs and wages.

A second implication of this binary framework was that dispute resolution could have only one of three outcomes. Either (i) the resolution must favor environmental protection and enhancement at the expense of economic interests; or (ii) it must favor economic interests at the expense of the environment; or (iii) there must be a compromise or saw-off where both parties both win and lose some of their demands. An ideal (i.e. fair) solution, is often projected as one in which the two parties gain and lose equally though in different ways by the compromise which results.

Interpretation of environmental disputes within this binary framework carries high costs. Three are particularly significant. The first consequence is that important values are excluded from public discussion.[20] Furthermore, values left out are likely to be those important to marginalized stakeholders.

In our study, for example, document analysis revealed that, in the cases in which everyone acknowledged that aboriginal interests were directly engaged, subsistence values played little or no role in the position statements of nonaboriginal stakeholders. In contrast, they were clearly a focus of real concern for aboriginal stakeholders and played a significant role in their justification of their positions on the issues being debated.

A second consequence: One of the quite striking findings emerging from our analysis was the importance of social values[21] in the thinking of the stakeholders involved in the four cases. Two examples will illustrate the point. Interviews with loggers who worked for companies involved in logging in Algonquin Park revealed significant anger over the way in which their values, i.e. what was important to them, were being interpreted by other stakeholders, for example, environmental groups who were actively involved in public debate over logging in the Park. What was resented was the suggestion that as loggers, their concerns were largely or exclusively economic, or specifically, a concern with protecting their jobs.

In contrast, interviews revealed that lying at the root of the position of the loggers were social values that defined a way of life. These were evidenced by a strong commitment to the social values around which life in the small towns in which they lived revolved. It was also clear from the interviews that respect for and a love of the natural environment was central to the matrix of values which defined that way of life. Failure on the part of environmental groups to recognize this commitment was the subject of considerable resentment and hostility.

Equally, both document analysis and interviews confirmed a central role for social values in the thinking of aboriginal stakeholders. Here the priority of social values resonated with the importance attached to subsistence values. That is to say, to ignore the importance of hunting and gathering for aboriginal communities was, in the view of aboriginal spokespeople, to ignore a crucial component in the matrix of activities and relationships central to their way of life. The fact that hunting and fishing had been supplanted by welfare and wage labor as the dominant economic support for the communities in question was simply irrelevant seen from their perspective. What was important was what I shall later describe as the symbolic role which subsistence activities continued to play in the life of the community.

To conclude, working with an impoverished values typology reduces the ability of those involved to understand the nature and the relative priority of the values that various stakeholders want to be taken into account by decision makers as decisions about the appropriate use of natural resources are being taken.

[20] For example, publicly mandated environmental assessments.

[21] See the appendix to this chapter for a definition.

Working with an impoverished values typology had a third consequence. The tendency to reduce debate to economic and environmental issues made it difficult to focus adequately on differences in values of a similar kind that different groups were bringing to the table. Thus, while the project proponent in the Mt. Milligan case acknowledged the importance of social and subsistence values for the aboriginal stakeholders in the area of the proposed development, the central concerns of the aboriginal communities with which they were negotiating were never adequately addressed seen from the perspective of the aboriginal stakeholders involved. The company recognized an obligation to take into account social impacts of the development being proposed. However, the structure of the values around which the company's response was constructed was conventional, urban, and poorly adapted to the concerns of the aboriginals with whom they were in discussion.

An example illustrates this point. The company was prepared to acknowledge that opening a mine in the area in question would probably exacerbate problems of substance abuse, particularly alcoholism. A typical company response, evolved in the industrial environment of labor agreements, was to provide discrete counseling for those affected. For the aboriginal communities, however, to address the problem this way was to treat the symptom and not the disease. What they wanted was recognition that to respond adequately to the social problems the mine was likely to precipitate required addressing the unique social values of their communities. To do this would require building community support systems, examining the way that work was assigned with a view to leaving the door open to traditional hunting and fishing activities, providing a place for traditional counseling on the part of elders in labor relations and company operations and so on. All of this suggested change in thinking and labor relations precedents that the company believed went well beyond its capacity to respond. What is important for present purposes, however, is not the lack of response but the difficulty faced by the aboriginal communities involved in having these issues addressed.

**Lesson Two**

There is a widely shared assumption that serious environmental conflicts are typically grounded on conflicts of principle. A related assumption on the part of conflict resolution practitioners is that conflicts of this kind are unresolvable.

Emerging from our research was the conclusion once again that this view rests on over-simplified assumptions about the nature of values-based conflict. In the cases we studied, disputes in which conflicts of principle were direct and explicit did occur. However, they were not the only or even the most important factor in the disputes to which our four cases gave rise. Understanding why this was so required first carefully distinguishing core and from use values and then analyzing the differing roles of both core and use values in environmental disputes and the interpretations and misinterpretations of those roles by the stakeholders involved.

What we discovered was that core values enter directly into environmental disputes in four quite different ways. Each involved conflicts of principle or core value conflicts. None of the conflicts were of a sort that clearly precluded meaningful negotiation or mediation.

There can be little doubt that disagreement over core values is in principle always a potential source of conflict. It should be obvious, however, that serious conflict does not inevitably flow from commitment to different, even radically different, and incompatible core values. If it did, pluralistic societies could not survive. Our findings illustrate this obvious but often ignored truth.

One of our cases, Algonquin Park, involved a clear example of core value conflict of this first sort. The raison d'être of the Algonquin Forest Authority was to ensure a reliable flow of logs to the local saw mills. The Wildlands League, on the other hand, believed that Algonquin Park should be recognized as a wilderness preserve. They believed that logging was incompatible with the Park's "wilderness" status. There was in this case, as a consequence, clear potential for values-based conflict. It may therefore seem surprising that of our four cases, the Algonquin Park case exhibited the lowest level of conflict.

An important factor in moderating the degree of conflict between these two groups was a shared core value. Both groups recognized that the Algonquin Park forest was something of great natural value. Further, both agreed that any logging permitted should be governed by sustainability values. Finally, they both agreed that central to sustainability was environmental protection and conservation. Environmental protection and conservation were therefore for both core values.

It is true that the two groups differed about what environmental conservation and protection required. For the Forest Authority, it required logging practices that disturbed as little as possible the prevailing forest ecology. For the Wilderness League, it required the elimination of logging in the Park. What the Wildlands League were prepared to acknowledge, however, was that if there was to be logging, the forest management practices of the Authority were the best available and did represent an honest and effective effort at sustainable forestry.

The result was disagreement mediated by mutual respect. What this in turn demonstrated was that respect is possible where core values diverge.[22]

Our case studies brought to light a second and distinct kind of dispute generated by a conflict of principle or core value conflict, namely misunderstandings about the values that another individual or group wanted to guide the resolution of the issues generating disagreement. In these cases, stakeholders simply misidentified, for whatever reason, the core values to which other stakeholders or stakeholder groups were committed. One characteristic form of this kind of conflict has already been described, namely the misidentification of values as one type rather than another, for example economic rather than social or subsistence. A typical example was the way in which the value attached by loggers to logging was described by third parties as an economic concern, a description that the loggers resented because it failed to recognize logging as an integral element of a way of life. This kind of conflict, we discovered, could generate real anger and bitterness. Furthermore, conflict generated by these kinds of misunderstandings gave every appearance of being more severe than genuine core value conflicts.

Unwillingness to accept that stated or publicly endorsed values were the real values motivating those involved in a dispute represented a third kind of core values conflict. This kind of response to the stated values of other stakeholders was particularly common where aboriginal stakeholders were involved. Thus, one response to native land claims was to re-describe them as a lever designed to ensure increased compensation, or access to jobs or some other political or economic benefit. However, this response was by no means restricted to aboriginal/nonaboriginal conflict. To the contrary, it was a basic response in two of our cases to the positions of the project proponents, namely Trout Lake and Mattagami. In the case of Trout Lake, the opposition of cottagers to the proposed Timber Management Plan was based on the belief that core values, environmental protection for example, around which the Ministry of Natural Resources officials claimed to have built the plan, were in fact just window dressing. The value that a number of cottagers believed was really driving the process was the need to ensure an adequate supply of logs for the local saw mills.

In the Mattagami case, a good deal of the conflict centered on a refusal on the part of the aboriginal stakeholders to accept at face value Ontario Hydro's new-found commitment to a form of sustainable development that included recognition of aboriginal interests and concerns.

Conflict generated by beliefs of this sort gave every appearance of being more intractable and bitter than conflicts of either the first or second sort. What conflicts of this sort reflected was a fundamental lack of trust. Integral to conflicts of this sort were charges of deliberate misrepresentation and

[22] The Mt. Milligan case illustrated this same conclusion though in a less clear way. The fundamental divergence occurred in this case between the company and two neighbouring Aboriginal bands. Analysis in this case was more complex, however, because the position of the two communities on the value of economic development for their two communities was divided. Some saw economic development as an opportunity to strengthen the viability of their way of life. Others saw economic development as a threat. What the Aboriginals bands and the company shared and accepted that they shared, however, was a commitment to environmental protection.

bad faith. This kind of core value conflict was largely (though not entirely) absent from two of our cases, Algonquin Park, and Mt. Milligan.

Simply ignoring or failing to take into account the core values of an individual or group was the fourth and last form of core value conflict that emerged from our cases studies. Where it occurred, it was typically interpreted as showing lack of respect or in many cases contempt for those espousing the values in question. This is hardly surprising. People's core values define in a very fundamental way who they are. To refuse to give any weight to someone's fundamental values in a particular decision making setting is to ignore that person. To deny status to someone's fundamental value commitments is to deny (moral) status to that person.

Of the potential sources of core value conflict, this was the hardest to identify.[23]

To conclude, our study pointed to four, distinct kinds of core value conflict, each important in its own right. None of the conflicts in question appeared to be unresolvable in principle. All had the potential for causing serious clashes between and among those involved. However, it was also apparent that serious conflict was more likely to be caused by core value conflict of the third and fourth variety. Given the role of core values in defining one's self identify, this "finding" is hardly surprising.

## Lesson Three: The Role of Noncore Values in Environmental Conflict and its Resolution

Analysis of use values is useful for understanding values based disputes for two basic reasons. First, the instrumental use value of something can vary from user to user. In the Mattagami case, for example, the value of redeveloping the Mattagami River to extract more of its potential for generating power derived from the company's mandate which was to produce power for the people of Ontario at the lowest possible cost. In contrast, fishing was highly prized by the Aboriginal population in part because of the reliance of members of the community on fishing as a source of food. Since there was a fear that redevelopment would negatively affect fish habitat, redevelopment was viewed with skepticism.

What we discovered, however, was that the most frequent clashes occurred when symbolic values were treated as though they were instrumental values. For example, in three of our cases, a number of people interviewed suggested that a concern with hunting and fishing on the part of aboriginal stakeholders should not be allowed to hold back development. Many of those who took this view made it clear that they did not want the interests of aboriginal stakeholders ignored. The solution they suggested in many cases was a promise of jobs, in the mine (Mt. Milligan) or with Ontario Hydro (Mattagami) that would ensure that the individuals who could no longer hunt and fish could none the less earn an adequate living. An alternative was to offer financial compensation. These suggestions were made by people who for the most part evinced real concern for the welfare of the individuals who would be affected. Their response, however, revealed a purely instrumental evaluation of the activities in question.

Interviews with aboriginal stakeholders, on the other hand, showed clearly that what was at stake for them was not simply income, or gainful employment, or food on the table. Rather, hunting and fishing symbolized a way of relating to the land as well as a way of living together. To argue that game or fish were of declining or little importance in the diets of the people involved was to miss the point and to misconstrue the value of the activities in question in what turned out frequently to be seriously offensive ways.[24]

[23] Note that differentiating between the third and the fourth source of core value conflict involved the interpretation and the imputation of motives. To simply ignore stakeholders' fundamental interests (i.e. core values) is to show disrespect or contempt. To misunderstand, on the other hand, may demonstrate insensitivity. But it may also suggest something significantly more innocuous, at least from a moral point of view, namely failure to take adequate time, for example, or simply human error.

[24] Two other examples illustrate this phenomenon. I include them as footnotes because they are not drawn directly from the four cases. Both are recent and drawn from hydroelectric development proposals in northern Canada. The first involved offering market value for flooded land where the land in question included burial grounds. The second involved offering to truck in frozen fish to replace the fish that could no longer be eaten safely because of mercury poisoning caused by flooding.

What emerged from our study was realization that the value of things as symbols was an integral but largely hidden, unnoticed, and frequently very difficult to discern element of all the cases we looked at. Failure to differentiate between instrumental and symbolic valuation was both common and a key element in misunderstandings, miscommunications, disagreements, and conflicts. Conflating instrumental with symbolic values therefore emerged as a significant source of conflict.

The same was true for prerequisite values. For example, one of the core values of the Wildlands League was the opportunity for wilderness experience. This was a key argument for eliminating logging from Algonquin Park. In the context of this core value, the sound of a chain saw, or a logging truck lumbering through the bush, or the sight of a clear cut or a logging road did not just distract from an experience of wilderness. It was incompatible with it. That is to say, freedom from the sights and sounds of "civilization" was not just a convenience. It was an integral part of the experience of wilderness.

In short, offense was given, often inadvertently, and anger generated when things of prerequisite or symbolic value were instrumentalized and treated as things that could be traded off, compromised, or exchanged and where value was typically measured in monetary terms.

## Methodological Conclusions for Business and Applied Ethics

It should be clear for our analysis of four Canadian resource-based economic development projects that methodological development in the domain of descriptive ethics has the potential to yield substantial practical value for business and management. However, what I have described as descriptive ethics also has significance for empirical and normative scholarly research focused on ethics and ethical decision making. It does, for example, support indirectly the normative contention that social science research is unavoidably value laden. However, the key methodological findings of this research lie elsewhere. Three stand out for their particular importance.

1. Descriptive ethics falls between the domains of empirical and normative research. Further its role with respect to both domains is complementary not antagonistic. It is a domain in which both empirical and normative research tools have a place and complement each other. As philosophers like Tom Scanlon have argued and human experience makes manifest, people typically have reasons for what they do. These reasons are structured around values that identify what is worth doing and why. They have both an explanatory and a justificatory role. The resulting explanations and/or justifications are not necessarily consistent or coherent. People and organizations make mistakes. The values guiding their decisions may be mistaken, limited in scope, inconsistently and incorrectly interpreted or applied. Nonetheless, people's values are real and do guide behavior.

A central function of applied ethics in general and business ethics more specifically is to critically assess the reasons people give for their actions, particularly where important issues are in play. Are the values guiding public policy the right ones? Are the values guiding public policy correctly understood? Are they being properly implemented? Clearly, critiques of positions people or groups are taking on important issues of the day will be of limited value if the positions being critically assessed are inaccurately set out. Perhaps more important, however, is that if positions being critically assessed are inaccurately set out, they can also generate unnecessary and avoidable misunderstanding, anger and conflict.

It follows that accurate descriptions of the positions people are taking on issues of importance are essential first steps in the critical evaluation of those positions. Further, as we have seen, accurately describing those positions has both empirical and normative elements.

2. Descriptive ethics bridges the empirical and normative study of values in general and ethical values in particular. Values by their nature have a normative character. They define for people and organizations what is good, worthwhile, useful, prudent, obligatory, right, and so on. But these normative features are also facts about the people who hold them. As such, values are influenced by

forces typically the subject of empirical research. It is not possible to provide accurate accounts of the values of people and groups that ignore their empirical as well as their normative features. The social scientific study of ethics is the study of a normative phenomenon. Equally the normative study of ethics has an unavoidably empirical component.

To illustrate this point with just one example, it is simply impossible to understand and critically evaluate the positions that Aboriginal communities or leaders take on economic development, while ignoring their history, their experience, and the settings which provide the context for their positions. The same is true wherever ethical values are brought to bear on practical issues. Ethics is in this sense intrinsically practical. Descriptive ethics is what links these two social and normative realities.

3. Descriptive ethics is not simply a bridge between two realities; it is also an interpretive tool. Empirical (i.e. social science) studies of ethics and normative studies of ethics are not uncommonly interpreted as mutually incompatible. Do people do what they do because of causal factors that are social or psychological or biological in nature? Or do they do what they do because of what they value and believe they ought to do? Reflection based on experience suggests that these two perspectives are not mutually nullifying but rather are complementary. History, setting, individual factors, and normative logic all impact human decision making. Neither social science nor the normative force of values can provide an adequate explanatory account of human behavior by itself. To accomplish this goal, descriptions of the ethical structure of positions and decisions that marry the empirical and the normative explanatory elements of human decision making are unavoidable. Combining the two explanatory tools opens the door to improved explanations of why people do what they do. It also has the potential to enhance the understanding and critical ethical evaluation of human behavior. This is perhaps the most important insight resulting from the four case studies at the center of this study. If one of the purposes of applied ethics in general, and business ethics as a branch of applied ethics in particular, is to enhance understanding while mitigating conflict, then we will have to give to the domain of descriptive ethics a higher priority than has been its lot over the past three quarters of a century.

## Appendix

### *Values*

**A List with Definitions**

- Aesthetic: Values having to do with beauty.
- Ecological: Values of nature independent of human use or enjoyment, e.g., the value of the existence of a plant, an animal, a species or an ecosystem for its own sake, even if it is of no use or benefit to people.
- Economic: Values having to do with the generation of material wealth.
- Educational: Values having to do with the passing on of knowledge and of skill in the use of knowledge.
- Environmental: Values having to do with features of environment that are useful or enjoyable to humans or that support human life, e.g., the value of clean air and water, of quiet, of wildlife that people enjoy, of protection from dangerous solar radiation, etc.
- Health/safety: Values having to do with human physical well-being and safety.
- Legal: Values having to do with laws, rules, and orders enforceable in a court, e.g., the value of acting within the law, of being law-abiding, or of deciding on the basis of legal principles.
- Moral: Values having to do with right and wrong, good and evil, and such virtues as justice and fairness.
- Personal: Values of a private or idiosyncratic character, such as sentimental attachments, individual tastes, personal preferences, etc.
- Political: Values having to do with legitimately authorized actions, procedures and decisions of governments and government agencies, and with efforts to influence governments and government agencies, e.g., the value of a government or government agency's acting within its mandate and jurisdiction, following proper

procedures, acting in a fair and democratic manner, etc., or the value of a lobby group's acting in an effective and appropriate manner.

- Recreational: Values having to do with pastimes whose goals are relaxation, amusement, refreshment etc.
- Religious/spiritual: Values having to do with what is thought, understood, or perceived to be sacred.
- Scientific: Values having to do with gaining knowledge through systematic observation and/or experimentation, e.g., the value of a forest or stream as a site for biological research.
- Social: Values having to do with human relationships such as families, friendships, communities, cultures, and ways of life.
- Subsistence: Values having to do with provision of the necessaries of life outside of a cash economy.

## References

Brandenburg, A. M. and Carroll, M. S. (1995) Your place or mine?: the effect of place creation on environmental values and landscape meanings. *Society and Natural Resources* 8(5):381–398.

Cragg, A. W. (1997) Teaching business ethics: the role of ethics in business and business education. *Journal of Business Ethics*, 16, (3).

Goodpaster, K. (1983) The concept of corporate responsibility. *Journal of Business Ethics*, 2, p. 1–22.

Kilby, R. W. (1993), *The Study of Human Values*. University Press of America.

Kim, T. W. & Donaldson, T. (2016) Rethinking right: moral epistemology in management research. *Journal of Bus Ethics*. doi:10.1007/s10551-015-3009-2.

Rokeach (1973). *The Nature of Human Values*. New York: The Free Press.

Scanlon, T. M. (2014). *Being Realistic About Reasons*. New York: Oxford University Press.

van Roojen, M. (2013). *Moral Cognitivism vs. Non-Cognitivism*. Stanford Encyclopedia of Philosophy.

Werhane, P. H. (1994). The normative/descriptive distinction in methodologies of business ethics. *Business Ethics Quarterly* 4: 175–180.

Wicks, A. C. (1996). Overcoming the separation thesis: the need for a reconsideration of business and society research. *Business & Society* 35: 89–118.

Wicks, A. C., & Freeman, R. (1998). Organization studies and the new pragmatism: positivism, anti- positivism, and the search for ethics. *Organization Science*, 9: 123–140.

CHAPTER 8

# Grounded Theory in Business Ethics

DAVID BEVAN and ANGELO CARLO S. CARRASCOSO

*Grounded theory marries two contrasting – and competing – traditions in sociology as represented by each of its originators: Columbia University positivism and Chicago school pragmatism and field research.*

(Charmaz, 2006, p. 6)

## Introduction

As you may have learned from this volume and your own training, one approach to business ethics research involves employing quantitatively oriented methods that utilize formal logic and hypothetico-deductive reasoning. We suggest that these may be regarded as research *technology*, to borrow and analogize from Claude Lévi-Strauss. In this chapter, we introduce the contribution of, and potential for, grounded theory in business ethics research. Grounded theory is a qualitative and interpretive approach, and can thus be regarded as research *craft* as opposed to technique.

From experimental origins in nursing during the 1950s, grounded theory was formally articulated in 1967; since then, it has been applied to psychology, education, and sociology. It has also been deconstructed and subdivided into varying and sometimes competing prescriptions; each of these is, in some way, a grounded theory. The formal use of grounded theory in management came later despite the predilection of this method for a thick conception of organizational reality. Karen Locke's work in 2001 was among the first to bring together the varied approaches to grounded theory for the interests of organization and management scholars. In this chapter, we hope to make a similar leap – from management and organization studies to Business Ethics research.

Grounded theory is an inductive general research method that can be systematically applied to qualitative and/or quantitative data to arrive at a conceptual core category. This core category is the goal (or more simplistically the single truth found at the center) of any grounded theory research. Thus, grounded theory is nominally both a research method, *and* the outcome or result of employing that method. As authors, we have grappled with the applicability of grounded theory to business ethics research, and firmly believe in this expansion. Here, we give you an opportunity to weigh up its value to your research.

We begin with the origins of grounded theory through its evolution in sociology through the late twentieth-century nursing and healthcare practice of Barney Glaser and Anselm Strauss (1967, 1971). We follow this with a broad description of how to perform and arrive at a grounded theory to ensure its acceptance and publication in outlets that may not fully appreciate its logic and value.

We then discuss works of grounded theory in management. Dutton and Dukerich (1991) explore the relationship between sense-making and identity through an in-depth study of a public utility in the 1980s. Christiansen (2006) asserts that business as an activity is definitively mere opportunizing. Lowe (1998) explores the strategies that banks undertake in dealing with clients in a postmerger scenario. Referring next to our own research in Business Ethics, we show how grounded theory reveals both the nature of corporate accountability (Bevan, 2007) and the immanence of moral hazard in SMEs (Carrascoso, 2009). Finally, we close with some thoughts about grounded theory in Business Ethics research, reflecting on the prospects of this distinctively *craft* approach.

## *Origins of Grounded Theory*

In the social sciences, the dominant mid-twentieth-century positivist paradigm stressed the scientific method and its demands for objectivity, statistical generalizability, and the falsification of competing theories and claims. Against this tradition, Glazer and Strauss (1965, 1968, 1971) wrote their seminal work in grounded theory. Together with a team of researchers, they investigated the patient / nursing professional relationship in intensive and palliative care situations. They initiated the practice of dialogically engaging with and observing "how people die" in a range of hospital and nursing home settings. In a world where the subject was seldom discussed or even acknowledged, they developed, through rigorous analysis, a theory of the social organization of the process of dying. As Charmaz (2006) notes in her invitation to grounded theory, this seminal "book made a cutting edge statement because it contested notions of the methodological consensus *and* offered systemic strategies for qualitative research practice" (p. 5, emphasis in original). Since their groundbreaking work, grounded theory has been extended to education (Glaser and Strauss, 1967, Munhall and Oiler, 1986), sociology (Strauss and Corbin, 1990), psychology (Moustakas, 1994), education (Jacob, 1987), and more widely across the social sciences and management (Denzin and Lincoln, 1994).

## *Characteristics of Grounded Theory*

Grounded theory is substantively grounded in symbolic interactionism and traceable back to the work of Charles Cooley and George Herbert Mead (Goulding, 2002, Alvesson and Sköldberg, 2000). It involves "the systematic generation of theory from data acquired by a rigorous research method" (Glaser and Strauss, 1967; p. 3) It is ideographic and particular in its focus (Locke, 2001), exploring individual situations and dialogically orienting the researcher and the research site/problem. Researchers will need to undertake their work inductively though a close interaction with the symbols of their research context.

Grounded theory repudiates the fallacy of categorical separations between theory and research, and data collection and interpretation/analysis. The research process is emergent, continuous and iterative (as opposed to fixed and determined). Data collection (i.e., interviews) and analysis/interpretation are simultaneous and co-mingled processes. At each stage, the opportunity to refine or refocus the theory is available and necessary to the research process. Grounded theory is also sparing and careful in its use of prior theorizing. Ideally, the researcher must have no preconceptions or hypotheses so that all coding and categorizing emerges from the context. The literature review is generally assembled after the grounded theory has started to emerge (and not fitted to a preconceived status quo).[1] If the use of existing theory cannot be avoided, then take care to exclude any data reductions that may be "removed from the empirical situations" (Locke, 2001: p. 104).

Finally, the goal of grounded theory is not statistical generalizability, or the application of the findings of a sample to a larger population. The method is not concerned with pseudoscientific quantification or compliance with sample sizes. Rather, the goal of theory generation is analytical generalizability, or the ability of the emergent theory to better explain or account for the experienced phenomena. The relevant question is not whether the theory applies to X group, but how the theory helps us better understand organizational realities.

Quite possibly, certain research supervisors will shudder at the "random impressionism" that this approach encourages. We assert that grounded theory challenges the belief that phenomenological data can be dismissed, and that qualitative methods are vague and incapable of generating substantive theory. In fact, *quantitative* analytic methods have built theory from *qualitative* data. In doing so, grounded theory demonstrates the validity of its theory-generating logic (Locke, 2001: p. 38–39)

[1] Grounded theory can be used to "enliven mature theorizing" (Locke, 2001; p. 96); accomplishing this requires some familiarity with the literature so that the theoretical gaps can be identified and addressed. Some researchers (e.g., Harris and Sutton, 1986; Eisenhardt and Bourgeois, 1988) have used prior theory to organize raw data.

and systemic approach to data analysis and interpretation. It is our hope that this summary will excite you enough to sustain your interest in this context-sensitive, symbolically-laden method for your research. The next section discusses the methodology of grounded theory.

## *How to Do, and How to Arrive at, a Grounded Theory*

There are many ways to describe the processes of grounded theory research. We identify the stages of grounded theory as suggested in Creswell (1997, 2003, 2008, 2012) who follows a conservative and scholarly research structure that would assure the quality of any grounded theory project. Bear in mind that nothing here is intended to be contradictory; this is a highly flexible methodology and open to extensive researcher eclecticism that reflects the diverse approaches of the originators and their respective students; Locke, 2001. Equally as important, grounded theory is iterative in nature as we indicated earlier; there is no clean separation between data collection, analysis, and interpretation. All told, you will have to work out a practical approach for theory generation as part of your research journey.

Broadly in common with the leading proponents of grounded theory, Creswell suggests that any first stage involves introducing and focusing your topic, identifying the problem and the purpose of your research, and explicating your research question(s) (i.e., the central question and any consequent corollaries).

The second stage involves data collection. In this phase, you design a data collection cycle, identify the research sites (individuals and *incidents*) while fully cognizant of access issues. You design a purposeful sampling strategy, consider how to conduct the interviewing and observations, and deal with the management of various data media. You also clarify any issues that concern the "field" of your research.

In a distinct but not so delineated third stage, you perform data analysis. This initially involves *open coding* of all data and the formulation of tentative categories. Then, through a constant and recursive comparison of the coded data with the emerging categories, you *saturate* the *categories* you have identified and their *properties*. Eventually, you identify a single *category* as the *central phenomenon*.

In the fourth stage, you narrate and present the data formally and identify the limitations and validity of your grounded theory. Creswell suggests illustrating how your research has complied with, and contributed to, the generation (or discovery) of an original grounded theory in the tradition that you have selected.

In their reflexive methodology handbook, Alvesson and Sköldberg (2000) propose a variant data collection approach. Here, the focus is on acquiring unconventional data sources. Where data are thin or inaccessible, they can be enhanced through library research which includes letters, biographies, memoirs, speeches; even fiction and autobiography is included in the parameters set by Glaser and Strauss (1967) along with participant or incident observations.

## *Assessing Grounded Theory*

Assessing the emergent theory is analogous to a progressive focusing toward and onto the "truth" of the core category or concept. Your grounded theory has been formalized to the point of theoretical saturation when it displays the following three characteristics:

a. Veracity. Stewart defines veracity as "devotion to and conformity with [descriptive] truth." (Stewart, 1998; p, 18) Veracity is achieved when a study "capably depicts what they claim to have observed" (Stewart, 1998; p. 15).
b. Objectivity. For Stewart, objectivity refers to the transcendence of perspectives beyond the current context which results from the actors' "intersubjective, often intercultural, communication" (Stewart, 1998: p 15). If the theory remains stuck within either the researcher's or informants' perspectives, objectivity is categorically not obtained.
c. Perspicacity. This refers to the "applicability of [the theory's] insights elsewhere" (Stewart, 1998; p. 17) beyond the current research setting. If this is not obtained, "findings are (at best) true

only in idiosyncratic settings, or (worse) there is no way to know where else, when else, or under what conditions, they would be applied." (Stewart, 1998; p. 18).

Theories that showcase these features are "pragmatically useful" (Locke, 2001: p. 59) in that people understand and apply the emerged theory's insights to a variety of contexts and conditions in the practice setting. In addition, because of the rigorous practices demonstrated by the theorists, the theory's credibility to academic and practitioners is enhanced.

### *Addressing the Limitations of Grounded Theory*

Upholding and explaining to others your study's veracity, objectivity, and perspicacity is easier than it seems. We have intimated that grounded theory has a degree of flexibility which could call its rigor into question. We also suggest how grounded theory leads to core variables that are at odds with mainstream (and perhaps sentimental) views of how ordered and static organizational life is perceived to be. Unfortunately, the unfamiliarity of reviewers and editors with the specifics of grounded theory in management, and their unintentional use of a hypothetico-deductive logic on emerging and undefined phenomena, is a problem that even its most seasoned and accomplished researchers face.

To address the concerns of readers, editors, and reviewers about grounded theory, Stewart (1998) proposes the following strategies to be observed throughout the research process. Please note that we only focus on the recommendations that Stewart (1998) considers as at least helpful, and not of questionable use.

1. Prolonged fieldwork. The rule of thumb for any research project is between 12 to 18 months to achieve a massive overdetermination of data, although a shorter period can be justified and compensated for with site revisits, virtual meetings, and other similar strategies.
2. Seeking out reorienting or disconfirming observations. You should actively search for these data elements enhance your study's perspicacity. A theory that stumbles with, or is overturned by such observations needs further clarification and refining to achieve theoretical saturation.
3. Good participative roles relationships. A good relationship between yourself as the researcher and the individuals in the field provides occasions for open inquiry and witnessing of a wide variety of events and occurrences.
4. Attentiveness to speech and interactional contexts. A properly derived theory concerns itself greatly with how messages are communicated, and in what environments the data are gathered and collected. Sometimes, you obtain the most valuable information outside of interviews, and in very informal settings where the individuals feel open and unhindered in their disclosure.
5. Multiple modes of data collection. You are advised to creatively and resourcefully obtain data through participant observation, interviews, insider and outsider documentation, artifacts, and photographs, surveys, and nonparticipative observation.
6. Trail of the Ethnographer's Path. To enhance the study's credibility, you should "depict the researcher's realized pattern of interaction with the actors (the ethnographer's path), whether ... by a reflexive writing style or in the methods discussion" (Stewart, 1998; p. 71). Attention is placed in showing how the researcher's interactions with insiders aided in data gathering.
7. Respondent validation. When possible, you should elicit the comments of insiders on draft versions of the report.
8. Outsider feedback. To complement respondent validation, you should obtain the insights of other field scholars and experts regarding the study to identify areas of further exploration and sampling.
9. Intense data consideration. You should painstakingly detail a "self-disciplined process of data transformation that, in broad outline, included indexing and coding of the data, decontextualizing, memoing, and recontextualizing ... [to show how] index words were prioritized and

clustered in the creation of higher-order constructs." (Stewart, 1998; p. 72).

10. Exploration. The sites that you chose for study must be rich in detail and complexity to allow for "contrast and reorientation" as the constructs are further refined to allow for theory emergence.

## *Manuscript Writing: Some Additional Reminders*

In addition to the steps just mentioned, you are strongly advised to remember the difference between presentation and process, and know your targeted journal's preferred presentation style.

Journals that are qualitatively oriented and familiar with grounded theory may not require you to adequately recount your data gathering and analysis steps. They may not even be interested in any literature review of your chosen phenomenon. However, a lot of US-based journals that are friendly to grounded theory require you to show how you demonstrated care and diligence throughout the data gathering and analysis, and theory generation steps. They may also require you to discuss the relevant literature first before making you extensively account for your methods and results. This presentation may conflict with your actual process for doing grounded theory research where any in-depth literature review is done after theoretical saturation is achieved. In this case, you should abide by the journal's preferred mode of formatting and presentation despite your personal reservations about how the discovery process unfolds in the exact opposite way that data are presented. It can spell the difference between a rejection of your work, and a revise and resubmit decision.

## *Examples of Grounded Theory in Management and Business*

To avoid speculating further, we now discuss completed grounded theory work in management, business, and business ethics. The articles discussed in the following section comprise what we believe to be exemplary work in grounded theory, some of them being the most cited works. The initial articles for your consideration are in management and business which provide an appropriate pathway to grounded theory use in business ethics, management being the mother discipline on which business ethics, broadly speaking, rests. Dutton and Dukerich's study of the Port Authority of New York and New Jersey is one of the most cited works in management, and its extensive and detailed use of grounded theory is thorough and noteworthy; it won the 2001 Best Journal AMJ Article award from the Academy of Management. Christiansen's work on opportunizing is both a thoughtful example of grounded theory applied to management, and an insightful manuscript that points to the significant amount of available opportunizing to business ethics researchers interested in breaking new ground in the field. Lowe is another example of notable grounded theory work for your consideration. As professors in the field of Business Ethics, we have also selected from our own research some indicative grounded theory approaches. This selection is circumstantially forced upon us by the relative absence of other contributors who use this approach.

### Dutton and Dukerich (1991)

Dutton and Dukerich's work on organizational sense-making in uncertainty and change utilized a single case study analysis of the Port of New York and New Jersey's experience in dealing with homeless people in the late 1980s. Open ended interviews of twenty-five employees were triangulated with internal documents ranging as far back as 1982, and publicly-available information from regional newspapers and magazines. Data were initially coded using a contact summary form which were subsequently used to develop a comprehensive theme list. Interview data were then coded onto the themes to create an issue history of the Port Authority during the 1980s that became the basis of the authors' theory on the role of image and identity in organizational adaptation. To them, identity influenced "image interpretations, emotions and actions. At the same time, the organization's image – how organization members thought others saw it – served as a gauge against which they evaluated and justified action on the issue. In addition, the organization's image was an important mirror for interpretations that triggered and judged issue action" (542).

### Christiansen (2006)

Christiansen's defended doctoral dissertation at the University of the Faroe Islands in 2006 is entitled "Opportunizing: A Classic Grounded Theory Study on Business and Management." It is an openly Glaserian grounded theory which focused on how companies maintain their growth or survive. We take an appreciative position on its significance as an orthodox and authoritative work.

Christiansen finds "opportunizing" to be the core category and main enterprise of management and business: "the current main concern that businesses have to continually resolve" (2006, p. 120) "Opportunizing is basically what business managers do, and do all the time" (*ibid.*). We emphasize this finding because it exemplifies a successful grounded theory. Whether it makes it morally any more attractive, the "opportunizing" that epitomizes all managers and business cycles through some clearly complementary behaviors which are an important contingency of grounded theory research. The core variable of manager and business behavior is "the recurrent creation and recreation of "convenient occasions" for the deliberate pursuit of competitive advantage in the business" (Christiansen, 2006; p. 123) and "the recurrent seizing of business opportunities." Christiansen was unable to find a single example of a manager behaving in a way that was not explained by this core variable.

In addition to the core category of opportunizing, the constitution of this opportunizing is deconstructed by reference to codes (facets) that arose during the research. These are subdivided into behavioral and organizational facets or subprocesses which continuously recreate managers' and business behavior. Christiansen lists these assiduously, and we need not follow that process through as it is easy enough to go direct to the document and see his deconstruction. Perhaps to the joy of some management faculty and business school deans, Christiansen suggests that his grounded theory is complementary to a range of already popular theories – some of which are well-known to critical business ethics scholars – including neoclassical economics, game theory, behaviorism, agency theory, evolutionary theory, etc.

For some people, Christiansen's grounded theory findings might foreclose any further useful discussion. Indeed, there is a temptation to explore the integrity of individuals whose activities are comprehensively characterized by such a universal term. But we resist pursuing that here, as our focus is methods for exploring and researching business ethics.

### Lowe (1998)

This paper is a grounded theory study of how a recently merged bank remodeled its relationships with its smaller corporate clients. In the postmerger aftermath, there is only one of the parties which emerges as being in the ascendancy. Clients of the organization, in this study, were treated very differently according to whether they were clients of the ascending or descending partner in the postmerger context.

In the initial part of the study, the researcher interviewed different members of a merged universal bank in Scandinavia, from board directors to front line bank officers to current and former clients. Following best practices in grounded theory research (careful journaling, maintaining close contact with insiders to ensure trust and continued access, and proper open and selective coding practices, among others), the research revealed that he bank redesigned its relationships with these clients in one of three main ways, With its preferred clients, the bank utilizes a cultivating approach where it "goes out of their way to be helpful and friendly" through "deal sweetening, customising … favouring … [and] being recognised and entitled to privileges." With clients that are deemed disadvantageous to the bank, it utilizes a terminating approach where it "systematically begins the process of freezing out the other party … as quickly as possible … [through] stigmatising, tainting and intimidating. When banks regard partners to be insufficiently important to their profitable operations, these clients are neglected through "benign denial, misunderstanding, distancing and impeding" (Lowe, 1998).

Having swiftly examined some useful milestones in the annals of grounded theory research in the field of management and business, we now feel confident in suggesting that we can explore grounded theory as a method for business ethics scholarship and research.

## *Examples of Grounded Theory in Business Ethics Research*

*To the best of our knowledge, there has been very little work in grounded theory in business ethics (emphasis ours).* One reason for this is the preponderance of academics whose methodological preferences lie elsewhere, either in philosophical logic or statistical analysis. Another, and perhaps related, explanation is the relatively significant time investment that a thoroughly done grounded theory manuscript involves. It is not uncommon for research projects to span a few years from start to finish, as time is spent gathering data and clarifying categories to the point of theoretical saturation. This consumes much of the researcher's time and attention. Given the prevalent publish-or-perish mentality in the academe, a great number of scholars would rather use methodologies with a much shorter publication cycle. The result has been that numerous business ethics phenomena have been either underexplored or unexamined. Applying the opportunizing of Christiansen (2006) here, we see a significant opportunity for those who seek to upend traditional business ethics paradigms or to explore new avenues and vistas for research inquiry. Here are some manuscripts that we offer as examples of our desire to expand business ethics research.

### Bevan (2007)

This doctoral dissertation in social accounting and accountability was examined by critical and social accounting professors at King's College London. Based on uniquely privileged access to managers at a FTSE100 firm, this exploratory thesis sought to contribute to corporate accountability new and potentially unsettling insights that were interpretively based on the contemporary accountability practice. In this circumstance, considerable effort was exerted to critically develop an appropriate framework to understand the rhetoric and reality of corporate discourses and the experience of accountability-in-practice. Two complementary research questions were asked: 1. What do the discourses of nonfinancial accountability and corporate social responsibility articulated by the transnational corporations actually propose, and; 2. What insights can be revealed from the experience of senior managers in such a transnational corporation to contribute to any understanding of such a proposal?

Responding to these questions involved a study of accountability and corporate social responsibility practice in a FTSE100 firm which is not known in advance. The dissertation aimed to provide a contextual analysis of accountability and corporate social responsibility by interpreting the objects of discourse discoverable from a field of such firms and the contrasting, or complementary, experiences of such accountability and corporate social responsibility by senior corporate managers in such a firm.(Bevan, 2007; p. 15)

To employ a distinction frequently offered in Glaser, this research is "grounded in data" and in practice, but it does not produce a grounded theory in the orthodox manner of Christiansen. Acknowledging the limitations of the method in the context of insights on accountability among FTSE managers, the author draws on GT for distinct strands of methodic practice. It borrows naturalistic interviewing processes for the extensive gathering of data from individual research sites. He then employs Glaser's (1998) interpretive/analytic method of text explication which challenges the data with a taxonomy of four categories:

1. First is baseline, which is the best description a participant can offer.
2. Second is proper line data, which is what the participant thinks it is proper to tell the researcher. It is what participants feel they are supposed to say, no matter what reality is. They have no stake in correct description, only in correct distortion.
3. Third is interpreted data, which is what is told by a trained professional whose job it is to make sure that others see the data his professional way, even though it alters the normal way of seeing it.

4. The fourth type of data is vaguing out. There is no stake for the participant in telling the researcher anything, so he just vagues out. (ibid., p. 9).

A definitive grounded theory was categorically excluded, both by reference to Glaser's terminology and method, and again by the delimitations of the author. A full grounded theory of management- or managerial accountability from such a small sample would not be plausible, when – on one hand Christiansen (2006) has shown that all managers are opportunists, and on the other hand Levinas (Levinas, 2004; 2005) proposes that accountability cannot be reduced to a theme (such as a grounded theory). While a definitive grounded theory is not the aim here, nonetheless this work is an exercise in developing an evaluative analysis from empirical observation; thus, it is a theory grounded in observation of practice in the world. Further, the ontologically compatible methodology of grounded theory based in Glaser (1998) and further diversified in Charmaz (2005) offers methods which entrain a valuable disciplinary rigor and thoroughness. (Bevan, 2007; p. 133)

Bevan (2007) can be considered to offer a qualitative and perhaps a morally pessimistic account of business ethics. The practice of managerial accountability appears to be constructed around the organizing principle of a genteel and legitimized self-interest. From this, taken as a principle – a core category – the attitude of senior managers is always understandable, there is little scope for wavering beyond such theorizations as that of Alain Badiou which sees commerce, in an ethical sense, as a practice of glib nihilism.

**Bevan (2008)**

This chapter was a contribution to a volume on Continental Approaches to Business Ethics (Painter-Morland and Werhane, 2008) in which a grounded theory "approach" is employed to discover insights on the label "Continental" philosophy as a distinct category to mainstream business ethics from literature. There is no account of "business ethics" in much of Continental Philosophy; it passes starkly-unmentioned in Foucault for example. Moreover, where there appears to be some engagement, as in Badiou mentioned above, it is not appreciative. It was for that pretext that grounded theory was used to inform the approach to this gap in the literature. Starting from one of the suggestions for future research in his doctoral dissertation (2007) the author asserts this to be the first attempt at employing grounded theory methods in the field of a Business Ethics textbook. He further claims that the use of grounded theory is called for given "that there is no complete account of the term *continental*" (Bevan, 2008: p. 138) in the field of business ethics.

This work used data from the texts and course designs for contributions to MBA and MSc Management curricula in 2006/2007 at HEC Paris (France) and Royal Holloway, University of London (UK). The research purpose was to find a core category of "business ethics" practice that might be explicated from teaching materials. The particular method employed is *explication de texte* which assists the researcher "who is doing constant comparisons to generate concepts that closely fit without imputation as to what is going on in the substantive area, while at the same time being able to claim authorship of the concept he generated" (Glaser, 1998: p. 28). The literature selected is a convenience sample of Continental authors, and from this sampling theory building is mediated by the author in excerpts. These excerpts are adduced to elicit and propose a distinct grounded theory of a Continental approach to business ethics quasi-symmetrically contrasted with a control sample of orthodox, traditional, or *classical* Enlightenment approaches to Business Ethics. Eschewing preconceptions in strict compliance with grounded theory protocols, Bevan (2008) carefully draws on Charmaz (2005) to emphatically avoid any bias by using his selected texts "as objects of scrutiny themselves rather than for corroborating evidence." (p. 39) Bevan suggests that *classical* business ethics informed indicatively by neoclassical economics, duty, rights, justice, virtue and formal logic are ***convenient business ethics*:** they convene upon and draw together in legitimate form the entire project of capitalism relying on classical ontology "for the achievement of pax mercatoria" (Bevan, 2008; p. 144) while Continental authors are *inconvenient* for the subject.

More fully, *convenient* ethics represent the classical business ethics frameworks which allow us to consider how, for example. the constituent firms of the Dow Jones Sustainability Index come to be considered as even sustainable. Perhaps it also tells us that sustainability, like corporate social responsibility which it has recently displaced as the palliative for ethical concerns, is merely more, bigger, newer, window dressing.

In addition, classical business ethics is *convenient* for writing and realizing codes of practice; theorizing all sorts of twenty-first century invisible hand substitutes like the triple bottom line and socially responsible investing behind which "normal business" can carry on apparently as usual. Finally, classical business ethics is not only *convenient*, but essential to legitimizing and structurally reinforcing the concept of business ethics. Meanwhile, continental ethics are ***inconvenient*** for most of the basic activities of the entire Global 500 firms, and inimical to the parochial project of classical business ethics. Continental writers are dismissed because they have nothing relevant to say to commerce or government.

### Carrascoso (2009, 2011)

This study began as a research project within a qualitative research methods course of Karen Locke where the author/researcher was interested in an in-depth empirical study of a business decision. He used Brickson's Organizational Identity orientation construct to understand how an organization's identity evolves as a firm internationalizes and "legitimates itself to a foreign partner or group, and what are the consequences and implications of such a [legitimation] process" (Carrascoso, 2009: p. 12). The study of such a process would reveal the ethically-laden nature of business decision-making, a key insight that the researcher wanted to highlight in his dissertation given the inadequacy of such ethical considerations in many businesses and industries.

Initial contact with large firms that were pursued through network contacts yielded no positive results because of intellectual property and security concerns that the researcher attributed to his lack of familiarity with key firm gatekeepers. This prompted him to pursue SMEs through his personal contacts. His initial contact with Triton (the SME under study) in April 2008 proved to be promising because of the owners' familiarity with him. The researcher utilized a variety of data sources to understand and explore "the company's identity orientation – how it is formed, interpreted and sustained" (Carrascoso, 2009: p. 38). Over a six-month period, he interviewed the owners of the firm, its key employees, and some of firm's partners. The owners and employees also allowed him to observe key firm events for which he took copious notes that detailed his observations and reflections. He complemented these data sources with archival data that the owners provided him to better understand Triton's operating procedures, financial position, and expansion plans.

Data analysis informally started after interview transcription. Following Locke's recommendation, data were fragmented into relevant chunks (Locke, 2001) so that they could be properly named and compared with one another. An initial set of seventeen provisional categories emerged after the transcription of the first three interviews. The iterative analysis process that occurred over the next few months and which included a second site visit, transcription of subsequent interviews and analysis of archival data and field notes, and further category refinement, reduced the number of viable categories to twelve, and finally to seven. The label "relationality" was chosen as the core category because of its ability to capture "an unending, complex interplay between various actors and forces unfolded and where social capital was given, received, and sometimes lost" Carrascoso (2011; p. 83). These seven categories were fit into a coding paradigm (Locke, 2001; p. 76) that specified how "founder characteristics and experiences and contextual factors ... influenced the network expansion strategies that Triton utilized in its internationalization initiatives" Carrascoso (2011; p. 76). The implications of the study are important given the frenetic pace of activity that small to medium enterprises encounter on a consistent basis. Internationalization is "a relationally-influenced and ethically-laden process that ... do not diminish one's responsibility for ethical behavior" (Carrascoso, 2011, p. 73). Subsequently, such firms need to "create an ethical infrastructure that, while cognizant of their resource constraints, enables them to develop and sustain a strong sense of character and integrity to deal with the challenges surrounding SME internationalization" (Carrascoso, 2011, p. 73).

## *Work Outside Management and Business*

Should our list of references prove inadequate, we suggest exploring groundedtheoryonline.com. It represents one of the best resources for articles and information on grounded theory that may be of help to your research. Work in nursing and healthcare may be found here.

## *Concluding Commentary*

We opened this chapter with a definition of grounded theory. A closer reading of at least of Glaser and Strauss's work may suggest the imposition of their preconceptions on the reader, renovating the orthodox position, and reasserting an unchallenged status quo. It was in this spirit of challenging orthodoxy and established practice that Glaser and Strauss brought a new understanding to the use of palliative care in the nursing of patients close to dying. This tension is a practical reminder of the potential of grounded theory to engage with business ethics issues, especially in cases where what passes for established and possibly even legitimate commercial practice is, by some of us, considered as indifference, injustice, or plainly wanton negligence. Equally in the context of a chapter on business ethics research, we could have more openly conducted a "grounded theory" of grounded theory. In this spirit, notwithstanding, the examples we have provided of our own research are indicatively well-enough differentiated to show the highly flexible and coherent nature of grounded theory.

We have also illustrated that grounded theory is a methodology in process. Since its inception, it is developmental and organic. It originated from the fragments of distinctly eclectic antecedents including philosophy, social sciences, and nursing. It has continued to develop through an array of social science practitioner craft since its first inscription some fifty years ago. We have shown examples of a grounded theory of management itself and illustrated from our personal research journeys the contribution that grounded theory has made to Business Ethics literature. Going forward, it is not an exaggeration to reiterate that grounded theory in business ethics is woefully underexplored; perhaps many researchers believe that such an in-depth approach is so time intensive that their efforts are better spent examining ethical phenomena using less consuming statistical and experimental methods that boost research productivity. However, as more and more fields of exploration become salient and accessible for theorizing, researchers should be aware of the massive opportunities afforded to grounded theory in expanding our understanding of organizations and ethical behavior in ways that other, quantitative methods cannot do as effectively. While writing his dissertation, one of this chapter's authors became pleasantly aware of the bright prospects for doing research on the ethics of SME internationalization. Very little has been written about it despite the sheer frequency of such a strategic move by SME entrepreneurs.

In closing this partial introduction to the use of grounded theory in business ethics, we repeat something that has emerged in other chapters here. As with any research methodology (and perhaps more especially so in the field of Business Ethics), one significant issue is the "fit" of any choice of methodology (i) with your research question(s), and of equal importance, (ii), with your access to research sites. These two must be mutually congruent to your methodological choice, even if, as in our own choices, grounded theory was one of an effective suite of methods chosen to achieve our research objectives.

## References

Alvesson, M. & Sköldberg, K. 2000. *Reflexive Methodology*, London: Sage.

Bevan, D. 2007. *Accountability and empire: insights from the experiences of senior managers at a FTSE100 firm.* PhD thesis, King's College London.

2008. Continental philosophy: a grounded theory approach and the emergence of convenient and inconvenient ethics. *In:* Painter-Morland, M. & Werhane, P. (eds.) *Cutting-edge Issues in Business Ethics: Continental Challenges to Tradition and Practice*. New York, NY: Springer.

Carrascoso, A. S. 2009. *The identity – strategy link: Context, driver and consequences for firm internationalization.* (Unpublished PhD dissertation in Business Administration). University of Virginia Darden School of Business, Charlottesville, Virginia.

2011. *The ethical issues surrounding network-expansion strategies in SME internationalization: an empirical investigation.* Business and Professional Ethics Journal, 30(1/2), 71–112.

Charmaz, K. 2005. Grounded theory in the twenty-first century: applications for advancing social justice studies. *In:* Denzin, N. K. & Lincoln, Y. S. (eds.) *The Sage Handbook of Qualitative Research.* London: Sage Publications.

2006. *Constructing Grounded Theory: A Practical Guide Through Qualitative Analysis*, London, UK: Sage Publications.

Christiansen, O. 2006. Opportunizing: a classic grounded theory study on business and management. *Grounded Theory Review*, 6, 109–133.

Creswell, J. W. 1997. *Qualitative Inquiry and Research Design: Choosing Among five Traditions*, London: Sage Publications.

2003. *Research Design: Qualitative, Quantitative and Mixed Method Approaches*, London: Sage Publications.

2008. *Research Design: Qualitative, Quantitative, and Mixed Methods Approaches*, London: Sage Publications.

2012. *Research Design: Qualitative, Quantitative, and Mixed Methods Approaches*, London: Sage Publications.

Denzin, N. K. & Lincoln, Y. S. 1994. *Handbook of Qualitative Research*, Thousand Oaks, CA: Sage.

Dutton, J. E. & Dukerich, J. M. 1991. Keeping an eye on the mirror: image and identity in organizational adaptation. *Academy of Management Journal*, 34, 517–554.

Glaser, B. 1998. *Doing Grounded Theory*, Mill Valley, CA: Sociology Press.

Glaser, B. & Strauss, A. 1965. *Awareness of Dying*, Chicago, IL: Aldine.

1967. *The Discovery of Grounded Theory*, Chicago, IL: Aldine.

1968. *Time for Dying*, Chicago, IL: Aldine.

1971. *Status Passage*, London: Routledge and Kegan Paul.

Goulding, C. 2002. *Grounded Theory: A Practical Guide for Management, Business and Market Researchers*, London: Sage.

Jacob, E. 1987. Qualitative research traditions: a review. *Review of Educational Research*, 57, 1–50.

Levinas, E. 2004. *Otherwise than Being – or beyond Essence*, Pittsburgh, PA: Duquesne University Press.

2005. *Totality and Infinity: An Essay on Exteriority*, Pittsburgh, PA: Duquesne University Press.

Locke, K. 2001. *Grounded Theory in Management Research*, London, UK: Sage.

Lowe, A. 1998. Managing the post-merger aftermath by default remodelling. *Management Decision*, 36, 102–110, https://doi.org/10.1108/00251749810204188.

Moustakas, C. 1994. *Phenomenological Research Methods*, Thousand Oaks, CA: Sage.

Munhall, P. L. & Oiler, C. J. (eds.) 1986. *Nursing Research: a qualitative perspective*, Norwalk, CT: Appleton-Century-Crofts.

Painter-Morland, M. & Werhane, P. (eds.) 2008. *Cutting-edge Issues in Business Ethics: Continental Challenges to Tradition and Practice.* New York, NY; Dordrecht, NL: Springer.

Stewart, A. (1998). *The ethnographer's method.* Thousand Oaks, CA: Sage Publications, Inc.

Strauss, A. & Corbin, J. 1990. *Basics of Qualitative Research: Techniques and Procedures for Developing Grounded Theory*, Newbury Park, CA: Sage.

CHAPTER 9

# Discourse Analysis as a Method for Business Ethics and Corporate Responsibility Research

ANNA HEIKKINEN, JOHANNA KUJALA, MATIAS LAINE, and HANNELE MÄKELÄ

## Introduction

Discourse, in the broadest sense, means a particular way of understanding and talking about a phenomenon (Jørgensen and Phillips 2002). In general, discourse analysis is a part of the social constructionist tradition. Accordingly, it relies on the ideas that knowledge is socially constructed and that our understanding of certain phenomena has material consequences (Burr 1995; Crotty 1998). Despite the varying understandings of what a discourse is, they all hold in general the belief that our ways of seeing, understanding, and talking about the world are not neutral reflections but actively shape it (Spence 2007) by organizing the relationships among objects, subjects, and concepts (Caruana and Crane 2008; Oswick et al. 2000). By intertwining with social practices in various social contexts, the language and the visual create discourses, which construct meanings and understandings of reality and have effects on our actions in societies. The discourse analytic approach allows a recognition and examination of the diverse and often paradoxical interests and demands within an organization (Nyberg and Wright 2012).

This chapter will discuss discourse analysis as a method for studying business ethics and corporate responsibility. Discourse analysis is approached as a qualitative research method that focuses on language use in social interaction. Discourse analytic research typically uses various types of empirical material, such as written documents, spoken words, nonverbal interaction, pictures, and other visual material. The research process is characterized as a reflexive process of several iterative rounds of reading and analysis between data and theory. We maintain that, through its interest in exploring how certain realities, or ways of seeing, are excluded and others included, discourse analysis offers opportunities for studying human interaction, organizations, and organizing, as well as the social world more broadly. The broad variety of existing discursive approaches allows investigating the social and organizational life on several levels, and facilitates explorations of the social and political interests inherent in the use of language (Vaara 2010). Discourse studies often takes an openly critical stance and focuses on analyzing, problematizing, and opening up seemingly neutral and taken-for-granted understandings. Moreover, power and power relations are at the core of critically oriented discourse studies (Caruana and Crane 2008; Fairclough 1992; Foucault 1972; Phillips and Hardy 1997).

This chapter proceeds as follows. We begin with an overview of the discursive approach, a brief introduction to the history of discourse studies and to the variety of approaches that exist within this research tradition. Thereafter, we continue with a discussion of the research process and different forms of data in discourse studies and give insights and practical examples of studies using discourse analysis as a method in the scholarly field of corporate responsibility. The final section concludes and highlights the key points of the article.

## Theoretical Approaches to Discourse Analysis

### *The Multidisciplinary Field of Discourse Studies*

Discourse studies is a highly heterogeneous field with roots in several disciplines and fields of science in which the interest in the use of language and communication has been developing in parallel since the 1960s (see Jørgensen and Phillips 2002; Van Dijk 2011; Wood and Kroger 2000). Among these were, for instance, scholars in linguistics and sociolinguistics who began to emphasize the importance of analyzing how language is used in the talk and text of real-life social settings. The field of philosophy saw the development of pragmatics, in which the focus extended from syntax and semantics into speech acts and contextually based language use more broadly. In sociology, the interest turned toward interaction and the use of language in the construction of social order and of the particular social settings. Likewise, in communication studies, interest began to be directed toward how language is used – for instance, in political communication and mass media – how talk and text in these settings take part in the constitution of social reality, and how the use of language has effects on the recipients of the messages and society as a whole. These parallel developments, as well as those in other disciplines – such as anthropology, cognitive psychology, and social psychology – first evolved separately, but over time began increasingly to overlap and merge. Today, the broad camp of discourse studies includes a wide variety of disciplinary backgrounds and methodological approaches. Van Dijk (2011) argues that the cross-disciplinary discourse studies have an established position throughout humanities and social sciences. The popularity of discourse studies is also evident in the number of readers and handbooks devoted to it (e.g., Angermuller et al. 2014; Van Dijk 2011).

Over the recent decades, discourse studies has increased in popularity, and the field, thereby, has developed swiftly in various directions. As the cross-disciplinary field was developing, scholars attempted to categorize the different approaches and perspectives within the field (e.g., Jørgensen and Phillips 2002; Phillips and Hardy 2002; Van Dijk 1997; Wood and Kroger 2000). These listings and hierarchies tend to appear in somewhat different forms, depending, for instance, on how much emphasis the authors have placed on methodological approaches, theoretical premises, or disciplinary backgrounds. The classifications and categories provided are influenced by the field and literature within which the respective authors have positioned themselves and the contribution in question. For instance, in a recent reader on discourse studies, Angermuller and colleagues (2014, p. 3) describe discourse studies to be "emerging as a new and fully-fledged field" in which several streams of work come together. Here, they classify past work as originating in structuralism and post-structuralism, pragmatics, interactionism, socio-pragmatics, historical work, and critical approaches. The diverse origins of discourse studies also are shown as differences in the emphasis given in the various approaches. The roots naturally have not disappeared, but the continuous development of discourse studies has made the construction of such categorizations increasingly complicated.

Despite acknowledging the complexity of providing any clear categories, we maintain that a brief broad-brush overview of four main approaches to discourse studies is in order for the purposes of this chapter. First, the micro-sociological approaches, or those based on sociolinguistics, are interested in the use of language in small-scale interaction. The emphasis is on exploring the use of text and talk in social settings, including, for instance, meetings, conversations, and presentations (Phillips and Hardy 2002).

Second, it is worth identifying the so-called Foucauldian discourse studies, which are strongly influenced by the work of Michel Foucault. Foucault's ideas have been influential in the development of discursive approaches in general (Jørgensen and Phillips 2002), but there is a subset of discourse studies that focuses on how language constructs issues such as knowledge and subjectivities (Phillips and Oswick 2012). Moreover, power and its productive role in society were key elements of Foucault's work. For Foucault, "power does not belong to particular agents such as individuals or the state or groups with particular interests; rather, power is spread across different social practices" (Jørgensen and Phillips 2002, p. 13).

Power is also a key element in the third category we identify here: critical discourse analysis. Here, research can be characterized as being interested in how discourses and the use of language constitute and sustain unequal power relations in societies (Fairclough 1992). Although the approach is somewhat ambiguous and avoids clear boundaries, critical discourse analysis has become a popular approach in organization studies (Alvesson and Kärreman 2011a). It is nonetheless worth noting that even though critical discourse analysis often is presented as a single category, the concept is somewhat ambiguous, and there is a considerable variety within studies described as belonging under its umbrella (see Jørgensen and Phillips 2002; Wodak and Meyer 2015). A common feature of critical discourse analysis is its interest in exploring the social and political consequences of language use.

Fourth, and finally, it is worth noting the poststructuralist theoretical approaches to discourse, which often draw on the work of Ernesto Laclau and Chantal Mouffe (1985). Laclau and Mouffe's theory is based on the idea that discourse constructs the social world in meaning, but since language is fundamentally unstable, no meaning will be fixed permanently. Discourses also are transformed constantly as they are in contact with and influenced by other discourses; thus different discourses represent different ways of understanding the social world. These various discourses "are engaged in a constant struggle with one other to achieve hegemony, that is, to fix the meanings of language in their own way" (Jørgensen and Phillips 2002, p. 7). This discursive struggle and the pursuit of hegemony is the key element in work drawing on Laclau and Mouffe (1985) and other subsequent poststructuralist discourse theoretical work. Recently, these approaches have been developed further, as scholars have sought new avenues through which discursive explanations could better be complemented with analysis of the nondiscursive elements. Cedeström and Spicer (2014), for instance, draw on the work of Ernesto Laclau and Slavoj Zizek to present a postfoundational approach, which they put forward to tackle some of the shortcomings they perceive in other approaches to discourse studies (see Glynos and Howarth 2007).

## *Organizational Discourse Analysis*

Together with the general diffusion of interest in discourse and the development of discursive studies, the field of organizational discourse studies also has burgeoned over the last 15 years. As is the case with broader discussion, in the late 1990s and early 2000s, there were several attempts to classify the different streams and approaches to discourse used in organizational studies (Alvesson and Kärreman 2000; Putnam and Fairhurst 2001; Phillips and Hardy 2002). One categorization was presented by Phillips and Hardy (2002), who classified discursive works based on their relationship to context and criticality toward the status quo; they ended up with four categories labeled social linguistics analysis, interpretive structuralism, critical linguistic analysis, and critical discourse analysis. Moreover, in their overview of the developing research field, Phillips and Hardy (2002) provided eight discourse analytical traditions present in prior organizational discourse, including Bakhtinian research, conversation analysis, critical discourse analysis, critical linguistics, discursive psychology, ethnography of speaking, Foucauldian research, and interactional linguistics. These traditions appear to have been identified on the basis of both the methodological emphasis and theoretical approaches used.

At around the same time, Putnam and Fairhurst (2001), in their review of discursive work in organizational studies looked at the ways prior studies had approached language and had understood the idea of organization. On this basis, Putnam and Fairhurst (2001) divided discursive research on organizations into categories, which included, for instance, cognitive linguistics, conversation analysis, critical language studies, literary and rhetorical analysis, postmodern language analysis, pragmatics and discourse analysis, semiotics, and sociolinguistics. It is worth pointing out that classifications often differ from one another, as the categories cannot be seen to be particularly clear-cut, nor are the logics of categorizing identical (see also Alvesson and Kärreman 2000).

Over recent years, the field of organizational discourse studies has continued to develop, and new debates and theoretical considerations have emerged, adding further to the diversity of the field. There is now considerable variety in the theoretical approaches and emphasis used by scholars across the field, making it both complex and also somewhat redundant to try and present a clear-cut classification of the current trajectories. A similar conclusion was presented by Fairhurst and Putnam (2014), who, reflecting on their prior review (Putnam and Fairhurst 2001) of organizational discourse studies, note that, at that time in 2001, the "field of organizational discourse analysis was still in its infancy" (Fairhurst and Putnam 2014, p. 271). They also point out that updating this earlier classification would be difficult, as it would be hard "to appreciate the stunning complexity of organizational discourse studies today" (*ibid.* pp. 273–274), highlighting hybrid theorizing, crossovers, and coalescing approaches as reasons for the diversity.

### *Levels of Discourse*

The most commonly used categorization of discourse studies is based on the level on which the study focuses (see Alvesson and Kärreman 2000; Phillips and Oswick 2012; Potter and Wetherell 1987). For the purposes of this article, we will draw on the classification of Phillips and Oswick (2012) of the types and forms of organizational discourse analysis. Phillips and Oswick (2012) present two often-used classifications: a levels-based and a methods-based classification. While we acknowledge that Phillips and Oswick (2012) do not view the use of these categorizations as particularly useful, we consider them to be helpful for the methodologically oriented purposes of this chapter. We will nonetheless also return to the concerns voiced by Phillips and Oswick (2012).

The micro-oriented, or micro-discourse, approaches are focused on conducting a very detailed analysis of language use, often based on an analysis of a single text, a conversation, or a talk within a particular context. Alvesson and Kärreman (2011a) characterize this approach as being based on the assumption that the social world is created from the bottom up, as people construct the social world though linguistic interaction on the local level. Thereby, for the most part, the micro-discourse is focused on studying the use of talk and text in social practices and, subsequently, the constructive effects and the variety of consequences that language use has there.

At the other end of the spectrum are located the macro-level approaches, which focus on exploring the big picture, including an analysis of institutions, ideologies, and meta-narratives. A well-known distinction between the micro and macro approaches is presented by Alvesson and Kärreman (2000), who talk of Discourse (with a capital "D") as exploring macro-level and grandiose topics with interest on long-range and macro-systemic themes and of discourse (with a small "d") as having a close-range interest in a very local context. Whereas the micro-level discursive work often draws on fields and methods of linguistics, research focusing on the broader macro-level discourses often draws on social theory, philosophy, and history. Phillips and Oswick (2012) maintain that Foucauldian discourse analysis would be the most popular approach, focusing on the macro-level discourses. Alvesson and Kärreman (2011a), in revisiting and refining their earlier work (Alvesson and Kärreman 2000), propose that research on macro-discourses, or capital D Discourse, could be called paradigm-type discourse studies. Here, the focus is not on real-time interaction nor on the specific details of a single text, but instead, such research is concerned, for instance, with how texts and language create and construct both subjectivities and objectivities and how the ways of talking constitute some authorities, institutions, and other matters as natural and true (see Alvesson and Kärreman 2011a).

The micro and macro approaches can be seen to form the endpoints of a spectrum, within which some intermediate positions also have been identified. In writing about organizational discourse studies, Phillips and Oswick (2012) speak of the meso-discourse approach (see Alvesson and Kärreman 2000; Potter and Wetherell 1987), which they position on the organizational level. Unlike the micro-level, the meso-discourse approach is not concerned with the development and interpretation of real-time interaction, but usually pays more attention to accounts and narratives of events within an organizational setting, or alternatively on a sample of texts providing a basis for an analysis.

One of the key arguments in the critique voiced toward such a level-based approach is that it reinforces the representation that social life would take place on isolated levels. Indeed, Phillips and Oswick (2012) emphasize how the different levels are intertwined and mutually implicated, and they further argue that it is both difficult and somewhat meaningless to approach them separately. They point out how, for instance, any micro-level interaction – such as those taking place in a meeting or laid out in a presentation – are influenced, shaped, and constrained by the macro-level discourses. Likewise, the macro-level discourse can be argued to be shaped and, to an extent, constituted by the micro-discourse taking place in local settings. Attempts to disentangle the various levels of discourse and to treat them analytically in isolation is, in the view of Phillips and Oswick (2012), hence, highly complicated and of limited use.

As one of the solutions for this challenge, Phillips and Oswick (2012) promote multilevel discursive work, which would overcome the problems faced by a single-level discourse study. Phillips and Oswick (2012) maintain that the most typical approach taken to integrate multiple levels of discourse in a single study is critical discourse analysis, the roots of which are attributed to the work of Norman Fairclough and his colleagues (e.g., Fairclough 1992). According to Phillips et al. (2008), the approach was developed as a response to earlier approaches, which tended to focus either narrowly on micro-level linguistics or, alternatively, solely on the very macro-level social aspects. Fairclough (1992, 1995) attempted to combine the micro and the macro levels by treating language use as a form of social practice. Here, discourse and social structures interact, as the discursive practices shape the social structures, which simultaneously constrain and shape the discourse. Thus, the relationships between social interaction, discourse and social structures are complex and recursive (see Phillips et al. 2008). To provide an approach to analyze such dynamics, Fairclough combined different methodological traditions and emphasized the need to work on three levels of analysis: text, discourse, and social context. A key element of critical discourse analysis lies in its interest in power and its use within societies. Discourse is seen to have a crucial role in the forming, constituting, and maintaining of political order and domination of society (Van Dijk 2011). Drawing on Fairclough (1995), Phillips and Oswick (2012) discuss how undertaking a critical discourse analysis necessitates approaching three levels by examining the language in use, identifying and analyzing the processes through which the text or language is produced and subsequently consumed, and also considering the broader macro-level institutional and social factors that have or could have influenced and shaped the discourse. Here, together with taking a multilevel approach to discourse, the studies based on critical discourse analysis are characterized by the emphasis given to the discussion of power and power relations.

To summarize, it is evident that there is wide variety of theoretical approaches to choose from within the broad tent of discourse studies, and as such we maintain that there is no single approach that could be considered as outright superior for those seeking to explore topics within the fields of business ethics or corporate responsibility. As for ourselves, we have tended to be interested in conducting critical research, in which questions of power and societal relations have often been key elements, and have hence considered it worthwhile to engage with, for instance, the work of Fairclough (1992) as well as Laclau and Mouffe (1985). The key point here, however, is that the choice of the theoretical approach should not be seen as an isolated decision, but something that is inherently intertwined with the questions one seeks to pursue and the data one is about to work with. We will now discuss these in more detail.

## Conducting Discourse Analysis

Newcomers to the field of discourse analysis often find themselves confused in trying to understand the research process of such studies. In addition to the lack of a shared understanding of what a discourse is, there is also a wide variety of ways to conduct discourse analysis (Grant and Hardy 2004; Jørgensen and Phillips 2002; Spence 2007). However, certain characteristics are in place every time one becomes immersed in discourse analysis. Generally speaking, discourse analysis means "[working] intensively with an important and manageable sample" of empirical material (Milne et al. 2009).

In discourse analysis, theory and method are fundamentally intertwined (Jørgensen and Phillips 2002; Spence 2007). Therefore, before starting the analysis, one should have an understanding of one's position and take on discourses in the form of questions such as "What is the author's theoretical approach on discourse analysis?" "What is the level of analysis (micro vs. macro-analysis)?" and "What is the theoretical framework and its role in the analysis?" These questions have underlying (and explicit) ontological and epistemological roots and implications, and hence, they guide the whole process of conducting discourse analysis. Naturally, one also must have a tentative understanding of the empirical material to be used in the analysis – although that understanding may well change later on while the author's understanding of the phenomenon in question expands. Typically, the process of discourse analysis involves several iterative and reflexive steps that consist of defining the research question, selecting the relevant empirical material, making decisions on the role of the context, developing the tentative interpretive frames of analysis, analyzing the material, and reflecting on the process. All the questions involve both epistemological and ontological considerations and, thus, are interlinked with the theoretical position on discourse adopted by the researcher.

The process of discourse analysis is iterative and reflexive, ongoing, and undoubtedly, very work-intensive (Milne et al. 2009; Spence 2007). Adjustments to the research design, as well as to the interpretive frames, often take place. The researcher's understanding of the research topic, context, and theory alters and evolves along the hermeneutic research process (Spence 2007). The tentative descriptive narratives develop along the reflexive process of several iterative rounds of reading and analysis between data and theory, emphasizing the self-critique by the researcher (Buhr and Reiter 2006; Spence 2007). Writing (research notes/diary, research manuscript, article revisions, etc.) in itself is "an integral part of the process" (Ailon 2013, p. 6), as is often the case in qualitative research in general. Hence, discourse analysis demands time and preparation, allowing room for the (critical) interpretation to emerge.

Similar to the considerable diversity that exists in the theoretical foundations of discourse analysis, also in practical terms, scholars have very different views on what it entails to conduct discourse analysis. Milne and colleagues (2009, p. 1244), for instance, state that "there is no recipe for interpretation." Usually, the more interpretive and critical one's approach is, the more difficult it is to add labels and order to the research process, as it essentially builds upon the critical interpretation of the researcher. Thompson (1990) emphasizes that no matter how detailed and rigorous the method, discourse analysis always and essentially relies on the subjective interpretation by the individual researchers. However, in retrospect, in addition to emphasizing the role of the context within which the discourses are situated, Milne et al. (2009) provide a well-documented and detailed description of their own research process. In their analysis of corporate sustainability disclosures, they describe the three phases of analysis, as well as the vital role of the researcher in producing interpretations and constructing knowledge. They rely on Mauthner and Doucet (2003), place emphasis on articulating the values and beliefs of the researchers, and highlight "the need to reflect on one's ontological and epistemological assumptions underlying the data analysis methods" (Milne et al. 2009, p. 1224).

Within a qualitative research setting, the role of the researcher and his or her constructions of meaning and knowledge are never totally free from biases, as the researcher is a situated person "characterised by feelings, imagination, commitments and particular pre-structured understandings" (Alvesson and Deetz 2000, p. 136). Hence, the author should be capable of reflecting on how his or her position impacts the types of knowledge produced. For instance, Buhr and Reiter (2006) greatly emphasize the role of the researcher, or researchers, that is, by emphasizing the need of having more than one researcher and of being very open about the backgrounds and characteristics of the researchers. They point to the biases and lived experiences of the researcher as an interpreter of the data and analysis and state that "a deeper and richer interpretation of the text could be achieved" by engaging several researchers, who would then share and discuss their individual interpretations until they reached a mutual agreement on their understanding of the analysis (Buhr and Reiter 2006, p. 15). In this manner, they point to the "soundness of analysis (i.e., reliability) that should be replicable in a broad-based sort of way" (ibid. p. 15).

## The Research Process

A typical feature of the discourse analytic research process is that the research tradition does not present a detailed method and process of analysis (Livesey 2002). However, the process can be described as including several iterative rounds of reading and writing. Thus, the first step often includes informal first-round readings of the empirical material to get to know the data, the phenomenon, and the context and to establish an understanding of "the totality" of what you are dealing with, as well as setting up a database of all your relevant data. You then may proceed by breaking down the data and coding it. For instance, Ailon (2013, p. 6) describes the example of a process of Foucauldian discourse analysis with three steps. Preliminary coding includes listing the themes and topics that emerge from the data. In a similar manner, Livesey (2002, p. 321) first codes all the data by "identifying and categorizing salient themes, metaphors, modes of expression, and argument structures" while paying "particular attention to nonconforming instances, variations, and changes over time." This iterative process occurs throughout and after the data collection. Coding of the data is an important part of the process, and it is even more helpful if done with more detail. Coding basically means categorizing the data, giving it "tags" according to the themes and meanings that the researcher sees as useful. This often involves some technical tools, such as Microsoft Excel or dedicated research tools such as NVivo, that have built-in coding functions. Of course, before coding, all data should be transformed into written form (see Hardy and Phillips 1999, for the use of visual data). However, discourse analysis is not only about text as such, but is also about "the bigger picture," about the rules, practices and institutions that constitute certain discourse (Mills 1997, as quoted in Prasad and Elmes 2005, p. 852).

The second step of the research process (Ailon 2013) involves a more detailed analysis of the ways of seeing the phenomena in question, including, for instance, making notes of the different ways of characterizing and describing it, of the rhetorical strategies used (such as metaphors or references to authorities), of the arguments and counterarguments, as well as of the "discursive resources that indicate particular ways of constructing [the topic]" (Livesey 2002, p. 321). In addition to analyzing what is said in the data, one should often also consider the silences in the text, the things that are left unsaid or marginalized (Laine 2009; Mäkelä 2013; Tregidga et al. 2013). In this way, preliminary interpretive frames, emerging discourses, or discursive practices can be constructed about the phenomenon in question.

The third step of the process consists of repeatedly re-evaluating the constructed frames of discourses by going back and forth to the data, allowing the researcher to recheck and elaborate the interpretations (Ailon 2013, p. 6). When conducting critical discourse analysis, in particular, this phase essentially includes intertextuality and consideration of the relationships between the micro-analysis of the empirical material and macro-analysis of the larger social context, power relations, and ideology (Brei and Böhm 2014; Fairclough 1995, 2003; Luke 2002; Vaara et al. 2006).

Finally, as the thinking process in discourse analysis is difficult to capture, one should aim at adhering to high research ethics in all the steps of the process, as well as at being as clear and well documented as possible (Milne et al. 2009; Tregidga et al. 2013). Documenting the research process greatly increases the possibilities of evaluating the quality of the research, as well as allows for an articulated reflection of the researcher's role. This includes, for instance, being precise about the empirical material: what does it consist of (e.g., how many and what type of articles and/or interviews), when and how was the data collected, and how was the data stored (see e.g., Ailon 2013; Brei and Böhm 2014). Documenting one's own thoughts along the reflexive research process is also essential;

this allows one to iterate and think back, re-evaluate original ideas, and develop them further.

## Different Types of Data

One of the practical questions in doing discourse analysis relates to data collection and management, that is, which texts should be used as data (Putnam and Fairhurst 2001). In discourse analysis, "text" is typically understood in a broad sense; the texts that embody discourse come in a wide variety of forms, for instance, written documents, spoken words, nonverbal interactions, pictures, symbols, and artifacts (Grant et al. 1998; Phillips and Hardy 2002). The relationship between text and discourse is multifold. On the one hand, texts represent a material manifestation of discourse, while on the other hand, discourse has an existence beyond any individual text from which it is composed (Chalaby 1996; Phillips et al. 2004). In practice, this means that discourse can be studied only by analyzing text, but a single text is unlikely to contain discourses in their entirety. Rather, various texts and bodies of text are analyzed to find clues about the nature of the discourse and the relations between texts, their production, and discourses (Phillips and Hardy 2002).

Method books on qualitative research and discourse analysis have presented various categorizations of data, including a classification into "naturally occurring" and "researcher-instigated material" (e.g., Phillips and Hardy 2002; Silverman 2001) as well as into "primary" and "secondary" materials (e.g., Eriksson and Kovalainen 2008). Naturally occurring data refers to texts that are constructed in the normal everyday activities of the research subject; they come into being "naturally" without the researcher's actions or intentions influencing their production (Eriksson and Kovalainen 2008; Joutsenvirta 2009). These kinds of texts include corporate reports, media texts, blog posts, diary entries, as well as other public and private texts. Typically, naturally occurring data is considered a particularly valid choice of data for conducting discourse analysis because it allows access to the actual examples of social interaction and language in use (Phillips and Hardy 2002). In the spirit of social constructionism; however, the notion of "natural" – something coming into being without human influence – is contestable. Rather, subjects and objects are seen as constructed and produced in social interaction; thus, all data and material is a result of such interaction (see Hacking 1999).

In comparison to naturally occurring data, researcher-instigated data appears as a result of the researcher interacting with the research subjects, typically by observing or interviewing them. The utilization of researcher-instigated data is somewhat contested in discourse analytic studies, as discussed by Phillips and Hardy (2002 p. 72):

> Although the talk of respondents in research interviews will bear some relation to the talk that they use to construct the organization, it is difficult to say exactly how much, and certainly the researchers' interests will have some bearing on the talk, regardless of how open-ended the interview is. As a result, some researchers eschew the use of interviews as data in discourse analytic studies. In contrast, we believe that interviews play a useful role in discourse analysis. At the very least, they are important for understanding the social context of the primary texts.

The categorization into primary and secondary data follows a similar logic of classification; the texts are categorized in terms of their production, that is, whether or not their production has been induced of influenced by the researcher(s). Primary data refers to material that has been generated by the researchers, while secondary data consists of material that exists irrespective of the research (Eriksson and Kovalainen 2008). In practice, a clear advantage of naturally occurring, or secondary, data is that it is already in transcribed format for the researcher to collect. This, however, requires the task of defining which texts to collect and acquiring access to the print or electronic databases or archives. Generating researcher-instigated data may be a more laborious process, including gaining access, making notes and audio recordings, and finally, transcribing the recordings.

Categorizations such as those presented above construct these types of data as remarkably different from one another, perhaps even implying that one type would be more adequate than the other because of the connotations of the terms "natural" and "primary." To add to this confusing terminology, discourse analytic studies also may use the terms primary and secondary to differentiate between data utilized as the primary source of findings and secondary material that provide the situational and historical context for the phenomenon under study (e.g., Joutsenvirta 2009). In the end, researchers should bear in mind that the empirical dataset is always a result of the researcher's activities and research aims. For example, researchers collecting media texts for the data make choices regarding the data sources and which articles, or parts of them, they include. Therefore, while these classifications may provide general guidelines regarding what kind of material to use, it is more important that researchers are aware of and reflect on the choices they make regarding the generation and use of the different types of empirical material. The following section will describe the use of different types of data in research by discussing business ethics studies to illustrate the use and advantages and disadvantages of different types of texts.

## *Media Texts, Websites, and Reports*

Media outlets – such as journals, newspapers, and other online and offline forums – produce a wide variety of texts, offering a resource-efficient access to rhetorically rich material (Joutsenvirta 2009). Another distinct advantage of media data is that media is one of the central arenas in society that construct and circulate discourses. Ailon (2013 p. 80) has presented media as "the main arena of 'discourse in action'" but notes, however, that it is still scarcely researched. This seems like a great shortcoming, as the media is not only a prime discursive engine in contemporary times but also a prime vehicle through which to observe and scrutinize the underlying grammar of the discursive moral dynamic (Ailon 2011, 2013). After all, the media does not simply or directly report events; media reports construct the meaning of events through patterned and historically contingent moral and ethical frameworks of meaning. They, therefore, provide an opportunity to study these frameworks in motion and to scrutinize the active constitution, negotiation, and articulation of moral "truths" and common sense.

This underlying dynamic of text production and framing for various audiences makes media a particularly interesting data source that requires the researcher to attune to the nuances of text and its intended audiences (Gamson and Modigliani 1989; Macdonald 2003; Walton 2007). Insightful findings can be reached with different kinds of media datasets as well as by combining media data to other texts. For instance, Lehtimäki and Kujala (2015) used media texts combined with company press releases as data. They follow the Foucauldian approach and use frame analysis as a tool to examine firm-stakeholder relations. The study concentrates on analyzing how stakeholder relationships are constructed through language and the ways language is used in different texts both to shape and reflect the dynamically changing nature of stakeholder relationships. The study shows that stakeholder relationships involve many meanings that are only partially shared by different actors, which is, at least to some extent, due to the fact that business seldom understands the role of language in managing stakeholder relationships (Lehtimäki and Kujala 2015). With the discursive approach, they are able to show that stakeholder relationships are constructed through language and that research on meaning making contributes to the understanding of the dynamics of stakeholder relationships.

Media data is often used in combination with other types of data to reveal contrasts and differing views. For instance, Joutsenvirta (2009, 2011) analyzed environmental writings by a forest company and by Greenpeace to examine how they debate over the use of forests. First, she used longitudinal discourse analysis and discursive-semiotic reading of the data and identified four main discourses: knowledge, responsibility, openness, and market (Joutsenvirta 2009). Later, she continued with critical discourse analysis and rhetoric analysis that resulted to recognizing five legitimation strategies: scientific, nationalistic, and commercial rationalization, as well as moralization and normalization (Joutsenvirta 2011). Using discourse analysis and placing attention to language allows for understanding how certain ways of talking hinder or facilitate efforts to create more balanced relationship among business, nature and society (Joutsenvirta 2009).

Herzig and Moon (2013) used the discursive approach to study how the financial and ethical media constructed corporate social responsibility and irresponsibility during the financial crisis. They identified four discourses, namely, market rationalization, moralization and ethical leadership, reconceptualization and professionalization, and political economy restructuring (*ibid.*). As a common feature to all these discourses, Herzig and Moon (2013) identify accountability, capacity, and reliability issues regarding corporate social responsibility. The discourses also share the view of the necessity for change but differ in their view of the nature and extent of the change required to guarantee a more accountable financial sector. Herzig and Moon (2013) concluded that with discourse analysis, they were able to identify different understandings of the reasons and prescriptions for the financial crisis.

Media texts also can be used to analyze representations of current phenomena. Lämsä and Tiensuu (2002), for instance, have examined representations of women leaders in Finnish business media articles with a dataset of fifty-one articles. The analysis followed a discourse analytic approach drawing on poststructuralism and language studies (Calas and Smircich 1999; Fairclough 1995; Gill 1993), with an emphasis on the functional and action-oriented nature of discourse (Potter and Wetherell 1987). Likewise, Ailon (2013) has analyzed the ethical discourse on managerial figures involved in corporate scandals by focusing on eighty-seven articles published in *BusinessWeek* and *Forbes*. The data was analyzed using a classificatory analysis that followed an inductive logic and utilized emergent coding. In addition to discussing the production, use, and change of the representations, these studies have highlighted the role of media in constructing and maintaining discourses that may even sustain the marginalizing of certain phenomena (Ailon 2013; Lämsä and Tiensuu 2002).

Media provides a rich source of other types of material as well, such as advertisements and advertorials. These texts and images convey, create, and reproduce images and constructions about what is good or bad, desirable or detestable. Livesey (2002) has analyzed advertorials on climate change published by ExxonMobil in *The New York Times* in 2000 to study the company's public discourse on climate change. Focusing on corporate communications, she has conducted a discourse analysis and a rhetorical analysis of the data, and in the article she compares the two approaches. Livesey (2002) concluded that these approaches offer researchers ways to examine how corporate public discourse maintains organizational legitimacy, further influencing social and institutional stability and change.

In addition to media data, corporate disclosures in the form of annual reports, CSR disclosures, and press releases offer an ample source of data, which scholars in business ethics and social accounting have made use of from a variety of discursive perspectives. The overall concern within these fields of study is how the understanding and knowledge of business ethics, corporate sustainability, and corporate social responsibilities are socially constructed, being strongly influenced by corporate talk in all forms, including accounting reports. Accounting scholars, for instance, have been interested in analyzing the varying discourses of sustainable development in corporate disclosure and financial and sustainability reports (e.g., Buhr and Reiter 2006; Laine 2005, 2010; Milne et al. 2009; Tregidga and Milne 2006). One such example is presented by Tregidga and colleagues (2014), who draw on Laclau and Mouffe's (1985) discourse theory to investigate how corporations have represented themselves in relation to sustainable development over the years and how they have managed to transform their identities and, thereby, maintain a right to speak within the debate over sustainable development. Likewise, corporate talk on corporate social responsibilities in general also has been studied with various discourse analytic approaches (Boyce 2009; Mäkelä 2013; Mäkelä and Laine 2011; Spence 2009), with datasets consisting of both reporting data as well as interviews with business managers. In regard to corporate responsibility, Siltaoja and Onkila (2013) draw on Fairclough (2003) and employ a critical discourse analysis to investigate the construction of discursive strategies in Finnish corporate responsibility reports. The rationale of examining corporate disclosures is well highlighted in their conclusion, in which they state that the "discursive processes have implications for how we come to understand not only the responsibilities of businesses but also the limits and terms of taking such responsibilities" (*ibid.* p. 369).

Websites of businesses and other institutions increasingly are acknowledged as sites of politics and controversy, and thus, a source of textual and visual material of interest for business- and society-oriented researchers (Brei and Böhm 2014; Caruana and Crane 2008; Gustavsson and Czarniawska 2004, p. 666). Websites contain a wide variety of public and private, formal and informal material offering researchers numerous possibilities for data generation. For example, Romani and Szkudlarek (2014) have studied how the professional community develops an ethical identity and codes of ethics using an extensive dataset, including observations, discussions from online forums, as well as various other documents – such as training material, newsletters, publications, and academic research – to situate the discourses in a broader historical and ideological perspective. The findings of the study show how a preexisting form of ethical identity can influence the early stage of the development of a code of ethics. In addition, the findings suggest that ethical identity construction may be subjected to the same mechanisms as organizational identity construction.

### Personal Interviews and Observations

As discussed above, researcher-instigated or primary data forms another group of datatypes for discursive scholars to explore. Personal interviews are a typical data-generation method in discourse analytic studies, as they provide the researcher with direct access to the specific informants and information on which the research focuses, assuming that issues regarding access have been resolved. Likewise, group discussions and focus groups can provide rich data, although these approaches seem to be less common than personal, one-on-one interviews. When planning for personal interviews and group discussions, the researcher is required to reflect on the interaction situation where the discussion is about to take place, as it is probably going to influence the type of material generated. Typically, personal interviews provide more personal accounts, whereas groups tend to discuss topics and issues that are common and shared by the members, while focusing less on personal emotions (Alasuutari 1995). Thus, group discussions provide material that can be utilized in analyzing group norms and dynamics, such as how the group negotiates and builds consensus, or in explicating how norms are constructed and followed by the members.

Walton (2007) has used interviews in combination with media texts in her study concerning a decision to site a mining operation in a conservation area in New Zealand and the dispute that ensued the decision. The media articles were used to select the first interviewees, while snowball sampling was used later to find more interviewees to gain access to insider views of the case. Altogether, twenty-seven interviews were conducted with key actors and community leaders. The interviews were designed as semistructured conversations in which the researcher sought to hear the participants' stories about the dispute. This research approach allowed the researcher to discuss the discursive strategies used by the participants and how dichotomies were used, such as jobs versus the environment as well as whether the environment should be managed or locked up (Walton 2007).

Another illustrative example is the study by de Graaf (2001), who discussed the relationship between discourse theory and business ethics by analyzing how bankers in Holland conceptualize their customers. The research data of ten interviews with local bank managers and documents published by the banks was analyzed with Q-methodology, which includes both qualitative and quantitative elements (Dryzek 1990; Stephenson 1953). According to the author, Q-methodology is used to "reconstruct the discourses, in their own words" (de Graaf 2001, p. 303). The findings present five discourses on customers within the banks and show how different customer understandings can coexist in the same industry, how we view and value things through discourses, and how the specific discourse a manager is in may have various consequences to banks, to their management, and to their customers (cf. de Graaf 2006).

Data generation through observation has roots in ethnography where the researcher traditionally has been immersed for months and years in a foreign culture. In business research, observation periods may vary from specific instances (e.g., meetings) to longer periods of time, a general feature, however, being that such an approach altogether requires quite a lot of time and effort. One of the key challenges is requiring access to the research site and the particular interaction situations in which the researcher is interested. Typically, the researcher may engage in participant observation (see e.g., Heikkinen 2014) or assume the role of a member of the organization. For example, in a study by Fyke and Buzzanell (2013) focusing on leadership ethics and conscious capitalism, one of the authors engaged in a field study for two months in an organization taking the role of an intern or a job shadower. This allowed a particularly wide access to the organization, and as a result, the study is based on a vast dataset, including sixteen interviews with the members of the organization and thirteen with its clients, over 500 pages of various documents, 100 hours of participant observation with field notes, and 120 pages of autoethnographic journaling. The data analysis has combined two methods: first, a constructivist grounded theory approach (Charmaz 2006) was conducted, resulting in identifying the key themes related to the case organizations' work; and second, a critical discourse analysis approach (Chouliaraki and Fairclough 2010) was taken to reflect further on the themes and to analyze specifically the issues of power, hegemony, and power relations. The authors note that the combination of these two methods allowed them to examine both surface-level and deeper meanings (Fyke and Buzzanell 2013).

In using data gathered through interviews, observations, or group discussions, the research needs to be particularly attentive to the role of the multiple layers of context. As noted above, context has an important role in discursive studies, as the results of the analysis always are presented and interpreted in relation to the study context. However, it is worth noting that the relevance of context differs from study to study and also is related to the type of data used. When using interviews or other such datasets and focus groups, researchers can gain first-hand access to the particular phenomenon in which they are interested. Here, however, it is paramount to pay particular attention to the interaction context, which refers to those characteristics of interaction that enable the interpretation of the themes, arguments, and other constructs used in talk (Heikkinen 2014; Siltaoja 2009). This includes considering the role of the researcher in the interaction, as well as considering the setting and other people present in the situation. Among other factors, these determine preconditions for the interaction that researchers should consider when planning the data generation as well as during it. Obviously, the interaction context can influence the contents of the data collected through interviews and group discussion. Thus, while this kind of material is unique in its ability to carry situated meanings and close-range interaction between two or more people and enables researchers to explicate how meanings become constructed and maintained in social interaction and in local settings, researchers should always reflect such material within its immediate interaction context when interpreting and analyzing it.

Likewise, the relevance of the cultural context is worth underscoring. Considering the importance of cultural context means paying attention to the issues often taken for granted in the culture in which the interaction takes place (Heikkinen 2014; Siltaoja 2009). When researchers belongs to the same culture from which the data is generated, they are better inclined to understand the cultural nuances than those approaching a new culture in their research. An outsider, however, may have the benefit of spotting those exact things that the researcher is no longer able to question. Thus, the cultural context and the researcher's role should be reflected prior to and during the study (Alasuutari 1995).

To summarize, the studies discussed here offer examples of what interviews and observations can contain and how these can be analyzed to examine business ethics and related phenomena. The micro/local-setting focus of the interview and observations data means that, as such, it offers only a limited insight into more general-level discourses, while it exemplifies how the societal-level discourses are constructed and reconstructed at the local level. However, as the studies presented in this chapter illustrate, it is characteristic of discourse analytic studies to combine different types of data. To conclude, the question of what kind of data to be used is crucial to consider in accordance with determining whether the study takes a micro or a macro approach, which in turn is related to the possible analysis methods for the study.

## Conclusions

The discursive approach is being used increasingly in the fields of business ethics and corporate responsibility. The broad variety of existing methods and approaches allows for examining various phenomena on several levels while facilitating the exploration of the social and political interests inherent in the use of language and of the interactions of language, social life, and social phenomena. The discursive approach maintains that by intertwining with social practices in social context, language and the visual create discourses that construct meanings and understandings of reality and impact our actions in societies. In discourse analysis, theory and method are fundamentally intertwined (Jørgensen and Phillips 2002; Spence 2007). Discourse analytic studies have multidisciplinary roots, and various traditions have been popularized within organization studies and, likewise, also in business ethics and corporate responsibility research. Thus, our discussion on conducting discourse analysis has highlighted a variety of methodological approaches.

Recently, several debates have taken place in the literature on some specific aspects of discourse studies as well as on the relationship the discursive approach has with other elements of the social world. Alvesson and Kärreman (2011a), for instance, discuss the spread of discourse in organizational studies over a ten-year span and ask whether discursive approaches have become too dominating and colonializing in the organizational studies literature. The provocation did not go unnoticed and was followed by several critiques and rejoinders (e.g., Alvesson and Kärreman 2013; Bargiela-Chiappini 2011; Hardy and Grant 2012; Iedema 2011; Mumby 2011). A detailed discussion of this debate is beyond the scope of this text, but it is nonetheless worth noting that, in their ultimate rejoinder to the debate, Alvesson and Kärreman (2013, see also 2011a) maintain that their original concerns, namely those of reductionism, overpacking and colonization, went to an extent unnoticed. To overcome these challenges, Alvesson and Kärreman (2013) argue that scholars should counter-balance concepts and avoid seeing everything as discourse, discuss the constitutive effects of discourses more openly, and be more specified in the use of concepts and discourse vocabulary. We acknowledge this discussion and maintain that it is worthwhile to consider many of the points taken up in the debate. These points, as well as a recent interest in discussions, highlight that researchers need be attentive to the relationship between discourse and materiality (e.g., Alvesson and Kärreman 2011b; Hardy and Thomas 2015; Orlikowski and Scott 2015; Phillips and Oswick 2012; Putnam 2015).

Overall, this chapter aimed to shed light on the research process in discursive studies and on the use of different datasets. For this purpose, we have also provided some exemplary studies using various types of methods to examine relevant phenomena in the field. All this was done for the purpose of offering practical insights for researchers beginning to use, or already using, the discursive approach in their empirical research. We hope the chapter will serve this purpose well.

### References

Ailon, G. (2011). Mapping the cultural grammar of reflexivity: The case of the Enron scandal. *Economy and Society*, *40*(1), 141–166.

(2013). From superstars to devils: The ethical discourse on managerial figures involved in a corporate scandal. *Organization*, *22*(1), 78–99.

Alasuutari, P. (1995). *Researching Culture: Qualitative Method and Cultural Studies*. London: Sage.

Alvesson, M. & Deetz, S. (2000). *Doing Critical Management Research*. London: Sage.

Alvesson, M. & Kärreman, D. (2000). Varieties of discourse: On the study of organizations through

discourse analysis. *Human Relations*, *53*(9), 1125–1149.
(2011a). Decolonializing discourse: Critical reflections on organizational discourse analysis. *Human Relations*, *64*(9), 1121–1146.
(2011b). Organizational discourse analysis – well done or too rare? A reply to our critics. *Human Relations*, *64*(9), 1193–1202.
(2013). The closing of critique, pluralism and reflexivity: A response to Hardy and Grant and some wider reflections. *Human Relations*, *66*(10), 1353–1371.

Angermuller, J., Maingueneau, D. & Wodak, R. (2014). *The Discourse Studies Reader: Main Currents in Theory and Analysis*. Amsterdam: John Benjamin's publishing company.

Bargiela-Chiappini, F. (2011), Discourse(s), social construction and language practices: In conversation with Alvesson and Kärreman. *Human Relations*, *64*(9), 1177–1191.

Boyce, G. (2009). *Critical, Social and Environmental Accounting: Prospects and Possibilities for Gramscian Intellectual Praxis in a Globalising World*. Doctoral thesis, Macquarie University.

Brei, V., & Böhm, S. (2014). "1L= 10L for Africa": Corporate social responsibility and the transformation of bottled water into a "consumer activist" commodity. *Discourse & Society*, *25*(1), 3–31.

Buhr, N. & Reiter, S. (2006). Ideology, the environment and one worldview: A discourse analysis of Noranda's environmental and sustainable development reports. *Advances in Environmental Accounting and Management*, *3*, 1–48.

Burr, V. (1995). *An Introduction to Social Constructionism*. London: Routledge.

Calas, M. B., & Smircich, L. (1999). Past postmodernism? Reflections and tentative directions. *Academy of Management Review*, *24*(4), 649–672.

Caruana, R., & Crane, A. (2008). Constructing consumer responsibility: Exploring the role of corporate communications. *Organization Studies*, *29*(12), 1495–1519.

Cedeström, C. & Spicer, A. (2014). Discourse of the real kind: A post-foundational approach to organizational discourse analysis. *Organization*, *21*(2), 178–205.

Chalaby, J. K. (1996). Beyond the prison-house of language: Discourse as a sociological concept. *British Journal of Sociology*, *47*, 684–698.

Charmaz K. (2006). *Constructing Grounded Theory: A Practical Guide through Qualitative Analysis*. London: Sage.

Chouliaraki L. & Fairclough N. (2010). Critical discourse analysis in organization studies: Towards an integrationist methodology. *Journal of Management Studies*, *47*(6), 1213–1218.

Crotty, M. (1998). *The Foundations of Social Research: Meaning and Perspective in the Research Process*. London: Sage.

de Graaf, G. (2001). Discourse theory and business ethics: The case of bankers' conceptualizations of customers. *Journal of Business Ethics*, *31*, 299–319.
(2006). Discourse and descriptive business ethics. *Business Ethics: A European Review*, *15*(3), 246–258.

Dryzek, J. S. (1990). *Discursive Democracy: Politics, Policy and Political Science*. Cambridge: Cambridge University Press.

Eriksson, P. & Kovalainen, A. (2008). *Qualitative Methods in Business Research*. London: Sage Publications Ltd.

Fairclough, N. (1992). *Discourse and Social Change*. Cambridge: Polity Press.
(1995). *Critical Discourse Analysis: The Critical Study of Language*. London: Longman.
(2003). *Analyzing Discourse: Textual Analysis for Social Research*. London: Routledge.

Fairhurst, G. T. & Putnam, L. L (2014). Organizational discourse analysis. In L. L. Putnam & D. K. Mumby (Eds.), *The Sage Handbook of Organizational Communication: Advances in Theory, Research and Methods* (3rd ed.) (271–296). London: Sage

Foucault, M. (1972). *The Archaeology of Knowledge*. New York: Harper and Row.

Fyke, J. P., & Buzzanell, P. M. (2013). The ethics of conscious capitalism: Wicked problems in leading change and changing leaders. *Human Relations*, *66*(12), 1619–1643.

Gamson, W. A., & Modigliani, A. (1989). Media discourse and public opinion on nuclear power: A constructionist approach. *American Journal of Sociology*, 1–37.

Gill, R. (1993). Ideology, gender and popular radio: A discourse analytic approach. *Innovation: The European Journal of Social Sciences*, *6*(3), 323–349.

Glynos, J. & Howarth, D. (2007). *Logics of Critical Explanation in Social and Political Theory*. New York: Routledge.

Grant, D. & Hardy, C. (2004). Introduction: Struggles with organizational discourse. *Organization Studies*, 25(1), 5–13

Grant, D., Keenoy, T., & Oswick, C. (Eds). (1998). *Discourse and Organization*. London: Sage.

Gustavsson, E., & Czarniawska, B. (2004). Web Woman: The on-line construction of corporate and gender images. *Organization, 11*(5), 651–670.

Hacking, I. (1999). *The Social Construction of What?*. Cambridge, MA: Harvard University Press.

Hardy, C. & Phillips, N. (1999). No joking matter: Discursive struggle in the Canadian refugee system. *Organization Studies, 20*(1), 1–24.

Hardy, C. & Thomas, R. (2015). Discourse in a material world. *Journal of Management Studies, 52*(5), 680–696.

Hardy, C. & Grant, D. (2012). Readers beware: Provocation, problematization and . . . problems. *Human Relations, 65*(5), 547–566.

Heikkinen, A. (2014). *Discursive Constructions of Climate Change Engagement in Business Organisations*. Tampere: Tampere University Press.

Herzig, C. & Moon, J. (2013). Discourses on corporate social ir/responsibility in the financial sector. *Journal of Business Research, 66*, 1870–1880.

Iedema, R. (2011). Discourse studies in the twenty-first century: A response to Mats Alvesson and Dan Kärreman's "Decolonializing discourse." *Human Relations, 64*(9), 1163–1176.

Jørgensen, M. & Phillips, L. (2002). *Discourse Analysis as Theory and Method*. London: Sage.

Joutsenvirta, M. (2009). A language perspective to environmental management and corporate responsibility. *Business Strategy and the Environment, 18*, 240–253.

(2011). Setting boundaries for corporate social responsibility: Firm–NGO relationship as discursive legitimation struggle. *Journal of Business Ethics, 102*(1), 57–75.

Laclau, E. & Mouffe, C. (1985). *Hegemony and Socialist Strategy: Towards a Radical Democratic Politics*. London: Verso.

Laine, M. (2005). Meanings of the term "sustainable development" in Finnish corporate disclosures. *Accounting Forum, 29*, 395–413.

(2009). Ensuring legitimacy through rhetorical changes? A longitudinal interpretation of the environmental disclosures of a leading Finnish chemical company. *Accounting, Auditing and Accountability Journal, 22*(7), 1029–1054.

(2010). Towards sustaining status quo: Business talk of sustainability in Finnish corporate disclosures 1987–2005. *European Accounting Review, 19*(2), 247–274.

Lämsä, A-M. & Tiensuu, T. (2002). Representations of the woman leader in Finnish business media articles. *Business Ethics: A European Review, 11*(4), 363–374.

Lehtimäki, H. & Kujala, J. (2015). Framing dynamically changing firm–stakeholder relationships in an international dispute over a foreign investment: A discursive analysis approach. *Business & Society*, doi: 0007650315570611.

Livesey, S. M. (2002). Global warming wars: rhetorical and discourse analytic approaches to Exxonmobil's corporate public discourse. *Journal of Business Communication, 39*(1), 117–148.

Luke A. (2002). Beyond science and ideology critique: Developments in critical discourse analysis. *Annual Review of Applied Linguistics*, 22, 96–110.

Macdonald, M. (2003). *Exploring Media Discourse*. London: Oxford University Press.

Mäkelä H. (2013). On the ideological role of employee reporting. *Critical Perspectives on Accounting*. *24*(4–5), 360–378.

Mäkelä, H. & Laine, M. (2011). A CEO with many messages: Comparing the ideological representations provided by different corporate reports. *Accounting Forum, 31*(4), 217–231.

Mauthner, N. S., & Doucet, A. (2003). Reflexive accounts and accounts of reflexivity in qualitative data analysis. *Sociology, 37*(3), 413–431.

Milne, M., Tregidga, H. and Walton, S. (2009). Words not action! The ideological role of sustainable development reporting. *Accounting, Auditing and Accountability Journal, 22*(8), 1211–1257.

Mumby, D. K. (2011). What's cooking in organizational discourse studies? A response to Alvesson and Kärreman. *Human Relations 64*(9), 1147–1161.

Nyberg, D. & Wright, C. (2012). Justifying business responses to climate change: discursive strategies of similarity and difference. *Environment and Planning A, 44*, 1819–1835.

Orlikowski, W. J. & Scott, S. V. (2015). Exploring material-discursive practices. *Journal of Management Studies, 52*(5), 697–705.

Oswick, C., Keenoy, T. W. & Grant, D. (2000). Discourse, organizations and organizing: concepts, objects and subjects. *Human Relations*, 53 (9), 1115–1123.

Phillips N. & Hardy C. (1997). Managing multiple identities: Discourse, legitimacy and resources in the UK refugee system. *Organization*, *4*, 159–185.

(2002). *Discourse Analysis: Investigating Processes of Social Construction*. London: Sage.

Phillips, N. & Oswick, C. (2012). Organizational discourse: Domains, debates, and directions. *The Academy of Management Annals*, *6*(1), 435–481.

Phillips, N., Lawrence, T. B. & Hardy, C. (2004). Discourse and institutions. *Academy of Management Review*, *29*(4), 635–652.

Phillips, N., Sewell, G. & Jaynes, S. (2008). Applying critical discourse analysis in strategic management research. *Organizational Research Methods*, *11*(4), 770–378.

Potter, J. & Wetherell, M. (1987). *Discourse and Social Psychology: Beyond Attitudes and Behaviour*. Sage, London.

Prasad, P. & Elmes, M. (2005). In the name of the practical: Unearthing the hegemony of pragmatics in the discourse of environmental management. *Journal of Management Studies*, *42*(4), 845–867.

Putnam, L. & Fairhurst, G. (2001). Discourse analysis in organizations: Issues and concerns. In F. Jablin & L. Putnam (Eds.), *The New Handbook of Organizational Communication* (78–136). Thousand Oaks, CA: Sage.

Putnam, L. L. (2015). Unpacking the dialectic: Alternative views on the discourse–materiality relationship. *Journal of Management Studies*, *52*(5), 706–716.

Romani, L. & Szkudlarek, B. (2014). The struggles of the interculturalists: Professional ethical identity and early stages of codes of ethics development. *Journal of Business Ethics*, *119*(2), 173–191.

Siltaoja, M. (2009). On the discursive construction of a socially responsible organization. *Scandinavian Journal of Management*, *25*, 191–202.

Siltaoja, M. E. & Onkila, T. J. (2013). Business in society: the construction of business-society relations in responsibility reports from a critical discursive perspective. *Business Ethics: A European Review*, *22*(4), 357–373.

Silverman, D. (2001). *Interpreting Qualitative Data: Methods for Analysing Talk, Text and Interaction*. London: Sage.

Spence, C. (2007). Social and environmental reporting and hegemonic discourse. *Accounting, Auditing and Accountability Journal*, *20*(6), 855–882.

(2009). Social accounting's emancipatory potential. *Critical Perspectives on Accounting*, *20*(2), 205–227.

Stephenson, W. (1953). *The Study of Behaviour: Q-technique and Its Methodology*. Chicago: University of Chicago Press.

Thompson, J. B. (1990). *Ideology and Modern Culture*. Stanford, CA: Stanford University Press.

Tregidga, H. & Milne, M. J. (2006). From sustainable management to sustainable development: A longitudinal analysis of a leading New Zealand environmental reporter. *Business Strategy and the Environment*, *15*, 219–241.

Tregidga, H., Kearins, K. & Milne, M. (2013). The politics of knowing "organizational sustainable development." *Organization & Environment*, *26* (1), 102–129.

Tregidga, H., Milne, M. & Kearins, K. (2014). (Re) presenting "sustainable organizations." *Accounting, Organizations and Society*, *39*(6), 477–494.

Vaara, E. (2010). Taking the linguistic turn seriously: Strategy as a multifaceted and interdiscursive phenomenon. *Advances in Strategic Management*, *27*(1), 29–50.

Vaara, E., Tienari, J., & Laurila, J. (2006). Pulp and paper fiction: On the discursive legitimation of global industrial restructuring. *Organization Studies*, *27*(6), 789–813.

Van Dijk, T. A. (1997). The study of discourse. In T. A. Van Dijk (Ed.), *Discourse as Structure and Process*, (1–34). London: Sage.

(2011). Introduction: The study of discourse. In T. A. Van Dijk (Ed.), *Discourse Studies: A Multidisciplinary Introduction* (2nd ed.) (1–7). London: Sage.

Walton, S. (2007). Site the mine in our backyard! Discursive strategies of community stakeholders in an environmental conflict in New Zealand. *Organization & Environment*, *20*(2), 177–203.

Wodak, R. & Meyer, M. (2015). *Methods of Critical Discourse Studies* (3rd ed.). London: Sage.

Wood, L. A., & Kroger, R. O. (2000). *Doing discourse analysis: Methods for studying action in talk and text*. Thousand Oaks, CA: Sage.

# Quantitative and Experimental Approaches

CHAPTER 10

# Quantitative Content Analysis as a Method for Business Ethics Research

IRINA LOCK and PETER SEELE

## Introduction

Business ethics as an academic field is a relatively young discipline. The well-established journals in the field, *Journal of Business Ethics, Business Ethics Quarterly*, and *Business Ethics: A European Review*, were founded as recently as the 1980s. Early research focused primarily on philosophical discussions of moral values, thereby relying heavily on its origins, namely ethics and philosophy, not so much on business and management studies. Today, the picture has changed, which is due to new emerging subdisciplines such as corporate social responsibility (CSR) or sustainability that are subsumed under the umbrella of business ethics. As these concepts are rooted in business studies, the normative and conceptual approach with which the discipline started is slowly being challenged by empirical, positivist paths. As one of the major concepts in business ethics (Ma et al. 2012), CSR accounts for 86% of the current empirical research (Taneja et al. 2011). Some researchers see this as a process of maturation of the field (Calabretta et al. 2011), while others speak of a marginalization of the theoretical approaches (van Liedekerke & Dubbink 2008). A trend toward more quantification of the research area, however, is not deniable, as the book *Empirically Informed Ethics* (Christen et al. 2014) describes.

Although in the *Journal of Business Ethics*, the percentage of empirical articles rose from 2.9% in 1982 to 35% in 2008 (Robertson 1993; Calabretta et al. 2011), the use of research methods is not very systematic – to say the least. The bulk of quantitative studies over the past 30 years consisted of survey methods, be it questionnaires or any type of interviews (Randall & Gibson 1990; Crane 1999). Qualitative research, on the other hand, was conducted using predominantly case studies. Those case studies were usually kept open and unstructured, with a low level of standardization (e.g. Brigley 1995). Thus, empirical studies in the field of business ethics borrowed either from ethics using case studies or from organizational research relying heavily on survey data. This rather limited application of research methods leaves the field vulnerable to criticism from other, more empirically oriented disciplines, and also restrains the gaining of intersubjectively comparable insights into business ethics questions.

That is why looking outside the business ethics box to neighboring disciplines may offer useful research methods for studying business ethics. Communication has already been addressed as an important driver and framework in conceptual business ethics research (Palazzo & Scherer 2006). In addition to the conceptual affinity, the authors move toward communication sciences, a field of research that may help looking beyond the familiar, as it maturely and creatively applies proven research methods. Borrowing from this field may help overcome the disadvantages of the limited use of empirical methods in business ethics, thereby expanding the opportunities to gain meaningful knowledge in the area.

There is one method in particular that appears decidedly suitable for the attainment of new insights into business ethics developments, viz. content analysis. Quantitative content analysis is a tool for the interpretation of usually written (corporate) communication. The method is rooted in communication sciences and may help understand and interpret the manifest as well as latent content of communication regarding a corporation's ethical understanding, conduct, and behavior.

Originally appeared in *Business Ethics: A European Review* Volume 24. Reprinted with kind permission of John Wiley & Sons Ltd.

Quantitative content analysis finds itself in a stage where software applications offer new possibilities for analysis, and in the future, might replace "handmade" human coding. As aforementioned, business ethics research is in a state of change due to the influx of study methods borrowed from other business fields, shifting the research paradigm from normative and conceptual to more positivist approaches. Both ongoing processes need to be closely examined to show the opportunities and pitfalls they hold for further development of the discipline and method. Therefore, the aim of this article is to introduce quantitative content analysis, previously applied in communication sciences, as a useful addition to the existing spectrum of business ethics research methods. While assessing its suitability for the business ethics field, this article draws attention to the challenges and opportunities of human and software-based coding.

## Business Ethics and its Affinity to Communication

The adoption of methods from communication sciences for the study of business ethics may seem farfetched. However, it is closer than it may be perceived in the first place: the fundaments of business ethics are grounded in social contract theory (Dempsey 2011), which implies that there is an invisible "social contract" between corporations and society, where firms have to fulfill or react properly to the norms and expectations of societal members (e.g., Donaldson & Dunfee 1999). "Any social institution – and business is no exception – operates in society via a social contract, expressed or implied, whereby its survival and growth are based on: 1. The delivery of some socially desirable ends to society in general and 2. The distribution of economic, social or political benefits to groups from which it derives its power" (Shocker & Sethi 1974: 67). Only if this is given will society grant the firm a license to operate, hence legitimacy. However, society's perceptions, norms, and expectations are changing over time and therefore businesses have to continuously demonstrate that their existence is (still) legitimate (Hooghiemstra 2000). To do so, communication is an essential means to convey to society in how far the social contract is upheld and maintained. In practice, this is communicated via ethical business conduct and, more recently and more explicitly, by means of CSR. CSR communication is therefore viewed as a reaction to stakeholders' expectations and to a firm's larger external environment (Dando & Swift 2003). In that sense, the license to operate of a company is formed by the communication about its actions (Schöneborn 2011).

The notion of CSR is inherently tied to business ethics with the mere terminology; the term responsibility within itself alludes to and implies "response." "Derived from the etymology, we understand responsibility as communication (literally *to respond*) of entities within a mutual relationship of obligation and governance. Responsibility is about not being indifferent or resigned. Responsibility is about caring and being accountable" (Heidbrink & Seele 2007). "Response"-ibility thus implies a discourse process, as a response can only be given if there was a request before. The naming connotes that there is a two-way communication process inherent in the notion of CSR and all other fields that have to do with the "response"-ibilities of companies (Heidbrink & Seele 2007). This idea of communication being the fundament of ethical business conduct comes as a response to the public's request for higher levels of transparency and more possibilities of engagement of corporations that arose from the myriad of corporate scandals over the last decade (Hooghiemstra 2000; Scherer & Palazzo 2007, 2011).

## Quantitative and Qualitative Research Streams and the "Paradigm War"

Given that business ethics roots in humanistic disciplines and was mainly characterized by conceptual, normative reflections, a dispute about empirical approaches did not take place. On the contrary, in the communication sciences, being part of the social sciences, such a discussion has been vividly held over the last decades.

The dispositions of researchers in communication sciences are different from the ones studying business ethics. This is mainly due to the discussion about the usefulness, quality, and suitability of quantitative or qualitative research methods for their specific fields, sometimes referred to as the "paradigm war" (Bryman 2008), which has been going on for decades. The debate, as the name indicates, was and is often times carried out in an unforgiving manner, although the arguments of both parties have been established in academia.

The main distinction between both notions lies in the fact that qualitative work studies the meaning and context of what is said, done, or intended by people. Hence, it concentrates on the interpretation of facts or their meaning. Thus, its nature of knowledge traces back to the constructivist view (Bryman 2008). For this approach, a main characteristic is the small sample size. Methods such as the aforementioned case study (e.g. Toppinen & Korhonen-Kurki 2013), focus groups (Vyakarnam 1995), observations (e.g., Bjerregaard & Lauring 2013), or discourse analyses (e.g., De Graaf 2006) are considered qualitative modes of inquiry.

Quantitative research, on the other hand, is characterized by bigger sample sizes, where the relationships of different variables are measured and tested statistically. This research stream is attributed more toward the positivist notion. The aim of quantitative research was to provide an objective method for studying phenomena of scientific interest (Benoit & Holbert 2008). Examples are large-scale surveys (Ramanathan et al. 2014), experiments (Moosmayer 2012), or quantitative content analyses (Farrell & Cobbin 2000).

With regard to business ethics, however, the distinction between both streams has one more connotation: Crane, for instance, holds that "understanding meaning must precede measurement" (Crane 1999: 245). He argues that the "functionalist paradigm" (referring to quantitative research, as opposed to the "interpretative paradigm") imposes the view that ethics are objective (Crane 1999: 242). Werhane, being more fundamental in her view, brings up the distinction between normative and empirical streams in business ethics, finding that there are neither purely empirical nor purely normative methods: "neither is singularly The Approach in business ethics" (Werhane 1994: 179). Qualitative research emphasizes the context, culture, and traditions and is already very well represented by the frequent use of case studies, theoretical, and conceptual papers, whereas quantitative research is underrepresented.

This pitfall, as the authors suggest in this article and with regard to the trend toward quantification in business ethics, can be overcome by adopting quantitative methods from neighboring disciplines such as communication sciences. Methods of this type deal with artifacts of communication such as texts or pictures along with qualitative connotations in an empirically informed way. Since ethical issues can be defined formally, also the operationalization and formal analysis of these ethical issues becomes feasible. By introducing more quantitative, numbers-based methods to the field, the process of (methodical) maturation of the discipline is advanced. The emergence of CSR as a new part of the discipline moreover contributes to the quest for more quantitative studies in business ethics. And given the fact that CSR is also strongly rooted in management and business studies, a move toward more quantitative approaches is evident (Taneja et al. 2011: 351).

## Mapping the Field of Content Analysis and Neighboring Concepts

Content analysis is a research technique that is applied in various academic fields, and particularly in the social sciences. First content analyses are attributed to Max Weber in 1911, and it was mostly within sociology that the use of the method gained popularity during the 1930s (Krippendorff 2013).

In political sciences, Harold Lasswell applied it to research on propaganda in the period between the two World Wars (1927). Still today, content analysis is used widely in the field of political research. A very well-established and widely used method for describing party positions is coding political party manifestos, which was advanced by the Comparative Manifestos Project that established a huge database of manifestos from political parties of several countries since 1945 (Budge et al. 2001). Laver & Garry (2000), in this tradition, use a human-based coding scheme to estimate policy positions from political parties in Ireland.

Slapin & Proksch (2008) further developed emerging software-based coding approaches and introduced a method named "wordfish" to electronically code and estimate party positions from political party manifestos, where human judgment in the coding process is no longer included.

In the last two decades the method also expanded more into business studies, because, according to Crane, "content analysis can provide important insights into the salience of particular social issues to the organization" (Crane 1999: 243). In the field of human resources, for instance, Mulla & Premarajan (2008) content analyzed chairpersons' speeches and directors' reports to study the range of strategic human resource management practices in Indian IT companies. To answer the question how public sector employers position themselves in the competition for talent on the job market, Waldner (2012) employed quantitative content analysis to job advertisements, finding that only few of the offers related to public service motivation factors. In accounting research, content analysis is a widely used method that is applied to all kinds of financial disclosure. Campbell (2003), for instance, studied the environmental disclosure of companies in the UK to test for inter- and intrasectoral differences in environmental sensitivity, applying human coding procedures. Further developing the technique, Beck et al. (2010) established their own mode of inquiry called consolidated narrative interrogation, a method that takes into account the depth and diversity of disclosure contents.

But content analysis is not a method singularly used in the social sciences; it also found its way into the humanities. In law, for instance, Evans et al. (2007) used software-based approaches from political science (Laver et al. 2003) to analyze amicus curiae reports. In religious studies, Hill et al. (2001) applied content analysis to media coverage of religion in the United States to see whether news outlets report in an unbiased and neutral way. They found that new religious groups are portrayed less neutrally than established ones.

This short overview shows how popular content analysis became in various disciplines. Its roots, however, lie in the field of communication research.

## (Quantitative) Content Analysis in the Communication Sciences

Content analysis is strongly rooted in mass communication and journalism studies, where it was used the most after World War II. In the last decades, the method became increasingly accepted in the scientific world, and some authors nowadays even call it *the* research method in communication and media science (Früh 2007: 13). Content analysis is a method that gives the researcher the opportunity to analyze secondary communication material and draw (statistically tested) meaning from manifest as well as latent content. Thereby it is not to be confused with discourse analysis. Discourse analysis is a purely qualitative approach that focuses on the meaning of a text with respect to its semantic, linguistic, and argumentative dimensions (Gee 2010).

One of the first definitions of content analysis was given by the US behavioral scientist Bernard Berelson as early as 1952. According to him, content analysis is "a research technique for the objective, systematic, and quantitative description of the manifest content of communication" (Berelson 1952: 18). This definition provides a helpful overview, however, it does not include all facets of content analysis. The "content" of communication is not defined further, although this can range from texts, sentences, or single words to visual content like videos or also pure acoustic pieces such as speeches or songs. Secondly, Krippendorff criticizes the use of the limiting word "manifest" content. Manifest content refers to objective meaning, one that everyone can agree upon. However, one of the major strengths of content analysis is the coding and interpretation of latent content, thus making it possible to empirically "read between the lines" (Krippendorff 2004: 20).

Content analysis can be conducted in a qualitative as well as quantitative mode, although this distinction is not always that easy to draw. According to Früh (2007) and Krippendorff (2013), content analysis binds up quantitative as well as qualitative levels of analysis. The strict separation made by many researchers (see e.g. Mayring 1993; Rössler 2005) between quantitative and qualitative content analyses is controversial.

Some authors even refrain from these dichotomous labels (Früh 2007). Krippendorff argues that qualitative as well as quantitative content analysts "sample text, in the sense of selecting what is relevant; unitize text, in the sense of distinguishing words, propositions, or larger narrative units and using quotes or examples; contextualize what they are reading in the light of what they know about the circumstances surrounding the texts; and have specific research questions in mind" (Krippendorff 2013: 88).

For the purpose of this article, we refer to a quantitative mode of application of content analysis. In line with Krippendorff (2013), we argue that quantitative content analysis does not neglect the context of texts. The transparent application of quantitative content analysis designs asserts the context-sensitivity of the method. The definition put forward by Riffe and colleagues is taken as a reference point, as it also refers to the interpretation of meaning of text: "Quantitative content analysis is the systematic and replicable examination of symbols of communication, which have been assigned numeric values according to valid measurement rules, and the analysis of relationships involving those values using statistical methods, in order to describe the communication, draw inferences about its meaning, or infer from the communication to its context, both of production and consumption" (Riffe et al. 1998: 20).

As we will argue here, quantitative content analysis as defined by Riffe et al. offers valuable insights into business ethics issues and has the potential to overcome the long-held critique of the poor scientific quality of business ethics methods. Social scientists often criticized business ethicists for the downsides of empirical research on ethics, which are usually referred to as a strong respondent's bias stemming from the perceived delicateness of ethical issues by the researcher and the researched person; a lack of attention to ethical theory; and a failure to address validity often accompanied by a poor description of methods in empirical business ethics articles (Randall & Gibson 1990; Bain 1995; Cowton 1998).

Quantitative content analysis has the power to address these downsides by the following four points:

- As it analyzes secondary data, hence data that have not been collected for the study's purpose, quantitative content analysis reduces the respondent's bias. It is considered an *unobtrusive method* (Krippendorff 2013).
- Validity and reliability checks (for instance intercoder tests) are usually easy to produce and therewith the *reliability* of the data collection *can be controlled.*
- Quantitative content analysis opens the door to *triangulation*, thus the use of multiple methods using one set of data (Harris 2001).
- However, the biggest advantage of the method is the *vast scope of application* that content analysis offers in business ethics – for instance, the study of news articles concerning a company's ethical behavior, internal codes of conduct, or CSR communication.

Quantitative content analysis has proven to be a suitable technique for the study of ethical issues, since it is applied quantitatively, but does not neglect the context. Its liminal nature makes it appear an appropriate method for the study of business ethics questions.

## Applying Quantitative Content Analysis to Business Ethics Research

The trend toward increasing quantification in business ethics research is not deniable. A book entitled *Empirically Informed Ethics* (Christen et al. 2014) indicates this recent development and proposes a "research program for the field." The emergence of CSR in the last years can certainly be seen as one of the main reasons for this development; but also the increasing publication of business ethics studies in journals of management (Aguinis & Glavas 2012), and of management articles in journals of business ethics leads to a blurring between the fields and a move toward more quantitative studies.

As indicated earlier, CSR in the last 20 years has emerged to be one of the most important subdisciplines in business ethics. While in 1990, only 3.2% of the articles published in the *Journal of Business Ethics* dealt with this topic (Robertson 1993), from

2003 to 2008, already more than 20% covered it, with an upward trend (Calabretta et al. 2011). Moreover, within the last 5 years, not only is CSR at the center of interest, but more and more also the communication of CSR by companies (Morsing & Schultz 2006; Reynolds & Yuthas 2008; Jahdi & Acikdilli 2009; Nielsen & Thomsen 2009; Fieseler 2011; Golob & Podnar 2014). Research in this area is usually conducted using quantitative methods; it explores the content, channels, and types of CSR communication such as CSR communication flows, web CSR content, or CSR reports. Quantitative surveys or quantitative content analyses are the most popular research methods governing this topic.

The bulk of studies published in recent years explore the website CSR communication of US-American companies (O'Connor & Shumate 2010; Gomez & Chalmeta 2011). Similar projects are also more and more to be found in Asia, with special emphasis on Chinese firms and their web-based CSR communication (Chapple & Moon 2005; Tang & Li 2009). In Europe, most publications focus on the country-level (UK: Sweeney & Coughlan 2008; Sweden: Frostenson et al. 2011; Germany and Switzerland: Lock & Seele 2015), on European Stock Indices (Gatti & Seele 2014), or analyze CSR reports in more detail (Maignan & Ralston 2002; Idowu & Towler 2004; Haniffa & Cooke 2005; Chen & Bouvain 2009). These projects on web CSR communication and CSR reporting often use quantitative content analysis to gain insights into the conduct and communication of CSR in companies. As already apparent from this short overview, quantitative content analysis is a frequently used research method when it comes to CSR communication. The next section will show how suited quantitative content analysis is for studies in business ethics in general.

## Quantifying Communication by Coding: Human versus Software Coding

Quantitative content analysis is, as seen before, a research technique for the study of communicational artifacts. When it was introduced in the 1950s, texts were available only in a printed format. Thus, content analyses were conducted by the researchers manually. With the increasing digitalization of media material and along with it corporate publications, human coding of content is nowadays no longer necessarily required. Advanced software solutions may substitute the process of human coding, allowing for the study of larger amounts of data with a reduction of costs and time (Popping 2000). However, computers at least today are not considered to be as language-skilled and sensitive as human coders. Software, for instance, has difficulties recognizing homonyms, distinguishing proforma, identifying irony, or categorizing synonyms (Früh 2007), if those were not programmed beforehand in a rather complex programming process. Furthermore, elaborate research questions that take into account the valuation of meanings, irony, or humor are difficult to be answered by software-based coding. Hence, relying on software-based coding alone does not seem to be adequate for all research questions at hand, especially in complex and challenging fields such as business ethics.

It is important to notice that quantitative content analyses can be conducted in many different ways, and the distinction between computer and human coding is not the only watershed. Some researchers have themselves developed modes of quantitative content analysis and offered alternative ways (e.g., Beck et al. 2010). However, the aim of this article is to give an overview of the method's application to business ethics research. Hence, the big picture with regard to the different modes of application of quantitative content analysis is presented. In the following sections, two ways of conducting quantitative content analysis are investigated, and selected examples of quantitative content analysis applied to business ethics are described and evaluated.

## Human Coding: Codebooks for Business Ethics and CSR Disclosure

The study of CSR and its communication to a corporation's stakeholders became an important sub-discipline in business ethics. CSR communication can take different forms and ranges from printed communication material such as CSR reports, over audio or video contents such as radio interviews to web-based communication, for instance on a corporation's homepage. CSR communication on the web became popular among companies (Dawkins 2004), and nowadays almost every corporation provides CSR information on their websites. This gives a good basis for researchers to study the communication of CSR, especially by applying content analysis.

Moreno & Capriotti (2009) used quantitative content analysis to study the websites of the top 35 Spanish corporations listed on the Madrid stock exchange. Their goal was to reveal which CSR issues and stakeholder groups were addressed by the companies and which control mechanisms were mentioned. The researchers developed a twofold coding scheme that was based on the content of the website communication and its presentation. Their findings indicate that the use of the web as a medium to convey CSR to the public is widespread; however, the issues covered are mainly limited to social and environmental action as well as human rights. Regarding the presentation of topics on corporate web pages, it was found that the content is rather dispersed, and, furthermore, interaction tools are rare, such that stakeholder dialog is not facilitated. Moreover, references to external parties, which would serve as assurance providers for the claims made regarding CSR, were missing. The analyzed corporations rather made use of self-regulation (Moreno & Capriotti 2009).

Another example shows that quantitative content analysis is not only highly suitable for the study of web-based CSR communication, but also for the examination of CSR reports. CSR reports have developed to be one of the most important tools for communicating CSR by corporations (Hooghiemstra 2000), and therefore the study of these publications provides important insights into the conduct of CSR. However, these reports, notwithstanding a high degree of standardization, differ very much in format and content. Moreover, they are often criticized for being marketing brochures prepared for public relations purposes, not for the communication of social and environmental business conduct (Jahdi & Acikdilli 2009).

Lock & Seele (2015) conducted a quantitative content analysis on the basis of CSR reports of corporations in Switzerland and Germany to reveal whether the information covered in these reports were actually relevant with regard to the companies' investors. Here, too, the codebook concentrated on the content and its presentation. The authors structured the codebook along three analytical units: the CSR report as a whole, the articles in these reports, and the photos. Furthermore, also the valuation of the articles (neutral, moderately judgmental, judgmental) and the pictures belonging to each were analyzed. The data analysis indicated that more than half of the content covered in the analyzed reports was actually irrelevant for the stakeholder group investors; thus, the critique of CSR reports being mere marketing brochures seems to be justified. Furthermore, the use of pictures throughout the reports is rather limited, and often does not refer to the topics treated. With regard to the question of human- or software-generated coding, the study included interpretative levels of coding that could not have been analyzed by a computer, such as the categories concerning the valuation of texts (from neutral to judgmental) and the pictures. On the other hand, the sample size of the study was relatively small, with 20 reports containing together 437 analyzed articles. Software coding may overcome this downside, as shown later.

## Software-Based Coding: The Use of the Software "Leximancer" and "Crawdad" in Business Ethics Research

Many studies so far used quantitative content analysis to analyze CSR communication of corporations, and the vast majority were conducted by human coders (Idowu & Towler 2004; Sweeney & Coughlan 2008; Moreno & Capriotti 2009; O'Connor & Shumate 2010; Gomez & Chalmeta 2011). But human coding implies, as mentioned earlier, certain disadvantages that can easily be overcome by a software-based coding procedure. Non-human coding looks back at a longer history, given that first applications date back to the 1960s, the very beginning of the computer era (Stone et al. 1966). Software packages for quantitative content analyses

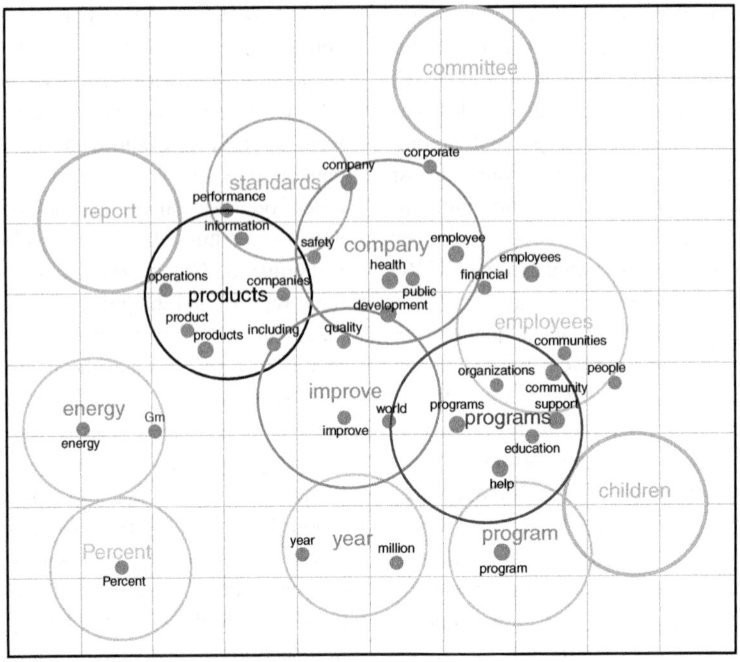


*Figure 10.1* Concept map of issues present in US–American corporate social responsibility (CSR) reports. (Chen & Bouvain 2009: 306)

have developed analogous to the way computers have over the last five decades. Already in the 1990s, researchers used elaborate programs (Weber 1990), ranging from mere word-counting packages over artificial intelligence software to programs that recognized the context of words (Nacos et al. 2009) or networks (Danowski 1993). Today, software specialists work on even more advanced programs that are able to code more complex and elaborate structures (Popping 2000), as the following studies on CSR reporting show.

Chen & Bouvain (2009) used the textual analysis software "Leximancer" (Leximancer Pty Ltd, Brisbane, Australia) to reveal whether membership to the United Nations (UN) Global Compact had an influence on CSR reporting in the USA, UK, Australia, and Germany. Another goal was to see whether membership had the power to overcome nation- and sector-specific differences. Using the textual analysis software, the researchers could not only recognize the most important topics of the reports, but also show the relationships among these terms by conceptual mapping. The most prominent issues for US-American companies centered on employees and local communities (see Figure 10.1).

German companies emphasized employee issues, too, but those related more to social and environmental topics. Furthermore, "Leximancer" distinguished the most important issues in every report, making it possible in a next step to draw cultural and sector-specific distinctions. The results, for instance, indicate that companies in the UK made much more use of third party assurance than US-American firms. Moreover, the sector and the multinationality of a company had a significant effect on the use of the term "environment." Regarding the UN Global Compact, Chen & Bouvain (2009) found that the framework significantly influenced the communication of CSR key figures.

The second example of software-based coding focuses on a specific type of quantitative content analysis called centering resonance analysis

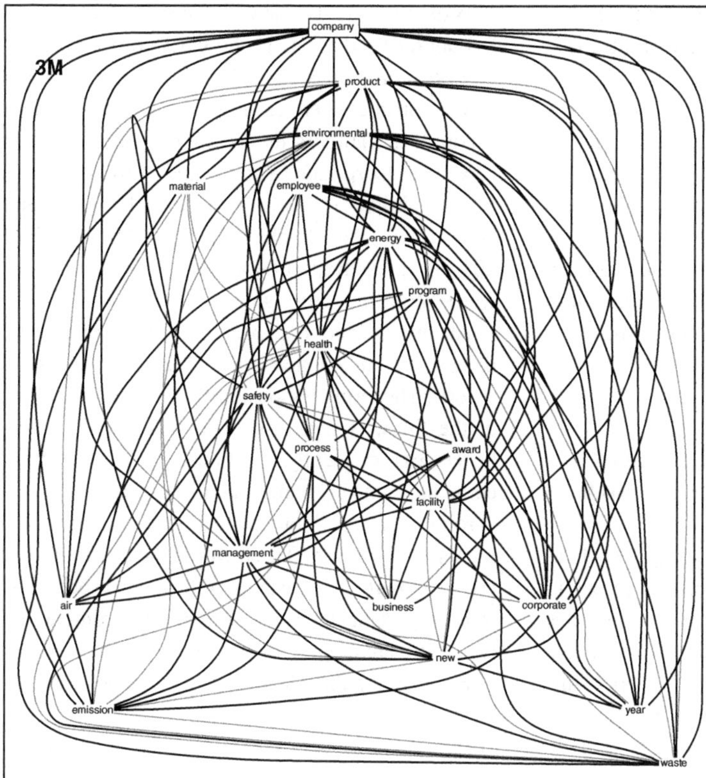


| Word | Value |
|---|---|
| Company | .33045 |
| Product | .07458 |
| Environmental | .05923 |
| Employee | .03783 |
| Energy | .03066 |
| Program | .02913 |
| Material | .02816 |
| Health | .02668 |
| Safety | .02356 |
| Process | .02159 |
| Award | .02034 |
| Facility | .01912 |
| Management | **.01910** |
| Corporate | .01897 |
| New | .01828 |
| Air | .01811 |
| Business | .01699 |
| Year | .01638 |
| Emission | .01618 |
| Waste | .01526 |
| Plant | .01385 |
| Good | .01338 |
| Organization | **.01320** |
| Pollution | .01239 |
| Result | .01183 |
| Performance | .01171 |
| United-States | .01163 |
| System | .01155 |
| Development | .01147 |
| Stakeholder | **.01120** |
| Sustainability | .01117 |

*Figure 10.2* "Crawdad" word network example. (Tate et al. 2010: 24)

(CRA). It "uses a combination of linguistics and network theory and methodology that builds upon inference, position of words and representation of concepts" (Tate et al. 2010: 24). In a study analyzing 100 CSR reports of leading sustainable companies with regard to supply chain management, Tate et al. applied the software "Crawdad" to conduct the quantitative content analysis (Corman & Dooley 2006). "Crawdad creates network maps of the words for each organization and then assigns influence values between 0 and 1 to words using the principles of CRA" (Tate et al. 2010: 24). Thereby, the influence capability of specific themes and thus their degree of significance can be measured. This software was in the past not only applied to CSR reporting studies, but also to content analyses of codes of conduct (Canary & Jennings 2008) or media press (Lee & James 2007). Figure 10.2 shows a word network example using the software "Crawdad," visualizing the relationships or networks between the single themes of a CSR report. "Crawdad" thereby opens the content analysis floor to advanced statistical data analysis by identifying word networks (see Figure 10.2) and the significant and influential themes in texts (Tate et al. 2010).

The authors' goal was to reveal the most influential words that were emphasized by the sampled corporations being so-called "leaders" in sustainability. Special consideration was given to supply chain issues. More than 10 themes (among them institutional pressure, community focus or risk management) were identified; it was also found that supply chain management had a large influence on the triple bottom line. Furthermore, Tate et al. uncovered that companies address institutional pressures in their reporting differently according to their country of origin and their size. Regarding the measurement of sustainability, US-American, European, and Japanese firms seemed to take on different points of view. Hence, US companies linked the measurement of sustainability to globalization, whereas European and Japanese businesses connected it more to supply chain figures. From this example, "Crawdad" appears to be a valuable tool for examining communicational artifacts such as CSR reports, introducing word network maps to the method's tool box of business ethics research.

## Software-Based Coding II: The Use of "Wordle" for Business Ethics Research

Apart from scientific software packages such as "Leximancer" or "Crawdad" other, less research-focused quantitative content analysis tools have appeared. An example is the open-space software "Wordle" (Developer: Jonathan Freiberg) that creates so-called "word clouds." This freely available online tool counts the frequency of words in texts and from these counts creates images, where the most frequent words appear in a bigger and bolder font, whereas the less used terms come out smaller. The application removes common words, which makes it possible to quantitatively analyze big amounts of texts. Hence, it is a useful software for rapidly visualizing the most frequently used terms in a given text. This is confirmed by the popularity the tool has enjoyed in recent years, where word clouds were found on many company publications and websites.

A widely discussed case concerning business ethics lately was the tragic series of suicides of workers at the Chinese electronic hardware manufacturer Foxconn (Seele 2012). Foxconn supplies electronic components to big corporations such as Apple, Dell, and Hewlett-Packard. The firm came under severe criticism for its poor working conditions and treatment of employees when in 2010, 14 employees committed suicide. In consequence, Apple, being one of Foxconn's major purchasers, was accused by nongovernmental organizations and other stakeholders of being at least partly responsible for the suicides.

With the aim to view the most common and frequently used terms in the CSR communication of both companies in 2010, and to see to what extent business ethics issues were taken into account, the authors used content analysis on the Foxconn Corporate Social and Environmental Responsibility (CSER) Report 2010 (Foxconn 2010) and the Apple Supplier Responsibility 2010 Progress Report (Apple 2010) using the software "Wordle" (see Figures 10.3 and 10.4).

At first glance it appears that the companies' names are mentioned most frequently in both reports. The term "responsibility," although included in the titles, is rather small in both word clouds, hence less frequently mentioned. Regarding Foxconn, the company name and fillers such as "report," "group," "CSER," or "annual" are the prevalent words in the report. These words, however, do not convey a particular meaning or thematic aspect. The most important stakeholder groups, according to the tag cloud, are employees and suppliers.

For Apple, the authors analyzed the Supplier Responsibility Progress Report, a report that specifically addresses one single stakeholder group. That is why thematic terms such as "facilities," "workers," "management," "audits," or the "suppliers" themselves are the most frequent ones, following the company's name.

The results obtained from the tag clouds indicate, especially in the case of Foxconn, that the content of such reports is not always as purposive as one might expect. While Apple's report seems to address the stakeholder group the publication is also intended for, it does not refer much to environmental or social issues. Foxconn's CSER report often uses "fillers," which indicates that the "hard" topics are rather avoided. Furthermore, the emphasis on suppliers and employees suggests that the report neglects other stakeholder groups such as local communities or financiers.

In brief, "Wordle" quantitatively measures the frequency of words used in defined texts and makes them visible at first glance. Thus, for the purpose of getting a quick overview of a large amount of text, it seems to be a good choice. However, the findings that can be obtained from the word clouds are rather limited and not suited for statistical analysis. Therefore, the software is

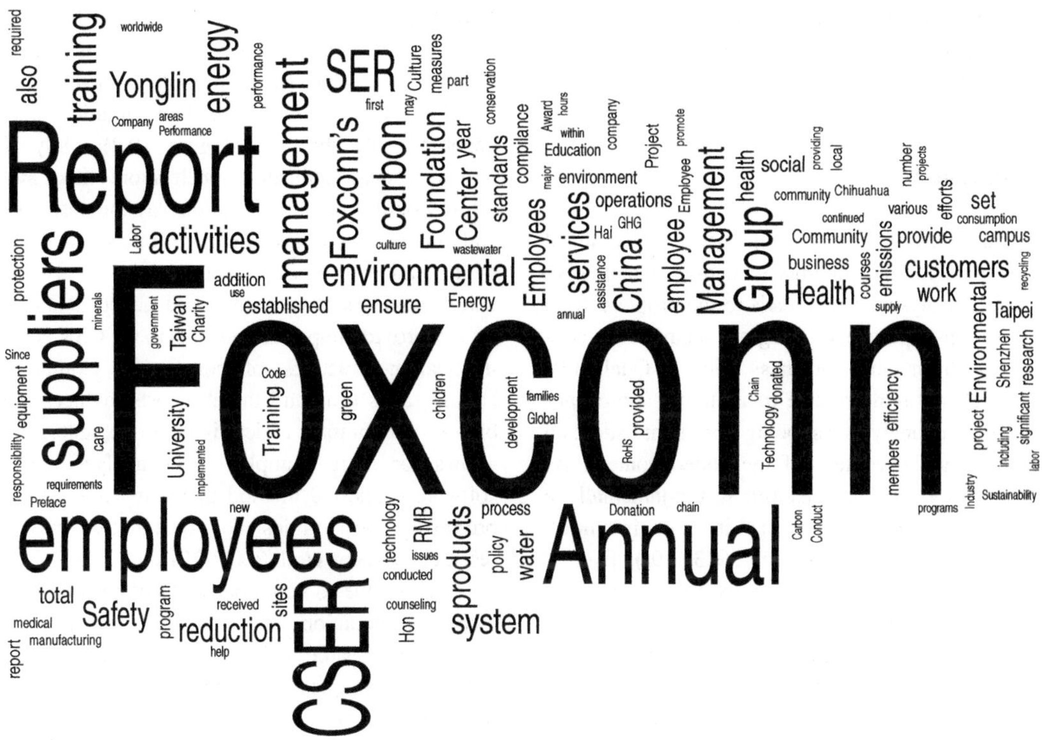


*Figure 10.3* Word Cloud Foxconn Corporate Social and Environmental Responsibility (CSER) Report 2010.

*Figure 10.4* Word Cloud Apple Supplier Responsibility Progress Report 2010.

not applicable to research purposes; it is rather to be considered a design tool than a serious quantitative content analysis method.

## Discussion

In the following we discuss the necessity of ethical reasoning for the findings gained by quantitative content analyses, which leads to the proposal for a three-step approach to integrate quantitative content analysis into business ethics. Qualitative researchers often criticize quantitative approaches to content analysis as being too simplistic and neglecting the context of the coded content. As Krippendorff holds, "reading is fundamentally a qualitative process, even when it results in numerical accounts" (Krippendorff 2013: 19f). Even if the "reading" of texts is taken over by a computer, the analysis of the output still underlies ethical reasoning and argumentation. It is not merely that the frequency of a word represents its importance; it is about the ethical interpretation of quantitative data resulting from quantitative content analyses. The method can therefore be regarded as a supplier of (numerical) data for ethical interpretation or sensemaking, addressing questions of normativity. Statistical significance, in the social sciences often the sole indicator for meaning or mistaken for causality, is not enough. Business ethics research necessarily requires ethical reasoning for the interpretation of data. However, the authors are well aware of the danger of stirring up a hornet's nest when using the term "quantitative," not only with regard to business ethicists, but also to communication researchers. That is why in addition to "quantitative content analysis" the term "formalized content analysis" is proposed by various scholars (Konkle 2004; Sachs et al. 2006; Caiani & Parenti 2011; Reinhard & Dervin 2012) to describe this mode of inquiry, as it accounts for the liminal nature of the method that carries qualitative notions despite being quantitative. This characteristic makes it an appropriate method for the study of business ethics phenomena.

The coding procedures in the course of quantitative content analyses are more and more conducted by computer software programs. Their biggest advantage is that the closeness or distance between single topics, countries, or also companies can be easily made visible (see Figure 10.1). Thereby, the networks of words, hence their relationships, become analyzable (see Figure 10.2). Only if human coders dedicated much more time and effort would it be possible to display the networks and connections between certain topics and show their relationships. Supplementary to the use of textual coding software, advanced statistical analysis can provide important insights to the CSR communication practices of companies. Computer coding saves time and thereby costs, reduces the bias of the human coder, is more reliable, and allows for larger samples to be analyzed. The software-supported method therefore "offers very promising possibilities for quantitative media research" (Nacos et al. 2009: 251).

However, the so far unique skills of human judgment, interpretation, and semantic attribution as required in research on business ethics dealing also with normative questions, cannot be entirely substituted by software-generated coding such as "Leximancer" or "Crawdad." Therefore, human coding of textual content turns out to be valuable, especially when judgment is required to make sense of communication. This is the case when, for instance, the valuation of a certain article or statement is to be analyzed or in case pictures are to be included in the content analysis (Lock & Seele 2015).

Thus, we suggest combining human as well as software coding in one research project to allow for the liminal nature of business ethics research. Furthermore, we propose a three-step approach (see Figure 10.5): business ethics research starts with a research objective from the field of business ethics. Then (communicational) artifacts are chosen to be analyzed by applying quantitative content analysis to business ethics. The quantitative data results are then used to supply and support the last and most important step: ethical reasoning, interpretation, and attribution of meaning.

This form of business ethics quantitative content analysis appears to be adequate when the presentation or accessibility of certain content, as shown in the example of website CSR communication (Moreno & Capriotti 2009), is to be coded. Quantitative content analysis through human coding therefore is

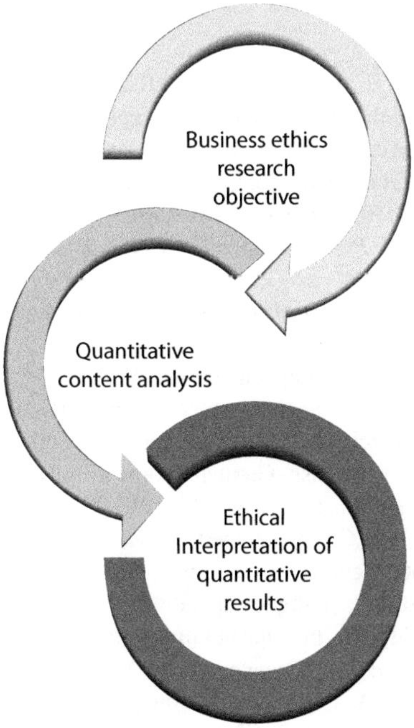


*Figure 10.5* Three-step process of quantitative content analysis in business ethics.

suitable for high context communication, where ambiguities, irony, sarcasm, or other latent meaning are to be revealed. Thus, it seems especially appropriate for the content of business ethics communication, given that studying business ethics requires "reading between the lines." Software-based coding, on the other hand, made important progress in the last decades. With the rise of the Internet and the digitalization of texts, software-based coding seems to become the future mode of conducting quantitative content analyses. However, the software package used is key. Open-space software such as "Wordle" that creates word clouds from defined texts based on the frequency of counts might be useful to get an overview of words frequently used in a specific piece. However, as shown by the examples, it is not applicable to research purposes as it allows only limited inferences.

## Limitations

It is obvious that quantitative content analysis, like any method, bears some limitations. Codebooks for a quantitative approach have to be internally valid, thus, the codes have to represent the specific topics/themes to be coded. Moreover, quantitative content analysis has to follow rigorous research designs. If coding is conducted by software, the technical progress on the one hand offers more and more sophisticated solutions for software-based coding. On the other hand, it might also crowd out the qualitative (meaning) dimension of the data analysis. With emerging computer programs that are able to recognize pictures, it might be that in the future, human coding is no longer necessary. Parametric models for text scaling or Poisson data models ("wordfish"; Slapin & Proksch 2008) transfer the data analysis from the human to the computer and limit ethical reasoning. Algorithms cannot address questions of normativity, which are crucial to the field of business ethics. If coding is conducted by humans, however, testing for intercoder reliability and consensus coding sessions are obligatory to assure reliability. Finally, quantitative content analysis has the advantage of being able to cover larger amounts of data, which implies that the interpretation for meaning of content can never be as profound and detailed as when using purely qualitative methods such as discourse analysis.

## Conclusions

The empirical maturation of business ethics research led to a shift from rather normative and conceptual to more positivist approaches. The electronic development of quantitative content analysis in the direction of sophisticated software solutions puts the idea of human coding on the spot. Both the method as well as the discipline reached a crossroads where it now becomes crucial to examine the challenges and opportunities both ways hold. In this article, we therefore took a close look at quantitative content analysis and the possibilities it offers for the advancement of the discussion of methods in business ethics.

This article has shown that content analysis applied quantitatively is an important technique to study questions of CSR and, more generally, business ethics. By introducing more quantitative research methods to the field, the process of methodical maturation is fostered (Calabretta et al. 2011). However, empirical research in business ethics will not, and should never, be seen as a substitute for ethical considerations and normative reflections (van Liedekerke & Dubbink 2008), as "neither is singularly The Approach in business ethics" (Werhane 1994: 179). That is why the authors depict a three-step process of applying quantitative content analysis to business ethics research that includes as the most important step the interpretation for meaning.

It was argued that communication is an essential part of business ethics, as it is considered the principal mean to establish and maintain the social contract between corporations and society. "Response"-ibility is seen as one of the fundaments of business ethics and, by its etymological meaning, appears to be close to communication and therefore to the discipline of communication sciences. In consequence, we argue that the application of communication sciences methods to business ethics is consistent.

Quantitative content analysis has proven to be a useful tool for analyzing business ethics phenomena, especially in the area of CSR and here particularly with regard to CSR communication. Human as well as software coding can be applied to systematize the content and the meaning of different CSR communication tools such as CSR disclosure.

Given the apparent advantages and limitations of human as well as software coding, in conclusion, we propose a more pluralistic, but research-specific approach, using human as well as software coding for conducting quantitative content analysis in business ethics. As (concurrent) mixed-methods research has become more popular in recent times in the social sciences, it allows capitalizing on the specific advantages each research technique holds. By including human and software coding within one research project, different cognitive notions are addressed and deeper insights may be provided to the field of business ethics, and CSR especially, without neglecting ethical reflections while being empirically informed.

## References


Aguinis, H. and Glavas, A. 2012. "What we know and don't know about corporate social responsibility: a review and research agenda." *Journal of Management*, 38:4, 932–968.

Apple 2010. *Apple Supplier Responsibility 2010 Progress Report*. Cupertino, CA: Apple.

Bain, W. A. 1995. "Ethical problems in ethics research." *Business Ethics: A European Review*, 4:1, 13–16.

Beck, A. C., Campbell, D. and Shrives, P. J. 2010. "Content analysis in environmental reporting research: enrichment and rehearsal of the method in a British–German context." *The British Accounting Review*, 42:3, 207–222.

Benoit, W. C. and Holbert, L. R. 2008. "Empirical intersections in communication research: replication, multiple quantitative methods, and bridging the quantitative–qualitative divide." *Journal of Communication*, 58:4, 615–628.

Berelson, B. 1952. *Content Analysis in Communications Research*. Glencoe, IL: Free Press.

Bjerregaard, T. and Lauring, J. 2013. "Managing contradictions of corporate social responsibility: The sustainability of diversity in a frontrunner firm." *Business Ethics: A European Review*, 22:2, 131–142.

Brigley, S. 1995. "Business ethics in context: Researching with case studies." *Journal of Business Ethics*, 14:3, 219–226.

Bryman, A. 2008. "The end of the paradigm wars?." In Alasuutari, P., Bickman, L. and Brennan, J. (Eds.), *The SAGE Handbook of Social Research Methods*: 13–25. Thousand Oaks, CA: Sage.

Budge, I., Klingemann, H.-D., Volkens, A., Bara, J., Tannenbaum, E., Fording, R., Hearl, D., Kim, H. M., McDonald, M. and Mendes, S. 2001. *Mapping Policy Preferences: Estimates for Parties, Electors and Governments 1945–1998*: Oxford: Oxford University Press.

Caiani, M. and Parenti, L. 2011. "The Spanish extreme right and the Internet." *Análise Social*, 46:201, 719–740.

Calabretta, G., Durisin, B. and Ogliengo, M. 2011. "Uncovering the intellectual structure of research in business ethics: A journey through the history, the classics, and the pillars of *Journal of Business Ethics*." *Journal of Business Ethics*, 104:4, 499–524.

Campbell, D. J. 2003. "Intra- and intersectoral effects in environmental disclosures: evidence for legitimacy theory? *Business Strategy and the Environment*, 12:6, 357–371.

Canary, H. E. and Jennings, M. M. 2008. "Principles and influences in codes of ethics: A centering resonance analysis comparing pre- and post-Sarbanes-Oxley codes of ethics." *Journal of Business Ethics*, 80:2, 263–278.

Chapple, W. and Moon, J. 2005. "Corporate social responsibility (CSR) in Asia: A seven-country study of CSR web site reporting." *Business & Society*, 44:4, 415–441.

Chen, S. and Bouvain, P. 2009. "Is corporate responsibility converging? A comparison of corporate responsibility reporting in the USA, UK, Australia, and Germany." *Journal of Business Ethics*, 87:1, 299–317.

Christen, M., Fischer, J., Huppenbauer, M., Tanner, C. and van Schaik, C. 2014. *Empirically Informed Ethics: Morality Between Facts and Norms*. Heidelberg: Springer.

Corman, S. R. and Dooley, K. 2006. *Crawdad Text Analysis System 2.0.* Chandler, AZ: Crawdad Technologies, LLC.

Cowton, C. J. 1998. "The use of secondary data in business ethics research." *Journal of Business Ethics*, 17:4, 423–434.

Crane, A. 1999. "Are you ethical? Please tick yes or no on researching ethics in business organizations." *Journal of Business Ethics*, 20:3, 237–248.

Dando, N. and Swift, T. 2003. "Transparency and assurance: minding the credibility gap." *Journal of Business Ethics*, 44:2/3, 195–200.

Danowski, J. A. 1993. "Network analysis of message content." In Richards, W. D. Jr. and Barnett, G.A. (Eds.), *Progress in Communication Sciences IV*: 197–221. Norwood, NJ: Ablex.

Dawkins, J. 2004. "Corporate responsibility: The communication challenge." *Journal of Communication Management*, 9:2, 108–119.

De Graaf, G. 2006. "Discourse and descriptive business ethics." *Business Ethics: A European Review*, 15:3, 246–258.

Dempsey, J. 2011. "Pluralistic business ethics: The significance and justification of moral free space in integrative social contracts theory." *Business Ethics: A European Review*, 20:3, 253–266.

Donaldson, T. and Dunfee, T. W. 1999. *Ties That Bind.* Boston, MA: Harvard Business School Press.

Evans, M., McIntosh, W., Lin, J. and Cates, C. 2007. "Recounting the courts? Applying automated content analysis to enhance empirical legal research." *Journal of Empirical Legal Studies*, 4:4, 1007–1039.

Farrell, B. and Cobbin, D. 2000. "A content analysis of codes of ethics from fifty-seven national accounting organisations." *Business Ethics: A European Review*, 9:3, 180–190.

Fieseler, C. 2011. "On the corporate social responsibility perceptions of equity analysts." *Business Ethics: A European Review*, 20:2, 131–147.

Foxconn 2010. "*Corporate social and environmental responsibility annual report 2010.*" Tucheng: Foxconn.

Frostenson, M., Helin, S. and Sandström, J. 2011. "Organising corporate responsibility communication through filtration: A study of web communication patterns in Swedish retail." *Journal of Business Ethics*, 100:1, 31–43.

Früh, W. 2007. *Inhaltsanalyse: Theorie und Praxis. [Content Analysis: Theory and Practice.]*. Konstanz: UVK.

Gatti, L. and Seele, P. 2014. "Evidence for the prevalence of the sustainability concept in European corporate responsibility reporting." *Sustainability Science*, 9:1, 89–102.

Gee, J. P. 2010. *An Introduction to Discourse Analysis: Theory and Method.* New York: Routledge.

Golob, U. and Podnar, K. 2014. "Critical points of CSR-related stakeholder dialogue in practice." *Business Ethics: A European Review*, 23:3, 248–257.

Gomez, L. M. and Chalmeta, R. 2011. "Corporate responsibility in U.S. corporate websites: A pilot study." *Public Relations Review*, 37:1, 93–95.

Haniffa, R. M. and Cooke, T. E. 2005. "The impact of culture and governance on corporate social reporting." *Journal of Accounting and Public Policy*, 24:5, 391–430.

Harris, H. 2001. "Content analysis of secondary data: A study of courage in managerial decision making." *Journal of Business Ethics*, 34:3/4, 191–208.

Heidbrink, L. and Seele, P. 2007. "Who responds to whom? Corporate culture and the question of communicating responsibility." CRR Working paper, 2/2007.

Hill, H., Hickman, J. and McLendon, J. 2001. "Cults and sects and doomsday groups, oh my: Media treatment of religion on the eve of the millennium." *Review of Religious Research*, 43:1, 24–38.

Hooghiemstra, R. 2000. "Corporate communication and impression management: New perspectives why companies engage in corporate social reporting." *Journal of Business Ethics*, 27:1/2, 55–68.

Idowu, S. O. and Towler, B. A. 2004. "A comparative study of the contents of corporate social responsibility reports of UK companies." *Management of Environmental Quality: An International Journal*, 15:4, 420–437.

Jahdi, K. S. and Acikdilli, G. 2009. "Marketing communications and corporate social responsibility (CSR): Marriage of convenience or shotgun wedding?" *Journal of Business Ethics*, 88:1, 103–113.

Konkle, B. E. 2004. "Scholastic journalism articles in school activities from 1934–1967: what many educators in the U.S. read about the student press." Paper for the AEJMC Scholastic Journalism Division Research Paper Competition, Midwinter meeting, St. Petersburg, FL, January 2005.

Krippendorff, K. 2004. *Content Analysis: An Introduction to its Methodology*, 2nd edn. Thousand Oaks, CA: Sage.

2013. *Content Analysis: An Introduction to its Methodology*, 3rd edn. Thousand Oaks, CA: Sage.

Lasswell, H. D. 1927. *Propaganda Technique in the World War*. New York: Knopf.

Laver, M. and Garry, J. 2000. "Estimating policy positions from political texts." *American Journal of Political Science*, 44:3, 619–634.

Laver, M., Benoit, K. and Garry, J. 2003. "Extracting policy positions from political texts using words as data." *American Political Science Review*, 97:2, 311–331.

Lee, P. M. and James, E. H. 2007. "She'E'Os: Gender effects and investor reactions to the announcements of top executive appointments." *Strategic Management Journal*, 28:3, 227–241.

Lock, I. and Seele, P. 2015. "Analyzing sector-specific CSR reporting: Social and environmental disclosure to investors in the chemicals and banking and insurance industry." *Corporate Social Responsibility and Environmental Management*, 22:2, 113–128.

Ma, Z., Liang, D., Yu, K. H. and Lee, Y. 2012. "Most cited business ethics publications: Mapping the intellectual structure of business ethics studies in 2001–2008." *Business Ethics: A European Review*, 21:3, 286–297.

Maignan, I. and Ralston, D. 2002. "Corporate social responsibility in Europe and the U.S.: insights from businesses' self-presentations." *Journal of International Business Studies*, 33:3, 497–514.

Mayring, P. H. 1993. *Qualitative Inhaltsanalyse: Grundlagen und Techniken. [Qualitative Content Analysis: Basics and Techniques.]*. Weinheim: Beltz/UTB.

Moosmayer, D. C. 2012. "Negativity bias in consumer price response to ethical information." *Business Ethics: A European Review*, 21:2, 198–208.

Moreno, A. and Capriotti, P. 2009. "Communicating CSR, citizenship and sustainability on the web." *Journal of Communication Management*, 13:2, 157–175.

Morsing, M. and Schultz, M. 2006. "Corporate social responsibility communication: stakeholder information, response and involvement strategies." *Business Ethics: A European Review*, 15:4, 323–338.

Mulla, Z. R. and Premarajan, R. K. 2008. "Strategic human resource management in Indian IT companies: development and validation of a scale." *VISION. The Journal of Business Perspective*, 12:2, 35–46.

Nacos, B. L., Shapiro, R. Y., Young, J. T., Fan, D. P., Kjellstrand, T. and McCaa, C. 2009. Comparing human coding and a computer-assisted method. In Krippendorff, K. and Bock, M. A. (Eds.), *The Content Analysis Reader*: 243–252. Thousand Oaks, CA: Sage Publications.

Nielsen, A. E. and Thomsen, C. 2009. "Investigating CSR communication in SMEs: A case study among Danish middle managers." *Business Ethics: A European Review*, 18:1, 83–93.

O'Connor, A. and Shumate, M. 2010. "An economic industry and institutional level of analysis of corporate social responsibility communication." *Management Communication Quarterly*, 24:4, 529–551.

Palazzo, G. and Scherer, A. G. 2006. "Corporate legitimacy as deliberation: A communicative frame-work." *Journal of Business Ethics*, 66:1, 71–88.

Popping, R. 2000. *Computer-Assisted Text Analysis*. London: Sage.

Ramanathan, R., Poomkaew, B. and Nath, P. 2014. "The impact of organizational pressures on environmental performance of firms." *Business Ethics: A European Review*, 23:2, 169–182.

Randall, D. M. and Gibson, A. M. 1990. "Methodology in business ethics research: A review and critical assessment." *Journal of Business Ethics*, 9:6, 457–471.

Reinhard, C. D. and Dervin, B. 2012. "Comparing situated sense-making processes in virtual worlds: application of Dervin's sense-making methodology to media reception situations." *Convergence: The International Journal of Research into New Media Technologies*, 18:1, 27–48.

Reynolds, M. and Yuthas, K. 2008. "Moral discourse and corporate social responsibility reporting." *Journal of Business Ethics*, 78:1/2, 47–64.

Riffe, D., Lacy, S. and Fico, F. 1998. *Analyzing Media Messages: Using Quantitative Content Analysis in Research*. Mahwah, NJ: Lawrence Erlbaum Associates.

Robertson, D. C. 1993. "Empiricism in business ethics: Suggested research directions." *Journal of Business Ethics*, 12:8, 585–599.

Rössler, P. 2005. *Inhaltsanalyse [Content Analysis]*. Konstanz: UVK.

Sachs, W., Dieleman, M., Fendt, J., Kaminska-Labbé, R., Thomas, C., and McKelvey, B. 2006. "Managing dilemmas in organizations: Irregular oscillation and coevolving causalities." Working Paper, Anderson School, UCLA.

Scherer, A. G. and Palazzo, G. 2007. "Toward a political conception of corporate responsibility: Business and society seen from a Habermasian perspective." *Academy of Management Review*, 32:4, 1096–1120.

Scherer, A. and Palazzo, G. 2011. "The new political role of business in a globalized world: A review of a new perspective on CSR and its implications for the firm, governance, and democracy." *Journal of Management Studies*, 48:4, 899–931.

Schöneborn, D. 2011. "Organization as communication: A Luhmannian perspective." *Management Communication Quarterly*, 25:4, 663–689.

Seele, P. 2012. "Triple-profitability-bottom line: Supplier responsibility in a multistakeholder perspective and the power of the markets in the Apple–Foxconn case." CRR Working papers, 11/2012.

Shocker, A. D. and Sethi, S. P. 1974. "An approach to incorporating social preferences in developing corporate action strategies." In Sethi, S.P. (Ed.), *The Unstable Ground: Corporate Social Policy in a Dynamic Society*: 67–80. Los Angeles, CA: Melville.

Slapin, J. B. and Proksch, S.-V. 2008. "A scaling model for estimating time-series party positions from texts." *American Journal of Political Science*, 52:3, 705–722.

Stone, P. J., Dunphy, D. C., Smith, M. S. and Ogilvie, D. M. (Eds.) 1966. *The General Inquirer: A Computer Approach to Content Analysis*. Cambridge, MA: MIT Press.

Sweeney, L. and Coughlan, J. 2008. "Do different industries report corporate social responsibility differently? An investigation through the lens of stakeholder theory." *Journal of Marketing Communications*, 14:2, 113–124.

Taneja, S. S., Taneja, P. K. and Gupta, R. K. 2011. "Researches in corporate social responsibility: a review of shifting focus, paradigms, and methodologies." *Journal of Business Ethics*, 101:3, 343–364.

Tang, L. and Li, H. 2009. "Corporate social responsibility communication of Chinese and global corporations in China." *Public Relations Review*, 35:3, 199–212.

Tate, W. L., Ellram, L. M. and Kirchoff, J. F. 2010. "Corporate social responsibility reports: a thematic analysis related to supply chain management." *Journal of Supply Chain Management*, 46:1, 19–44.

Toppinen, A. and Korhonen-Kurki, K. 2013. "Global reporting initiative and social impact in managing corporate responsibility: A case study of three multinationals in the forest industry." *Business Ethics: A European Review*, 22:2, 202–217.

van Liedekerke, L. and Dubbink, W. 2008. "Twenty years of European business ethics: Past developments and future concerns." *Journal of Business Ethics*, 82:2, 273–280.

Vyakarnam, S. 1995. "FOCUS: Focus groups: Are they viable in ethics research?" *Business Ethics: A European Review*, 4:1, 24–29.

Waldner, C. 2012. "Do public and private recruiters look for different employees? The role of public service motivation." *International Journal of Public Administration*, 35:1, 70–79.

Weber, R. P. 1990. *Basic Content Analysis*. Newbury Park, CA: Sage.

Werhane, P. H. 1994. "The normative/descriptive distinction in methodologies of business ethics." *Business Ethics Quarterly*, 4:2, 175–180.

# CHAPTER 11 Experiments in Business Ethics

HELET BOTHA

## Introduction

Two friends were walking in Cape Town's Company Gardens when they encountered a family of ducks. They were used to seeing these particular ducks in the Gardens. The one friend pointed out that the ducklings that had hatched but a few months earlier, had grown so much that their appearance was now indistinguishable from their mother's. Familial ties were easy enough to infer from the manner in which they waddled around together. But who was the mom?

One of the friends made a sudden advance in the direction of the flock. All but one retreated. The duck that did not retreat, instead, flapped its wings, made a spectacular noise and (!) advanced right back in the direction of the curious friend. *This* was the mother.

The above scene serves as a vivid embodiment of the spirit of experimentation. People – researchers, entrepreneurs, managers, parents, preschoolers – experience having questions, the answers to which can best or, perhaps, only be discovered by initiating change in the social world, and then observing the effect.

Why should you, the reader, care to examine experimentation more closely? Life lends itself to lab-like procedures. Incidents that involve disturbing ducks can be grouped with all sorts of attempts that, in essence, are about *acting in order to know*, as opposed to knowing in order to act. Consider two examples: one involving children's play and the other involving the start of a new business.

In a study by Schulz and Bonawitz (2007), preschoolers could distinguish between mixed and clear causal evidence for how mechanical toys operate, or move. In a case of mixed, or confounded evidence, it was not clear which out of two possible actions were actually causing the toy to move. The researchers found that the kids preferred to explore causally confounded toys – toys where the cause and effect relationship was not clear – over matched unconfounded toys – toys where the cause and effect of their operation was clear. Kids even liked playing with the causally ambiguous toys better than brand new toys! This indicates that young children want to figure out cause and effect, and that they do so through exploratory play.

Next, consider the "experiment" that effectively propelled the company (and the product) Dropbox into existence. The founder, Drew Houston, had an idea for software that would enable people to share files effortlessly. The product he envisioned would, however, be very expensive to develop and although he suspected it he did not know for a fact whether people would value the yet-to-exist product. Instead of developing the software, he made and published a video explaining its features and essentially presold the product to test whether people would be interested. The response to the video was such that Houston's hunch was validated (Ries, 2011). In 2014, Dropbox was valued at $10 billion (Tonner, 2016).

Of course, the specific focus of this chapter is the use of controlled experiments as a formal research method. The scholarly use of experiments to address social scientific questions has become ubiquitous ever since Wilhelm Wundt opened the first psychology laboratory at the University of Leipzig in 1879 (Rieber & Robinson, 2001). Experiments capture our attention and imagination. Think of the fame of Walter Mischel's marshmallow test (Mischel, 2014) and the controversy around Milgram's obedience experiments (Milgram, 1963). Experiments have the potential to influence organizational and public policy, as well as the way individuals think about themselves and others.

In short, experiments in their lived and scholarly forms are a real phenomenon. The relative simplicity of conclusions reached through experiments can be very alluring, not least because quantified results tend to be seen as objective and (therefore) authoritative. The allure of simplicity and quantification persists in the case of experiments that suffer from poor conception, imagination, and design. We must therefore be vigilant when it comes to *how* experimentalists employ their methods. As members of society and especially as ethics scholars, we ought to care about the quality of experimentation, regardless of the extent to which our own academic projects rely on empirical analysis.

The primary goal of this chapter is to discuss the ways in which business ethicists may use experiments (section 2). To serve this goal, I will:

1. Briefly present the high-level distinctive features of experimentation as social research method;
2. Develop an indication of the degree to which experimental methods are being employed in business ethics currently;
3. Deal with some of the ideological complexities involved in using experiments in business ethics;
4. Directly address some of the ways in which business ethicists could put experiments to productive use;
5. Argue that for the sake of business ethics being an intellectually vigorous discipline, it is important that business ethicists are capable of critically engaging experimental design.

The two secondary goals of this chapter are to discuss the components of a controlled experiment in somewhat more detail (section 3), and to outline a set of questions that ethicists may use to establish their own stance on the validity of experimental findings (section 4). Some scholars, especially students, may very well command the kind of reasoning that is required to engage experiments, but they may not yet possess the technical language. Understanding the basic terminology would not only help ethics scholars to evaluate experiments more efficiently, but may also enable more fruitful conversations across disciplines.

## Using Experiments in Business Ethics

The phrase "experiments in business ethics" could be interpreted in different ways. This discussion will not focus on how the denotation of "experiments in business ethics" is different from or similar to, say, experiments in behavioral ethics or moral psychology. Instead, the overarching question is *how* experiments may serve business ethicists in their thinking, regardless of whether said experiments are published in psychology, organizational behavior, or business ethics outlets. In other words: In what ways may experiments be useful for those scholars who identify with the field of business ethics? Before tackling this question it is necessary to make some high-level remarks about the use of experiments in general.

### *Controlled Experiments: Distinctive Features and Appropriate Application*

#### Distinctive Features

How are controlled experiments different from the examples of "lived" experiments at the start of this chapter? In controlled experimental designs, researchers develop explicit, measurable hypotheses prior to collecting data. Hypothesis statements concern a specific variable of interest (the independent variable) and its causal relationship to another variable (the dependent variable).[1]

Experiments are "controlled" in the sense that they are designed so as best to isolate independent and dependent variables from any other confounding variables that may bear on the hypothesized relationship. An important part of the control is introduced by *manipulating* the independent variable, via the administration of different treatment conditions, either to different groups of participants (in a between-subjects design), or to the same participant (as per a within-subjects design).

In between-subject designs it is important that subjects are randomly assigned to different

[1] To speak practically, researchers may study multiple independent and dependent variables simultaneously. They may also study variables that mediate and moderate the relationship between the independent and dependent variables.

treatment conditions. Random assignment ensures that variables *other than the treatment condition*, which have to do with participants' personalities, abilities, or circumstances, do not systematically vary *with* the treatment condition. To make the problem clear, let us say that variable X (e.g., an individual trait) varies systematically with the treatment condition. In such a case, we will not be able to know whether it was the independent variable (the treatment condition) or variable X that actually caused the difference in the dependent variable.

Control also comes from measuring other, potentially confounding variables that could vary systematically *with* either the dependent or independent variable. By measuring such "nuisance" variables, researchers are able to effectively check for and cancel out the possibility that a confound exists.[2]

### Appropriate Application

Researchers have a variety of methods to their disposal when it comes to tackling questions about the social world, e.g., case studies, correlational survey studies, interviews, conceptual analysis. My aim here is to offer guideposts as to what to take into account in deciding whether experiments are an appropriate method in a particular situation.

Firstly, controlled experiments are particularly useful when researchers are interested in discovering causal relationships. If scholars were purely interested in establishing whether a correlation exists between certain variables, manipulating the independent variable (IV) may be redundant or premature. It is very important to note that the term "experiment" is sometimes used to designate studies where the IV was not actually manipulated (see, e.g., study 2, Xu & Ma, 2016). This usage is not wrong, but it could be misleading. Scholars should thus determine whether the IV was manipulated before inferring causal evidence. The term "experiment" does not in and of itself indicate evidence for causation.

Secondly, when very little is known about a phenomenon, it may be hard to generate the reliable quantitative measures that are necessary to conduct experiments. Researchers may at first conduct some surveys, or some qualitative work to determine what needs to be measured and how.

Thirdly, when experiments are designed and executed well, they have *high internal validity*. That is, potential confounding variables are dealt with effectively and therefore the message that materializes from the study is clear and certain, relative to other methods. However, because the nature of experimental settings is contrived, and because experiments seldom make use of random sampling (that is, the sample is not randomly drawn from the population), some scholars are inclined to think that there exists no grounds for extending the experimental results beyond the boundaries of the actual experiment. The participant's experience in the lab is unlikely to reflect their experiences in the world. The sample is unlikely to accurately represent the diverse people in the world. Therefore, we cannot generalize the findings to social phenomena in the world. The shorthand of this criticism is to say that experiments have *low external validity*. I would like to make two remarks regarding external validity.

There is a distinction to be made between statistical generalization and nonstatistical generalization (Keppel, 1991: 18). The former is dependent on statistical considerations, such as random sampling.[3] Nonstatistical generalization, on the other hand, depends on intimate knowledge of theory and extant empirical work on the subject matter. That is, with careful inductive reasoning, researchers could actively build a valid case for the generalization of experimental results.

Lack of external validity is often cited as a weakness, or limitation of experimental procedures. This way of thinking puts us at risk of not seeing how a variety of empirical methods and, per implication, multiple studies are necessary to shed light on relationships that exist in the world. It is less a question of relative strength and weakness

[2] Note that a more detailed discussion on experimental design and internal validity is offered in section 3.

[3] Random sampling is not to be confused with random assignment, which was discussed earlier.

and more a question of appropriateness to where we find ourselves in process of understanding a phenomenon. Just because experiments indicate a causal relationship does not make their results more correct than, say, the results of a survey that reliably showed correlational relationships. These respective results constitute *different kinds* of contributions to our understanding of a given phenomenon.

In summary, experiments are appropriate when we care to uncover causal relationships and when we are confident that we can measure dependent variables in reliable ways. If an experiment is conducted with a convenience sample, i.e., a sample that is not randomized, it is incumbent upon the researcher to argue conceptually for generalization.

## *The State of Experiments in Business Ethics*

Let us now look at whether and how experiments have been and are being used by Business Ethicists. Since my arguments in this chapter are addressed to scholars who identify with the field of business ethics, I decided to limit the scope of our review to outlets that focus on business ethics per se. Specifically, we reviewed the journal of the Society for Business Ethics, *Business Ethics Quarterly*, as well as another high ranking ethics journal, the *Journal of Business Ethics* (Beets et al., 2016; Wicks & Derry, 1996; Serenko & Dohan, 2011; Albrecht et al., 2010). Experiments that could potentially be relevant to business ethicists are published in a wider variety of journals. However, it is not clear that scholars who publish in these journals identify with being ethicists, as opposed to psychologists and/or behaviorists.

Our first step was to consult review papers that respectively cover: (1) all of the papers published in *Journal of Business Ethics* from its inception up to 1999 (Collins, 2000); and (2) a selection of empirical papers on the topic of ethical beliefs in organizational settings that were published in various journals between 1972 and 1990 (Randall & Gibson, 1990).

These review papers indicate that experiments were used relatively seldom, especially in the decades before 1990. Lab experiments were used in less than 6 percent of the empirical studies reviewed by Randall & Gibson (1990: 465). Collins' classification of research methodologies published in JBE up to 2000 does not include experiments. The author lists the following as "methodologies" that were used: essays, model building (theory papers), interviews, case study, surveys that report percentages, surveys that report statistical analysis of variance (ANOVA) results, databases that report percentages, and databases that report ANOVA results. Now, if experiments were published in JBE before 2000, they would fall within the "surveys that report ANOVA results" category.

From 1982 through 1990, the average percentage of survey ANOVA papers published per year was 9 percent. The overwhelming majority of studies that were published during this time were essays, that is, they were not empirical papers. From 1991 through 1999, the average percentage of survey ANOVA papers published per year goes up to almost 28 percent. Clearly, the ratio of empirical to conceptual efforts is shifting. The problem with the 9 percent and 28 percent figures is that conducting an ANOVA does not automatically mean conducting an experiment. As stated in the previous subsection, researchers often use ANOVA to compare scores across groups when they did not in fact manipulate the independent variable. Thus, we cannot judge how many of these papers actually employed controlled experiments designs. The very fact that no clear categorical designating of experiments exists, is telling. Experiments were a rare phenomenon in business ethics up to the year 2000.

To establish a sense of the most recent state of experimentation in business ethics, we reviewed publications in *BEQ* and *JBE*. For *BEQ*, we reviewed all of the papers that were published from 2011 through 2015: 105 papers in total. Eighteen percent included empirics and only 3 percent reported on controlled experiments. For *JBE*, we focused on a shorter time period, because of the large volume published by the journal. We focused on all of the papers that were published in 2016, with the exception of special issues. This meant that we worked through 234 papers overall. Of these 234 papers, 74 percent included some sort of empirics (i.e., they had "methods," "data," or "sample" sections). Despite the considerable publication of empirical work, only 8 of the 234 papers (3.4 percent) constituted clear examples of (controlled) experiments.

To impart a sense of the qualitative nature of the eleven papers we did find (eight from *JBE* and three from *BEQ*), I include two tables at the end of this chapter. Table 11.1 summarizes sample sizes, number of studies conducted, whether experiments were conducted online or in a physical lab space and whether the experimental design was employed to test the effectiveness of an intervention in practice. Only two of the eleven papers used experimental design to test for the effectiveness of interventions, processes, or codes aimed at enhancing ethics in practice. Most papers reported on a single experiment, although others did report on two or three studies.

Table 11.2 summarizes the independent and dependent variables in three of the papers.[4] The main goal with this table was to offer a concrete sense of how independent variables were manipulated. In all three cases, researchers were interested in seeing how different beliefs or knowledge about a specific situation would influence the ethicality of subsequent decision-making or behavior. The different treatment conditions thus consisted of injecting different *ideas* into the conscious experience of the participants.[5]

When it comes to experiments, where can business ethicists go from here? What is there to be cautious of? And why should they bother?

## *Ideological Complexities*

It is necessary to acknowledge that some scholars would not agree that ethicists stand much to gain from experiments at all. In fact, some scholars aver that there is a fundamental mismatch between (1) the reasoning we employ in arguments about ethics and (2) experimental logic, or any form of descriptive reasoning for that matter. Opponents of the notion that business ethicist may put experiments to good use tend to affiliate with either or both of the following ideas:

> **The Fact/Value Dichotomy**
> Analytical tools (techniques and instruments that allow us to measure and statistically describe phenomena) cannot be used in arguments about ethics. Ethics centers on normative arguments, or arguments that deal with what we ought to, or should do. Analytical tools support descriptive thinking. It is impossible for "is"-statements to feed into or become "ought" statements. See, e.g., Blasi (1990) for a contemporary example of a subscription to this idea, known as Hume's guillotine (Hume, 1739). At best, analytical tools can tell us about what people *sense* or *feel* they ought to or should do. What they *sense* they ought to do is not necessarily what they ought to do.
>
> Not only are analytical tools inappropriate to the task of normative theorizing, but the aim of normative theorizing may also threaten empirical rigor. (Blasi, 1990: 55)
>
> We can call this idea the fact/value dichotomy. See Putnam (2002) for a thorough philosophical exposition and a critique.
>
> **The Threat of Naturalism**
> By developing an ethics based on natural scientific approaches we are endorsing and promoting determinism. In a paper aimed at critiquing behavioral ethics, within a section on "Mechanistic Explanations," Ellertson, Ingerson and Williams (2016: 150) state the following: "The central problem encountered in these aforementioned popular models of moral action[6] is that by attributing behavior to a mechanistic or some other type of structure or process to which human beings themselves do not actively contribute, behavioral ethicists are unable to account for human action in a manner that preserves its essentially meaningful, moral

[4] Note that I deliberately selected these three studies for the sake of their simplicity.

[5] Note that this is just one general way in which experience could be manipulated. I will address other general ways of manipulating in section 3.

[6] Here, the authors refer to theories of moral personality, or personhood that are preoccupied with understanding the gap between moral judgment and moral action, as well as human beings more primitive moral tendencies. They refer to work by: Aquino and Reed (2002) and Narvaez and Lapsley (2009) on moral identity; and Bazerman and Gino (2012) and Tenbrunsel and Smith-Crowe (2008) on behavioral ethics.

> character." Thus, situating ethics within mechanistic models undermines the notion that our ethics are a result of our free will.
>
> We can call this idea the threat of naturalism. This concern is not particular to the field of business ethics. Dennett makes the argument that when naturalism is opposed within the larger discipline of Philosophy, it is mostly in defense of moral agency (or free will) (2004). He also argues that the very inquiry into how morals served us in our evolutionary past, does *not* mean that the purpose and meaning of our ethical beliefs in the present has to do with successful reproduction.

While some scholars have voiced fundamental issues with the idea of experimentation (and the quantification that is an integral part of it), other philosophers have actively called for empirical scientific attempts (Harris, 2010), and experiments more specifically to inform our ethics (Appiah, 2008; Dewey, 1920; 2004).[7]

Appiah (2008) basically avers that an ethics that is ignorant of human capabilities is not worth developing. In other words, to think properly about what we should do, we should know what we can do. (I will return to this idea shortly.) Dewey, in *Reconstruction in Philosophy* (1920; 2004), makes a completely different argument for why ethics should take experiments seriously. Since I find this idea particularly compelling, I provide a brief account of it here.

In a text aimed at evaluating the (moral) philosophical project, Dewey argued that, at the time (1920), the discipline of philosophy had not yet responded to how modern societies relate to and create knowledge. The idea that knowledge is a body of universal, abstract truths, only to be accessed by those among us with deep reflective abilities (*à la* Plato) is diminishing due to the ubiquity of laboratory experiments. Dewey originally made this point about 40 years after psychology first started to be studied through controlled experimentation.

What does experimental procedure imply for how we understand knowledge? Simply put: it causes a shift from understanding knowledge as an outcome of reflection to an outcome of hands-on activity. We develop knowledge to the extent that we initiate change and then observe the effect of our initiative. Change no longer obscures knowing, as Plato would have us believe, but enables it.

According to Dewey, it is appropriate that the way we develop knowledge about ethics is in keeping with the way we develop knowledge in other spheres. He pointed out that philosophical attempts (which for our purposes can be understood as normative thinking) are *of* a society, *of* a place and time. It is therefore problematic that an action-based way of developing knowledge had not yet affected moral issues, "matters of supreme human significance," to the extent that it had been brought to bear on "physical and . . . physiological conditions" (p. xvii).[8]

In summary, an ethics that claims to be about *knowing* how to act, cannot divorce its way of reaching that knowledge from what society understands knowledge to be. Experiments are one of the major ways in which our society continues to develop knowledge.

Let us return to the bases on which an ethics scholar may object to using experiments in one way or the other. I will focus on the fact/value dichotomy, since I think that a proper engagement with the treat of naturalism position falls outside of the scope of this chapter.

If an ethics scholar subscribes to the fact/value dichotomy, they will have difficulty reconciling ethics with the use of experiments. Scholars in such a position are required to:

(a) Make a clear case for why an ethics that deliberately avoids engaging human capacities is worth developing.
(b) Argue for why our knowledge about ethical decision-making and action should be

[7] Indeed, this call has been heeded in the form of experimental philosophy. See the work of Joshua Greene (2014), Jesse Prinz (2009), and Shaun Nichols (2007) for examples that are relevant to ethics.

[8] What is more, Dewey recognizes that experimentation does not only exist in its formal, scholarly form. He urged the individual to apply moral imagination *as they experiment* to figure out the moral value that needs to be pursued in any given ethical dilemma.

divorced from other forms of knowledge that human beings care to develop.

If, on the other hand, a scholar does not subscribe to the fact/value dichotomy, they are *ideologically* open to drawing from experimental methods and findings – in principle. The absence of ideological tension, however, does not imply the absence of practical tension. It is not plain or obvious as to how exactly ethicists might engage practically in experimentation without *either* compromising empirical rigor *or* refraining from actually making "normative" arguments.

For example, prominent behavioral ethicists explicitly maintain neutral positions on the normative implications of their findings (see, e.g., Bazerman and Tenbrunsel, 2011: 8, 26).[9] This is potentially problematic since it could amount to the reduction of "ought" to "is" by definition (Ellertson et al., 2016: 146–147). Note, however, that this reduction is not a *logical outcome* of a behavioral ethicist's publically neutral normative stance toward empirical findings. Rather, it is what ensues *in practice* if scholars who have intimate knowledge of specific, ethically relevant behavior, motivations and traits are not willing to engage in the discussion about how people in business should tackle ethical problems. What emerges is something of a strict division of labor between those scholars who understand the intricacies of people's experiences of ethical dilemmas and those scholars who aim to develop processes for dealing with these dilemmas.

Indeed, the practical *challenge* that is cultivating and employing sophisticated experimental logic, while also engaging in applied prescriptive thinking, is at the heart of this chapter.

[9] It may be that behavioral ethicists are disinclined to engage in normative argumentation, because they assume that normative theorizing necessarily culminates in overarching, logically coherent theories about the difference between Good and Bad, Right and Wrong. Indeed, this is the perception of philosophical normative theorizing as it is put forth by Blasi (1990) and it is this very same perception of the moral philosophical project that is criticized by American pragmatists philosophers (see Chapter 18 of this volume).

## *Ways of Using Experiments in Business Ethics*

Before turning to the discussion on how business ethicists could use experiments, an important caveat needs to be made explicit. Experimental results are best leveraged:

(1) In conjunction with results from a series of other studies. A single experiment, or even a coherent set of experiments, is highly unlikely to furnish the business ethicists with the full answer to their question(s).
(2) As part of conceptual arguments that are aware of their moral philosophical underpinnings and implications.

Let us now look at three ways in which business ethicists could put experiments to productive use

### Understanding Human Cognitive and Motivational Constraints

The vast body of experimental findings on human cognitive and motivational limitations is a rich resource for business ethicists who subscribe to the idea that "ought implies can" (see Griffen, 2015: chapters 2 & 3).

The experimental work on behavioral ethics (Zhang, Gino & Bazerman, 2014; Tenbrunsel & Smith-Crowe, 2008) shows that there are often differences between the way in which people reason about ethical issues, and the way in which they act in the context of these very same issues. Work on bounded ethicality (Bazerman & Moore, 2008: chapter 8; Bazerman & Tenbrunsel, 2013) explores the ways in which people are unaware of the implications of their decisions for their own ethical values. Forms of bounded ethicality include in-group favoritism, implicit prejudice, self-serving biases. It also refers to the way in which we discount the future consequences, or are not able to accurately predict them.

Ethicists may use these bodies of work to (1) make a case for what can and cannot be reasonably expected of individuals in particular organizational settings. They may also (2) conduct studies that speak to the ways in which individuals may capable of deliberate improvement along these various dimensions provided that, in each case, scholars make an argument for the ethicality of learning.

Assuming that people are relatively partial toward people who are close to them, it is also the case that individuals can become relatively more impartial if they choose to apply themselves to the matter (Griffin, 2015: 39). It is a matter of growth and degree, more so than a matter of can and cannot. How much can a person improve when they apply themselves and what does applying oneself entail? As an example of work along these lines, Bazerman and Tenbrunsel (2008: chapter 8) offer courses of action through which individuals may "narrow the gap" between their ethical intentions and their actions.

Notice that the questions of whether and how people can learn and grow within various sub-areas of ethics implies knowledge about causal relationships. To say that an individual can or cannot, at any given point in time, be held accountable requires strong causal evidence.

### Understanding Human Evolutionary Capacities

By studying experimental findings within evolutionary moral psychology – (see Tomasello, 2016 for a comprehensive review and integration of experiments in this field) – business ethicists can develop an understanding of how features of our evolutionary history play into our capacities for ethical decision-making and action. Evolutionary moral psychology illustrates well the tensions within ethical experiences, and accounts for them (Tomasello, 2016: 7): human ethicality is layered; our ethical concerns are various (e.g., caring for family and friends; concern with the fair treatment of distant others). These concerns emerged at different stages in human history, and – today – they often compete with each other. It is thus inevitable that people today experience ethical failure, because competing moral requirements may be impossible to meet simultaneously. (See Tessman, 2014 for a comprehensive treatise on this phenomenon.)

Experiments in the previous subsection typically hone in on one individual's ethical judgments in one particular moment in time; experiments within moral evolutionary psychology (including those on early child development) hone in on our ethical behavior as having emerged over millennia *in the context of pair-bonding and, later, bigger and bigger social groups.*

Griffin (2015: chapter 5) holds that the findings within evolutionary moral psychology are too indiscriminate to really help ethicists think about right versus wrong in practical settings. Apart from this, we might also think that other primates and human children in laboratory settings are too far away from people in business environments for us to draw parallels. Even so, this work gives us (1) a set of findings that we could bring to bear on our thinking about ethical dilemmas, particularly the kind that involves competing ethical requirements. Experimental findings in evolutionary psychology help us to construct[10] the problem of ethical dilemmas in a new way. It also gives us (2) tools for thinking about how, for example, group size may play into how difficult or easy it may be for employees to behave according to ethical standards.

Without experiments, we would have had much less of an intellectual grip on our species' history with respect to ethics: our world has changed and therefore we need to intervene to create situations that may mirror the ones our ancestors experienced; we also need to study other species and young children under highly controlled conditions at very young ages to be able discover their capacities for doing good (or bad).

### Testing for the Effects of Prescriptions and Interventions

The previous two subsections focused on how experimental findings could contribute to arguments that ethicists may want to make. Let us shift to thinking about the ways in which conducting experiments may be useful.

The field of business ethics may be strengthened considerably if more attention were paid to testing prescriptive procedures and tools for making better decisions. This testing could be done by applying rigorous experimental designs to practical settings, or it could be done in the lab. I suspect that one of the primary contributors to the sparseness of work

[10] See Werhane et al.'s (2011) discussion on the construction of ethical decisions through mental models.

along these lines is that business ethics as a field still operates from the armchair, to a large extent. When it concerns itself with empirics, these empirics are seldom produced in controlled laboratory settings. When empirics are produced *in the lab*, the variables under study hardly ever pertain to business ethics and the practice of ethics, specifically. Rather, they are most likely instruments and manipulations borrowed from (organizational) behavioral science and personality and social psychology. (Consider summaries in Table 11.1 and Table 11.2 of this document. I have no doubt that these experiments could be put to good use in arguments within business ethics. They are useful in much the same way as experiments published in the fields of behavioral ethics, moral psychology, and evolutionary moral psychology. My point is that such experiments do not test or even directly deal with the processes, tools, and heuristic rules for ethical business practice, which business ethicists (aim to) develop.

The field has not taken to the idea that initiating change in the practice of ethics, and observing the effect, is a legitimate way of developing our knowledge-base. As indicated earlier, conceptual work as well as work on field data is also important. My claim is that there exists significant, underutilized opportunity to conduct rigorous tests of tools and processes that aim to enhance ethics in practice.

Behavioral ethicists often claim that, despite wide adoption, the effects of "ethics training programmes" and value-based mission statements are, at the very least, not clearly positive (Bazerman and Tenbrunsel, 2013: chapter 1). If any scholarly community should be busy developing more sophisticated tools and forms of support for ethical practice it should be business ethicists. The onus rests on this very same group of scholars to do controlled testing for the conditions under which the designed tools and processes are effective. That is: we should do experiments in order to endorse the adoption of techniques or tools that are meant to support ethical practice. We can adapt Karl Popper's (1963) famous idea of our theories dying in our stead, to say that laboratory testing is a way for our tools to fail on our behalf. Labs allow us to "play" with ideas for tools and techniques that could support the practice of ethics in business.

Let us take an in depth look at one recent study that was aimed at evaluating an ethics intervention. Of the eight controlled experiments that were published in *JBE* in 2016 (see Table 11.1 and Table 11.2), only one investigated an intervention which was aimed to improve the practice of ethics. Arfaoui et al. (2016) attempted to test the effect of an educational ethics course on accounting students' level of moral development. The most prominent way in which moral development was measured was with the "defining issues test" (DIT) (p. 165). The treatment was administered to forty-five students. A strength of this study was that the authors did include data on a control group consisting of thirty-nine students. Another strength of the study is that authors did measure both groups' DIT before and after the ethics course, or intervention. The results indicated that there was no difference between the treatment and control conditions on the posttest of the DIT (p. 167). This suggest that an ethics training intervention has no effect on moral development.

Now, two factors may lead us to doubt the validity of this result. Firstly, we cannot be sure that the DIT is an appropriate way to measure the effectiveness of moral growth of adult populations in applied settings. The authors state that this test was inspired by Kohlberg (1976) and Rest (1986), and that it has been used widely. Yet, they do not refer to instances of where this instrument was used toward understanding ethics in organizational settings in the past. The authors make no argument for why the DIT is an appropriate way to measure the effects of an intervention of this kind. Indeed, they do not even indicate where – exactly – the reader can see this exact six-scenario instrument. (Ideally, this instrument should have been included in the addenda to the paper.) The following questions need to be answered if we are to take this specific result seriously: (1) What reason do we have to believe that a person's level of moral development as captured by the DIT can change within the course of four weeks? I.e., is this not a measure that captures a relatively stable trait? (2) Is this particular measure truly testing for the understanding that the course, or intervention, aimed to develop?

Secondly, only 37 percent of the eighty-one participants across the two groups submitted complete and undistorted answers, leaving us with a very small overall sample.

My criticism of this study should be seen in the context of my project: I have just argued that this kind of testing is exactly the kind of work that the field should be doing more of.

**Summary**

Business ethicists could use experimental methods and results to:

1. Enhance their understanding of human cognitive and motivational constraints. This understanding, in turn, could be used to design experiments that would reveal the ways in which individuals can learn and grow in terms of ethical practice.
2. Enhance their understanding of human moral capabilities that are a result of our evolutionary history. This understanding, in turn, could be used to design experiments that center on how our layered morality influences our experience of ethical dilemmas in organizational contexts.
3. Design and test the effectiveness and the effects of tools and procedures that are meant to enhance ethics in practice.

### *An Alternative Title: Business Ethics in a World of Experiments*

At the start of this section, we considered that the title of the chapter could be interpreted in different ways. It is also important to consider the inverted word order of the title: we need to situate business ethics within the context of experiments.

Whether business ethicists feel particularly inclined to pay close attention to experimental results and conduct experiments or not, it should be recognized that academia and the media is rife with reporting on controlled experiments in both social and natural science. As I argued in the introduction, our lived experience is also rife with forms of experimentation: from a young age, we learn that by acting on an object or on a social situation, we are better able to figure out what is going on.

Given this larger reality, and given the rise of moral psychology over the last few decades,[11] it is paramount that business ethicists are capable of critically engaging with social scientific experiments, regardless of their stance on the fact/value dichotomy. Experiments are an important and prominent feature of the social world, which is a world of knowledge creation, after all, even outside of formal educational and research institutions.

Not all experiments have high internal validity. Some are poorly designed. Some implication sections suffer from poor imagination and deterministic interpretations where they are not warranted. It is the scholarly community's responsibility to participate in the discussion so that credible findings may "travel further" than those that are less credible. This responsibility does not dissolve if, from a personal intellectual stance, we choose *not* to rely on experimental procedures or results in our own academic arguments.

In service of promoting this critical engagement that I argue is our responsibility, the next section discusses the basic components of experimentation in somewhat more detail. The fourth and final section outlines a set of questions that business ethicists can use to help them evaluate experiments. Note that a sensitivity to potential confounds is something of a stand-alone skill which takes years to hone.[12] This list, or any text book, for that matter, cannot substitute for the apprenticeship model followed by so many disciplinarians and their students. In my personal experience, weekly, or bi-weekly discussions of fresh experiments with senior colleagues, has contributed most to my learning.

## The Components of Experimentation

I have already offered commentary on the distinctive features and appropriate use of experiments. This section will add more detail, by devoting extra attention to each of the four component parts of

[11] See Haidt (2012) for a discussion of how this field grew.
[12] Keppel makes a similar point (1991: 12).

experimentation as discussed by Keppel (1991):[13] hypotheses, treatment, statistical analysis, and assimilation of the outcomes.

## Hypothesis Statement

An experimental study starts with a hunch about how one aspect of human experience (the independent variable, or the IV) might affect another aspect of human experience (the dependent variable, or the DV). The formalized and theoretically supported version of the hunch is, of course, called the hypothesis.

The hypothesis is the motivating force that drives experimental design (Keppel, 1991:4). A research question in and of itself is not enough to make progress toward an experimental design. The researcher must also offer a prediction as to what the answer might be. The researcher must argue how and why their prediction is supported by existing theory and must formulate it in a measurable way.

## Treatment Condition

To be able to study the hypothesized relationship between the IV and the DV, the experimenter deliberately exposes the participants to carefully designed treatment conditions. Treatment condition is thus the experimenter's method of intervening in the social world, such that the IV becomes part of the participant's experience. Note that some authors refer simply to either "condition" or to "treatment." Yet others refer to the treatment as the "manipulation," or the factor.

In practical terms, the treatment could be an exposure to a specific (educational) message or idea, e.g., by asking participants to read an article as is often done when manipulating mindset (Dweck, 2006; e.g., Schumann and Dweck, 2014). We saw that manipulation via ideas is very common among the experiments published in *JBE* in 2016 (see Table 11.2).

A treatment could also be a set of instructions for how to behave. It could take up the form of a writing task. It could be about introducing a certain feature into the participant's physical environment. See Kaufman & Libby (2012) for an example of a manipulation that worked through physical environment: to enhance the salience of the self-concept, researchers included a mirror in the experimental condition, which was not there in the control condition. Very often in psychology experiments, part of what it takes for the treatment to have an effect is that the participant must not be aware of the treatment as such.

Up to this point we have said that the treatment condition is the way in which the researcher intervenes to introduce variance into the experience of the participants. More needs to be said to about the researcher's *control* over the variance they introduce. To this end, I now address confounds that arise due to: (1) IV's that are not manipulations; (2) variance as it relates to the participants themselves.

Let us suppose that a team of researchers is trying to uncover whether gender has an influence on unethicality. Such a study was undertaken recently by Suar and Gochhayat (2016). Let us suppose further that they find a statistically significant[14] difference across the two experimental groups: males and females. Females exhibited "higher corporate responsibility values" than men (Suar and Gochhayat, 2016).

We could then claim that gender *predicted* the degree to which participants exhibited concern with corporate social responsibility. We would not be able to claim that gender *caused* the degree of concern. The IV (gender) was not manipulated. Gender may happen to coincide with a host of other variables, the variance within which may be the actual driving force behind the effect on our DV (concern with corporate responsibility).

Confounds can arise even if we *do* manipulate the independent variable. We have already considered that random assignment is one of the ways in which researchers can control for latent (or nuisance) variables. If each participant is equally

[13] Note that I rely on Keppel (1991) to determine the specific areas of the discussion, but apart from where I reference Keppel explicitly, the argumentation is my own.

[14] I will say more about the meaning of statistical significance in another part of this section.

likely to be assigned to one of our conditions, then that lowers the chance of an unaccounted for factor varying systematically across groups (Keppel, 1991:17).

Another particularly powerful way to control for potentially confounding variables that have to do with predispositions or circumstances of the participants, is by using a within-subjects design. We have seen that a between-subjects design refers to the practice of treating every participant in the study with only one of two, or more, differential conditions. A *within-subjects* design, also referred to as a repeated measures design, sees each participant receive all of the possible treatments. The relationship between the IV and the DV is then assessed by looking at whether there is a systematic, directional difference in how participants respond to the one treatment vs. the other(s). Depending on the nature of the treatment, within-subject designs may not be practically feasible: the narrative spell of the treatment might be broken if a participant has to go through it multiple times. Participants may also suffer from fatigue, and this could affect the results.

### Statistical Analysis

Researchers use a variety of statistical analytical techniques to determine whether a treatment condition does have a significant influence on the dependent variable. There is a vast body of literature on the various techniques and I will not attempt to summarize them here.[15] Rather, my aim is to give the reader a perspective on what statistical analytical results represent.

Researchers conduct statistical analysis so that they may know how likely it is that the difference between treatment conditions will transpire repeatedly, if we were to run the experiment repeatedly. Thus, statistical analysis helps us to gage the significance of the finding beyond the spatio-temporal bounds of a single experiment. Said significance is expressed in probabilistic terms.

[15] For a comprehensive and detailed account, see *An introduction to statistical concepts* (Lomax, R. G., & Hahs-Vaughn, D. L.) and *Applied multivariate statistics for the social science* (Stevens, 2009).

Let us consider the *p*-value as it is often reported most prominently when researchers have found a difference between treatment conditions. The *p*-value is the probability that that specific difference between treatment conditions in the researcher's data would be found, *if the null hypothesis were true*. The null hypothesis is the theoretical assumption that there is no difference between the treatment groups. In other words, if we assume, theoretically, that the DV scores across our treatment conditions should be the same, what are the chances of us seeing the practical difference that we are seeing? If those chances are really small, say, less than 5 percent ($p < .05$), it is a good indication that the difference between treatment conditions is not merely due to chance.

Note that the p-value speaks to the confidence with which we can claim that the same causal relationship will result if we were to run the experiment over and over again (provided that we hold the null hypothesis to be true). It does not speak to the direction of the causal influence, nor does it say anything about the magnitude of the independent variable's impact on the dependent variable. It is thus not a definitive test (Nuzzo, 2014), and it follows that effect sizes as well as raw mean scores and standard deviations must be reported and considered.

At present, the social research community is becoming increasingly aware of the biases that could result of an overemphasis on p-value reporting. The phenomenon called "p-hacking" has raised concern (Simmons, Nelson & Simonsohn, 2013; Simonsohn, Nelson & Simmons, 2014; Nuzzo, 2014; Head, Holman, Lanfear, Kahn & Jennions, 2015). To quote from Head et al. (2015): "p-hacking," occurs when researchers collect or select data or statistical analyses until nonsignificant results become significant."

### Assimilation of the Outcomes

The *meaning* of experimental results are not simply given. The researchers who conducted the study are responsible for relating their findings to the theoretical body of work used to justify their research hypothesis. This process leads to more hypotheses being generated and more experiments being run (Keppel, 1991: 5). Hypotheses lead to experimentation, which lead to results being assimilated, which leads to hypotheses. Researchers cycle through deductive and inductive reasoning. This cycle is indicative of the fact that no single experiment, or even a collection of experiments, has a final say on the nature of relationships between phenomena.

## Evaluating Experiments

When evaluating experiments, ethicists can use the following set of questions to help them arrive at their own sense of the validity of the results.

1. What are the hypotheses statements? What are the researchers' predictions?
2. Was the independent variable manipulated? I.e., did the experimenters design different treatments, which were then administered according to a between-subjects or within-subjects design?
3. Are you convinced of the connection between the manipulation and the independent variable? I.e., is the treatment a good operationalization of the independent variable? If one is not an expert on the subject matter, one could check for this is by ascertaining whether the particular manipulation has been used and published before.
4. Are you convinced of the connection between existing theory and the hypothesis statement(s)?
5. Do the researchers provide evidence that the manipulation worked? I.e., did they do a manipulation check?
6. Is the independent variable truly independent of other variables that have to do with the participants? Or is there a potential confound between the independent variable and some variable that has to do with the participants' predispositions, abilities, or circumstances?
7. Were the participants randomly assigned to treatment conditions in the case of between-subjects design?
8. In the case of a factorial design – a design where more than one independent variable is being manipulated – are the two (or more) manipulations truly independent of each other?
9. Are the dependent variable measures validated measures that have been published or used before?
10. Was the dependent variable measured in more than one way? (See Table 11.2 for examples of how the DV may be measured in multiple ways in one study.) Do the results across the different measures all support the hypotheses? If not, do the researchers attempt to account for this discrepancy?
11. In the case of an experiment that involves multiple measures and/or tasks on the dependent variable side, is there the potential for serial order bias? I.e., could the order of the tasks be impacting participant responses?
12. Did the researchers use a convenience sample? If so, how strong is their theoretical argument for generalizability?
13. Consider the relevant $p$-values, effect sizes, and absolute mean scores jointly. Are you convinced that the statistical results are compelling?

## Conclusion

In this chapter, I have showed that up to now, business ethicists have underutilized experimental methods. I have discussed some of the ideological factors that bear on the use of experimental design and experimental results in business ethics. Even in the absence of ideological barriers, cultivating, and employing sophisticated experimental logic, while also engaging in applied prescriptive thinking remains a practical challenge.

Business ethicists could use experimental methods and results to enhance their understanding of (1) human cognitive and motivational constraints, and (2) human moral capabilities that are a result of our evolutionary history. Experimental design may also be used to test for the effectiveness and the effects of tools and procedures that are meant to enhance ethics in practice.

Regardless of how business ethicists orient themselves toward the use of experiments, they are a real phenomenon in moral psychology, Behavioral Ethics, and lived experience. It is therefore incumbent upon business ethicists to actively develop the capacity for critical engagement with experiments.

## References

Ackert, L. F., Church, B. K., Kuang, X. J., & Qi, L. (2011). Lying: an experimental investigation of the role of situational factors. *Business Ethics Quarterly*, 21(04), 605–632.

Albrecht, C., Thompson, J. A., Hoopes, J. L., & Rodrigo, P. (2010). Business ethics journal rankings as perceived by business ethics scholars. *Journal of Business Ethics*, 95(2), 227–237.

Appiah, A. (2008). *Experiments in ethics*. Cambridge, MA: Harvard University Press.

Aquino, K., & Reed II, A. (2002). The self-importance of moral identity. *Journal of Personality and Social Psychology*, 83(6), 1423.

Arfaoui, F., Damak-Ayadi, S., Ghram, R., & Bouchekoua, A. (2016). Ethics education and accounting students' level of moral development: experimental design in tunisian audit context. *Journal of Business Ethics*, 138(1), 161–173.

Bazerman, M. H., & Gino, F. (2012). Behavioral ethics: Toward a deeper understanding of moral judgment and dishonesty. *Annual Review of Law and Social Science*, 8, 85–104.

Bazerman, M. H., & Moore, D. A. (2008). *Judgment in managerial decision making*. 8th Edition. NY: John Wiley & Sons.

Bazerman, M. H., & Tenbrunsel, A. E. (2011). *Blind spots: Why we fail to do what's right and what to do about it*. Princeton, NJ: Princeton University Press.

Beets, S. D., Lewis, B. R., & Brower, H. H. (2016). The quality of business ethics journals: an assessment based on application. *Business & Society*, 55(2), 188–213.

Blasi, A. (1990). How should psychologists define morality? Or, the negative side effects of philosophy's influence on psychology. *The moral domain: Essays in the ongoing discussion between philosophy and the social sciences*, 38–70. Edited by Thomas E. Wren. The MIT Press. Cambridge Massachusetts.

Burger, J. M. (2009). Replicating Milgram: Would people still obey today? *American Psychologist*, 64(1), 1.

Collins, D. (2000). The quest to improve the human condition: the first 1500 articles published in *Journal of Business Ethics*. *Journal of Business ethics*, 26(1), 1–73.

Dennett, D. C. (2004). *Freedom evolves*. Penguin London, UK.

Dewey, J. (1920; 2004). *Reconstruction in philosophy*. Mineola, NY. Dover Publications.

Dweck, C. S. (2006). *Mindset: The new psychology of success*. NY: Penguin Random House LLC.

Ellertson, C. F., Ingerson, M. C., & Williams, R. N. (2016). Behavioral ethics: a critique and a proposal. *Journal of Business Ethics*, 138(1), 145–159.

Greene, J. (2014). *Moral tribes: Emotion, reason and the gap between us and them*. Penguin Books Ltd. New York.

Griffin, J. (2015). *What can philosophy contribute to ethics?*. Oxford: Oxford University Press.

Gromet, D. M., & Okimoto, T. G. (2014). Back into the fold: The influence of offender amends and victim forgiveness on peer reintegration. *Business Ethics Quarterly*, *24*(03), 411–441.

Haidt, J. (2012). *The righteous mind: Why good people are divided by politics and religion*. Vintage. New York.

Harris, S. (2011). *The moral landscape: How science can determine human values*. Simon and Schuster.

Hayibor, S., & Collins, C. (2016). Motivators of mobilization. *Journal of Business Ethics*, 139(2), 351–374.

Head, M. L., Holman, L., Lanfear, R., Kahn, A. T., & Jennions, M. D. (2015). The extent and consequences of p-hacking in science. *PLoS Biol*, 13(3), e1002106.

Hume, D. (1978). 1739. *A treatise of human nature*. London: John Noon.

Kaufman, G. F., & Libby, L. K. (2012). Changing beliefs and behavior through experience-taking. *Journal of Personality and Social Psychology*, 103(1), 1.

Keppel, G. (1991). *Design and analysis: A researcher's handbook*. Prentice-Hall, Inc. Upper Saddle River, NJ.

Kohlberg, L. (1976). Moral stages and moralization: the cognitive-developmental approach. *Moral development and behavior: theory, research, and social issues*, 31–53. NY: Holt, Rinehart and Winston.

Lavelle, J. J., Folger, R., & Manegold, J. G. (2016). Delivering bad news: How procedural unfairness affects messengers' distancing and refusals. *Journal of Business Ethics*, 136(1), 43–55.

Lee, J. S., & Kwak, D. H. (2016). Consumers' responses to public figures' transgression: Moral reasoning strategies and implications for endorsed brands. *Journal of Business Ethics*, 137(1), 101–113.

Lomax, R. G., & Hahs-Vaughn, D. L. (2013). *An introduction to statistical concepts*. Routledge. NY.

Milgram, S. (1963). Behavioral study of obedience. *The Journal of Abnormal and Social Psychology*, *67*(4), 371.

Mischel, W. (2014). *The marshmallow test: understanding self-control and how to master it*. NY: Little, Brown and Company.

Narvaez, D., & Lapsley, D. K. (2009). *Personality, identity, and character: explorations in moral psychology*. NY: Cambridge University Press.

Nichols, S. (2004). *Sentimental rules: on the natural foundations of moral judgment*. NY: Oxford University Press.

Niven, K., & Healy, C. (2016). Susceptibility to the 'dark side'of goal-setting: does moral justification influence the effect of goals on unethical behavior? *Journal of Business Ethics*, 137(1), 115–127.

Nuzzo, R. (2014). Statistical errors. *Nature*, 506 (7487), 150.

Popper, K. R., & Hudson, G. E. (1963). Conjectures and refutations. NY: Routledge Classics.

Prinz, J. (2009). *The emotional construction of morals*. Oxford: Oxford University Press.

Putnam, H. (2002). *The collapse of the fact/value dichotomy and other essays*. Harvard University Press.

Randall, D. M., & Gibson, A. M. (1990). Methodology in business ethics research: a review and critical assessment. *Journal of Business Ethics*, 9(6), 457–471.

Rest, J. R. (1986). *Moral development: Advances in research and theory*. NY: Praeger.

Rieber, R. W., & Robinson, D. K. (2001). *Wilhelm Wundt in history: The making of a scientific psychology*. NY: Springer Science & Business Media.

Ries, E. (2011, Oct 19). *How Dropbox started As a minimal viable product*. Retrieved from https://techcrunch.com/2011/10/19/dropbox-minimal-viable-product/.

Rittenburg, T. L., Gladney, G. A., & Stephenson, T. (2016). The effects of euphemism usage in business contexts. *Journal of Business Ethics*, 137(2), 315–320.

Schulz, L. E., & Bonawitz, E. B. (2007). Serious fun: Preschoolers engage in more exploratory play when evidence is confounded. *Developmental Psychology*, 43(4), 1045.

Schumann, K., & Dweck, C. S. (2014). Who accepts responsibility for their transgressions? *Personality and Social Psychology Bulletin*, 40(12), 1598–1610.

Serenko, A., & Dohan, M. (2011). Comparing the expert survey and citation impact journal ranking methods: Example from the field of artificial intelligence. *Journal of Informetrics*, 5(4), 629–648.

Shehu, E., Becker, J. U., Langmaack, A. C., & Clement, M. (2016). The brand personality of nonprofit organizations and the influence of monetary incentives. *Journal of Business Ethics*, 138(3), 589–600.

Simonsohn, U., Nelson, L. D., & Simmons, J. P. (2013), Life after p-hacking, in – *Advances in Consumer Research* 41, eds. Simona Botti and Aparna Labroo, Duluth, MN: Association for Consumer Research.

(2014). p-Curve and effect size: correcting for publication bias using only significant results. *Perspectives on Psychological Science*, 9(6), 666–681.

Stevens, J. P. (2012). *Applied multivariate statistics for the social sciences*. Routledge. NY.

Suar, D., & Gochhayat, J. (2016). Influence of biological sex and gender roles on ethicality. *Journal of Business Ethics*, 134(2), 199–208.

Tenbrunsel, A. E., & Smith-Crowe, K. (2008). ethical decision making: Where we've been and where we're going. *The Academy of Management Annals*, 2(1), 545–607.

Tessman, L. (2014). *Moral failure: On the impossible demands of morality*. Oxford University Press.

Tomasello, M. (2016). *A natural history of human morality*. Harvard University Press.

Tonner, A. (2016, Jun 11). *Should Dropbox really be worth more than Box Inc.?* Retrieved from www.fool.com/investing/2016/06/11/should-dropbox-really-be-worth-more-than-box-inc.aspx.

Warren, D. E., Gaspar, J. P., & Laufer, W. S. (2014). Is formal ethics training merely cosmetic? A study of ethics training and ethical organizational culture. *Business Ethics Quarterly*, 24(01), 85–117.

Werhane, P. H., Hartman, L. P., Moberg, D., Englehardt, E., Pritchard, M., & Parmar, B. (2011). Social constructivism, mental models, and problems of obedience. *Journal of Business Ethics*, 100(1), 103–118.

Wicks, A. C., & Derry, R. (1996). An evaluation of journal quality: The perspective of business ethics researchers. *Business Ethics Quarterly*, 6(03), 359–371.

Xu, Z. X., & Ma, H. K. (2016). How can a deontological decision lead to moral behavior? The moderating role of moral identity. *Journal of Business Ethics*, 137(3), 537–549.

Yam, K. C., & Reynolds, S. J. (2016). The effects of victim anonymity on unethical behavior. *Journal of Business Ethics*, 136(1), 13–22.

Zhang, T., Gino, F., & Bazerman, M. H. (2014). Morality rebooted: Exploring simple fixes to our moral bugs. *Research in Organizational Behavior, 34*, 63–79.

**Table 11.1 Summary of recent experiments published in business ethics journals: setting of experiment, the number of studies conducted, and sample sizes reported.**

| | Authors | Journal | Title | Lab or practical intervention | Number of studies | Sample |
|---|---|---|---|---|---|---|
| 1. | Lavelle, J., Folger, R., & Manegold, J. | *JBE*, 2016 | *Delivering bad news: how procedural unfairness affects messengers' distancing and refusals* | Lab | 2 | Study 1: n = 52<br>Study 2: n = 51, used 50 |
| 2. | Arfaoui, F., Damak-Ayadi, S., Ghram, R., & Bouchekoua, A. | *JBE*, 2016 | *Ethics education and accounting students' level of moral development: experimental design in tunisian audit context* | Effective-ness of practical intervention, or policy aimed at enhancing ethicality in a particular context<br><br>*Note that the researchers did collect data on a control group | N/A | Contacted: n = 84<br>Used: n = 31 |
| 3. | Rittenburg, T., Gladney, G., & Stephenson, T. | *JBE*, 2016 | *The effects of euphemism usage in business contexts* | Lab | 1 | n = 159 |
| 4. | Niven, K., & Healy, C. | *JBE*, 2016 | *Susceptibility to the 'dark side' of goal-setting: does moral justification influence the effect of goals on unethical behavior?* | Lab | 1 | n = 106 |
| 5. | Shehu, E., Becker, J., Langmaack, A., & Clement, M. | *JBE*, 2016 | *The brand personality of nonprofit organizations and the influence of monetary incentives* | Lab (online) | 2 | Study 1: n = 111<br>Study 2: n = 418 |
| 6. | Yam, K., & Reynolds, S. | *JBE*, 2016 | *The effects of victim anonymity on unethical behavior* | Lab (combination of online & physical) | 3 | Study 1: n = 138<br>Study 2: n = 72<br>Study 3: n = 159 |
| 7. | Lee, J., & Kwak, D. | *JBE*, 2016 | *Consumers' responses to public figures' transgression: moral reasoning strategies and implications for endorsed brands* | Lab (combination of online & physical) | 3<br>*Note that the independent variable was not manipulated in study 3 | Study 1: n = 97<br>Study 2: n = 259<br>Used: n = 218<br>Study 3: n = 237<br>Used: n = 219 |
| 8. | Hayibor, S., & Collins, C. | JBE, 2016 | *Motivators of mobilization* | Lab | 1 | n = 333 |
| 9. | Warren, D. E., Gaspar, J. P., & Laufer, W. S. | BEQ, 2014 | *Is formal ethics training merely cosmetic? A study of ethics training and ethical organizational culture* | Effective-ness of practical intervention, or policy aimed at enhancing ethicality in a particular context<br><br>*Note that there was no control group | N/A | n = 392<br>(18% of the whole of the organization) |
| 10 | Gromet, D. M., & Okimoto, T. G. | BEQ, 2014 | *Back into the fold: the influence of offender amends and victim forgiveness on peer reintegration* | Lab (online) | 3 | Study 1: n = 501<br>Study 2: n = 725<br>Study 3: n = 159 |
| 11 | Ackert, L. F., Church, B. K., Xi (Jason), K., & Li, Qi. | BEQ, 2011 | *Lying: an experimental investigation of the role of situational factors* | Lab | 1 | n = 244 |

**Table 11.2 Summary of the manipulations and measures employed by three recent experimental studies in JBE.**

| | Authors, title, and prediction | How was the independent variable manipulated? | How were the dependent variables measured? | What were some of the main findings? |
|---|---|---|---|---|
| 1. | Lavelle, J., Folger, R., & Manegold, J.<br><br>*Delivering Bad News: How Procedural Unfairness Affects Messengers' Distancing and Refusals*<br><br>The researchers predicted that procedural fairness of a decision made by upper management will impact explanation offering (or refusal) by lower-management, or "the messenger." | The independent variable in study 1 was the procedural justice of a decision. Participants were placed in the role of a manager that had to deliver the news of having been laid off to other employees. The decision about the layoff had come from upper-level management. Procedural fairness of the layoff decision was manipulated in a between-subjects design: one group read a paragraph about questionable decision-making procedures leading up to the decision, while a second group read a paragraph about fair decision-making procedures leading up to the decision.<br><br>A manipulation check was done to make sure that participants actually did perceive the hypothetical procedure as fair or unfair.<br><br>*Past literature was used to develop the paragraphs on fair vs. unfair procedure. | The dependent variable in study 1 was the behavior of the participants were placed in the role of "the messenger." The dependent variable was captured both as a continuous and as a dichotomous variable.<br><br>Participants were asked to indicate how much time (on a scale) they would spend explaining the decision to the employee being laid off (continuous variable). They were also asked to write what they would say to the employee. These responses were coded for whether or not a participant made any attempt to explain the layoff (dichotomous variable).<br><br>A 3-item measure was developed to tap into how easy it would be for the participant to be open and honest while delivering the bad news.<br><br>*Note that none of the measures had been used prior to this study. | Participants reporting on fair procedures reported that they would spend more time explaining to employees why they were being laid off. Significantly more participants (58%) in the fair condition were willing to offer explanations at all, as compared with the unfair condition (21%). |
| 2. | Niven, K., & Healy, C. *Susceptibility to the 'Dark Side' of Goal-Setting: Does Moral Justification Influence the Effect of Goals on Unethical Behavior?*<br><br>The researchers predicted that individuals will be more inclined to act unethically in order to meet specific goals in the workplace, as compared with vague goals. | The independent variable is goal specificity. This was manipulated by randomly assigning participants to one of two goal conditions. In the specific goal condition, participants were given a specific target goal before two tasks. In the vague condition goal, participants were simply informed to "do their best" before the same two tasks. | The dependent variable was unethical behavior. It was captured both as a continuous and as a dichotomous variable.<br><br>Participants were asked to complete an anagram task. This task had been developed and published prior to this study. Participants were tasked with either completing a specific number of anagrams in a limited amount of time, or they were told to simply to their best, in the same limited amount of time. Afterwards, participants were asked to report on their own performance. The bigger the delta between the reported performance and their actual performance, the higher the degree of unethicality. | When the scores of the two DV measures were combined, goal type (or condition) did predict the level of unethical behavior. However, when the effect of the condition was studied for each of the two measures respectively, goal type only significantly predicted the participants' scores on the vignette decisions. The specific goal condition did show significantly higher levels of unethicality than the "do your best" condition. This difference also existed when comparing the overstatement of scores on the |

| | | | | |
|---|---|---|---|---|
| | | | For the second "task," the authors compiled a set of three vignettes, each of which presented the participants with a choice between an ethical or an unethical course of action. Prior to this study, the vignettes had not been applied together to form one measure, however, all three had been used in previous publications, and were therefore based on previous work. Each of the choices were scored with a 1 (in the case of unethical behavior) or a 0 (in the case of ethical behavior).The scores across the three vignettes were added together to form a measure of a participant's propensity for unethical behavior while striving for a goal. | anagram task, yet it was not statistically significant. |
| 3. | Yam, K., & Reynolds, S. *The Effects of Victim Anonymity on Unethical Behavior*<br><br>The researchers predicted that people will engage in more self-interested behavior and generally unethical behaviors when victims are anonymous compared to when they are identifiable. | The independent variable in study 1 was the anonymity of victims, or people affected by a particular decision.<br><br>Participants were presented with a scenario from the pharmaceutical industry. The participant's hypothetical company developed a drug that could cure a specific disease. Participants were presented with the number of people in Africa being affected by said disease. It was also conveyed that it would be financially beneficial for the company to withhold the drug in the current moment and to release it later.<br><br>In the control condition, participants read about thousands of people suffering from the disease, without the piece including any identifying information. In the experimental condition, the name of a specific victim was also added to to the content.<br><br>*Researchers cited a specific paper that manipulated anonymity in a similar way. | The dependent variable in study 1 was unethical behavior, and was captured both as a continuous and as a dichotomous variable.<br><br>Participants were asked whether or not they would release the drug. Not releasing was coded as "unethical," whereas releasing was coded as "ethical." Participants were also asked about the quantity of the drug they were unwilling to release in the current moment. This captured the degree of unethicality: the more units they were unwilling to release, the higher the level of unethicality. | Participants in the experimental condition – where the name of one victim was included – were willing to release significantly more units of the drug. They were also more likely to release any amount of drugs than those participants in the control, or the anonymous condition. |

# Contemporary Approaches

CHAPTER 12

# Mixed Methodologies, Full-Cycle Research, and the Shortcomings of Behavioral Ethics

SCOTT SONENSHEIN and KATHERINE DECELLES

Behavioral ethics is "the social scientific study of ethical and unethical behavior in organizations" (Treviño, Weaver, and Reynolds, 2006: 952). It is a subset of business ethics research focused on describing and explaining how individuals make decisions involving issues with potential ethical implications.

As behavioral ethics research has grown in popularity, it is important to step back and examine the way that scholars conduct their research. There is a strong appeal of this type of research because it allows scholars to examine causal relationships, make use of quantitative data (which sometimes comes with the convenience that it is already collected), and allows for generalizing to a population of interest.

In this chapter, we focus on the common approaches scholars use in their empirical research, point out some of its limitations, and advocate for a perspective based on full-cycle research (Chatman and Flynn, 2005). We begin with a review of experimental approaches in behavioral ethics, which have proliferated during the past decade. Afterwards, we examine field research, which compensates for some of the weaknesses in experimental approaches but raises different kinds of concerns. We will then propose how mixed-methods studies, using what we call quasi-full-cycle approaches, can provide a potent design that builds from the strengths of any single approach while compensating for their limitations. By conducting studies that meet criteria of both internal and external validity, behavioral ethics scholars offer the possibilities of richer theorizing for scholars and more relevant insights for practitioners.

## Experimental Approaches in Behavioral Ethics

The last decade has seen a surge of behavioral ethics research that has used experimental methods. This research has led to several significant theoretical advances in the literature, including a focus on the antecedents of unethical behavior and the contextual conditions that shape unethical behavior (Kish-Gephart et al., 2010). For example, scholars using experimental approaches have helped teach us about enablers of unethical behavior as diverse as psychological anonymity (Zhong, Bohns, and Gino, 2010) and using counterfactuals (Shalvi et. al., 2011).

It is straightforward to understand the appeal of these methods. First, it is relatively simple to get access to data. Common approaches within this paradigm use undergraduate samples, typically relying on students taking an introductory course who are brought into a university laboratory conveniently nearby. Physical laboratory samples are especially helpful because they allow researchers to manipulate important aspects of context that are part of natural organizational settings but difficult to assess through other means. They also allow for a strong control over the design that is often challenging outside of a lab setting and allow for creative experimental methodologies to be implemented. For example, experimentalists have used physical props such as sunglasses or various levels of lighting, as well as altered the dirtiness and smell of the environment to examine how the physical and psychological context both can shape unethical behavior (Liljenquist, Zhong, and Galinsky, 2010; Zhong et al., 2010).

In other experimental approaches, researchers rely on online samples. These samples are both inexpensive and fast to obtain. Using services such as MTurk, researchers can run large enough studies (multiple times) to satisfy increasing calls for greater statistical power (e.g., Funder et al., 2013). For example, Welsh and Ordonez (2014) used a sample of 315 MTurk members to complement their much smaller, undergraduate lab study to examine the effects of subconscious priming on ethical behavior.

The strengths of experimental approaches for the study of behavioral ethics include establishing internal validity and causality, as well as unobtrusively measuring unethical behavior that, in organizations, is hard to access and measure (Trevino, 1992). The controllability of a lab or online setting, along with random assignment, helps eliminate many alternative explanations. As such, they have, and will continue to have, an important role to play in behavioral ethics.

As much progress as lab-based experimental approaches have made, there are three drawbacks. First, the studies often use undergraduate students, whose moral viewpoints may not be as fully developed as executives, middle managers, or even line employees. This leaves some important doubts about the generalizability of these studies. Although research using MTurk draws from a broader population, and offers the ability to screen people for criteria such as age and work experience, it too has some key limitations. For example, MTurk workers are often not paid very well (Dholakia, 2016), meaning that they might put a minimal effort to complete the task, whereas in natural settings, people might more deliberately consider the ethical implications of their actions.

Second, most ethical issues in business take place in strong organizational contexts that shape how people understand and respond to them (Ashforth and Anand, 2003; Sonenshein 2007). As Mischel (1977) pointed out, strong situations are likely to minimize individual differences, and individual differences also play a key role in how people respond to ethical issues (Trevino, 1986). Accordingly, what happens in an artificial setting may not represent what happens in an organization full of real relationships and power dynamics.

Third, the stakes of unethical behavior are often lower in experimental studies – as are the consequences of getting caught. Cheating to earn a few dollars is very different than bilking shareholders out of millions of dollars or bribing a government official. For experimental studies, there are few, if any, practical consequences for a research participant to engage in unethical behavior. Beyond a short debrief, research participants simply exit the situation, leaving the unethical behavior unresolved or even unnoticed by them. Research ethics standards themselves also likely make it that the participant experience limited moral shame or guilt after the study has concluded, something that likely won't happen in natural settings. These issues raise serious questions about the generalizability to real life settings of findings in this paradigm as they speak to both the motivations of participants and the aftermath of committing ethical transgressions.

## Field Research in Behavioral Ethics

Field research involves studies conducted in natural organizational settings. They are especially helpful for establishing external validity because researchers observe, describe, and analyze ethical issues actually confronted by people and organizations. In this manner, they offer an important complement to experimental methods not well-suited for external validity.

Field research typically uses one of two approaches. First, some scholars use ethnographic accounts to explain how organizations create situations that spur decision making about ethical issues. For example, Jackall's (1988) ethnography provides an in-depth look at the complex moral mazes people have as they navigate practical challenges that obscure the ethical content of their choices. Such research provides scholars with a deep understanding of processes around critical ethical issues not possible in a laboratory environment.

Even without full-blown ethnographic accounts, researchers can collect qualitative data using interviews and observations to unpack the processes of how unethical issues evolve. For example, Sonenshein (2009) traces the meaning-making that transforms strategic issues from managerial perspectives into issues of ethical import. This research is especially useful for examining how something becomes an ethical issue in the first place as it gets shaped by an organization's meaning-making system.

A second way of conducting field research involves surveys, which can be paired with more objective data from organizations themselves such as turnover or performance metrics. Research on ethical leadership has frequently used survey methodology, helping unpack the leader, and organizational conditions that foster unethical behavior. For example, research on ethical leadership examines how behaviors at the top of the organization can trickle down to those employees on the front line, influencing how ethical line employees act (e.g., Mayer et al., 2009). Given a focus on how leaders shape ethical behaviors on the front line, this research would be difficult to examine using laboratory methods where existing relationships and power dynamics are hard to emulate in less natural settings. DeCelles and colleagues (2013) used survey methodology paired with archival research to assess organizational climate and leadership and across prisons, and the dynamics underlying staff insubordination. While performing an experiment in the prison context would be difficult if not impossible, the quantitative method allowed for organization-level comparisons and examination of multiple levels of analysis.

Survey and qualitative based field research is not without its own limitations. The main drawback is that because the field tends to have lots of uncontrollable factors, this research is frequently subject to alternative explanations – something that threatens internal validity. Furthermore, in the absence of longitudinal data, it is hard to establish causality and getting survey responses multiple times at an organization is challenging. Organizational leadership often rejects using long surveys, precluding the inclusion of full established measures. Furthermore, field experiments are often incredibly difficult to implement given organizational constraints and a general lack of concern for the scientific method among managers. Additionally, when studying issues of unethical behavior among employees, employees likely will not be entirely forthcoming in a survey, particularly if it is not anonymous; however, tying the data to secondary sources of data, including follow up surveys, requires the identification of individuals by researchers. Yet, collecting multiple waves of data and/or linking a survey to existing data is usually critical for publication in top journals that often do not accept manuscripts with only same source, cross sectional data.

Another major limitation of field research is that it is often difficult to obtain site access, particularly when it comes to studying unethical behavior. Many organizations, for legal or reputational risks, tend to avoid having researchers study ethical violations. When they do allow researcher access, it is often shallow access – not the deep kind of access necessary for rich field studies (Feldman, Bell, and Berger, 2003).

In some cases, ethical issues might emerge from inductive studies but are not the explicit focus of the research going in. This "back door" approach to using field work to study ethical issues is promising, but unpredictable. Researchers might not ask a comprehensive set of questions to fully understand the unethical/ethical issue or decision. Furthermore, it might not be ethical itself to propose research that is decoupled from its true purpose.

Working in the field also brings up issues of social desirability bias (Randall and Fernandes, 1991). Informants may not candidly disclose information to present themselves in a more positive light, skewing the results. This is also especially the case when there are potential sanctions for the person engaging in the ethical transgression. However, those who excel at ethnographic and interview based qualitative work can often establish trust between the subjects and the researcher to help overcome these concerns.

Finally, there are legal challenges that create ethical quandaries for researchers themselves. Discovering something unethical, and especially illegal, raises the question of what the researcher should do. Confidentially agreements mandated by university ethics boards, and nondisclosure agreements with field sites sometimes required for field access, may limit what a researcher can report. At the same time, being a bystander while something unethical or illegal unfolds not only creates ethical quandaries for the researcher but also permits others to be harmed.

## Quasi-Full-Cycle Research and Behavioral Ethics

Both experimental and field research have significant strengths but also key limitations. We argue that one way of building on the strengths and minimizing the weaknesses of any one approach is to conduct mixed-methods, full-cycle research. Chatman and Flynn (2005) argue that mixed methodologies are an important design approach that can reach both internal and external validity, but they also point out that the cyclical use of diverse methodologies provides an even more powerful approach. By assigning the responsibility of an iterative set of studies and using diverse methodologies to individual researchers or research teams (and not to the field writ large), it is possible to more effectively and quickly build an accumulating knowledge base. Chatman and Flynn propose four stages of full-cycle organizational research: (1) field observations of a phenomenon, (2) theorizing about its cause, (3) experimentally testing the theory, and (4) additional observations to deepen understanding and spark additional research.

Chatman and Flynn intend the full-cycle approach to unfold over multiple papers, and the example they use in the paper – Staw's escalation of commitment research – spanned over two decades. Although there is tremendous merit in their approach, we advocate a less ambitious but more practical approach in behavioral ethics research: quasi-full-cycle research. Quasi-full-cycle research takes the spirit of what Chatman and Flynn argue for, and the work they build on (e.g., Cialdini, 1980), to set up three principles for behavioral ethics research intended for a single paper. By condensing existing approaches, we present a more pragmatic approach to research, especially for questions involving business ethics where methodological flexibility (as we propose, in our second stage) is critical. In behavioral ethics, it is sometimes more difficult to get access to data or get informants to provide candid responses due to legal repercussions or social desirability bias.

I. Primary or secondary observation of a phenomenon to refine research focus.
II. Use of multiple methodologies to explain the development of the phenomenon and/or its consequences.
III. Theorizing about the phenomenon, using either additional data or the compilation of studies.

It is often very hard to directly observe ethical improprieties in organizations, absent a long-term and deep engagement with a field site (e.g., Jackall, 1988). Accordingly, quasi-full-cycle behavioral ethics research can start with a secondary observation of a phenomenon of interest: learning about a corporate scandal such as Enron or even observing something unethical in one's own life. Ethical issues might also come to light from initial discussions or observations in "closet qualitative research" (Sutton, 1997), which might not even make the final cut of a paper but can stimulate theoretical ideas about phenomena.

The second step is to bring multiple methodologies to explain a phenomenon and some of its consequences. Keeping in mind that our approach is geared for a single paper (and not a decades-plus stream of research), it is important to set realistic expectations. Creswell and Plano Clark (2011) describes several mixed-methods approaches to complete this step. Two especially helpful designs for behavioral ethics are what they call the explanatory sequential design and the exploratory sequential design.

In the former, researchers collect and analyze quantitative data and then use qualitative data to explain and deepen the initial quantitative results (even though in management journals, the norm for mixed-methods favors the presentation of qualitative before quantitative studies). The qualitative study also can add external validity to a quantitative study. The second approach, the exploratory sequential design, uses qualitative research to generate most of the theory but then tests the theory, and builds toward internal validity, using quantitative methods. For example, in their paper Bunderson and Thompson (2009) developed much of their theory from an interview based study of zookeepers, and then designed a follow up observational quantitative study that provided more generalizability of the results and examination of multiple objective dependent variables. These are not exhaustive designs and it is possible to bring multiple methodologies using a single type of data, such as experiments, observations, and surveys.

The third step of our quasi-full-cycle approach is to theorize about the phenomenon considering all the results of the study. This involves a deeper reflection on a paper's findings, treating it as data itself to draw out conclusions and point out patterns and unanswered questioned. Each study can serve as a single case in a multiple case study approach, allowing researchers to follow methodologies of theory building typically associated with inductive approaches (Eisenhardt, 1989). Under this type of research, instead of viewing a series of studies as moving to an increasingly narrow test of hypotheses, researchers view their studies like clues in an ongoing mystery they are trying to solve. Each study provides a new source of information – with some studies better geared at helping establish causality and others better suited for generalizing to natural settings. The result is an induced theory that accounts for all the data and reports the overall pattern of findings.

## Examples of Quasi-Full-Cycle Research in Behavioral Ethics

Unfortunately, there are not that many mixed-methods studies in behavioral ethics – let alone those that follow the spirit of our three steps. We outline three examples that come closest to illustrating the power of quasi-full-cycle behavioral ethics research.

Gino and Pierce (2010) examined the extent to which a customer's wealth influences the likelihood an employee will engage in unethical (and illegal) behavior. Using the context of vehicle emissions testing, they first relied on a field dataset from archival sources of all emissions testing done in a large northern state. They found that most inspectors favored unethically helping customers of lower wealth by letting them disproportionately pass emissions tests. They followed up this field study with a laboratory experiment, using a student sample that responded to a scenario that tried to replicate some key findings from the field study. This design offered several benefits. First, the field data was obtained from a state's Department of Motor Vehicle's office, something that didn't require organizational access. Second, by using a lab study, the authors could test for mechanisms to explain some of their findings in the field (in their case, empathy leads inspectors to favor less wealthy people, and envy leads them to not want to help wealthier people). They conclude their paper by considering how the field and lab study complement each other and give the reader a fuller picture of how the wealth of the customer shapes unethical behavior.

Barnes and colleagues (2011) rely on several methodologies to unpack the relationship between sleep and unethical behavior. Drawing from the ego depletion model, they hypothesize that a lack of sleep will positively relate to unethical behavior. To examine their hypotheses, the researchers started with two experiments – one, using undergraduate students, which was designed to validate the way they measured sleep and the other which was used to test how lower levels of sleep negatively related to cognitive self-control. For this last experiment, researchers compared a participants' level of sleep to their ability to exert cognitive control by persisting on a difficult task. The next study also used undergraduates but focused on examining the degree of sleep the previous night and cheating, which was incentivized through money. Study 3 brought the research into the field. Using an online panel, participants completed a survey about how much sleep they typically had in the previous three months. Participants' supervisors independently completed a questionnaire, evaluating their employees' unethical behaviors over the same period. After controlling for some alternative explanations, the researchers found that sleep accounted for 6 percent of the variation of unethical behavior. A fourth study used an experience sampling methodology. Using students who worked, the researchers asked during the beginning of the work shift about sleep quality and quantity and asked near the end of the work shift about unethical behavior. By using experiments, field samples, and experience sampling, the researchers could build on the limitations of each single study and test their hypotheses in a more comprehensive way. At the end, they could draw broader conclusions by considering the full portfolio of studies, allowing them to theorize how sleep impacts unethical behavior.

A third example using mixed methods doesn't involve formal hypothesis testing and follows more closely to our quasi-full-cycle approach. In our own work examining environmentalists trying to be greener (Sonenshein, DeCelles, and Dutton, 2014), we started off with an inductive study of environmentalists compiled from a sample from a university program that focused on creating environmental change agents. The research was sparked by both of our interests in environmental activism, and in the case of Katy, by her personal experiences in the program we studied.

Our qualitative study led us to induce a theoretical model that identified the mix of self-assets and self-doubts environmentalists had. It also allowed us to dive deeper into the context of how these self-doubts emerged, such as through relational, cognitive, and organizational challenges.

Our second study did not directly test the entire theoretical model we developed in the first study but rather was meant to complement it by asking how self-doubts and self-assets shaped ethical behaviors (in this case, doing something good for the environment). We first conducted a pilot study to assess the reliability and validity of our self-assets and self-doubts scales. We next moved to our main observational study, in which we recruited ninety-one issue supporters who were active in environmental groups. We had participants come to a computer lab where they took a survey which measured self-assets and self-doubts. Incorporating some of our study's measures naturally, we provided participants with a drink, three slices of pizza, vegetables, and strawberries. We left the green tops on the strawberries, reasoning that even hungry people wouldn't eat them. We also had a compost bin commonly found in the city conveniently located. Participants then left the computer lab, believing the study was over. Close by, we had street activists engage with participants and used video recording to help identify which participants agreed to sign up for a campaign for a real, upcoming environmental event. We tallied the number of ethical issues participants did from three sources (1) whether they composted their leftovers and/or dishware, (b) wrote feedback to us about some of our design choices that implied an ethical issue (for example, not serving locally produced snacks and using drinks from a company with some questionable ethical practices), and (c) signed the pledge offered by the street activists. We then used these data to theorize three profiles of environmental issue supporters – self-affirmers, self-critics, and self-equivocators – and examined how these profiles related to their environmental behaviors.

Our goal of using mixed methods was to continue to keep inductively developing theory, rather than to develop and then test theory. Our observational study served as the final part of the puzzle that allowed us to induce a pattern of how self-evaluations shape ethical behaviors.

## The Challenges and Promises of Quasi-Full-Cycle Research in Behavioral Ethics

The reason why quasi-full-cycle research is so scarce is that it is incredibly hard to do for several reasons. First, it is a challenge to master a single method, let alone multiple ones. Combining multiple methodologies is also time consuming and takes up valuable pages. Many journals expect each study to stand on its own, plus relate in some meaningful way to each other. Two mediocre studies usually fail to meet the bar of many journals.

Second, it is challenging to satisfy reviewers who might be accustomed to only one of the methods used, and have unfamiliarity, or even biases, against the other methods. An experimental reviewer might not understand a qualitative study, and may want the authors to use the space to run another experiment. Likewise, a qualitative researcher might not understand a lab study. Scholars from the different paradigms may also have incommensurable epistemologies, with qualitative researchers often favoring interpretive epistemologies that are at odds with the positivism of many experimentalists. It takes a strong and open-minded editor to shepherd a mixed-methods paper through this thorny process.

Third, in an era of counting papers, and not fully reading them, it is tempting to conduct a more limited number of studies for a single paper to increase publications. Two excellent studies often tempt authors to split their research into different papers to increase their perceived productivity. We think this approach is unfortunate because a full-cycle approach allows for a much deeper examination of a phenomenon that is harder to do when the work is distributed across different research teams (Chatman and Flynn, 2005), or even over long periods of times.

If researchers can overcome these challenges, they can truly unpack a phenomenon, relentlessly using each study as data to theorize deeper. This will allow researchers to achieve more insightful findings that go beyond incremental contributions as well as offer the benefits of a phenomenon that is more grounded in natural settings, something important for practitioners as well as scholars.

## References


B. E. Ashforth, and V. Anand, "The Normalization of Corruption in Organizations," *Research in Organizational Behavior*, 25 (2003), 1–52.

C. M. Barnes, J. Schaubroeck, M. Huth, and S. Ghumman. "Lack of Sleep and Unethical Conduct," *Organizational Behavior and Human Decision Processes*, 115(2) (2011), 169–180.

C. B. Zhong, V. K., Bohns, and F. Gino, "Good Lamps Are the Best Policez; Darkness Increases Dishonesty and Self-interested Behavior." *Psychological science*, 21(3) (2010), 311–314.

D. C. Funder, J. M. Levine, D. M. Mackie, C. C. Morf, C. Sansone, S. Vazire, and S. G. West. "Improving the Dependability of Research in Personality and Social Psychology: Recommendations for Research and Educational Practice." *Personality and Social Psychology Review*, 18 (2013), 3–12, 10.1177/10888683 13507536.

D. M. Mayer, M. Kuenzi, R. Greenbaum, M. Bardes, and R. Salvador, "How Low Does Ethical Leadership Flow? Test of a Trickle-down Model," *Organizational Behavior and Human Decision Processes* 108 (2009), 1–13.

D. M. Randall and M. F. Fernandes, "The Social Desirability Response Bias in Ethics Research," *Journal of Business Ethics*, 10(11) (1991), 805–817.

D. Welsh, and L. Ordonez, "Conscience Without Cognition: The Effects of Subconscious Priming on Ethical Behavior," *Academy of Management Journal*, 57(3) (2014), 723–742.

F. Gino and L. Pierce, "Robin Hood Under the Hood: Wealth-based Discrimination in Illicit Customer Help," *Organization Science*, 21(6) (2010), 1176–1194.

J. A. Chatman, and F. J. Flynn, "Full-cycle Micro-organizational Behavior Research," *Organization Science*, 16(4) (2005), 434–447.

J. J. Kish-Gephart, D. A. Harrison, and L. K. Treviño, "Bad Apples, Bad Cases, and Bad Barrels: Meta-analytic Evidence About Sources of Unethical Decisions at Work," *Journal of applied Psychology*, 95(1) (2010), 1.

J. S. Bunderson, and J. A. Thompson, "The Call of the Wild: Zookeepers, Callings, and the Double-edged Sword of Deeply Meaningful Work," *Administrative Science Quarterly*, 54(1) (2009), 32–57.

J. W. Creswell and V. L. P. Clark, *Designing and Conducting Mixed Methods Research*, 2nd ed., Thousand Oaks, CA: Sage Publications, (2007).

K. Liljenquist, C. B. Zhong, and A. D. Galinsky, "The Smell of Virtue: Clean Scents Promote Reciprocity and Charity," *Psychological Science*, 21(3) (2010), 381–383.

K. M. Eisenhardt, "Building Theories from Case Study Research," *Academy of Management Review*, 14(4) (1989), 532–550.

L. K. Trevino, "Ethical Decision Making in Organizations: A Person–situation Interactionist Model," *Academy of Management Review*, 11(3) (1986), 601–617.

"Experimental Approaches to Studying Ethical-unethical Behavior in Organizations," *Business Ethics Quarterly*, 2(2) (1992), 121–136.

L. K. Treviño, G. R. Weaver, and S. J. Reynolds. "Behavioral Ethics in Organizations: A Review." *Journal of Management*, 32(6) (2006): 951–990.

M. S. Feldman, J. Bell, and M. T. Berger, *Gaining Access: A Practical and Theoretical Guide for Qualitative Researchers*, new edn. (Altamira Press, 2003).

R. B. Cialdini, "Full-cycle Social Psychology," L. Bickman ed. *Applied Social Psychology Annual*, Vol. 1, (2009), 21–47.

R. I. Sutton, "Crossroads: The Virtues of Closet Qualitative Research." *Organization Science*, 8 (1) (1997), 97–106.

R. Jackall, "Moral Mazes: The World of Corporate Managers." *International Journal of Politics, Culture, and Society*, 1(4) (1988), 598–614.

S. Shalvi, J. Dana, M. J. Handgraaf, and C. K. De Dreu, "Justified Ethicality: Observing Desired Counterfactuals Modifies Ethical Perceptions and Behavior," *Organizational Behavior and Human Decision Processes*, 115(2) (2011), 181–190.

S. Sonenshein, "Emergence of Ethical Issues During Strategic Change Implementation," *Organization Science*, 20(1) (2009), 223–239.

"The Role of Construction, Intuition, and Justification in Responding to Ethical Issues at Work: The Sensemaking-Intuition Model," *Academy of Management Review*, 32(4) (2007), 1022–1040.

S. Sonenshein, K. A. DeCelles, and J. E. Dutton, "It's Not Easy Being Green: The Role of Self-Evaluations in Explaining Support of Environmental Issues," *Academy of Management Journal*, 57(1) (2014), 7–37.

U. Dholakia, "My Experience as an Amazon Mechanical Turk (MTurk) Worker," LinkedIn, 2016, https://www.linkedin.com/pulse/my-experience-amazon-mechanical-turk-mturk-worker-utpal-dholakia.

W. Mischel and N.S. Endler, (1977). *Personality at the Crossroads: Current Issues in Interactional Psychology* (Hillsdale, NJ: Lawrence Erlbaum, 1977), pp. 333–352.

CHAPTER 13

# Applying Neuroscience to Business Ethics

FILOMENA SABATELLA, NICOLA M. PLESS, and THOMAS MAAK

## Introduction

Understanding the mind has always been one of the main interests of humanity. Over the past decades, there has been a surge of interest in the human brain, especially in decision making and behavior. The developments of neuroimaging technologies have allowed researchers to measure brain patterns as individuals feel and think. Building on early structural imaging technologies such as computer tomography (CT) or magnetic resonance imaging (MRI), which can only provide structural information about the brain, a variety of functional imaging technologies have been introduced. Among these technologies, the functional magnet resonance imaging (fMRI) has boosted the advance of neuroscience in medicine, psychology, and psychiatry by providing new possibilities to gain insights into the functioning of the human brain. These recent advances have sparked the interest of research outside of the traditional clinical setting, such as economics (Fehr and Rangel, 2011), law (Jones, Marois, Farah and Greely, 2013), marketing (Lee, Broderick and Chamberlain, 2007), or business ethics (Robertson, Voegtlin and Maak, 2016).

We also witness a steadily growing interest in the application of neuroscience as a method in the management discipline in general and business ethics in particular. A database search of ABI info shows that more than 3000 articles have been published in peer-reviewed management journals. Seventy of these articles have been published in leading business ethics journals such as *Business Ethics Quarterly* and *The Journal of Business Ethics*.

In this chapter we will provide a brief overview of neuroscience methodology and provide selected examples of its application in business ethics. After having introduced the most frequently used neuroimaging technologies, we review neuroscience as a research method analyzing its advantages and raising possible concerns. We then provide examples of contributions that neuroscience has made to business ethics research, in particular the role of emotions in ethical decision making. In the last section we focus on a newly emerging line of research that investigates the relationship of mindfulness and ethical decision making through the process of *reperceiving*. We will exemplify how neuroscience can help understand and examine this process.

## Neuroimaging Technologies

The visualization of the brain has reached new dimensions thanks to neuroimaging technologies which allow to collect information about the brain ranging from the individual molecule to several brains working together as a group. For the purpose of this chapter, and from the many available neuroimaging technologies, we will focus on fMRI and EEG (electroencephalography). While structural imaging technologies (such as CT, MRI, etc.) provide information about the brain anatomy, they cannot discern its physiology or behavioral correlates. Since this is where we see the contribution from neuroscience to business ethics research, we choose to present two functional instruments in greater detail.

### *fMRI Technology*

fMRI is a noninvasive metabolic imaging technology built upon MRI. The following principle is crucial for fMRI: changes in neural activity are coupled with changes in regional cerebral blood flow. When we engage a specific brain area, blood flow increases and oxygen-rich blood displaces oxygen-depleted blood a few seconds later since all body cells neurons need oxygen to function. The oxygen neurons need to perform is carried by hemoglobin. Deoxygenated hemoglobin is more magnetic than oxygenated hemoglobin, this difference in magnetism leads to an improved MR signal. The hemodynamic response reaches its peak after 4–6 seconds before returning to its baseline. This process discovered by Ogawa in 1990 is called *Blood Oxygenation Level Dependent contrast* or BOLD signal and is one of the most used methods in fMRI research. It is important to note that the hemodynamic change described here takes some time to occur, and hence the BOLD signal is an indirect measure of neuronal activity. This leads us to one of the main disadvantages of fMRI: its poor temporal resolution. Further disadvantages are the price of fMRI equipment and the fact that it is impossible to record group processes – at least for the time being. However, its advantages prevail: it is a noninvasive method and can therefore be used without a medical team, its spatial resolution is excellent (about 2 mm) and it can examine brain processes associated with empathy (Singer et al., 2004), moral dilemmas (Greene, Sommerville, Nystrom, Darley, and Cohen, 2001), decision making (Heekeren, Wartenburger, Schmidt, Schwintowski, and Villringer, 2003) and other human cognitions. For a more detailed description on how fMRI works and the analysis of fMRI data see for example Lindquist (2008) or Kable (2011).

### *EEG Technology*

Whereas fMRI is based on coupling neural and vascular response, EEG reflects directly the electrical activity of neurons. This electrical activity is the result of neurons in the brain communicating via electrical impulses. Thus, it is not the activity of one single neuron that is recorded, but the activity of multiple neurons results in a measureable electrical field outside the brain. To measure this field multiple electrodes are placed on the scalp. The resulting brainwaves are analyzed in various ways. Compared to fMRI, EEG spatial resolution is poor, but EEG has a lot of advantages: it is not as expensive as fMRI and it can be used nearly everywhere. Like fMRI the use of EEG doesn't imply the collaboration of a medical team. Its main advantage is its excellent temporal resolution milliseconds after the neural activity has started. Recent technological developments have also made it possible to record wireless EEG signal. Waldman et al. (2013; 2015) used wireless EEG technology to assess multiple team members simultaneously in real time as they solved a case as a team. This opens new possibilities for research and contributes to increased external validity.

## Neuroscience in Business Ethics Research

Neuroscience has made important contributions to business ethics research in recent decades. One of them is to substantiate the role of emotions in ethical decision making. For a long time philosophers have recognized emotions as being important for making moral judgments. Moreover, empirical research shows that emotions play a key role in moral decision making (Haidt, 2001). Neuroscience has provided scientific evidence for these important insights. In 1994, Damasio proposed the somatic marker hypothesis. In his theory emotions result from changes in the body. These bodily states are elicited during decision making and mark options as advantageous and disadvantageous. While these principles were initially observed in patients with focal lesions they are now applied to nonclinical human decision making sciences. In the following we provide examples of neuroscience insights relevant to understand the role of emotions in ethical decision making.

Brain areas such as the orbitofrontal cortex, the amygdala, and the anterior cingulate cortex play a critical role in emotional processes. These parts of the brain have been found to have higher levels of activation when individuals encounter stimuli that are morally relevant versus stimuli that are not. In an fMRI study of basic and moral emotions by Moll et al. (2002) designed to examine the neural substrates of moral awareness, subjects were randomly assigned to view one of six sets of pictures.

Some of the pictures evoked emotional responses and others didn't. Among the participants who viewed the "emotionally charged" pictures, some were designated to look at images involving moral issues (e.g., street children) and moral violations, such as war scenes and physical assaults; whereas others observed nonmorally related pictures (e.g., dangerous animals). The fMRI results indicated the following: Participants who viewed the morally relevant pictures, had a higher level of activation in parts of the brain associated with emotional processing. Participants who viewed pictures that were not morally relevant, whether these pictures were emotionally charged or not, had significant less activation in brain parts associated with emotion regulation. These results highlight the involvement of emotions when humans are exposed to situations involving moral violations and they strengthen the assumption that moral appraisal is linked to an emotional experience.

Neuroscience has also revealed the existence of neural mechanisms linking moral judgment with particular emotions. De Quervain, Fischbacher, Treyer and Schellhammer (2004) studied processes in the brain of people who altruistically punished social norm violators (e.g., for cheating in an economic exchange). An altruistic punishment is a punishment for which the punisher does not receive any material benefit or even accepts an economic cost. The authors discovered that when individuals engage in altruistic punishment, the dorsal striatum, that is the part of the brain associated with the emotional experience of satisfaction for being rewarded, is activated. In other words, when people exercise social norm-enforcing actions (e.g., regarding fairness and cooperation) and have the chance to "do the right thing," they are internally rewarded by satisfaction. Such findings help understand the motivation of moral behavior; in this case why people engage in altruistic norm-enforcing action. This in turn not only provides insights into reward-related regions of the brain but can also serve as a predictor for future behavior.

Further studies have found evidence that judgments about other fairness related tasks (e.g., unfair monetary offers) are processed in the ventral prefrontal cortex (VPFC), a brain region associated with emotional regulation (Tabibnia, Satpute, and Lieberman, 2008). In a study Tabibnia and colleagues tested participants' fairness using the ultimatum game. The ultimatum game is often used in economic experiments to study rational decision making. In the game the first player (proposer) receives a sum of money and chooses how to divide the sum between himself and the other player. The second player (responder) can either accept or reject the offer. If the responder accepts, the money is split according to the offer. If the responder rejects, neither of the two receives any money. During the game, Tabibnia et al. (2008) found a recurring activity pattern of the VPFC. This pattern suggests that the VPFC plays a key role when subjects make a normative decision. By accepting the unfair offer, the subjects have to control their negative emotions (e.g., anger about the offer) and let reason prevail (accepting the offer and getting some reward as opposed to receiving no reward at all).

While the research described above emphasizes the involvement of emotions in ethical decision making, traditional theories of decision making and moral development focused more on the role of controlled cognition (e.g., Kohlberg, 1969). Neuroscience research has identified the dorsolateral prefrontal cortex (DLPFC) to be a decisive area for the cognitive component of decision making. This part of the prefrontal cortex is active when we consider multiple sources of information to make a decision. The DLPFC is often active during tasks requiring working memory (Curtis and D'Esposito, 2003), an executive function responsible for holding, processing, and manipulating information relevant for decision making.

In an fMRI study, Heekeren et al. (2003) investigated ethical decision making using simple, nonemotional scenarios which did not contain any direct bodily harm or violence. They chose these type of stimuli because studies applying complex moral decision making dilemmas or salient emotional stimuli (e.g., violence and direct bodily harm) suggest that the ventromedial prefrontal cortex (vmPFC), the left posterior superior temporal sulcus (pSTS) and the posterior cingulate cortex are engaged during decision making. In contrast, Heekeren et al. wanted to investigate, which of these brain region is active during simple ethical decision making. They report that "simple moral decisions compared to semantic decisions resulted in activation of left pSTS and middle temporal gyrus, bilateral temporal poles, left lateral PFC and bilateral vmPFC." (Heekeren et al., 2003, p. 1215). The activation of the pSTS and the vmPFC, suggests that simple ethical decision making and more complex ethical dilemmas involving emotional processing, rely on a similar neural substrate. These findings are important, because they underline two things: First, in complex mental processes like ethical decision making, there is not a single brain area involved, but a networking of different brain areas is required. Second, cognition and emotion are equally important and may also have a common neural substrate. Thus, ethical decision making requires explicit deliberation and integration of diverse sources of information both, cognitive and emotional.

Greene and colleagues (2009) developed a theoretical model to emphasize the importance of the interplay of emotion and cognition, the *dual process theory of moral judgment*. In their theory, the authors synthesize emotion and cognition into one model. They link controlled cognitive processing to utilitarian moral judgment aimed at promoting the "greater good," and emotional response to deontological judgment aimed at respecting individual rights, duties, and obligations that may trump utilitarian considerations. To test the model they used moral dilemmas like the *switch case* and the *footbridge case*.[1] The authors assume, that due to the higher personal involvement, a personal dilemma like the footbridge case elicits an emotional response, whereas a more impersonal dilemma like the switch case does not. Therefore, they set up an fMRI study using various personal dilemmas and a contrasting set of impersonal dilemmas. As expected, during the personal dilemmas brain regions involved in emotional processing like the medial prefrontal cortex, the posterior cingulate cortex and the amygdala (Greene, Nystrom, Engell, Darley, and Cohen, 2004) showed more activation. In contrast, exposure to impersonal dilemmas elicited more activity in the DLPFC.

These are some examples showcasing how neuroscience may inform and indeed support research in Applied Philosophy and Business Ethics. We hope that these examples also provide inspiration for designing neuroscience-based studies in the field.

## Benefits of the Use of Neuroscientific Methods

Neuroscience has started to be widely used to investigate a broad range of phenomena in management research. Specifically, the field of leadership is at the forefront of adopting neuroscientific methods. Researchers apply neuroscience to enhance understanding of leadership as a phenomenon and to investigate whether "good leaders" may be differentiated by particular neuropathways. Moreover, evolving wireless EEG technology enables researchers to study leader-follower effects in dynamic settings.

Following Powell (2011) and Senior, Lee and Butler (2011), Waldman, Wang, and Fenters (2016) identify three key advantages of using neuroscientific methods and thus engage in organizational cognitive neuroscience. The first advantage is a better understanding of the ontological basis of constructs of interest. Understanding how brain structure and functioning relate to important phenomenon for business ethics such as ethical decision making and moral judgment can form a deeper appreciation and comprehension of what occurs within the mind. The second advantage leads to the creation of more precise measures. With the use of neuroscience, researchers have the possibility to measure ethical phenomena in a more direct way. For example, researchers have found that moral decisions with high personal involvement are processed in areas of the brain

[1] "Switch case": A runaway trolley is about to run over and kill five people, but the decision maker can save five people by hitting a switch that will divert the trolley onto a side track, where it will run over and kill only one person.

"Footbridge case": A runaway trolley threatens five people. Here, the only way to save the five people is to push a large person off a footbridge and into the trolley's path, stopping the trolley but killing the person pushed.

pertaining to emotions (Greene et al., 2001), confirming David Hume's (1738) and Adam Smith's (1759) visionary conceptualization of "moral emotions" and highlighting that emotions play a crucial role in moral decisions with high involvement and a certain level of complexity.

Accordingly, neuroscientific evidence has not only the potential to move the field forward and add reliability to more traditional survey methods; more importantly it may help business ethics research to a better approximation of the 'real' interplay of emotions and cognition in moral decision making and thus to more accurate predictions of the nature of managerial decision making which in turn may lead to better training in business ethics, linking rational analysis, emotional involvement, and contextual depth. This leads to the last point: the enhanced ability to predict important organizational phenomena. The external validity of a study can be increased by the assessment of the brain in addition to more traditional research methods. Such a validity increase is due to the fact that brain activity cannot be manipulated by the subject, since it is not prone to biases such as social desirability (Pless, Sabatella, and Maak, in press). Therefore, variables derived from neurological data can help explain variance in outcome measures and lead to more accurate predictions of moral action.

Nevertheless, following Lindebaum and Zundel (2013) and Robertson et al. (2016), we want to acknowledge two important considerations as such applications move forward in the future: (a) the potential for excessive reductionism through neuroscience and (b) ethical concerns. Neuroscience is one potential form of inquiry, and in our view should always be combined with other research methods. Neuroscientific data as such does not capture complex social phenomena; only when paired with social and psychological theories it adds substantial explanatory value. Thus, careful attention must be paid to research design. Regarding ethical concerns, researchers need to be aware that we now have the possibility to identify brain processes that are related to experiences and concepts such as free will, agency, and moral judgment. This development raises ethical questions: What are the social and cultural consequences of technologies that enable humans to manipulate their own minds? What impact will neuroscience have on our self-understanding and our concept of being human in general? What conclusions can or should be drawn from neuroscience data in regards to moral agency and free will? These are questions researchers have to keep in mind as the field advances to avoid both, simplistic explanations of moral behavior and ill-guided conclusions about moral determinism. If anything, recent advances in applied neuroscience have shown that more complex moral decisions are the outcome of an equally complex interplay of emotions, cognition, contextual, and personality factors – and that there is a need to study integration effects of these factors. Put differently, despite significant advances we still know relatively little about how exactly the relevant subregions in our brain interact with each other.

In sum, while we recognize the current limitations surrounding neuroscientific methods, and while caution is required in their application and interpretation of results, we also believe that there are clear advantages in incorporating them into business ethics research. In the next section, we introduce the emerging topic of mindfulness to ethical decision making in management and give an example how neuroscience can contribute to a nascent field of interest.

## Neuroscience, Mindfulness, and Ethical Decision Making

Neuroscience has been applied as a research method in ethical decision making. With the growing interest in the role of mindfulness and its role in decision making, neuroscience provides a potential method to better understand the different brain regions and processes involved.

Over the past decades mindfulness has been developed as a theory and practice in medicine and health for stress reduction. Reducing stress and reactivity in decision making is discussed as an important quality for better decision making. Eisenbeiss, Maak and Pless (2014) and Pless, Sabatella and Maak (in press) highlight the process of reperceiving as a particular relevant link between mindfulness and ethical decision making.

Therefore, we will discuss this relationship in more detail and examine how neuroscience may advance our understanding of the mechanisms involved.

Mindfulness meditation-based interventions are increasingly well-regarded in the psychological and medical literatures for their therapeutic efficacy in reducing distress (Greeson, 2009). The popularity of mindfulness in Western societies is mainly due to the increasing interest in the approach and work of Jon Kabat-Zinn (1994). Mindfulness is a concept originating in Buddhism, which was applied by Kabat-Zinn in the clinical setting and developed into a well researched clinical intervention called mindfulness based stress reduction (MBSR). For the purpose of this paper we build on this stream of research and define mindfulness as a *state of being in the present moment with a nonjudgmental, accepting attitude*.

Research has shown that the practice of mindfulness leads to a number of positive outcomes. Practicing mindfulness can lead to greater well-being (Bränström, Duncan, and Moskowitz, 2011), reduce stress and anxiety (Khoury, Sharma, Rush, and Fournier, 2015), enhance focus and attention (Smallwood and Schooler, 2015), increase working-memory capacity (Roeser et al., 2013; Stanley and Jha, 2009), and emotional regulation (Glomb, Duffy, Bono, and Yang, 2011). These, in turn, are all qualities relevant for effective decision making. An important characteristic of mindfulness is its potential to help shift perspective; that is to say it allows decision makers to witness themselves and occurring events impartially and with more distance, clarity, objectivity, and flexibility. Therefore, Eisenbeiss et al. (2014) see mindfulness as a precondition for complex problem solving and better decision making and Karelaia and Reb (2014) stress the positive connection between mindfulness and improved moral reasoning in decision making.

However, so far the interface of mindfulness and managerial decision making has been examined only by few authors (Eisenbeiss et al., 2014; Good et al., 2015; Karelaia and Reb, 2014; Kirk et al., 2016; Ruedy and Schweitzer, 2010; Shapiro, Jazaieri, and Goldin, 2012). To understand how mindfulness might affect ethical decision making, Eisenbeiss et al. (2014) suggest to examine this relationship through the meta-mechanism of reperceiving (Kabat-Zinn, 1990; Shapiro, Carlson, Astin, and Freedman, 2006). *Reperceiving*, or decentering, implies the capacity to witness oneself and occurring events impartially. It is described as the "ability to take a step back and to see oneself from a 'balcony'" (Kareleia and Reb, 2014, 165). It involves the ability to maintain a certain reflective distance from one's own emotions and thoughts, to witness them impartially, and to respond without being fully absorbed by them (ibid, 165). As such it involves attention to, and processing of, internal (e.g., emotion or thought) or external experiences (Good et al., 2016). Eisenbeiss et al. (2014) introduced a tripartite structure of reperceiving. It encompasses the human functions of (1) cognition (cognitive flexibility and insight), (2) emotions (compassion and interbeing), and (3) regulation (integrated functioning). Drawing on a child labor case (Pless and Maak, 2012), the authors argue that the process of reperceiving can support the development of innovative, values-based, and stakeholder-oriented solutions, important for business leaders when faced with complex moral dilemmas (see also Pless et al., in press). This is a particularly important quality as ethical decisions often have a broader impact on society requiring the abitity to pause, step back, and see the broader picture and considering the perspectives of other constituencies – of those involved in the dilemma and/or affected by the decision to be made. However, to understand how mindfulness can influence ethical decisions through reperceiving we need more insight into the different domains of human functioning. In the next section, we will review neuroscientific studies that provide supporting evidence for elements of the process of reperceiving, such as cognition and emotion.

## Cognition

Mindfulness and attentional qualities have been associated with cognitive performance by different authors (Eisenbeiss et al., 2014; Smallwood and Schooler, 2015; Good et al. 2016). Cognitive flexibility is the ability to respond in a nonhabitual fashion (Moore and Malinowski, 2009), to shift attention, and to consider more options. These are important skills for informed decision making. In neuroscience, cognitive flexibility has been examined in task-switching studies where subjects disengage from one task to undertake another. Task-switching studies using fMRI have identified a distributed and often left-lateralized network in the fronto-parietal part of the brain, including DLPFC, ventrolateral prefrontal cortex (VLPFC), fronto-polar cortex (FPC), presupplementary motor area (pre-SMA) and posterior parietal cortex (PPC) (Braver, Reynolds, and Donaldson, 2003).

In regards to problem solving neuroscience research (Heeren, Van Broeck, and Philippot, 2009) shows that there is a positive relation between mindfulness and cognitive flexibility with regard to cognitive processing and the creation of alternative options. Ding et al. (2015) conducted a study with randomly assigned participants who took part in a brief 5-hour mindfulness intervention. The study showed that the randomly assigned participants were more likely to look for alternatives when faced with a problem compared to the control group; their neural patterns indicated that cognitive flexibility is related to greater introspection (the ability to regulate thoughts or emotions) and attentional control.

In addition to above-mentioned studies, neuroscience has also provided evidence that in ethical decision making subconscious and intuitive processes play a crucial role. Therefore, we will discuss these aspects more in detail.

### *Emotion*

Emotions play a crucial role in decision making. According to neuroscience findings (Burns and Bechara, 2007) individual decision making is substantially influenced by unconscious, implicit processes in the brain. Decety, Michalska, and Kinzler (2011) stress the tight relationship between moral cognition and related affective and emotional processing. Regarding emotions, it is useful to distinguish between positive and negative emotions since they have different effects on decision making. Negative emotions (anger, guilt), may have disruptive effects, as discussed by some authors (e.g., Hofmann and Baumert, 2010). Others have focused more on the influence of positive emotions (e.g., empathy, compassion) on decision making. Positive emotions have been seen as particularly relevant to mindfulness and ethical decision making (Eisenbeiss et al., 2014). Empathy is defined as the ability to understand the emotional experiences of others (e.g., happiness or sadness) and feel with them. Mencl and May (2009) understand empathy as a "moral emotion" and suggest that higher levels of empathy potentially lead to greater awareness of negative decision making consequences for stakeholders by opening up, seeing issues from a different perspective and potentially developing alternatives for better stakeholder-sensitive decision making.

Neuroscience research has been of great benefit for understanding the role of emotions in ethical decision making processes by providing insights into the neurobiological foundations of emotions in such processes. A pioneering role in the drive of neurobiological research, was the case of Phineas Gage. Phineas Gage was a 19th century worker who survived a traumatic brain injury. Gage suffered a frontal lobotomy, which is a damage to the prefrontal cortex caused by a dynamite tramping iron penetrating his skull. He survived the accident and the neurological brain functions and intellectual faculties such as logical thinking and problem solving remained intact. However, his ability to process and regulate emotions, including empathy, and to make ethical decisions in social life were severely compromised (Damasio, 1994). The Phineas Gage case shows how fundamental emotions are for moral decision making. It also demonstrates that cognitive and ethical decision making are two distinct but connected processes in the brain. More recent case reports suggest that damages to the ventral and medial prefrontal cortex lead to deficits in social and moral decision making (Anderson, Bechara, Damasio, Tranel, and Damasio, 1999; Bechara, Damasio, and Damasio, 2000).

This pioneering case and subsequent neuroscience studies (see also Robertson et al., 2016) suggest that empathy plays a crucial role in ethical decision making. Eisenbeiss et al. (2014) argue that empathy and compassion are important emotions required for ethical decision making, in particular for developing compassionate solutions to moral dilemmas. With regard to the aforementioned child labor case they show that it was the manager's ability to tune into the situation, and to feel with the affected stakeholders – in this case, working children and their families – that enabled him to come up with a realistic and compassionate solution.

In sum, neuroscience can help us to better understand the different mechanisms involved in ethical decision making and the interplay between different brain regions. Further research is required to understand the potential of mindfulness for ethical decision making. This is particularly relevant in light of the growing need of a more responsible approach to business and the potential of the mindfulness concept to make a positive contribution to ethical decision making in business.

## Conclusion

In this chapter we have explored how advances in neuroscience research can add value to the field of business ethics and discussed examples of how neuroscientific methods can be incorporated in future research. We have considered advantages and disadvantages and raised possible concerns. By exploring the link of mindfulness and ethical decision making we provided an example of novel and promising research – especially given a fast growing mindfulness movement and its proposed positive link to ethical decision making. While there is growing awareness among management scholars that mindfulness has implications for ethical behavior (Dane, 2011) and managerial decision making (Good et al., 2015; Karelaia and Reb, 2014; Kirk et al., 2016; Ruedy and Schweitzer, 2010), knowledge of the mechanisms of mindfulness in ethical decision making is still in its infancy. Traditional research methods such as interviews and survey studies reach their limits in light of complex constructs such as mindfulness and ethical decision making. More specifically, the subjective nature of self-report data and the difficulty for research participants to describe internal processes and mechanisms accurately and objectively in interviews pose explicit challenges. Given the limits of traditional research methods, neuroscience research can help to illuminate the black box of ethical decision making by providing a better understanding of brain functioning, neural pathways involved in mindfulness and ethical decision making and unravel such complex processes (Hölzel et al., 2011).

We conclude this chapter with some thoughts on a potential research approach addressing the selection of neuroscience technology, research collaborations, and publication outlets. First, we note that although neuroscience is starting to examine moral reasoning and the specific neural circuitry involved with morality (Decety et al., 2011), most of the research is done using fMRI technology. For management and organizational research, Waldman et al. (2016) particularly suggest the use of qEEG technology for the following reasons: 1. The technology is very cost effective (the hardware costs are a fragment of the fMRI technology) and practical since EEG headsets are portable and can be used for studies outside the lab and in the workplace. 2. The technology can be used both for individual assessments and for team studies and produces highly ecologically valid assessments. 3. qEEG technology can be applied in interactive settings allowing for the examination of natural stimuli (e.g., effects of team members on each other) and alternatively the use of manipulated stimuli (e.g., a trained confederate could introduce stimuli in an ethical decision-making situation).

Second, the use of neuroscience methodology brings an interdisciplinary stance to management research. While the use of EEG does not require collaboration with medical researchers, the knowledge and expertise of neuroscientists is invaluable for setting up and conducting successful research projects (Waldman et al., 2013). Collaboration partners can not only be found in university departments (e.g., medicine, neuroscience, psychology), but also in firms specializing in neuroscience research and application (Waldman et al., 2016). However, due to the discipline specific vocabulary the challenge within such interdisciplinary research teams is the generation of a common language and the dissemination of research results in the discipline specific language of journals, so that findings can be understood and accepted by the respective group of reviewers and readers.

Third, regarding publication outlets management scholars are not restricted to publish their findings in neuroscience-based journals. As we noted at the beginning of the chapter, there is an increasing number of peer-reviewed management and business ethics journals that publish articles which apply neuroscience theory and methods. This is as trend that according to Waldman et al. (2016) will continue into the future; including and perhaps more frequently in the field of business ethics.

## Acknowledgments

Nicola Pless acknowledges the financial support by an internal grant of the University of South Australia for the project "Unlocking the potential of mindfulness for responsible leadership: An investigation into decision making, well-being and cognitive function outcomes" (0000035244).

### References

Anderson, S. W., Bechara, A., Damasio, H., Tranel, D., and Damasio, A. R. (1999). Impairment of social and moral behavior related to early damage in human prefrontal cortex. *Nature Neuroscience*, *2*(11), 1032.

Bechara, A., Damasio, H., and Damasio, A. R. (2000). Emotion, decision making and the orbitofrontal cortex. *Cerebral Cortex*, *10*(3), 295–307.

Bränström, R., Duncan, L. G., and Moskowitz, J. T. (2011). The association between dispositional mindfulness, psychological well-being, and perceived health in a Swedish population-based sample. *British Journal of Health Psychology*, *16*(2), 300–316.

Braver, T. S., Reynolds, J. R., and Donaldson, D. I. (2003). Neural mechanisms of transient and sustained cognitive control during task switching. *Neuron*, *39*(4), 713–726.

Burns, K., and Bechara, A. (2007). Decision making and free will: A neuroscience perspective. *Behavioral Sciences and the Law*, *25*(2), 263–280.

Curtis, C. E., and D'Esposito, M. (2003). Persistent activity in the prefrontal cortex during working memory. *Trends in Cognitive Sciences*, 7(9), 415–423.

Damasio, A. (1994). *Descartes' error: Emotion, reason and the human brain*. New York: Putnam and Sons.

Dane, E. (2011). 18 Capturing intuitions "in flight": Observations from research on attention and mindfulness. *Handbook of intuition research*, 217.

Decety, J., Michalska, K. J., and Kinzler, K. D. (2011). The developmental neuroscience of moral sensitivity. *Emotion Review*, *3*(3), 305–307.

De Quervain, D. J., Fischbacher, U., Treyer, V., and Schellhammer, M. (2004). The neural basis of altruistic punishment. *Science*, *305*(5688), 1254.

Ding, X., Tang, Y.-Y., Cao, C., Deng, Y., Wang, Y., Xin, X., and Posner, M. I. (2015). Short-term meditation modulates brain activity of insight evoked with solution cue. *Social Cognitive and Affective Neuroscience*, *10*(1), 43–49. www.doi.org/10.1093/scan/nsu032.

Fehr, E., and Rangel, A. (2011). Neuroeconomic foundations of economic choice: recent advances. *The Journal of Economic Perspectives*, *25*(4), 3–30.

Eisenbeiss, S.. Maak, T., and Pless, N. M. (2014). Leader mindfulness and decision-making. In: Linda Neider and Chester Schriesheim (Eds.). *Research in Management*, Vol. 10: Authentic and ethical leadership, pp. 191–208, Information Age Publishing.

Glomb, T. M., Duffy, M. K., Bono, J. E., and Yang, T. (2011). Mindfulness at work. *Research in Personnel and Human Resources Management*, *30*, 115.

Good, D. J., Lyddy, C. J., Glomb, T. M., Bono, J. E., Brown, K. W., Duffy, M. K., … Lazar, S. W. (2015). Contemplating mindfulness at work: An integrative review. *Journal of Management*, 0149206315617003.

Greene, J. D., Sommerville, R. B., Nystrom, L. E., Darley, J. M., and Cohen, J. D. (2001). An fMRI investigation of emotional engagement in moral judgment. *Science*, *293*(5537), 2105–2108.

Greene, J. D. (2009). The cognitive neuroscience of moral judgment. In M. S. Gazzaniga (Ed.), *The cognitive neurosciences* (4th edn, pp. 987–999). Cambridge, MA: MIT Press.

Greene, J. D., Nystrom, L. E., Engell, A. D., Darley, J. M., and Cohen, J. D. (2004). The neural bases of cognitive conflict and control in moral judgment. *Neuron*, 44(2), 389–400.

Greeson, J. M. (2009). Mindfulness research update: 2008. *Complementary Health Practice Review*, 14(1), 10–18.

Haidt, J. (2001). The emotional dog and its rational tail: a social intuitionist approach to moral judgment. *Psychological Review*, *108*(4), 814–834.

Heekeren, H. R., Wartenburger, I., Schmidt, H., Schwintowski, H. P., and Villringer, A. (2003). An fMRI study of simple ethical decision-making. *Neuroreport*, *14*(9), 1215.

Heeren, A., Van Broeck, N., and Philippot, P. (2009). The effects of mindfulness on executive processes and autobiographical memory specificity. *Behaviour Research and Therapy*, *47*(5), 403–409.

Hofmann, W., and Baumert, A. (2010). Immediate affect as a basis for intuitive moral judgement: An adaptation of the affect misattribution procedure. *Cognition and Emotion*, *24*(3), 522–535.

Hölzel, B. K., Carmody, J., Vangel, M., Congleton, C., Yerramsetti, S. M., Gard, T., and Lazar, S. W. (2011). Mindfulness practice leads to increases in regional brain gray matter density. *Psychiatry Research: Neuroimaging*, *191*(1), 36–43. https://doi.org/10.1016/j.pscychresns.2010.08.006.

Hume, D. (1738). *A treatise of human nature*.

Jones, O. D., Marois, R., Farah, M. J., and Greely, H. T. (2013). Law and neuroscience. *The Journal of Neuroscience*, *33*(45), 17624–17630.

Kabat-Zinn, J. (1990). *Full catastrophe living: The program of the stress reduction clinic at the University of Massachusetts Medical Center*. New York: Delta.

(1994). *Wherever you go, there you are: Mindfulness meditation in everyday life*. New York: Hyperion.

Kable, J. W. (2011). The cognitive neuroscience toolkit for the neuroeconomist: a functional overview. *Journal of Neuroscience, Psychology, and Economics*, *4*(2), 63.

Karelaia, N., and Reb, J. (2014). Improving decision making through mindfulness. Working paper, INSEAD.

Khoury, B., Sharma, M., Rush, S. E., and Fournier, C. (2015). Mindfulness-based stress reduction for healthy individuals: a meta-analysis. *Journal of Psychosomatic Research*, *78*(6), 519–528.

Kirk, U., Gu, X., Sharp, C., Hula, A., Fonagy, P., and Montague, P. R. (2016). Mindfulness training increases cooperative decision making in economic exchanges: Evidence from fMRI. *NeuroImage*, 138, 274–283.

Kohlberg, L. (1969). *Stage and sequence: The cognitive-developmental approach to socialization*. New York: Rand McNally.

Lee, N., Broderick, A. J., and Chamberlain, L. (2007). What is "neuromarketing"? A discussion and agenda for future research. *International Journal of Psychophysiology*, *63*(2), 199–204.

Lindebaum, D., and Zundel, M. (2013). Not quite a revolution: scrutinizing organizational neuroscience in leadership studies. *Human Relations*, *66*(6), 857–877.

Lindquist, M. A. (2008). The statistical analysis of fMRI data. *Statistical Science*, *23*(4), 439–464.

Mencl, J., and May, D. R. (2009). The effects of proximity and empathy on ethical decision-making: an exploratory investigation. *Journal of Business Ethics*, *85*(2), 201–226.

Moll, J., de Oliveira-Souza, R., Eslinger, P. J., Bramati, I. E., Mourao-Miranda, J., Anjelo Andrejuolo, P., and Pessoa, L. (2002). The neural correlates of moral sensitivity: a functional magnetic resonance imaging investigation of basic and moral emotions. *Journal of Neuroscience, 22*(7), 2730–2736.

Moore, A., and Malinowski, P. (2009). Meditation, mindfulness and cognitive flexibility. *Consciousness and Cognition*, *18*(1), 176–186.

Robertson, D. C., Voegtlin, C., and Maak, T. (2016). Business ethics: the promise of neuroscience. *Journal of Business Ethics*, 1–19.

Roeser, R. W., Schonert-Reichl, K. A., Jha, A., Cullen, M., Wallace, L., Wilensky, R., . . . Harrison, J. (2013). Mindfulness training and reductions in teacher stress and burnout: Results from two randomized, waitlist-control field trials. *Journal of Educational Psychology*, *105*(3), 787.

Ruedy, N. E., and Schweitzer, M. E. (2010). In the moment: The effect of mindfulness on ethical decision making. *Journal of Business Ethics*, *95*(1), 73–87.

Pless, N.M. and Maak, T. (2012). Levi Strauss & Co.: Addressing child labour in Bangladesh. In Mendenhall, M. E., Oddou, G. R. and Stahl, G. K. (Eds.) *Readings and cases in international human resource management and organizational behavior*. 5th ed., London, New York: Routledge, 446–459.

Pless, N. M., Sabatella, F. and Maak, T. (2017). Mindfulness, Reperceiving, and Ethical Decision Making: A Neurological Perspective. In *Responsible Leadership and Ethical Decision-Making* (pp. 1-20). Emerald Publishing Limited.

Powell, T. C. (2011). Neurostrategy. *Strategic Management Journal*, *32*(13), 1484–1499.

Senior, C., Lee, N., and Butler, M. (2011). Organizational cognitive neuroscience. *Organization Science*, *22*(3), 804–815.

Shapiro, S. L., Carlson, L. E., Astin, J. A., and Freedman, B. (2006). Mechanisms of mindfulness. *Journal of Clinical Psychology*, *62*(3), 373–386.

Shapiro, S. L., Jazaieri, H., and Goldin, P. R. (2012). Mindfulness-based stress reduction effects on moral reasoning and decision making. *The Journal of Positive Psychology*, *7*(6), 504–515.

Singer, T., Seymour, B., O'Doherty, J., Kaube, H., Dolan, R. J., and Frith, C. D. (2004). Empathy for pain involves the affective but not sensory components of pain. *Science*, *303*(5661), 1157–1162.

Smallwood, J., and Schooler, J. W. (2015). The science of mind wandering: Empirically navigating the stream of consciousness. *Annual Review of Psychology*, *66*, 487–518.

Smith, A. (1759). *The theory of moral sentiments*. New York: Garland, 1971.

Stanley, E. A., and Jha, A. P. (2009). Mind fitness and mental armor: enhancing performance and building warrior resilience. *Joint Force Quarterly*, *55*, 144–151.

Tabibnia, G., Satpute, A. B., and Lieberman, M. D. (2008). The sunny side of fairness preference for fairness activates reward circuitry (and disregarding unfairness activates self-control circuitry). *Psychological Science*, *19*(4), 339–347.

Waldman, D. A., Wang, D., and Fenters, V. (2016). The added value of neuroscience methods in organizational research. *Organizational Research Methods*, 1094428116642013.

Waldman, D. A., Wang, D., Stikic, M., Berka, C., Balthazard, P. A., Richardson, T., Pless, N. M., and Maak, T. (2013). Emergent leadership and team engagement: an application of neuroscience technology and methods. In *Academy of Management Proceedings* (Vol. 2013, p. 12966). Academy of Management.

Waldman, D. A., Wang, D., Stikic, M., Berka, C., and Korszen, S. (2015). Neuroscience and team processes. *Organizational Neuroscience*, 277–294.

# Case Study Approaches

CHAPTER 14

# Wide Reflective Equilibrium as a Case-Based Research Approach to Business Ethics

PATRICIA H. WERHANE

## Introduction

In business ethics research, one commonly uses real-life or fictional cases to explain, illustrate, and strengthen one's arguments. This strategy involves a number of approaches. Often, researchers apply traditional ethical principles such as virtue ethics, Kantianism, or utilitarianism to the case. In a second approach, one might use a case as an exemplar to illustrate reoccurring themes, such as deception, transparency, whistleblowing, environmental sustainability, social responsibility, community involvement, visionary decision-making, globalization, or even avarice. In qualitative research or grounded theory, a case is often the centerpiece from which one derives theoretical considerations. See Chapter 8 on grounded theory for details about this approach to business ethics research.

In this chapter we will give examples of a number of these case approaches and we will introduce a promising and effective approach, wide reflective equilibrium. In following the approach of wide reflective equilibrium or WRE, the researcher analyzes a series of cases, studying their background conditions and the appropriate principles they reveal for moral judgment. Typically, one will compare the tentative conclusions reached in the first case to those reached in the second, and so on. By studying the evolution of moral principles used in these analyses, one may come to a tentative conclusion on a set of considered moral judgments that can be reiterated in other scenarios. That ideal is seldom achieved, but the process is very useful in business ethics research.

## Some Standard Approaches to Case Analysis

When contemporary business ethics was a nascent discipline, case analysis simply used traditional ethical theories to examine a particular scenario. For example, in thinking about the well-known Merck and river blindness case, using this technique, one would approach that case and its managerial decision-making processes through the utility: the costs, and/or benefits, of developing and producing ivermectin, the drug for river blindness. This is often coupled with a stakeholder analysis: how and in what ways might each primary stakeholder affect or be affected by the possible outcomes this case might produce. Then one would appeal to Immanuel Kant's categorical imperatives that seemingly require producing this drug despite the virtual impossibility of a monetary return on Merck's investment. Another, a rights approach, would list and analyze in what ways each set of stakeholders have claims to basic rights. A fourth approach might appeal to an Aristotelian idea of character: What kind of company is Merck? Does it follow the mission of its founder, who was quoted as saying, "We try never to forget that medicine is for the people. It is not for the profits. The profits follow, and if we have remembered that, they have never failed to appear" (Bollier, Weiss and Hansen, 1991). How does Merck want to be perceived as a company by its researchers and managers, in the market, or by the public? The utilitarian response is likely to be quite different from a Kantian decision since the costs of producing and marketing ivermectin outweigh its benefits to Merck, and Merck could just as easily work on other important life-saving drugs that will have market value as well. A rights approach wherein one measures the equal rights claims of Merck, its patients who have benefited from Merck's drugs, and those infected with river blindness might produce even different conclusions.

Cases in research can also be used as exemplars or models for judging reoccurring similar cases. For example, the explosion of the Challenger, due to the burnout of its o-rings, was administratively caused by siloed thinking and a strict managerial hierarchy. Because there was no communication between engineers at NASA and its managers, each thought about the launch of Challenger through a different mindset. Engineers were worried because they could not verify that the o-rings would withstand the low atmospheric temperatures predicted for the launch day. Placing safety first, they did not want to sign off on the launch. Managers at NASA, having no proof that the o-rings *would* fail, saw little risk. And because of the hierarchical structure at NASA, engineers, who saw themselves as working for their managers, did not blow the whistle before the launch even when, in theory, there were avenues for that (Rogers Commission Report, 1987).

Because siloed thinking and strict hierarchies are prevalent in many firms, this case becomes an exemplar or model for how not to organize and engage in organizational decision-making. Following this approach one could imagine finding a series of cases where these two phenomena were prevalent. For instance, one could compare the Challenger explosion to the later Columbia shuttle explosion and to earlier shuttle incidents to see parallels and differences in each case. Indeed, although the Columbia explosion was due to tiles that pierced the shuttle capsule, not from o-ring failure, documented evidence shows mentalities where engineers and managers simply did their jobs and managers did not consider the mindsets of the others, as well as a hierarchical culture that virtually guaranteed no one would blow the whistle. From these series of incidents, one could draw some general conclusions about reoccurring themes and their possible antidotes. This kind of analysis is the approach of WRE.

## Wide Reflective Equilibrium

WRE is a model introduced by the late John Rawls and developed by Norman Daniels. In a very early essay, Rawls begins his thinking by declaring that "ethics must, like any other discipline, work its way piece by piece" (Rawls, 1951, 189). He suggests that one begins with a specific case and works toward what he calls "a considered moral judgment." To make such a judgment, Rawls argues, one needs to be as impartial and reasonable as possible, trying to disregard emotions and personal influences. In making a considered moral judgment, Rawls argues, "it is necessary to specify the kind of situation in which the problem [in the case] . . . and the action consequent thereto arises" (191). Rawls then introduces principles by which one evaluates this considered moral judgment. However, this is not the end of the process, since, as we saw in the Merck case, there may be conflicts as to which principles are the most applicable, and how they are to be operationalized in evaluating the judgment.

Later, in *A Theory of Justice* Rawls elaborates the next step, which involves "going back and forth, sometimes altering the conditions of the circumstances and withdrawing our judgments and confirming them to principle." The goal is to reach "principles which match our considered judgments duly pruned and adjusted . . . A set of cases is in equilibrium when our principles and judgments coincide; and it is reflective since we know to what principles our judgments conform and the premises of their derivation" (Rawls, 1971;1999, 18). But Rawls also adds a proviso, that these "considered moral judgments" are not absolute or "necessarily stable," because changing background conditions and/or introducing other cases may change our judgments or revise our principles (see also Daniels, 1996, 338).

Working off Rawls's theory, Norman Daniels expands the idea of reflective equilibrium to what he calls wide reflective equilibrium (WRE). "WRE entails testing one's considered judgments and principles against a wide range of ethical and nonethical beliefs in the aim of arriving at some long-term consensus. Wide reflective equilibrium . . .requires that we develop support for our moral beliefs by working back and forth among judgments about particular cases, moral principles, and other theoretical considerations. We are to revise them [our moral beliefs and particular judgments] whenever appropriate, aiming for the system of the strongest mutual support among them." (Daniels, 1996, 10).

In his theoretical essay, "Wide Reflective Equilibrium and Theory Acceptance in Ethics" (1979), Daniels frames this idea in more formal terms.

> The method of wide reflective equilibrium is an attempt to produce coherence in an ordered triple of sets of beliefs held by a particular person, namely, (a) a set of considered moral judgments, (b) a set of moral principles, and (c) a set of relevant background theories ... working back and forth, making adjustments to his considered judgments, his moral principles, and his background theories until he arrives at an equilibrium point that consists of the ordered triple (a), (b), (c). (1979, 258–259)

Both Rawls in *A Theory of Justice* and Daniels contend that this methodology can apply to many levels of generality, not merely to particular individual decision-makers (Rawls, 1971, 1999; Daniels 1979; 1996). Thus, this methodology is suitable for business ethics when we analyze not only with individual decision-making but also organizational and more systemic ethical issues in commerce.

Implied but not explicit in Rawls and Daniels writings on WRE is that engaging in this process requires stepping back from the contexts of the cases or issues involved and taking as impartial or disinterested a perspective as is possible in case analysis. This step enables or can enable a clearer judgment or set of judgments that approach considered consensus or equilibrium.

## WRE and Research Approaches in Business Ethics

### *A Starting Place*

Let us assume that a viable method for research in business ethics begins with or engages a case, a vignette, a story, or a narrative that while not an actual case, resembles a scenario that makes sense in commerce, for example using literature that has clear analogies to "real life" characters, events, or behavior to illustrate ethical issues in business. I shall refer to these as "cases." Whatever example is used, any jumping off point for research comes with its own baggage, e.g., the point of view of the author, limited amounts of information, and the context in which the narrative of the case occurs.[1]

To begin, one describes the context, the background conditions of the case (e.g., locale, traditions, and customs of those involved or affected, the nature of the focal organization, etc.) Then one lists the ethical issues in the case, noting that sometimes these issues may be intertwined with marketing, finance, other divisions of the organization, and similar organizations. Do the goals and mission of the organization involved in this case and its culture or dominant logic affect the issues at stake and the company's decision?

Then one lists and analyzes those stakeholders who are most affected by or contribute to the case. At this stage of the analysis one introduces ethical theory. What are the interests of the primary stakeholders in the outcome of the case? Are any human rights at threat for any of these stakeholders? Who will benefit and who might be harmed, depending on the outcome of the case? What are the moral minimums, those very basic, sometimes negatively framed, moral principles that appear to be widely, if not globally agreed upon? For example, murder, torture, lying, cheating, and stealing, in all but the most egregious instances, are considered morally reprehensible

[1] It is this context that cannot be dismissed, although that is often ignored. For example, in thinking though British Petroleum's oil spill in the Gulf of Mexico, the focus is usually on the importance of the lives lost on the rig, the lives, culture, local practices, and well-being of residents and fishermen in the region who were negatively affected by the explosion. The case writers then focus most of the responsibility on BP, and rightly so. But one sometimes forgets the other players in this scenario. The the rig was built by Hyundai, a Korean firm, owned by Transocean, and leased to BP who operated this rig under a Marshall Islands flag. This is to hold BP accountable for this accident and to suggest that other players had roles in the rig's failure as well. BP lost 12 workers in the blast, who, too, are sometimes neglected in the pressing urge to emphasize the environmental disaster that resulted from the spill. Stakeholder analysis helps to mitigate this neglect, so that piece of methodology is crucial.

A similar analysis is conducted on the issues. Given the issues in each case, one could ask, what are the viable options? How does each issue affect each stakeholder, including shareholders? How does each affect the company and its long-term goals? Who benefits, and who might be harmed by each option? Are any human rights at threat? How might each option affect the communities touched by this case? How might it affect the ecosystem system? Can we decide on the right thing to do, all things, considered, or are there only options that are the least bad? If there are professionals involved, such as engineers, medical teams, accountants, or lawyers, how does each option fit with their codes of ethics? Can one come up with a decision that will not violate their codes? And of course, is each option legal? Is each option viable or possible to operationalize given the circumstances and context? What kind of precedent does each option set both within the organization and for the industry? How does each option affect the reputation of that company and its leaders? When doing business globally, how would this decision be received in one's home country? Then one can compare responses to these questions to similar inquiries surrounding the next case.

Taking the perspective of a noninvolved spectator in the case, what would that person decide? Given the choice (which, again, may be the least bad), how does one operationalize that choice in this context and circumstances? Initially, then, going back and forth between ethical theories, moral standards, or moral minimums, stakeholders, and the issues in this case, one arrives at a tentative decision. If one is dealing with a case whose outcome has been determined, one uses this methodology pathologically to reanalyze and critique the decision and lessons learned.

But that is only the beginning. In a well-organized use of WRE, one would analyze a series of cases, using what was learned from each to hone the analysis and, at least ideally, arrive at a tentative consensus. In evaluating just two cases, Challenger and Columbia explosions, for example, one can make tentative but worthwhile conclusions on organizational distress and how that can be avoided. But in most instances, more cases are useful, and consensus is seldom achieved. Still, by examining a series of cases in their contexts, the principles to which one appeals, and the moral judgments we engage in in each case, the researcher may be led to develop new approaches to commerce. Figure 14.1 represents this process graphically.

## *Some Other Examples*

To illustrate, let me give a simple example – American political history of voting and two more complex contemporary set of cases that are less easily resolved.

### The Right to Vote

When the United States was founded and the Constitution and Bill of Rights were formulated, one of the incorporated rights was the right to vote. This was, from the beginning, an equal right with only one-vote-per-adult person in any election, and that democratic principle has remained unaltered. However, initially the right to vote was extended only to white male adult (21 years old and older) land-holding Protestants (except in Maryland where Catholics could vote.) While there was consensus on the importance of this right, the extent to which only white adult land-holding males, usually Protestants, were included was challenged, particularly by land-holding non-Protestants.

Because of pressures from wealthy land-holding white men of other religions, these men were given the right to vote in most states. Then, going back and forth from the initial principle, stated in the Constitution and the Bill of Rights, grounding the right to vote, as well as societal changes, by 1865 men of color and indigenous males were given this right.

Since that time, because it was recognized that not every sane male adult held property, the property-holding proviso was lifted in every state. Yet there still was not consensus because half the adult population in this country, women, could not vote.

Finally, due to endless protests and lobbying mostly by adult women, in 1922 women were granted the right to vote. Even later, when people over the age of eighteen were in the armed services, the voting age was changed to eighteen

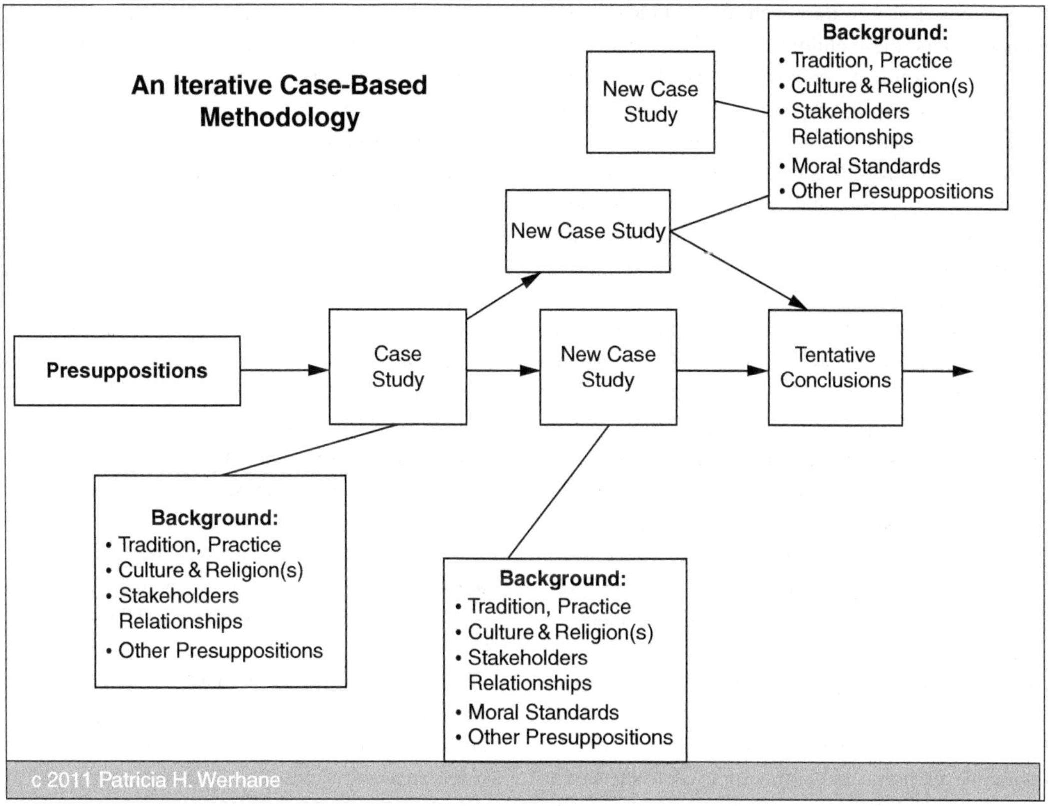


*Figure 14.1* An iterative case-based methodology.

years. Today in most states one has to have some sort of residence in order to vote, and we are now worrying about how to give the homeless and former convicted felons such a right. Thus, the United States has reached a consensus on operationalizing this right to reach as many individual adults as possible, but the consensus is provisional, as the extension of voting rights continues (Carroll et al., 2012).

Of course, using this methodology does not always produce consensus, or, like voting in the United States, it may take centuries. But by comparing cases and the various dimensions of ethical theories in practice, researchers may discover how to mitigate incompatible either-or dilemmas and, for example, siloed mentalities and bureaucratic hierarchies such as those that thwarted choices in the Challenger and Columbia cases.

**Either-Or Dilemmas**

Let us look at a set of cases involving either-or dilemmas, instances where the company or manager seems to be faced with an intractable moral dilemma. Often neither alternative is satisfactory and neither will produce a satisfactory outcome.

A few years ago, the German transnational company, Bayer, acquired an Indian company, CropScience, which was able to provide Bayer with linseeds, a product that Bayer needed for some of its chemical production. The best source of these seeds were small farms spread throughout India. However, Bayer subsequently discovered that the seeds were harvested by children, a customary practice throughout most of the farms in the region, but patently against Bayer's mission, which explicitly states that child labor will not be condoned anywhere throughout the company's operations. Because they were in the fields during school hours, these children fell behind their peers in the government schools and usually dropped out. Bayer's employees were highly critical of the purchase because of the child labor, the German media was outraged, and there were strong arguments that Bayer should get rid of CropScience. Bayer was seemingly faced with an either-or situation. Should they remain in India, providing much-needed jobs for rural people and linseeds for the company? Or should they pull out because of their principled mission not ever to condone child labor?

Part of this either-or dilemma entailed moral risk. In this essay, we define moral risk as a phenomenon that occurs in situations in which there is uncertainty about whether one's choices will produce, on balance, positive or negative outcomes. Moreover, in engaging in a morally risky proposition, one may have to sacrifice some ideals in order to achieve other outcomes or one might have to violate an important human right in order to achieve another equally important moral goal (Werhane, 2004). Thus, is analyzing this case the principle of moral risk, sometimes defined as the principle of double effect (Werhane, 2004) can be introduced into the analysis.

If Bayer were to sell CropScience, they would not only miss an opportunity for the valued linseeds, they also risked harming their thriving chemical business and their ability to improve the status of the children. However, attempting to improve the status of children would be a risky endeavor as well. After all, child labor had been part of the culture of these farms for hundreds of years; would Bayer be practicing a form of neocolonialism if they intervened in this age-old practice? Moreover, child labor was such an ingrained tradition that Bayer might not be able to change it anyway. On the positive side, withdrawing would bolster the morale of Bayer's employees and meet the criticisms of the media. This seemingly back-and-forth dilemma also introduces another dimension to ethical decision-making, that of moral imagination. That is, can a case analysis produce a resolution that is not merely the choice of lesser evils?

In the Bayer CropScience seemingly insolvable dilemma Bayer, neither succumbed to the child labor practices at the Indian farms nor did it sell CropScience. In fact, it did not even imagine this as a dilemma. It could have engaged in siloed thinking where either principle (selling) or profitability was the trump. But it did not. Rather, the company developed a process that satisfied its mission, created job availability in many parts of rural India, and achieved its need for the linseeds. Bayer created a strategy that was beneficial to the children, the farmers and to its bottom line. It partnered with an Indian NGO that provided remedial schooling for the children of the farmers, children who formerly worked in the fields, so that they would be prepared to enter government schools, and it paid the farmers a premium to use adult labor. The farmers soon found that their efficiency was improved with adult labor, the children went to school, children's families did not suffer income loss, and the company gained a valuable product (Dhanaraj, Branzei, and Subramanian, 2011; Subramanian, Dhanaraj, and Branzei, 2011).

This case illustrates that merely analyzing a case from a utilitarian or from a Kantian perspective or allowing oneself to become mired in what seems to be an impossible either-or situation can create a morass of decision dilemmas. A more nuanced approach can often produce more satisfying solutions. That creative approach (which involves stepping back from the particular dilemma to search for a creative solution) can be useful in analyzing a series of cases.

For example, another seemingly either-or dilemma is illycaffè's quality initiatives in Brazil, an initiative that began as an economic pursuit of better coffee beans. Illy is a high-end Italian producer that is in constant search of good beans. But in Brazil, its main source of coffee, coffee beans had become a commodity. Because the beans were not sorted by quality, illycaffè had to discard thirty-nine of every forty bags it purchased. Should the company continue this expensive practice or withdraw from the Brazilian market? This either-or dilemma presented two solutions, neither of which was satisfactory to the Brazilians not to illy, who had been in Brazil for a long time.

Stepping back from the dilemma rather than miring itself in these issues, illycaffè began by pursuing a singular and deliberate economic strategy, without any intent toward social action. It offered Brazilian farmers monetary rewards for their best beans. This competition resulted in finding farmers who had incentives to grow the best beans, for which the company paid them a premium. But illycaffè unexpectedly engaged in social action that resulted in positive economic value for multiple stakeholders and also positive social value for Brazilian farmers. In the course of that pursuit for the best beans, the firm inadvertently created social benefits for the Brazilian coffee farmers through paying the farmers higher premiums for good beans and through the establishment of an education program designed to improve productivity. These initiatives have improved the economic well-being of these farmers and the bottom line at illycaffè.

This case also illustrates how a corporate dominant logic, a concentration on creating the best quality coffee, can be amended by circumstances, just as what appears to be an intractable dilemma can often be ameliorated by new thinking. Ernesto Illy admits that "[t]he impact of [the company's] initiative has been much greater than what we had foreseen. We simply wanted to solve our problem but, in fact, we changed the mentality of the Brazilian market" (Andriani, Biotto, and Ghezzi, 2012, pp. 198–202).

In both cases the companies faced moral risk – the risk of creating more harm than good in their decision-making – because of their power as multinational companies (they could be perceived as neocolonialists) and because the outcomes of their decisions were unclear. By introducing the notion of moral risk as well as the process of stepping back to consider creative alternatives in a set of cases one can reach a provisional consensus that illustrates how an "either-or" dilemma does not have to result in a stalemate if managers examine the context and local conditions in which they propose to operate carefully and think imaginatively about some creative solutions.

Another dimension of these two cases (and there are others with similar issues) is that they each model corporate strategies or partnering with unlikely partners, such as Brazilian small coffee growers and Indian small farmers. By engaging in a WRE approach with sets of cases such as these we can challenge biased mindsets that perceive poor people as incapable or lazy, all of which is mistaken as these growers and farmers illustrate. Thus, one can reach a tentative set of moral judgments concerning moral risk, the challengeability of ethical dilemmas, and a revised set of moral judgments about those living in poverty.

### Social Media in China

Research on moral risk presents a useful model for examining corporate behavior in challenging settings. For instance, when Motorola decided to develop manufacturing in China some years ago, they faced the following dilemma: By attempting to set up a model for responsible corporate behavior and provide good technical jobs for Chinese citizens, were they, in fact, condoning one-child-per family rules that were mandatory at the time for all companies to enforce, and by operating in a country that does not have a good human rights record were they implicitly condoning that behavior? (Werhane, 2004). That latter issue has not been resolved; foreign companies operating in China today still face these moral risks, as exemplified in the LinkedIn, Facebook, and Google cases. Studying those cases in tandem and building a WRE approach on each yields interesting conclusions, although not equilibrium.

In 2006 Google, known for its mission statement, "don't be evil," entered the China internet market,[2] aware of the moral risk that entailed. It accepted the Chinese censorship practices and made that transparent to its users. Nevertheless, Google found the enormous Chinese internet market appealing and had, we surmise, hoped that transparency of information rather than censorship would prevail. Google overlooked the fact, however, that the Chinese are also well known for tapping into internet users' files and/or hacking emails. In 2010 the Chinese government hacked

[2] Google's original mission statement was "to organize the world's information and make it universally accessible and useful." Its unofficial motto was "Don't be evil," a phrase which appears on its Code of Conduct page for employees and investors (Google, 2016).

into the Google email of some Chinese human rights dissidents, who were subsequently arrested. Outraged, Google withdrew from the Chinese market, despite the presence of its chief competitor, Yahoo!, who was and is still there.

Facebook and Twitter were banned by the Chinese government in 2009, barely a year after they entered that market because riots in the Chinese Western province of Xinjiang were reported on these social media and the rioters were allegedly using Facebook. The Chinese authorities accused these sites of abetting the rioters and the riots (Woollaston, 2013). The *New York Times* has been blocked since its reporting that the family of then-Premier Wen Jiabao had amassed a huge fortune.[3]

In the meantime, LinkedIn, despite being aware of the censorship restrictions of the Chinese government, entered the Chinese social media market in 2014. Today it is the major source of communication among business persons and other professionals throughout China and this turns out to be a great service to that economy and its professionals who had no previous way to communicate efficiently. However, as an American company, LinkedIn had to compromise the basic principle of free speech that Americans claim as their most valued principle. Its justification is that "it is only dealing with professional content, job postings, and management practices so that most all of its content is not controversial" (Benner, 2014). "LinkedIn is a window onto, and in some cases a passport to, the middle class, white-collar professional world that Chinese citizens have craved ever since they traded in their Mao suits for Levis in the 1980s" (Bloomberg, 2014). At the end of 2015 it had over 13 million Chinese users to its site. Still, according to Bloomberg, the content of some users has been blocked by censors and by LinkedIn Chinese-based managers themselves (Benner, 2014).

According to the LinkedIn website, "Our mission is simple: To connect the world's professionals to make them more productive and successful. When you join LinkedIn, you get access to people, jobs, news, updates, and insights that help you be great at what you do" (LinkedIn, 2016). But does that mission guarantee uncensored access? Apparently not.

Is LinkedIn's service to Chinese business people worth the trade-off? Even though it violates the principle of freedom of speech, might it lead to more open communication and information sharing in the future? That is the risk that LinkedIn has taken on, and this LinkedIn case provides a good illustration of what is at stake in moral risk – freedom of speech v. censored communication and information sharing.

Finally, in 2016, Google has decided to reenter the Chinese market, acknowledging the censorship restrictions. Google justified its decision with the argument that providing even censored information is an important service to the Chinese internet users that now number hundreds of millions of people. According to this reasoning, the interests of those stakeholders take priority over the possibility of hacking and the always present threat of Chinese discovery of dissenters. Google has insisted that this is the most ethical option given the number of users and their need for information. Still, this is a morally risky proposition, particularly given Google's stated mission of "doing no evil." It is also a case of moral compromise, balancing the need for information against the ideal of unfettered freedom of speech (Waddell, 2016).

These cases, Google, LinkedIn, Facebook, Twitter, and the *New York Times* work well together in research analysis. They illustrate the value of transparency, they challenge free speech as an overriding basic right. Each case illustrates how each company faces the moral risk of partnering that may create more harm than good, and each case brings up the thorny question as to the limits of profitability and the question of who is harmed and who benefits as a result of this pursuit. Notice that LinkedIn, and Yahoo!, and now Google, are

[3] Interestingly, since 2013 a small selection of people living and working in the 17-square-mile free-trade zone in Shanghai, China are now able to access these banned sites including Facebook, Twitter, and other 'politically sensitive' links, despite the general censorship of these social media for the rest of China. There are also unverifiable rumors that clever internet users have learned to go around the censors. (Woollaston, 2013).

compromising their mission and the American ideal of free speech in order to serve a very large market. Perhaps each hope that eventually censorship will be lifted and communication without compromise will be restored to this market. This is their either-or dilemma and they chose the more profitable, less-principled approach.

## Conclusion

Most cases and sets of cases in commerce do not reach equilibrium. Nevertheless, the methodology is very useful. Engaging with a series of cases that build on each other one can learn from each with tentative conclusions that carry forward to the next case and point to issues that might not be patently evident. Each of the cases we briefly summarized in this chapter illustrates new or otherwise worn-out approaches. Siloed thinking, obedience to hierarchies, either-or thinking, moral risk, moral compromise, and unsolvable dilemmas challenge us to be even more creative. These are just illustrations of what a case-based WRE approach can contribute to business ethics research. Using cases in business ethics research helps to clarify issues and links theory to practice. Using a series of cases can advance ethical thinking beyond utilitarianism, Kantianism, and virtue theory, with the introduction of other dimensions of moral judgments. Thus, WRE is a viable and enriching approach to business ethics research.

### References

Andriani, P., Biotto, G., and Ghezzi, D. M. (2012). "The Emergence of Trust-Based Knowledge Ecosystems: The Case of illycaffè in Brazil. In F. Belussi and U. H. Staber (Eds.), *Managing Networks of Creativity* (pp. 191–211). London, UK: Routledge.

Benner, Katie. 2014. "How LinkedIn Cracked the Chinese Market." *Bloomberg View.* www.bloomberg.com/view/articles/2014-1 Accessed July 10, 201

Bollier, D., Weiss, S., and Hanson, K. O. 1991. *Aiming Higher*. New York: American Management Association.

Clark, Che, Greniuk, Holly, Riherd, Jacob, Rome, Brendan and YU, Jessica. 2010. "The Great Fire Wall of China: Google's Market Entry into China." *Forbes India.*http://forbesindia.com/article/thunderbird/the-great-fire-wall-of-china-googles-market-entry-into-china/16472/1#ixzz4F1bCoZ8o Accessed July 22, 2016.

Columbia Accident Report. 2003. *Report of Columbia Accident Investigation Board.* www.nasa.gov/columbia/home/CAIB_Vol1.html Accessed February 24, 2015.

Daniels, Norman. 1979. "Wide Reflective Equilibrium and Theory Acceptance in Ethics." *Journal of Philosophy.*76: 256–282.

1996. *Justice and Justification*. New York: Cambridge University Press.

Dhanaraj, C., Branzei, O., and Subramanian, S. (2011). Bayer CropScience in India (A): Value-Driven Strategy. *Ivey Case Publishing, Case No. 9.* Retrieved from www.iveycases.com/ProductView.aspx?id=45590. Accessed January 14, 2016.

GOOGLE. 2016. www.google.com/about/company/. Accessed July 12, 2016.

LinkedIn. 2016. www.linkedin.com/about-us. Accessed July 27, 2016.

Mozur, Paul and Goel, Vindu. 2014. To reach China, LinkedIn plays by local rules. *New York Times.* October 5. www.nytimes.com/2014/10/06/technology/to-reach-china-linkedin-plays-by-local-rules.html Accessed July 14, 2016.

Pallardy, Richard. 2016. "Deepwater Horizon Oil Spill of 2010." *Encyclopedia Britannica.* www.britannica.com/event/Deepwater-Horizon-oil-spill-of-2010 Accessed August 2, 2016.

Rawls, John. 1951. "Outline of a Decision Procedure for Ethics." *Philosophical Review.* 60: 177–197.

1971; 1989. *A Theory of Justice*. Cambridge, MA: Belnap Press.

Rogers Commission Report. 1986. The Report of The Presidential Commission on the Space Shuttle Accident. www.ksc.nasa.gov/shuttle/missions/51-l/docs. Accessed June 3, 2014.

Waddell, Kaveh. 2016. "Why Google Quit China and Why It's Heading Back." *The Atlantic*, January 19, 2016.

Werhane, Patricia H. 2004. "The Principle of Double Effect and Moral Risk: Some Case Studies of US Transnational Corporations," in *Responsibility in World Business: Managing Harmful Side-effects of Corporate Activity.* ed. Lene

Bomann-Larsen and Oddny Wiggin. New York and Japan: United Nations University Press, pp. 105–120.

Woollaston, Victoria. 2013. "China lifts ban on Facebook – but only for people living in a 17 square mile area of Shanghai." www.dailymail.co.uk/sciencetech/article-2431861/China-lifts-ban-Facebook–people-living-working-small-area-Shanghai.html September 23. Accessed July 27, 2015.

CHAPTER 15

# Casuistry as a Case-Based Research Approach to Business Ethics

MARTIN CALKINS

Derived from the Latin *casus* meaning "case," *casuistry* is an inductive method of moral deliberation that uses previously settled truth-bearing cases arranged in a taxonomy in a back-and-forth fashion according to fit to determine the best course of action in a particular and immediate situation.

As a research tool for business ethics, casuistry's descriptive and normative qualities help to define the circumstances, motives, behaviors, and values that people use in moral argumentation. In this way, it facilitates a fuller understanding of the sentiments and reasoning of people as they form judgments. As a normative instrument, casuistry provides users with an ordered set of cases in which moral judgments have already been rendered so they can make defensible decisions in present similar circumstances.

While the term admittedly has negative connotations in everyday language (as clever but unsound reasoning) as well as philosophy (as a method prone to sophistry), casuistry has long been a viable research approach with a wider and different meaning than lay individuals or philosophers attribute to it. In the following we will see how casuistry's long enduring and unflattering reputation for promoting lax reasoning, sophistry, and equivocation is rooted in the political and theological disputes of the seventeenth century. As a scholarly method, however, casuistry remains an excellent approach for describing, dissecting, and nuancing information about people and places so as to reach defensible moral judgments.

## Casuistry's Uniqueness

Although other case-based approaches such as the business case method provide the same sort of descriptive information as casuistry, casuistry is unique in that it focuses on the established *moral* judgments of the past for the purpose of reaching defensible judgments in the present.

For one, casuistry captures the inclination to reason by means of analogy. As such it is an inductive moral method, drawing exclusively from multiple resolved (settled) truth-bearing cases and inferring general norms and specific actions from narratives that capture past particular instances of right or wrong. Casuistry in this way is a "bottom up" approach that begins with the particular and concrete and proceeds upward to general judgments by means of analogical reasoning.

As a method, casuistry is similar to common law and the diagnostic practices used in clinical medicine (Arras, 1990; Hunter, 1989; Johansen, 1995; Jonsen, 1986, 1991; Tomlinson, 1994). Its relationship to common law – the sort of law practiced in many of the countries that trace their legal heritage to England – is well established and based on the same practice of retrieving precedent cases for the purpose of building up an argument that will sway listeners to a judgment about a present problem. In both, the new judgment and its proceedings become a new case that is included in a compilation of cases and then used as a reference in subsequent court proceedings. In both casuistry and common law then, settled cases are retrieved from a case taxonomy by means of analogy according to the cases' relevance to the present circumstance. In both cases are then used for their ability to guide users to a defensible judgment and retained for future application.

Not unlike common law, casuistry has also been extended into new realms. In casuistry's case, it has found its way into a variety of applied ethical approaches such as bioethics (especially medical and clinical ethics), computer ethics, and the ethics of journalism (Boeyink, 1992; Coleman, 2007; McLaren, 2006).

Although casuistry has been explored in general terms in business ethics, it has been applied less deeply there than in other areas of applied ethics (Brinkmann and Ims, 2004; Ciulla, 1994; Drucker, 1981; McMahon, 1986; Velasquez, 1994). More recently, however, the author of this chapter has expanded upon some of the earlier general descriptions of casuistry within business ethics research and bridged various outside applications to show how casuistry can be a valuable tool for moral decision making in business, especially when casuistry is twinned with virtue ethics (Calkins, 2001, 2002, 2014).

In addition, casuistry is advantageous for having cases ordered according to their ability to convey moral certitude. Casuistry's case ordering (or case taxonomy) is formal, having at its foundation paradigm cases that convey unambiguous moral certitude. Those that are more ambiguous (or marginal) are then arranged in relation to the foundational cases according to their ability to convey moral certainty.

When employed in moral problem solving, cases are withdrawn systematically from the taxonomy according to fit, that is, in terms of the similarity of the present situation to settled cases of the past. Since, however, present and past situations rarely dovetail, the casuist returns repeatedly to the taxonomy, systematically drawing from it and employing other more or less related cases by means of a back-and-forth process of analogy and rebuttal. Put another way, after first drawing on an obvious paradigm case that turns out not to fit precisely, the casuist then turns to marginal cases in an organized way, bringing each forward according to their fit and relevance to the present situation.

Throughout, cases are summoned to support, nuance, or refute a position. Cases and their attendant judgments are layered upon each other – stacked one atop the other as in a *pousse-café* or layered drink. In this way, just as a glass of various liqueurs delivers a stronger punch than any single ingredient in the drink, so the arrangement of an aggregate of settled cases produces a judgment that is multifaceted, practical, defensible, and more potent than any single case or argument used in isolation.

When applied to business, casuistry is helpful in showing a continuum of similar moral problems and judgments over time. For example, the question about how to deal with a costly HIV medication needed by an impoverished population can be shown to be similar to past cases such as Merck and Co.'s decision to freely distribute ivermectin to combat river blindness in less developed countries and Johnson & Johnson's decision to pull a tainted product off the shelves during the Tylenol Crisis.[1] With these prior cases, decision makers have a resource for making responsible decisions in the present.

In addition, the prudent use of cases can enhance the numbers-based risk management processes of business actuaries in investment banking and insurance. Here, cases can be weighted in the same way as legal hazards and then factored into the risk probability modeling associated with certain speculative ventures – buying a business, trading particular stocks, underwriting specific losses, and so forth. In these situations, casuistry is more useful than an appeal to a single case because of the changing nature of risk. By this is meant that a cluster of cases is more helpful where the risk can mutate and the probability of realizing a hazard can change sufficiently over time due to the shifting sentiments of society. In these risk modeling situations, multiple cases are more beneficial than a single case with more or less fit with the present shifting circumstances (Calkins, 2014, chapter 14).

## Comparisons to Other Approaches

Although unique, casuistry is sometimes confused with other incremental deliberative approaches such as the process to achieve reflective equilibrium, applied principles approaches, and the

[1] (Calkins, 2014, 317–319). For details about the Merck & Co. river blindness case, see Reporter, 1987, 78; Hanson and Weiss, 1991; Donaldson and Werhane, 1999, 148–153; Cavanagh, 1998, 235–236).

For the Johnson & Johnson Tylenol case, see (Buchholz, 1989, 212–232; Cavanagh, 1998, 237–238; De George, 1999, 3–5).

business case method. These, we shall see, appear similar to casuistry but are actually distinctly different in their own ways.

### *Casuistry Versus the Process to Achieve Reflective Equilibrium*

Casuistry seems similar to the process to achieve reflective equilibrium, for one, because the two methods have similar dialectical dynamics. In fact, the resemblance of reflective equilibrium and casuistry processes seem so alike that casuistry has been called a watered down or incomplete version of reflective equilibrium (Sunstein, 1993).

Although the two processes do rely on the same back-and-forth dialectical processes to derive considered and defensible judgments, they nevertheless differ in terms of their definitions, manner of use, and objectives.

At its foundation, reflective equilibrium is best described as a balanced state of beliefs derived through a deliberative process of mutual adjustments among general principles. As a process, it is directed toward principle formation and focused upon the abstract and formal aspects of situations with an overarching objective of settling upon a reasonable mix (or balance) of the formal qualities associated with particular circumstances.

Popularized and promoted by political philosopher John Rawls, the process to achieve reflective equilibrium is a coherentist and pragmatic method of achieving consensus (Rawls, 1971, 1980; van der Burg and van Willigenburg, 1998, 145). Advocated for use in pluralistic societies, it was later parsed into "narrow" and "wide" varieties, with the narrow version being a simple balance of moral judgments deemed acceptable to a given person/society/cluster of societies. The wide or broad version is now regarded as a process to account for the facts and functions of human nature beyond the realm of narrow reflective equilibrium.

In both narrow and wide varieties, the process of seeking reflective equilibrium involves a back-and-forth exchange of ideas or principles having as its goal the eventual settling upon a balance (or equilibrium) between competing positions. Though seemingly similar to casuistry and other dialectical thesis-antithesis-synthesis processes, the process here is more closely aligned with the Kantian-inspired quest for formal adherence to moral principles. Not unlike the Rawlsian exercise of a veil of ignorance, for example, where rational and self-interested individuals are stripped of their knowledge of particular differences to stand in a so-called "original position" of ignorance for the purpose of settling upon a principle (here, a principle of justice), the process to achieve reflective equilibrium attempts to forge objective guiding moral principles by means of an exercise of pure reason. The overall objective in doing so is to settle upon one or more abstract principles that are reasonable, objective, and morally binding.

Although the process to achieve reflective equilibrium can consider the particulars embedded in cases, cases remain illustrative rather than central to the process. Deliberations remain throughout more concerned with the abstract qualities associated with principle formation and so the similarity of the process to achieve reflective equilibrium to casuistry is weak. Although both are balance seeking, alternating, corrective, and reconciling deliberative processes, the concentration on abstract theories combined with the use of cases as illustrations of secondary importance to the primary drive to establish objective principles make the process to achieve reflective equilibrium different from that of casuistry.[2]

On close inspection then, the assertion that casuistry is some sort of watered down version of reflective equilibrium is shown to be conceptually inaccurate and chronologically backward. Although the two methods do share certain features, the process to achieve reflective equilibrium is more accurately described as a distilled version of casuistry. It would be more proper to describe reflective equilibrium as a modern reductionist endeavor along the lines of Jeremy Bentham's reduction of the ancient Greek notion of *eudaimônia* to happiness as pleasure or the absence of pain because in both the older process is more comprehensive than the modern version. From this perspective, with casuistry we have a more

[2] For more on casuistry versus reflective equilibrium, see "Reflective Equilibrium and Casuistry" in (Calkins, 2014).

wide-ranging and richer method than the simpler and reduced contemporary method to achieve reflective equilibrium. It is therefore more precise to describe reflective equilibrium as a watered down form of casuistry than the reverse.

## Casuistry Versus Applied Principles Approaches

In addition to reflective equilibrium, casuistry also differs significantly from applied principles and "top down" deductive analytic approaches where principles or theories are drawn out from cases and then examined and used to form judgments about particular present problems. In these other approaches, cases are again used to illustrate a preferred abstraction, that is, a favored preordained moral theory or principle. Here as in the process to achieve reflective equilibrium, cases are simply situation-based narratives to be deconstructed for other analytical purposes. In this consideration, however, the goal is to locate and isolate the abstract inner principle(s) and then apply those according to a prescribed formula. In the process, cases are shorn of their power to convince in favor of an attempt to settle on a principle to be used in moral deliberations (utilitarianism's "greatest good for the greatest number" or deontology's mandate to "treat others always as ends and never as a means," as examples).

Casuistry, in contrast, is a "bottom up" approach that maintains the power and integrity of narratives. In it, moral principles remain fully contextualized and amalgamated with each other, within cases, within the taxonomy, and (always) within the present circumstances. Although principles are not the primary focus, principles remain always present and are never extracted for use as didactic tools of judgment. Instead, they remain embedded and fully integrated, always part of an intricate admixture of particulars and principles where principles overlap each other and stay deeply rooted within concrete situations.

While it might seem that *not* isolating moral principles would diminish the importance of principles (and normativity itself), the opposite is actually true. With casuistry, normative strength is not associated with how well a principle *per se* shines forth, but how well the amalgam of fully contextualized principles within cases informs the judgment at hand. Here it should be remembered that casuistry relies upon *settled* cases, that is, situations in which norms have been identified and applied. The use of past cases in this way evidences the application of prevailing moral standards, with paradigm cases being the clearest examples and marginal cases proportionately less so.

Of course such a normative approach confounds many principle-oriented moralists. Casuistry's general lack of concern with abstractions, epistemic purity, rules, certainty of judgments, and so forth upends their principlist values and views of morality. Nevertheless, casuistry is more successful in facilitating practical moral judgments than abstract approaches and its outcomes are more defensible in terms of the prevailing standards of society. Perhaps more important, unlike complex theoretical or principle-based approaches that require the guidance of so-called ethical experts, casuistry focuses on the concrete by means of cases that are easy enough to understand and capable of being used by those actually charged with making moral decisions.[3]

## Casuistry Versus the Business Case Method

In addition to these other moral approaches, casuistry has also been confused with nonmoral methods such as the business case method. While it is true that casuistry and the business case method concentrate similarly on cases, the type of cases that casuistry uses as well as the ways cases are used and the goals that it seeks make casuistry distinctively different from case-based nonmoral methods.

To begin, casuistry and the business case method both use cases to facilitate judgments. The business case method cases, however, are open-ended and designed "to give each individual

[3] For more on casuistry versus applied principles approaches, see "Casuistry versus Ethical Pluralism with Applied Principles," "Normativity and Analogy in Casuistry," and The Role of Principles in Casuistry" in (Calkins, 2014).

student a practical and professional training suitable to the particular business he (or she) plans to enter."[4] Its cases, moreover, have certain well-documented identifiable features that make them easy to use in a prescribed way, mostly for instructional purposes.[5] In addition, their classroom use is fairly regimented, following a protocol developed at Harvard University's law and business schools in the late-nineteenth and early-twentieth centuries.[6] Far from a moral method, business case-method cases are used to advance discussion about the "possibilities, probabilities, and expedients – the possibilities of the combinations of very intricate facts, the probabilities of human reactions, and the expedients most likely to bring about the responses in others that lead to a definite end" (Dewing, 1954, 4).

The purpose of case use in the business case method is to help future managers sharpen their analytical skills, enhance their ability to put order into unstructured situations, identify problems, develop conclusions, and recommend actions in complex business situations (Rotch, 1996). Cases are therefore framed to highlight a pressing dilemma faced by a manager – and students are placed in the role of that manager and then asked, "What would YOU do if you were the manager in this case?"

In these ways, the business case method and casuistry are alike. Both compare present circumstances to incidents of the past, rely upon cumulative arguments, and strive to establish the high probability of good judgments. In both, discussion and argumentation are not embraced as purely intellectual pursuits, but used to guide action. In both, practicality and probability are emphasized over certainty and a quest to establish formal proofs.

In other ways, however, the business case method and casuistry differ significantly. Casuistry's cases are resolved or settled whereas the business case method's cases are open-ended and inconclusive. In addition, casuistry maintains a case taxonomy while the business case method's cases float freely without any particular order. Further, with the business case method there is no consensus or even necessary concern about the moral rightness or wrongness of an action. Although particular business cases may be used heavily, they are not deemed "paradigmatic" in the sense of conveying moral certitude. Instead, cases are used for illustrative purposes to highlight theory, a truism, a principle, or cluster of principles related to business or economics.

Thus, while both methods rely on cases and can be used for instructional purpose, casuistry's central purpose is more didactic, moral in nature, and purposely driven toward one sort of judgment (a moral one) than the business case method.[7]

## Casuistry Combined with Virtue Ethics

As we have seen, casuistry is a unique and robust method for making moral judgments. As a stand-alone method it upholds conventional morality,

4 C. R. Christensen quoted in (Lundberg, 1993, 45).

5 Although there seems to be agreement about the general characteristics of the business case, there is little consensus about the case's proximity to reality.
Lundberg, for one, distinguishes between "true" cases based on real experiences and "near cases" that are fictional accounts of particular situations. In the latter category, he includes sets of actual organizational data and instances derived from business articles, journals, and newspapers. In his view, research that "explore(s) or elucidate(s) some phenomenon of theoretic or pragmatic significance" of real situations may enhance classroom discussion, but such research cannot be considered to be on par with actual experience (Lundberg, 1993, 47).

William Rotch, for another, seems to care little for such distinctions. He asserts that business cases may be based on interviews or observation in the field, obtained from readily available published resources (newspapers, magazines, court records, government documents, and so forth), or derived from one's own experiences. (Rotch, 1992)

James W. Culliton adopts the middle position that "at times cases are written exclusively from published sources; but experience indicates that, by and large, they are not so satisfactory as cases secured in whole or in part from personal interviews." (Culliton, 1954, 256)

6 For excellent summaries of the early history of the business case method, see Beauchamp, 1998; Copeland, 1954, 25–33; Barnes, Christensen, and Hansen, 1994, 38–50

7 For more on casuistry and the business case method, see (Calkins, 2001) and "Casuistry's Revival in Medicine and Now, Business" and "Bringing Casuistry and the Business Case Method Together" in (Calkins, 2014).

helps the user develop defensible moral judgments, and is easily accessible by those responsible for making moral decisions in real world contexts. At the same time, casuistry retains an unflattering reputation for promoting lax reasoning, sophistry, and equivocation. As Jonsen and Toulmin have shown, however, this disrepute is ill deserved and more accurately the result of an abuse of a method caught up in attacks against Jesuits as part of a series of seventeenth century theological disputes.[8] While the disparagement continues, casuistry as a method is no more remiss than other moral approaches that can also be shown to be wanting. Unlike these others, however, casuistry can benefit from being twinned with a moral approach that offsets its shortcomings while also strengthening its benefits. That other approach is virtue ethics.

## *Pairing Casuistry with Virtue Ethics*

In many ways, casuistry and virtue ethics are similar in orientation and approach. Both emphasize practical reason (Gk. *phronēsis*), strive for highly probable rather than epistemically pure moral judgments, and have similar histories of growth, rejection, and redemption.

That two distinct moral methods are similar is not particularly unusual. William James in dedicating his summative book on pragmatism, for example, claims that pragmatism is so close to utilitarianism that John Stuart Mill would be "our leader were he alive to-day."[9] Similarly, "the moderns" of western tradition developed many of their notions of process and ends from their ancient forebears.

In examples such as these, newer theories grow out of older ones. In other instances, new theories develop in stubborn opposition to dominant or older approaches. Immanuel Kant, for one, developed his absolutist deontology in part because of his strong opposition to consequentialism. Kant abhorred the hubris of measuring ends that may or may not occur.[10] John Stuart Mill, on the other hand, defended consequentialism by arguing for the usefulness of considering ends in moral discourse. In countering Kant, Mill argued that if one followed Kant's commendation to make moral judgments in terms of overarching principles while ignoring the consequences of those applications, rational people would be free to adopt "the most outrageously immoral rules of conduct" (Mill, 1906, 5).

Casuistry and virtue ethics have neither of these contentions in their backgrounds. Instead, the two have a certain tacit compatibility. Both are old and once widely practiced deliberative methods that developed within the same general culture and were modified by theologians and philosophers for the purposes of moral teaching and preaching. Virtue ethics, for one, was interpreted and then integrated into Christian teachings with the works of Aurelius Ambrosius, Augustine of Hippo, and others. Thomas Aquinas' *Summa Theologica* epitomizes Aristotelian virtue theory woven into Catholic moral teaching (Aquinas, 1947). Later "modern" philosophers such as David Hume and Adam Smith also modified ancient virtue theory and their work, not unlike that of theologians, was used casuistically in sermons, sermons, and so forth.[11]

The two approaches also have a shared history, with distinct periods of ebb and revival. Although virtue ethics never suffered casuistry's devastating reputational loss, it was overshadowed by other moral approaches for years until its revival in the late twentieth century with Alasdair MacIntyre's

[8] (Jonsen and Toulmin, 1988).

[9] William James' dedication states, "To the memory of John Stuart Mill from whom I first learned the pragmatic openness of mind and whom my fancy likes to picture as our leader were he alive to-day" (James, 1969, Author's Dedication of Pragmatism).

[10] Kant clearly excised consequentialism from his moral theory in his "second proposition," arguing that "an action done from duty derives its moral worth, not from the purpose which is to be attained by it, but from the maxim by which it is determined, and therefore does not depend on the realization of the object of the action, but merely on the principle of volition by which the action has taken place, without regard to any object of desire" (Kant, 2004, First Section: Transition from the common rational knowledge of morality to the philosophical).

[11] For examples of these points, see Aquinas, 1984; Aristotle, 1962; Donahue, 1990; Keenan, 1996; Porter, 1990; Statman, 1997.

*After Virtue* (MacIntyre, 1984). Moreover, just as with casuistry, virtue ethics' revival led to its subsequent integration into many areas of contemporary applied ethics.

Perhaps most important, casuistry and virtue ethics have similar identifiable conceptual traits. Both are grounded in the concrete rather than the abstract, rely upon practical decision making, are social group specific, refer obliquely rather than directly to principles or theories, account for the effects of judgments on those making decisions, are reflective approaches, emphasize narratives, and are convenient, understandable, and easy to use by ordinary people.

First, as similarly grounded in the concrete rather than the abstract, casuistry and virtue ethics concentrate on tangible specifics rather than intangible abstractions, theories, or principles. As we have seen, casuistry relies upon cases that are comprehensive, independent, and practical accounts of situations wherein a variety of moral precepts are played out. Similarly, virtue ethics promotes virtues that are formed and performed in real world settings such that they become habitual. The notion of moderation that is key to virtue ethics is also defined and honed my means of direct interface with concrete everyday circumstances.

Second, as approaches that emphasize practical decision making, casuistry, and virtue ethics similarly build to defensible if not epistemically pure judgments. The practical aspects of casuistry are evident in its cases, which are fundamentally narratives that recount practical instances of right and wrong. These are then ordered according to their ability to convey moral clarity in similar practical circumstances rather than by their coherence with a steadfast principle or theory-based norm. In like manner, virtue ethics emphasizes practical wisdom or prudence (Gk. *phronēsis*) each time balance is sought between inclinations toward the extreme practical behaviors.[12] Not only is this golden mean of virtue practically determined, but prudence is itself considered a moral virtue.

Third, as social group specific approaches, casuistry and virtue ethics operate under the similar premise that an ability to deliberate well is constructed by and for society and realized only within specific social contexts. Casuistry's settled cases, we have seen, reflect the moral standards (norms) of identifiable groups of people, that is, particular religious groups, tribes, cultures, or communities. Virtue ethics' virtues, in like manner, are social group specific with each virtue taking on different manifestations according to social context. As a result, the virtue of courage can be as widely different in the contexts of nineteenth century Japan versus contemporary Europe as modern American and jihadist notions of justice are today.

Fourth, as approaches that refer obliquely rather than directly to moral principles and theories, casuistry and virtue ethics do not eschew principles so much as they insist that principles remain embedded within the context where they apply or are found. In casuistry, appeals to principles and theories are embedded in the judgments about case fit, that is, in the agreement that certain cases contain elements of normativity. In other approaches this normativity would be extracted, examined in terms of their underlying abstract qualities, then framed in terms of principles or theories. In casuistry such embedded normativity is expressed in terms of the case taxonomy, where cases are ordered in terms of their ability to convey moral certainty.

Ancient Greek virtue theory also refers obliquely rather than directly to moral principles and theories by strongly promoting ill-defined notions of good moral character. Its notion of virtue as a shifting "golden" mean between two vices dances on the edge of principlism without formalizing the notion being expressed the

[12] *Phronēsis* (Greek) is practical wisdom or sound judgment in everyday life, a trait of good deliberation, excellent understanding, and an ability to judge well (Aristotle, 1962, VI 9–13). It is a learned habit. In ancient Greece, young people (the boys of aristocrats) were placed alongside men of practical wisdom (Gk. *phronimos*) who taught them the ways of the world. Mentor, the figure in Greek lore, was this sort of prudent figure. A trusted advisor and wise friend of Odysseus, Mentor and Odysseus developed a *phronimos-protégé* relationship that effectively transferred an understanding of practical wisdom from the elder to the younger person.

way modern theories such as utilitarianism or deontology do. Put another way, while we might understand what a shifting mean is and might know what is commonly considered excessive enough to be regarded a vice, we would be hard pressed to define that moving middle ground and the exact point when actions become vices in touchstone principles. Similarly, that virtuous action is directed toward a formal final good end (Gk. *telos*) of happiness (Gk. *eudaimônia*) and is decided in terms of "a rational principle, such as a man of practical wisdom would use to determine it," suggests that principles are fluid and open to interpretation (Aristotle, 1962, II 6 1106b 1136).[13] As such, principles are not discounted or discarded but rather used as tools in a decision-making process focused upon the nuances of the situation at hand rather than those of the moral principles employed.

Fifth, as approaches that account for the effects of judgments on those making decisions, casuistry and virtue ethics draw attention to the character of the agent in ways that other methods do not. In casuistry, the selection of cases from a cache of cases reveals the values and priorities of the decision-maker. Put another way, as an individual chooses one case over another, he or she reveals a personal hierarchy of values that mirror his or her moral character.

Virtue ethics similarly links moral choice with the character of the individual insofar as the virtues (or lack of the virtues) define the person. As characteristic habits of the person, virtues reflect not just the choices of the individual but also the sort of person (character) he or she is and is striving to become. In this way, virtues establish one's reputation – define the individual as a particular sort of person that has been developed over time – and indicate the moral trajectory of the individual (the sort of person he or she will become through repetition of such action.

[13] *Telos* means "end" or "conclusion." It is the perfection or complete actuality of a thing. Applied to the human being, the proper *telos* is happiness (Aristotle, 1962, 315). Aristotle defines the good "as that to which all things aim" (Aristotle, 1962, 1094a).

Sixth, as reflective approaches, casuistry and virtue ethics are driven less by prescriptive principles than reflective discernment of the agent. Casuistry does so by having the user reflect upon the cases of a case taxonomy before settling upon those that fit the present situation.

Virtue ethics, in contrast and as we have seen, defines virtue itself as something defined by a principle as it is interpreted by a person having practical wisdom. In this way, virtues contain one or more principles that are to be interpreted by the agent. Principles therefore retain their position and relevance within specific circumstances rather than floating outside of situations and exerting their authority over agents.

Seventh, as narrative-based approaches to moral decision making, casuistry and virtue ethics rely on stories. Casuistry, a case-based method, relies most obviously upon truth-bearing narratives that are simply accounts of past situations in which people faced moral quandaries and made judgments. As stories, these cases have an ability to capture the user's imagination so he or she can grasp the nuances of both the past and the present situation and thereby come to a defensible judgment about a real-life moral dilemma.

Virtue ethics, in like manner, advocates the advancement of moral character by means of repetitive or habitual practices encapsulated, enlivened, nurtured, and made relevant by means of narratives. One learns what it is to be prudent, for example, from the stories of prudent others and the power of these stories correlates to how well they resonate with the individuals recounting and listening to them.

Finally, casuistry and virtue ethics are accessible approaches that are handy, readily understandable, and easy to use by ordinary people. Their reliance upon familiar narratives makes them appealing to those tasked with making moral judgments in everyday practical contexts without access to moral experts. This ease of use and accessibility makes it more likely that those who should make moral judgments will actually attempt to do so when they otherwise might not.

It should be recognized, however, that while casuistry and virtue ethics share certain identifiable traits, the two are different in significant ways. For one, they have different functions, with casuistry acting as an instrument for moral decision making and virtue ethics being a way to consider virtuous character and how to work toward moral objectives. Casuistry and virtue ethics differ as well in terms of their objectives, with casuistry's goal being the derivation of a defensible moral judgment and virtue ethics' goal being the articulation of a *telos* particular to the individual. Finally, casuistry and virtue ethics differ in terms of their orientation toward time. As a method that uses narratives rooted in the past, that is, precedent cases, casuistry bridges past and present by considering the ways that the present and past compare and differ. Virtue ethics, in contrast, is directed toward a consideration of the individual's character, that is, the sort of person an individual is and will become as a result of certain actions. It turns to the past for guidance for the purpose of inspiring future excellence on the part of the individual.

When combined in "virtue-imbued casuistry," casuistry and virtue ethics create a synergy that strengthens their individual effects and offsets their particular weaknesses. In tandem, the two approaches emphasize the concrete over the abstract, nuance and fortify moral norms within practical situations, provide a flexible hermeneutic for the interpretation of principles, stress the imaginative and aspirational aspects of ethics, enliven and strengthen moral narratives, and enhance the likelihood that the ordinary people charged with making moral decisions in real contexts will do so. While casuistry alone is a helpful method for researchers, virtue-imbued casuistry, as we have seen, is an even more powerful tool for moral deliberation.

## Conclusion

In sum, casuistry is an inductive method of moral deliberation useful to business ethics researchers. It is a method that uses previously settled truth-bearing cases arranged in a taxonomy in a back-and-forth fashion according to fit to determine the best course of action in a particular and immediate situation. As such, casuistry can be used as a method to establish expedient moral judgments that are practical and defensible. While it appears to be similar to other case-based approaches and continues to suffer an ill-deserved reputation for promoting equivocation, casuistry – especially when combined with virtue ethics – is more grounded in the concrete, more conservative in its retention of the nuance of principles as they relate to each other and the situation at hand, and more user-friendly and likely to be used than other business and theory-based case methods.

## References


Aquinas, Saint Thomas. *Treatise on the Virtues*. Notre Dame: University of Notre Dame Press, 1984.

Aquinas, Thomas. *Summa Theologica*. Translated by Fathers of the English Dominican Province. 3 vols. New York: Benziger Brothers, Inc., 1947.

Aristotle. *Nicomachean Ethics*. Translated by Martin Ostwald. Englewood Cliffs, New Jersey: Prentice Hall, Inc., 1962.

Arras, John D. "Common Law Morality." *Hastings Center Report*, July/August (1990): 35–37.

Barnes, Louis B., C. Roland Christensen, and Abby J. Hansen. *Teaching and the Case Method: Texts, Cases, and Readings*. 3rd ed. Boston: Harvard Business School Press, 1994.

Beauchamp, Tom L., ed. *Case Studies in Business, Society, and Ethics* 4th ed. Upper Saddle River: Prentice-Hall, Inc., 1998.

Boeyink, David E. "Casuistry: A Case-Based Method for Journalists." *Journal of Mass Media Ethics* 7, 2 (1992): 107–120.

Brinkmann, Johannes and Knut J. Ims. "A Conflict Case Approach to Business Ethics." *Journal of Business Ethics* 53 (2004): 123–136.

Buchholz, Rogene A. *Fundamental Concepts and Problems in Business Ethics*. Englewood Cliffs: Prentice-Hall, Inc., 1989.

Calkins, Martin. "Casuistry and the Business Case Method." *Business Ethics Quarterly* 11, 2 (April 2001): 237–259.

"How Casuistry and Virtue Ethics Might Break the Ideological Stalemate Troubling Agricultural Biotechnology." *Business Ethics Quarterly* 12, 3 (July 2002): 305–330.

"Developing a Virtue-Imbued Casuistry for Business Ethics." *Vol. 42 Issues in Business Ethics*. New York: Springer Science and Business Media, 2014.

Cavanagh, Gerald F. *American Business Values with International Perspectives*. 4th ed. Upper Saddle River: Prentice-Hall, Inc., 1998.

Ciulla, Joanne B. "Casuistry and the Case for Business Ethics." In *Business as a Humanity*, ed. Thomas J. Donaldson and R. Edward Freeman, 167–183. New York: Oxford University Press, 1994.

Coleman, Kari Gwen. "Casuistry and Computer Ethics." *Metaphilosophy* 38, 4 (July 2007): 471–488.

Copeland, Melvin T. "The Genesis of the Case Method in Business Instruction." In *The Case Method at the Harvard Business School: Papers by Present and Past Members of the Faculty and Staff*, ed. Malcolm P. McNair, 25–33. New York: McGraw-Hill Book Company Inc., 1954.

Culliton, James W. "Writing Business Cases." In *The Case Method at the Harvard Business School: Papers by Present and Past Members of the Faculty and Staff*, ed. Malcolm P. McNair. New York: McGraw-Hill Book Company, Inc., 1954.

De George, Richard T. *Business Ethics*. 5th ed. Upper Saddle River: Prentice Hall, Inc., 1999.

Dewing, Arthur Stone. "An Introduction to the Use of Cases." In *The Case Method at the Harvard Business School: Papers by Present and Past Members of the Faculty and Staff*, ed. Malcolm P. McNair, 1–5. New York: McGraw-Hill Book Company, Inc., 1954.

Donahue, James A. "The Use of Virtue and Character in Applied Ethics." *Horizons* 17 (1990): 228–243.

Donaldson, Thomas and Patricia H. Werhane, eds. *Ethical Issues in Business: A Philosophical Approach* 6th ed. Upper Saddle River: Prentice-Hall, Inc., 1999.

Drucker, Peter F. "What is 'business ethics'?" *National Affairs* 63 (Spring 1981): 18–36.

Hanson, K. O. and S. Weiss. *Merck & Co., Inc.: Addressing Third-World Needs*. Cambridge: Harvard Business School Publishing, 1991, no. 9–991-021 to 024.

Hunter, Kathryn Montgomery. "A Science of Individuals: Medicine and Casuistry." *Journal of Medicine and Philosophy* 14, April (1989): 193–212.

James, William. *Pragmatism and Four Essays from The Meaning of Truth*, ed. Ralph Barton Perry. Cleveland: Meridian Books, 1969.

Johansen, Baber. "Casuistry: Between Legal Concept and Social Praxis." *Islamic Law and Society* 2, 2 (1995): 135–156.

Jonsen, Albert R. "Casuistry and Clinical Ethics." *Theoretical Medicine* 7 (1986): 65–74.

"Casuistry as Methodology in Clinical Ethics." *Theoretical Medicine* 12, December (1991): 295–307.

Jonsen, Albert R. and Stephen Toulmin. *The Abuse of Casuistry: A History of Moral Reasoning*. Berkeley: University of California Press, 1988.

Kant, Immanuel. *Fundamental Principles of the Metaphysics of Morals*. Trans. Thomas Kingsmill Abbott, 2004. Accessed 30 August 2016. Internet. Available from http://philosophy.eserver.org/kant/metaphys-of-morals.txt.

Keenan, S. J., James F. *Virtues for Ordinary Christians*. Kansas City: Sheed & Ward, 1996.

Lundberg, Craig C. "Case Method." In *Mastering Management Education: Innovations in Teaching Effectiveness*, ed. Charles M. Vance, 45–52. Newbury Park: Sage Publications Inc., 1993.

MacIntyre, Alasdair. *After Virtue: A Study in Moral Theory*. 2nd ed. Notre Dame: University of Notre Dame Press, 1984.

McLaren, B.M. "Computational Models of Ethical Reasoning: Challenges, Initial Steps, and Future Directions." *Intelligent Systems, IEEE* 21, 4 (July-August 2006): 29–37.

McMahon, Thomas F. "Creed, Cult, Code and Business Ethics." *Journal of Business Ethics* 5, 6 (1986): 453–463.

Mill, John Stuart. *Utilitarianism*. Chicago: The University of Chicago Press, 1906.

Porter, Jean. *The Recovery of Virtue: The Relevance of Aquinas For Christians*. Louisville: Westminster/John Knox Press, 1990.

Rawls, John. *A Theory of Justice*. Cambridge: The Belknap Press of Harvard University Press, 1971.

"Kantian Constructivism in Moral Theory." *Journal of Philosophy* 77 (1980).

Reporter. "Miracle Worker." *Time*, 2 November 1987, 78.

Rotch, William. *Casewriting*. Charlottesville: University of Virginia Darden School Foundation, 1992, no. UVA-G-0364.

"Casewriting Workshop Handout." Charlottesville: Unpublished, 20 May 1996.

Statman, Daniel, ed. *Virtue Ethics: A Critical Reader*. Washington, D.C.: Georgetown University Press, 1997.

Sunstein, Cass R. "Commentary on Analogical Reasoning." *Harvard Law Review* 106, January (1993): 741–791.

Tomlinson, Tom. "Casuistry in Medical Ethics: Rehabilitated, or Repeat Offender?" *Theoretical Medicine* 15, March (1994): 5-20.

van der Burg, Wibren and Theo van Willigenburg, eds. *Reflective Equilibrium: Essays in Honour of Robert Heeger*, Dordrecht: Kluwer Academic Publishers, 1998.

Velasquez, Manuel G. "Some Lessons and Nonlessons of Casuist History." In *Business as a Humanity*, ed. Thomas J. Donaldson and R. Edward Freeman, 184–195. New York: Oxford University Press, 1994.

CHAPTER 16

# Building on Actor-Network Analysis to Study Corporate Social Responsibility

## *Conceptual and Methodological Insights*

JEAN-PASCAL GOND and MARION LIGONIE

## Introduction

It may seem paradoxical at first to dedicate a chapter to actor-network theory (ANT) in a handbook focused on research approaches and methods in the domains of business ethics (BE) and corporate social responsibility (CSR). First, according to its early promoters (Latour, 1999, 2005; Law, 2008), ANT is neither a unified theory nor, strictly speaking, a methodological approach, and the ANT acronym could be best described as an "umbrella construct" for sociological works grounded in the social studies of science (SSS) and society and technology society (STS) studies that share common assumptions about how to conduct inquiries in the world, such as, for instance, the need to consider both human and nonhuman entities to provide fair accounts of the phenomena under study (Callon, 1986).

Second, ANT is certainly not a well-established perspective in the CSR field of study, despite a few pioneering studies (e.g., Bergström & Diedrich, 2011; Gond & Nyberg, 2017; Pasquero, 1996) and growing attention to this approach by students of social and environmental accounting (e.g., Barter & Bebbington, 2013; Malsch, 2013) and management control (e.g., Ligonie, 2016). To date, CSR scholars have rarely built on ANT, even though ANT research has delivered insights about multiple phenomena of high relevancy to CSR scholarship, such as the status of "nature" in the political and social worlds (Latour, 2004, 2017), the importance of bringing back material entities within the scope of analysis to appreciate ethical decision making (Latour, 1992), the influence of economic and financial theories within contemporary societies (Callon, 1998a; MacKenzie & Millo, 2003) or the social construction of ecological externalities (Callon 1998b).

This chapter addresses this paradoxical situation by clarifying some of the underlying assumptions of ANT and discussing their theoretical and methodological implications for CSR scholarship. Our aim in doing so is not only to provide students of CSR with a new set of analytical tools and original ideas about how to conduct their empirical inquiries, but also to enable the cross-fertilization of ANT and CSR studies.

We first introduce three key assumptions of ANT – the focus on the assembling of actor-networks, materiality, and performativity – and explain how they can help address lasting conceptual issues in CSR scholarship. We then derive the methodological implications of these assumptions for conducting ANT-inspired studies in the CSR field, providing illustrations from ANT and CSR research. We finally review and discuss critically the different forms of theoretical and methodological engagement with ANT assumptions, and propose some suggestions for exploiting further the potential of ANT in future CSR research.

## Reconsidering Corporate Social Responsibility through Actor-Network Theory

Although CSR scholars have built on multiple disciplinary sources to develop their understanding of phenomena located at the interface of business, society and the natural environment (Aguinis & Glavas, 2012; Bansal & Song, 2017), they have mainly been inspired by economics and the structure-functionalist sociological traditions, leading to relative neglect of poststructural approaches to CSR such as ANT (Gond & Nyberg, 2017; Scherer & Palazzo, 2007), beyond the reliance on Habermasian framework by some of the promoters of "political CSR" (Scherer & Palazzo, 2011; Scherer, Rasche, Palazzo & Spicer, 2016).

ANT provides a unique set of conceptual and methodological resources for further exploration of CSR from a poststructural perspective. Specifically, by relying on a distinct set of ontological and epistemological assumptions, ANT can give a new impulse to CSR scholarship as it focuses researchers' attention on the ongoing social construction processes underlying the *assembling* CSR activities and phenomena, the role of *materiality* and nonhuman entities in the analysis of CSR and the potentially *performative* quality of CSR theories and concepts—i.e. the capacity of these theories and concepts to transform social reality according to their own assumptions and representations.

## Assembling Corporations, Society, and Responsibility

Challenging traditional sociologists' assumption according to which social is a property of some phenomena – i.e. things being regarded as social *by nature* –, ANT conceives the social as a "movement of association" (Latour, 2005), through which various entities are connected to each other to form and maintain social orders. This assumption means that in researching social phenomena, ANT scholars should not assume the social existence of what they wish to explain (e.g., the existence of social structures or of macro-actors, such as the state or an organization) (Law, 1992) but rather seek to provide accounts of how *the social is assembled* (Latour, 2005), notably by tracing the connections through which elements are mobilized and intertwined in the making of social orders.

Social actors are thereby defined as "any element which bends space around itself, makes other elements dependent upon itself" (Callon & Latour, 1981, p. 286). Actors (or, in the ANT terminology borrowed from semiotics, "actants") are entities of any nature (from humans to objects, animals or discourses) that can contribute "to make a difference" in the existing state of affairs or the process of assembling (Latour, 2005).

Actors play off each other in order to fulfill their own views of the world (Callon, 1986). As a result, an actor does not only orient others' paths but is also made to act in certain ways by many other actors. ANT thus foregrounds a relational view of reality, in which "entities achieve their form as a consequence of the relations in which they are located" (Law, 1999, p. 4). It follows that one can only fully understand an actor and the role it plays by accounting for the associations it is subjected to, i.e. by examining the networks in which it is embedded and investigating how this network has been assembled into being.

The notion of network used in ANT differs radically from the structural approach to network adopted by "social network analysis" scholars such as Burt (1995) or Granovetter (1985) as it focuses on the construction network approaches as a permanently ongoing process. Networks refers for ANT scholars to the array of traces left by actors' connections (Latour, 2005). Networks point to these associations of heterogeneous elements (human and nonhuman) that together produce actions, establish meanings, and lead to the temporary stabilization of social orders. Accordingly, agency lies in the networks: actors necessarily are networks, and networks are actors within reality, which is why ANT scholars use the term "actor-network." The process through which the interests of a set of autonomous entities are redefined in order to be aligned and hence to become stabilized as a network is called "translation" (Callon, 1986; Law, 1992; for recent reviews of this concept and its use in management, see: Van Grinsven, Heusinkveld & Cornelissen 2016; Wæraas & Nielsen, 2016). Translation thus differs from a purely linguistic metaphor and corresponds to a highly political process, as suggested by the definition that follows:

> [By] translation, we understand all the negotiations, intrigues, calculations, acts of persuasion and violence, thanks to which an actor or force takes, or causes to be conferred on itself, authority to speak or act on behalf of another actor or force. ... Whenever an actor speaks of "us", s/he is translating other actors into a single will, of which s/he becomes the spokesman. (Callon & Latour, 1981, p. 279)

Considering networks as composed of heterogeneous interconnected actors, each of which trying to align the others' actions and interests with its own, basically comes down to depicting social orders as the sites of endless battles of power, where actors with divergent interests might resort to violence and persuasion to mobilize others into shaping the actor-network in accordance with their worldviews (Latour, 1986; Law, 1986). Therefore, ANT approaches social reality as always in the making and thus necessarily "incomplete," "contested" and "temporary" (Law, 1992). As such, translation processes never are complete and fully immutable (Callon, 1986).

Such theoretical insights offer opportunities to address the under-examined social construction of CSR by shedding a different light on the organizing processes underlying CSR practices. Following ANT's insights, CSR can be viewed both as an outcome and as an element of actor-networks, bringing together human and nonhuman elements from corporations, societies and theories about responsibility (Pasquero, 1996). *As an outcome of actor-networks*, CSR is best understood when the internal connections and power struggles leading to the stabilization of a specific definition (e.g., Ählström & Egels-Zandén, 2008) or "glocal" practice that associate entities from various scales (e.g., Gond & Boxenbaum, 2013), are revealed. *As an element of an actor-network*, CSR can be itself provided with agency and conceived as an "actant" that makes other actors do something in its name, mobilizing other actors to realize its worldview as well as being mobilized by them to serve their interests (Bergström & Diedrich, 2011). Although CSR concepts and practices are often "black-boxed" when used by scholars and practitioners alike, ANT calls to mind the instability of such arrangements and foregrounds their underlying negotiations and battles (Bled, 2010; Füssel & Georg, 2000).

## Materializing Corporate Social Responsibility

Materiality plays a central role in ANT because it is what maintains networks together (Law, 1992). Networks are inherently heterogeneous and both humans and nonhumans might participate in their stabilization (Callon, 1991). Material elements actively participate in the course of actions and are granted the capability of bending other actors' trajectories. They might orient actions in certain ways, encouraging or forbiding them, making them possible, or impeding them. For instance, speed bumps force car drivers to slow down when approaching a school (Latour, 2005), tides can be obstacles to scallops' anchorage to collectors (Callon, 1986), limitations of current technologies in coping with new demands favor accounting change (Briers & Chua, 2001) and financial spreadsheets or electronic computing devices facilitate the adoption of specific financial models for option pricing (MacKenzie & Millo, 2003).

This distribution of agency across humans and nonhumans is one of ANT's distinctive premises as organizational studies usually attribute agency and power to humans only. According to Latour (2005, p. 72):

> What is new is not the multiplicity of objects any course of action mobilizes along its trail – no one ever denied they were there by the thousands; what is new is that objects are suddenly highlighted not only as being full-blown actors, but also as what explains the contrasted landscape we started with, the overarching powers of society, the huge asymmetries, the crushing exercise of power.

Despite the increasing materialization of CSR through the development of metrics, tools and practices (Gond & Nyberg, 2017), only a few studies have used the analytical potential of ANT's insights on materiality. In a research domain primarily concerned with environmental issues, it is strange that nature and environmental elements rarely are visible (for an analysis of the relevance of ANT to the study of social and environmental reporting, see, however, Barter & Bebbington, 2013). For example, the intervention of fossil fuels and carbon emissions are agential in framing corporations' environmental accountability (Callon, 2009). This is especially significant because bringing materiality into the CSR realm has the potential to challenge current power asymmetries, democratizing decision making, and reviving CSR's political potential (Gond & Nyberg, 2017).

ANT studies have also stressed the inherent link between materiality and ethics. Although morality and ethics have been traditionally associated with "humans," Latour (1992) showed – in his piece about an engineering device that does not allow a car to start if the driver does not wear a security belt, that objects could also embody moral rules by restricting behaviors and preventing potential consequences of neglecting moral rules. Humans may be forced to behave "ethically" (e.g., respect the speed limit) not because they deliberately decide to but because their material environment embeds such ethical rules. Because other actors do not follow the moral rule of limiting the car speed – either the drivers who shouldn't be trusted in willingly limiting their speed, or the car itself, which can go much faster than the speed limit –, morality is transferred to devices such as road bumpers in streets near primary schools. To protect their cars, drivers will slow down, and in this sense the moral rule "you shouldn't drive too fast" is inscribed in the street's material design. Jensen et al. (2009), provide similar evidence in the CSR domain about how corporate codes of ethics change the meaning of ethics and influence humans' moral practices.

These two illustrations suggest that by neglecting the sociomaterial dimension of morality and ethics, CSR studies have made invisible an important side of the phenomena. Beyond these cases, many ethical, CSR or sustainability-related controversies or attempts at radically changing society question the boundary between what is regarded or defined as human and nonhuman (Descola, 2013; Latour, 2004). Such is the case, for instance, of the medical uses of stem cells, the discussions as to whether a fetus or an embryo actually already is a social or a human being (Boltanski, 2013), or the struggle from activists to attribute political rights to animals (Whelan & Gond, 2017).

### *Performing Corporate Social Responsibility*

A third important assumption of ANT deriving from its focus on the constitution of "actor-networks" points toward the notion of performativity. As explained by Law (2008, p. 13), "the webs of relations only hold if they are enacted, enacted again, and enacted yet again – which may or may not happen in practice. But if we think in this way then we're no longer on the metaphorical equivalent of a building site. Instead we are in a world of performance or enactment." It follows that an underlying principle inherent to ANT is its attention to the simultaneous constitution of reality and of representations of this reality.

> It is about performativity. It is arguing that *realities* (including objects and subjects) and *representations* of those realities are being enacted or performed simultaneously. It is, as I noted above, poststructuralist in inclination, albeit in a particular and materially-oriented mode. This means that it is also profoundly nonhumanist (beware, performance here has nothing to do with Erving Goffman's sociology). Shift the verb from making to doing – to *doing* realities – and we catch what is at stake. To put it in formal language, what is at stake is not simply epistemological. We are also in the realm of *ontology*. Law (2008, p. 13)

The concept of performativity encompasses a variety of approaches and meanings developed after Austin's (1962) foundational insight according to which some utterances have the capacity to bring about what they describe (Gond, Cabantous, Harding & Learmonth, 2016). Performativity studies are grounded in a tradition of social and philosophical studies of sciences that has drastically reconsidered the notion of science as a neutral "representation" of an "external" reality to approach instead the production of science as the result of constant interventions in reality (Hacking, 1983).

Building on this "antirepresentationalism" position, ANT scholars have more specifically investigated how a variety of scientific discourses – such as economics, management, or finance – contribute to "bring into being" the very entities they describe, and in so doing to shape the world according to specific assumptions (Callon, 1998a; Latour, 1996). For instance, MacKenzie and Millo (2003) have shown how options prices converged toward the prices predicted by the Black–Scholes–Merton options pricing formula as this formula became used by traders and then embedded within the computer devices used in the trading room; Cabantous and Gond (2011) show rational choice theory assumptions became embedded within organizations in ways that orient decision making toward rationality.

In the domain of CSR, a performativity approach suggests to reflect on how the academic and practical discourses about CSR are intertwined with each other and co-produced in ways that may reflect or not the promoters of CSR. On the one hand, performativity calls for closely considering the conditions that make possible the production of academic discourses (theories and concepts) related to CSR, and invites to question and investigate which actors make possible the production of CSR theory. This would encourage for instance, analyses of how actors measuring CSR – such as for instance "CSR rating organizations" such as KLD (now MSCI) or Arese (now Vigeo) – to contribute to bringing into being the entities they describe and in so doing make possible the development of CSR-related products – such as "responsible financial products" (Déjean, Gond and Leca, 2004) – while allowing the conducting of quantitative empirical studies linking measures of CSR to other outcomes.

On the other hand, a performativity analysis of CSR suggests considering whether and how CSR theory and concepts – such as the notion of creating shared value (Ligonie, 2017) or corporate citizenship – contribute to reshaping organizational and social realities. Marti and Gond (2017), for instance, adopt such a performativity approach to discuss whether and how the positive relationship between corporate social and financial performance could become a self-fulfilling prophecy within financial markets.

Together, the consideration of *CSR assembling*, *CSR materiality* and *CSR performativity* not only contribute to reintegrate within the scope of CSR scholarship a processual ontology, nonhumans, and self-reflexivity, but also invite the adoption of a slightly distinct style of research because they have specific methodological implications that we will now discuss.

## Some Methodological Implications of Actor-Network Theory Studies

Although there is no such a thing as a toolkit methodological approach to ANT research (Latour, 2005; Law, 2008), it is nevertheless possible to highlight some key methodological implications that derive logically from the adoption of ANT assumptions such as the importance of following actors, providing accounts about the constitution of connections, and engaging reflexively with the effects produced by theory. Each of these three methodological implications are introduced and then illustrated in a CSR research context.

### *Following the Actors, Unpacking the Making of their Networks*

ANT research focuses on explaining how the heterogeneous elements of networks are assembled and maintained together to produce and stabilize social orders, and thus involves uncovering the "traces" left by actors' activities in forming and dismantling networks, and mapping out the "web of connections" underpinning these activities (Latour, 2005). To do so, ANT scholars have often engaged in qualitative inquiries enabling the researcher's close engagement within the research field. Tellingly, most famous ANT empirical studies are either case studies or ethnographies (Latour, 2005; Law, 2004).

When conducting empirical studies, ANT researchers:

> have "to follow the actors themselves", that is try to catch up with their often wild innovations in order to learn from them what the collective existence has become in their hands, which methods they have elaborated to make it fit together, which accounts could best define the new associations that they have been forced to establish. (Latour, 2005, p. 12)

This methodological approach has two implications. The first one is that ANT essentially focuses on micro-level relationships (Callon & Latour, 1981), placing the emphasis on the array of local activities and interactions. Following actors is not necessarily restricted to human individuals but can be carried out for any type of actor: Cabantous and colleagues (2010) followed rational choice theory within organizations, Bled (2010) followed the Convention on Biological Diversity, and Jensen and colleagues (2009) followed a corporate code of conduct throughout its enactment in the Swedish subsidiary of an American company. ANT narratives aim to grasp how actors are drawn together, and how they mobilize each other and fight each other to bring their visions of the world into being.

The second implication of the focus on actor-network assembling is that ANT-driven empirical studies are usually inductive and interpretative. To "learn from [the actors] what the collective existence has become in their hands" (Latour, 2005, p. 12), researchers ought not to make any assumption or impose preestablished grids of analysis upon the reality they examine but should give voice to the actors and understand how they make sense of their reality (Callon, 1986).[1] Surely, giving voice to technical artifacts that do not speak for themselves can represent a challenge (Larssaether & Nijhof, 2009) and in this case, crossing multiple sources of information might be helpful. Researchers should get accustomed to juggling multiple frames of reference coexisting in the field and should learn to shift from one to another in order to gain a prismatic understanding of reality (Latour, 2005).

In focusing the analysis on the interconnections between micro-level actors to explain the stabilization of social orders, ANT scholars circumvent the micro-macro dichotomy. The analysis centers on processes of organizing in which there are not any "institutions" or "social structures" (they would be all treated as actants in an actor-network or as the outcome of successful translation processes), only actors, connected to each other, and bending networks in particular ways. In so doing, actors may produce new entities (groups, organizations, nation states) that positivist scholars would usually describe as referring to a macro-social level of analysis. Accordingly, ANT scholars regard actors as engaged in efforts to "macro-structure" the reality (Callon & Latour, 1981, p. 277). With this in mind, Latour (2005) engages ANT researchers to "flatten the social."

Michel Callon's (1986) seminal study on the scallops of St Brieuc offers an exemplary illustration of ANT's methodological approach. While examining the experimentation of scallops' cultivation at the St Brieuc Bay in the 1970s, he narrates the constitution of scientific knowledge attempted by three researchers and brings to light their efforts to build an actor-network that would support their undertakings. Through evidencing three moments in the actor-network constitution, Callon traces how actors and their identities were moved along with the definition of the problem (the *problematization* moment), including other researchers and the fishermen but also the scallops themselves, their predators, and the cultivation nets; how actors were made allies and locked into the network (the *interessement* moment), either through persuasion – convincing the fishermen that their interests were aligned with the researchers' attempts at scallops' cultivation –, or through more violent means – for example placing scallops' larvae into collectors, physically dissociating them from predators and tides turbulences; and how actors were "enrolled" (the *enrolment* moment) (Callon, 1986, p. 211), that is, how they accepted their respective roles and coordinated with each other, so that their alliance was secured. Box 1 offers an illustration of an ANT account.

Gond and Boxenbaum (2013) provide a different illustration of an ANT empirical account. To study the "glocalization" of responsible investment practices – the concomitant local transformation and global diffusion of responsible investing

[1] In this regard, ANT share strong similarities with the epistemological positioning of ethnomethodologists such as Harold Garfinkel (1967), by considering that social scientists should not impose on the social phenomena their own pre-conceived categories or objects (e.g. social classes, macro structures). However, ANT scholars derived distinct implications from this approach, by making the analysis of the constitution of such macro-objects or categories one of their main topic of inquiry (see, e.g., Callon & Latour, 1981).

**Box 16.1: An Illustration of ANT Account**

"The towline and its collectors constitute an archetype of the interessement device. The larvae are "extracted" from their context. They are protected from predators (starfish) which want to attack and exterminate them, from currents that carry them away where they perish, and from the fisherman's dredge which damages them. They are (physically) disassociated from all the actors who threaten them. In addition, these interessement devices extend and materialize the hypothesis made by the researchers concerning the scallops and the larvae: (1) the defenseless larvae are constantly threatened by predators, (2) the larvae can anchor, (3) the Japanese experience can be transposed to France because St. Brieuc's scallops are not fundamentally different from their Japanese cousins. The collectors would lose all effectiveness if the larvae "refused" to anchor, to grow, to metamorphose, and to proliferate in (relative) captivity." (Callon, 1986, p. 209).

This narration of an *interessement* dynamic clearly manifests some of ANT's fundamental tenets. First, it renders visible the central role played by materiality in building the network, as the towline and collectors are agential in making the researchers' experiment possible. This citation also accounts for these devices' agency, in that they not only embody ("materialize") the assumptions made by the researchers and on which the network they are trying to stabilize is grounded, but also contribute to the success or failure of the researchers' attempts – they extract the larvae and protect them.

Second, this quote clearly uncovers the interdependences between the actors associated within the network. The collectors act on the larvae and play a role in the researchers' undertaking, but the network might break down if the larvae refused to anchor and grow, if the fishermen refused to play along or if the researchers abandoned the experiment.

Finally, this excerpt gives a sense of the tensions undergoing among the actors, each of which striving to satisfy their interests – the fishermen to fish the scallops, the predators to feed, the collectors to protect the larvae, the larvae to live, the researchers to conduct their experiment. Accordingly, in a few lines, this citation offers a glance at the negotiations and instability underpinning the constitution of an actor-network.

practices – they draw on a comparative case study between two settings, France and Québec, in which a US practice of responsible investment was adopted. Engaging within each setting through interviews and document analysis, these authors followed the moves of this practice across different local contexts, tracking the "contextualization work" undertaken by the actors that enabled stabilization of a network supporting the performance of this new practice. Gond and Boxenbaum's (2013) study thus uncovers the transformations that the practice itself had to undergo in order to fit the technical, cultural, and political specificities of its adoptive contexts as well as the underground negotiations through which actors mobilized, or on the contrary disentangled, some of the practice's components to achieve fit.

## *Writing Social Accounts of the Connections*

ANT accounts aim to map out the connections and the related power forces that underlie and constitute the social. They take the form of dramatic stories, i.e. detailed textual narrations of what concretely happens or has happened. Without any prior conceptions of what they analyse, they give voice to the actants themselves and put forth their activities, conflicts, and interdependencies in rendering the canvas of social orders. More importantly, these accounts make visible the *movement* of the social. As explained by Latour (2005, p. 128):[2]

> A good ANT account is a narrative or a description or a proposition where all actors *do something* and don't just sit there. Instead of simply transporting effects without transforming them, each of the points in the text may become a bifurcation, an event, or the origin of a new

[2] Latour (2005) distinguishes mediators from intermediaries. Intermediaries do not make a difference: they "transport meaning or force without transformation" (Latour, 2005, p. 39). In contrast, mediators "transform, translate, distort, and modify the meaning or the elements they are supposed to carry." (Latour, 2005, p. 39).

translation. As soon as actors are treated not as intermediaries but as mediators, they render the movement of the social visible to the reader.

As Latour emphasized, ANT accounts are first and foremost stories of movements and transformations. They seek to evidence the web of individual and collective agencies, and resulting displacements, shaping the social in one way or another. ANT accounts stress power dynamics and conflicts, shedding light on how the tensions emerge and are silenced among actors (Law 1992). These renditions draw particular attention to actors' hesitations, struggles, and identities fluctuations as a result of their association into actor-networks (Callon, 1986). As such, ANT narratives always are multifaceted stories.

A compelling illustration of this approach is Latour's (1996) book *Aramis or the Love of Technology*. Analyzing a project of automated underground which was never brought into action, this study brings to light the processes underlying technological innovations. The author articulates actors' different voices by alternating sections of dialogs, of actors' internal reflections, of excerpts from documents and interviews, of exchanges between the researchers, and, more importantly, gives voice to the main "actant" by letting the project-in-the-making provide its own perspective and account of process (one of the reasons why this book has been described as a form of "scientifiction"). In so doing Latour (1996) draws attention to the ongoing discussions, negotiations and hesitations that underpinned both the project itself and the researcher's analysis and includes the researcher as well as the main object under study (the project itself) into the setting as actants on their own right.

In a domain closer to CSR, Bled's (2010) study of international negotiations on the Convention for Biological Diversity (CBD) offers an interesting empirical account of an actor-network stabilization. Following the CBD, Bled describes how actors with diverse interests – the scientific community and NGOs, the preservation of biodiversity; States, the protection of their sovereignty; Monsanto, the exploitation of new technologies – coalesced around a common concern, the need to stop biological diversity loss, and mobilized other actors (conferences, reports, narratives of success stories and alliances) to transform this concern into an action plan. The study reveals the shifts in actors' positions as well as in the framing of the issue (from biodiversity preservation to sustainable development and to the fight against bio-piracy) as a result of actors' efforts. By using multiple voices, Bled's (2010) study offers a striking narrative of the multiple "displacements" underlying the CBD's life.

## Engaging Reflexively with CSR Issues and Theories

The performativity dimension of ANT calls for an increased researchers' attention to the various effects produced by the entities they analyse, the concept and theory they develop as well as their own research practice in the field within which they operate. In regard to the first implication of performativity, Wright and Nyberg's (2014) analysis of the performativity of climate change risk offers a good illustration of how the performativity of entities – here risks related to climate change – emerged unexpectedly from a field study.

> While the initial aim of our research was not to study risk per se, the concept of "risk" emerged early on in our data analysis as a key discourse for managers and corporations in their engagement with climate change. (p. 622)

In their methods, the authors explain further how "risk" was then coded in their multiple sources of data, and how this coding uncovered various modes of "climate change risk enactments" that corresponded to multiple ways for corporate actors to "naturalize" this new form of risk by bringing it into being.

Other research in the domain of CSR has started to unpack the process by which the concept of CSR itself has transformed or shaped reality, notably through the activity of social reporting. In their analysis of the genesis of the French laws about social information reporting – the 1977 Law on the "*Bilan Social*"(that made mandatory the reporting of information about human resources as well as a predefined set of social indicators) and the 2001 Law on "New Economic Regulations" (that made mandatory the reporting of environmental and social information for listed companies in their financial report), Gond, Igalens and Brès (2013) identified how specific concepts of CSR and dominant CSR-related ideologies were together involved in the debates preceding the adoption of each legal framework. By tracking the proceedings and debates surrounding both legal processes, their study reveals how the concepts of CSR shaped the legal outcomes of these negotiations and made differences resulting in specific compromises about the nature of reporting.

Finally, a performativity approach invites researchers to beware of the effects produced by CSR entities and/or academic concepts and theories when developing them, and to aim at capitalizing on some of the effects produced by CSR theory. Schaefer and Wickert (2016) recently proposed a concept of progressive performativity aiming at harnessing the CSR concept to enhance change through "micro-engagement" with managers within organizations and to develop a "reflexive conscientization" of actors (pp. 117–122); whereas Gond and Nyberg (2017) invite to mobilize the effects produced by materialized forms of CSR in order to recover the social and environmental purpose of CSR activities. Both papers call for a more reflexive conduct of research in the CSR space that could leverage the potentially performative effects of CSR.

## Discussing the Uses of Actor-Network Theory in CSR Research

Strictly following the spirit and letter of ANT assumptions may raise tricky challenges, especially in a disciplinary field such as CSR that has borrowed its insights and methods from multiple research traditions beyond sociology. It is therefore no surprise that scholars have engaged with different levels of depth with ANT fundamental assumptions and methodological implications. This diversity is illustrated by Table 16.1 that provides an overview of studies from a range of journals in organization theory, management, and CSR, specifying their key topic of inquiry, approach to ANT, key findings, and discussing their specific use of ANT.

In what follows, we first review briefly and then discuss critically how ANT assumptions and ideas have been performed through this representative sample of CSR studies, and discuss how ANT could be further leveraged to advance CSR scholarship.

### *How Has ANT Been Used in Prior CSR Studies?*

ANT has been appropriated by a few researchers in the CSR domain, usually to be combined with a variety of other theories and frameworks in empirical studies, such as stakeholder theory (e.g., El Abboubi & Nicolopoulou, 2012), institutional theory (Caron & Turcotte, 2009) or sensemaking (e.g., Füssel & Georg 2000). Combining ANT with other theoretical frameworks creates important epistemological and ontological challenges as ANT typically considers entities like actor-network to have potentially "variable ontologies," and neither stakeholder theory nor institutional analysis, for instance, share such assumptions. Accordingly, most authors tend to simply "import" an ANT concept (e.g. contextualization, translation, actor-network) within another framework, without necessarily adopting the corresponding underlying assumptions about the nature of this concept. This approach, though useful, does not necessarily exploit the full potential of the three characteristics of ANT we have described earlier.

In contrast, other studies build on ANT as an alternative to mainstream frameworks such as new institutional theory and recognize it as a theoretical perspective "on its own" to unpack their phenomenon of interest. For instance, Bled (2010) relies on ANT to complement social network analysis, and Åhlström and Egels-Zandén (2008) suggest that ANT can bring power back into the analysis of CSR, in contrast to prior institutional studies. Although such an approach brings CSR scholars closer to build on ANT assumptions, it may create difficulties to position the analysis and outcomes of the studies in relation to prior studies of the same phenomenon adopting a distinct set of epistemological and ontological assumptions.

**Table 16.1. Illustration of some corporate social responsibility studies using actor-network theory.**

| Article | Empirical focus | Methods (Type and Data sources) | Argued theoretical contribution of ANT | Main empirical insights and/or contributions to CSR | Limitation in the use of ANT assumptions and potential to develop further the analysis |
|---|---|---|---|---|---|
| Åhlström and Egels-Zandén (2008) | Definition of CSR | Type: Case study of the redefinition of Swedish garment retailers' responsibilities between 1996 and 2004<br>Data sources: 29 interviews between 2002 and 2004 and document analysis. | ANT is presented as an alternative to institutional theory enabling a greater focus on power, micro-level actions and on analyzing processes. | Battles of interpretation occur where pluralism is silenced.<br>Nondominant actors can use other actors' power to direct the negotiations, where others are silenced.<br>Definitional processes do not necessarily unfold in democratic and transparent ways. | The paper focuses on negotiations between human actors while understating other types of actors (e.g. the agency of CSR itself, or of the codes of conducts that were designed).<br>Further analysis could investigate CSR performative dynamics in making a certain definition to prevail. |
| Bergström and Diedrich (2011) | Definition of CSR | Type: Case study of a Swedish high-tech company, over a one-year period<br>Data sources: observations of daily work and meetings, thirty-one interviews, and document analysis | ANT is used in combination with stakeholder theory, enabling to account for the complexities of power relations. | This paper offers a processual understanding of stakeholders' interactions in CSR. It shows the micro-political dynamics through which the organization and its stakeholders influenced and shaped one another until the organization's definition of social responsibility was accepted. | The analysis downplays the power dynamics undergoing the negotiations and the leverages mobilized by actors to get their worldviews succeed.<br>Further analysis could direct attention onto if, and how, actors which contested the organization were silenced. |
| Bled (2010) | International environmental governance | Type: Case study of the development of the Convention on Biodiversity<br>Data sources: literature review, documentation, and archival analysis fieldwork observations and interviews. | ANT is presented as an alternative to social networks analysis, enabling to better account of the sociomaterial genesis of agency. | Forming alliances plays a crucial role in international environmental processes<br>Power, rather than being predetermined, emerges from actors' capability to reconcile their interests with practical actions.<br>International environmental governance is | The account provided does not really consider the full set of performative effects produced by the negotiation.<br>Further analysis could investigate how the negotiations produce new entities that shape reality. |

**Table 16.1.** ***(cont.)***

| Article | Empirical focus | Methods (Type and Data sources) | Argued theoretical contribution of ANT | Main empirical insights and/or contributions to CSR | Limitation in the use of ANT assumptions and potential to develop further the analysis |
|---|---|---|---|---|---|
| | | | | focused on aligning commercial interests with environmental priorities. | |
| Caron and Turcotte (2009) | Sustainability reporting | Type: Secondary data analysis<br>Data sources: Analysis of ten sustainability reports using mixed methods (quantitative-qualitative, deductive-inductive) | ANT is used in combination with institutional theory to analyse sustainability reports as artifacts in an innovation process. | Both path dependence and path creation dynamics are found in the innovation process in which sustainability reports are embedded and are in tension in determining the process direction.<br>Path dependence dynamics considerably limit the reports content and make them suboptimal for stakeholders' evaluation of firms' sustainability performance. | The paper accounts for a very linear process of GRI adoption without allowing full agency to the sustainability reports.<br>Further analysis could show more clearly the interdependences and power forces between actors of the network (e.g. how the reports shaped GRI itself). |
| El Abboubi and Nicolopoulou (2012) | International accountability standards | Type: Longitudinal case study of a multinational company in Belgium<br>Data sources: 24 interviews and document analysis. | ANT is used in combination with stakeholder theory, enabling to highlight the involvement process of salient stakeholders. | The analysis evidences the micro-political dynamics involved in multistakeholders involvement processes.<br>Organizations may mobilize stakeholders external to those identified by the standards and legitimize their involvement by a participative approach. | The paper offers a rather disincarnated account of the interactions under study grounded on a single standpoint, that of the corporation.<br>Further analysis could provide a more nuanced story by (1) giving voice to the individual actors themselves; and (2) confronting the voices of the various stakeholders. |
| Füssel and Georg (2000) | Green accounting | Type: Case study of a Danish hospital<br>Data sources: observation of meetings, interviews, and document analysis. | ANT is used in combination with sensemaking and presented as an alternative to institutional theory, enabling to study technologies as | The paper shows the greening process as an effect of multiple interactions around the construction of green accounting. | Nonhuman actants are silenced in the analysis.<br>Further analysis could investigate how the materiality of green accounts |

**Table 16.1. (*cont.*)**

| Article | Empirical focus | Methods (Type and Data sources) | Argued theoretical contribution of ANT | Main empirical insights and/or contributions to CSR | Limitation in the use of ANT assumptions and potential to develop further the analysis |
|---|---|---|---|---|---|
| | | | subject to multiple interpretations and contestation. | | (e.g. the material supports of the accounts) act in the greening process. |
| Gond and Boxenbaum (2013) | Responsible investment (RI) | Type: Comparative case study between two cases of importation of RI practices<br>Data sources: interviews and document analysis. | ANT is used in combination with institutional work, allowing to render visible the purposeful selection of elements through which actors deliberately make a new practice fit their local institutional context. | The paper introduces three types of contextualization work through which individuals fit the RI practice to their contexts: filtering, repurposing, and coupling. | The paper does not describe how the work of contextualization changes local institutional contexts.<br>Further analysis could investigate the performative effects through which the diffusion of RI changes local institutions. |
| Jensen, Sandström and Helin (2009) | Corporate codes of ethics | Type: Case study of the Swedish subsidiary of an American company, over two years.<br>Data sources: 48 interviews and document analysis | ANT departs from previous research on the role of codes of conducts by granting artifacts agency and conceiving morality as both a human and nonhuman matter. | The paper depicts the code of ethics as "bending moral space" and creating different moral possibilities.<br>The meaning of ethics was transformed under the combined influence of human, material, and discursive actors. | The analysis insufficiently exhibits the power dynamics at play in the adoption of the code of ethics.<br>Further analysis could shed more light on the power struggles underlying this change. |

Table 16.1 also highlights the diversity of CSR-related topics such as the process of CSR definition (e.g., Bergström & Diedrich, 2011), the international governance of biodiversity (e.g., Bled, 2010), sustainability reporting and standards (e.g., Caron & Turcotte, 2009) or responsible investing practices (e.g., Gond & Boxenbaum, 2013). To this diversity of topics also correspond a diversity of methodological protocols, as few studies have actually applied to the letter Latour's (2005) idea of "following the actors," which requires an excellent level of access to the field, and most studies propose case studies, sometimes retrospective. These case studies usually reconstruct – through historical analysis, archival material and/or interviewing and observations – the assembling of actor-networks, the production of CSR relevant entities (reporting), or the political processes underlying the negotiation of specific social or environmental issues.

As a whole, and thanks to its reliance on the aforementioned assumptions and methods, ANT research has contributed to shed light on subtle processes often neglected in more structural-functionalist analyses of CSR. Several of the studies reviewed highlight unnoticed micro-level power dynamics (Bergström & Diedrich, 2011;

Bled, 2010) or address paradoxical phenomena, such as the global diffusion and differentiation of responsible investing practices across multiple regions of the world (Gond & Boxenbaum, 2013), or the role of material entities such as reporting systems (Caron & Turcotte, 2009).

## How Can ANT Be Leveraged in Future CSR Studies

In sum, our analysis of prior research using ANT provided in Table 1 suggests that CSR researchers rarely capitalize on the whole set of ANT assumptions. Few scholars engage with ANT's underlying assumptions beyond the reliance on one or two key concepts, and when they do so, they do not necessarily assume the three principles we introduced earlier in this chapter. When *assembling dynamics* are carefully unpacked to uncover power dynamics, actants became silent or not accounted for (e.g., Bergström & Diedrich, 2011). When *materiality* is the center of the study, power dynamics crucial to the making of actor-network remain often ignored (e.g., Caron & Turcotte, 2009). And finally, when materiality and assembling are accounted for, the *performative dimensions* usually remain uncovered (e.g., Bled, 2010; Gond & Boxenbaum, 2013).

This lack of deep engagement with ANT epistemological and ontological assumptions is problematic, as it suggests that the full potential of ANT for CSR has not yet been captured. However, this situation also creates unique opportunities to further contribute to CSR through ANT. In the last column of Table 1, we provide illustrations of how these missing assumptions can encourage the development of further research.

As a whole, it thus resorts from our analysis of a sample of studies that CSR researchers are far from having fully exploited the possibilities offered by the consideration of the three assumptions of *assembling*, *materiality*, and *performativity*, alone or in combination, to uncover empirically CSR-related phenomena. Through its relational ontology, ANT research allows to address multiple tensions (micro vs. macro, normative vs. prescriptive) that remain profoundly anchored in most CSR scholarship (e.g., Aguinis & Glavas, 2012; Donaldson & Preston, 1995), offers a renewed understanding of how power plays through material devices within and across organizations (Bergström & Diedrich, 2011; Gond & Nyberg, 2017), enables to bring nonhuman entities (climate, animals, ecosystems) with the analysis (Latour, 2004) and ultimately suggests engaging more reflexively with the meaning and significance of CSR theory and concepts for the rest of society through the notion of performativity.

Although addressing these issues involves multiple methodological challenges that we have introduced, we hope this chapter will offer "would-be ANT scholars" operating in the CSR field some of the necessary resources, and we hope, a relevant starting point, to adopt a different approach to the entities they study, the theory they seek to develop, and the world they wish to bring about.

## References

Aguinis, H., & Glavas, A. (2012). What we know and don't know about corporate social responsibility a review and research agenda. *Journal of Management*, 38(4): 932–968.

Ählström, J., & Egels-Zandén, N. (2008). The process of defining corporate social responsibility: A study of Swedish garment retailers' responsibility. *Business Strategy and the Environment*, 17: 230–244.

Austin, J. L., (1962). *How to Do Things with Words*. Oxford: Oxford University Press.

Bansal, P., & Song, H-C. (2017). Similar but not the same: Differentiating corporate responsibility from sustainability. *Academy of Management Annals*. 11(1): 105–149.

Barter, N., & Bebbington, J. (2013). Actor-network theory: a briefing note and possibilities for social and environmental accounting research. *Social and Environmental Accountability Journal*, 33(1): 33–50.

Bergström, O. & Diedrich, A. (2011). Exercising social responsibility in downsizing: Enrolling and mobilizing actors at a Swedish high-tech company. *Organization Studies*, 32(7): 897–919.

Bled, A. J. (2010). Technological choices in international environmental negotiations: an actor–network analysis. *Business & Society*, 49(4): 570–590.

Boltanski, L. (2013). *The Foetal Condition: A Sociology of Engendering and Abortion*. John Wiley & Sons.

Briers, M., & Chua, W. F. (2001). The role of actor-networks and boundary objects in management accounting change: a field study of an implementation of activity-based costing. *Accounting, Organizations and Society*, 26(3): 237–269.

Burt, R. S. 1995. *Structural Holes: The Social Structure of Competition*. Cambridge, MA: Harvard University Press.

Cabantous, L., & Gond, J. P. (2011). Rational decision making as performative praxis: explaining rationality's éternel retour. *Organization Science*, 22(3): 573–586.

Callon, M., (1986). Some elements of a sociology of translation: Domestication of the scallops and the fishermen of St Brieuc Bay. In J. Law (ed.), *Power, Action and Belief: A New Sociology of Knowledge*: 196–223. London: Routledge.

(1991). Techno-economic networks and irreversibility. In J. Law (ed.) *A Sociology of Monsters: Essays on Power, Technology and Domination*: 132–161. London: Routledge and Keegan Paul.

(1998a). Introduction: The embeddedness of economic markets in economics. In M. Callon (ed.), *The Laws of the Markets*: 1–58. Oxford: Blackwell.

(1998b). An essay on framing and overflowing: Economic externalities revisited by sociology. In M. Callon (ed.), *The Laws of the markets*: 244–269. Oxford: Blackwell.

(2009). Civilizing markets: Carbon trading between in vitro and in vivo experiments. *Accounting, Organizations and Society*, 34(3): 535–548.

Callon, M., & Latour, B. (1981). Unscrewing the big Leviathan: How actors macro-structure reality and how sociologist help them to do so. In K. Knorr-Cetina & A.V. Cicourel (eds) *Advances in Social Theory and Methodology: Towards an Integration of Micro- and Macro Sociologies*: 277–303. Boston, MA: Routledge.

Caron, M. A., & Turcotte, M. F. B. (2009). Path dependence and path creation: Framing the extra-financial information market for a sustainable trajectory. *Accounting, Auditing & Accountability Journal*, 22(2): 272–297.

Déjean, F, Gond, J.-P. & Leca, B. (2004). Measuring the unmeasured: An institutional entrepreneur strategy in an emerging industry. *Human Relations*, 57(6): 741–764

Descola, P. (2013). *Beyond Nature and Culture*. University of Chicago Press.

Donaldson, T., & Preston, L. E. (1995). The stakeholder theory of the corporation: Concepts, evidence, and implications. *Academy of Management Review*, 20(1): 65–91.

El Abboubi, M., & Nicolopoulou, K. (2012). International social-related accountability standards: Using ANT towards a multi-stakeholder analysis. *M@n@gement*, 4(15): 392–414.

Füssel, L., & Georg, S. (2000). The institutionalization of environmental concerns: Making the environment perform. *International Studies of Management & Organization*, 30(3): 41–58.

Garfinkel, H. 1967. *Studies in Ethnomethodology*. Polity Press.

Gond, J.-P., & Boxenbaum, E. (2013). The glocalization of responsible investment: Contextualization work in France and Québec. *Journal of Business Ethics*, 115(4): 707–721.

Gond, J.-P., Cabantous, L., Harding, N., & Learmonth, M. (2016). What do we mean by performativity in organizational and management theory? The uses and abuses of performativity. *International Journal of Management Reviews*. 18(4): 440–463.

Gond, J.-P., Igalens, J., & Brès, L. (2013). Rendre compte du social. *L'art du compromis performatif. Revue Française de Gestion*, 237: 201–238.

Gond, J.-P. & Nyberg, D. (2017). Materializing power to recover corporate social responsibility. *Organization Studies*. 38(8), 1127–1148.

Granovetter, M. (1985). Economic action and social structure: The problem of embeddedness. *American Journal of Sociology*, 481–510.

Hacking, I. (1983). *Representing and Intervening: Introductory Topics in the Philosophy of Natural Science*. Cambridge, MA: Cambridge University Press.

Jensen, T., Sandström, J., & Helin, S. (2009). Corporate codes of ethics and the bending of moral space. *Organization*, 16(4), 529–545.

Larssaether, S., & Nijhof, A. (2009). Moral landscapes: Understanding agency in corporate responsibility initiatives. *Corporate Social Responsibility and Environmental Management*, 16: 228–236.

Latour, B. (1986). The power of association. In J. Law (ed.), *Power, Action and Belief: A New Sociology of Knowledge?* 264–280. Boston: Routledge.

(1992). Where are the missing masses? The sociology of a few mundane artifacts. W. E. Bijker,

J. Law (eds), *Shaping Technology/Building Society: Studies in Sociotechnical Change*: 225–258. MIT Press, Cambridge, MA: Harvard University Press.

(1996). *Aramis, or the Love of Technology*. Cambridge, MA: Harvard University Press.

(1999). On recalling ANT. *The Sociological Review*, *47*(S1), 15–25.

(2004). *Politics of Nature: How to Bring the Sciences into Democracy*. Cambridge, MA: Harvard University Press.

(2005). *Reassembling the Social: An Introduction to Actor-Network Theory*. Oxford University Press.

(2006). *Petites leçons de sociologie des sciences*. Paris: La Découverte.

(2017). *Facing Gaïa. Eight Lectures on the New Climatic Regime*. London: Polity Press. Forthcoming.

Law, J. (1986). On the methods of long-distance control: Vessels, navigation and the Portuguese route to India. In J. Law (ed), *Power, Action, and Belief: A New Sociology of Knowledge?*: 234–263. London: Routledge & Kegan Paul.

(1992). Notes on the theory of actor-network: ordering, strategy and heterogeneity. *Systems Practice*, 5(4): 379–393.

(1999). After ANT: Complexity, naming and topology. In J. Law and J. Hassard (eds) *Actor Network Theory and After*: 1–14. Oxford: Blackwell.

(2004). *After Method: Mess in Social Science Research*. London: Routledge.

(2008). On sociology and STS. *Sociological Review*, 56: 623–649.

Ligonie, M. (2016). *Management Control for Sustainability. A Practice-based Approach to Corporate Social Responsibility*, PhD dissertation, ESSEC Business School.

(2017). The "forced performativity" of a strategy concept: Exploring how shared value shaped a gambling company's strategy. *Long Range Planning*. Published online. DOI: 10.1016/j.lrp.2017.04.001

MacKenzie, D., & Millo, Y. (2003). Constructing a market, performing a theory: The historical sociology of a financial derivatives exchange. *American Review of Sociology*, 109(1): 107–145

Malsch, B. (2013). Politicizing the expertise of the accounting industry in the realm of corporate social responsibility. *Accounting, Organizations and Society*, 38(2), 149–168.

Marti, E. & Gond, J.-P. 2017. When do theories become self-fulfilling? Exploring the boundary conditions of performativity. *Academy of Management Review*. Published online. DOI: 10.5465/amr.2016.0071.

Pasquero, J. (1996). Stakeholder theory as a constructivist paradigm. In: *Proceedings of the International Association for Business and Society*, 7: 1153–1164.

Schaefer, S. M., & Wickert, C. (2016). On the potential of progressive performativity: Definitional purity, re-engagement and empirical points of departure. *Human Relations*, 69(2): 215–224.

Scherer, A. G., & Palazzo, G. (2007). Toward a political conception of corporate responsibility: Business and society seen from a Habermasian perspective. *Academy of Management Review*, *32*(4), 1096–1120.

(2011). The new political role of business in a globalized world: A review of a new perspective on CSR and its implications for the firm, governance, and democracy. *Journal of Management Studies*, 48(4), 899–931.

Scherer, A. G., Rasche, A., Palazzo, G., & Spicer, A. (2016). Managing for political corporate social responsibility: New challenges and directions for PCSR 2.0. *Journal of Management Studies*, 53 (3), 273–298.

Van Grinsven, M., Heusinkveld, S. & Cornelissen, J. (2016). Translating management concepts: Towards a typology of alternative approaches. *International Journal of Management Reviews*, 18(3): 271–289.

Wæraas, A. & Nielsen, J. A. (2016). Translation theory 'translated': Three perspectives on translation in organizational research. *International Journal of Management Reviews*, 18(3): 236–270.

Whelan, G., & Gond, J. P. (2017). Meat your enemy: Animal rights, alignment and radical change. *Journal of Management Inquiry*. 26(2): 123–138.

Wright C, & Nyberg D. (2014). Creative self-destruction: corporate responses to climate change as political myths. *Environmental Politics*, 23: 205–223.

PART III

# A Researcher in the Spotlight

CHAPTER 17

# Social Construction as Background for Research in Business Ethics

JOHN J. PIRRI and PATRICIA H. WERHANE

> [T]he seemingly objective social world is constructed by human action and interaction.
> (Berger and Luckmann,1966, 1, 78)

As human beings, we are born into a socially constructed world where we frame and deal with our experiences through mindsets or mental models. Indeed, we cannot escape nor can we experience the world except though these mindsets, which, although socially learned and incomplete, frame and focus all our experiences. Moreover, the corporate cultures or dominant logics that pervade organizational thinking and decision making are themselves the products of organizationally constructed mindsets.

As researchers in business ethics, these socially constructed incomplete mindsets frame our approaches to the topic and our critiques of individual and organizational moral behavior. By studying these mindsets and their positive and adverse effects, we are better able to analyze individual managerial decision making and the worldview that we call corporate culture or the corporate dominant logic that usually pervades organizational thinking and decision making. And what we will call a piecemeal constructive methodology is also useful in studying particular phenomena. We conclude, therefore, that in research approaches to business ethics, it is critical to become aware and to get at the root of the socially constructed frames we use as researchers to approach a topic, and, in turn, to study these pervasive individual and organizational phenomena.

Parts of this chapter are revisions from chapter 2 of Werhane et al., 2013 Reprinted by permission of Cambridge University Press and the authors.

## Social Construction

We begin by outlining a version of social constructionism and mental models suited to business ethics research and social responsibility. The origins of constructionism can be traced to Immanuel Kant's critique of a *tabula rasa* construct of the mind (Kant, 1787, cited in 1965). Kant hypothesizes that our minds do not mirror experience. He argues that the *tabula rasa* thesis does not explain how we are able to communicate and understand each other while having different experiences. Rather, Kant argues, our minds project, constitute and/or reconstitute phenomena, the raw data of all experiences, into a structured, ordered coherence. He concludes that all human beings order and organize their experiences through identical sets of formal concepts, and while the content of our experiences may be quite different for each of us, we all structure and order these experiences in the same ways.

Today many thinkers challenge Kant's concept of how our minds are hard wired. Nevertheless, his description of mentally constitutive interactions between the perceiver and the perceived (what we call 'experience') is retained and explained within a social constructionist perspective. According to this thesis, each of us perceives, frames, orders, and organizes the data of our experiences through a lens, from a point of view, or within a set of frames. The social constructionist separates from Kant in arguing that these data are socially acquired and developed.

According to Ian Hacking and other proponents of social constructions, we are born into and depend on a world that is historically situated, linguistically, socially, and culturally defined, and is usually in some process of evolution or change. We neither create nor choose these particular sets of embedded historical, political, economic, and social narratives. They frame our early mental models and define our roles, as children, as women or men, as tribal members, as worshippers, as citizens (Hacking, 1999). These narratives and the language in which they are embedded are the background for individual experiences. They provide the initial conditions for the conceptual schema that frame all our experiences, and they often direct, influence, or confine the range of mental models we learn and adapt.

We further construct new meanings through lenses and frames, which are conceptual schema or mental models that serve as filtering and focusing mechanisms. These models are "mental representations, cognitive frames, or mental pictures through which all human beings interact with experience, developing narratives, observations, and scientific content, which is then called 'knowledge'" (Werhane, 1999, 53; see also, Gorman, 1992, Goldman and Blanchad, 2015; Gentner and Whitley, 1997, 210–211).

In the social constructionist paradigm, such mental models frame all our experiences. They schematize and otherwise facilitate and guide the ways in which we recognize, react to, and organize the world. Various scientific methodologies are themselves mental models through which scientists discover, predict, and hypothesize about what we then call reality. How we define the world is dependent on such schema and thus reality is socially structured. In the socially constructed paradigm, the multivariate mental models or conceptual schema are the means and mode through which we constitute our experiences. Because these schema are socially learned, fragile, transient, and changeable, each is always incomplete or unfinished, such that one never gets a holistic world view (Werhane, 1999; Gorman, 1992; Senge, 1990).

Still, it is one thing to claim that one cannot get at reality, the world, or even experience, except through some mental model, and quite another to conclude that reality or experience *itself* is merely created or solely socially constructed. Contending that the incomplete and disparate ways in which we present and distill experiences are socially constructed is different from arguing that experience or reality itself is socially created. The latter is a form of strong constructionism. "Strong social constructionism claims not only that representations are socially constructed, but that the *entities themselves* to which these representations refer are socially constructed" (Goldman, 2010). A strong or universal constructionist would argue that "... every object whatsoever, is in some nontrivial sense socially constructed. Not just our experience of them, our classifications of them, our interests in them, but *these things themselves*" (Hacking, 1999, 24; emphasis added). Ian Hacking and others contend that strong social constructionism is not tenable because it creates a form of regress regarding the status of the constructionism thesis itself.

The conclusion that we do not construct reality or the data of our experiences is part of a weak constructionist conclusion; however, we only access that data through framing models and language. These framing perspectives or mental models interpret the data of our experiences, and it is this data that we call "facts." What we normally call "reality" or the world is socially construed in certain ways such that one cannot get at the source of the data except through these construals.

One version of social constructionism is what Karl Weick and others call "sensemaking." (see Weick, 1995) "Sensemaking involves the ongoing retrospective [and prospective] development of plausible images that rationalize what people are doing" (Weick, Sutcliffe, and Obstfeld, 2005, 409). Sensemaking is in part habitual, describing the implicit ways in which we socially frame and order our experiences. But, according to Weick et al., sensemaking can also be proactive. We may deliberately reframe or reorder our experience in an effort to give meaning or new meaning to those experiences. In this way, we can order or reorder and shape organizations, as well as our personal experiences. "A central theme in both organizing and sensemaking is that people organize to make sense of equivocal inputs and enact this sense back into the world to make that world more orderly" (Weick et al., 2005, 410). Sensemaking can also be actively retrospective. We can look back at the ways in which we have framed or interpreted an experience, and we can then reinterpret that experience or test new perspectives on those mindsets.

A standard critique of proposing that social construction is ubiquitous of all our experiences is that that conclusion itself is a general one. Is it too socially constructed? One is reminded of the apocryphal story of the well-known psychologist William James. The legend is that one day one of his students declared to him that the world was held up by a giant turtle. Asking what held up that turtle, the student replied, "Well, another turtle." And when James asked what held up the second turtle, the student replied confidently, "Professor, it is turtles all the way down." If Rorty and Putnam are correct that "'Elements of what we call language or mind penetrate so deeply into what we call reality that the very prospect of representing ourselves as mappers of something 'language-independent' is fatally compromised from the start." (Rorty, 1993, 443 quoted from Putnam, 1990, 28) then it is "language all the way down," and there is no getting around that.

Nevertheless, as social linguistic beings we are constantly interacting with, thus affecting and being affected by, others' mental models. These in turn are historically and culturally situated and at least partly constructed from this situational context. Out of these interactions we often come to consensus on our views, for example, about the scientific method, the validity of historical models, etc.

Moreover, the background narratives, which themselves function as revisable mental models, are neither static nor incommensurable with each other. Thus, none of us is identified merely with our socially connected selves; nor are we merely determined by our historical social narratives. We are at once byproducts of, characters in, and authors of our own stories (e.g., Werhane, 1999; Johnson, 1993, 153; Sartre, 1956). Because all mental models or mindsets are incomplete, we can be proactively reshaping our interpretations of experiences, as Weick suggests, and we can also engage in second-order studies, evaluations, judgments, and assessments about our own and other operative mental models. Of course, this is a complex process since the act of reflection is itself a further framing or reframing.

This process is what Amartya Sen (1993) calls "positional objectivity." Positional objectivity defines the way in which a phenomenon or an event appears "from a delineated somewhere" (Sen, 1993, 127). According to Sen, any person in that position will make similar observations. Sen assumes that from a certain point of view we are able to observe and process the same data similarly. We would add that the parameters of the phenomenon of positional dependency entail shared mental models and similar or identical historical and cultural contexts. However, a positionally objective point of view that does not account for relevant available information could be misleading. Almost any position has alternatives as well as critics. Even positionally objective phenomena have been filtered through the social sieve of a shared mental model or narrative, and are neither infallible nor complete.

## Two Levels of Social Construction: A Macro Level and Piecemeal Approaches

If social construction is ubiquitous in all our experiences and in the ways, we frame our experiences, then it descriptive of the totality of all approaches in which a researcher frames a topic or phenomena she studies. But if one is not a thoroughly committed to social construction as a worldview, it is useful for piecemeal studies of certain kinds of phenomena.

On the macro level, in a seminal article published in 1992 Mark Granovetter persuasively argues that economic institutions are social constructions. In a strong critique of neoclassical economics, Granovetter contends that it is just one of a number of possible socially constructed economic theories, one that fails to be relevant in communities where "economic activity comes to be coordinated by groups of people rather than carried out by isolated individuals ... [such as in] [f]irms in developing countries, business groups, origins of the electrical industry in the United States" (Granovetter, 1992, 3).

In business ethics, if one frames that research primarily from a financial lens, where shareholder returns drive that thinking, then how one does research on business ethics will be framed by that focus. So, for example, recent massive layoffs of large American firms in pursuit of lower-waged workers elsewhere can be defended on the basis of increased shareholder returns. Pushing that analysis further, sweatshops, which do provide jobs, albeit terrible ones from a worker perspective, can be defended as providing shareholder returns and in the long run economic growth (See Maitland, 1997 for that defense).

On the other hand, framing research in stakeholder terms takes into account value added for the primary stakeholders of a firm including shareholders or owners, thus presenting a more complex analysis of value-added. If one then reworks stakeholder maps to reflect a view that all stakeholders have equal claims, and if one takes the firm out of the center of the standard stakeholder graphic, as Freeman implied in his original 1984 book, one's research agenda may be still more nuanced (Freeman, 1984). And, if one adds the idea that each group of stakeholders is a collection of distinct individuals, the McVea/Freeman idea of giving each member of each class a "name and face," (McVea and Freeman, 2005) one's research agenda will be further complicated, but quite different from a traditional preoccupation with shareholder value-added.

Similarly, a preoccupation with research concentrating on corporate social responsibility may focus attention on corporate external relationships, while an ethics perspective may focus primarily on internal stakeholder relationships. In either case the research agenda and thus the analyses and outcomes will be different. An empirical descriptive quantitative approach to managerial or organizational issues is important to lay out cause-and-effect relationships. On the other hand, a purely normative approach might concentrate on what companies and their managers ought to do, sometimes fairly abstractly. In another essay in this volume, Wes Cragg argues that a better way to socially construct one's research is to engage in a hybrid technique that does not separate the normative from the descriptive (a separation that is theoretically questionable anyway. See Werhane, 1994) More generally, the very way one frames a research agenda affects the kinds of analyses that can be generated from that agenda. Being aware of that framing is critical if one is to be able to critique one's own and others's thinking.

## Piecemeal Approaches

Without committing to the claim that social construction is a comprehensive world view, a number of researchers use the idea of social construction as a piecemeal device in their research approaches. For example, in a recent unpublished paper, Shadnam, Crane, and Lawrence, in an analysis of moral failure, argue that there is a "Significant role of social construction in a wide variety of moral phenomena . . . Moral failure is . . . a multi-faceted concept that is open to multiple discursive [social] constructions that in turn prompt a range of interpretive schema." (Shadnam, Crane, and Lawrence, forthcoming) So if one approaches organizational moral failure as noncompliance, for instance, one's analysis of that failure will be different from arguing that it could be due to unethical managerial or organizational behavior.

In another older paper, Richard Whitley studied the institutional environment in each of four East Asian countries, Japan, Korea, China, and Hong Kong. He noticed that each institutional environment created by a socially constructed framework was different in each community, and that framework, in turn, structured how business is conducted. Those differences are sometimes ignored when researchers study "East Asian commerce" as if that were one sort of phenomenon. Whitley's point is that one must understand these differences in order to engage in comparative research analyses (as well as in doing business in these various communities.) (Whitley, 1991).

These examples are just two of hundreds of articles that use social construction as a piecemeal jumping-off point for research into understanding various specific managerial and organizational dimensions of commerce.[1] As a researcher, then, engaging in piecemeal appeals to the social construction of various phenomena is very useful. In addition, we would argue, that being aware of these different frames or social constructions as

[1] A search for the term "social construction" in the *Journal of Business Ethics* alone produced 1773 results. A search for "Social construction of corporate responsibility" produced 1430 citations. And this is only in ONE journal.

incomplete constructions is very important as well, to avoid making generalized conclusions from specific schema and for comparative analyses that do not ignore these differences.

## Another Research Agenda: The Role of Social Construction in Managerial Thinking

One other important agenda for business ethics researchers is to study and make transparent the socially constructed dominant logics that pervade organizational thinking. According to Weick, Sutcliffe, and Obstfeld, sensemaking occurs at the organizational level as well as individually. (Weick, et al., 1995). This phenomenon is evidenced in a firm's dominant logic. "[A] dominant logic is a mindset or a world view or a conceptualization of the business and [the conceptualization of] the administrative tools to accomplish goals and make decisions in that business. It is stored as a shared cognitive map (or set of schemas) among the dominant coalition ... as the way in which managers conceptualize the business and make critical resource allocation decisions—be it in technologies, product development, distribution, advertising, or in human resource management" (Prahalad & Bettis, 1986, pp. 485, 490). This cognitive orientation governs how and why decisions are made. A corporate dominant logic predisposes managers toward the strategic choices they make as they engage in problem-solving behavior. Ultimately, this orientation, which becomes an integral part of all of the firm's decision-making processes and includes reward systems, promotion, and critical resource allocation decisions, sometimes reinforces behavior that is not ethical.

When a dominant logic becomes deeply embedded in an organization for a long time, those mindsets instill habits, and "dominant logics tend to become rigid ideologies, reducing strategic adaptability and locking firms in existing business models." (Fawcett & Waller, 2012, p. 175). If managers become indoctrinated in this way to certain organizational mindsets, they may accept those mindsets as determinate and thus fail to engage in the sort of proactive sensemaking that would enable them to anticipate media influences, new regulatory forces, public changes in mindsets, or unforeseen pressures from the public.

An excellent example of static reactive sensemaking is that of the recent case of Volkswagen's creative design of its software to meet American emission standards in its diesel autos. In an effort to meet production goals the company apparently falsified the software. Although managers and engineers at Volkswagen had access to much of the same data about this protocol, no one there questioned the decision or challenged this choice. From a positionally objective point of view, Volkswagen could be defended; it was committed to the positionally objective belief of the value of corporate efficiency in achieving its production goals and to a shared organizational mental model of corporate secrecy. Indeed, the Chairman of the VW Supervisory Board contended that one of the causes of this scandal was a corporate "mindset in some areas of the company that tolerated breaches of the rules" (Pötsch, 2015 quoted by Goodman, 2015). Pötsch admitted, "We are not talking about a one-off mistake, but a whole chain of mistakes that was not interrupted at any point along the timeline" (Goodman 2015). Outsiders, however, e.g., American owners of diesel automobiles and U.S. government regulators, processed the same information differently. They operated under a belief system that placed mandated emission standards safety concerns ahead of economy. These two perspectives are analogous to the views of the Copernicans and Ptolemaists, who, at least initially, processed the same data about the universe, but processed it differently, resulting in different conclusions and thus conflicting positionally objective points of view.

No positionally objective phenomenon is immune from challenge. But according to Sen (1993), in addition to taking positionally objective points of view, we are able to engage in "transpositional" assessments. A transpositional view is a constructed critique of a positionally objective phenomenon. This assessment compares various positionally objective points of view to determine whether one can make coherent sense of them and develop some general theories about what is being observed. From a transpositional point of view, mental models themselves can be questioned on the basis of their coherence or their explanatory scope. Transpositional assessments are constructed views, because they too depend on the schema of the assessors. Although the challenge can be conducted only from another mental model, the assessment can take into account more than one point of view. Revisions of the schema in question might produce another mental model that more comprehensively explains a range of phenomena or incidents. Although one can never begin with pure unconstituted data, one can, at least, in principle, achieve a limited, dispassionate perspective.

Thus, one set of research agendas in business ethics research is to uncover and expose flawed dominant logics. In short, studying *sets* of perspectives or organizational dominant logics can reveal how certain events are experienced and reported and even bring into view the mental models that are shaping the narratives about these experiences. As researchers, we do this all the time, but being aware that each perspective, each dominant logic, and even each research approach is socially constructed adds a new dimension to research thinking.

If one is doing research on organizations, one has to take into account institutional theory. Institutional theory argues that "no organization can properly be understood apart from its wider social and cultural context" (Scott, 1995, cited in 2001, 151). An institutional theory of organizations argues that organizations, like individuals, are created and determined by their social and political contexts. Moreover, according to this theory, while it is true that human beings construct institutions, "institutions… are socially constructed to make life stable and meaningful, and they both constrain and enable action … [Thus] human action is largely conditioned by institutions" (Van de Ven and Hargrave, 2004, 259; Scott, 1995, cited in 2001). However, these contexts are not fully determinate of all organizational behavior and can and should be continually evaluated and revised. Organizations are created by and made up of individuals or groups of individuals, the decision makers, who have flexible mindsets and are capable, in Sen's words, of making transpositional assessments. Thus, individuals and organizations can revise their dominant logics and change the direction of the organization. It is the work of researchers to make these assessments.

## Sensemaking, Dominant Logics, and Moral Imagination

One challenge in the research of organizational sensemaking is to demonstrate whether and how an organization can redefine itself, change its mission, or reinterpret its purpose in order to change its identity or dominant logic. We shall argue that one viable approach to this process is to engage in the processes of moral imagination.

"Moral imagination . . . is the ability in particular circumstances to discover and evaluate possibilities not merely determined by that circumstance, or limited by its operative mental models, or merely framed by a set of rules or rule-governed concerns" (Werhane, 1999, p. 93; see also Werhane, 2008; Johnson, 1993). Moral imagination entails heightening one's awareness of situational contexts or schemas, envisioning and evaluating different cognitive frameworks, reframing the situation, and creating solutions that are feasible, economically viable, and morally justifiable (Werhane, 1999). In the study of evaluating firms, in short, moral imagination requires that researchers assess, in as disengaged a manner as possible, a given situation, recognize its strategic and moral components, step back from its particular schema, and suggest different paradigms or revised dominant logics.

At least four processes are involved in moral imagination: recognition, disengagement, envisioning novel perspectives, and evaluation. By recognition we mean the ability to identify the operative dominant logic and underlying schemas in an organization. To achieve recognition, one must first understand that dominant logics are operative in any organization; then one may engage in a transpositional assessment to analyze its operative habits and procedures. Because one tends to be tightly embedded in an organization's dominant logic, as we have seen in the VW case, recognition does not come easily.

According to Bower and Christensen (1995), firms frequently fail at this effort because, stuck in their context or situation, they evaluate new technology through their existing financial and customer models rather than framing new possibilities. These companies fail to challenge their existing dominant logics. The ability to disengage from one's context or situation is the most important step in developing moral imagination. If managers are unable to disengage and evaluate a firm's practices and principles, they become mired in habit and this can lead the firm to eventually atrophy. Managers are frequently urged to "think out of the box." But in order to do so, one must first be aware of what is *in* the box. This ability to disengage enhances our power to take an alternate organizational perspective, partially freeing us from our own dominant logic, and helping us to understand that our particular set of circumstances and schemas is but one of many. The breakthrough that sparks awareness of and disengagement from an embedded dominant logic often occurs when there is some sort of triggering event that threatens or otherwise affects an organization or when there is an internal or external threat to a company's products, future, or wellbeing (Weick, 1993; Isabella, 1992).

The process of disengagement—becoming cognitively detached from the dominant logic and immersed in a more critical perspective–enables us to make a transpositional assessment of that logic. It may turn out that the operative dominant logic is in fact flexible and adaptable to new environments, but such an evaluation is nevertheless necessary to ensure that the organization not become mired in nonproductive habitual behaviors.

The third important dimension of moral imagination is to become truly imaginative – to play with new ideas and to envision novel perspectives. The creative imagination allows researchers to envision organizations selves as different organizations, in different situations, even as living in different time/ space continua, with different needs and desires. Through the ability to disengage, the creative moral imagination can evaluate new possibilities as well as critique present dominant logics.

All three of these steps in employing moral imagination are necessary to evaluate organizational structures and dominant logics. Moral imagination helps us see the strategic and moral components of a particular situation and to assess contextual factors. It also helps us categorize a particular dominant logic. As part of the process of moral imagination, transpositional assessments provide further tools to evaluate both existing dominant logic and new perspectives as adaptive, viable, and socially acceptable. Creative imagination generates and helps us to evaluate novel solutions integral to this process (Werhane, 1999, 2002). This evaluative dimension of moral imagination is vital to judge the viability of proposed new strategies and value creation so that researchers can propose what might be adaptable to new markets, and ultimately improve performance, and also, sometimes at least, to help firms avoid some of the pitfalls of creative but mismatched ideas. Moral imagination, we conclude, is essential to those sorts of processes.

## Conclusion

Along with exposing the researcher to the notions of social construction, dominant logics, and moral imagination, this chapter aims to show why these concepts are important to business ethics research. At the beginning of the chapter, we argued that mindsets or mental models are ubiquitous to human perception and cognition. If that is the case, and if, as we have argued, these mindsets are socially created, incomplete but universal sense-making methods, then it is essential to acknowledge this in business ethics research. No researcher has perfect knowledge. Sometimes in the pursuit of certain conclusions, researchers have what Bazerman, Tenbrunsel, and Moberg have called "blind spots" (Bazerman and Tenbrunsel, 2012; Moberg, 2006). As researchers, we sometimes miss something important in our analyses. Often this is not deliberate. We all miss or do not notice dimensions of our research that perhaps should have been evident. Blind spots are, in part, the result of unexamined or habitual thinking, and as researchers, just as in organizations, we sometimes fail to understand the obvious or fail to study a particular social construction as just that, an incomplete framing. In business ethic research, we must recognize that blind spots are a frequent element of our studies.

We suggested earlier that because companies are made up of human individuals and groups of individuals who can initiate change through transpositional assessments as part of an imaginative process, there is no excuse for stale or outworn dominant logics. Van de Ven's institutional theory needs to be augmented by this sort of thinking. From a research point of view, an analysis of the limitations of institutional theory, as well as analyses of these logics, should be part of ongoing research.

Finally, in other venues, Werhane has argued tirelessly for the importance of developing a robust moral imagination. Tim Hargrave reminds us that there is much more work to be done on theory development, particularly at the organizational level. (Hargrave, 2016). We strongly encourage research in these areas.

## References


Bazerman, M and Tenbrunsel, A. 2012. *Blind Spots*. Princeton: Princeton University Press.

Berger, P. and Luchmann, T.. 1966. *The Social Construction of Reality*. New York: Penguin.

Bettis, R. A., & Prahalad, C. K. (1995). "The Dominant Logic: Retrospective and Extension." *Strategic Management Journal, 16*(1), 5–14.

Bower, J., & Christensen, C. (1995). "Disruptive technologies: Catching the wave." *Harvard Business Review, Jan-Feb*, 43–53. Retrieved from https://hbr.org/1995/01/disruptive-technologies-catching-the-wave. Accessed May 12, 2016.

Fawcett, and Waller, M. 2012. "The Implications of Supply Chain Management Research: You Cannot Unring a Bell." *Journal of Business Logistics*. 33: 259–261.

Freeman, R. E. 1984; 2010. *Strategic Management: A Stakeholder Approach*. Cambridge: Cambridge University Press.

Gentner, D. and Whitley, E. W., 1997. "Mental Models of Population Growth." In *Environment, Ethics, and Behavior*.ed.. M Bazerman, D. Messick, A. Tenbrunsel, and K. Wade-Benzoni. San Francisco: New Lexington Press. 209–233.

Goldman, A. and Blanchard, T. 2015. "Social Epistemology." *Stanford Encyclopedia of Philosophy*. Ed. E. N. Zalta. http://plato.stanford.edu/entries/epistemology-social/ Accessed May 14, 2016.

Goodman, Leah M. 2015. "Why Volkswagon Cheated." *Newsweek* December 15. www.newsweek.com/2015/12/15/why-volkswagen-cheated-404891.html Accessed May 13, 2016.

Gorman, Michael. 1992. *Simulating Science*. Bloomington IN: Indiana University Press.

Granovetter, Mark. 1992. "Economic Institutions as Social Constructions: A Framework for Analysis." *Acta Sociologica*. 35. 3–11.

Hacking, Ian. 1999. *The Social Consruction of What?* Cambridge, MA: Harvard University Press.

Hargrave, Timothy. 2016. "Building on Werhane's foundation: Toward a Theory of the Morally Imaginative Organization. "Forthcoming in *Essays in Honor of Patricia H. Werhane*.

Isabella, L. A. 1992. Managing the Challenge of Trigger Events: The Mindsets Governing Adaptation to Change. *Business Horizons*. September–October: 59–66.

Johnson, M. (1993). *Moral Imagination: Implications of Cognitive Science for Ethics*. Chicago, IL: The University of Chicago Press.

Kant, Immanuel. 1787; 1965. *Critique of Pure Reason*. Trans. Norman Kemp Smith. New York: St. Martins Press.

Maitland, Ian. 1997. "The Great Non-Debate Over International Sweatshops," *British Academy of Management Annual Conference Proceedings*, September, pp. 240–265.

McVea, John, and Freeman, R. E. 2005. "A Names-and-Faces Approach to Stakeholder Management." *Journal of Management Inquiry*. 14: 57–69.

Moberg, Dennis. 2006. "Ethical Blind Spots in Organizations." *Organizational Studies*. 27: 413–428.

Prahalad, C. K., & Bettis, R. A. (1986). The dominant logic: A new linkage between diversity and performance. *Strategic Management Journal*, *7*(6), 485–501.

Putnam, Hilary. 1990. *Realism with a Human Face*. Cambridge, MA: Harvard University Press.

Rorty, Richard. 1993. "Putnam and the Realist Menace." *Journal of Philosophy*. 90: 443–461.

Sartre, Jean-Paul. 1956. *Being and Nothingness*. trans. Hazel Barnes. New York: Philosophical Library.

Sen, Amartya. 1993. "Positional Objectivity." *Philosophy and Public Affairs*. 22: 119–131.

Senge P. M. 2006. *The Fifth Discipline: The Art & Practice of the Learning Organization*. Doubleday: New York.

Shadnam, M., Crane, A. and Lawrence, T., forthcoming. "Who Calls It? Agents of the Social

Construction of Organizational Moral Failure." Presented at the biannual meeting of the Transatlantic Business Ethics Conference (TABEC), St. Galen Switzerland, September 30, 2016.

Van de Ven, Andrew and Hargrave, Timothy. 2004. "Social, Technical and Institutional Change." *in Handbook of Organizational Change and Innovation*. ed. Marshall Scortt Poole and Andrew Van de Ven. New York: Oxford University Press. 2590–2303.

Weick, KE. 1993. "The Collapse of Sensemaking in Organizations: The Mann Gulch Disaster." *Administrative Science Quarterly* 38(4), 628–652.

1995. *Sensemaking in Organizations*. Sage: Thousand Oaks, CA.

Weick K. E., Sutcliffe K. M., Obstfield D. 2005. "Organizing and the Process of Sensemaking." *Organization Science* 16(4), 409–421.

Werhane, P. H. 1994. "The Normative/Descriptive Distinction in Methodologies of Business Ethics." *Business Ethics Quarterly*, 4: pp. 175–180.

(1999). *Moral Imagination and Management Decision Making*. Oxford, UK: Oxford University Press.

(2002). "Moral Imagination and Systems Thinking." *Journal of Business Ethics*, *38*, 33–42.

(2008). "Mental models, moral imagination and system thinking in the age of globalization." *Journal of Business Ethics*, *78*(3), 463–474.

Werhane, P. H., Hartman, L. P., Archer, C., Englehardt, E. and Pritchard, M. 2013. *Obstacles to Decision-Making*. Cambridge: Cambridge University Press.

Whitley, R. D. 1991. "The Social Construction of Business Systems in East Asia." *Organizational Studies*. 12: 1–28.

CHAPTER 18

# A Pragmatist Approach to Business Ethics Research

BIDHAN L. PARMAR, ROBERT PHILLIPS, and
R. EDWARD FREEMAN

## Introduction

The purpose of this chapter is to give an introductory account of the main tenets of a philosophical approach called "pragmatism." Pragmatism has its origins in the late nineteenth and early twentieth century in the work of the American philosophers Charles S. Pierce, William James, John Dewey, and others. It has experienced a renaissance in recent years under the auspices of modern philosophers such as Richard Rorty, Richard Bernstein, Hilary Putnam, and increasingly, many others. These more recent philosophers have established a myriad of connections to other intellectual movements and to other philosophers. For instance, Rorty writes a great deal about the connections between Dewey and so-called Continental philosophers such as Nietzsche, Heidegger, Derrida, and others.

There is a stream of pragmatist work in business ethics especially in what has come to be called "stakeholder theory" (Freeman, et al., 2010), and the beginnings of a stream of work in organization theory (Kelemen & Rumens, 2013; Wicks and Freeman, 1998). In section II we give a brief historical view of the development of pragmatism. In section III we explain some central pragmatist ideas, even though not all pragmatists will agree. In section IV we argue why these ideas are important for business ethicists.

This chapter draws significantly from our chapter, "Pragmatism and Organization Studies" published in Mir, R., Willmott, H., & Greenwood, M. (Eds.). (2015). *The Routledge companion to philosophy in organization studies*. Routledge.

## A Brief History and Key References

It is important to note that pragmatism has been developed as a way to understand a set of traditional philosophical problems, rather than as a way to understand how human beings create value and trade with each other (business and management). However, we believe that a pragmatist approach to business and management offers great potential in practice and in theory.

Pragmatism developed in opposition to some traditional philosophical claims. The first kind of claim – typical of Cartesian and Kantian philosophy – is that thinking must be somehow founded on *a priori* first principles. So, when James defends his "radical empiricism," he is pitting it against the sort of theorizing that assumes thought to be prior to any empirical observation. For example, while science and the scientific method play vital roles, the authority of science can be overstated (e.g., positivism). Pragmatists are (generally) at great pain to demonstrate the relevance of moral thinking alongside scientific thinking. As we read the sample passages below, we may have cause to recognize this reductionist vice that pragmatist authors seek to pry open.

Pragmatism shares, broadly, the features described below in III. At the margins, however, pragmatism comes in as many flavors as there are scholars writing about it. In 1908, Arthur O. Lovejoy isolated thirteen different variations of pragmatism – a number Richard Bernstein called "far too conservative" (2010: 5). At the periphery there are arguments about who should be included in the Pantheon and who was (or is), a closet pragmatist whether they claimed the mantle or not. We will not attempt to summarize or adjudicate these questions here. The authors we summarize here were all quite wide-ranging in their interests and writings. We have isolated representative passages from each writer to give the reader a sense of each author's style.

While Charles Sanders Peirce[1] is typically regarded as the first pragmatist, later in life, Peirce began describing his own work as "pragmaticism" ("a word ugly enough to be safe from kidnappers") in order to distinguish it from what pragmatism had grown into. This quasi-apostasy notwithstanding, Peirce is credited by the other early pragmatists as the originator. Durand and Vaara (2009) adapt some of Peirce's work for uses in understanding strategic management research. Here is a taste of Peirce's (1878/1965) work:

> From all these sophisms we shall be perfectly safe so long as we reflect that the whole function of thought is to produce habits of action; and that whatever there is connected with a thought, but irrelevant to its purpose, is an accretion to it, but no part of it. (p. 256)
>
> To develop its meaning, we have, therefore, simply to determine what habits it produces, for what a thing means is simply what habits it involves. (p. 257)

William James, considered the father of experimental psychology, is among most accessible and reader-friendly of the early pragmatists. Combining a capacity for deep thought with remarkable writing skills and an eschewal of jargon, his work was able to speak to both scholarly and popular audiences alike. Margolis and Walsh (2008) make good use of James's work in their influential discussion of businesses' social initiatives. Here are representative passages from James (1907/2014):

> In other words, the greatest enemy of any one of our truths may be the rest of our truths. Truths have once for all this desperate instinct of self-preservation and of desire to extinguish whatever contradicts them. My belief in the Absolute, based on the good it does me, must run the gauntlet of all my other beliefs. Grant that it may be true in giving me a moral holiday. Nevertheless, as I conceive it, - and let me speak now confidentially, as it were, and merely in my own private person, - it clashes with other truths of mine whose benefits I hate to give up on its account. It happens to be associated with a kind of logic of which I am the enemy, I find that it entangles me and metaphysical paradoxes that are inacceptable, etc., etc. But as I have enough trouble in life already without adding the trouble of carrying these intellectual inconsistencies, I personally just give up the Absolute. I just *take* my moral holidays to me; or else as a professional philosopher, I try to justify them by some other principal. (p. 78)

A prominent public intellectual with a long-time interest in education, John Dewey emphasized the role that humans have in creating our world, not merely acting and reacting within it. Dewey consistently emphasized the role of art, literature, and morals – in addition to science – in co-creating our world. Dewey's work was deeply influential on the later work of Richard Rorty (see below); Mahoney (1993) relies on Dewey and others to examine the role of determinism in strategic management. The following passages (Dewey, 1908) are representative of his critique of prior philosophizing and his beliefs in the centrality of values:

> If we suppose the traditions of philosophic discussion wiped out and philosophy starting afresh from the most active tendencies of to-day, – those striving in social life, in science, in literature, and art, – one can hardly imagine any philosophic view springing up and gaining credence, which did not give large place, in its scheme of things, to the practical and personal, and to them without employing disparaging terms, such as phenomenal, merely subjective, and so on. (p. 125)
>
> To frame a theory of knowledge which makes it necessary to deny the validity of moral ideas, or else to refer them to some other and separate kind of universe from that of common sense and science, is both provincial and arbitrary. The pragmatist has at least tried to face, and not to dodge, the question of how it is that moral and scientific "knowledge" can both hold of one and the same world. And whatever the difficulties and his proffered solution, the conception the scientific judgments are to be assimilated to moral is closer to common sense than is the theory that validity is to be denied of moral

[1] Though resembling Pierce, it is homophonous with "purse."

> judgments because they do not square with a preconceived theory of the nature of the world to which scientific judgments must refer. (p. 127)

After a bit of a lull in philosophical interest in the middle part of the twentieth century, pragmatism was forcefully revived with the writings of Richard Rorty.[2] Controversial among mainstream philosophers, Rorty considered language as the medium for making sense of the world and the poet (in a broad sense) as the one who shows us new and better ways to live. As with others on our list, Rorty was an apostate in analytic philosophy. Wicks & Freeman's (1998) work bear the marks of Rorty's influence. The following passages give a sense of Rorty's (2010) distinctive writing style:

> communities are held together by agreement on what counts as coherent, but make progress only when linguistic innovators break this agreement. One of their strategies is by talking about objects that we have no agreed-upon ways of talking about . . . Without a consensus to break, innovation would be pointless. Without innovation the crust of convention would never be broken. The alternation between the two has made it possible for human beings to move from poem to poem, from language game to language game, and from poorer to richer forms of life. (p. 194)

Like Peirce, Hilary Putnam is a mathematician as well as a pragmatist philosopher. Richard Rorty (1991) calls him "the most important contemporary philosopher to call himself a pragmatist." Purnell & Freeman (2012) rely on Putnam's collapsing of the fact/value distinction in assessing the quality of ethics conversations among investment bankers. While Putnam's writing has perhaps less lyrical quality (poetry) to it than James or Rorty, it is less technical and jargon-laden than Peirce, it is clear, careful, and precise. This is evident in the passages below (Putnam, 2002):

> There are a variety of reasons why we are tempted to draw a line between "facts" and "values" – and to draw it in such a way that "values" are put outside the realm of rational argument all together. For one thing, it is much easier to say, "that's a value judgment," meaning, "that's just a matter of subjective preference," and to do what Socrates tried to teach us: to examine who we are and what our deepest convictions are and hold those convictions up to the searching test of reflective examination . . . The worst thing about the fact/value dichotomy is that in practice it functions as a discussion-stopper, and not just a discussion-stopper, but a thought-stopper. (p. 43ff)

More recently, Hilary Putnam calls Richard J. Bernstein's *The Pragmatic Turn*, "by far the best and most sophisticated account of recent and present-day pragmatist thought." With chapters centrally focused on Peirce, James, Dewey, Hegel, Putnam, and Rorty among others, this book is an excellent critical introduction to the history of pragmatism, the surface of which is barely scratched here.

Many, many others could have been on this list including, but not limited to O.W. Holmes, R.W. Emerson, C.I. Lewis, W.V.O. Quine, L. Wittgenstein, and C. West. And there are pragmatist interpretations of many others besides (e.g., Bernstein has a chapter entitled "Jürgen Habermas's Kantian Pragmatism"). But any serious investigation into pragmatism and its potential role in the study of organizations must eventually contend with the work of the authors above.

## What Do Pragmatists Believe?

While there are almost as many versions of pragmatism as there are pragmatist philosophers, there is a great deal of agreement on a few general principles, many of which are about what counts as doing work in philosophy that is useful. We isolate the following commonalities:

(1) All "theory" is based in experience and practice.
(2) Most dualisms and dichotomies are at best misleading.
(3) Framing and language use is central to understanding the world.
(4) Hope and freedom should be the goals of discourse rather than "truth."

[2] Freeman (2004) has written a book review essay entitled, "The Relevance of Richard Rorty to Management Research" in *Academy of Management Review*.

### All "Theory" Is Based in Experience and Practice

The founders of pragmatism, Pierce, James, and Dewey, all believed that good thinking was rooted in experience. They talk about the primacy of both practice and experience. And, they all had an idea of experience as a primary conceptualization of humans encountering the world. Dewey especially thought that our conceptual apparatus evolved to solve problems. We became language users somewhere in our evolutionary history as it gave us an ability to solve complex problems, and an advantage over some of our natural competitors and predators. Dewey (1998) writes:

> Mankind has hardly inquired what would happen if the possibilities of experience were seriously explored and exploited. There has been much systematic exploration in science and much frantic exploitation in politics, business, and amusement. But this attention has been, so to say, incidental and in contravention to the professedly ruling scheme of belief. It has not been the product of belief in the power of experience to furnish organizing principles and directive ends. (p. 23)

These pragmatists eschewed the idea of theorizing for the sake of theorizing that characterizes so much of contemporary philosophy, not to mention much of management theory. Pragmatists see the point of intellectual life as solving real problems that come from experience.

Gregory Pappas (2008) suggests that another related hallmark Dewey's thought is "seeing problems from the inside." What does this problem feel like if you are experiencing it yourself? It is often too easy to intellectualize a problem away, or simply use one of our favorite theories to understand the problem. Pappas suggest that this is seeing the problem as a spectator, and that doing so loses most of what we gain when we actually have an experience.

A good example is Dewey's approach to ethics where he does not begin with a theory like utilitarianism, or deontology, or virtue, but he begins by trying to understand the particular aspects of a moral problem from the inside. As we see how these aspects are related to one another, and to other problems we have had, we can draw on these more theoretical ideas to help solve the problem. But, we are not trying to prove the theories in any case. Every situation is different, but there are common aspects. The pragmatists look for the particularity as well as the generality in experiences.

### Most Dualisms and Dichotomies Are at Best Misleading

Much of modern philosophy depends on a set of dichotomies or dualisms that contrast ways of seeing the world. For instance, "mind vs. body," "external world vs. internal world," "things as they appear vs. things in themselves," "theoretical vs. empirical," "science vs. nonscience," "self interest vs. altruism," "facts vs. values," etc. The list is almost endless and it has been said that Dewey never met a dichotomy that he didn't want to collapse.

Quine (1951) identified two of these dualisms as important dogmas of empiricism that are regrettably present in current management thinking as well. The first was the theory–observation distinction, or what philosophers would call "analytic–synthetic" distinction. Analytic sentences were true by definition and synthetic sentences were true by virtue of their relationship to the world. The idea from the positivists was that certain terms were theoretical terms while other terms were observational (data), and that data stood in a relationship of confirmation or disconfirmation to the theoretical terms. Quine argued that there was no way to enforce this distinction without appealing to a set of terms that were circular in their meaning.

Dewey's version of the same argument was that the data that you look for are already at least partially contained in how you frame a hypothesis. Theory does bear a connection to the world, but only in terms of theory as a whole, not particular hypotheses. Quine's dictum is that "[O]ur statements about the external world face the tribunal of sense experience not individually but only as a corporate body." (1951: 38) People always bring their background theories, disciplines, ideas, etc. with them.

In a similar way, Hilary Putnam has argued that facts and values are entangled (see quoted passage above), much in the way that theory and data are entangled. Putnam's example is that to call someone "cruel" is to state a fact, if they are acting cruelly, and it is to make a value judgment at the same time, since calling someone cruel is to disapprove of them. Much of our language works this way. Putnam and Bernstein would argue that facts and values are interwoven with theory and practice, so that facts, values, and interpretations are always relevant to some interpretive community or other.

## *Framing and Language Use Is Central to Understanding the World*

Most pragmatists would agree with Wittgenstein when he argued that we should not look to a world of meanings of words to understand language, but we should look to how the words are used. When children learn a language they learn what the words will do, what problems they will solve, and what problems they will not solve. Meanings emerge out of these uses and problems solved, as "short hands" or "rules of thumb." They are not a representation of the relationship of language to the world. Indeed, most modern pragmatists would argue that many people (philosophers) misunderstand the nature of language.

As language using primates we managed to coordinate our behavior in powerful ways to become the dominant species on the planet. Indeed, Tomasello and his colleagues (2012) have suggested that human evolution selects for being "good collaborators." We coordinate our behavior by making marks and noises that indicate what we are doing. Of course this is now very sophisticated, yielding many vocabularies in fields as diverse as mixing concrete and quantum mechanics.

According to Donald Davidson, language is an unbroken whole. By that he means that we can't divide up language into different "mind sets" or "conceptual schemes" that are wholly different from each other. He argues that one of the main mistakes in both science and social science is the idea that such a "scheme-content distinction" is possible. He articulates the problem of conceptual relativism as follows (Davidson, 1984):

> Conceptual schemes, we are told, are ways of organizing experience; they are systems of categories that give form to the data of sensation; they are points of view from which individuals, cultures, or periods survey the passing scene. There may be no translating from one scheme to another in which case the beliefs, desires, hopes, and bits of knowledge that characterize one person have no have no true counterparts for the subscriber to another scheme. Reality itself is relative to a scheme: what counts as real in one system may not in another. (p. 183)

Davidson then argues the idea of a total failure to translate from one conceptual scheme to another makes no sense, and then shows how even a partial failure to translate doesn't imply separate conceptual schemes. Language is all we have.

Even though we may not know how to navigate from one mindset to the other, it has to be possible, even if sometimes it isn't very useful. For instance, what does the vocabulary of nineteenth century romantic poetry have to do with the vocabulary of twenty-first century business ethics? One might find that the passion present in the stanzas of nineteenth century romantic poetry is simply missing in current business ethics. Such a comparison might lead to a question about why that is the case, and a call for a renewed vocabulary for understanding our humanity in organizations. The pragmatist program of seeing what problems vocabularies solve and why some are better than others, and how some can be enriched by comparison with others, yields very different methods for studying business than are currently used in most scholarship on management and organizations.

## *Hope and Freedom Should Be the Goals of Discourse Rather Than "Truth"*

When many scholars hear the word "pragmatism" they immediately associate it with the idea that "truth is what is useful." This often cuts against the very reasons that scholars have chosen their field, i.e., to "get to the truth of the matter." In fact, many pragmatists have a far more nuanced view of "truth," and there has been substantial philosophical debate about the idea in the literature among pragmatists. For instance, Davidson believes that even if we give up the idea of an "uninterpreted reality" to be approximated by language, a view of objective truth is still possible. Davidson writes (1984):

> Of course truth of sentences remains relative to language, but that is as objective as can be. In giving up the dualism of scheme and world, we do not give up the world, but re-establish unmediated touch with the familiar objects whose antics make our sentences and opinions true or false. (p. 198)

Rorty on the other hand, thinks that the idea of truth is best understood as reminding us that any belief that we have is potentially revisable. Knowledge for Rorty is the idea of warranted assertability, and whether a claim is warranted is largely a matter of an interpretive community. The idea of an assertion being true reminds us that all the evidence for assertion may not be in. Rorty argues that vocabularies can be useful ways to solve problems or not. In that spirit, Hilary Putnam suggests that if you want to know why a square peg won't fit into a round hole, the vocabulary of molecular structure won't work very well (atoms and molecules being mostly empty space). There are lots of ways to talk about the world, and no one of them gets at the world "as it really is."

Rorty has gone further than most here by claiming that hope and freedom are more tangible goals than Truth. By this he means engaging in the search for solidarity with others, seeing "them" as "us" rather than some outside "other." He writes (Rorty, 1999):

> The trouble with aiming at truth is that you would not know when you had reached it, even if you had in fact reached it. But you can aim at ever more justification, the assuagement of ever more doubt. Analogously you cannot aim at "doing what is right," because you will never know if you have hit the mark. Long after you are dead, better informed and more sophisticated people may judge your action to have been a tragic mistake, just as they may judge your scientific beliefs as intelligible only by reference to an obsolete paradigm. But you can aim at ever more sensitivity to pain, and ever greater satisfaction of ever more various needs. Pragmatists think that the idea of something nonhuman luring us human beings on should be replaced with the idea of getting more and more human beings into our community – of taking the needs and interests and views of more and more diverse human beings into account. (p. 82)

What these ideas mean for research is that we need to engage in a conversation that at once moves across vocabularies. When researchers embrace a plurality of metaphors it can unsettle the dominant paradigm and provide a broader toolkit from which to craft a better world. In order to generate a plurality of metaphors and stories, researchers would be better served to relax assumptions about truth and focus instead on conversation. Conversation is where different perspectives encounter on another and form the basis for a constructive dialog about the cash-value of particular metaphors.

## Pragmatism, Positivism, and Business Ethics

In 1959 the Ford and Carnegie Foundations issued separate reports on the state of university-based business schools in the US. These reports were highly critical of the low standards and rigor in a majority of business schools and sought to instigate change by infusing these institutions with a dose of the newly emerging "management science" – including a methodology for managerial decision making honed during the World War II. This new decision making science included tools such as decision analysis, game theory, and insights from emerging behavioral science. The hope was that knowledge from these new disciplines would allow managers to make decisions using reason and analysis rather than intuition and judgment.

To realize the vision of a scientifically-based business school and management profession, a new kind of faculty was needed, "one focused more on fundamental research than on descriptive analysis, and deriving decision making principles more from theory than from existing practice."

(Khurana, 2007: 271). Therefore, new faculty were trained in behavioral sciences, particularly economics, and were encouraged to increase research productivity and publish in academic journals to raise the research profile of their institutions. Just five years after the publication of the Ford report, faculty at the twenty-five leading business schools in the US were significantly more research oriented and published more in academic journals.

This new emphasis on science brought with it a positivist epistemology, rather than a science based on Dewey's pragmatic experimentation. Positivism makes the assumption that the study of business and organizations can occur through a scientific approach that is value free and is superior to nonscientific methods because it corresponds to objective reality. Astley (1985:497) argues that positivism embraces a conventional model of scientific progress as cumulative discovery of objective truth, where knowledge grows linearly as new data are added to the existing stock of research findings.

Positivism, and its newer incarnations postpositivism and neopositivism, are all attempts to uncover objective Truth or True Reality. Postpositivism differs from positivism in holding that reality can be known only probabilistically, and hence verification is not possible. Neopositivism asserts that science must deal in exact descriptions and generalization, both of which require "the quantitative statement." Both post- and neopositivism share the belief that science should not – and cannot – deal with value statements.

Throughout the latter half of the twentieth century and the early twenty-first century, little changed in university-based business schools as faculty continued to publish research and focus on quantitative methods as a vehicle for discovering Truth. In the late twentieth century the introduction of programmatic rankings for graduate business schools (and similar ranking for journals) accelerated and focused these trends in ways that reduced the diversity of research published in these journals and increased the dominance of positivism. Rankings of business school programs typically include surveys of stakeholders such as students, alumni, and recruiters but also count the number of articles that faculty have in a finite number of journals deemed "A" journals. By constraining the space in which research publications "count" as good research rankings such as *BusinessWeek* and *US News & World Report* increase competition for publishing in the journals they deem worthy as more faculty aimed for these journals to get tenure and increase their own research reputation.

This increased competition in turn serves to strengthen "normal" science and reinforce the dominant theoretical and epistemological perspectives as academic reviewers fall back on their own assumptions about epistemology and truth to make judgments on papers and ideas that they think are "True" and therefore worth publishing. Constrained space for what counts as "good" research makes new ideas and different approaches more difficult to publish, because those authors have to compete with authors who publish "normal" science that fits dominant assumptions and expectations about how science should look.

Given this background on the current state of theory and scholarship, we now turn to several ways in which a pragmatist may seek to improve this situation.

## *Practice-Focused Research*

Pragmatism sees theory as a tool for doing things better in the world. For Dewey, the role of thought and knowledge is not to passively reflect a preexisting world, but to change and improve reality. The outcome of a successful inquiry is a "transformation of the situation." On Dewey's account, the most "basic conception of inquiry" is "as determination of an indeterminate situation" (Dewey, 2008) or, to use another term, sensemaking.

Pragmatism encourages scholars to show how theoretical differences make a real difference to practice. This focus on practice shifts the focus on theory building in management science away from insular conversations between academics and toward practice-relevant research. Research that is focused on theory only for the sake of theory makes the assumption that good theory is a value-neutral and objective view of the world from which many different purposes can be achieved.

Therefore academics focus on proof and evidence as mechanisms for creating Truth. This emphasis crowds out discussion of practical relevance and stacks the deck in favor of "an entrenched vocabulary which has become a nuisance" rather than "a half-formed new vocabulary which vaguely promises great things" (Rorty, 1989). Positivist assumptions direct research toward those questions that can be more easily "proved" with statistics rather than questions that impact how we should live, but may not be as easily measurable.

Organizational scholars have debated their relevance to practice in journal articles, books, and conferences: (i.e., *Administrative Science Quarterly* 1982, Vol. 27, No. 4; *Academy of Management Journal*, 2001, Vol. 44, No. 2; Lawler et al, 1985; Murphy and Saal, 1990; Larwood and Gattiker, 1999; Mowday, 1997; Hitt et al., 1998; Huff, 2000a). Some scholars argue that academics and practitioners hold irreconcilably different views about research that is relevant and of high quality (Shrivastava and Mitroff, 1984). Others have called for practically relevant research and isolated (modest) zones of agreement between practitioners and academics about what constitutes interesting research (Baldridge et al., 2004). Yet the actual practice of publishing work that has practical relevance remains difficult.

If "management science" is to become focused on practice, there are several prescriptions based on Dewey's pragmatic experimentation that can make it more relevant and useful. First, publishing null findings is a useful practice so that researchers and practitioners know what does *not* work. Publishing only positive findings that fit existing theory are not practices that foster the sensemaking necessary to create more useful explanations. Rather it is an artificial way to limit the kind of research that "counts." By not publishing null findings current research practice reinforces the ideas of Objectivity and Truth because there is less emphasis placed on the boundary conditions of a theory, and theoretical limitations are less salient when only positive findings are published with a small paragraph about hypothesized limitations.

Additionally, according to Dewey, the scientific spirit requires seeking out new problems that are not widely known or experienced. Pragmatism would encourage management science to look for novel problems and develop new and distinct processes for evaluating novel work. Treating new ideas in the same way as old established ideas is a sure way to kill innovation and experimentation.

Finally, inquiry is based in particular perspectives and theoretical lenses. These lenses were crafted for particular purposes and to address specific problems. Scholars must become clearer about the purposes for which their explanations were created, to encourage more careful use and experimentation with theory. Research is not an objective map of reality that can be used for any purpose, but itself is a purpose-driven activity, that must be clear about the uses it has been developed for so that others can pick up the right tool for the right job. For example, using economic assumptions to narrowly describe the corporate objective is to use a theory in a way that creates negative outcomes for companies and their stakeholders. Forgetting the purpose for which a particular theory is created can lead to what Daniel Dennett calls, "greedy reductionism," where, "in their eagerness for a bargain, in their zeal to explain too much too fast, scientists and philosophers … underestimate the complexities, trying to skip whole layers or levels of theory in their rush to fasten everything securely and neatly to the foundation" (Dennett, 1995: 82).

## Bringing Back Knowing-How

According to Dewey, knowing-that is a kind of knowledge that "involves reflection and conscious appreciation." It is our ability to consciously reason about things. Dewey sees knowing-that as a kind of reflective thinking which is an:

> active, persistent and careful consideration of any belief or supposed form of knowledge in light of the grounds that support it, and the further conclusions to which it tends. (Kreuger, 2009: 36)

Dewey sees most of everyday human action and interaction as involving a different sort of knowledge – knowing-how, or the

> experiential or embodied learning that is activated prior to, or without the invocation of, reflective

> thinking. This sort of knowledge is a pre reflective coping or skill-knowledge that enables us to navigate our world with a high degree of expert interaction. (Kreguer, 2009: 37)

This distinction is important for management theory and business ethics because it largely focuses on "knowing-that" and assumes that "knowing-that" is sufficient to cope with the world in better ways. This distinction is connected to the need for practice-focused research. Theories and concepts solve problems. When they no longer solve problems they are discarded in favor of other theories and concepts that do a better job. For instance, astrology once solved a problem about why certain events occurred, and what we should do in the future given these astrological predictions. Ultimately, better explanations emerged, from biology, physics and psychology, and astrology has been largely discarded. It does not help us to solve the problems of what we should do in the future nearly as well as the theories and concepts of these more modern disciplines. When children learn language, they do not learn the meanings of the words. Rather they learn what the words do, including sometimes irritating their parents. We do things with words. This distinction helps us to see that much work must be done to build "knowing-how."

Business ethicists must think differently about how they teach and research, so that their students build the capacity to know how to live better. The problem a great deal of published research seems to solve is the problem of "how do faculty get published in A journals," which has nothing to do with the kinds of problems that organizational members experience.

### Fetish Around Perfect Definitions

As research becomes more insular, there is a growing emphasis on tight definitions and constructs. Tightly defined constructs are seen as necessary for science to accurately measure phenomena and to more closely reflect reality. Suddaby argues that, "For positivists, construct clarity helps them test theory, since precisely defined constructs are easier to operationalize and test (Schwab, 1980) and it is easier for researchers to compare and contrast results (Bagozzi & Edwards, 1998) ... in some instances constructs become so clearly defined, measurable, and operationalized over time that they lose relevance with the empirical world and, ultimately, reappear under a different name." (2010: 353)

A pragmatist does not see these constructs as reflective of the world, but as shared assumptions and expectations within a community of scholars, trying to solve a set of real world problems. Increased precision in constructs can be helpful as shared meaning about a construct increases understanding and coordination between the author and her readers. Suddaby (2010: 352) agrees when he argues that, "The creation of a common vocabulary avoids the "Tower of Babel" effect, in which subcommunities of researchers have no common means of communication. In the absence of common and well-articulated constructs, the boundaries between subcommunities become more sharply defined and organizational knowledge becomes increasingly fragmented." But these expectations about construct clarity can be also be a detriment when expectations about the precision of constructs gives license to scholars to reject work that does not share their personal (sometime idiosyncratic) definitions. Suddaby continues, "finding a single exception is often fatal to a construct because it implies that any proposition associated with the construct is false. Reviewers may take this position even in cases where there is substantial positive empirical support for a construct, largely because most reviewers have been oversocialized to accept falsification as the basis of scientific truth" (Suddaby, 2010: 349). The meaning of these constructs are negotiated in conversation, but in the journal review process the burden of translating new ideas into the old vocabulary is placed on the new author not the incumbent, thereby significantly decreasing the likelihood that novel work will be published in "A" journals.

Additionally, the assumption that research is an endeavor to produce Truth can give license to reviewers to reject work that does not fit their world view instead of engaging in conversation with the authors. It also disadvantages new vocabularies from being published when they contain constructs that are defined and used in a consistent and logical way, but may fall short of empirical testing.

### *Seeing Problems from the Inside*

Another important aspect of pragmatism is the focus on lived experience and seeing problems from the inside. When theorists develop descriptions of problems, their perspective and goals are different from those of the people who experience the problem. To help those successfully address the problem, it is important to see the issues from the perspective of individuals who experience those problems. For example, in the study of ethics, John Dewey argues that traditional moral theories have abstracted out the qualitative experience of moral problems and the social context in which they occur. In his own masterwork, *The Varieties of Religious Experience*, James (1902/1985) sees matters of religion and faith in terms of common, if difficult to explain, experiences. By disregarding the lived experience of ethical issues, scholars increase the likelihood that their theories will be less useful to those individuals.

In organization studies, taking the lived experience seriously can mean several things. For example, in social psychological work on ethics we can examine not just on how context shapes behavior, but on how people experience and interpret context differently. Across disciplines, we may work to understand how people experience and apply the theories we generate, rather than assume that their application is straightforward or obvious. Attending to how people experience and apply theories can shed light on how to make them more useful and applicable.

One way to take experience seriously is highlight that organizational phenomena are socially constructed. In addition to redescribing phenomena as contingent and created, pragmatism encourages organizational scholars to pay attention to the effects of different social constructions. Each way of construing a situation or problem has benefits and costs that are differentially distributed across stakeholder groups. Therefore we must not stop at describing a process of social construction or at claiming that something is socially constructed, but also examine the effects of those constructions, how those effects themselves are created and maintained, and how they shape the ability of others to live better. These questions are inseparable from ethics and morality and therefore hold promise for business ethicists.

## Conclusion

We believe that pragmatism holds great promise in shaping business ethics and organizational studies in ways that can help organizational actors live better lives. In this paper we have provided a brief history of pragmatist thought, outlined several of its central tenets, and provided a few directions which the studies of organizations and management can take if scholars want to take pragmatist ideas seriously. It is important to note that ideas are only the beginning, and while a growing number of academics now sympathize with pragmatist thought and decry the narrow view of science that pervades our journals, action is important. To change existing practice is difficult, but necessary if we are serious about living and helpings others to live better lives through our scholarship.

### References


Astley, W. G. (1985) "Administrative Science as Socially Constructed Truth," *Administrative Science Quarterly*, 30: 497–513.

Bagozzi, Richard P., and Jeffrey R. Edwards. "A General Approach for Representing Constructs in Organizational Research." *Organizational Research Methods* 1.1 (1998): 45–87.

Baldridge, David C., Steven W. Floyd, and Lívia Markóczy. "Are Managers from Mars and Academicians from Venus? Toward an Understanding of the Relationship between Academic Quality and Practical Relevance." *Strategic Management Journal* 25.11 (2004): 1063–1074.

Bernstein, R. J. (2010). *The Pragmatic Turn*, (Cambridge: Polity).

Davidson, D. (1984) *Inquiries into Truth and Interpretation*, (Oxford: Oxford University Press).

Dennett, Daniel C. (1995) "Darwin's Dangerous Idea." *The Sciences* 35.3: 34–40.

Dewey, J. (1908/1998) "Does Reality Possess Practical Character?" *The Essential John Dewey Volume 1*, L. Hickman and T. Alexander (eds.), (Bloomington: Indiana University Press).

(1930/1998) "What I Believe" *The Essential John Dewey Volume 1*, L. Hickman and T. Alexander (eds.), (Bloomington: Indiana University Press).

Dewey, John. *Experience and Education*. Kappa Delta Pi, 1998.

*The Later Works of John Dewey*, Volume 7, (2008) 1925–1953: 1932, *Ethics*. Vol. 7. SIU Press.

Durand, R., and Vaara, E. (2009) "Causation, Counterfactuals, and Competitive Advantage," *Strategic Management Journal*, 30(12), 1245–1264.

Freeman, R. E., Harrison, J. S., Wicks, A. C., Parmar, B. L., and De Colle, S. (2010). *Stakeholder Theory: The State of the Art*. Cambridge University Press.

Freeman, R. E. (2004) "Book Review Essay: The Relevance of Richard Rorty to Management Research," *Academy of Management Review*, 29(1): 127–144.

Hitt, Michael A., Javier Gimeno, and Robert E. Hoskisson. (1998)."Current and Future Research Methods in Strategic Management." *Organizational Research Methods* 1.1: 6–44.

Huff, Anne Sigismund. (2000) "1999 Presidential Address: Changes in Organizational Knowledge Production." *Academy of Management Review* 25.2: 288–293.

James, W. (1902/1985) *The Varieties of Religious Experience*, Cambridge, MA: Harvard University Press.

(1907/2014), *Pragmatism*, (New York: Cambridge University Press).

Khurana, Rakesh. (2007). "From Higher Aims to Hired Hands: The Social Transformation of American Business Schools and the Unfulfilled Promise of Management as a Profession." (Princeton, NJ: Princeton University Press).

Krueger, J. W. (2009). "Knowing Through the Body: the Daodejing and Dewey." *Journal of Chinese Philosophy*, 36:1. 31–52.

Larwood, Laurie, Urs E. Gattiker, (1999) eds. *Impact Analysis: How Research Can Enter Application and Make a Difference*. Psychology Press.

Lawler, Edward E., ed. *Doing Research that is Useful for Theory and Practice*. Lexington Books, 1999.

M. Kelemen and N. Rumens, (2013) (eds.) *American Pragmatism and Organization*. (Surrey, England: Gower)

M. Tomasello, Melis, A.P., Tennie, C., Wyman, E. and Herrman, E. (2012) "Two Key Steps in the Evolution of Human Cooperation: The Interdependence Hypothesis," *Current Anthropology*, 53(6): 673–692.

Mahoney, J. T. (1993) "Strategic Management and Determinism: Sustaining the Conversation," *Journal of Management Studies* 30(1): 173–191.

Margolis, J. D., and Walsh, J.P. (2003) "Misery Loves Companies: Rethinking Social Initiatives by Business," *Administrative Science Quarterly*, 48: 268–305.

Mowday, Richard T. (1997). "Celebrating 40 Years of the *Academy of Management Journal*." *Academy of Management Journal* 40.6: 1400–1414.

Murphy, Kevin R., and Frank E. Saal, eds. (2013) *Psychology in Organizations: Integrating Science and Practice*. Psychology Press, 2013.

Pappas, G. F. (Ed.). (2008). *John Dewey's Ethics: Democracy as Experience*. (Bloomington: Indiana University Press.

Peirce, C. S. (1878/1965) "How to Make Our Ideas Clear," *Collected Papers of Charles Sanders Peirce* (Vol. 5) (Cambridge, MA: Harvard University Press).

Purnell, L. S. and Freeman R. E. (2012) "Stakeholder Theory, Fact/Value Dichotomy, and the Normative Core: How Wall Street Stops the Ethics Conversation, *Journal of Business Ethics*, 109(1): 109–116.

Putnam, H. (2002). *The Collapse of the Fact/Value Dichotomy and Other Essays*. (Cambridge, MA: Harvard University Press).

Quine, W.V. (1951) "Main Trends in Recent Philosophy: Two Dogmas of Empiricism," *The Philosophical Review*, 60(1): 20–43.

Rorty, R. (1991) "Feminism and Pragmatism: The Tanner Lectures on Human Values," (Ann Arbor: University of Michigan).

(1999) *Philosophy and Social Hope*, (New York: Penguin Books).

(2010) "Reply to Aldo Giorgio Gargani," *The Philosophy of Richard Rorty*, R.E. Auxier and L. E. Hahn, (eds.) (Chicago: Open Court), pp. 193–195.

Rorty, Richard. (1989) *Contingency, Irony, and Solidarity*. Cambridge University Press.

Schwab, D. P. (1980). "Construct Validity in Organizational Behavior." In B. M. Staw & L. L. Cummings (Eds.), *Research in Organizational Behavior* (Vol. 2). Greenwich, Conn.: JAI Press, 3–43.

Shrivastava, Paul, and Ian I. Mitroff. (1984) "Enhancing Organizational Research Utilization: The Role of Decision Makers' Assumptions." *Academy of Management Review* 9.1: 18–26.

Suddaby, Roy. (2010)."Editor's Comments: Construct Clarity in Theories of Management and Organization." *The Academy of Management Review*, 346–357.

Wicks, A. C., and Freeman, R. E. (1998). "Organization Studies and the New Pragmatism: Positivism, Anti-Positivism, and the Search for Ethics." *Organization Science*, 9(2), 123–140.

CHAPTER 19

# Rethinking Right

## *Moral Epistemology in Management Research*

TAE WAN KIM and THOMAS DONALDSON

### Introduction

Over fifty years ago, Herbert Simon (1957) remarked,

> an administrative science, like any science, is concerned purely with factual statements. There is no place for ethical assertions in the body of a science. (p. 253)

More recently in a 2015 interview with the *Financial Times*, Jeffrey Pfeffer remarked:

> I'm not a moral philosopher, I'm a social scientist . . . So I'm going to teach you the social science, and hopefully somewhere along the line, in religion or [from] your parents or your peers or something you've read, you've learned how to use the power that you're going to get for good rather than evil. (Hill 2015)

Most modern management researchers, at least those who publish primarily in American mainstream management journals, would agree with these statements. The reasons for pausing at the threshold of right and wrong are obvious. Values imply a "subjective" and personal dimension. Empirical research is capable of discovering that people and organizations in fact have certain values, and it can correlate those values with other variables. But, presumably, a scientist should not assume that one value can be objectively better than another, or that any values are objectively "right" or objectively "wrong." Beware the unsupported premise! Value propositions lie beyond the realm of empirical research and, worse, invite moral and religious interference in empirical work. One must not forget the lessons of the European Renaissance, the trials of moral heretics such as Galileo, and the final intellectual triumph of the scientific method. Science must fight to stay free from moral and religious hegemony.

And yet, is there nothing at all "objective" about moral[1] notions? Most of us, whether academics or not, behave in our daily lives as if they possess some form of objectivity. We defend democracy over tyranny, compassion over insensitivity, and the protection of life over murder. Most of us believe that even though the terrorists who ruthlessly killed 118 people in the Bataclan concert hall in Paris in November of 2015 may have believed that their massacre was justified, there was objective reason not to commit the act. Social scientists sometimes acknowledge objective moral failure, as for example, when psychologists critiqued – too late – the post-9/11 psychological research on torture. On August 7, 2015, the American Psychological Association moved belatedly to ban any ties by psychologists to US National Security Interrogations (Risen 2015). If there was nothing objectively wrong or at least objectively problematic about torture, then the Association's ban seems misguided.

So *are* values objective? Are there sometimes objectively good reasons for moral actions? And if so, what are the implications for research? Perhaps it is time to rethink the widespread hesitation about accepting moral objectivity in management research. This article argues that there are at least three distinct ways in which assuming an epistemic orientation that warrants objective reasons,

Originally appeared in *Journal of Business Ethics* DOI 10.1007/s10551-015-3009-2, reprinted with kind permission of Springer.

[1] In this paper, we follow standard practice in moral philosophy and use the terms "ethics" and "morality" as synonyms. We acknowledge that, however, Aristotelians sometimes use the two terms often differently, where "ethics" primarily concerns the issue of "What is it for a life to go well?" and "morality," in contrast, concerns issues such as "What do we owe to each other?"

i.e., moral objectivity, can benefit management research. These are 1. by guiding the practice of management research; 2. by using patterns of moral objectivity as clues for formulating empirical hypotheses and explanations; and 3. by adding prescriptive power to empirical theories. Our aim in this paper is not to engage professional philosophers but to engage colleagues in management for whom empirical research is the dominant approach. For this reason, we give special emphasis to management examples and management literature.

## The Values Quandary

No one can accuse management researchers of fully neglecting values issues. Quite the contrary. Researchers have invoked values frequently in explanations of organizational behavior. In the 1990s and early 2000s, many business academics referenced values both when analyzing management behaviors and when critiquing dominant economic models of corporate governance, e.g., Transaction cost economics (TCE) and agency theory. They argued that limits exist for the purely "selfish" interpretations of human behavior that economic models assumed. They stopped short, however, of taking a last, bold step – namely, of legitimating objective accounts of "right" and "wrong," or "good" and "bad."

In other words, such criticisms targeted prior theories' positive or empirical failings but not their failure to incorporate objective accounts of intrinsic moral value. For example, it was alleged that TCE discourages alternative social controls in favor of "rational" controls that are "bad for practice" (Ghoshal and Moran 1996, p. 24); that TCE oversimplifies complex phenomena (Perrow 1986, p. 236); that agency theory often fails to predict corporate performance because of its excessive emphasis on self-interested mechanisms of monitoring, independence, and incentives (Dalton et al. 2003, 1999; Westphal 1999; Zajac and Westphal 1994); that theories of organizational economics neglect historical realities of culture and local morality (Guillen 2001); and that adopting a traditional view of the corporation in which shareholders are the sole residual claimants misses the underlying reality of economic value creation and the distribution of value to stakeholders (Asher et al. 2005; Coff 1999; Zingales 2000).

While such criticisms may expose failings in economic theories of governance, and have implications for the relevance of values in explaining corporate behavior, they accept the theories' empirical epistemological assumptions. That is to say, they target empirical failings such as factual accuracy, psychological assessment, and problems of achieving preestablished objectives, such as curbing opportunism and shirking. They stop short, however, of assigning independent or epistemic[2] "rightness" or "goodness" to the values in question. Thomas Jones's well-known article, "Instrumental Stakeholder Theory: A Synthesis of Ethics and Economics" (1995) is a case in point. Jones argues that if managers subscribe to a subset of ethical intrinsic values (trust, trustworthiness, and cooperativeness), they may well create competitive advantage for their firms. Here the issue of whether those values are objectively "good" does not arise. At issue, rather, is the empirical correlation between certain kinds of management behavior and a firm's competitive advantage. At issue, in other words, is whether certain corporate outcomes flow from behaving in certain ways.

One might well ask what an objective "morally normative claim" amounts to, and who, if anyone, endorses such a claim? In this article, we use the word "normative" in the strong sense used by most moral philosophers, although we grant that other uses of the term are possible. We use "normative" as a synonym for the expression, "morally normative," and not in the weaker sense adopted by many social scientists, i.e., meaning merely practical guidance. "Normative" in the strong sense refers to concepts that are prescriptive or action-guiding in a categorical

[2] By "epistemic" we refer to the structure of knowledge or its justification.

rather than hypothetical way. The proposition, "If you want good barbecue, then eat at Tuco's," is action-guiding but only in a hypothetical sense. It is meant in a hypothetical way because its guidance is conditioned by the hypothetical, "If you want good barbecue." In contrast, most morally normative propositions are categorically action-guiding. The proposition, "You ought to do the right thing" and its twin imperative, "Do the right thing," are intended as all-things-considered, nonhypothetical guides to action. For this reason, such imperatives qualify as "normative" in the strong sense.

In this article, we use the word "objective" to characterize a moral claim or reason that is justifiable by moral reasoning rather than by empirical etiology.[3] Forms of moral reasoning vary, and different schools of philosophy endorse different accounts. Consequentialist (e.g., utilitarian) reasoning differs from nonconsequentialist or principled (e.g., Kantian or deontological) moral reasoning, and both from Aristotelian virtue ethics, which identifies concepts of virtue and happiness (Sison 2014). But all forms of moral reasoning share one important feature: Their own objectivity, as well as the objectivity of the moral propositions they aim to justify, is not a function of empirical correlation or causation, nor is such objectivity reducible without remainder to empirical states of affairs. The distinction between reasons and causes, of something being an objective, justifying reason for something in contrast to its being the cause of something, is sharply drawn in moral philosophy. This is despite the fact, as we shall see later, that some philosophers argue that reasons can themselves function as causes.[4] Moral reasoning identifies acts, character, and states of affairs as good or right in themselves, not good or right in virtue of some empirical fact, such as the fact that they happen to be endorsed by Person A.[5]

Although social scientists seldom speak of objective, morally normative reasons, moral philosophers often do. The alternative view, that ethics is *not* objective, is labeled "normative ethical relativism," and has never fared well among professional philosophers (Brandt 1967; Wellman 1963).[6] Normative ethical relativism holds that "If someone thinks it is right (or wrong) to do A, then it is right (or wrong) for him to do A." As Richard

[3] The moral reasoning, however, may make reference to empirical or "natural" states of affairs, as with Aristotle (1962).

[4] According to some theorists, subjective reasons can be "causes" of intentional action (Davidson 1963). For more philosophical discussions about the distinction between objective and subjective reasons, see Harman (2015) and Sepielli (Forthcoming).

[5] In this article, we do not defend a particular view of moral objectivity, an activity already undertaken by several moral philosophers (e.g., Enoch 2011; Scanlon 2014; Setiya 2015; Skorupski 2010). One widely accepted account of moral objectivity is "reflective equilibrium" (Goodman 1955; Rawls 1971). Reflective equilibrium represents an *attempt* to justify moral values by achieving a state of coherence in a dynamic process of reasoning, which involves moving back and forth between, on the one hand, (a) considered moral judgments and (b) relevant background theories (Daniels 1996; Bambrough 1979; DePaul 1993; McMahan 2004). It works back and forth between (a) and (b), making incremental adjustments to existing beliefs about cases and particular principles in the light of background theories, and then moves to the other side, making incremental adjustments to theories in light of moral intuitions. The culmination of the reasoning process is an equilibrium point where incremental change is no longer necessary. The underlying idea behind reflective equilibrium is that rational and informed people's substantive convergence can be an important *proxy* for moral objectivity. But as Rawls himself points out, convergence is not itself moral objectivity. Note that divergence of normative views by itself does not refute moral objectivity. First, rational disagreement can exist even when discussing empirical fact (McMahon 2009). Second, the fact that reflective equilibrium cannot explain how to fundamentally resolve a genuine moral conflict should not be considered a defect. Any adequate theory must reflect rather than dissolve conflicts if intrinsically difficult. Third, the moral skepticism based on divergence itself assumes a certain moral objectivity because the critic purports the criticism to be objectively true. For more comprehensive discussions about this matter, see McGrath (2010).

[6] Normative ethical relativism is typically distinguished from metaethical relativism. The latter deals primarily with the epistemic basis for moral judgments rather than the objective status of the judgments themselves. Metaethical relativism, in contrast to normative ethical relativism, is frequently defended by moral philosophers.

Brandt (1967) notes, despite its rather wide popular acceptance, moral relativism is thought to be absurd and self-defeating by philosophers because it implies "that there is no point in debating with a person [about] what is right for him to do unless he is in doubt himself" (p. 76).

Notably many empirical researchers flirt with moral objectivity even as they resist outright endorsement. Work by the behavioral economist Dan Ariely (Gino and Ariely 2012; Gino et al. 2013) is a case in point. Ariely's hypotheses are often cast in a manner that suggests moral objectivity. He implies, for example, that a particular kind of action is straightforwardly immoral (such as intentionally miscounting dots in an experiment) insofar as he labels the behavior "cheating" or "unethical." He then proceeds to identify empirical factors that correlate with such "cheating" behavior. For example, in recent research, he and other colleagues show that people "cheat" more when others can benefit from their cheating and when the number of beneficiaries of wrongdoing increases (Gino et al. 2013). Yet at no point does Ariely describe "cheating" as objectively wrong. At no point does he offer moral reasons for specifying how miscounting dots in an experiment qualifies as "unethical."[7] This omission, as we shall see later, can expose an experiment's operational constructs as well as their prescriptive power, to challenges of accuracy and relevance.

Another study by Edwards and Rothbard (1999) fits the same mold. The target of Edwards and Rothbard's theoretical construct is "well-being." The operational measures for "well-being" are ratings about affective responses to work and family (e.g., "In general, I am satisfied with my job") and ratings of symptom frequency about anxiety, depression, irritation, and somatic symptoms. It is noteworthy that the construct and the measures suggest an implied morally normative claim about "well-being." The authors do not develop their definition of well-being from a survey of what people think is well-being. Rather, they propose it. Well-being, most of us assume, is objectively good and its absence objectively bad. But the authors are careful to stop short of ascribing moral objectivity to their conclusions, and no moral justification for the "well-being" construct is offered.

Interestingly, Richard Ryan, one of the authors of self-determination theory, along with his colleagues (DeHaan, Hirai and Ryan 2015) recently proposed an account of "human wellness" drawing upon the philosopher Martha Nussbaum's well-known normative account of capabilities. Ryan, thus, seems to recognize the inescapably normative nature of well-being, and also problems of purely subjective accounts of it (Parfit 1984; Sison 2014).

## Empirical Methodologies Stumble over Objective Values

Research methodologies differ in their treatment of values, but the dominant views converge in their skepticism of what we have called "objective values." Central to the debate is the issue of the relative superiority of different research methods, an issue lying at the center of what management scholars call the "paradigm wars" (Burrell 1997; Deetz 2009; Fabian 2000; Hassard and Kelemen 2002; Moldoveanu and Baum 2005; Shepherd and Challenger 2013). Which of many competing research methods is the most powerful? Which is the best fit? Management scholars already acknowledge that questions about methods can entail ones about epistemology, i.e., about the nature of knowledge and justified or warranted belief (Alvesson and Willmott 2012; Bechara and Van de Ven 2007; Easterby-Smith et al. 2012; John and Duberley 2000; Westwood and Clegg 2002). This acknowledgment is not surprising, because appropriate methodologies in organizational research must build upon an accurate understanding of the nature of the knowledge sought.

Management scholars often characterize the two dominant contemporary camps interpreting the epistemology of management research as "positivist" and "subjectivist" (see Baum 2014

[7] Deception is not always unethical. For circumstances under which deception can be unethical, see, for example, Strudler (2005).

for reviews).[8] The positivist camp is also sometimes given the label, "scientific" or "realist," and the subjectivist sometimes "constructive" or "interpretive." As we shall see, however, both camps stumble over objective values. The positivist believes that researchers can objectively observe, validate, and transfer knowledge (Baillie and Meckler 2012; Hunt 2004; Donaldson 1985, 2003, 2005; Simon 1977). The subjectivist believes that researchers cannot objectively codify knowledge using the positivist's scientific method, because researchers subjectively perceive organizational reality and pluralistically construe it (Astley 1985; Astley and Zammuto 1992; Gioia 2003; Mitroff 1972; Van Maanen 1995a, b; Weick 1979, 1995). Arguments for both positivism and subjectivism have been coherently developed by theorists, and both are able to cite allied arguments in philosophical epistemology (Leplin 1984; Sosa 1991; Steup and Sosa 2005).[9]

Recent alternative approaches, in particular "Practice Theory," appear more open to integrating objective notions of moral value with research objectives (Feldman and Orlikowski 2011; Bourdieu 1977, 1990; Giddens 1986; Schatzki 2002). Let us briefly analyze the challenges posed by positivism, subjectivism, and practice theory.

### Positivist Management Research

From the standpoint of moral values, taking the "positivism" side is tantamount to banishing value judgments from research except when they are treated as measurable data. All objectivity for the positivist is empirical objectivity. Certain data, however, can reflect moral attributes and can constitute proper objects of knowledge. These are the moral opinions, behaviors, and attitudes that can be studied using empirical methods (Tenbrunsel and Smith-Crown 2008; Treviño et al. 2006; Weaver et al. 2014). A management researcher who identifies herself as a positivist in the paradigm wars can use survey data, for example, to test the hypothesis that "Fewer than fifty percent of young Germans believe that what Hitler did was morally acceptable." But observation and experiment alone are impotent to confirm the objectivity of the moral proposition itself, i.e., "What Hitler did was morally wrong." Of course, organizational theorists defending positivist management research also could conceivably adopt a "meta-moral" posture that equates moral objectivity with particular empirical relationships – but they almost never do. For example, a positivist management theorist in the epistemic debates could adopt the view that what is morally correct is what a majority of people believe is morally correct, and in this way allow the objectivity of moral propositions to be tested by empirical methodologies that assess the prevalence of moral belief. But, again, management researchers almost never adopt theories of moral/empirical equivalence, and for good reason. Empirical equivalence views are rejected by both common sense and moral philosophy. In the Antebellum South of the United States, where a majority of people accepted slavery, that majoritarian view hardly confirmed the moral proposition "Slavery is morally acceptable."

Because, then, positivist management research limits itself to a conception of objectivity that relies entirely on empirical description, cause, and correlation, positivist management researchers have

8 The positivist and the subjectivist division can be articulated in much greater detail, and the division itself is open to challenge, especially by philosophers of science. For the purposes of this article, however, we accept the simple division. It is one commonly made by management scholars.

9 At this point, one might note a possible difference between management research and moral reasoning, asking whether or not, in the domain of moral propositions, there exist what David Armstrong calls "truth makers" – "something in the world which makes it the case that serves as an ontological ground, for this truth." (1997: p. 155). Social scientists, both positivists and subjectivists, assume that truth makers, such as stock values, currency changes, job stress, or motivation exist, but different camps have different views about what they can know about the facts. A certain version of moral objectivity, especially that of some correspondence theorists (e.g., Boyd 1988; Shafer-Landau 2003), is committed to the view that there must exist truth-makers for moral propositions, and they attempt to explain the existence of moral facts using metaphysics or evolutionary biology. But, more recently, important moral realists (e.g., Scanlon 2014); Setiya 2015) argue that even without truth-makers, moral propositions can be objectively true or false.

sometimes marginalized moral values in organizational research, a fact already noted by many observers (Ghoshal 2005; Keeley 1983; Wicks and Freeman 1998; Zald 1991, 1993). The marginalization of values, in part, derives from an "old sociology of morality" (Abend 2010), which assumes that only positive statements are capable of being objectively defended, and which, as Abend notes, does not properly reflect recent metaethical development on moral cognitivism (Dworkin 1996; Enoch 2011; Scanlon 2014; Setiya 2015; Skorupski 2010; Smith 1994).[10] Wicks and Freeman (1998), too, take a strong stand on this issue: "Avoiding discussion of ethics and trying to remain agnostic on the subject does not allow positivist researchers to make organization studies value-free. Such a strategy entails that they, in effect, do ethics badly" (p. 124).

## *Subjectivist Management Research*

The "subjectivism" side of the epistemological debate in business school research also has difficulty with moral objectivity. Although subjectivist management researchers have often been more aware of moral values in organizational scholarship than their positivist counterparts, they tend to relegate those values to soft epistemic relevance. Their relevance is "soft" because it stops short of affirming value objectivity. To be sure, ethnographic or narrative-oriented research designs associated with subjectivism can directly reference moral values more easily than can the positivist's narrower, largely quantitative methods of data analysis. For this reason, they are able to lift values to greater prominence. But by jettisoning true objectivity for soft objectivity, the subjectivist interprets moral values as part of a narrative, while never qualifying them as genuinely "objective."

Of course, moral values can be personally interpreted, but it does not follow that moral reasons are themselves merely subjective. This becomes more obvious when one thinks about moral issues that hold significant human consequences.[11] Consider examples of morally normative propositions whose epistemic confidence level is high and that play crucial roles in many real world institutions. The status of such propositions is more objective than that of a mere element in a subjective narrative or "story." Take, for example, the proposition, "The harm caused by corporate lawbreaking must be an important factor in determining the level of a sanction applied by a judicial authority." Courts regularly endorse this fairness-based criterion when sanctioning corporate behavior (Dworkin 1975). Now, should someone challenge this proposition, arguing instead that the harm caused by an offense is unrelated to the determination of a fine or other sanction, then the very act of arguing against it – an act meant to offer a rational justification for a contrary proposition – assumes the possibility of some moral objectivity, just as one assumes the possibility of some empirically objective truth when arguing on behalf of the proposition "the Mississippi River is the second longest river in the United States." If either the proposition about corporate sanctions or about the Mississippi's length is disputed, the disputant implies that the proposition is capable of being believed or doubted, i.e., capable of being objectively justified or not. Both propositions, moreover, are typically subject to the norms of logic, and the principle of noncontradiction, "It is not the case that S and not S," applies to both statements (Hooker 2010). In short, if there were nothing "objective" about moral values, then efforts to arrive at morally

[10] Most but not all moral philosophers accept moral objectivity. For instance, those who hold expressivism (Blackburn 1984; Gibbard 1990) hold that moral value statements are simply expressions of one's noncognitive attitudes, such as personal approval or disapproval. But the expressivist has several difficult problems to solve. One of them is the Geach-Frege problem (Geach 1960; Searle 1962), which has stubbornly resisted solution from anti-objectivist positions (Drier 1996; Sinnott-Armstrong 2000). Today, most current anti-objectivists have softened their views. (See van Roojen 2009, for reviews.) Contemporary anti-objectivists accept, at least, the epistemic features of moral objectivism (Blackburn 1984; Gibbard 1990).

[11] For more philosophical discussion about the objective status of moral knowledge, see Boyd (1988), Brink (1989), Enoch (2011), Hampton (2012), Scanlon (2014), Setiya (2015), Skorupski (2010), Smith (1994), Shafer-Landau (2003).

correct answers about courts' endorsement of such principles would amount to a charade (Dworkin 1977, 1986).[12]

This basic insight about objectivity in moral dialog, however, is difficult to explain using the existing epistemics of subjectivism. While subjectivist management research elevates the status of values in explanation, it nonetheless stops short of endorsing moral objectivity, as does its rival, positivism. The late New York University Law School professor Ronald Dworkin summarizes his advice to any who would deny moral objectivity, including both the subjectivists and objectivists: "You'd better believe it" (1996).

### *Practice Theory: A Bridge to the Subjectivism/Positivism Dichotomy?*

In management research, a recent alternative to the subjectivism/positivism dichotomy is "Practice Theory" (Feldman and Orlikowski 2011; Bourdieu 1977, 1990; Giddens 1986; Schatzki 2002). Practice theory rejects the simple dichotomy between subjective agency and objective structure, and may hold promise for capturing objective value. "Central to a practice lens," write Feldman and Orlikowski, "is the notion that social life is an ongoing production and thus emerges through people's recurrent actions" (p. 1240). Issues of knowledge (epistemology) are treated as offshoots of practice. The practice perspective rejects the dichotomy traditionally set up between knowledge that exists "out there" (encoded in external objects, routines, or systems) and knowledge that exists "in here" (embedded in thoughts, bodies, or communities). Rather, "knowing is an ongoing social accomplishment, constituted and reconstituted in everyday practice" (Feldman and Orlikowski, p. 1243). Actual practice, thus, drives knowledge. The resulting view is an interesting amalgam of a social-construction view of reality and traditional philosophical pragmatism. "[T]he tangible fact at the root of all our thought-distinctions, however subtle, is that there is no one of them so fine as to consist in anything but a possible difference of practice" (1975: 29), wrote the American Pragmatist, William James. Because practice is the common denominator for all reality, values, and states of affairs in the world alike, practice theory promises pragmatic objectivity for values. Whether it can fulfill this promise remains to be seen.

## Tipping the Hat to Objective Value

Outside the paradigm wars in business school research, some management theorists advance the need for objective moral values in business theory. Some argue that, for example, management activities must be understood as "value creation," by which they mean not only financial value, but also intrinsic values for human flourishing (Donaldson and Walsh 2015; Freeman 1984; York et al. 2013; Mahoney and Kor 2015); that management research needs to be reconceptualized as a humanistic as well as a scientific area of study because many problems in management studies are not value-free issues (Alvesson and Willmott 1992; Ezzamel and Willmott 2014; Melé 2003; Zald 1993); that because business and morality cannot be separated (Freeman 1994, 2000; Robertson 1993; Sandberg 2008; Wicks 1996), epistemology in management research that is not adequately selected for its inherent moral aspect may risk rendering the research morally illegitimate (Donaldson 2012; Wicks and Freeman 1998); and that morally illegitimate ideologies entrenched in management theories result in socially destructive impacts, with the implication that research needs to be more firmly based on an adequate understanding of moral values (Preston 1986; Swanson 1999).

Business ethicists have also debated the fact-value distinction. Thomas Donaldson (1994) supported Hume's thesis that a value proposition cannot be drawn in any simple manner from a set of purely factual propositions, i.e., that an "is" cannot be simply derived from an "ought," even as Pat Werhane (1994) and Linda Treviño and Gary Weaver (1994) claimed that there are no purely factual, i.e., value-free, statements. The positions of the two camps are not necessarily

[12] More metaphysical discussion about how moral deliberation, acceptance of moral mistake, and correction can philosophically demonstrate objectivity of moral propositions can be found in Brink (1989).

inconsistent. Werhane means that because there are no purely factual statements, most management statements must have some normative justification, a position that acknowledges Hume's "is-ought" gap. At the same time, Donaldson never denies that factual propositions can be entangled with values. His point is rather that a set of purely factual statements cannot by themselves be normative, and for this reason any management statements or concepts that are value-laden need clarification in order to exhibit their normative aspects. Both camps agree that moral values are deeply reflected in management research.

However, such endorsements of ethics in management research say little about how traditional empirical research should understand moral objectivity or use it to its *advantage*. Hence, although we admire the spirit of such attempts, we admit the need to identify and explain the specific roles that moral objectivity should play in empirical research.

## Three Roles for Moral Objectivity in Management Research

Selectively assuming moral objectivity can benefit empirical management research in three ways: 1. guiding the practice of research; 2. providing clues for empirical hypotheses; and 3. adding prescriptive power to empirical theories.

## Guiding the Practice of Management Research

Objective values can guide the practice of management research by prescribing research standards and anchoring discussions of meaningful research. Intrinsic moral values serve in particular to establish ethical limits on experimentation and data gathering, to provide ethical canons for research quality, and to help identify meaningful research projects.

### *Establishing Ethical Limits on Experimentation and Data Gathering*

This particular role for objective values is well-accepted, even if often unacknowledged. Principles and procedures that establish the parameters for ethical research and that invoke values such as dignity, bodily integrity, autonomy, and privacy, themselves reflect professional support for some nonrelative, "objective" character to morality. Earlier we referenced the decision by the American Psychological Association to ban any ties by psychologists to US National Security Interrogations (Risen 2015), which was made out of fear of professional psychologists' involvement in torture. Additionally, business school professors who conduct human experiments are already familiar with the mandated moral guidelines (e.g., informed consent) of the Institutional Review Board, which has served as the academic community's response to morally controversial experiments such as the Milgram obedience experiments (Milgram 1963) and the Zimbardo prison experiments at Stanford (Zimbardo 1971). Here, the guidance extends to the identification of organizations that qualify as off-limits for the activities of professional researchers. Notice, too, that the very use of moral values such as autonomy, privacy, and the avoidance of torture, presumes an objective moral status for such values.

### *Providing Ethical Canons for Research Quality*

Some objective values are crucial for establishing research quality. The virtues of integrity, independence, and honesty – including the proper acknowledgment of sources and the allocation of research credit – are widely recognized (National Academy of Sciences 2009). Spurious data, biased measurement, and conflicts of interest can wreck scientific discovery. Plagiarized research should not qualify as good research, a point few researchers would deny.

Both philosophers of social science (Cartwright and Hardie 2012; Root 1991; Rosenberg 2012) and management researchers (Mantere and Ketokivi 2013; Nystrom and Starbuck 1977) agree that epistemic values such as validity, accuracy, rigor, objectivity, or robustness are crucial to the formation of knowledge. Of course, there is room for constructive debates about exactly what those values mean in the context of management research, but there exists significant convergence (e.g., standard validity test in psychological experiments). Epistemic values are akin to other values in the sense that they prescribe standards whose objectivity is not subject to empirical verification. In fact, the renowned psychometrician Samuel Messick (1980, 1989, 1995) admits that validity in psychometrics is fundamentally a normative concept. No imaginable experiment could disprove the value of "accuracy" or "honesty" in measurement and hypothesis testing. Indeed, any experiment attempting to disprove such a value would need to assume such values *a priori* as essential in its own experimental process. Notably, such values are maintained even by the most extreme empiricist philosophers of science, i.e., those labeled "logical positivists" (Putnam, 2002). "Bad" research is, by definition, research that flouts precepts such as accuracy, robustness, and validity. In this sense, "scientifically valid, value-free research" is an oxymoron (Putnam).[13]

We recall Jeffrey Pfeffer's insistence that he is a social scientist and not a moral philosopher. Yet even Pfeffer emphasizes evidence-based research in ways that reflect values such as integrity and honesty. The very title of Pfeffer's (2015) book, *Leadership BS: Fixing Workplaces and Careers One Truth at a Time*, reflects his concern for speaking "truth" to business managers, in contrast to half-truths that managers may sometimes prefer to hear.

## Helping to Identify Meaningful Research Projects

Researchers often select topics with moral significance, such as gender discrimination in the workplace, or perceptions about workplace injustice, because of those topics' moral relevance. Researchers sometimes choose a topic because they believe that discoveries about their topic could both add to factual knowledge and make the world *better*. In doing so, they implicitly appeal to an objective conception of "better."

Some topics have greater moral significance than others, and the investigation of some topics carries moral risks. In 2013, Ann Tsui (2013) called on the community of management researchers to create socially responsible scholarship. Hollensbe et al. (2014) offer a passionate call for a renewed focus on corporate purpose. They encourage researchers to find "how corporate purpose and the values that drive it might best be brought together in the service of society" (p. 1228).

Professional researchers often encourage one another to explore topics with moral significance. The themes chosen for the annual Academy of Management Meetings often carry clear value import. The theme for the 2016 Meeting was "Making Organizations Meaningful." Earlier themes included "Doing Well by Doing Good" (2007); "Dare to Care" (2010); and "Green Management Matters" (2009).

Clear cases of evil are reminders that full impartiality may be impossible. The well-known sociologist, Zygmunt Bauman (1989), insightfully claims that insofar as we should not forget the Holocaust, any intellectual approach holding that no moral propositions can be objectively graded must be rejected. Bauman writes, "Were the distinction between right and wrong or good and evil fully and solely at the disposal of the social grouping able to 'principally co-ordinate' the social space under its supervision (as the dominant sociological theory avers), there would be no legitimate ground for proffering a charge of immorality against such individuals as did not breach the rules enforced by that grouping" (1989: p. 176). And as Abend (2010) explains, if a sociologist writes a book about the Holocaust assuming that the moral accusations against Hitler simply amount to a culturally determined view, something about that assumption is deeply wrong. One might reasonably respond that "it's impossible to *really* understand the Nazi worldview, ideology, or belief system – its rise, success, causes, consequences, etc. – if one

[13] One can argue that values about how research ought to be done can be reduced to usefulness. First, usefulness is itself a value, rather than an empirical fact, since what is useful is based on a more fundamental value like well-being. Second, what is true is not always equivalent to what is useful. In some contexts, a scientifically untrue theory or story may be more pragmatically useful than a true theory. Indeed, Alvin Plantinga (1993) argues that epistemic values cannot be well explained by evolutionary biology or survival alone, in part because untrue stories can sometimes benefit our survival better than true stories.

doesn't understand that it was a wicked one, perhaps the most wicked that has ever existed" (p. 574; italics added). Indeed, an attempt to describe the Nazi worldview while being indifferent to its moral vice might be construed as another value-laden view, albeit dressed in camouflage.

## Using Patterns of Moral Objectivity as Clues for Formulating Empirical Hypotheses

Good explanations of moral/immoral behavior and of how people are affected by moral principles are the ones that sometimes make use of the objective structure of moral reasoning. This is not to confuse moral structures with empirical relations or to equate what "ought" to be with what "is." Normative morality is not a positivistic domain. But it is to say that because people think in pattered ways about ethics, those patterns may be revealed in their actual behavior. Take a simple example related to the value of fairness. Countless experiments have shown that people respond to issues of "fairness" in patterned ways that reflect underlying "deontic" structures, i.e., structures whose logic is deontic and that deal with obligation and permissibility rather than more familiar "instrumental structures," i.e., the ones involving means and ends. One of the most famous is the "Ultimatum Game," in which player pairs respond in predictable ways when asked to divide a sum of money. One player announces the exact structure of the division, and the other player either accepts or rejects the division. In the event of rejection, neither receives any money. The patterns of play in the game often reflect deontological, principle-based reasoning, not instrumental reasoning. Players frequently reject offers in which they receive less than 50 percent, despite the fact that doing so means that they are foregoing money, and the dominant explanation is that the counterparty behaved "unfairly." The Ultimatum Game evokes reference to an assumed norm of "fairness," namely, to treat everyone more or less equally, something reflected in the fact that the most common division in the game is 50–50. Most players believe that it is impermissible (unfair) to move too far from this mark, although what they think constitutes "too far" varies (Cameron 1999; Kahneman et al. 1986).

An additional deontic concept is also in evidence in the game: that of the permissibility or obligation to punish unfair behavior. This is seen when players explain their rejection of an "unfair" offer as itself an act of punishment in response to an unfair act by the counterparty. The same principle of the permissibility (sometimes even obligation) to punish unjust behavior has been illustrated in many other game-theoretic experiments that involve more than two players, especially the so-called trust game. One of the first such experiments to do so (Kahneman et al. 1986) showed that game participants would pay money in order to punish an unfair allocator and to reward a fair one.

Perhaps management researchers' hesitation to refer to moral principles when explaining behavior stems from the assumption that moral reasons or principles can never serve as causal explanations of behavior. In this vein, Donald Davidson's (1963) famous defense of reasons as a form of causal explanation is relevant. As mentioned earlier, the idea of reasons serving as explanations is widely accepted in philosophy of action. But Davidson goes further; he argues that reasons can serve as "causes." Of course, not all actions should be interpreted as caused by reasons. But when someone believes, for example, that she has a reason to treat the other in a fair manner and she acts on that reason, it can be correct for Davidson to say that the moral reason "caused" her to perform the action. Davidson's complex arguments on behalf of reasons as causes lie beyond the reach of the present analysis. But they open the door to considering good reasons in general, and morally good reasons in particular, as powerful explanations – and perhaps even causes – for human behavior.

Davidson himself hints at how good reasons have a privileged place in behavioral explanation through his introduction of the principle of "rational accommodation" (sometimes also called the principle of "charity"). This principle of rational accommodation, similar to one articulated earlier by Quine, is a normative and epistemic injunction about explaining human behavior, asserting that when one is assessing the causes of a given behavior, one should presume, just as the actor herself no doubt does, that true beliefs lie behind bringing the action about, and not false ones (Davidson 1973, 1991).

Among other things, this principle of rational accommodation affirms the special status of good reasons when interpreting human behavior. It is a short step from there to affirming the special status of good *moral* reasons. Gary Weaver in a panel discussion at the Society for Business Ethics' Annual Meeting in 2014 aptly makes this point:

> scholars need to recognize that part of the reason or explanation as to why an actor acts ethically is that the actor in some way grasps the ethical quality of the action. That even a perfect correlation between, say, shoe size and ethical behavior explains nothing about the behavior *as ethical* is, I suspect, uncontroversial. But my question is whether a behavioral explanation of ethical behavior (distinct from unethical behavior) that is adequate from the standpoint of "pure" explanatory social science (i.e., no normative theory or assumption is invoked) fails in some way if the ethical propriety of the act is not in some sense part of its explanation. And if such propriety is explanatorily implicated, then scholars cannot claim to be able to ignore normative business ethics even when teaching or studying behavioral business ethics.[14]

Weaver's remarks seem persuasive. Some instances of management research already recognize the explanatory power of moral reasons, for example, the "deontic justice" perspective advanced by organizational justice scholars Cropanzano et al. (2003). "Deontic," again, is a philosophical term used to refer to categories of permission and obligation in ethics, and of necessity and possibility in logic. The older, more traditional explanatory framework for organizational justice research holds that just or unjust (fair/unfair) behaviors are caused by economic self-interest – the same explanation that many economists think is an inductively established law of human behavior. Hence, the prior organizational justice research literature has mostly explored relationships between fair or unfair behaviors on the one hand, and self-seeking motives on the other. These studies do not extend, morally speaking, beyond the identification and analysis of behavioral and psychological states in relation to self-interest, albeit to "self-interest" in an expanded sense related to group-based identity.

However, as Folger and Salvador (2008) argue, exclusively relying on the construct of self-interest may be a misleading and incomplete behavioral account that can place "theoretical blinders on us" (p. 1148). Indeed, Cropanzano et al. offer striking instances of justice behaviors that cannot be explained by self-interest. They propose instead that justice behaviors are often better explained by particular good reasons, "good" because they are presumed to be morally just, that people use when they behave. In this way, Cropanzano et al. also affirm the importance of moving beyond traditional self-seeking motives when explaining the phenomenon of organizational justice. A person's fair or just behavior or negative response to unfair or unjust behavior can be caused by "principled moral obligations" (Cropanzano et al. p. 1019), distinct from egocentric personal desires.[15] The authors appeal for more theoretical and empirical investigation of "the role of morality" (Cropanzano et al. p. 1022) in the ethical decision-making process.

Making reference to the objectivity and underlying logic of moral reasoning can be especially helpful when constructing empirical hypotheses. Without much fanfare, this approach has been often used in the construction of theories and hypotheses about topics such as "moral development" (Kohlberg 1981), "firm responsibility" (Quinn and Jones 1995), and "corporate moral maturity" (Andreas 2004). Kohlberg's well-known structure of moral development is a striking example of using objective moral notions to frame hypotheses and, in Kohlberg's instance, to justify theory. He hypothesizes, and then uses empirical evidence to confirm, the existence of progressive "stages" of moral development, beginning with

[14] This quote is from an unpublished manuscript (De los Reyes, Kim and Weaver, Unpublished).

[15] This view, interestingly enough, is similar to the one defended by the so-called school of moral realism in moral philosophy (e.g., Scanlon 2014; Setiya 2015).

"conventional" levels and moving finally to "postconventional" levels (most people never reach the highest levels). It is not accidental that the highest, postconventional levels – specifically, "social contract orientation" and "universal ethical principles" – match precisely well-recognized interpretations of moral reasoning that appear in many moral theory textbooks. The interpreted deontic structures discussed by philosophers play an important role in the construction of the empirical hypotheses utilized by Kohlberg, and Kohlberg himself often discusses the connections. He writes, for example, that notions of morality such as social contract are natural structures that emerge in ordinary people's thinking as they "reflect upon customary morality in varied cultural settings" (Kohlberg 1973, p. 634). Elsewhere, he is even more specific: "Our psychological theory as to why individuals move from one stage to the next is grounded on a moral-philosophical theory which specifies that the later stage is morally better or more adequate than the earlier stage" (p. 633). For Kohlberg, there is an "isomorphic" relation between what empirical evidence shows and what moral reasoning demonstrates.

Kohlberg's theory has been criticized for neglecting other moral approaches, including virtue ethics and Confucian ethics. Our aim in this article is not to defend Kohlberg's theory's selection of one version of moral objectivity over another, but simply to note that its potential contribution to the psychological interpretation of moral behavior relies upon its underlying assumption of moral objectivity. Indeed, the criticism that his theory would have been better were it not for its deontological moral bias implies that better normative thinking would improve the construction of his empirical hypothesis. The moral controversy surrounding Kohlberg's moral development theory, thus, is clear evidence of how moral objectivity can play an important role in empirical research. Were Kohlberg's theory merely empirical, only empirical criticisms would be relevant.

Thomas Jones (1991) offers yet another instance of drawing inspiration from moral reasoning. He hypothesizes in his well-cited "Ethical Decision Making by Individuals in Organizations," that "moral intensity" influences every component of moral decision making and behavior, and he defines "moral intensity" in terms of a well-known concept from consequentialist moral theory: "magnitude of the consequences." Here, too, the normative quality of the "magnitude of consequences" concept becomes a plus (or minus) for evaluating his empirical theory.

To put the idea of hypothesis construction in perspective, consider a partial analogy to mathematical behavior. Mathematical truth is often assumed to be the canon of "objectivity." Without attempting to equate moral objectivity with mathematical objectivity, it is noteworthy that both morality and mathematics cannot be empirically or etiologically grounded (Enoch 2011; Hampton 2012; Putnam 2002; Scanlon 2014; Setiya 2015; Shafer-Landau 2003). Neither morals nor mathematics are subject to hypothetical falsification by observation or experiment. No matter how many times our eyes witnessed two objects and two objects adding up to five objects, it would not overturn the truth that "2 + 2 = 4." We simply would not believe our eyes. Morality is similar in defying hypothetical falsification by observation or experiment. Ask yourself: What empirical experiment could possibly dissuade people of the view that torturing infants for fun is wrong, or that humans deserve to be treated with dignity?

Notice, too, that patterns of mathematical reasoning, just as patterns of moral reasoning, can serve as clues to the formulation of empirical hypotheses. Again, we are not conflating morals with math, but only drawing on a particular relevant similarity. Suppose a grade school student writes the number "4" on the whiteboard alongside the written expression, "2 + 2 = ." A good explanation of her behavior may involve reference to the structure of mathematical validity. Suppose the answer "4" had been whispered to the student by a classmate while walking up to the whiteboard. This explanation for writing the number "4" would be different from an explanation that referred to the epistemic validity of the concept of mathematics. Suppose that the student is asked later to write the answer to "6 + 6 = ." What prediction might a good psychologist make about the student's ensuing behavior? If the cause of the earlier writing of "4" was not a whisper, but an understanding of simple integer calculation in mathematics, then we can predict that the student will write the answer "12" (We might find evidence for this hypothesis by looking at previous answers the student has given to questions about other problems of simple addition). As obvious as it may seem, our behavioral explanation/prediction must refer implicitly to the objectively rational structure of mathematical calculation. That is, in order to predict that the student will write the number "12," the researcher must calculate (in addition to the student calculating) the answer to the question "6 + 6 = ."

Moral insights often arrange themselves in rational patterns that can serve as hypotheses for explaining behavior in ways that moral falsity does not. Again the partial analogy with mathematics is instructive. If someone understands mathematics, we can make predictions about their answers even to novel problems. Mathematics is rationally defensible and "objective," despite the fact that its truths are established through rational reflection and not empirical methods (Putnam 2002). But to the extent someone fails to understand mathematics and behaves irrationally, making predictions about their answers becomes more difficult. Indeed, explanations of mathematical failures, in contrast to successes, must derive from data outside the concepts of mathematics, and can be found in an almost infinite set of possible causal explanations: for example, neural failure, anxiety, strategic deception, bad teaching, etc. Hence, just as the internal objectivity of mathematics can serve as a tactic for explaining behavior, so too the structure of morality can serve as a tactic for explaining organizational and individual ethical behavior.

Explaining moral irrationality is often as important as explaining moral rationality. The need to explain irrational or failed moral behavior has launched a new, promising subfield of business ethics, whose prominent contributors include Daniel Ariely (2008), David Messick (Messick 1995), Bazerman and Watkins (2004), and Bazerman and Tenbrunsel (2011). These writers examine "blind spots" and "predictable surprises" in moral behavior, using the tools of psychology, organizational psychology, and sociology to expose and explain failures in ethical decision making. With impetus from the pioneering work of decision theorists such as Daniel Kahneman, this academic subfield has affinities with the area of behavioral economics. It successfully illuminates many of the dark spaces lurking behind more "rational" or "theoretical" approaches to ethics, with obvious significance for practitioners. Just as behavioral economics seeks to explain the failures of "rational" economic presumptions, so too does behavioral morality seek to explain the failures of ethical motivation. Hence, ironically, this new subfield also serves to underscore the primary power of rational or "good" moral reasoning, the very reasoning that serves, using Davidson's expression, as the default "rational accommodation." This coin has two sides.

## Adding Prescriptive Power to Empirical Theories

Economic theories are often used as if their embedded moral notions entailed moral objectivity, despite their authors stressing the moral neutrality of their underpinnings. Minus a concept of the right to property, economic theory is sterile except as a mode of description and prediction (Donaldson and Preston 1995). That is to say, economic theory requires some conception of "mine" vs. "yours" that extends beyond a regime of communal, mutually shared ownership, and beyond (what amounts to nearly the same thing) a regime of no ownership at all. And while it is technically possible to interpret economic theory so as not to imply that respecting another's property is a good thing to do, most economists act and talk as if they believe that improving efficiency while not violating ownership rights is a good thing. Moreover, were the moral objectivity of property rights not assumed, it would follow that any normative (in the hard sense) guidance from economic theory, such as "behave efficiently" or "optimize" would carry no authority. Such words would amount to a fully contingent, hypothetical suggestion: something like, "If you happen to want efficiency defined in a particular way and happen to accept a regime that recognizes personal property rights, then you should optimize according to the following formula."

Consider "rights," a classic moral concept. Neoclassical economic theory implies that a moral right to property exists and possesses objective relevance. Notably, the moral right remains even when the legal right is missing. States such as the former Soviet Union failed to create and enforce a legal right to property, but in doing so they opened themselves to criticism for having failed to protect the more basic moral right to property. A moral right to property exists regardless of whether or not it is recognized by a given government (Dworkin 1984; Feinberg 1992; Thomson 1990; Waldron 1984; Wenar 2005, 2008).

Defenders of empirical theories of the firm often seek prescriptive relevance for their theories, which is understandable. Yet, when giving advice about the "right thing to do," underlying moral commitments should be acknowledged. If the advice is to remove conflicts of interest in governance systems and thereby better serve the legitimate property rights of owners, then the underlying commitment to the moral rights to property (and also the moral duties of agents to principals) should be acknowledged. But they are barely acknowledged, at least in mainstream economics and much organizational theory. Agency theorists and other defenders of particular conceptions of the firm frequently move beyond claims that their conceptions are accurate descriptions of how firms do behave, to advocate governance reforms such as enhancing the power of shareholders. And they often do so with political zeal. There's nothing wrong with advocacy, at least so long as the claim about what is objectively the "right thing to do" is acknowledged to rest upon certain objective – and often well-accepted – moral values.

Some concepts combine descriptive relevance with moral objectivity. Aristotle (1962) lays out the conditions for "arête," virtue/excellence, using words with hybrid meaning, such as "phronesis," or practical wisdom. Contemporary philosophers Hilary Putnam (2002) and Bernard Williams (1985) follow Aristotle's lead and refer to "thick ethical concepts," ones that cannot be fully understood unless interpreted in both descriptive and normative ways. Consider Putnam's example, "cruelty." To call a person cruel is both to describe his moral character and to evaluate him normatively. Thick ethical concepts are pervasive in management research. Take, for example, Oliver Williamson's (2005) use of the term "workable" in TCE. Williamson's use of the term can be assigned two meanings. The first sense of "workable" evokes the ordinary meaning of the term, which is clearly normative. This sense implies that a given act or policy is "workable" in that it can achieve desirable or desired goals and is not in conflict with other firmly held objectives and values. The second sense is a descriptive and technical sense, meaning a transaction cost-economizing result that can be predicted from the interplay of market forces and market actors.

Obviously, "virtue" is another thick ethical concept. Thus, it is futile to examine virtue through a purely descriptive lens. Many management scholars who study virtue or moral character acknowledge that the object of their study is, at least in part, a normative concept. Taya Cohen, for instance, (Cohen 2014), investigates what it means to have moral character and how levels of moral character are related to unethical and ethical behaviors. In doing so, her work stands in stark relief to so-called philosophical "situationism," i.e., the view that humans are blocked from displaying moral character by situational forces (e.g., Doris 2002; Harman 2002).

If virtue is a thick ethical concept, then any adequate understanding of virtue must consist of both descriptive and normative studies. Social psychologists who study virtue might enrich their research by paying attention to moral philosophers' normative analysis of virtue. Recently, Miguel Alzola (2015) contrasted what social psychologists mean by virtue with what moral philosophers mean. Alzola points out that social psychologists' current understanding of virtue is in need of greater philosophical sophistication, and that many even recognize this fact. Social psychologists today often interact with moral philosophers in workshops and seminars, and often co-edit books on the topic of virtue. It is no surprise that the recent John Templeton Foundation's grant for moral character went to a team consisting of a philosopher and a psychologist (Nancy Snow and Darcia Narvaez). Because social psychologists use other thick concepts such as guilt, shame, blame, etc., they can similarly strengthen the normative aspect of their research by paying attention to virtue ethicists' normative analysis of specific thick concepts.

Also consider the widely used concept of "legitimacy," interpreted as "a generalized perception or assumption that the actions of an entity are desirable, proper, or appropriate within some socially constructed system of norms, values, beliefs, and definitions" (Suchman 1995, p. 574). The term "legitimacy" can describe a society's shared opinions that certain organizational actions are desirable or appropriate, and, as Suchman explains, these sorts of shared perceptions or opinions are constructed through public discussions. At the same time, however, "legitimacy" can be interpreted as what is objectively legitimate rather than what people merely happen to believe is legitimate. Here, notice the implicit moral premise that public deliberation seeks to warrant the creation of value perceptions that are objectively correct (Scherer and Palazzo 2007).

Earlier we explained how some researchers flirt with moral objectivity, and may even cross the line into objectivity, without acknowledging that they have crossed it. The notion of a "thick ethical concept" just described can be used to rescue such attempts. Consider again the work of behavioral economist Dan Ariely (Gino and Ariely 2012; Gino et al. 2013). Ariely's use of the term "cheating" or "unethical" reveals "thick" ethicality. It is at once meant as having a measurable empirical component and also as possessing objective moral content. By using such "hybrid" or "thick" concepts, researchers can acquire enhanced normative relevance. Their conclusions can carry normative authority about what, under certain circumstances, will help people to do the objectively "right thing." Thick ethical concepts, with their component of objective moral meaning, can thus enhance the reach and relevance of empirical research.[16]

One more example is Edwards and Rothbard's (1999) study discussed earlier. Again, the key construct for their study is "well-being," and in the study, ratings about affective responses to work and family serve as operational measures for well-being. Here again, by using "well-being" in a hybrid manner that includes moral objectivity, it is possible to extend the relevance of the results into the moral realm. Used in this way, the authors' findings would have relevance to attaining "well-being" – the very moral question that moral philosophers such as Aristotle, Jeremy Bentham, John Stuart Mill, and Amartya Sen have struggled to answer. Many of Edwards and Rothbard's characteristics, interestingly enough, are key concepts in the tradition of normative utilitarian moral theory (e.g., Parfit 1984).

In a similar vein, Alejo J. Sison's book, *Happiness and virtue ethics: the ultimate value proposition* (Sison 2014) covers issues closely tied to that of "well-being." "Happiness" in Sison's sense and "well-being" are almost synonyms. Sison surveys economic and neuro-scientific approaches to happiness, identifying strengths, and weaknesses. A problem of such studies, he notes, is that they frequently ignore objective morality in favor of emphasizing merely what people subjectively perceive as happiness. Drawing on Aristotelian virtue ethics, Sisson stresses the importance of genuine or what we have called "objective" happiness in contrast to the mere utilitarian satisfaction of preferences. If management scholars who study well-being or happiness would address this normative issue, their studies might well be enriched.

[16] Another example is Gino and Pierce's (2009) study about "unethical" behavior. In one experiment, when piles of cash (about $7000 in real $1 bills) were present on a table before participants, the participants were more likely to behave unethically – to cheat – on the task than when less money (only the cash necessary to pay participants) was visually available. Note that what the authors want to explain is the nature of a certain "unethical" behavior – not merely behavior that the subjects perceive as unethical. This follows from the fact that their hypothesis is that "the presence of abundant wealth increases the likelihood of individuals to behave unethically for personal gain" (p. 143). Therefore, the experiment suggests that cheating in the experiment is an "objectively unethical" behavior. Again, by treating the concept of cheating as a "thick" or hybrid concept, the experiment can be interpreted as relevant to the general question of how people ought, objectively, to behave.

## Conclusion

The fundamental claim in this article is that confused ethics, spurred by confused epistemology in management research, begets academic naiveté. Moral objectivity is denied sometimes to the detriment of research quality. True, the lessons of the European Renaissance must not be forgotten, and moral concepts must know their place in science. Yet, as we have argued, objective moral concepts can find *some* place in empirical research. Both the dominant epistemological camps of positivism and subjectivism stumble over the notion of moral objectivity, often to their detriment. Accepting at least limited moral objectivity through an objectivity-seeking research orientation, as we have shown, can benefit management research by guiding its practice by means of patterns of moral objectivity as clues for formulating empirical hypotheses, and by adding prescriptive power to empirical theories.

Clearly then, Herbert Simon's (1967) famous remark that "[t]here is no place for ethical assertions in the body of a science" shortchanges both ethics and science. However, a final irony arises for this remark. A close look at Simon's broader writings reveals surprising sympathy for at least one form of objective values. Khurana and Spender (2012) show that Simon wanted business schools to serve as the "intellectual context" in which "both methodological openness and a diversity of normative, ethical and intellectual commitments to socially meaningful and useful theory" are maintained (p. 18). We are reminded that by "theory," in fact, Simon does not mean purely scientific explanation. Instead, he means both empirical explanation and design, where the former involves pure positive explanation and the latter involves normative prescription and, hence, intrinsic moral values.[17] In this way, the "real" Simon, and not the Simon of the single quote, urges management scholars to incorporate moral values into the objective activity of management research.

[17] In fact, the GSIA (Graduate School of Industrial Administration) of Carnegie Institute of Technology – the former name of the Tepper School of Business, Carnegie Mellon University, was one of the earliest business schools that incorporated ethics into a curriculum (Modzelewski 2001). Ethics has been taught at the GSIA and the Tepper School since 1966 – one year before the publication of Simon's article (Simon 1967).

## References


Abend, G. (2010). What's new and what's old about the new sociology of morality. In S. Hitlin and S. Valsey (Eds.), *Handbook of the sociology of morality*. New York: Springer.

Alvesson, M., and Willmott, H. (1992). On the idea of emancipation in management and organization studies. *Academy of Management Review*, *17*, 432–464.

(2012). *Making sense of management*. London, UK: Sage.

Alzola, M. (2015). Virtuous persons and virtuous actions in business ethics and organizational research. *Business Ethics Quarterly*, Online First.

Andreas, W. F. (2004). When in Rome... moral maturity and ethics for international economic organizations. *Journal of Business Ethics*, *54*, 17–32.

Ariely, D. (2008). *Predictably irrational: The hidden forces that shape our decisions* (1st ed.). New York: Harper.

Aristotle. (1962). *Nicomachean ethics* (M. Ostwald, Trans.). New York: Macmillan Publishing Company.

Asher, C. C., Mahoney, J. M., and Mahoney, J. T. (2005). Towards a property rights foundation for a stakeholder theory of the firm. *Journal of Management and Governance*, *9*, 5–32.

Astley, W. (1985). Administrative science as socially constructed truth. *Administrative Science Quarterly*, *30*, 497–513.

Astley, W., and Zammuto, R. F. (1992). Organization science, managers, and language games. *Organization Science*, *3*, 443–460.

Baillie, J., and Meckler, M. R. (2012). Truth and objectivity regained. *Journal of Management Inquiry*, *21*, 248–260.

Bambrough, R. (1979). *Moral skepticism and moral knowledge*. London: Routledge.

Baum, J. C. (2014). European and North American approaches to organizations and strategy research: An Atlantic divide? Not. *Organization Science*, *22*, 1164–1679.

Bauman, Z. (1989). *Modernity and the Holocaust*. Ithaca: Cornell University Press.

Bazerman, M. H., and Tenbrunsel, A. E. (2011). *Blind spots: Why we fail to do what's right and what to do about it*. Princeton: Princeton University Press.

Bazerman, M. H., and Watkins, M. (2004). *Predictable surprises: The disasters you should have seen coming, and how to prevent them*. Boston: Harvard Business School Press.

Bechara, J. P., and Van de Ven, A. H. (2007). Philosophy of science underlying engaged scholarship. In A. H. Van de Ven (Ed.), *Engaged scholarship: A guide for organizational and social research*. New York: Oxford University Press.

Blackburn, S. (1984). *Spreading the word*. New York: Oxford University Press.

Bourdieu, P. (1977). *Outline of a theory of practice* (R. Nice, Trans.). New York: Cambridge University Press.

(1990). *The logic of practice* (R. Nice, Trans.). Stanford, CA: Stanford University Press.

Boyd, R. N. (1988). How to be a moral realist. In G. Sayre-McCord (Ed.), *Essays on moral realism*. Ithaca: Cornell University Press.

Brandt, R. (1967). Ethical relativism. In P. Edwards (Ed.), *The encyclopedia of philosophy*. London: Macmillan.

Brink, D. (1989). *Moral realism and the foundations of ethics*. Cambridge: Cambridge University Press.

Burrell, G. (1997). Organization paradigms. In A. Sorge and M. Warner (Eds.), *The handbook of organization behavior*. London: International Thompson Business Press.

Cameron, L. A. (1999). Raising the stakes in the ultimatum game: Experimental evidence from Indonesia. *Economic Inquiry*, *37*, 47–59.

Cartwright, N., and Hardie, J. (2012). *Evidence-based policy: A practical guide to do it better*. New York: Oxford University Press.

Coff, R. W. (1999). When competitive advantage doesn't lead to performance: The resource-based view and stakeholder bargaining power. *Organization Science*, *10*, 119–133.

Cohen, T. R. (2014). Moral character in the workplace. *Journal of Personality and Social Psychology*, *107*, 943–963.

Cropanzano, R., Goldman, B., and Folger, R. (2003). Deontic justice: The role of moral principles in workplace fairness. *Journal of Organizational Behavior*, *8*, 1019–1024.

Dalton, D. D., Daily, C. M., Certo, S. T., and Roengpitya, R. (2003). Meta-analysis of financial performance and quality: Fusion or confusion? *Academy of Management Journal*, *46*, 13–16.

Dalton, D. D., Daily, C. M., Johnson, J. L., and Ellstrand, A. E. (1999). Number of directions and financial performance: A meta-analysis. *Academy of Management Journal*, *42*, 674–686.

Daniels, N. (1996). *Justice and justification*. New York: Cambridge University Press.

Davidson, D. (1963). Actions, reasons, and causes. *The Journal of Philosophy*, *60*, 685–700.

(1973). Radical interpretation. *Dialectica*, *27*, 314–328.

(1991). Three varieties of knowledge'. In A. Phillips Griffiths (ed.), *A. J. Ayer memorial essays: Royal institute of philosophy supplement*, vol. 30. Cambridge: Cambridge University Press.

Deetz, S. (2009). Organizational research as alternative ways of attending to and talking about structures and activities. In D. Buchanan and A. Bryman (Eds.), *The Sage handbook of organizational research methods*. London: SAGE.

De los Reyes, G., Kim, T. W., and Weaver, G. (Unpublished). Teaching ethics in business schools: A conversation on disciplinary differences, academic provincialism, and the case for integrated pedagogy.

DeHaan, C. R., Hirai, T., and Ryan R. M. (2015). Nussbaum's capabilities and self-determination theory's basic psychological needs: Relating some fundamentals of human wellness. *Journal of Happiness Studies*, Online first.

DePaul, M. R. (1993). *Balance and refinement*. New York: Routledge.

Donaldson, L. (1985). *In defense of organization theory*. Cambridge: Cambridge University Press.

Donaldson, T. (1994). When integration fails: The logic of prescription and description in business ethics. *Business Ethics Quarterly*, *4*, 157–169.

(2003). Organization theory as a positive science. In H. Tsoukas and C. Knudsen (Eds.), *The Oxford handbook of organization theory*. New York: Oxford University Press.

(2005). For positive management theories while retaining science: Reply to Ghoshal. *Academy of Management Learning and Education*, *4*, 109–113.

Donaldson, T. (2012). The epistemic fault line in corporate governance. *Academy of Management Review*, *37*, 256–271.

Donaldson, T., and Preston, L. E. (1995). The stakeholder theory of the corporate concepts, evidence, and implications. *Academy of Management Review*, *20*, 65–91.

Donaldson, T., and Walsh, J. P. (2015). Toward a theory of business. *Research in Organizational Behavior*. doi:10.1016/j.riob.2015.10.002.

Doris, J. (2002). *Lack of character: Personality and moral behavior*. New York: Cambridge University Press.

Drier, J. (1996). Expressivist embeddings and minimalist truth. *Philosophical Studies*, *83*, 29–51.

Dworkin, R. (1975). Hard cases. *Harvard Law Review*, *88*, 1057–1109.

(1977). *Taking rights seriously*. Cambridge, MA: Harvard University Press.

(1984). Rights as trumps. In J. Waldron (Ed.), *Theories of rights*. New York: Oxford University Press.

(1986). *Law's empire*. Cambridge, MA: Harvard University Press.

(1996). Objectivity and truth: You'd better believe it. *Philosophy and Public Affairs*, *25*, 87–139.

Easterby-Smith, M., Thrope, R., and Jackson, P. (2012). *Management research*. London: Sage.

Edwards, J. R., and Rothbard, N. P. (1999). Work and family stress and well-being: An examination of person–environment fit in the work and family domains. *Organizational Behavior and Human Decision Processes*, *77*, 85–129.

Enoch, D. (2011). *Taking morality seriously: A defense of robust realism*. New York: Oxford University Press.

Ezzamel, M., and Willmott, H. (2014). Registering 'the ethical' in organization theory formation: Toward the disclosure of an 'invisible' force. *Organization Studies*, *35*, 1013–1039.

Fabian, F. H. (2000). Keeping the tension: Pressures to keep the controversy in the management discipline. *Academy of Management Review*, *25*, 350–371.

Feinberg, J. (1992). In defense of moral rights. *Oxford Journal of Legal Studies*, *12*, 149–169.

Feldman, M. S., and Orlikowski, W. J. (2011). Theorizing practice and practicing theory. *Organization Science*, *22*, 1240–1253.

Folger, R., and Salvador, R. (2008). Is management theory too "selfish"? *Journal of Management*, *34*, 1127–1151.

Freeman, R. E. (1984). *Strategic management: A stakeholder approach*. Boston: Pitman.

(1994). The politics of stakeholder theory: Some future directions. *Business Ethics Quarterly*, *4*, 409–421.

(2000). Business ethics at the millennium. *Business Ethics Quarterly*, *10*, 169–180.

Geach, P. T. (1960). Ascriptivism. *Philosophical Review*, *69*, 221–225.

Ghoshal, S. (2005). Bad management theories are destroying good management practices. *Academy of Management Learning and Education*, *4*, 75–91.

Ghoshal, S., and Moran, P. (1996). Bad for practice: A critique of the transaction cost theory. *Academy of Management Review*, *21*, 13–47.

Gibbard, A. (1990). *Wise choices, apt feelings*. New York: Oxford University Press.

Giddens, A. (1986). *The constitutions of society*. Malden: Polity Press.

Gino, F., and Ariely, D. (2012). The dark side of creativity: Original thinkers can be more dishonest. *Journal of Personality and Social Psychology*, *102*(445), 459.

Gino, F., Ayal, S., and Ariely, D. (2013). Self-serving altruism? The lure of unethical actions that benefit others. *Journal of Economic Behavior and Organization*, *93*, 285–292.

Gino, F., and Pierce, L. (2009). The abundance effect: Unethical behavior in the presence of wealth. *Organizational Behavior and Human Decision Processes*, *109*, 142–155.

Gioia, D. A. (2003). Give it up: Reflections on the interpreted world. *Journal of Management Inquiry*, *12*, 285–292.

Goodman, N. (1955). *Fact, fiction, and forecast*. Cambridge, MA: Harvard University Press.

Guillen, M. (2001). *The limits of convergence: Globalization and organizational change in Argentina, South Korea, and Spain*. Princeton: Princeton University Press.

Hampton, J. E. (2012). *The authority of reason*. New York: Cambridge University Press.

Harman, G. (2002). No character or personality. *Business Ethics Quarterly*, *13*, 87–94.

Harman, E. (2015). The irrelevance of moral ignorance. In Russ Shafer-Landau (Ed.), *Oxford studies in metaethics* (Vol. 10). New York: Oxford University Press.

Hassard, J., and Kelemen, M. (2002). Production and consumption in organization knowledge. *Organization*, *9*, 331–355.

Hill, A. (2015). Scorpions, cockroaches and the reality of unpleasant leaders, *Financial Times: September 9*. London: FT.Com.

Hollensbe, E., Wookey, C., Hickey, L., George, G., and Nichols, V. (2014). Organizations with purpose. *Academy of Management Journal, 57*, 1227–1234.

Hooker, J. (2010). *Business ethics as rational choice*. Boston: Prentice Hall.

Hunt, S. D. (2004). For truth and realism in management research. *Journal of Management Inquiry, 20*, 2004.

John, P., and Duberley, J. (2000). *Understanding management research: An introduction to epistemology*. London: Sage.

Jones, T. M. (1991). Ethical decision making by individuals in organizations: An issue-contingent model. *Academy of Management Review, 16*, 366–395.

Kahneman, D., Knetsch, J. L., and Thaler, R. (1986). Fairness as a constraint on profit seeking: Entitlements in the market. *American Economic Review, 76*, 728.

Keeley, M. (1983). Values in organizational theory and management education. *Academy of Management Review, 8*, 376–386.

Khurana, R., and Spender, J. C. (2012). Herbert A. Simon on what ails business schools: More than 'a problem in organizational design'. *Journal of Management Studies, 49*, 619–639.

Kohlberg, L. (1973). The claim to moral adequacy of highest stage of moral judgement. *Journal of Philosophy, 70*, 630–646.

(1981). *Essays on moral development* (1st ed.). San Francisco: Harper and Row.

Leplin, J. (1984). *Scientific realism*. Berkley: University of California Press.

Mahoney, J. T., and Kor, Y. (2015). Advancing the human capital perspective on value creation by joining capabilities and governance approach. *Academy of Management Perspectives*, Online First.

Mantere, S., and Ketokivi, M. (2013). Reasoning in organization science. *Academy of Management Review, 38*, 70–89.

McGrath, S. (2010). Moral realism without convergence. *Philosophical Topics, 38*, 59–90.

McMahan, J. (2004). Moral intuition. In H. LaFollette (Ed.), *The Blackwell guide to ethical theory*. Malden: Blackwell.

McMahon, C. (2009). *Reasonable disagreement: A theory of morality*. New York: Cambridge University Press.

Melé, D. (2003). The challenge of humanistic management. *Journal of Business Ethics, 44*, 77–88.

Messick, S. (1980). Test validity and the ethics of assessment. *American Psychologist, 35*, 1012–1027.

(1989). Meaning and values in test validation: The science and ethics of assessment. *Educational Researcher, 18*, 5–11.

(1995). Validity of psychological assessment. *American Psychologist, 50*, 741–749.

Milgram, S. (1963). Behavioral study of obedience. *Journal of Abnormal and Social Psychology, 67*(4), 371–378.

Mitroff, I. I. (1972). The myth of objectivity or why science needs a new psychology of science. *Management Science, 18*, 613–618.

Modzelewski, E. (2001). CMU's Tom Kerr retiring after teaching business ethics for 35 years. *Post-Gazette, April 17*.

Moldoveanu, M. C., and Baum, J. A. (2005). Contemporary debates in organizational epistemology. In J. A. Baum (Ed.), *The Blackwell companion to organizations*. Malden: Blackwell.

National Academy of Sciences. (2009). *On being a scientist: A guide to responsible conduct in research*. Washington, D.C.: The National Academic Press.

Nystrom, P. C., and Starbuck, W. H. (1977). Why prescription is prescribed. *TIMS Studies in Management Studies, 5*, 1–5.

Parfit, D. (1984). *Reasons and persons*. New York: Oxford University Press.

Perrow, C. (1986). *Complex organizations: A critical essay*. New York: McGraw-Hill.

Pfeffer, J. (2015). *Leadership BS: Fixing workplaces and careers one truth at a time*. New York: Harper Business.

Plantinga, A. (1993). *Warrant and proper function*. New York: Oxford University Press.

Preston, L. E. (1986). Business and public policy. *Journal of Management, 12*, 261–275.

Putnam, H. (2002). *The collapse of the fact/value dichotomy*. Cambridge, MA: Harvard University Press.

Quinn, D. P., and Jones, T. M. (1995). An agent morality view of business policy. *Academy of Management Review, 20*, 22–42.

Rawls, J. (1971). *A theory of justice*. Cambridge, MA: Harvard University Press.

Risen, J. (2015). Psychologists approve ban on role in national security interrogations, *New York Times: August 7*.

Robertson, D. (1993). Empiricism in business ethics: Suggested research directions. *Journal of Business Ethics, 12*(8), 585–599.

Root, J. (1991). *Philosophy of social science*. Malden: Blackwell.
Rosenberg, A. (2012). *Philosophy of science*. New York: Routledge.
Sandberg, J. (2008). Understanding the separation thesis. *Business Ethics Quarterly*, *18*, 213–232.
Scanlon, T. M. (2014). *Being realistic about reasons*. New York: Oxford University Press.
Schatzki, T. R. (2002). *The site of the social: A philosophical account of the constitution of social life and change*. University Park: Pennsylvania State University Press.
Scherer, A. G., and Palazzo, G. (2007). Toward a political conception of corporate responsibility: Business and society seen from a Habermasian perspective. *The Academy of Management Review*, *32*(4), 1096–1120. doi: 10.2307/20159358.
Searle, J. (1962). Meaning and speech acts. *Philosophical Review*, *71*, 423–432.
Sepielli, A. (Forthcoming). Subjective and objective reasons. In Daniel Star (Ed.), *Oxford handbook of reasons and normativity*. Oxford University Press.
Setiya, K. (2015). *Knowing right from wrong*. New York: Oxford University Press.
Shafer-Landau, R. (2003). *Moral realism: A defense*. Oxford: Oxford University Press.
Shepherd, C., and Challenger, R. (2013). Revisiting paradigm(s) in management research: A rhetorical analysis of the paradigm wars. *International Journal of Management Reviews*, *15*, 225–244.
Simon, H. A. (1957). *Administrative behavior*. New York: Free Press.
(1967). The business school: A problem in organizational design. *Journal of Management Studies*, *4*, 1–16.
(1977). *Models of discovery: And other topics in the methods of science*. Boston: D. Reidel.
Sinnott-Armstrong, W. (2000). Expressivism and embedding. *Philosophy and Phenomenological Research*, *61*, 677–693.
Sison, A. J. G. (2014). *Happiness and virtue ethics in business: The ultimate value proposition*. Cambridge: Cambridge University Press.
Skorupski, J. (2010). *The domain of reasons*. New York: Oxford University Press.
Smith, M. (1994). *The moral problem*. Oxford: Blackwell.
Sosa, E. (1991). *Knowledge in perspective: Selected essays in epistemology*. New York: Cambridge University Press.
Steup, M., and Sosa, E. (2005). *Contemporary debates in epistemology*. Malden: Blackwell.
Strudler, A. (2005). Deception unraveled. *Journal of Philosophy*, *102*(9), 458–473.
Suchman, M. C. (1995). Managing legitimacy: Strategic and institutional approaches. *Academy of Management Review*, *20*, 571–610.
Swanson, D. L. (1999). Toward an integrative theory of business and society: A research strategy for corporate social performance. *Academy of Management Review*, *24*, 506–521.
Tenbrunsel, A. E., and Smith-Crown, K. (2008). Ethical decision-making: Where we've been and where we're going. In J. P. Walsh and A. P. Brief (Eds.), *Academy of Management Annals, 2* (pp. 545–607). New York: Routledge.
Thomson, J. J. (1990). *The realm of rights*. Cambridge, MA: Harvard University Press.
Treviño, L. K., and Weaver, G. R. (1994). Business ETHICS/BUSINESS ethics: One field or two? *Business Ethics Quarterly*, *4*, 113–128.
Treviño, L. K., Weaver, G. R., and Reynolds, S. J. (2006). Behavioral ethics in organizations: A review. *Journal of Management*, *32*, 951–990.
Tsui, A. S. (2013). The spirit of science and socially responsible scholarship. *Management and Organization Review*, *9*, 375–394.
Van Maanen, J. (1995a). Fear and loathing in organization studies. *Organization Science*, *6*, 687–692.
(1995b). Style as theory. *Organization Science*, *6*, 133–143.
Waldron, J. (Ed.). (1984). *Theories of rights*. New York: Oxford University Press.
Weaver, G. R., Reynolds, S. J., and Brown, M. E. (2014). Moral intuition: Connecting current knowledge to future organizational research and practice. *Journal of Management*, *40*, 100–129.
Weick, K. E. (1979). *The social psychology of organizing*. New York: Addison Wesley.
(1995). *Sensemaking in organizations*. Newbury Park: SAGE.
Wellman, C. (1963). The ethical implications of cultural relativity. *Journal of Philosophy*, *60*, 169–184.
Wenar, L. (2005). The nature of rights. *Philosophy and Public Affairs*, *33*, 223–253.
(2008). The analysis of rights. In M. Kramer, C. Grant, B. Colburn, and A. Hatzistavrou (Eds.), *The legacy of H.L.A. Hart*. New York: Oxford University Press.

Werhane, P. H. (1994). The normative/descriptive distinction in methodologies of business ethics. *Business Ethics Quarterly*, *4*, 175–180.

Westphal, J. D. (1999). Collaboration in the boardroom: Behavioral and performance consequences of CEO-board social ties. *Academy of Management Journal*, *42*(1), 7.

Westwood, R., and Clegg, S. (2002). *Debating organization: Point-counterpoint in organization studies*. Malden: Blackwell.

Wicks, A. C. (1996). Overcoming the separation thesis: The need for a reconsideration of business and society research. *Business and Society*, *35*, 89–118.

Wicks, A. C., and Freeman, R. (1998). Organization studies and the new pragmatism: Positivism, anti-positivism, and the search for ethics. *Organization Science*, *9*, 123–140.

William, J. 1975 (1907). *Pragmatism: A new name for some old ways of thinking*. Cambridge, MA: Harvard University Press.

Williams, B. (1985). *Ethics and the limits of philosophy*. Cambridge, MA: Harvard University Press.

Williamson, O. E. (2005). The economics of governance. *American Economic Review*, *95*, 1–18.

York, J. G., Sarasvathy, S. D., and Wicks, A. (2013). An entrepreneurial perspective on value creation in public-private ventures. *Academy of Management Review*, *35*, 307–309.

Zajac, E. J., and Westphal, J. D. (1994). The costs and benefits of managerial incentives and monitoring in large U.S. corporations: When is more not better? *Strategic Management Journal*, *15*, 121–142.

Zald, M. N. (1991). Sociology as a discipline: Quasi-science and quasi-humanities (pp. 165–187). Fall/Winter: *The American Sociologist*, Fall/ Winter 165–187

(1993). Organization studies as a scientific and humanistic enterprise: Toward a reconceptualiza. *Organization Science*, *4*, 513–527.

Zimbardo, P. G. (1971). The power and pathology of imprisonment. *Congressional Record*. (Serial No. 15, October 25, 1971). Hearings before Subcommittee No. 3, of the Committee on the Judiciary, House of Representatives, 92nd Congress, First Session on Corrections, Part II, Prisons, Prison Reform and Prisoners' Rights: California. Washington, DC: U.S. Government Printing Office.

Zingales, L. (2000). In search of new foundations. *Journal of Finance*, *55*, 1623–1653.

CHAPTER 20

# Another View from China

## *Daoist Thought as an Approach to Global Business Ethics*

KATHLEEN M. HIGGINS

## Introduction

Western philosophy has served business ethics as a source of models, drawn from such luminaries as Aristotle and Adam Smith. While these Western thinkers have many disagreements, they have tended to share certain assumptions, such as the idea that stasis is more basic than change and the view that individuals constitute society, not the other way around. In an era of globalization, however, when those involved in business routinely interact with people from different cultural backgrounds, Westerners cannot assume that their presuppositions are shared by everyone with whom they deal. In this context, models from other philosophical traditions can help provide insight into the perspectives of some of those with whom they do business. These non-Western ethical models can valuably complement Western ones by emphasizing features of the business situation that have been underappreciated in the West.

The business ethics literature has given some discussion to Confucian ethics, particularly in connection with Chinese business practices, but much less emphasis has been placed on the ethical viewpoint of another school of Chinese thought, that of the Daoists.[1] Daoist thought contrasts with much of what is taken for granted in Western business practice, which encourages a go-getter ideal and a "take charge" approach to management. Daoists, by contrast, emphasize receptive attentiveness and restraint until circumstances warrant intervention.

The Daoist approach bears affinity to the "negative capability" approach that certain theorists in leadership ethics have proposed as an antidote to the excesses of certain Western ideals. In what follows I will consider the philosophical notion of "*wu-wei*" (無 為, literally "non-action"), particularly as characterized in Daoist thought. Because it offers a well-developed conception of the sort of "negative capability" that these theorists defend, the Daoist account of *wu-wei* can help elucidate this under-appreciated aspect of ethical management, which affects the well-being of both the individual and the organization.

Several authors who discuss the importance of negative capability have noticed the relevance of Daoism and cite the *Tao Te Ching* to underscore their points (French 2001; Suen, Cheung & Mondejar 2007; Wang & Juslin 2009: 445; Saggurthi & Thakur 2016: 191). Suen, Cheung, and Mondejar even mention *wu-wei* specifically, describing it as "a Chinese version of Ockham's Razor – entities or principles should not be unnecessarily multiplied ... While Ockham's razor is directed primarily toward purely metaphysical and epistemological issues, the Taoists are concerned with an economy of action and a simplicity of life" (Suen, Cheung, & Mondejar 2007: 262). This characterization draws attention to the overall ethical system of the Daoists, which discourages needless and unproductive exertions and calls for appreciation of the basics: life, health, and satisfaction in what is present at hand, whether or not it furthers one's agenda.

If the connection between the Daoist outlook and negative capability has already been acknowledged,

[1] Both the Wade-Gilles and the Pinyin scheme (the one I am using) remain in use. However, Pinyin is the official Romanization system at use in mainland China and it is currently the most frequently used system in Western journals. Because I am using the Pinyin system, I will refer to "Daoists" and "the Dao," as opposed to "Taoists" and "the Tao."

why give it, and in particular *wu-wei*, further consideration? I see three reasons for doing so. First, the ancient discussions of *wu-wei* can add further dimensions to an understanding of negative capability as it has thus far been elaborated. Second, consideration of the Daoist texts can enrich our understanding of the worldview on which Chinese business practice is premised. Third, the ancient texts, with their striking images and stories, can provoke experiences of negative capability, against which we can test the claims that have been made about its value.

## The Daoist Approach and Negative Capability

### *Negative Capability*

The term "negative capability" was originally coined by romantic poet John Keats in a letter to his brother. There he describes negative capability as evident "when man is capable of being in uncertainties, Mysteries, doubts, without any irritable reaching after fact & reason." Keats notes that it is the "quality went to form a Man of Achievement especially in Literature & which Shakespeare possessed so enormously" (Keats 1970, p. 43). What is "negative" here is the avoidance of certain default tendencies in attitude and action. In business these might include tendencies to rush to conclusions, engage reflex responses, view relentless effort as a virtue, avoid risk and uncertainty, and pursue one's goals without interruption. Paradoxically, Keats points out that the negative, in the form of avoidances, is essential to positive accomplishment.

Although Keats's characterization of negative capability is terse, theorists in many fields have found it suggestive and useful for bringing into focus both means and obstacles to obtaining creative results. These researchers have highlighted both "negative" capabilities (toleration of uncertainty and ambiguity, non-defensiveness, detachment from the ego, pausing to ponder the possibilities, and openness) and the positive characteristics of the person who has such capability (being present-centered, emotionally empathetic, aesthetically sensitive, and creative) (Cornish 2011; Simpson, French & Harvey 2002: 1210, 1215; French 2004; Saggurthi & Thakur 2016: 183–184). Peter Simpson, Robert French, and Charles Harvey, emphasize the importance of negative capability in the context of dealing with complicated and high risk situations such as international negotiations (Simpson, French & Harvey 2002:1224). French also stresses the value of being able to "contain" one's anxious emotions in the face of uncertainties, as opposed to dispersing energies into avoidance strategies and anxious behavior (French 2004). Sally Cornish points out that negative capability involves "imaginative openness of mind" and "keen attention to process," noting that these are incompatible with an ego-driven approach (Cornish 2011: 138).

Suneetha Saggurthi and Munish Thakur argue that the high value placed on "speed, control, and performativity" in most discussions of organizations "has disabled critical thought," encouraged neuroses, and undermined business people's ability to feel passion for their work. They define negative capability as

> the ability to delight in doubt and revel in uncertainty without feeling compelled to rationalize half-knowledge or to reach for facts or fall back on existing knowledge structures, resisting conceptual closure and in a state of diligent indolence and passive receptivity, move toward a knowing with the power of one's imagination, sensations, and intuition

Negative capability, they argue, can provide a means of moving "from the ego to the eco" by virtue of the stance of responsiveness and relational thinking that it involves (Saggurthi & Thakur 2016: 180, 181, 185, 189; cf. Simpson, French & Harvey 2002). They also maintain that negative capability helps managers maintain a sense of mission in their work and approach the challenges they encounter in a spirit of creative play. These adduced virtues of negative capability, I will contend, are precisely what the Daoists see as the benefits of approaching one's life and one's undertakings in a spirit of *wu-wei*.

## *Wu-wei* as Negative Capability

The term *wu-wei* is a compound of two characters: *wu* (無), a negating term, and *wei* (為), which means "acting" or "doing." Translating the term straightforwardly, then, "*wu-wei*" means "non-action," "no action," or "doing nothing" (see Graham 1989: 232). Like "negative capability," *wu-wei* conceived as an ideal has a paradoxical ring. Aspiring requires doing things to reach one's goal, but *wu-wei* involves not doing. Indeed, Edward Slingerland speaks of "the paradox of *wu-wei*" in just this connection (Slingerland 2003: 6–7).

Slingerland mitigates the appearance of contradiction by translating *wu-wei* as "effortless action" (Slingerland 2003: 6–7). He points out that the person who is *wu-wei* is not, or not necessarily, motionless or "inactive" in an everyday sense. The concept is not so much about what is happening as it is about the actor's state of mind. *Wu-wei* "describes a state of personal harmony in which actions flow freely and instantly from one's spontaneous inclinations – without the need for extended deliberation or inner struggle – and yet nonetheless accord perfectly with the dictates of the situation at hand" (Slingerland 2003: 7).

Whether or not one exemplifies *wu-wei* depends on what causes one to move. The persons who display *wu-wei* do not move assertively or willfully, but in accordance with the larger flow of energies with which they are connected. Chinese thought since antiquity has considered reality to be in constant transformation, in contrast with most of the ancient Greek philosophers, who (with the notable exception of Heraclitus) assumed stasis as the normal condition (Hall & Ames 1995: 24, 215; Hershock 2012: 11). The term "Dao" (道, or "way") is used to indicate the "way" the world operates, as a dynamic flow of energies that exhibit patterns but also produce unpredictable changes. "Dao" in this sense is referenced in the term "Daoism." Human beings are part of the Dao, this large dynamic system in which all things, beings, and energies interact. When one acts in a manner that is *wu-wei*, one allows the prevailing energies within the Dao to use one as a vessel. But because one is part of the Dao oneself, it is one's own nature that has acted. In contemporary Western parlance, one's actions bear the perfection stemming from "flow" (Csikszentmihalyi 1990).

*Wu-wei*, in fact, yields optimal results. It leads to what Slingerland describes as "an almost supernatural efficacy" (Slingerland 2003: 7, 8), while also according with moral ideals, creating harmony among persons and the broader world.[2] Even though *wu-wei* involves abandonment of explicit effort in a particular direction, it is the presupposition of consummate effectiveness. As A. C. Graham expresses the idea, "the way to attain a goal is to cease to aim at it deliberately" (Graham 1989: 232). This seems to be precisely Keats's point when he says that negative capability characterizes the "Man of Achievement."

## *Wu-wei* in Schools of Chinese Thought

Various schools of ancient Chinese thought have linked *wu-wei* with their own interpretation of optimal outcomes. Legalism is concerned with the best methods for maintaining power, and it emphasizes *wu-wei* in the sense of non-interference on the part of a ruler. The legalist plan, articulated by Han Fei Zi (c. 280–233 BCE), is to institutionalize roles, ensure that laws are clear and known to everyone, punish infractions harshly and without exception, and incentivize good behavior with predictable rewards. Rewards and punishments should be doled out automatically, so it would be counterproductive for the ruler to intervene. Refraining from overt action also intensifies the ruler's inscrutability, thereby facilitating the ruler's hold on power by enhancing the mystique of the office (see Watson, in Han Fei Tzu 1964: 10).

Like Han Fei Zi, Sunzi recommends *wu-wei* as a means of being inscrutable, though with respect to an enemy as opposed to subjects being ruled.

[2] The connection between *wu-wei* and morality can be approached in various ways, and it is somewhat differently considered by particular Confucians and particular Daoists. Peter Hershock, however, suggests a common tendency among them tracing to their shared dynamic perspective on reality, which made them tend toward "a moral inclination toward adaptive, harmonizing engagement with continuously changing circumstances" (Hershock 2012: 93).

Sunzi's *Art of Warfare* has often been applied to business, and many of its strategies involve *wu-wei*. Strikingly, given his topic, Sunzi urges literal non-action to the extent possible. "To win a hundred victories in a hundred battles is not the highest excellence; the highest excellence is to subdue the enemy's army without fighting at all" (Sun Tzu 1993: 111). If one does go to war, one should utilize whatever strategic advantages the circumstances afford. Sunzi stresses that commanders should not allow personal desires or ambitions to interfere with sound strategy, a view in keeping with the notion of negative capability as a non-ego-dominated approach. Sunzi urges commanders to be still and attend to the minute details of the situation, spontaneously responding when opportunities present themselves rather than formulating a grand plan and aggressively pursuing it. Sunzi's approach emphasizes non-action, non-exertion, receptivity, responsiveness, exploitation of the energies within one's situation, and the avoidance of willful interventions. Maintaining a posture of stillness and attentiveness is a negative capability of the sort French describes, putting restraint on inner tendencies to dissipate emotional tension into anxiety-prompted behavior.

Confucian texts also make use of *wu-wei*. The term itself only appears once in the *Analects*, the work that gives us the most extensive portrait of Confucius (551–479 BCE), but that passage suggests its conceptual importance. Confucius uses the term in describing one of his heroes from history, the Sage-King Shun:

> The Master said, "If anyone could be said to have effected proper order while remaining nonassertive, surely it was Shun. What did he do? He simply assumed an air of deference and faced due south". (*Analects* 15.5, in Ames and Rosemont 1998: 185)

For Shun to "face due south" was to play his role as emperor, for the emperor was always seated facing south when dealing with subordinates in an official capacity. *Wu-wei* is translated as "nonassertive" here, and this emphasis is reinforced by the mention of deference (cf. Hall & Ames 1998: 52). Instead of indulging in displays of his power, Shun attuned himself to his role and responded appropriately to circumstances; and as a result of this exemplary practice, he had moral charisma that encouraged his subjects' cooperation, making assertive rule unnecessary (see Slingerland 2003: 44). In general, the Confucian texts encourage negativity on the part of leaders in the form of not acting on ego-dominated motives. As Ames describes it, "the ruler 'does nothing' inasmuch as he concerns himself with the fulfilment of his own nature without projecting any artificial and arbitrary demands on his subordinates" (Ames 1981: 194–195).

Despite its widespread use in Chinese philosophy, *wu-wei* is given a particularly rich treatment in Daoist thought. "Daoist" is a very general category, applied to a variety of non-orthodox (non-Confucian) philosophical perspectives that share certain broad views. Probably the most influential Daoist texts are the *Dao De Jing* (*Tao Te Ching*, also called the *Laozi*, in reference to its author, 570–510 BCE) and the *Zhuangzi* (the name of its author, 369–298 BCE).[3] Both reject the Confucian emphasis on ritual behavior as a means of creating a harmonious society in favor of *wu-wei*.

The Daoists emphasize *wu-wei* understood as attunement to the movements of the Dao and responding in accordance with every change of circumstance. This responsive stance links *wu-wei* with another, more "positive" concept, that of *ziran* (自然). *Ziran* is often translated "spontaneity," but other translations, such as "so-of-itself" (Slingerland 2003) and "self-so-ing" (Hall & Ames 1998) have also been proposed, bringing out the idea that *wu-wei* enables one's true, "original" nature to operate (cf. Slingerland 2003: 35). When one's behavior manifests *wu-wei*, one is free of the constraints imposed by pre-given conceptions of how best to achieve one's goals. The *Dao De Jing* compares this optimal state to the condition of "the newborn babe": "its harmony is at its height" for its actions emerge without forethought or deliberate effort (Lao Tzu 1963, 55: 62). And this accounts for the efficacy of *wu-wei*: "The way

[3] Contemporary scholars believe that most ancient Chinese texts are products of multiple authors. However, I will follow convention in referring to the authors to whom these Daoist works are attributed.

[*Dao*] never acts yet nothing is left undone" (Lao Tzu 1963, 37: 42).

The person acting with *wu-wei*, on this view, is unencumbered by the impediments that commonly obstruct one's efforts, and this makes the Daoist interpretation of *wu-wei* useful for analyzing problems confronted in business, often diagnosing them as linked to an attitudinal stance. Approaching one's situation without the blinders of fixed expectations may be essential to dealing effectively with the fluid circumstances in which managers commonly find themselves. Such openness makes possible fresh observations that can inform creative solutions to challenging issues. The situation itself can also throw up obstacles that resist the energies one has summoned in pursuit of a project, much as the flow of traffic can stymy a driver's attempt to reach a destination. François Jullien points out the value of being flexible in one's attitude and tapping the energies already at work in one's situation, noting the utter pointlessness of doing otherwise:

> It is impossible to go against the propensity inherent in the regular unfolding of processes. This does not, of course, mean that one should completely desist from action; instead, one should simply understand how to put aside all "activism" and disregard one's own desire to take the initiative. Having done so, one should go along with the flow of the phenomena, profit from their dynamism, and induce them to cooperate. (Jullien 1995: 223–224)

This is precisely what is involved when a person acts with *wu-wei*:

> All he does is respond and react to whatever reality prompts within him. And this he does not do partially or at particular moments, when it is in his interest to do so, but in all situations and continuously. In this way his power to change reality is checked by no obstacles or limits. He does not "act," does nothing himself (on his own initiative), and the degree of the efficacy of this behavior is determined by the extent to which he refrains from trying to manage things. (Jullien 1995: 263–264)

Jullien's point that relinquishing control can be the best way to affect one's situation is illustrated by an example from Eugen Herrigel's *Zen and the Art of Archery*. (Zen, we should note, derives from a school of Chinese Buddhism, Chan, that was strongly influenced by Daoism.) Herrigel, a German who went to Japan to study archery with a Zen master, reports an interaction as follows, beginning with his own analysis of a problem he was having with timing:

> "When I have drawn the bow, the moment comes when I feel: unless the shot comes at once I shan't be able to endure the tension. And what happens then? Merely that I get out of breath. So I must lose the shot whether I want to or not, because I can't wait for it any longer."
>
> "You have described only too well," replied the Master, "where the difficulty lies. Do you know why you cannot wait for the shot and why you get out of breath before it has come? The right shot at the right moment does not come because you do not let go of yourself. You do not wait for fulfillment, but brace yourself for failure. So long as that is so, you have no choice but to call forth something yourself that ought to happen independently of you, and so long as you call it forth your hand will not open in the right way – like the hand of a child. Your hand does not burst open like the skin of a ripe fruit". (Herrigel 1953:30)[4]

The master's instruction here points to negative capabilities that allow one to attune one's action to the situation, such as the avoidance of an ego-dominated perspective and the refusal to be determined by some preselected strategy. The relevance of this approach to dealing with challenges in business is obvious. If timing is often everything in business, *wu-wei* is everything in timing.

## *Wu-wei* in the *Dao De Jing*

The *Dao De Jing* can be read as a handbook of leadership ethics, and many of its suggestions to leaders center on *wu-wei*: "The best of all rulers is but a shadowy presence to his subjects . . . When his task is accomplished and his work is all done/ The people all say, 'It happened to us naturally'" (Lao Tzu 1963, 17:31). Those who seek

[4] My thanks to Sarah Canright for first drawing my attention to this passage.

ego-gratification are unlikely to desire any such strategy, but the *Dao De Jing* takes the very lack of recognition for one's efforts as a sign that one is doing something right. Showy initiatives that sound impressive more often than not disrupt what has been working well. The *Dao De Jing* resoundingly endorses the policy of "if it's not broke, don't fix it." Non-interference is the policy that has the best results:

> Hence the sage says,
>
> I take no action and the people are transformed of themselves;
> I prefer stillness and the people are rectified of themselves;
> I am not meddlesome and the people prosper of themselves;
> I am free from desire and the people of themselves becomes simple like the uncarved block. (Lao Tzu 1963, 57: 64)

The "uncarved block" is one that has not been shaped by coercive methods, and so it is able to be what it is, developing in accordance with its own nature. The *Dao De Jing*'s ideal manager allows for "thinking outside the box" because he or she does not insist that matters proceed in accordance with a plan specified in advance.

The very process of fixing ideas in words distorts the subtle and dynamic character of reality, according to the Daoists, and one can be misled by these distortions. The *Dao De Jing* begins with this insight: "The way that can be spoken of/Is not the constant way;/The name that can be named/is not the constant name" (Lao Tzu 1963, 1:6). Such seemingly self-contradictory statements aim to disrupt thinking in terms of straightforward binaries. Zhuangzi makes similar suggestions: "The fish trap exists because of the fish; once you've gotten the fish, you can forget the trap ... Words exist because of meaning; once you've gotten the meaning, you can forget the words" (Chuang Tzu 1964, 140). Whatever is expressed in words focuses attention on some aspects of things at the expense of others, and we should recognize that we may miss something important if we take verbal formulations too seriously. The Daoist texts suggest that we should not consider our concepts as more important than what we observe and that we should beware of using black-and-white categories as the bases for programs and projects. The Daoists are dubious of labels in general, and they would be dubious of buzzwords and any policy too much premised on the outlook that buzzwords encourage us to adopt.

## *Wu-wei* in the *Zhuangzi*

The *Dao De Jing*'s vision of *wu-wei* emphasizes non-intervention, a straightforwardly negative capability. Zhuangzi, whose writing abounds with colorful vignettes, draws greater attention to the positive side of negative capability, the creative approach to undertakings that it makes possible and the sort of playfulness Saggurthi & Thakur emphasize. By enabling "free and easy wandering," an unscripted approach to thinking and feeling, *wu-wei* allows one to recognize valuable resources in what one had previously dismissed as useless. Though he explicitly renounces the pursuit of worldly success as one's overarching goal, Zhuangzi praises entrepreneurial imagination, which depends on an attitude of *wu-wei*. In one vignette he describes a friend telling him about being given some seeds that have produced large gourds and reaching the conclusion that they are useless since they are too big to use as dippers. Zhuangzi responds with a story about a member of a family of silk-bleachers who invented a salve to prevent chapped hands. For many years the inventor had kept the salve recipe a family secret, but he was persuaded by a traveler to sell it to him for a large sum of money. The traveler showed the salve to the King of Wu and was given a military commission and later a fief. Zhuangzi concludes,

> The salve had the power to prevent chapped hands in either case; but one man used it to get a fief, while the other one never got beyond silk bleaching – because they used it in different ways. Now you had a gourd big enough to hold five piculs. Why didn't you think of making it into a great tub so you could go floating around the rivers and lake, instead of worrying because it was too big and unwieldy to dip into things! Obviously you still have a lot of underbrush in your head. (Chuang Tzu, 1964: 29)

Zhuangzi gives examples of artists and athletes who succeed because they do not impose their preconceptions and binary categories on their perceptions or actions. He describes "Artisan Ch'ui" as a master in drawing "because his fingers changed along with things and he didn't let his mind get in the way . . . You forget your feet when the shoes are comfortable. You forget your waist when the belt is comfortable. Understanding forgets right and wrong when the mind is comfortable." (Chuang Tzu 1964: 128). This last line underscores Zhuangzi's conviction that binary thinking interferes with the kind of spontaneous thought that comfortably "fits" the problem it addresses.

Zhuangzi's most detailed account of a person acting with *wu-wei* is his story of Cook Ding, who worked for a duke. The duke visits Cook Ding in his kitchen and marvels at the grace with which the cook butchers an ox. The duke notes that he moves "in perfect rhythm," as if he were engaged in a dance or musical performance. Cook Ding explains that when he first started butchering, he saw the whole ox in front of him, but later his awareness changed. Now, he says, "I go along with the natural makeup" and "follow things as they are." "There are spaces between the joints, and the blade of the knife has really no thickness. If you insert what has no thickness into such spaces, then there's plenty of room – more than enough for the blade to play about in." He mostly refrains from thinking: "I go at it by spirit and don't look with my eyes. Perception and understanding have come to a stop and spirit moves where it wants." However, if there is a complicated place, he attends to the difficulties, concentrates, and works slowly: "I . . . move the knife with the greatest subtlety, until – flop! The whole thing comes apart like a clod of earth crumbling to the ground" (Chuang Tzu 1964: 46–47).

Cook Ding's story sums up the method of behaving with *wu-wei*, which it presents as efficacious precisely because of what it does *not* do. Cook Ding does not let his mental understandings and theoretical constructs (e.g. the image of the whole ox or conceptions of what cuts of meat he should produce) direct his course. He defers to the natural patterns before him, moving his knife as they direct him. He has emptied himself of ego, not forcing his way on things, and yet he justifiably takes satisfaction when his task is accomplished.

In summary, *wu-wei* as characterized by the Daoists represents a form of negative capability of the sort recently discussed in the business ethics and leadership literature. The *Dao De Jing* encourages abandonment of certainties, cliché notions, presupposed hierarchies, and scripted behaviors, instead urging an appreciation of the subtle dynamics of the Dao and the power of allowing useful insights to materialize when they will. The free and easy wandering of the *Zhuangzi* is premised on *wu-wei* as an open and receptive stance toward the world, free of defensiveness and the dominance of ego. More positively characterized, this condition involves experiential immediacy, enabling artistic prowess, aesthetic sensitivity, and responses attuned to the specificities of the situation, which it reflects without prejudice. Although the Daoist texts do not focus directly on emotion as such, as do some recent discussions of negative capability (French 2001; Saggurthi & Thakur 2016), the *Zhuangzi* celebrates exuberant and responsive engagement with reality and embodies a sense of play (cf. Saggurthi & Thakur 2016: 182). I will proceed to indicate how the ancient Chinese and especially Daoist accounts of *wu-wei* can further contemporary discussion of negative capability.

## Benefits of the Daoist Approach

### *Refining Our Thoughts about Negative Capability*

Chinese philosophy's long interest in *wu-wei* can contribute to contemporary theorizing about negative capability. First, because the competing schools of Chinese thought took somewhat different views of the value of *wu-wei*, comparing these approaches can help us to recognize that there might be a range of possibilities for making use of negative capability, with different mixes of elements in this notion being particularly serviceable for different purposes and situations.

The Legalists and Sunzi saw *wu-wei* as a vehicle of subterfuge. For the Legalists, it could prevent subordinates from being capable of manipulating a ruler, while Sunzi saw it as a means through which a commander could confuse the enemy. The negative capability of the Legalist ruler is made possible by an organizational set-up that is in good working order. Intervention is necessary or desirable only when something breaks down, and then only to restore the good functioning of the bureaucratic machine. Negative capability here is a matter of restraint.

By contrast, *wu-wei* in the Confucian *Analects* is a marker of having achieved the ethical ideal through self-cultivation, as exemplified in Confucius and Shun. Being *wu-wei* reveals that one's character does not resist moral propriety in any respect. Although Zhuangzi similarly takes operating with *wu-wei* as an indicator of greatness (as is shown in his story of Cook Ding), he focuses on mastery in the concrete practices of daily life, such as those manifest in one's work. He places accent on the positive consequences of this negative capability. Which particular conceptions of *wu-wei* is most useful depends on the ends in view. The "free and easy wandering" of Zhuangzi does not seem particularly relevant to the project of maintaining power; it may, however, be the optimal means for overcoming an impasse in a project or for reformulating what is currently at stake in a negotiation.

Recognizing the dissonances among the different perspectives the Chinese traditions take to *wu-wei* might also help us to recognize tensions among recent analyses of negative capability. The characterizations of negative capability within recent discussions bear family resemblances to each other, but they vary in which features are foregrounded and which are underplayed. For example, Suen and his colleagues' aforementioned comparison of *wu-wei* with Ockham's razor brings out the Daoist emphasis on letting go of superfluous judgments and attending to the basics. However, this comparison may give the impression that *wu-wei* is primarily a matter of abstinence or eliminating the extraneous, without much attention to what *wu-wei* adds to experience (such as greater appreciation of textural nuance, complexity, and the range of possibilities within in a situation). Saggurthi and Thakur make the general observation that many recent discussions of negative capability similarly place emphasis on uncertainty and what one refrains from doing, while leaving other aspects of negative capability (such as its aesthetic and playful character) implicit or entirely hidden (Cf. Saggurthi and Thakur 2016: 182). The different tendencies that they note are paralleled in the different emphases of the *Dao De Jing* and the *Zhuangzi*. Our understanding of negative capability is likely to benefit from focusing greater attention on these differences. Perhaps like their ancient Chinese predecessors, these distinct understandings of negative capability each have merit, but one may be preferable to another in a particular context at hand.

Attending to some of the characterizations of *wu-wei* in the ancient texts can also suggest issues related to negative capability that might be given greater attention. One of these is whether or not everyone can cultivate negative capability. Robert French affirms that some are born with a gift for negative capability and that this talent admits of degrees, but he thinks that others can develop negative capability through learning (French 2001: 483; cf. Simpson et al. 1220). Determining the extent to which an aptitude for relinquishing control is inborn may be a nature/nurture debate that cannot be definitively resolved, though most discussions focus (quite reasonably) on the desirability of developing the skills that negative capability involves.

Saggurthi and Thakur, however, suggest that some people might not be able to develop negative capability. They cite people with low self-esteem, who may be "incapable of handling the degree of loss of self that NC requires," and the emotionally color-blind, who often compensate by being highly action-oriented (Saggurthi and Thakur 2016: 190). Their view seems to differ from that of French (and of Simpson et al, 2002). It is also in apparent disagreement with the *Dao De Jing*'s suggestion that the condition of *wu-wei* arises when a person returns to the state of infants, who are spontaneous and unselfconscious in their behavior. This comparison of *wu-wei* with the infant's condition suggests that negative capability could in principle be developed by anyone, since it depends on a person's reviving abilities previously demonstrated.

Saggurthi and Thakur, proposing questions for further research, also suggest that negative capability may be different in different cultures (Saggurthi and Thakur 2016:189). While this is an empirical issue, attention to ancient discussions of *wu-wei* may help to focus empirical investigations by suggesting differences that are significant and testable. If Saggurthi and Thakur's suggestion proves correct, we should ask about different uses of negative capability within cultures as well. If there are different negative capabilities, moreover, the means of developing them might also vary. The *Dao De Jing* and the *Zhuangzi* indicate the value of meditative practices for this purpose, and both texts convey the idea that negative capability reflects spiritual attainment. This is far from the kind of negative capability that we see in the calculated avoidance of overt action and the hands-off policy of the Legalist ruler.

If there are different types of negative capability, consideration might be given to the question of whether there is a hierarchy among them, and if so, on what basis it should be determined. However, this question itself might be out of keeping with the orientation that the idea of *wu-wei* is designed to encourage, one in which one is open to reassessing what one has taken to be the value of a particular thing. Nevertheless, we might be interested in formulating a typology of different negative capabilities, and asking whether some versions are in certain ways deficient, and in this, the ancient texts might help us. For instance, does harnessing *wu-wei* to the specific goals of the Legalist ruler render it too qualified to count as full-fledged negative capability? Certainly, *wu-wei* in this vision seems too restricted to enable non-linear leaps of creative imagination. Should efforts to cultivate negative capability be of the "no holds barred" variety that Zhuangzi encourages, or should the goal be skill at using negative capability within constraints? Presumably in the context of business, an extreme "no holds barred" version would be too open-ended to be compatible with the positive aims of a business enterprise. but if that is the case, what is the right degree of negative capability? All of these are questions that the models provided by the Chinese texts might help us to pursue.

## *Wu-wei* and Chinese Business Practice

A second way in which consideration of *wu-wei* can contribute to discussions of negative capability in the context of business ethics is that it provides a fuller picture of the cultural context within which Chinese business practices have developed. By and large, discussions of the intellectual roots of Chinese business have tended to focus on Confucian values to a greater extent than Daoist ones. While certain attitudes are shared by Confucianism and Daoism, such as the ideal of harmony, the two traditions bring different emphases to the fore (Suen, Cheung, & Mondejar 2007). Thus, even though Confucian texts acknowledge that one who has reached the ethical ideal need not act assertively, they can be read as accentuating achievement as such and the diligent practice of self-cultivation required. The Daoist texts, by contrast, more pervasively stress the spontaneous and non-effortful character of *wu-wei*, and this emphasis, too, is part of the intellectual matrix that informs Chinese business practice. Greater attention to Daoist perspectives will provide a fuller awareness of the context in which Chinese business has developed and the way these perspectives influence the values evident in within it.

A frequently mentioned contrast between Chinese and Western approaches in both business and political policy is that the Chinese take a longer-term view than do their Western counterparts. The Chinese worldview since ancient times has attended to transformation and flows of energies. These ways of thinking are basic to Chinese thought about matters from physical health to good architecture and interior design. The idea of *wu-wei* draws on the presupposition that when one stops aggressively trying to direct things, the larger field of energies will be reflected in one's actions and this will make them superlatively efficacious. Chinese thinkers of diverse schools of thought share the conception of the world as a dynamic energy field in which tendencies flow into and affect one another. It is plausible that the habits of mind promoted by this worldview promote analysis in terms of long-term developments and more remote consequences of steps taken at present. The Daoist treatment of *wu-wei* would also encourage cultivation of timing of a sort that is seldom analyzed in the West.

We might consider the emphasis on *wu-wei* and natural development to be at work in other tendencies within Chinese business behavior as well. Daryl Koehn makes a convincing case that the Confucian ethic, with its focus on trustworthiness and good will as bases for good relationships, helps to explain the Chinese reluctance to spell out the details of business relationships in contracts. Contracts deflect attention away from being guided by a spirit of good will toward taking one's bearings from the details of the contract. Focus on contractual obligations also distracts attention from the bigger picture of "the economic, psychological, and cultural factors at work" (Koehn 2001:420).

As important as Confucian ideas are for shaping the aims of Chinese business, the Daoist perspective and its emphasis on *wu-wei* should also be recognized as among these cultural factors. Cultivating relationships in an open spirit, without stipulating precise demands and restrictions, is continuous not only with Confucian ideals, but with the Daoist emphasis on the kind of natural, spontaneous development for which *wu-wei* allows. In a climate nurtured by the Daoist vision, mutually advantageous ways of partnering might emerge spontaneously from the parties attuning themselves to their common goals and the situation. This, too, stands in contrast to a conception of negotiation in which each side is trying to make the best possible deal for itself.[5]

The case that Simpson and colleagues describe as showcasing negative capability serves as an illustration. They describe progressive stages of an international business negotiation, arguing that success in this context depended on making room for spontaneous synergies. According to Nicholas, one of the negotiators, "We didn't try to be impartial – although we had to be. We were just trying to focus on what could happen if this could succeed" (Simpson et al. 2002: 1219). The Daoist contribution to the Chinese mindset would encourage such an orientation in negotiations – one in which the accent is on positive possibilities, and it would in itself disincline Chinese negotiators from taking contracts as the basis for interaction.

One might also see the *wu-wei* approach of making space for spontaneous development to be a factor in the phenomenon of *guanxi*, the informal networks of interpersonal connections that have been basic to business activity in China for centuries (Zhang & Zhang 2006: 375; Su, Sirgy &Littlefield 2003: 303). Although many Western ethicists take *guanxi* to be conducive to or coextensive with corruption and bribery, it can also be seen as ethically positive. Han and Altman acknowledge *guanxi*'s potential for negative consequences within the workplace, but they itemize many "meaningfully and ethically positive reciprocal exchanges" that convey mutual support, caring, recognition, and concern for fairness (Han & Altman 99). Chenting Su and his colleagues Sirgy and Littlefield go so far as to characterize *guanxi* as itself amounting to an ethical approach:

> People exchange favors to develop extensive networks of interpersonal relationships to share scarce resources and cope with uncertainties. Therefore, *guanxi* can be viewed as the Chinese way of doing business based on friendship and trust. (Su et al. 2003: 303–304)

It should be noted that Su and colleagues distinguish favor-seeking *guanxi*, doing favors as gestures of reciprocity and appreciation of previous favors, from the undesirable "rent-seeking *guanxi*," which involves "social collusion based on power exchange in a hybrid Chinese socialist market economy" for the purpose of personal gain (Su et al. 2003: 310).

Zhang and Zhang contend that *guanxi* is an outgrowth of Confucianism's relational and particularistic orientation (Zhang & Zhang 2006: 377). However, we might also consider the informal and long-term character of favor-seeking *guanxi* and the networks it cultivates as reflecting an orientation that is geared to building on relationships that evolve spontaneously, as opposed to more abstractly

[5] My thanks to Peter Hershock for suggesting this way of seeing business negotiation.

structured connections. What amounts to providing favors depends on the particular circumstances, and thus favor-seeking *guanxi* can respond to new developments in a situation more straightforwardly than a policy based on conforming to prior stipulations of mutual obligations.

### *Exercise in Negative Capability*

To note the "positive" contributions of the "negative" capability of *wu-wei* draws attention once again to the seemingly oxymoronic character of these notions. A third benefit of considering the way that the Daoist texts approach *wu-wei* is that it can help us see past this apparent paradox. The Daoist texts remind us of that our use of binary judgments has its limitations. In so far as one of the values of negative capability is that it frees the imagination and makes fresh insights possible, negativity and positivity go hand-in-hand. The reciprocity of negative and positive capabilities is, indeed, a point that some of the recent theorists of negative capability have made central to their discussion (Cornish 2011; Simpson et al. 2002; Saggurthi & Thakur 2016). The Daoist texts reflect the view of binaries embedded in the well-known yin-yang symbol: the "positive" and the "negative" are always transforming into each other, and each already contains elements of its opposite.

The Daoist texts do more than help us to see beyond simplistic judgments of what is positive and negative. They can also spur us to draw on our own negative capability by offering images and stories that are initially perplexing. In the *Zhuangzi*, for example, we find a character remarking, "Men claim that Mao-ch'iang and Lady Li were beautiful, but if fish saw them they would dive to the bottom of the stream, if birds saw them they would fly away, and if deer saw them they would break into a run. Of these four, which knows how to fix the standard of beauty for the world?" (Chuang Tzu 1964, 41). The idea that deer running from beautiful women makes the standard of beauty seems so ludicrous that one might wonder if one really gets the point. We might have a similar reaction to *Dao De Jing*'s claim that the newborn babe is at the height of virility. To make any sense of these ideas, we have to reconfigure the way we are thinking. To read these texts in their entirety is to put oneself again and again in a state of uncertainty, and the only way forward is to explore imaginatively what the author(s) could have meant and how it relates to our own experience and problems.

The Cook Ding story ends with the cook's employer, the Duke, exclaiming, "Excellent! I have heard the words of Cook Ting and learned how to care for life!" (Chuang Tzu 1964, 47). The idea of a duke learning the secrets of life from his cook is unexpected, as well as absurd in the context of hierarchical ancient China. What does the Duke take away from his encounter with Cook Ding? And what can we take away from this story? Certainly, the answers are not straightforward. But our quandary is precisely the kind of impasse that resists our usual analytic approaches and forces us to reconsider. In this respect, we are led to an experiential context in which we are left to ponder without any assurance of the correctness of any interpretation we formulate. We are led, in other words, into a situation in which we require negative capability to move forward, and thus we gain experiential awareness of how negative capability can be useful in a quandary.

Our very grappling with the interpretive situation puts us in experiential touch with the sort of context in which our well trained "positive capabilities," which usually guide our efforts, are not serviceable, potentially leading us to pause in our efforts and allow space for a new approach to dawn on us. The Daoist texts' resistance to easy interpretation and their potential to force us to explore to our own negative capability is a third benefit of considering the Daoist texts that deal with *wu-wei.*

## Conclusion

Doing business in a globalized economy involves encounters among members of different cultures. The prevalence of international consumer goods and the widespread global movement of technologies can mislead us into assuming more homogeneity of outlook and experience than there actually is. Business ethicists and managers have reason to be interested in the philosophical orientations that shape traditions outside their own cultures, for awareness of them can help make sense of differences in culturally grounded expectations of how business dealings should proceed. In particular, recognition of the Daoist contribution to Chinese perspectives on timing, spontaneity in relationships, circumstances in which assertion is not warranted, and *guanxi* can provide foreigners with some awareness of ways in which their own approach may not be shared by the Chinese.

A second reason for learning more about the Daoist orientation, in particular, is that it counters the current business emphasis on speed and performance, which taken to extreme can lead to malfunction, harming both the well-being of businesspeople and the results achieved by their work. Certain theorists who consider negative capability see it as a focus that can help to address the imbalance that results from exclusive emphasis on the performativity ideal. The Daoist explorations of *wu-wei* can help to further identify practices of negative capability that can counteract burnout, tunnel vision, and impasse. In an analogue to the maxim "less is more," the Daoists claim that negative exertion is positive, and attention to *wu-wei* helps to reveal the grounds for this view.

Finally, Daoist images and stories confound our expectations. They do so deliberately, in this way shaking up our typical assumptions. The ancient Daoist texts can help us develop negative capability, which can be a corrective to harmful excesses within the status quo. Sunzi's relevance for business has been recognized. Those concerned with good practice in business should turn their sights to Zhuangzi and Laozi as well.

## References


Ames, Roger T. (1981). "Wu-wei in 'The Art of Rulership' Chapter of the Huai Nan Tzu: Its Sources and Philosophical Orientation." *Philosophy East and West* 31: 2 (April 1981): 193–213.

Ames, Roger T., and Henry Rosemont, Jr., translators (1998). *The Analects of Confucius: A Philosophical Translation*. New York: Ballantine Books.

Chuang Tzu (1964). *Basic Writings*. Translated by Burton Watson. New York: Columbia University Press.

Cornish, Sally (2011). Negative capability and social work: Insights from Keats, Bion, and business. *Journal of Social Work Practice*, 25(2): 135–148.

Csikszentmihalyi, Mihalyi (1990). *Flow: The Psychology of Optimal Experience*. New York: Harper and Row.

Fingarette, Herbert (1972). *Confucius: The Secular as Sacred*. New York: Harper Torchbooks.

French, Robert B. (2004). "Negative Capability." In *Encyclopedia of Leadership*. Edited by George R. Goethals, Georgia J. Seroenson, and James MacGregor Burns, III (1077–1080). Thousand Oaks: Sage.

(2001). "'Negative Capability': Managing the Confusing Uncertainties of Change". *Journal of Organizational Change Management* 14(5): 480–492.

Graham, A. C. (1989). *Disputers of the Dao: Philosophical Argument in Ancient China*. La Salle, IL: Open Court.

Hall, David L., and Roger T. Ames (1995). *Anticipating China: Thinking through the Narratives of Chinese and Western Culture*. Albany: State University of New York Press.

(1998). *Thinking from the Han: Self, Truth, and Transcendence in Chinese and Western Culture*. Albany: State University of New York Press.

Han Fei Tzu (1964). *Basic Writings*. In *Basic Writings of Mo Tzu, Hsün Tzu, and Han Fei Tzu*. Translated by Burton Watson. New York: Columbia University Press.

Han, Yong, & Yochanan Altman (2009). "Supervisor and Subordinate *Guanxi*: A Grounded Investigation in the People's Republic of China." In *Journal of Business Ethics* 88, Supplement 1: Business Ethics in Greater China: 91–104.

Herrigel, Eugen (1953). *Zen and the Art of Archery*. Trans. R. F. C. Hull. New York: Random House.

Hershock, Peter D. (2012). *Valuing Diversity: Buddhist Reflection on Realizing a More Equitable Global Future*. Albany: State University of New York Press.

Hsün Tzu (1964). *Basic Writings*. In *Basic Writings of Mo Tzu, Hsün Tzu, and Han Fei Tzu*. Translated by Burton Watson. New York: Columbia University Press.

Jullien, François (1995). *The Propensity of Things: Toward a History of Efficacy in China*. Translated by Janet Lloyd. New York: Zone Books.

Keats, John (1970). *The Letters of John Keats: A Selection*. Edited by R. Gittings. Oxford: Oxford University Press.

Koehn, Daryl (2001). "Confucian Trustworthiness and the Practice of Business in China." *Business Ethics Quarterly* 11: 415–429.

Lao Tzu (1963). *Tao Te Ching*. Translated by D. C. Lau. New York: Penguin Books.

Loy, David (1985). "Wei-Wu-Wei: Nondual Action," *Philosophy East and West* 35: 73–86.

Mencius (1970). *Mencius*. Translated by D. C. Lau. London: Penguin.

Mo Tzu (1964). Basic Writings. In *Basic Writings of Mo Tzu, Hsün Tzu, and Han Fei Tzu*. Translated by Burton Watson. New York: Columbia University Press.

Ou, Li (2009). *Keats and Negative Capability*. London: Bloomsbury.

Saggurthi, Suneetha, & Thakur, Munish K. (2016). "Usefulness of Uselessness: A Case for Negative Capability in Management." *Academy of Management Learning and Education*, 15(1): 180–193.

Skaja, Henry (1998). "How to Interpret Chapter 16 of the *Zhuangzi*: 'Repairers of Nature (Shan Xing).'" In *Wandering at Ease in the Zhuangzi*, edited by Roger T. Ames (101–124). Albany: State University of New York Press.

Simpson, Peter, Robert French & Charles E. Harvey (2002). "Leadership and Negative Capability," *Human Relations*, 55(10): 1209–1226.

Slingerland, Edward. *Effortless Action: Wu-Wei as Conceptual Metaphor and Spiritual Ideal in Early China*. New York: Oxford University Press, 2003.

Su, Chenting, M. Joseph Sirgy and James E. (2003). "Is *Guanxi* Orientation Bad, Ethically Speaking? A Study of Chinese Enterprises." *Journal of Business Ethics* 44: 303–312.

Su, Chenting, Ronald K. Mitchell, and M. Joseph Sirgy (2007). "Enabling *Guanxi* Management in China: A Hierarchical Stakeholder Model of Effective *Guanxi*." *Journal of Business Ethics* 71: 301–319.

Suen, Henry, Sai-On Cheung, & Reuben Mondejar (2007). "Managing Ethical Behavior in Construction Organizations in Asia: How Do the Teachings of Confucianism, Taoism and Buddhism and Globalization Influence Ethics Management?" *International Journal of Project Management* 25: 257–265.

Sun-Tzu (1993). *The Art of Warfare*. Translated by Roger T. Ames. New York: Ballantine Books.

Warden, Clyde A., and Judy F. Chen (2009). "Chinese Negotiators' Subjective Variations in Intercultural Negotiations," *Journal of Business Ethics* 88: 529–537.

Wang, Cheng Lu, and Xiaohua Lin (2009). "Migration of Chinese Consumption Values: Traditions, Modernization, and Cultural Renaissance. *Journal of Business Ethics* 88: 399–409.

Wang, Lei, and Heikki Juslin (2009). "The Impact of Chinese Culture on Corporate Social Responsibility: The Harmony Approach," *Journal of Business Ethics* 88: 433–451.

Watson, Burton, translator (1964). *Basic Writings of Mo Tzu, Hsün Tzu, and Han Fei Tzu*. New York: Columbia University Press.

Zhang, Yi, and Zigang Zhang (2006). "Guanxi and Organizational Dynamics in China: A Link Between Individual and Organizational Levels. *Journal of Business Ethics* 67: 375–392.

# Index